Cases on Responsive and Responsible Learning in Higher Education

Nor Aziah Alias
Universiti Teknologi MARA, Malaysia

Sharipah Ruzaina Syed-Aris
Universiti Teknologi MARA, Malaysia

Hamimah Hashim
Universiti Teknologi MARA, Malaysia

A volume in the Advances in Higher Education and Professional Development (AHEPD) Book Series

Published in the United States of America by
IGI Global
Information Science Reference (an imprint of IGI Global)
701 E. Chocolate Avenue
Hershey PA, USA 17033
Tel: 717-533-8845
Fax: 717-533-8661
E-mail: cust@igi-global.com
Web site: http://www.igi-global.com

Copyright © 2023 by IGI Global. All rights reserved. No part of this publication may be reproduced, stored or distributed in any form or by any means, electronic or mechanical, including photocopying, without written permission from the publisher. Product or company names used in this set are for identification purposes only. Inclusion of the names of the products or companies does not indicate a claim of ownership by IGI Global of the trademark or registered trademark.
   Library of Congress Cataloging-in-Publication Data

Names: Alias, Nor Aziah, 1961- editor. | Syed Aris, Sharipah Ruzaina, 1971-
   editor. | Hashim, Hamimah, 1975- editor.
Title: Cases on responsive and responsible learning in higher education /
   Nor Aziah Alias, Sharipah Ruzaina Syed Aris, and Hamimah Hashim, editors.
Description: Hershey, PA : Information Science Reference, 2023. | Includes
   bibliographical references and index. | Summary: "The book attempts to
   introduce responsive and responsible learning as an upshot to the
   expected and unexpected massive changes in higher education globally.
   Indeed, the acronym VUCA has precisely illustrated the situation in the
   last two years and in many years to come. Higher Education management,
   academics and students are inadvertently diverting their attention from
   a structured three or four year program on campus as the proliferation
   of courses and just in time learning are now being attractively and
   excitingly packaged and offered by other corporations and industry than
   the universities. The premise for the book is a psychologically inclined
   construct, centring on the SELF that is, responsive and responsible
   learning. It extends the notion of self directed learning and heutagogy.
   The book will focus on how the concepts of responsive and responsible
   are translated into practice by the instructors, learning facilitators
   and higher education managers. The book will deal more on the
   practicalities and strategies ; existing frameworks for the 21st century
   learning will be adopted and adapted by the writers. New and appropriate
   technologies will be able to perpetuate and generate both responsive and
   responsible learning. Hence, the book will include aspects of
   technology, learning environment, lifelong, connected learning and also
   policies. A chapter on under represented learners and how they are
   nurtured for responsive and responsible learning is also expected"--
   Provided by publisher.
Identifiers: LCCN 2022039770 (print) | LCCN 2022039771 (ebook) | ISBN
   9781668460764 (hardcover) | ISBN 9781668460801 (paperback) | ISBN
   9781668460771 (ebook)
Subjects: LCSH: Education, Higher--Malaysia. | Educational
   change--Malaysia.
Classification: LCC LA1238 .C37 2023 (print) | LCC LA1238 (ebook) | DDC
   378.595--dc23/eng/20221007
LC record available at https://lccn.loc.gov/2022039770
LC ebook record available at https://lccn.loc.gov/2022039771

This book is published in the IGI Global book series Advances in Higher Education and Professional Development (AHEPD) (ISSN: 2327-6983; eISSN: 2327-6991)

British Cataloguing in Publication Data
A Cataloguing in Publication record for this book is available from the British Library.

All work contributed to this book is new, previously-unpublished material. The views expressed in this book are those of the authors, but not necessarily of the publisher.

For electronic access to this publication, please contact: eresources@igi-global.com.

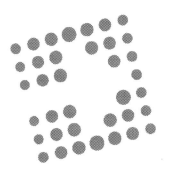

Advances in Higher Education and Professional Development (AHEPD) Book Series

Jared Keengwe
University of North Dakota, USA

ISSN:2327-6983
EISSN:2327-6991

Mission

As world economies continue to shift and change in response to global financial situations, job markets have begun to demand a more highly-skilled workforce. In many industries a college degree is the minimum requirement and further educational development is expected to advance. With these current trends in mind, the **Advances in Higher Education & Professional Development (AHEPD) Book Series** provides an outlet for researchers and academics to publish their research in these areas and to distribute these works to practitioners and other researchers.

AHEPD encompasses all research dealing with higher education pedagogy, development, and curriculum design, as well as all areas of professional development, regardless of focus.

Coverage

- Adult Education
- Assessment in Higher Education
- Career Training
- Coaching and Mentoring
- Continuing Professional Development
- Governance in Higher Education
- Higher Education Policy
- Pedagogy of Teaching Higher Education
- Vocational Education

IGI Global is currently accepting manuscripts for publication within this series. To submit a proposal for a volume in this series, please contact our Acquisition Editors at Acquisitions@igi-global.com or visit: http://www.igi-global.com/publish/.

The Advances in Higher Education and Professional Development (AHEPD) Book Series (ISSN 2327-6983) is published by IGI Global, 701 E. Chocolate Avenue, Hershey, PA 17033-1240, USA, www.igi-global.com. This series is composed of titles available for purchase individually; each title is edited to be contextually exclusive from any other title within the series. For pricing and ordering information please visit http://www.igi-global.com/book-series/advances-higher-education-professional-development/73681. Postmaster: Send all address changes to above address. Copyright © 2023 IGI Global. All rights, including translation in other languages reserved by the publisher. No part of this series may be reproduced or used in any form or by any means – graphics, electronic, or mechanical, including photocopying, recording, taping, or information and retrieval systems – without written permission from the publisher, except for non commercial, educational use, including classroom teaching purposes. The views expressed in this series are those of the authors, but not necessarily of IGI Global.

Titles in this Series

For a list of additional titles in this series, please visit: www.igi-global.com/book-series

The Impact of HEIs on Regional Development Facts and Practices of Collaborative Work With SMEs
Susana Rodrigues (Polytechnic Institute of Leiria, Portugal) and Joaquim Mourato (Polytechnic Institute of Portalegre, Porugal)
Information Science Reference • © 2023 • 315pp • H/C (ISBN: 9781668467015) • US $215.00

Cases on Teacher Development, Personalized Learning, and Upskilling the Workforce
Sriya Chakravarti (Higher Colleges of Technology UAE)
Information Science Reference • © 2023 • 300pp • H/C (ISBN: 9781668455180) • US $215.00

Best Practices and Programmatic Approaches for Mentoring Educational Leaders
Amanda Wilkerson (University of Central Florida, USA) and Shalander Samuels (Kean University, USA)
Information Science Reference • © 2023 • 320pp • H/C (ISBN: 9781668460498) • US $215.00

Global Perspectives on the Internationalization of Higher Education
John D. Branch (University of Michigan, USA) and Mehmet Durnali (Ereğli Faculty of Education, Zonguldak Bülent Ecevit University, Turkey)
Information Science Reference • © 2023 • 335pp • H/C (ISBN: 9781668459294) • US $215.00

Handbook of Research on Revisioning and Reconstructing Higher Education After Global Crises
Shalin Hai-Jew (Kansas State University, USA)
Information Science Reference • © 2023 • 493pp • H/C (ISBN: 9781668459348) • US $270.00

Co-Constructing and Sustaining Service Learning in a Doctoral Program
Rabia Hos (University of Rhode Island, USA) and Brenda Santos (University of Rhode Island, USA)
Information Science Reference • © 2023 • 300pp • H/C (ISBN: 9781668465332) • US $215.00

Elevating Intentional Education Practice in Graduate Programs
Abeni El-Amin (Fort Hays State University, USA & Shenyang Normal University, China)
Information Science Reference • © 2023 • 293pp • H/C (ISBN: 9781668446003) • US $215.00

Handbook of Research on Developments and Future Trends in Transnational Higher Education
Gareth Richard Morris (Perse School Suzhou, China) and Li Li (Exeter University, UK)
Information Science Reference • © 2023 • 499pp • H/C (ISBN: 9781668452264) • US $270.00

701 East Chocolate Avenue, Hershey, PA 17033, USA
Tel: 717-533-8845 x100 • Fax: 717-533-8661
E-Mail: cust@igi-global.com • www.igi-global.com

Table of Contents

Foreword xviii

Preface xix

Acknowledgment xxiii

Section 1
Concept and Facets of Responsive and Responsible Learning

Chapter 1
Postulating Responsive and Responsible Learning.. 1
    Nor Aziah Alias, Universiti Teknologi MARA, Malaysia
    Sharipah Ruzaina Syed-Aris, Universiti Teknologi MARA, Malaysia
    Hamimah Hashim, Universiti Teknologi MARA, Malaysia
    Khalid Ismail Mustafa, Koya University, Iraq

Chapter 2
"Response-Able" Education for Sustainable Employability Aligned With Sustainable
Development Goals: SOARing to Success 15
    Arti Kumar, Independent Researcher, UK

Chapter 3
Responsive and Responsible Learning in the Malaysian Education System: A Game Changer 42
    Sheela Jayabala Krishnan Jayabalan, Universiti Teknologi MARA, Malaysia

Chapter 4
Meaningful Learning Didactic Strategies in Higher Education.. 54
    José G. Vargas-Hernández, Posgraduate and Research Department, Tecnológico Mario
        Molina Unidad Zapopan, Mexico
    Omar C. Vargas-González, Tecnológico Nacional de México, Ciudad Guzmán, Mexico
    Selene Castañeda-Burciaga, Universidad Politécnica de Zacatecas, Mexico
    Adlet D. Kariyev, Kazakh National Women's Teacher Training University, Kazakhstan

Chapter 5
Humanistic Teaching During the Pandemic: Education Beyond the Lesson 73
    Nadia Ainuddin Dahlan, Universiti Teknologi MARA, Malaysia
    Melissa Malik, Universiti Teknologi MARA, Malaysia
    Khadijah Said Hashim, Universiti Teknologi MARA, Malaysia
    Fatin Aliana Mohd Radzi, Universiti Teknologi MARA, Malaysia
    Farhana Wan Yunus, Universiti Teknologi MARA, Malaysia

Chapter 6
Creating a Responsive and Responsible Learning Environment: Bookopolis@UiTM Malaysia 92
    Norshiha Saidin, Universiti Teknologi MARA, Malaysia
    Nur Hidayah Md Yazid, Universiti Teknologi MARA, Malaysia
    Sakinatul Ain Jelani, Universiti Teknologi MARA, Malaysia
    Leele Susana Jamian, Universiti Teknologi MARA, Malaysia

Section 2
Pedagogy and Strategies in Responsive and Responsible Learning

Chapter 7
Collaborative Pedagogy for Global Learners: Adaptive Teaching for Borderless Learning 103
    Malai Zeiti Sheikh Abdul Hamid, Universiti Teknologi Brunei, Brunei
    Khadijah Said Hashim, Universiti Teknologi MARA, Malaysia
    Kriscentti Exzur P. Barcelona, Lourdes College Inc., Cagayan de Oro City, Philippines
    Rene II Mediana Babiera, University of the Immaculate Conception, Philippines

Chapter 8
Engaging Responsive and Responsible Learning Through Collaborative Teaching in the STEM
Classroom 120
    Mawarni Mohamed, Univeristi Teknologi MARA, Malaysia
    Nor Syazwani Mohd Rasid, Universiti Teknologi MARA, Malaysia
    Norezan Ibrahim, Universiti Teknologi MARA, Malaysia
    Padmanabhan Seshaiyer, George Mason University, USA

Chapter 9
Creativity and the Self: A Higher Educational Praxis for Responsive Learning 134
    Mohd Hafnidzam Adzmi, Universiti Teknologi MARA, Malaysia
    Zainuddin Ibrahim, Universiti Teknologi MARA, Malaysia
    Suriati Saidan, Universiti Teknologi MARA, Malaysia

Chapter 10
Songs in the Key of Life: Cultivating the Student qua Artist to Empower Authentic Becoming 144
    Daniel Christopher Blackshields, University College Cork, Ireland

Chapter 11
Cultivating and Nurturing an Empathy-Ready Mindset Through Value-Based Innovation 177
    Serit Banyan, Taylor's University, Malaysia
    Zaim Azizi Bin Abu Bakar, Taylor's University, Malaysia
    Fadhilah Raihan Binti Lokman, Taylor's University, Malaysia

Chapter 12
The Determinants of Potential Volunteering Among Moroccan Students: An Empirical Analysis 198
    Jabrane Amaghouss, Faculty of Law, Economics, and Social Sciences, Cadi Ayyad University, Morocco
    Aomar Ibourk, Faculty of Law, Economics, and Social Sciences, Cadi Ayyad University, Morocco

Chapter 13
Mathematics Preservice Teachers' Responsiveness in Microteaching Using 21st Century Skills 217
    Teoh Sian Hoon, Universiti Teknologi MARA, Malaysia
    Priyadarshini Muthukrishnan, HELP University, Malaysia
    Geetha Subramaniam, SEGi University, Malaysia
    Nor Azah Mohd Rathi, Universiti Teknologi MARA, Malaysia
    Nurshamshida Md Shamsudin, Universiti Teknologi MARA, Malaysia
    Koo Ah Choo, Multimedia University, Malaysia

Chapter 14
Responsive and Responsible Preservice Teacher Reflective Thinking Towards Chemistry for Life 236
    Canan Koçak Altundağ, Hacettepe University, Turkey

Chapter 15
Multiple-Multimodal Skills Through Responsive and Responsible Learning: Audiovisual Media Communications Classifications 256
    Constantinos Nicolaou, Aristotle University of Thessaloniki, Greece

Chapter 16
The Environmental Commitment of Moroccan Students: Measures and Determinants – Case of Cadi Ayyad University 280
    Jabrane Amaghouss, Faculty of Law, Economics, and Social Sciences, Cadi Ayyad University, Morocco
    Younes Elguerch, Faculty of Law, Economics, and Social Sciences, Cadi Ayyad University, Morocco

Chapter 17
Framing Responsive and Responsible Learning in Project-Based Assessment: A Study on the Malaysian General Studies Subject 305
    Aiedah Abdul Khalek, Monash University, Malaysia

Chapter 18
Assessment Strategies in Empowering Self-Regulated Learning in Higher Education: A
Systematic Review 323
    Zuraimi Zakaria, Universiti Teknologi MARA, Malaysia
    Adibah Abdul Latif, Universiti Teknologi Malaysia, Malaysia

Section 3
Related Matters in Responsive and Responsible Learning

Chapter 19
Ethics of Hybrid Learning in Higher Education 339
    Lin Chen, Universiti Putra Malaysia, Malaysia
    Nur Surayyah Madhubala Abdullah, Universiti Putra Malaysia, Malaysia

Chapter 20
Factors to Consider When Moving a Cooperative Academic Literacy Activity Online 360
    Chris Harwood, Sophia University, Japan

Chapter 21
Exploring Lecturer and Student Readiness on Flexible Learning Pathways Toward SDG4 380
    Rafidah Abd Karim, Universiti Teknologi MARA, Malaysia
    Ramlee Mustapha, Sultan Idris Education University, Malaysia

Chapter 22
SoTL for Responsive Teaching: Managing Issues and Challenges 404
    Nurahimah Mohd. Yusoff, Universiti Utara Malaysia, Malaysia
    Aizan Yaacob, Universiti Utara Malaysia, Malaysia

Compilation of References 415

About the Contributors 469

Index 481

Detailed Table of Contents

Foreword xviii

Preface xix

Acknowledgment xxiii

Section 1
Concept and Facets of Responsive and Responsible Learning

Chapter 1
Postulating Responsive and Responsible Learning... 1
    Nor Aziah Alias, Universiti Teknologi MARA, Malaysia
    Sharipah Ruzaina Syed-Aris, Universiti Teknologi MARA, Malaysia
    Hamimah Hashim, Universiti Teknologi MARA, Malaysia
    Khalid Ismail Mustafa, Koya University, Iraq

In the past 10 years, the world witnessed two significant phenomena: the ascent of the fourth industrial revolution and the breakout of the COVID-19 pandemic. The two events posed different challenges, but as the world pulls through, one valuable lesson for educators prevails. The pandemic together with a heightened higher education readiness for technology ushers in a new brand of learners and learning. Learners and learning are inherently active. Nurturing a culture of responsiveness is the current narrative as we navigate the bends and nooks of change and uncertainty. This chapter serves as a prelude to the other chapters in this book. It helps redefine and set the context for responsiveness in (individual) learning and learning delivery. Since learners are learning in a multifaceted realm and the aim of learning goes beyond the academic transcript, being responsible is indisputably necessary. The chapter is written with an author from a different end of the globe to signify the most significant way forward for educators around the world (i.e., to work collaboratively).

Chapter 2
"Response-Able" Education for Sustainable Employability Aligned With Sustainable
Development Goals: SOARing to Success 15
    Arti Kumar, Independent Researcher, UK

'The SOAR model' (as it has come to be used in the UK and abroad) is in effect a conceptual metamodel that scaffolds pedagogy, andragogy, and heutagogy in its design and delivery of response-able, equitable, and empowering learning for all students. SOAR invokes personally meaningful interconnections within and between the dimensions of self, opportunity, aspirations, and results through inbuilt requirements for self-reflection, action and interaction, research, analysis, and synthesis. It is inclusive while it values diversity, and its practical methodology enables all learners to become response-able while developing employability and sustainability for effective functioning in the diverse contexts of learning, work, and life in a changing, challenging world. This chapter shows how SOAR integrates and implements an 'inside-out' systemic approach that teachers can adapt to deliver several key and currently siloed strategic agendas under one umbrella, thereby encompassing the much broader agenda of response-able transformational education that is sorely needed in contemporary times.

Chapter 3
Responsive and Responsible Learning in the Malaysian Education System: A Game Changer.......... 42
Sheela Jayabala Krishnan Jayabalan, Universiti Teknologi MARA, Malaysia

Responsive and responsible learning connects the learner to the content. It is grounded in the teacher's understanding of the subjects taught and connects with each student to not only comprehend the subject but also apply the knowledge to real-life situations. Responsive and responsible teaching should help students build on prior learning to develop skills, mold attitudes, and cultivate independent learning. The pedagogies of teaching, therefore, should be attuned to a student-centered learning approach instead of teacher-centered, which is the practice in most educational institutions around the world including Malaysia. However, the process of teaching should start with early childhood education. Only then can the effectiveness of nurturing students to be independent learners and thinkers, which is the foundation of responsive and responsible learning, be achieved. This chapter, therefore, discusses the weaknesses of the current teaching and learning approaches (pedagogies) practiced in Malaysia and the reasons why a change is desirable (i.e., a game changer).

Chapter 4
Meaningful Learning Didactic Strategies in Higher Education... 54
José G. Vargas-Hernández, Posgraduate and Research Department, Tecnológico Mario Molina Unidad Zapopan, Mexico
Omar C. Vargas-González, Tecnológico Nacional de México, Ciudad Guzmán, Mexico
Selene Castañeda-Burciaga, Universidad Politécnica de Zacatecas, Mexico
Adlet D. Kariyev, Kazakh National Women's Teacher Training University, Kazakhstan

This work aims to analyze and explain the didactic strategies used to achieve meaningful learning. It begins under the assumption that if meaningful learning is created and students are given freedom and confidence, they can find their own answers and develop their knowledge both in the classroom and in practical life. The method used is the analytical-descriptive one of the reviews of the literature of the main authors who have given rise to this approach, its elements, and the didactic strategies used. It is concluded that the design and implementation of didactic strategies focused on meaningful learning with the application of active didactic methodologies and strategies in meaningful learning processes depending on the context in which it takes place obtains better results in the training of professionals.

Chapter 5
Humanistic Teaching During the Pandemic: Education Beyond the Lesson.. 73
Nadia Ainuddin Dahlan, Universiti Teknologi MARA, Malaysia
Melissa Malik, Universiti Teknologi MARA, Malaysia
Khadijah Said Hashim, Universiti Teknologi MARA, Malaysia
Fatin Aliana Mohd Radzi, Universiti Teknologi MARA, Malaysia
Farhana Wan Yunus, Universiti Teknologi MARA, Malaysia

During the COVID-19 crisis, teaching and learning activities were largely conducted online through open and distance learning (ODL). As a result, educators and students lacked the personal warmth and emotional support usually found in face-to-face classes, which affected the quality of the teaching and learning process. Therefore, what could educators do to facilitate the teaching and learning process during the pandemic? This chapter features narratives on humanistic practices in teaching that were carried out during the pandemic by five university lecturers. The narratives shed light on how they embedded humanistic elements in either one or several of these aspects of teaching: delivery, content, consultation, and assessment. Their pedagogical approaches indicate that education is not a rigid domain, but it can be extended beyond the four walls of the classroom and executed from the sincere heart.

Chapter 6
Creating a Responsive and Responsible Learning Environment: Bookopolis@UiTM Malaysia......... 92
    Norshiha Saidin, Universiti Teknologi MARA, Malaysia
    Nur Hidayah Md Yazid, Universiti Teknologi MARA, Malaysia
    Sakinatul Ain Jelani, Universiti Teknologi MARA, Malaysia
    Leele Susana Jamian, Universiti Teknologi MARA, Malaysia

New ideas about learning spaces offer a significant opportunity for higher education to transform learning. The creation of a reading-friendly space and a book exchange program, 'Bookopolis', offered UiTM Foundation Centre an opportunity to encourage active learning and create a responsive learning environment. 'Bookopolis' fulfilled the reading needs of the students in an economic and innovative way. Creativity and necessity provided the impetus to transform a non-functional space into an accessible and exciting area for reading and discussions. A flexible system of self-check in and out inculcates the values of trust and integrity, thus heightening a sense of responsibility. The redesigned learning space optimizes the current learning theory to support and extend students' learning environment. This chapter shares the journey and experience in creating a responsive learning space, encouraging a reading culture and literacy skills in a demanding one-year foundation program.

Section 2
Pedagogy and Strategies in Responsive and Responsible Learning

Chapter 7
Collaborative Pedagogy for Global Learners: Adaptive Teaching for Borderless Learning 103
    Malai Zeiti Sheikh Abdul Hamid, Universiti Teknologi Brunei, Brunei
    Khadijah Said Hashim, Universiti Teknologi MARA, Malaysia
    Kriscentti Exzur P. Barcelona, Lourdes College Inc., Cagayan de Oro City, Philippines
    Rene II Mediana Babiera, University of the Immaculate Conception, Philippines

Collaborative pedagogy is one of the teaching approaches that focuses on students' engagement and teamwork in classroom activities to develop critical skill sets such as socio-emotional skills, intercultural communication skills, leadership skills, and problem-solving skills. This study explores students' experiences and reflections on collaborative pedagogy. The objectives of this study are to (1) identity the challenges of online learning, (2) uncover students' insights on collaborative learning, (3) explore significance of collaborative learning, and (4) examine implementation of collaborative pedagogy. This study employed a qualitative design involving 11 college/university students from three different ASEAN countries: Philippines (n=6), Brunei (n=2), and Malaysia (n=2). The primary findings revealed themes including lack of focus and social isolation as the main challenges faced by students. The implication of this study is crucial to optimise learning through the practice of collaborative pedagogy.

Chapter 8
Engaging Responsive and Responsible Learning Through Collaborative Teaching in the STEM Classroom 120
    Mawarni Mohamed, Univeristi Teknologi MARA, Malaysia
    Nor Syazwani Mohd Rasid, Universiti Teknologi MARA, Malaysia
    Norezan Ibrahim, Universiti Teknologi MARA, Malaysia
    Padmanabhan Seshaiyer, George Mason University, USA

This chapter explores how the elements of responsive and responsible learning were adopted in the first STEM education classroom through collaborative teaching with external experts in a public university in Malaysia. The objectives for the introduction of the course were to enable students to apply the knowledge of mathematical and pedagogical aspects in the teaching of science and mathematics to solve problems in a scientific and systematic manner and to demonstrate the ability to seek new knowledge independently. Three class projects involving collaborators fulfilled 8 weeks of lectures. These included Training of Trainers (ToT), Green Energy Project – Solar Panel and the University Centre for Innovative Delivery and Learning Development (CIDL) focused on Internet of Things (IoT) content. Collaborative teaching in the STEM education classroom has successfully served the specific technical requirements of industry using the design-thinking framework into the university classroom setting.

Chapter 9
Creativity and the Self: A Higher Educational Praxis for Responsive Learning 134
    Mohd Hafnidzam Adzmi, Universiti Teknologi MARA, Malaysia
    Zainuddin Ibrahim, Universiti Teknologi MARA, Malaysia
    Suriati Saidan, Universiti Teknologi MARA, Malaysia

This chapter conceptualizes the approach to nurturing creativity in higher education. The chapter begins by describing the creative self based on personality theories discussed in the creativity research literature. This chapter then engages in the discussion of the contradiction between the concept of the creative self and some aspects of the current educational policies in Malaysia, in particular the implementation of outcome-based education (OBE) as outlined by the Malaysian Qualifications Agency (MQA). This chapter ends with the discussion of proposing the activity theory as a framework for creative education.

Chapter 10
Songs in the Key of Life: Cultivating the Student qua Artist to Empower Authentic Becoming 144
    Daniel Christopher Blackshields, University College Cork, Ireland

Twenty-first century uncertainties privilege creative action. Creativity is an emergent property of dynamic relationships between individuals and their environment. Adopting a structured uncertainty curriculum design embodying the student qua artist and classroom qua creative recording studio, students experience actionable uncertainty. Such experiences foster intrapersonal insights. Giving expression to emerging self-concepts cultivates students' authentic voices, nurturing investment in care for who they are, who they are endeavouring to become, and to perceive their potentiality as they transition from university.

Chapter 11
Cultivating and Nurturing an Empathy-Ready Mindset Through Value-Based Innovation 177
    Serit Banyan, Taylor's University, Malaysia
    Zaim Azizi Bin Abu Bakar, Taylor's University, Malaysia
    Fadhilah Raihan Binti Lokman, Taylor's University, Malaysia

The Social Innovation Project focuses on developing and implementing innovative solutions to impact students and the community positively. In this module, students are engaged in an interdisciplinary and collaborative setting to identify opportunities in today's global and local environments that create and capture values. The project-based learning activities for this module emphasize situated learning, which deals with authentic and unique real-world issues. Students will be involved in collaborative decision-making and problem-solving as they have to discuss, consult, collaborate, and solve the problem to provide services or create a product for the desired community. After taking this module, students are able to enhance their creativity and instill values, such as leadership, teamwork, communication, and interpersonal skills, among students through the completion of the group's project.

Chapter 12
The Determinants of Potential Volunteering Among Moroccan Students: An Empirical Analysis... 198
> *Jabrane Amaghouss, Faculty of Law, Economics, and Social Sciences, Cadi Ayyad University, Morocco*
> *Aomar Ibourk, Faculty of Law, Economics, and Social Sciences, Cadi Ayyad University, Morocco*

The aim of this chapter is to measure the potential for volunteering and to analyze and understand the determinants of participation in volunteering. The data comes from a survey of students enrolled at two open-access institutions of the Cadi Ayyad University in Morocco. Using Tobit model, which combines both continuous and discrete variables, the results show a high potential supply of volunteering compared to the supply actually realized and a high potential supply of female students compared to that of male students. The potential volunteering supply comes much more from students from a low socioeconomic status as measured by the level of education of the parents. Student members of associations are predisposed to perform voluntary tasks, and this offer increases with seniority in the association. Age is positively correlated with the potential supply of volunteering. The motivational framework can strengthen the potential supply of volunteering.

Chapter 13
Mathematics Preservice Teachers' Responsiveness in Microteaching Using 21st Century Skills..... 217
> *Teoh Sian Hoon, Universiti Teknologi MARA, Malaysia*
> *Priyadarshini Muthukrishnan, HELP University, Malaysia*
> *Geetha Subramaniam, SEGi University, Malaysia*
> *Nor Azah Mohd Rathi, Universiti Teknologi MARA, Malaysia*
> *Nurshamshida Md Shamsudin, Universiti Teknologi MARA, Malaysia*
> *Koo Ah Choo, Multimedia University, Malaysia*

The development of 21st century abilities necessitates satisfying students' needs. Preservice teachers may find it difficult to meet the criteria. Responsive teaching needs to take precedence to effectively meet student needs. As a result, it is essential to consider how preservice teachers view this issue. This chapter first sets to highlight some of the issues preservice teachers face during microteaching in a mathematics classroom. Next, it looks at possible ways to promote responsiveness by using 21st century skills. It further discusses some solutions, suggestions, and recommendations based on the highlighted issues. Specifically, this chapter aims to identify ways for preservice teachers to contribute to teaching mathematics in a more creative way based on their responsiveness in microteaching. Finally, input is provided to educators on how to meet the output of responsive teaching by applying classroom microteaching strategies.

Chapter 14
Responsive and Responsible Preservice Teacher Reflective Thinking Towards Chemistry for
Life 236
    Canan Koçak Altundağ, Hacettepe University, Turkey

This study aims to determine the relationship between preservice teachers' responsive and responsible learning skills attained in their university education along with their reflective thinking tendencies. The participants of this research were preservice teachers from the Education Faculty at Hacettepe University. Data were collected through the reflective thinking scale, and metaphors of preservice teachers about chemistry of daily life were collected through a diagram prepared according to the lotus flower technique. Both qualitative content analysis and statistical analysis were employed. It was found that most of the preservice teachers have basic reflective thinking at least at the intermediate level (habitual action, understanding, reflection, and critical reflection). This research also illustrates the need for practices such as responsive teaching and differentiated instructional practices. However, the limited studies on responsive and responsible learning poses a significant problem for chemistry education.

Chapter 15
Multiple-Multimodal Skills Through Responsive and Responsible Learning: Audiovisual Media
Communications Classifications 256
    Constantinos Nicolaou, Aristotle University of Thessaloniki, Greece

This chapter investigates and highlights the multiple-multimodal skills from and through literature review that can be acquired in the educational path using audiovisual media technologies and audiovisual content (henceforth, audiovisual media communications) through technology-enhanced learning perspective. Specifically, an attempt is made to present how audiovisual media communications help both learners and educators to achieve these multiple-multimodal skills under the lens of responsive and responsible learning. The chapter also presents and comments indicative ways in which audiovisual media communications can be used in technology-supported learning environments to support teaching, professional learning, and effective educator-learner communication. Nowadays society is highly visualized and requires all of us, in addition to being receptive to the continual use of audiovisual media communications, to somehow maintain a positive outlook for every emerging cutting-edge innovation, and to possess a plethora of skills in order to survive in this digital technological world.

Chapter 16
The Environmental Commitment of Moroccan Students: Measures and Determinants – Case of
Cadi Ayyad University 280
    Jabrane Amaghouss, Faculty of Law, Economics, and Social Sciences, Cadi Ayyad
        University, Morocco
    Younes Elguerch, Faculty of Law, Economics, and Social Sciences, Cadi Ayyad University,
        Morocco

The aim of the chapter is to investigate the factors that motivate Moroccan students to engage in pro-environmental behavior. In this study, the authors tried, within the framework of the theory of the motivation towards protection, to measure the degree of the environmental commitment and to explain the pro-environmental behavior of the students of Cadi Ayyad University Marrakesh, the FLESS. In this case, the authors took a sample of 415 students on which they proceeded to an analysis of their pro-environmental behavior through structural equation modeling. The major findings of this study support the notion that students' pro-environmental conduct is positively influenced by their environmental attitudes. Additionally, the escalating severity of environmental issues motivates individuals to accept environmentally friendly behaviors. Given the significance of environmental attitudes, it is possible to raise the likelihood of pro-environmental activities among students by using strategies and incentives aimed at enhancing their environmental attitudes.

Chapter 17
Framing Responsive and Responsible Learning in Project-Based Assessment: A Study on the Malaysian General Studies Subject 305
    Aiedah Abdul Khalek, Monash University, Malaysia

This chapter aims to reimagine learning and teaching general studies by embedding responsive and responsible learning elements in the project-based assessment. The author unfolds the educator's reflective experiences in carrying out the assessment and the student's experiences in completing the project. Data are collected through the educators' reflective journals and students' evaluations, including students' evaluation reports and qualitative feedback. The findings include a discussion on strategies and challenges in curating responsive and responsible learning in a project-based assessment, and how the project-based assessment creates an affective and effective learning environment. This study aspires to serve as evidence-based practice and reflections to develop responsive and responsible learning in the project-based assessment.

Chapter 18
Assessment Strategies in Empowering Self-Regulated Learning in Higher Education: A Systematic Review 323
    Zuraimi Zakaria, Universiti Teknologi MARA, Malaysia
    Adibah Abdul Latif, Universiti Teknologi Malaysia, Malaysia

Self-regulated learning (SRL) is essential to higher education. An increasing body of knowledge has attested to the significance of assessment activities in promoting SRL strategies. However, the influence of assessment practices on SRL in higher education is considered a neglected research area. Aimed to fill this gap, this paper presents a systematic review of six peer-reviewed articles focusing on the effective employment of assessment strategies to promote SRL. Five key features of the compelling interplay between assessment activities and SRL strategies were noted in the review: feedback-driven, discussion-focused, specific assessment designs that provide continuous SRL opportunities, and learning contexts that influence motivation and purpose, with educators' assessment competency as a pre-requisite for successful implementation.

Section 3
Related Matters in Responsive and Responsible Learning

Chapter 19
Ethics of Hybrid Learning in Higher Education 339
    Lin Chen, Universiti Putra Malaysia, Malaysia
    Nur Surayyah Madhubala Abdullah, Universiti Putra Malaysia, Malaysia

The issue of unethical behavior in academic work is more severe in hybrid learning in the context of responsive and responsible learning. This study conducted a qualitative research method and a case study design. It used the semi-structured interview to determine the college students' understanding and motivations for unethical behavior in academic work in hybrid learning, in the context of responsive and responsible learning. The findings showed that participants noticed unethical behavior contrary to ethical norms but could not come up with a sound definition of unethical behavior in academic work. Participants pointed out some types of unethical behavior. Still, they were mainly unsure about the different types of unethical behavior. Besides, nine categories of motivations for students' unethical behavior were revealed.

Chapter 20
Factors to Consider When Moving a Cooperative Academic Literacy Activity Online 360
    Chris Harwood, Sophia University, Japan

This chapter focuses on cooperative learning in an undergraduate English for academic purposes context and discusses the pedagogical factors that educators should consider when moving a face-to-face cooperative learning activity online. In the discussion, a text-based academic literacy activity is used to illustrate how the principles of cooperative learning should incorporate pedagogic concepts and approaches from group-based online learning to facilitate cooperative learning online. Factors within task structure, and the importance of teaching presence and social presence in fostering cognitive presence in an online learning environment are discussed. Then, recommendations for how to cultivate positive interdependence, promotive interaction, individual accountability, interpersonal and small group skills, and group processing in online activities are proposed.

Chapter 21
Exploring Lecturer and Student Readiness on Flexible Learning Pathways Toward SDG4 380
    Rafidah Abd Karim, Universiti Teknologi MARA, Malaysia
    Ramlee Mustapha, Sultan Idris Education University, Malaysia

This chapter presents a study about flexible learning pathways towards SDG4 in Malaysian higher education. The purpose of the study was to explore the lecturers' perception on flexible teaching and the students' readiness for flexible learning pathways to achieve the Sustainable Development Goal 4 (SDG4) in Malaysian higher education institutions (HEIs). The study employed a survey method. An online questionnaire was designed and distributed to a total of 167 students and 60 lecturers from selected higher education institutions in Malaysia. Data were analysed using the SPPS version 27, and the findings were presented using descriptive statistics. The study found that the tertiary students were ready for flexible learning pathways. In terms of teaching, the lecturers agreed that they have implemented flexible teaching modes. Based on the empirical findings, several suggestions for future research are presented.

Chapter 22
SoTL for Responsive Teaching: Managing Issues and Challenges... 404
    Nurahimah Mohd. Yusoff, Universiti Utara Malaysia, Malaysia
    Aizan Yaacob, Universiti Utara Malaysia, Malaysia

While many studies have acknowledged the positive impact of the scholarship of teaching and learning, also known as SoTL, issues and challenges in implementing SoTL at public universities, particularly in Malaysia, are not fully understood. Building on this gap, it is felt that there is a need to conduct a study on the SoTL grant recipients in Universiti Utara Malaysia (UUM). This study chose the samples who could provide "rich and relevant information" to answer the research questions. The findings include issues related to (1) time constraints, (2) understanding SoTL concept, (3) SoTL inquiry, (4) student learning, (5) publication as an output, (6) difficulty in convincing others to change, (7) workload and (8) reflective practice. It is recommended that more trainings be given to SoTL recipients from various discipline areas, to ensure completion of the project and continuous mentoring be provided for them to ensure sustainability of SoTL. SoTL in UUM, it can be concluded, has empowered academicians in pursuing their academic endeavor.

Compilation of References 415

About the Contributors 469

Index 481

Foreword

The concept of responsive and responsible learning has not been rigorously deliberated but has garnered interest in post pandemic higher education where voice, choice and personalized learning proliferate with the help of the internet and advanced technologies. It gives me immense pleasure to write a short foreword to this book, *Cases on Responsive and Responsible Learning in Higher Education,* co-edited by three innovative practitioners and researchers in curriculum and delivery. In the past two years, new forms of learning have surfaced; efforts made to keep abreast of the changing landscape of our education must indeed be valued and supported.

I am especially impressed with one feature of the collection of cases and chapters in this book which is the collaborative case-writing by authors from various parts of the world. This illustrates our common concerns, as well as the possibility of arriving at a common solution to educational problems despite our geographical and cultural context. The pandemic has taught us well. Working collaboratively with a culture of responsiveness and heightened global awareness is the way forward. Overall, the chapters and cases are written by authors from Malaysia, Brunei, the Philippines, Japan, Turkey, Greece, Ireland, Mexico, Morocco, Republic of Kazakhstan, Iraq, Ireland, United Kingdom, and the United States of America. I applaud the editors who have successfully put together chapters that deliberate on the concepts, pedagogical strategies, assessments, delivery practices that can be emulated, and concerns surrounding the notion of responsive and responsible learning.

Responsive and responsible learning may not be a totally new concept but its application in higher education requires a clearly defined framework that encompasses the learners, the instructors, and the learning environment. What are the attributes of a responsive and responsible learner? What does a responsive learning environment entail? How does the role of the instructor change (or not)? In the wake of a more advanced internet capability, AI and mixed realities, students have access to tools and devices that instigate learning beyond the textbook and the walls of the lecture halls on campus. The skills attained through exhilarating learning experiences such as collaborative learning, volunteerism, global learning, involvement in social innovation projects and many more become the pivotal point of exploration in most of the cases presented. In addition, a few chapters are written to highlight related concerns such as ethics of hybrid learning and reflective practice among instructors.

I feel honored and privileged to contribute to this book. I thank the editors for allowing me to briefly share my thoughts on the subject matter and to include me in the production of such valuable academic work.

All the best!

Wan Zuhainis Saad
Department of Higher Education, Ministry of Higher Education, Malaysia

Preface

We take great pleasure in introducing *Cases on Responsible and Responsive Learning in Higher Education* as a response to the unprecedented pandemic related education experiences and the emergence of the VUCA (Volatile, Uncertain, Complex, Ambiguous) and the BANI (Brittle, Anxious, Non-Linear, Incomprehensible) world. The book provides us, the editors and the authors, the opportunity to reframe the nature of learning in the light of post pandemic higher education and the task of nurturing future change-ready graduates. We believe it is in fact, the right time to re-evaluate the physical classroom-based, didactic teacher-know all teaching and to restore learning that heavily focuses on students' voice, experience, spiritual strength, learner centeredness, and not forgetting global, society and environment focus.

This book was conceptualized and developed following the editors' involvement in managing a large Malaysian university teaching and learning program from the onset of the pandemic until 2022. It introduces responsive and responsible learning as an upshot to the expected and unexpected massive changes in higher education globally. It specifically aims to highlight learning that has taken an even more personalized stance and how instructors and academic managers support the change through various policies, strategies, and activities.

The premise for the book is a psychologically inclined construct, that is, responsive and responsible learning. It extends the notion of self-determined learning and heutagogy. The book focuses on how the concepts of responsive and responsible are translated into practice by the instructors, learning facilitators and higher education managers. The book deals more on the practicalities and strategies ; both new and existing frameworks for learning in higher education are adopted and adapted by the writers. The book also includes include aspects of technology, assessments, learning environment, meaningful and connected learning and also scholarship of teaching.

There are several approaches taken by authors in presenting the chapters in this book, most of whom presented well conducted research findings while others deal with a more conceptual treatment of the theme. However, all of them propounded a more enriching learning experience for the students. The book is unique in the sense that it does not dwell on learning that occurs in a structured academic environment alone. As we probe deeper into the notion of being responsive and responsible for one's own learning, we do not ignore the instructors and the context in which the learning takes place. The chapter by Saidin et al. for instance, illustrates the importance of setting up a flexible learning space that supports responsive and responsible learning.

The rest of the book deals mainly with the dimensions of responsive and responsible learning; in particular, notions of empathy, collaboration, peer learning, partnership, SDG, volunteerism and global learning are explicated the chapters. This book is targeted for higher learning educators; the different experiences that go beyond the four walls of the college lecture halls promulgated by the authors from different parts of the world make this book a good reference in designing for responsive and responsible learning. Chapters are also written collaboratively across countries; this signifies the universality of our principles and practices as we strive to attain a common goal – to educate and to do it well in a new demanding era.

ORGANIZATION OF THE BOOK

The cases in the book are arranged according to three foci: (1) Deliberations on the concept of responsive and responsible Learning, (2) Pedagogies and strategies in nurturing responsive and responsible Learning, and (3) Issues and matters related to responsive and responsible Learning.

In the early part of the book, the authors introduce contextual and conceptual matters that inform responsive and responsible learning. A preliminary discussion on the different elements that make up responsive and responsible learning such as agency, agility, mindfulness, connectedness, resourcefulness, active and seamless learning, and regulation of learning is incorporated at the beginning of the book. The introductory chapter also sets the construct within the currently used terms such as responsive education and responsive teaching. This will help the readers comprehend the notion-its similarities and differences to current concepts being used.

Kumar in her chapter proposes a conceptual metamodel that scaffolds pedagogy, andragogy and heutagogy in its design and delivery of response-able, equitable and empowering learning for all students. SOAR invokes personally meaningful interconnections within and between the dimensions of Self, Opportunity, Aspirations and Results (SOAR). Jayabalan poses reasons why a change is now desirable i.e., a game changer that promotes responsive and responsible teaching that should help students build on prior learning to develop skills, mold attitudes, and cultivate independent learning. Her concern is independence.

Vargas-Hernández and team explain didactic strategies used to achieve meaningful learning. The chapter is based on the assumption that meaningful learning is created if students are given freedom and confidence, they can find their own answers and develop their knowledge, both in the classroom and in practical life. Freedom and independence play a pertinent role in shaping the responsive and responsible learner.

Ainudin et al. illustrates pandemic influenced teaching that embed humanistic elements in either one or several of these aspects of teaching - delivery, content, consultation, and assessment. Their pedagogical approaches indicate that education is not a rigid domain, but it can be extended beyond the four walls of the classroom and be executed from the sincere heart.

Saidin et al. share the journey and experience in creating a responsive learning space, encouraging a reading culture and literacy skills in a demanding one-year foundation program. They demonstrate how creativity and necessity provided the impetus to transform a non-functional space into an accessible and exciting area for reading and discussions. They describe a flexible system of self-check-in and out that inculcates the values of trust and integrity, thus heightening a sense of responsibility.

The second part of the book consists of cases on further strategies to promote responsive and responsible learning. Sheikh Abdul Hamid and authors from three countries espouse collaborative pedagogy as one of the teaching approaches which focuses on the importance of students' engagement and teamwork in classroom activities, learning tasks or projects. A similar practice is described by Mohamed et al., who explore how the elements of responsive and responsible learning were adopted in the first STEM

Preface

education classroom through collaborative teaching with external experts. These two chapters illustrate learning that can be easily designed to incorporate experiences in a global classroom. The innovative teaching approach brings a paradigm shift to classroom delivery and it helps students to explore different worldviews, cultures and life experiences, globally and boundlessly.

In the light of the student attributes and competencies, the chapters that ensue focus on the learner dimensions. Adzmi, et al. conceptualize the approach to nurturing creativity in higher education. They propose a framework for creative education and relate creativity and self as a higher educational Praxis for Responsive Learning.

Blackshields adopts a structured uncertainty curriculum design embodying the student qua artist and classroom qua creative recording studio students experience. Such experiences foster intrapersonal insights. Giving expression to emerging self-concepts cultivates students' authentic voices, nurturing investment in care for who they are, who they are endeavoring to become and to perceive their potentiality as they transition from university.

Banyan and team on other hand, promotes social innovations through which students are engaged in an interdisciplinary and collaborative setting to identify opportunities in today's global and local environments that create and capture values. In lieu of nurturing responsible learners, Amaghouss and Ibourk analyze and seek to understand the determinants of participation in volunteering. In their chapter, Teoh et al sets to highlight some of the issues preservice teachers face during microteaching in a mathematics classroom. They also look at possible ways to promote responsiveness by using 21st Century Skills.

Altundag reports preservice teachers' responsive and responsible learning skills attained in their university education along with their reflective thinking tendencies. This is indeed an important attribute of responsive and responsible learning. Being able to reflect and act is the mark of a responsive learner. This is further brought forward by Amaghouss and Elguerch who investigate the factors that motivate students to engage in pro-environmental behavior. They measure the degree of environmental commitment and explain the pro-environmental behavior of the students within the framework of motivation theory.

Earlier in chapter 16, Nicolaou stipulates how audiovisual media communications help both learners and educators acquire multiple-multimodal skills under the lens of responsive and responsible learning. The chapter presents ways in which audiovisual media communications can be used in technology-supported learning environments to support teaching, professional learning, and effective educator-learner communication.

Assessments play an important role in validating responsive and responsible learning. In their systematic review, Zakaria and Abdul-Latif highlighted the importance of self-regulated learning which is also a feature of responsive and responsible learning. They noted the interplay between assessment activities and SRL strategies viz feedback-driven, discussion-focused, specific assessment designs that provide continuous SRL opportunities, and learning contexts that influence motivation and purpose, with educators' assessment competency as a pre-requisite for successful implementation.

Abdul Khalek reimagines learning and teaching General Studies by embedding responsive and responsible learning elements in the project-based assessment. The author unfolds the educator's reflective experiences in carrying out the assessment and the student's experiences in completing the project.

The third section of the book discusses issues and matters related to the provision of responsive teaching and learning. The chapters on ethics in hybrid learning and Moving a Cooperative Academic Literacy Activity Online echo the less conventional teaching stipulated in the earlier chapters. Going online and/or hybrid is very much the way forward in perpetuating responsive teaching and learning. Lin Chen and Abdullah used semi-structured interview to determine the college students' understanding and motivations for unethical behavior in academic work in hybrid learning in the context of responsive and responsible learning. In a more positive light, Harwood shares ways to cultivate positive interdependence, promotive interaction, individual accountability, interpersonal and small group skills, and group processing in online activities.

Further deliberations on flexible learning pathways towards Sustainable Development Goals (SDG4) in Higher Education are made by Abdul Karim and Mustapha in Chapter 22. The authors studied the readiness of both students and the lecturers, and found tertiary students were ready for flexible learning pathways. The lecturers they surveyed have, in fact, implemented flexible teaching modes. This signifies responsive teaching among lecturers who are aware of the changes necessary in delivering post pandemic higher education.

Educator's reflective practice is the focus of the last chapter on issues and challenges in implementing SoTL (scholarship of teaching and learning) written by Mohd. Yusoff, and Yaacob. In order to promote students' reflective experience, educators need to be trained first. They found issues related to (1) Time constraints, (2) Understanding SoTL concept, (3) SoTL inquiry, (4) Student learning, (5) Short term grant, (6) Publication as an output, (7) Difficulty in convincing others to change, and (8) Workload.

The chapters give numerous accounts of responsive and responsible learning, responsive teaching, and responsive learning environment. Nurturing learners to be responsive and responsible in a challenging world is the mainstay of the book. Designing learning experiences and driving the learning process that goes beyond the conventional textbook based, on-campus learning is the way forward as educators and learners navigate a progressive world with ubiquitous technology. Readers who are researchers will benefit from the evidence-based reports while practitioners will find the many facets discussed an interesting mix to be implemented in their own context. We foresee the book will serve as a guide as we move into a less conventional, more dynamic era .

Thank you.

Nor Aziah Alias
Universiti Teknologi MARA, Malaysia

Sharipah Ruzaina Syed-Aris
Universiti Teknologi MARA, Malaysia

Hamimah Hashim
Universiti Teknologi MARA, Malaysia

Acknowledgment

We would like to acknowledge the time and effort spent by the reviewers listed below who have worked to ensure chapters written are of quality and within the scope of the book.

1. Adzura Elier Ahmad
2. Elia Md Johar
3. Haida Umiera Hashim
4. Ika Camelia
5. Lina Mursyidah Hamzah
6. Maftuhah Damio
7. Munirah Mohd Izam
8. Nabilah Abdullah
9. Nik Mastura Nik Ismail Azlan
10. Norazah Abdul Aziz
11. Nurizah Md Ngadiran
12. Rohaya Abdul Wahab
13. Roslinda Alias
14. Sharifah Muzlia Syed Mustafa
15. Sorhaila Latip-Yusoph

We would also like to thank the authors and co-authors who have assumed the role of peer reviewers and have immensely contributed to the success of the book.

Special thanks to the members of the editorial advisory board for assisting us with the chapter reviews and supporting us in completing the book.

Thank you

Editorial Advisory Board

Handoko, *Universiti Andalas, Indonesia*
N. B. Jumani, *International Islamic University, Pakistan*
Sherouk J. Kadhm, *E-Institute for 21st Century Skills, Germany*
Senol Orakci, *Aksaray University, Turkey*
Vandana Tulsidas Veeraragoo, *Mauritius Institute of Education, Mauritius*

Section 1
Concept and Facets of Responsive and Responsible Learning

Chapter 1
Postulating Responsive and Responsible Learning

Nor Aziah Alias
https://orcid.org/0000-0002-6405-1400
Universiti Teknologi MARA, Malaysia

Sharipah Ruzaina Syed-Aris
Universiti Teknologi MARA, Malaysia

Hamimah Hashim
Universiti Teknologi MARA, Malaysia

Khalid Ismail Mustafa
Koya University, Iraq

EXECUTIVE SUMMARY

In the past 10 years, the world witnessed two significant phenomena: the ascent of the fourth industrial revolution and the breakout of the COVID-19 pandemic. The two events posed different challenges, but as the world pulls through, one valuable lesson for educators prevails. The pandemic together with a heightened higher education readiness for technology ushers in a new brand of learners and learning. Learners and learning are inherently active. Nurturing a culture of responsiveness is the current narrative as we navigate the bends and nooks of change and uncertainty. This chapter serves as a prelude to the other chapters in this book. It helps redefine and set the context for responsiveness in (individual) learning and learning delivery. Since learners are learning in a multifaceted realm and the aim of learning goes beyond the academic transcript, being responsible is indisputably necessary. The chapter is written with an author from a different end of the globe to signify the most significant way forward for educators around the world (i.e., to work collaboratively).

DOI: 10.4018/978-1-6684-6076-4.ch001

INTRODUCTION

In the past ten years, the world witnessed two significant phenomena: the ascent of the fourth industrial revolution and the breakout of the Covid 19 pandemic. The two events posed different challenges but as the world pulls through, one valuable lesson for educators prevails. The pandemic together with a heightened higher education readiness for technology ushers in a new brand of learners and learning. Learners and learning are inherently, active. Nurturing a culture of responsiveness is the current narrative as we navigate the bends and nooks of change and uncertainty. This chapter serves as a prelude to the other chapters in this book. It helps redefine and set the context for responsiveness in (individual) learning and learning delivery. Since learners are learning in a multifaceted realm and the aim of learning goes beyond the academic transcript, being responsible is indisputably necessary.

Why the Need for This Chapter?

Learners are currently learning and are expected to thrive in a VUCA (volatile, uncertain, complex, ambiguous) and BANI (Brittle, Anxious, Non-Linear, Incomprehensible) world once they stepped out of the campus regimes. They must be responsive, responsible, and resilient enough to navigate swift and amorphous changes. This chapter puts forward the attributes of responsive and responsible learners and how these learners strategize and flourish in their learning environment. It will focus mainly on the concepts of responsive and responsible in the context of learning, post pandemic and in future endeavours. The chapter will begin with discussing the two terms and proceeds to highlight the characteristics that define responsive and responsible learning. Responsive education, responsive learning environment and responsive teaching will be discussed in tandem to provide a bigger picture. The chapter then briefly relates responsive and responsible learning to existing related theories, in particular, heutagogy and self-determined learning. Recent student and teaching cases related on responsive and responsible learning will be embedded to provide clarity to the concept and to frame the notion of such learning. The term postulating is chosen to signify an act or attempt to explore and evoke an unconventional way of looking at learners and facilitators of learning.

What Does It Mean to Be Responsive? What Should a Learner be Responsive To?

The Cambridge Dictionary describes the term "responsive" as *saying or doing something as a reaction to something or someone, especially in a quick or positive way*. It connotes a fast action but in contrast to being reactive, responsiveness implies thoughtful action that is typically an informed one. Often, reactive is tagged to an action driven with less controlled emotion whereas responsive is a conscious thought. In this chapter, responsiveness is discussed in the context of education and learning. Akin to business responsiveness which means getting back to customers quickly with solutions to their problems, responsiveness in education and learning deals with the learners as the ultimate recipient of educational services.

A learner who is responsive is someone who has knowledge of all the different elements of learning in his or her environment, is aware of changes and react in a way to enhance his or her learning process and experience. If we were to illustrate these elements, it may lead to at least five main ones; (1) the learner himself (or herself); (2) the content; (3) the environment; (4) the learning experience and (5) the assessment and attainment of learning outcomes. Being responsive thus means the learner must be able to monitor his/her own learning needs, gauge the dynamics of the environment within which content and knowledge are delivered, stay aware of the expected outcomes, attentive to how one will be assessed to signify outcomes achieved and respond to the changes that ensue by curating a meaningful learning experience without being dependent on an instructor or the program coordinator. The learner must be responsive to the growing knowledge base and skills needed to fulfil the learning outcomes, or else one finds gaps and disparities once out in the workplace, and in the society one lives.

Figure 1. Major elements associated with learning

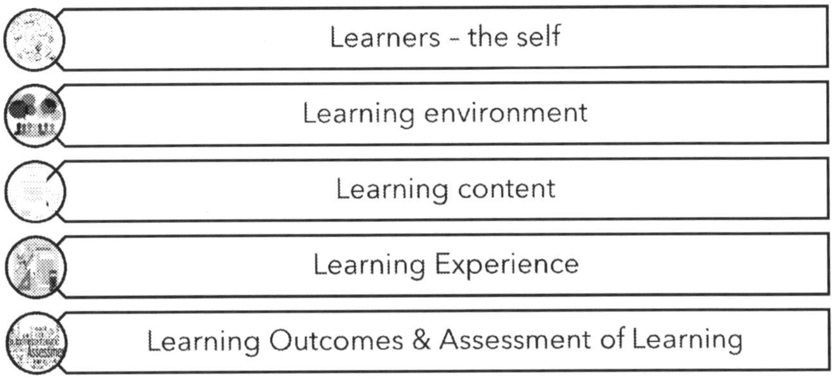

- Learners – the self
- Learning environment
- Learning content
- Learning Experience
- Learning Outcomes & Assessment of Learning

When postulating the multi-faceted attributes of the responsive learner, it is also crucial to point out that in this chapter, learning is basically defined as an active acquisition of knowledge and skills (cognitive, psychomotor, affective) that instigate change in one's awareness, behaviour, and actions. Thus, learning can be attained through study, instruction, and experience. The ultimate aim is for the person to indulge in learning according to the four pillars posited by UNESCO's commission headed by Delors (1996): (1) Learning to know, (2) Learning to do, (3) Learning to be, *to become* and (4) Learning to live together.

Before we deliberate further on responsive learning, it is pertinent to review the notion of responsiveness in the context of education, teaching, and learning.

RESPONSIVE EDUCATION, RESPONSIVE LEARNING ENVIRONMENT AND RESPONSIVE TEACHING

Responsiveness in education has been conveyed in government policies and research especially following the Covid 19 pandemic. The Organisation for Economic Co-operation and Development (OECD) Education Policy Outlook 2021 put forward a Framework for Responsiveness and Resilience in Education Policy that aims to support development of eco-systems that adapt to change (resilience), and the *important* challenge of navigating the ongoing evolution (responsiveness). Responsive Education is also the focus of an ongoing Worldbank project that responds to school disruptions caused by the COVID-19 pandemic; seeking to recover access and improve education quality with a focus on disadvantaged areas and vulnerable populations in Pakistan (Worldbank, 2020). Earlier, the OECD *Government at A Glance* documents responsiveness in education as involving

.... adapting teaching methods to the needs of different students, but also maintaining good communication with parents (or guardians of children) and interactions with community groups that might also provide support to the successful completion of basic education for all children.

OECD (2015)

In addition, OECD Reviews of School Resources (2018) focuses on responsive school systems as a significant feature in the context of changing demand for school places and evolving student needs. (https://www.oecd.org/education/school-resources-review/ResponsiveSchoolSystemsENG.pdf). In terms of higher education responsiveness, most research are basically on curriculum development and undertaken to enhance relationship between educational institution, the community, and the industry (Kruss, 2004; Dutta& Islam, 2017; Fomunyam & Teferra, 2017).

Responsive Learning Environment

Another area much discussed is responsive learning environment. The United States Department of Health Services via the Early Childhood Learning & Knowledge Center (December 2021) put forward research notes on responsive learning environment that include

1. Responsive learning environments are tailored to the individual needs and interests of all children.
2. Learning environments include classrooms, play spaces, homes, and outdoor areas, including areas visited by a child during their daily life.
3. Responsive adults are the most important part of any learning environment. This includes teachers, home visitors, families, and caregivers.

(Early Childhood Learning & Knowledge Center, 2021)

In higher education, researchers have dwelled on the notion of the responsive learning environment, typically in the context of online and open learning (Hicks, Reid, & George, 2001; Buchan, 2011; Kaban, Adiguzel & Özaydın, 2019) Hicks, Reid, and George (2001) for instance, focused on learning support in an online learning environment. A more rigorous treatment would be that of Fruhmann, Nussbaumer, and Albert (2010) who presented a psycho-pedagogical framework for self-regulated learning in a responsive open learning environment (ROLE). ROLE was a four-year project that supported learning by propounding the concept of personalised self-regulated learning. Responsiveness is developed through a learner-centred tasks, tools, resources, and strategies within the learner's own learning environment. ROLE was also investigated by Kaban, Adiguzel and Özaydın (2019) who found that the implementation of ROLE posed challenges on the psycho pedagogical as well as the technical aspects. The researchers focused on the technology that support PLE (personalized learning environment). However, designs were based on instructional design models rather than a more flexible learning design approach. Wallin, Reams, Veine and Anderson (2018) deliberated on formative assessments and students' reflective capacity in a responsive learning environment. These and several other articles presented lifelong learning and personalization as the mainstay of the responsive environment. In relation to e-learning, Trimer (2016) limits responsive e-learning to imply responsive design of the online system and delivery. This is frequently embodied in many online and e-learning design blogs and articles. There is still a need to examine the whole concept, framework and design of a responsive learning environment that suits learners in the current higher education era.

The Responsive Classroom

In contrast to responsive learning environment, the responsive classroom is barely a learning space. It is an approach initiated by the Northeast Foundation for Children; Inc. (NEFC) founded in 1981. Kiser (2020, updated 2022) describes a responsive classroom as a student-centered and evidence-based approach to teaching and discipline with principles developed to help with social skills with academic learning. (https://www.graduateprogram.org/2020/07/what-is-a-responsive-classroom/). Students need to learn a set of social-emotional competencies that include cooperation, assertiveness, responsibility, empathy, and self-control. In this instance, responsive classroom stresses classroom management at school level. Responsive classroom thus focuses on (1) creating optimal learning conditions for students to develop the academic, social, and emotional skills needed for success in and out of school, and (2) building positive school and classroom communities where students learn, behave, hope, and set and achieve goals (https://www.responsiveclassroom.org/wp-content/uploads/2018/07/RC-Approach-Handout.pdf)

Responsive Teaching

Wood (2018) describes responsive teaching as (1) setting clear goals and planning learning carefully, (2) identifying what students have understood and where they are struggling and (3) responding, adapting teaching to support students to do better. The idea of responding to the diverse students' learning needs perpetuates in Wood's and many other authors' work (Torrecampo, 2020). Most research on responsive teaching, however, has taken place at the school or K 12 level. At the higher education level, responsive teaching has been very much centered on culturally responsive teaching (Larke, 2013; Abdul Jabbar & Hadaker, 2013; O'Leary, Shapiro, Toma, Sayson,, Levis-Fitzgerald, Johnson, & Sork, 2020; Day & Beard, 2019; Benediktsson,, Wozniczka, Tran, & Ragnarsdóttir, 2019; Hutchinson & McAlister-Shields, 2020) which is basically a student-centered approach to teaching that includes cultural references and recognizes the importance of students' cultural background and experiences in all aspects of learning (Pinto-López,, Montaudon-Tomas, Muñoz-Ortiz, & Montaudon-Tomas, 2020).

Apart from that, researchers in higher education have related responsive teaching to teacher discourse and student thinking in STEM education (Richards, & Robertson, 2015). Gehrtz, Brantner, & Andrews, 2022; Bishop, 2021). In their review of responsive teaching in Science Education (approach to instruction that centralizes student thinking), Gouvea and Appleby (2022) highlighted that it is not sufficient to focus on student's ideas alone, a more holistic approach is necessary.

attention to and engagement with all that students bring with them to learning environments—their many varied ideas, strategies, feelings, values, and modes of expression. (p.3)

Four main points can be highlighted from the above discussion.

1. Responsiveness has always been tagged to differences, changes, and uncertainties. As indicated at the beginning of the chapter, changes may happen to the learner, the learning environment, the learning experience, and the content to be delivered thus affecting the learning outcomes.
2. Responsive education, teaching and/or learning deals with lifelong learning and personalization.
3. Educators have thus far, place responsive teaching as crucial. We place less emphasis on responsive learning, perhaps due to our ingrained, conventional teaching paradigm. The concepts of responsive and responsiveness in education are generally deliberated at the system, platform, and teaching level. Rarely has the idea of responsive learning at the learner's level been discussed directly in depth.
4. Responsive teaching must take a holistic approach.

RESPONSIVE AND RESPONSIBLE LEARNING

Very few authors deliberate on responsive learning as a process or as an action by the learner. Nonetheless the 21st Century learning requires quick informed action by the learner to drive success in his/her campus learning endeavours. The globalised world with its borderless possibilities including learning from an expert across the globe, learning anytime, anywhere, through any mode and alongside massive data and rapidly evolving knowledge, necessitates the learners to seek opportunities and to move fast.

Apart from that, the recent global pandemic has placed the learner in need of the following:

Competence and capability

This involves the desire of feeling capable of performing a determined task; being skilful and having a perception of confidence and effectiveness

Autonomy

Basically, this is about making decisions by one's own will, based on one's own needs and values. It means engaging in learning activities because one wants to, freely choosing to devote time and energy to one's studies

Relatedness

This means the need for belongingness or connectedness with significant others, being accepted and valued by people surrounding us, such as fellow students, and instructors

Resilience

This is about "bouncing back" from these difficult experiences, involving profound personal growth and staying positive.

Responsive learning can, hence, be postulated as the moment-to-moment decisions that the learner makes as he or she observe and analyses the dynamics of his or her environment and the four other dimensions discussed in the earlier paragraphs. It is through the observation and analysis that the learner strategizes learning. It is very much related to the notion of the expert learner, self-regulated learning, self-determined learning and learning agility. Subsequently, the responsive learner will need to be a responsible learner as well.

What constitutes a responsive and responsible learner?

Responsiveness requires attentive, adaptive action and charting one's own course to address one's needs. The illustration in Figure 2 below provides four dominant characteristics of a responsive learner.

Postulating Responsive and Responsible Learning

1. A responsive learner is a mindful learner. The learner is aware of oneself, one's ability, one's needs, one's surrounding and one's place in the system
2. A responsive learner thus sees learning as seamless. Each experience and event that one encounters is an opportunity for learning.
3. A responsive learner is instinctively networked and automatically connected. The learner has access to the latest updates in the field; seeks information profusely and relies on evidence-based assessments
4. A responsive learner is an active and agile learner. Spoon feeding or waiting to be provided for has no place in the responsive learner's vocabulary. Being active. resourceful and swift in making learning decision forms the core attribute of a responsive learner.

The responsive learner ultimately will go beyond the lecture halls and textbooks to learn.

Figure 2. The attributes of a responsive learner

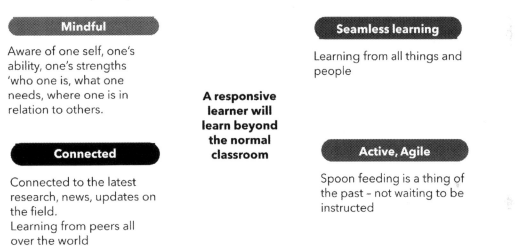

The Oxford Dictionary describes being responsible to simply mean being the person that causes something to happen. An agentic learner is undoubtedly a responsible learner. Being responsible in learning with notions of self-regulation and self-control has been deliberated much earlier by Bacon (1991). Gautam, Jangam and Kai (2018) associate a responsible learner with a person who has ownership over one's own learning, wanting to engage in academic tasks with more vigour and taking responsibility for one's learning. To demonstrate the idea of responsible learners, Gautam, Jangam and Kai (2018) propose students to be given an opportunity to be part of grading can enable them to see themselves as active builders of their own grades—providing them with intrinsic motivation to take responsibility for their learning. Pendoley (2019) posits responsible learners as those who "define the purpose of their learning and determine how they will wield it in their relationships with themselves and the world". In an earlier module, McCombs (2015) suggests development of autonomous and responsible learners through giving learners choices to allow them to feel empowered. Having control or ownership over their own learning will ultimately develop a sense of responsibility and self-motivation. In the context of this book, a responsible learner is seen as a person who will drive one's own learning. He or she is (1) agentic, (2) resourceful, and continuously seeks to (3) regulate and (4) sustain learning. A responsible learner charts his or her own learning process and manages the tools and strategies required to uphold the process. A responsible learner also accepts the fact that he/she is accountable for his/her actions, thoughts and ideas. A responsible learner thus, demonstrates ethical behaviour and decision making in both personal and social realm.

Figure 3. The Responsible Learner

The above discussion brings into focus the elements of heutagogy and self-determined learning as the precursor to responsive and responsible learning. Self-determined learning is defined as learning processes in which learning is initiated, planned, organized, and evaluated by learners starting from their individual experiences, deciding for themselves what, why, how, when, where and with whom together is learned; in doing so, learners are aiming at self-imposed goals, above all the enhancement of abilities to act (Blascke, 2012; Hase & Kenyon, 2013). Much of the idea of responsive and responsible learning rest on the attributes of self-determined learning and the idea of an agentic learner; one with a sense of personal empowerment involving both knowing and having what it takes to achieve goals (Wehmeyer & Little, 2013; Blaschke, 2018). In other words, it is concerned with learner-centred learning that sees the learner as the major agent in their own learning, which occurs as a result of personal experiences (Hase & Kenyon, 2007; Blaschke, Kenyon, & Hase, 2014).

Mini Case 1

Remote learning during the pandemic required learners to be actively responsible and responsive. Anna (pseudonym) was a first-year university student studying teacher education when Covid 19 was first detected. When resources were tight, Anna quickly resorted to the online platform despite her internet connectivity being less stable. When assigned a task to experience learning using a MOOC, Anna completed the full course even though the task required only three weeks of engagement. She gained a certificate from the University of California, San Diego. Anna even registered for another MOOC and completed learning a few months later. As she moved to a higher semester, Anna sought the university assistance to allow her to be back on campus to secure a more stable internet connection. She stayed at the residential college and studied online while her peers were at home with their families. Anna depicts a responsive and a responsible learner. She went beyond the assigned task to learn on her own and strived to solve her learning problems, making sacrifices to ensure she learned well. Anna graduated after four semesters of remote learning claiming several awards to mark her success. To support learners like Anna, task options were given to encourage interest in learning. Students are also given tasks that foster self-direction with appropriate and timely feedback. Above all, these learners must be given the opportunity to learn on their own.

The preceding section has provided an initial idea of responsive and responsible learning. The discussion will be flawed if the teacher, instructor, or facilitator is not brought into the picture of responsive and responsible learning. The next section will reiterate the point made earlier that is responsive education, teaching and/or learning deals with lifetime learning and personalization.

CULTIVATING RESPONSIVE AND RESPONSIBLE LEARNING THROUGH RESPONSIVE PEDAGOGY

How does an instructor, a teacher or a learning facilitator encourage responsive and responsible learning? This section investigates teaching strategies that nurture the responsive and responsible learner whose attributes are based on the definitions given in the earlier sections. In this context, several pertinent pedagogical approaches and tactics must be considered by the instructor, teacher or learning facilitator. These include

1. Supporting student voice and choice
2. Letting go of teacher reverence
3. Advocating self-determined learning
4. Comprehending learning in the connected world
5. Instigating collaborative learning
6. Designing the experience rather than delivering a content centric curriculum
7. Curating learner centred tasks and activities
8. Playing multiple roles
9. Ensuring an adaptive learning environment
10. Continuously assessing learning in context and authentic situation

An instructor, a teacher or a learning facilitator who understands responsive and responsible learning will definitely promote voice and choice among the learners. The notion of the instructor as the only source of information and knowledge on the area is no longer valid when learning resources are bounteous and accessible. Learners learn with peers; they seek experts and scholars to help them make sense of the materials they are studying. The sage on the stage is almost obsolete as the responsibility to learn is turned to the learner (Sadonik, 2022; Stover, Heilmann & Hubbard, 2018; Dougan, 2015; Rajalekshmi, Chikwa, & Bino, 2015). Methods and approaches such as flipped learning, active learning and participatory learning inevitably enhances responsible learning (Huang, 2020; Urquiza-Fuentes, 2020; Nouri, 2016).

With reference to the earlier stated definition of learning, learning through experience and collaboratively is germane to developing the responsive and responsible learner. It not only elevates an awareness and understanding of theories in context; it allows the learner to reflect on one's own conviction with respect to others. An instructor, a teacher or a learning facilitator will promote experiential learning in and off campus by bringing students to the community and the industry. Collaborative experience gained through small task collaboration, project collaboration, volunteering, learning groups and learning communities must be supported and curated by the instructor or learning facilitator. Additionally, learning environments can be designed and created to facilitate responsive and responsible learning. The notion of connectedness needs to be imbued; a learner must be connected to the learning environment, learning resources, peers, instructors, learning facilitators, experts, practitioners, industry players and community/social groups via technology platform or in person (service learning, community-based learning, field experience, internships and many more). Place-responsive pedagogy espoused by researchers and authors such as Mannion, Fenwick and Lynch (2013), Stewart (2020) and Boyd (2020) must be seriously considered for this purpose.

Mini case 2: Packaging the Experience

An Instructional Technology course is taught to first year students at a Malaysian university. Students are basically preservice teachers with hardly any school experience. During the pandemic, the course was delivered online and in packages, rather than a week-by-week scheduling of topics to be covered. In one instance, students learned spreadsheet together with planning on how to integrate technology in the classrooms, considering infrastructural constraints and financial implications. This was done over two weeks. They first explored the learning management system through an online treasure hunt. The students then interacted online with a schoolteacher who implemented video-based games for learning English at a rural school for indigenous pupils. Despite the movement control order, the students were connected to a brilliant practitioner. Their level of awareness and interest increased, they were motivated, and they experienced an authentic case; learning was definitely not textbook based. They successfully conducted needs analyses and calculated ROI using Microsoft Excel to complete a scenario-based assessment on technology integration in a rural school. They were also able to empathetically comprehend the limitations and challenges in integrating technology.

The preceding paragraphs discuss the notion that a learner must be made responsible for his/her learning. An instructor may support this by curating learning experiences, advocating constant self-evaluation and by finding the avenues to the learner fulfil his/her learning needs. It is also imperative to note that learners are fundamentally different. Learner diversity and learner preferences must be supported through varied teaching strategies that can be rotated or conducted interchangeably to address such differences. An understanding of universal design of learning (UDL) when formulating these strategies is thus unavoidable and espoused by many authors and researchers (Cressey, 2020; Kieran & Anderson, 2019; James, 2018). It is not within the scope of this chapter to discuss universal design of learning framework at length. Suffice it to say that an instructor, a teacher, or a learning facilitator must address learner differences and provide multiple means of 1) engagement, 2) representation, and 3) action and expression. Learning is designed from the perspective of students' diversity as strengths rather than shortfalls. There is an abundance of literature discussing culturally responsive pedagogy and UDL that are directed at nurturing strengths and promoting an open-minded, supportive environment celebrating cultural differences which will certainly aid the instructor and learning facilitator.

CONCLUSION

There are many other relevant aspects of responsive and responsible learning. The chapter attempts to frame and discuss such form of learning in relation to both the student and the instructor. Some of the salient points discussed are captured in the table below.

Table 1. Students and Lecturers' Roles in Responsive and Responsible learning

	Role(s)	Description of tasks (examples)*
Students	Agent of own learning, Accountable/Hold responsibility for own achievement and success	Be aware, identify, search, seek, direct and establish information and knowledge base, resources, expertise, network, opportunities etc Reflect, regulate, drive own learning, and conduct environmental restructuring Plan for achievement of learning outcomes and more
Lecturers/instructors	Designer, curator and facilitator	Be creative, stay abreast of advances in the field and in learning technology Utilize responsive pedagogy, Design learner-centred activities in and out of campus, extend learning to the community and industry, collaborate with others outside the university and at the global front to develop students' program and projects

* Non-exhaustive

As mentioned in the earlier sections, this chapter is a pre-amble to the other chapters in the book. The deliberations in the following chapters encompass the delivery strategies, assessments, faculty initiatives and institutional themes that encapsulate responsive pedagogy and innovative fostering of the responsive and responsible learner. On the cusp of a volatile and uncertain technologically advanced era, these learners are poised to be ones who are prepared and equipped to navigate their learning pathways triumphantly.

REFERENCES

Bacon, C. S. (1991). Being Held Responsible versus Being Responsible. *The Clearing House: A Journal of Educational Strategies, Issues and Ideas, 64*(6), 395–398. doi:10.1080/00098655.1991.9955903

Bahoo-Toroodi, T., Yousefi-Saidabadi, R., & Saffarian Hamedani, S. (2020). The role of leading professors and responsive teaching on development of third generation university and presenting a model in Mazandaran University of Medical Sciences. *Majallah-i Danishgah-i Ulum-i Pizishki-i Mazandaran, 30*(188), 116–124.

Benediktsson, A. I., Wozniczka, A. K., Tran, A. D. K., & Ragnarsdóttir, H. (2019). Immigrant Students' Experiences of Higher Education in Iceland: Why Does Culturally Responsive Teaching Matter? *Nordic Journal of Comparative and International Education, 3*(2), 37–54. doi:10.7577/njcie.2850

Bishop, J. P. (2021). Responsiveness and intellectual work: Features of mathematics classroom discourse related to student achievement. *Journal of the Learning Sciences, 30*(3), 466–508. doi:10.1080/10508406.2021.1922413

Blaschke, L. M. (2012). Heutagogy and Lifelong Learning: A Review of Heutagogical Practice and Self-Determined Learning. *International Review of Research in Open and Distance Learning, 13*(1), 57–70. doi:10.19173/irrodl.v13i1.1076

Blaschke, L. M. (2018). Self-determined Learning (Heutagogy) and Digital Media Creating Integrated Educational Environments for Developing Lifelong Learning Skills. In D. Kergel, B. Heidkamp, P. Telléus, T. Rachwal, & S. Nowakowski (Eds.), *The Digital Turn in Higher Education*. Springer VS. doi:10.1007/978-3-658-19925-8_10

Blaschke, L. M., Kenyon, C., & Hase, S. (2014). *Experiences in self-determined learning*. CreateSpace Independent Publishing Platform.

Boyd, S. (2020). *Place-responsive principles of sustainable networked learning*. Paper presented at International Conference on Networked Learning 2020, Kolding, Denmark. https://www.networkedlearning.aau.dk/digitalAssets/826/826402_20.-boyd---place-responsive-principles-of-sustainable-networked-learning.pdf

Brennan, K., Feng, F., Hall, L., Kim, J., Kojima, D., & Petrina, S. (2007, June). Methodologies for Researching Cognition and Technology: Dynamically Responsive Learning Environments. In EdMedia+ Innovate Learning (pp. 4069-4073). Association for the Advancement of Computing in Education (AACE).

Cressey, J. (2020). *Universal Design for Learning: Culturally Responsive UDL in Teacher Education*. doi:10.4018/978-1-7998-1770-3.ch008

Day, L., & Beard, K. V. (2019). Meaningful inclusion of diverse voices: The case for culturally responsive teaching in nursing education. *Journal of Professional Nursing, 35*(4), 277–281. doi:10.1016/j.profnurs.2019.01.002 PMID:31345507

Delor, J. (1996). *Learning: the treasure within; report to UNESCO of the International Commission on Education for the Twenty-first Century, EFA Global Monitoring Report*. UNESCO.

Dougan, N. (2015). From Sage on the Stage to Guide on the Side. An Action Research Project using a 'flipped classroom' model. *Practice and Research in Education University of Bolton Education Research Journal, 67*.

Dutta, B., & Islam, K. M. (2017). Responsiveness of Higher Education to Changing Job Market Demand in Bangladesh. *Higher Education for the Future, 4*(1), 60–81. doi:10.1177/2347631116681218

Fomunyam, K. G., & Teferra, D. (2018, April 18). Curriculum responsiveness within the context of decolonization in South African higher education. *Perspectives in Education*. Advance online publication. doi:10.18820/2519593X/pie.v35i2.15

Fruhmann, K., Nussbaumer, A., & Albert, D. (2010, July). A psycho-pedagogical framework for self-regulated learning in a responsive open learning environment. In *Proceedings of the International Conference eLearning Baltics Science (eLBa Science 2010)* (pp. 1-2). Fraunhofer.

Gautam, S., Jangam, S., & Kai, C. K. (2018, Winter). Developing Responsible Learners. *Chemical Engineering Education, 52*(1), 23–30. doi:10.18260/2-1-370.660-29477

Gehrtz, J., Brantner, M., & Andrews, T. C. (2022). How are undergraduate STEM instructors leveraging student thinking? *International Journal of STEM Education, 9*(1), ar18. doi:10.118640594-022-00336-0

Hicks, M., Reid, I., & George, R. (2001). Enhancing on-line teaching: Designing responsive learning environments. *The International Journal for Academic Development, 6*(2), 143–151. doi:10.1080/713769258

Huang, H. (2020). Learner Autonomy and Responsibility: Self-learning Through a Flipped Online EFL Course. In M. Freiermuth & N. Zarrinabadi (Eds.), *Technology and the Psychology of Second Language Learners and Users*. Palgrave Macmillan. doi:10.1007/978-3-030-34212-8_8

Hutchison, L., & McAlister-Shields, L. (2020). Culturally Responsive Teaching: Its Application in Higher Education Environments. *Education Sciences, 10*(5), 124. Advance online publication. doi:10.3390/educsci10050124

Jabbar, A., & Hardaker, G. (2013). The role of culturally responsive teaching for supporting ethnic diversity in British University Business Schools. *Teaching in Higher Education, 18*(3), 272–284. doi:10.1080/13562517.2012.725221

James, K. (2018). Universal Design for Learning (UDL) as a Structure for Culturally Responsive Practice. *Northwest Journal of Teacher Education, 13*(1), 4. Advance online publication. doi:10.15760/nwjte.2018.13.1.4

Kaban, L. A., Adiguzel, T., & Özaydın, M. (2019). Responsive Open Learning Environment in a Higher Education Institution: A Case Study. In Student Support Toward Self-Directed Learning in Open and Distributed Environments. IGI Global. doi:10.4018/978-1-5225-9316-4.ch011

Kieran, L., & Anderson, C. (2019). Connecting Universal Design for Learning with Culturally Responsive Teaching. *Education and Urban Society, 51*(9), 1202–1216. doi:10.1177/0013124518785012

Kruss, G. (2004). Employment and employability: Expectations of higher education responsiveness in South Africa. *Journal of Education Policy, 19*(6), 673–689. doi:10.1080/0268093042000300454

Larke, P. (2013). *Culturally responsive teaching in higher education: What professors need to know* (Vol. 391). Counterpoints.

Mannion, G., Fenwick, A., & Lynch, J. (2013). Place-responsive pedagogy: Learning from teachers' experiences of excursions in nature. *Environmental Education Research, 19*(6), 792–809. Advance online publication. doi:10.1080/13504622.2012.749980

McCombs, B. L. (2015, March 9). *Developing responsible and autonomous learners: A key to motivating students*. American Psychological Association. https://www.apa.org/education-career/k12/learners

Nouri, J. (2016). The flipped classroom: For active, effective, and increased learning – especially for low achievers. *Int J Educ Technol High Educ, 13*(1), 33. doi:10.118641239-016-0032-z

O'Leary, E. S., Shapiro, C., Toma, S., Sayson, H. W., Levis-Fitzgerald, M., Johnson, T., & Sork, V. L. (2020). Creating inclusive classrooms by engaging STEM faculty in culturally responsive teaching workshops. *International Journal of STEM Education, 7*(1), 1–15. doi:10.118640594-020-00230-7 PMID:32647597

OECD. (2015). *Government at a Glance 2015.* OECD Publishing. doi:10.1787/gov_glance-2015-

OECD. (2021). *Education Policy Outlook 2021: Shaping Responsive and Resilient Education in a Changing World.* OECD Publishing. doi:10.1787/75e40a16-

Pendoley, R. (2019). *Owning the Responsibility for Learning.* https://medium.com/age-of-awareness/owning-the-responsibility-for-learning-19a5261d428b

Pinto-López, I. N., Montaudon-Tomas, C. M., Muñoz-Ortiz, M., & Montaudon-Tomas, I. M. (2020). Culturally responsive teaching to empower indigenous student communities. In *Culturally responsive teaching and learning in higher education* (pp. 1–30). IGI Global. doi:10.4018/978-1-5225-9989-0.ch001

Rajalekshmi, K. G., Chikwa, G., & Bino, D. (2015). *The end of the "sage on the stage": Assessing the impact of flipping classrooms on teaching and learning practice across multiple disciplines at a higher education institution in Oman.* 8th International Conference of Education, Research and Innovation, Seville, Spain.

Richards, J., & Robertson, A. D. (2015). A review of the research on responsive teaching in science and mathematics. *Responsive Teaching in Science and Mathematics*, 54-73.

Robertson, A. D., Atkins, L. J., Levin, D. M., & Richards, J. (2016). What is responsive teaching? In Responsive teaching in science and mathematics (pp. 1–35). Routledge.

Sadownik, S. (2022). *Sage on the Stage to Guide on the Side: The Changing Perception of Teachers' Role and Subsequent Worth.* doi:10.31124/advance.19383692.v1

Sobe, N. W. (2021). *Reworking Four Pillars of Education to Sustain the Commons.* UNESCO Futures of Education Ideas Lab. Retrieved from https://en.unesco.org/futuresofeducation/ideas-lab/sobe-reworking-four-pillars-education-sustain-commons

Stover, S., Heilmann, G. & Hubbard, A. (2018). Learner-Centered Design: Is Sage on the Stage Obsolete? *Journal of Effective Teaching in Higher Education, 1*(1).

Torrecampo, R. M. (2020). *Responsive and Inclusive Education in the New Normal: A Case Study of Adaptive Curriculum Implementation in a Philippine Tertiary Classroom.* British Council. https://www.teachingenglish.org.uk/sites/teacheng/files/Rosella%20Torrecampo_DOI_v3.pdf

Urquiza-Fuentes, J. (2020). Increasing Students' Responsibility and Learning Outcomes Using Partial Flipped Classroom in a Language Processors Course. *IEEE Access: Practical Innovations, Open Solutions, 8*, 211211–211223. doi:10.1109/ACCESS.2020.3039628

Wallin, P., Reams, J., Veine, S., & Anderson, M. K. (2018). Creating responsive learning environments to develop students' reflective capacity. *Integral Review, 14*(1), 167–186. https://integral-review.org/issues/vol_14_no_1_wallin_reams_veine_andersen_creating_responsive_learning_environments.pdf

Wehmeyer, M. L., & Little, T. D. (2013). Self-Determination. In The Oxford Handbook of Positive Psychology and Disability. Oxford Library of Psychology. doi:10.1093/oxfordhb/9780195398786.013.013.0010

Wood, H. F. (2018). *Responsive Teaching: Cognitive Science and Formative Assessment in Practice.* Routledge. doi:10.4324/9781315099699

Chapter 2
"Response–Able" Education for Sustainable Employability Aligned With Sustainable Development Goals:
SOARing to Success

Arti Kumar
Independent Researcher, UK

EXECUTIVE SUMMARY

'The SOAR model' (as it has come to be used in the UK and abroad) is in effect a conceptual metamodel that scaffolds pedagogy, andragogy, and heutagogy in its design and delivery of response-able, equitable, and empowering learning for all students. SOAR invokes personally meaningful interconnections within and between the dimensions of self, opportunity, aspirations, and results through inbuilt requirements for self-reflection, action and interaction, research, analysis, and synthesis. It is inclusive while it values diversity, and its practical methodology enables all learners to become response-able while developing employability and sustainability for effective functioning in the diverse contexts of learning, work, and life in a changing, challenging world. This chapter shows how SOAR integrates and implements an 'inside-out' systemic approach that teachers can adapt to deliver several key and currently siloed strategic agendas under one umbrella, thereby encompassing the much broader agenda of response-able transformational education that is sorely needed in contemporary times.

DOI: 10.4018/978-1-6684-6076-4.ch002

"Response-Able" Education for Sustainable Employability Aligned With Sustainable Development Goals

INTRODUCTION

Teachers have a responsibility to teach.

Learners have an equal responsibility to learn.

Teachers can and should enable students to response-ably develop employability skills and attributes for transfer to sustainable global futures.

Some of the complexities inherent in the three fundamental statements above are unravelled and explored in this chapter, with reference to 'the SOAR model' or framework, as it has come to be known and used in the UK and abroad, and hereafter referred to in this chapter as SOAR, for brevity. **SOAR** is a simple and positive acronym that offers teachers and students a way of animating the recursive interconnections between *Self, Opportunity, Aspirations* and **Results**. These universal interrelationships are innovatively interpreted by the author into a pedagogy and an andragogic process of personalised learning, enabling students to develop their skills, knowledge, attributes, and experiences in a broad holistic frame, and to do this with more intrinsic motivation, sense of direction and destination. The author's implementation of SOAR is not to be confused with other uses of the same acronym in other contexts.

The SOAR process and praxis of personalized development is implicitly underpinned by the conceptualization of 'responsibility' as 'response-ability' – the unique human metacognitive ability to reflect and choose responses mindfully and purposefully in relation to both external demands and personal needs and aspirations. *SOARing to Success* methods and resources have been tried and tested with diverse cohorts of students, at different levels and programmes of study, including mature and international students. Evaluations consistently show positive benefits in terms of integrated personal, social and employability development, broadly defined as the behavioural competencies that are needed for individuals to be effective and productive in our challenging times. The concepts and methods are comprehensively described and available in a series of publications by this author[1] for teachers to implement in their own context (also see references and footnotes later). This chapter provides further clear and explicit understanding with reference to the SOAR methods as a novel application in relation to response-able education for sustainable development.

'Responsibility' is a term that implies an external imposition, such as in job descriptions which itemise the responsibilities a jobholder is expected to undertake in performing certain tasks at a particular level of ability, whereas 'response-ability' is the intrinsic creative and critical decision-making power of a jobholder in response to performance demands. A key power of teachers lies in the response-ability to decide what to include and what to exclude in the design of curricula and how best to deliver it. Teaching the knowledge and technical skills content of subject disciplines must take priority. Additionally, successive UK national agendas have called for teachers to develop employable graduates with transferable personal and professional skills. At the time of writing, a combination of personal, social, academic and career development capabilities are needed by everyone – staff and students – in response to complex intersecting contemporary challenges. For instance, education for sustainable development is a new agenda that is rapidly gaining ground in the UK, requiring teachers to respond with innovative pedagogies. This raises the question for all in educational roles: how are we responding to these urgent and important needs and challenges?

In this endeavour, response-ability' (and its related intrinsic characteristics such as self-efficacy beliefs, personal agency, values, multiple intelligences), are implicitly and explicitly developed throughout the SOAR process as critical outcomes in response-able education, alongside a range of essential transferable skills.

According to well-established models (Dacre Pool and Sewell 2007; Kumar 2007), graduate employability requires developing a wealth of attributes, skills and knowledge which will assist graduates in applying their disciplinary knowledge in the workplace; as well as technical expertise, career development skills and engaging in extra-curricular activities and work experience... Understanding the importance of lifelong learning; self-confidence and high self-esteem; ability to transfer learning across different contexts and disciplinary expertise all feature prominently in dominant employability models and are considered vital for future personal growth and career success. They do not, however, always appear in national or institutional generic skill frameworks and their importance may therefore not be sufficiently appreciated by relevant stakeholders. (Jackson, 2014: 359)

The importance of such intrinsic attributes is not usually appreciated or acknowledged in evaluations, Quality Assurance Agency (QAA)'s quality standards, graduate outcomes (GOs) and other metrics in traditional education, even though these personal and professional qualities are essential for self-awareness and self-development aligned with the mindset and heartset needed for sustainable employability in a sustainable world. This chapter therefore spotlights some of the main features and enablers in **SOAR** pedagogy, andragogy and heutagogy that provide ways of appreciating and cultivating the qualities of being response-able.

Whatever external circumstances, challenges and demands teachers (and students) face, there is a gap between the external stimulus and the individual response. It is in that gap where power lies to choose an informed response driven by positive values. While knowledge and skills content in a core curriculum is essential and can be conveyed by traditional pedagogies, equally important are the range of personal attitudes, values, interests and priorities that make knowledge useable *in the right way*. For example, Mahatma Gandhi gave the world wise principles for preventing problems when he said that it is perilous for humanity to convey knowledge without developing character; apply science without humanity; pursue pleasure without conscience; generate wealth without work; conduct business without ethics; engage in politics without principle; and follow religious rituals without right action. He was an inspiring role model in what he advocated: *be the change you want to see in the world.*

All teachers should see themselves as changemakers and teach the change they want to see in education and in the world at large. Gandhi's principles are relevant for the personal development of sustainable employability in alignment with the global development of sustainable futures and require teachers to think BIG – in a metacognitive sense, beyond disciplinary knowledge, and beyond narrow definitions of employability. Universities play a central role in social, cultural and economic transformation as they nurture future leaders and thinkers. If students are to be and become their best selves in best possible global futures, they will need to respond *in the right way* to 'the world of work and the work of the world'[2]. Socio-economic and ethical principles can and should be integrated, animated and role modelled in curricula as they are relevant for students' current learning, future life-career choices and sustainable employability in all occupational areas. Moreover, they also offer powerful potential for teachers and students to work in partnership to align their self-development and self-fulfillment with much-needed regeneration as formulated in the UN's Sustainable Development Goals (SDGs).

In this endeavour, SOAR offers in effect a practical meta-model – an overarching model and framework that encompasses other models and their resources, designed to motivate students to discover and build their unique identities positively and proactively through a process of **S**elf-discovery, effective participation in learning **O**pportunities both within and outside the formal curriculum, the formation of realistic, implementable career **A**spirations and the achievement of more intentional **R**esults as they move towards and beyond transition points into life and work. All learners are empowered to identify, critically appreciate and develop their strengths and address their development needs through inbuilt requirements for reflection, action, interaction, collaboration, analysis, synthesis and lateral thinking (see Figure 1).

Figure 1. SOAR as a metamodel engages everyone in a developmental cycle

In this educational process, self-reflective tools and follow-up activities are central in developing meta-skills such as self-awareness and opportunity-awareness. Cultivating the metacognitive quality of response-ability in ways that engage the whole person (integrating skillsets, mindsets and heartsets), enables behaviours and actions to become more psychosocially aligned with professional, socio-economic and environmental needs, and moral codes for effective, regenerative functioning across all major domains of life and work in a challenging, changing world.

The exploration of outer space has sparked widespread interest and an international space race, but it is far more relevant, salient (and difficult) to take a deep dive into one's inner space. Many problems arise when we act without thinking or think without acting. Response-able education, using SOAR concepts and tools, can spark reflection, action and collaboration in facing the unprecedented challenging circumstances and difficult decisions that need to be made, individually and collectively.

BACKGROUND: THE CONTEXT AND ISSUES AGAINST WHICH SOAR EVOLVED

SOAR is a prime example of response-able and responsive education. It evolved by responding creatively to the needs and expectations of staff, students and employers, initially through the design and delivery of accredited and assessed Career Development Learning (CDL) modules that were options for students of any degree discipline. SOAR therefore started as the author's broad, eclectic interpretation and practical application of the conceptual DOTS model, underpinned by social science theories that have evolved over the past century while attempting to explain career choice and identity in relation to changing times and perspectives (Watts, 1999). DOTS is widely understood by UK careers professionals as an acronym for Decision learning, Opportunity-awareness, Transition skills and Self-awareness. In practice, the 'DOTS' are not usually 'joined up' in this order, however. A more logical way of introducing students to the theoretical underpinnings of careers programmes is usually in the following sequence, which assumes that students need to develop skills and knowledge in these four areas:

1. **Self-awareness:** 'awareness of the distinctive characteristics (abilities, skills, values and interests) that define the kind of person one is and the kind of person one wishes to become.'
2. **Opportunity-awareness:** 'awareness of the possibilities that exist, the demands they make and the rewards and satisfactions they can offer.'
3. **Decision learning:** 'increased ability to make realistic choices based on sound information.'
4. **Transition skills:** 'increased ability to plan and take action to implement decisions.'
5. (Watts and Hawthorn, 1992)

The following is an extract from Tony Watts's review of SOAR (after its first edition was published in 2007), in the *British Journal of Guidance & Counselling*:

The conceptual model for the book is based around the four concepts of Self, Opportunity, Aspirations and Results, which translate into the arresting acronym SOAR. In many respects this is a recasting of the DOTS model developed by Bill Law and myself, but refreshed and reshaped into a more logical sequence (the correct sequence for DOTS was SODT, which sometimes morphed into SODIT!). It also seeks to extend the framework so that it provides a basis for personal and academic as well as career development. Nonetheless, 'career' is at its heart. (Watts, 2008:217)

The second edition (Kumar, 2022) further extends SOAR and aims to:

1. refocus DOTS in line with contemporary concepts and needs
2. broaden the CDL framework to integrate personal, social, professional and academic development, thereby enhancing employability, enterprise and sustainable development goals
3. interpret SOAR elements against a broader range of theories, case studies and survey findings
4. link theoretical concepts with practical examples (all available as eResources) for teachers to experiment with, in class and online
5. show how appropriate pedagogy can develop a range of skills and attributes without diluting academic standards.

SOARing to Success[3] is the subtitle of the book / eBook that was first published in 2007 and is fully updated in its second edition (2022) with additional material that addresses essential needs for strengthening mental health, wellbeing, resilience, self-efficacy, information literacy, and much-needed sustainable regeneration in contemporary times. The tools and techniques are comprehensively described so that teachers can contextualise them within or alongside a core curriculum and students can personalise their learning and development. The second edition comes with eResources that make it easier for teachers to download and deliver the student activities, either in person or via digital platforms.

When Personal Development Planning (PDP), the Progress File and Employability agendas were phased in from 2001-2006 onwards, the SOAR framework expanded and integrated the principles, values and intended outcomes of these agendas. At the University of Bedfordshire (UoB), the entire curriculum was revised at a whole institution level during 2005-2010, and SOAR became the framework of choice for implementing broad-based 'employability development' as an integral part of every degree programme. The upward trajectory of SOAR was upscaled and elevated in this way to faculty and institutional level, with coordinated collaboration amongst academic and support staff, students and employers.

It is important to note that SOAR does not devalue the teaching of subject-based or occupation-specific disciplines or make careers guidance redundant; rather it serves as a transdisciplinary, complementary, enhancement approach that teachers can contextualise and operationalise within or alongside a core curriculum. Congruently, students can more response-ably use relevant support, resources and feedback, engage more developmentally in learning opportunities and apply their achievements to the diverse demands of real-world situations.

SOAR for Employability[4] describes the innovative and integrative features of *SOAR* and references action research undertaken with MBA students at University of Bedfordshire. It is significant to note that the majority were international students from India, and this was a pilot project in two postgraduate courses. In this case the core MBA curriculum had no room for innovative additions, so a series of SOAR-framed optional workshops were designed to be delivered alongside. These were closely linked with the MBA knowledge content and a reflective written assessment required each student to undertake an in-depth evaluation of SOAR experience and outcomes. Students consistently reported very positive personal and professional gains and significantly increased employability skills and attributes that they could flexibly transfer to the evolving needs of business in India (see student comments published in Kumar, 2015; and an example below).

I personally felt SOAR is one of most effective self-assessment forms. It actually helped to realise where I stand and where I am heading towards. It also clearly helped me to identify what are my weaknesses and potential threats that could halt my career progress. It is important to know as an individual, weaknesses within you and external factors. It helped me to make long terms plans that align with my aspirations and analyse constraints in achieving the aspirations.

(MBA student comment[5]*, used with permission. He goes on to articulate explicitly the strengths and areas for improvement he identified through SOAR)*

The SOAR framework has since been used in the UK and abroad in diverse contexts, principally by academic staff and careers professionals. Cycles of action research and evaluations with several cohorts of students from diverse backgrounds, subjects and levels of study have consistently proved that SOAR methodology delivers equitable and empowering learning for all students, regardless of their background, subject and level of study. It is therefore inclusive while it simultaneously values staff, student and subject diversity, and is responsive to the changing needs of key stakeholders in a rapidly changing world. As just one example, this is evidenced in two papers that report findings from two courses delivered at Griffith University, Brisbane, Australia by Gregory Reddan, Director of Education and Senior Lecturer in Exercise Science, and Maja Rauchle, who worked in the Careers and Employment Service. This resulted in an effective collaboration. The courses combined quality work-integrated learning and career development learning using the SOAR model to develop employability.

The SOAR model and the resources in Kumar's text were found to be of significant benefit in the organization of student activities in the curriculum of both Work-integrated Learning (WIL) and Career Development Learning (CDL) courses. (Reddan, 2017)

Since employability is a common concern in a global economy, higher education institutions (HEIs) the world over are attempting to create a skilled workforce capable of wealth creation. Advancing digital technologies have brought new possibilities to globalisation, which is reflected in possibilities for the 'comprehensive internationalisation' of HE (Hudzik, 2011)[6]. Additional challenges arise for everyone needing to educate for effective and productive functioning in a Volatile, Uncertain, Complex, Ambiguous (VUCA) world that urgently needs to find and apply solutions to the intersecting crises of climate change, global inequities, social unrest, collapsing ecologies and economies. Education for sustainable development is an essential agenda for contemporary times.

Correspondingly, teachers generally have the intrinsic drive and desire to develop students more holistically, so that they are prepared for life beyond their studies. For example, a recent survey[7] with 7,000 teachers and school leaders in English schools reveals that the vast majority of teachers wish to see a range of topics incorporated into the national curriculum that give parity to life skills such as social and emotional development, communication skills, resilience, health and wellbeing, developing sustainability mindsets and global citizens – in short a curriculum that develops children's characteristics and response-abilities for future personal success in life and work while also in dealing effectively with complex socio-economic and global issues.

Such perspectives and ambitions have already changed the role of HEIs, academic and support staff, and students. Teachers now widely and response-ably accept that more self-regulated academic learning, personal development, career management, employability and sustainability development should lead to broader graduate outcomes. Despite such values, good intentions and innovative pedagogies, many issues are still discussed and debated as overwhelming problems looking for solutions. The sector is clearly still learning how to navigate this changing landscape.

In this respect, Iain Patton's comments in his article *Embedding sustainability in universities*[8] (2014) are pertinent. He points to excellent collaborative initiatives following the UN Earth Summit Rio+20. For example, the Higher Education Sustainability Initiative (HESI) was set up by a group of UN partners and perceived by Ban Ki-moon (UN Secretary General) as "transformative, global in reach and could reach thousands of graduates from universities and business schools." However, Patton highlights the need for transformational leadership in universities to realize the potential of such initiatives:

We need transformational leadership that can vision and shape a different future – a low carbon future. With their teaching, research, community engagement and campuses, universities are exceptionally well placed to generate a better economy, society and planet. And if they don't – who on earth will?...

That leaves me with the question: how do we achieve a truly sustainable campus? Perhaps we need a new approach in which we abandon 'stand-alone sustainability' and move to one in which we embed the principles and values of sustainability into the sectors' existing policy infrastructure. Perhaps it's not so surprising that the sector struggles to embrace what it sees as an additional, separate agenda (Patton, 2014:1).

So that leaves us here and now with the question: how does and how can SOAR offer the powerful potential of this 'new approach' that Patton suggests is needed by HEIs to envision and create a different future, but is proving difficult to implement?

SOLUTIONS AND RECOMMENDATIONS: KEY PRINCIPLES IN SOAR

Interconnectedness: Integrating the Intended Outcomes of Agendas

Picking up on Patton's concluding comment "*that the sector struggles to embrace what it sees as an additional, separate agenda*", it is indeed problematic when these agendas are approached as multiple, complex, siloed requirements, to be debated and delivered through policy and strategy 'from the outside in'. To give just one recent example, Dr Emily Beaumont writes[9]:

Employability, enterprise, and entrepreneurship (commonly referred to as the 3Es) are frequently addressed 'as distinct, if not mutually exclusive concepts' (Dean, 2010:21), existing in silos... This session intends to explore this wicked problem and consider potential 'work arounds' in an environment where a solution seems unachievable.

SOAR offers a different approach: it *integrates* the transdisciplinary skillsets, principles and values of personal, social, academic and career development, employability, enterprise, entrepreneurship (the 3 Es), and sustainable development (Kumar, 2022). This integrated approach does not perceive these agendas and goals as polemical or mutually exclusive. Their intended benefits and outcomes are interconnected and transferable across all the diverse contexts of learning, life and work, and can be brought together in the Self-awareness and Opportunity-awareness of each student as personal and collective development goals. Such an ethically integrated approach enhances the ability of students to choose principled and mindful responses to their study, work and life choices. As an MBA coordinator observed while co-designing a set of workshops for her students, 'The SOAR model demands internal integrity between its four elements and also external integration with real-life socio-economic conditions.'

This is big picture thinking, seeing the whole forest and not just the trees, as it were. For instance, Ban Ki-Moon perceives the integrated nature of the UN's sustainable development goals (SDGs):

Saving our planet, lifting people out of poverty, advancing economic growth... these are one and the same fight. We must connect the dots between climate change, water scarcity, energy shortages, global health, food security and women's empowerment. Solutions to one problem must be solutions for all[10]. (Ban Ki-moon, Red Sea Economic Development, undated)

The difficulty of integrating agendas and 'connecting the dots' is understandable for a variety of reasons. Teachers usually focus their time and energy on teaching and research in one domain, and even that is complex and multi-faceted. They have little time to consider strategies for teaching, learning and assessment in other (multiple) domains and sort through myriad conceptual approaches and practical resources for implementing them. Many have not explicitly considered what success looks like for their students, and in fact it may look very different for each student. So, seeing all this through the lens of interconnectedness can be a gamechanger. Dr Doug Cole, who has used and endorsed SOAR, articulated the problem and the solution perfectly on a LinkedIn post on 26 August 2022:

What is needed but commonly missing is a recognition of the value of the wider curriculum, and the pedagogies that can be employed across all courses in developing student identity and the human capabilities essential to flourish in a future and complex world. The value of this practice may be implicit and therefore the value students recognise and articulate remains at a surface level. We all need to be making this much more explicit with our students through the language we use on a daily basis, asking the right questions and ensuring we have transformative reflective practice, scaffolded and developmental across all levels of study.

We know a job is no longer for life and we know that skills soon become outdated. Therefore, a focus on these more sustainable personal qualities, attitudes and behaviours are equally, if not more, important. Incidentally these same areas not only underpin learning for employability but also retention, attainment, progression, sustainability and wellbeing. Collectively this presents an opportunity for smarter and more integrated approaches, breaking down silos often created by parallel strategic agendas… In order to be successful, shifting the narrative beyond knowledge and skills alone is crucial, and should underpin how we support our students as lifelong and lifewide learners.

(Dr Doug Cole, Deputy Director of Employability at Nottingham Trent University)

Concepts such as 'career' 'employability' and 'sustainability' are redefined as multi-dimensional, complex, recursively interlinked skillsets and mindsets that can be incorporated within the humanistic systemic approach of SOAR. This encompasses the much broader agenda of response-able transformational education that is sorely needed in our times and enables teachers to meet the requirements of multiple key and currently siloed strategic agendas simultaneously.

At the heart of the ***SOAR*** framework are the recursive connections between 'Self-awareness' and 'Opportunity awareness'. Enabling students to critically appreciate how their inner world of *Self* interacts with the external world of Others and ***O****pportunity* is a psychosocial approach to developing an individual's behavioural competencies in relation to social and cultural experiences in diverse environments. SOAR methods include specific career and work-related learning experiences which enable students to generate, clarify and test their ***A****spirations* so that they become more realistic and implementable. As an important graduate outcome at the point of transition, students can articulate, promote and demonstrate the range of ***R****esults* (skills and attributes) that employers require and recruit. Congruently, various individual and collaborative activities explicitly require students to align their personal and professional goals with sustainable development goals, using the UN's SDGs as reference points.

Figure 2. Constructive alignment of Self with Results

Developing 'The Whole Person from The Inside Out' Using Constructive Alignment

Figure 2 shows an individual at the start of a learning journey where part of the pathway is set out, typically in a course or module description. Further on there is a significant gap in the path, which represents potential pitfalls and ambiguity which the student must bridge across to achieve their personal vision of Success. The people on the right carrying jigsaw pieces can help to put in place a bridge to build the pathway, with each piece representing opportunities, resources and support. The student must take ownership and complete his or her own journey with personal agency, self-motivation and self-management, critical and creative thinking and a whole host of other skills and values – all components of response-ability – and all implicit or explicit in the SOAR process of development.

SOARing to Success does not pre-conceive or encourage visions of 'success' in terms of selfish opportunism, wealth creation, status or fame – nor does it promote an isolated view of Self. Although SOAR is not didactic or judgemental, it is based on ethical assumptions about invoking positive human potential for sustainable living rather than materialistic goals. It is important for students to self-develop in accordance with moral codes required for effective and regenerative functioning across all aspects of life-careers in a challenging, changing world. Employability is therefore redefined from a learner-centric viewpoint and in a broader sense than just securing employment at the end of a course:

Employability development is a personal journey with staged outcomes, requiring a set of positive values, beliefs and dispositions that drive performance and behaviour conducive to developing relevant competencies and experiences, finding and engaging with suitable **opportunities,** *implementing realistic* **aspirations***, demonstrating and learning from* **results** *through multiple contexts and identities. (Kumar, 2022:39)*

A student's vision of success may focus on any or all of the following results: graduating with best possible qualifications, entry to an occupation, job or employer organisation of choice, enterprise and entrepreneurship skills for self-employment, making an impact on people and planet, or simply realising one's potential for a fulfilling personal life.

Recent surveys and studies in the USA indicated that 80% of graduates' work values were focused on finding meaningful, purposeful and interesting work (Gallup, 2017, 2019) but only 34% reported that they were 'deeply interested in the work they do', and only 26% agreed that they 'do something interesting every day'. Experiencing disengagement and lack of job fulfilment impacts the wellbeing and productivity of workers as well as the organisations they work in. This should be a matter of grave concern for HE and for the corporate sector.

Connecting *Self* with *Results* (the **S** and **R** of **SOAR**) enables teachers to design a structured and supported SOAR module that 'begins with the end in mind'[11] – that is, to first formulate learning and performance outcomes (the requisite skills, knowledge, experiences and standards that students need to achieve) and then cast back to constructively align the learning methods and objectives with the outcomes. SOAR implements the twin principles of constructivism and alignment (Biggs and Tang, 2011), in the sense that each individual personally and response-ably constructs his or her own pathway in alignment with the achievement of given outcomes. The constructive alignment approach recognises "knowledge is constructed by the activities of the learner" (Biggs, 2014: 9), rather than being directly transferable from teacher to student.

This is neatly illustrated in the self-assessment questionnaire (SAQ) *It's My Journey through Life: am I in the driving seat?* which is congruent with *Me plc*[12] This student exercise (like all SAQs in SOAR) requires students to reflect and act on what is needed in order to work with complete response-ability, self-leadership and creativity for oneself (as in Figure 3). This is very apt for today's less supported environments in HE and the workplace as it alerts students to take response-ability and self-develop in preparation for their life-career journeys, giving them ownership and placing them at the heart of their learning.

Changing the Role of Teachers and Students

The academic tendency to approach teaching expertise as the ability to convey knowledge and develop academic skills reinforces the responsibility of teachers to know more, do more, and understand students. On the other hand, an 'inside-out approach' (Kumar 2013) invokes the pragmatic response-ability of students to understand themselves more analytically through combining intellectual understanding with lived experience: who they are, the characteristics and capabilities that define their unique identity, who they want to be(come) and what they need to do and develop to implement their aspirations realistically. Students are then empowered to learn better, know more and do more to develop their characteristics, capabilities and experiences in congruence with externally defined needs and expectations.

In a nutshell, the *SOAR* process of holistic learning and development requires all learners to identify and make response-able and meaningful interconnections within and between the essential, mutually supportive and dynamically related dimensions of *Self*, *Opportunity*, *Aspirations* and *Results*. It then simply remains for teachers to use the SOAR process to animate the synergy in 'connecting the dots' between the SOAR elements, using the constructively aligned tools that are relevant and applicable for all. This is inclusive and innovative practice while it simultaneously values the diversity of students, whatever their age, background, subject or level of study.

Figure 3. Connecting teachers' and students' concerns and needs

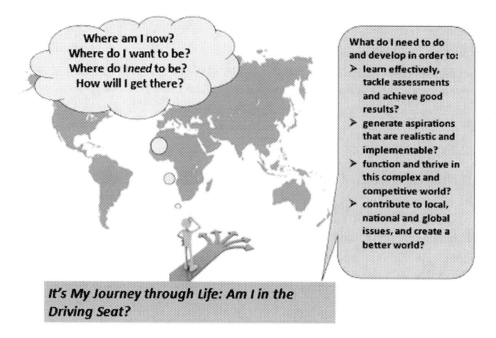

The questions in the callout on the left and the rectangle on the right in Figure 3 are overarching 'inside out' questions that typify some universal and personal needs that are largely relevant and applicable to address the common concerns and needs of teachers as well as students. For example, to function effectively and productively, everyone must update knowledge and skills to cope with advancing technologies, at various ability levels according to need. Everyone needs to take stock of a current position and plan ahead in relation to both personal aspirations and external demands, but how often do such questions structure a programme of study?

In the post-pandemic world, everyone has become more sensitised to risk and more averse to it, so everyone needs to maintain and strengthen health, wellbeing and resilience. For this purpose, the SANE exercise conceptualises Self as an integrated physical, mental, emotional and spiritual entity, and enables individuals to reflect, discuss and act on their personal needs for Sleep, Attitude, Nutrition and Exercise. Many development needs are shared by teachers and students. These may be unspoken expectations or unacknowledged needs while everyone is busy with daily routines and challenges. They are however important and central within the structured and supported process of *SOARing to Success*.

Inherent in Figure 3 are career and employability-linked person-environment interactions and adaptations implicit in career construction theories. SOAR is congruent with the Australian Blueprint for Career Development (ABCD) that progressively recast concepts of 'career':

Career' involves one's whole life, not just occupation… It concerns him or her in the ever-changing contexts of his or her life … self and circumstances – evolving, changing, unfolding in mutual interaction. (Wolf and Kolb, 1980, cited in McMahon et al., 2003: 4).

A subjectively experienced 'life-career' is inclusive of skills, values, interests and experiences from different life stages and life roles. All are subject to change, and all are important as they are the unique, portable intrinsic possession of each individual. The ability to identify, critically appreciate and articulate them, especially when self-promotion is called for, is of paramount importance, yet many find themselves unprepared. As such, they are relevant in particular for students when they go through employers' application and selection procedures and draw upon evidence to demonstrate suitability for a job; and for teachers when they go through performance appraisals, apply for promotions or change jobs in mid-career.

The career management paradigm is not so much about making the right occupational choice as it is about equipping people with the skills to make the myriad choices necessary throughout their lives to become healthy, self-reliant citizens, able to cope with constant change in rapidly changing labour markets and maintain balance between life and work roles. (Jarvis, 2000:3)

Switching to this perspective changes the role of teachers and students. *SOARing to Success* endorses the dual benefits of a partnership approach: teachers can realise the potential of SOAR in tandem with students. It is powerful when they share their experiences (successes and failures) and role model a positive and responsive approach, so that everyone critically appreciates and develops their inner goals in constructive alignment with externally defined requirements. Teachers can apply the methodology to their requirements in continuous professional development (CPD) or the Professional Standards Framework. The boundaries become blurred as teachers are learners too, and learners can be teachers.

To engage students in this process of 'mindful being and becoming' requires scaffolded pedagogy, andragogy and heutagogy that is not addressing the subject of career management, employability or sustainability as such but foregrounding the developmental needs of each individual Self from a person-centred, inside-out perspective. (Kumar, 2013:222)

Relational Pedagogy and Appreciative Inquiry

Enhancing self-awareness for inner development cannot be 'taught' in any traditional sense but needs to be facilitated with appropriate tools and techniques to motivate, engage and enable students in their self-discovery and self-development. Expertise then lies in the artistry of relational pedagogy that gives a voice and value to each *Self* as 'the subject', and in creating appropriate environments to encourage a response-able growth mindset and heartset. The positive psychology of Appreciative Inquiry methods[13] honours the physical, mental, emotional and spiritual Self as a whole system, and engages head, heart and hands.

This works best when teachers flip power to students with an attitude of humility, using words to the effect that: "We are at different stages in our lives, but I will be learning in tandem with you, using some of the same tools and methods in this course for our discovery learning together. The module will include self-assessments and activities that require us to reflect and research, think critically and creatively, collaborate actively and with respect for each other, so I am here to inform, guide and support you but we will all need to take personal responsibility for what and how we achieve here."

In the journey towards career maturity, the positive psychosocial principles of AI are used throughout as a motivating and enabling force in engaging students with the concept of *Self as hero in the journey of life*. SOAR reframes the SWOT analysis that is often used in business to assess and analyse Strengths, Weaknesses, Opportunities and Threats. The focus on Strengths is right and good but an appreciative inquiry into Self in SOAR enables the critical appreciation of strengths *and* 'development needs' (rather than 'weaknesses'). Instead of the advice to 'find your flaws and fix them', the self-assessment tools enable students to find their natural strengths first and foremost, to use and cultivate them so that they 'appreciate in value'. Self-assessment tools simultaneously invoke and surface their development needs, blind spots, the shadow side of strengths, and ways of addressing them in real life. Secure in the identification, articulation and application of their strengths, students are then more energised to acknowledge and deal with the difficult development needs that draw them out of their comfort zones.

Appreciative Inquiry is not a touchy-feely approach with the clichéd feel-good vocabulary of forced positivity. A sense of optimism does not provide false hope that everything will be fine but role-models what can be done by taking response-able action with a positive mental attitude, real-life resources, collaborative working and support. These qualities are implicit in an educator's relational pedagogy, compassionate care, and the creation of safe and supportive learning environments that help to strengthen appropriate confidence, self-efficacy beliefs, a growth mindset – and the so-called 'soft skills' that are transferable and desirable throughout life and work.

KEY ENABLERS IN DEVELOPING SUSTAINABLE EMPLOYABILITY

Begin with End Results in Mind: An Assessment Centres Project

In the spirit of beginning with the end in mind, viewing the DVD *At the Assessment Centre* (AGCAS, 2009) is an excellent way at the start of any skills development programme, to introduce and motivate students (and staff) to see how employers expect applicants to demonstrate their suitability for the position they are applying for. Though a little dated, the DVD brings to life the range of activities that employers typically use in an Assessment Centre (AC) to observe and assess applicants, either in person at a physical venue or at virtual ACs. (Digital platforms have been used due to pandemic restrictions and may continue as they offer some advantages).

The DVD shows real students and graduates from many diverse universities and fields of study participating in the activities set up by real recruiters for general management positions. This viewing is therefore relevant for a whole range of different subject areas, and for the methodology of SOAR. 'Skills and attributes' are intrinsic qualities, so they can only be observed when they turn into behaviours and actions.

Behavioural competency descriptors (that are such an important hallmark of ACs and the lexicon of SAQs in the SOAR process) create shared understanding between staff and students, clarify expectations and outcomes, and provide criteria for observation, feedback and assessment related to employability... It can take students from initial awareness-raising through a clear line of sight to the practical benefits associated with SOAR methodology. (Kumar, 2022: 283)

Figure 4. An Assessment Centres project bridges across transitions

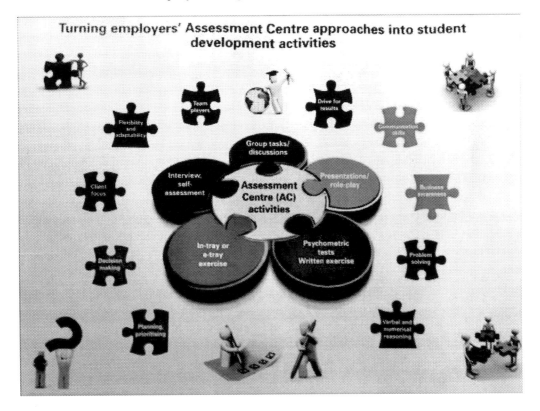

Viewing the video should be followed with discussion so that students and staff create shared understanding of the 'skills and attributes' employers are looking for and how they observe and assess 'them as behavioural competencies' through AC activities. Students then appreciate the significance and relevance of the competencies they need to cultivate and are more motivated to engage with SOAR methodology. Such behaviours are evidence of key transferable competencies for effective functioning across most aspects of life and work, even if students never encounter a real-life AC.

Self-Assessment Questionnaires (Saqs)

Accordingly, back casting from the 'skills' that are typically required and recruited by employers, in the spirit of constructive alignment a range of self-assessment questionnaires (SAQs) were developed in the language of behavioural competency descriptors. The SAQs prompt initial individual reflections for students to identify their current behaviours, and simultaneously appreciate potential behaviour change towards the achievement of ideally effective behaviours in the whole range of skillsets you see represented in the jigsaw pieces in Figure 7. Together with follow-up discussions, activities and assessments SAQs raise awareness of skills and motivate students to reflect, develop, articulate, record and evidence their personal possession of 'skills' in terms of what they actually do and what they intend to develop.

Self-assessment as formulated in SAQs is a key enabling method if understood and used as part of a developmental process. The potential benefits of SAQs will be lost if they are administered as quantitative checklists for students to use as superficial tick-box exercises and left at that…They should be briefed and debriefed, extended into reflective, active and collaborative learning – I give many examples throughout this book… SAQs are interdependent and weave together as essential threads in the SOAR process. The symbiotic nature of the skills they develop means that they have equal weight in the holistic development of all students, together building up to graduate level employability and identity. (Kumar, 2022:44)

Figure 5 indicates how students should approach a SAQ, in this example the SAQ for *Learning and Improving*. This format can easily be adapted for administering other similar SAQs, such as *Groupwork and team effectiveness* (Figure 6). Students are encouraged to see that simply recognising and planning a needed behaviour change means they are on the learning pathway, with many opportunities and support to practice new habits that can be slow and sometimes difficult to develop.

Throughout the process of development, the competencies assessed at ACs are particularly useful as behavioural frames of reference for end-goals and the criteria for achieving them. They are distributed through a module or programme of study and serve as a spine of consistency – a thread running through which students can finally pull together to present as evidence of suitability for a position they are applying for.

Figure 5. Approaching self-assessment with self-care

Self-assessment Questionnaire
Learning and Improving : *How can I be effective?*

Caution!

- This SAQ is expressed in terms of an ideal world where perfect people conduct themselves perfectly in learning behaviours. Arguably there is no such thing

- Please consider each statement as potential for improving towards being more effective and productive, and not in terms of expecting perfection. Low ratings are not to be viewed as failure but as raw material for development and success.

- It can damage your sense of well-being as a learner if you evaluate your abilities harshly and use any SAQ as a stick to beat yourself up with!

Realising the potential of this SAQ:

- It alerts you to actions you can take in order to perform and achieve better results as you learn and develop (similar to marking criteria and rubrics that show what it takes to achieve a top A+ grade)

- Use it as a self-diagnostic tool at the start (Time 1) and then return to it at a later stage (Time 2) to evaluate how your behaviours may have changed

- At any stage of the process it serves as a frame of reference

- You can identify those behaviours that are important for you to develop, and seek opportunities, support and resources to develop them, including other activities in the SOAR process.

Figure 6. An indicative Self-Assessment Questionnaire for improving groupwork / team effectiveness

In relation to groupwork, ask yourself:		
To what extent do I (a) consider these actions important; (b) act in this way? Rate yourself from 1 to 4 (4 = high and 1 = low)	a) Ratings 1–4 importance	b) Ratings 1–4 frequency
I express myself confidently and assertively		
I contribute ideas and suggestions relevant to the task		
I take on a specific role when required		
I listen respectfully to others		
I support others' positive contributions		
I focus (or re-focus) the group on its tasks and goals		
I help the group to achieve its goals within a given timeframe		

The behaviours I consider most important are…

My highest ratings:…

Evidence that I do this in real life…

Behaviours I need to practice…

Opportunities and resources I will use in order to be more effective…

Assessment Methodology

A triangulated assessment regime was carefully set up at the start of a SOAR module, which involved students in homework between each session. This usually required individual reflection and interpretation around a SAQ, other activity or resource, and brief written notes which they could use to prepare and present a 5-minute presentation. Each week they presented in turn on different set topics in small groups of 3 or 4. The risk of students' ratings and claims being far-fetched or understated was countered by peers seeking real-life evidence and examples, but doing so with respect, maintaining appropriate confidentiality.

Students were trained in giving and receiving feedback and the ethical use of criterion referencing to use in peer assessment and feedback. SAQs could double up as criteria to be used in peer observations, feedback and peer / tutor assessments. These were low stakes activities which prompted discussions to clarify words, ideas and theories, with input from tutors. Over time this formative, ipsative and summative assessment regime built up to more professional high-stakes presentations, interviewing and communication skills, collaborating in groupwork, time management, attendance and engagement.

Building Self-Maps as A Regenerative Process in Life-Career Journeys

Know yourself, know your future was an inscription above the Greek Oracle at Delphi. This sentiment is echoed in many cultural traditions, in many variations, and in contemporary praxis. Kumar's version of this is *Know yourself, create your future*. Let's start with the premise that everyone has an inner map that interacts subconsciously with the external world from birth onwards, resulting in the formation of unique identities. This map drives our career aspirations, the opportunities we engage with, the attraction we feel to friends and lovers, and the results we achieve, personally and professionally. We need to understand the regenerative workings of our internal drives and not simply allow them to determine our lives.

The metacognitive process of *Self-MAPing* is a key enabler in bringing internalized maps to conscious awareness so that we are not just blown around by the winds of chance and circumstance. Humans have response-ability – the ability to use awareness more meaningfully, to choose responses, to change perspectives and beliefs as needed – so that decisions, behaviours and actions become more aligned with realistic, implementable personal aspirations, collective needs and moral codes required for effective functioning in the diverse contexts of learning, work and life in general.

Scaffolding pedagogy, andragogy and heutagogy supports students in growing proactively, becoming more capable of self-regulation and self-development as they progress. The mix of metacognitive, cognitive and affective methods used in SOAR engages the minds, hearts and hands of students as an interconnected capacity spanning across three main dimensions of personal identity and response-ability: motivation, ability and personality.

Building authentic, holistic, positive Self-**MAP**s engages students in a process of identifying, critically appreciating, developing and articulating three interlinked, equally important personal dimensions: **Mo**tivation (interests, values, priorities)**; A**bility (knowledge, multiple intelligences, competencies, talents); **P**ersonality (preferences and styles of interacting with others and with different situations). Much human potential is sadly overlooked, undervalued and under-developed when traditional education focuses on intellectual ability and academic skills, whereas employers value the broad range of characteristics and capabilities inherent in Self-MAPs.

Given that MAP strengths are transferable and essential for success, all students should have opportunities to develop them within or alongside any curriculum. Students are apt to say, "I never knew I had so much substance!" or positive evaluative comments to that effect. Finding harmony between every aspect of the MAP and using it to find congruent directions and destinations in life-career journeys is an imperfect lifelong quest but engaging deeply with our inner selves has multiple, regenerative, proven benefits.

Aspiration for the long term: To be a top-notch executive in a well-known financial service company. Then later go on to start my own firm of consulting. My personal MAP is aligned with my aspirations, as I am motivated which is why I have undertaken this MBA program. My abilities are such that they can be developed to hold the position I seek, and my personality is very forward. (MBA student's comment, used with permission)

Figure 7. Building a positive, authentic Self-MAP for the life-career journey

*The assessment, Building My MAP, endorses the unique subjectivity of students while also defining objective criteria for grading this important piece of work as part of an accredited module. Self-awareness progressively provides the building blocks for students to create their Self-**MAP**, as **M**otivation, **A**bility and **P**ersonality are essential dimensions of a personal profile. The MAP then serves as both a map and a compass along the pathways of each life-career journey. (Kumar, 2022:78)*

Self-Opportunity Awareness and Aspirations

At the next stage of development, students take their psychosocial MAPs into the external world and interact more meaningfully with Others and Opportunities, which creates awareness of options in a vast field of pure potential for learning both formally and informally, in co- and extra-curricular activities. Collaborative work with others develops intra-personal and interpersonal skills in tandem. An in-depth understanding of innate preferences and styles of interaction with others, and in different situations, is an excellent way to develop communication skills and emotional, social and intercultural competencies, to name but a few.

An in-depth Job Study assessment requires and enables students to analyse the extent of congruence between their MAP and their Aspirations in relation to the requirements of their chosen job, occupation or employer organisation. The choice is wide, and can include a job abroad, self-employment or other Aspiration. The requirements and tools enhance academic ability to tackle assessments with research, digital and information literacy, critical, analytical and creative thinking, concise report-writing, interviewing and networking skills. The benefits connect personal, social, academic, career and employability development (see Figure 8).

Figure 8. Psychosocial interactions between Self and Opportunity

The SOAR attempt to be inclusive while also valuing diversity acknowledges that everyone has ability and disability in some form or another, along a spectrum, and Opportunity is differentially available, depending on where one stands in relation to it. For example, Kumar (2022:183) turns Opportunity structure and Community Interaction theories into a student exercise that links reflective self-assessment with a 'Lifeline' activity that enables students to identify the various influences in their lives (expectations, feedback, support, modelling and information). These influences come from a range of sources: parents, extended family, neighbourhood, peer group, ethnic group, teachers at school and at university, employers, work experience providers and other contacts.

In follow-up discussions, students understand how such influences affect them and, importantly, how negative impacts can be overcome or reduced through positive experiences that compensate for limitations or meet specific needs. They should be referred and encouraged to use university and community services and available opportunities that can support them, for example in health issues, finding a mentor, organising work experience and placements, and much more according to their needs.

Sustainable Employment as a Key Aim And 'Result' Of Soaring

Seeking and obtaining 'graduate jobs' or training schemes with large employers has consistently been a main important aspiration for the majority of students and may simply be a need for all to transfer their learning into earning. This strikes home with force at the point of transition into work beyond university. For many it is daunting to promote themselves and present convincing evidence of suitability for a specific job, initially through CVs, letters, applications, LinkedIn profiles, then at interviews (which may be in person, on the telephone or virtual platforms) – and finally at Assessment Centres (ACs), which are usually used at the last stage in the selection and recruitment process by some employers. Viewing the DVD *At the Assessment Centre* (AGCAS, 2009) again at this stage reinforces the need to demonstrate performance behaviours that they may need to develop further (see Figure 10).

Figure 9. Capabilities needed and developed for implementing Aspirations

The demanding and 'testing' nature of selection procedures requires high level capabilities and personal attributes, which in principle students will have developed through their academic studies and the SOAR process of connecting Self and Opportunity with Aspirations – and now focusing on Results. They will have gathered specific evidence of suitability for whatever they are aspiring to if they have engaged with the SOAR methodology and assessments. The learning tools for success in gaining employment are more specifically given in the Results section of the book (Kumar 2022) and should ideally be used in the final year curriculum when transition is looming large. Additionally, most employment sectors and organisations are tasked with and committed to action for climate change and social justice, Net Zero emissions and the creation of a green economy. They are actively seeking graduates with technical and occupation-specific knowledge, and the skillsets, mindsets and values to co-create solutions for the complex intersecting global challenges of contemporary times.

FUTURE RESEARCH DIRECTIONS

Conducting An 'Appreciative Inquiry' Into Sustainable Development

While the SOAR framework has already proven its capacity to develop a range of transferable skills, in its second iteration (Kumar, 2022) SOAR provides additional activities for students to align their response-ability and aspirations with the urgent and important global needs that are formulated in the UN's sustainable development goals (SDGs). This is a novel application which requires teachers and students, preferably in partnership, to think about what needs to change. The SDGs are useful reference points in discussing, exploring and researching what is being done and what can be done. This works ef-

Figure 10. Transition skills for success in employers' recruitment procedures

fectively in cross-disciplinary contexts and in collaboration with other universities. International students can be given a valued voice in researching across national boundaries as they can bring in perspectives from their home countries.

The world is at a crossroads where complex problems are seeking solutions. Appreciative Inquiry is essential for creating a positive 'can do' attitude in the face of multiple shockwaves: the global Covid-19 pandemic, extreme climate events, the war in Ukraine, the rising cost of living, growing inequities – all brought home by negative media reports and images – leaves individuals thinking, "what can I do about any of this?". Presenting the SDGs as 17 separate goals is overwhelming for students, so it is imperative for them to see the interconnected nature of the goals while focusing on a goal that is likely to be subject-related, personal or professionally meaningful for them. Even small personal changes can add up to a huge collective change since there are so many of us on this planet. While raising Opportunity-awareness, teachers should encourage students to respond to threats, challenges obstacles, pitfalls, failures and feedback as opportunities for the development of competencies such as adaptivity and creative problem solving in relation to achieving the SDGs.

Appreciative Inquiry has no place for vitriol and blame games. Response-able and responsive education can bring in success stories, what is, can and should be done by individuals, communities, business, industry and government, at different levels of granularity. There are also many examples from the global South, and international students should be given a voice and value in contributing from their perspectives, collaborating to find workable solutions for achieving Net Zero, neither catastrophising nor bright siding the intersecting realities of life today. It is highly relevant to use Gandhian principles (mentioned earlier in this chapter) as a moral compass and take the right actions to achieve environmental protections, a viable green economy and a just society.

This is an underpinning thread running through SOAR (Kumar, 2022) and made explicit in some sections. For example, mindset and values are key determinants of response-able actions and behaviours in sustainable development. Both the ability to adapt and the ability to be adaptive are important in responding to global needs. In the spirit of 'starting with the end in mind', a glimpse of Utopia prompts progress towards the kind of future world that everyone can aspire to. An ambitious multidimensional capstone project is suggested for final year students to take responsibility in co-creating, researching and collaborating across national boundaries to find and implement solutions, using the UN's SDGs as reference points for transformative regeneration. This further applies, develops and showcases all the gains from previous development.

The positive narrative, structure and praxis of SOAR can form a connecting thread running through all levels of a programme of study, and beyond, into personal learning, continuous professional development and life experiences in general. So, SOAR has come full circle in this iteration, but it is to be hoped that it will carry into lifelong and life wide learning as an upward spiral of continuous development, (as in Figure 11), becoming a recurrently used life skill – or rather an automatic habit of self-reflection for the purposes of choosing the right actions and interactions in response to the complex Results needed in complex life-careers. *Self-awareness* linked with *Opportunity-awareness* is the one constant recursive dynamic, the connective glue through lifelong and life wide learning, which is an overarching need for everyone in an unstable world of rapid change.

In the journey of life, bridges to success are always under construction, and success is not a destination but a journey. Reaching an end-goal is just the start of building a further pathway towards other life-career goals. If students graduate successfully into their dream job and stay in it happily their whole life, they would be the fortunate exception. Values, interests, priorities and circumstances change, and everyone must learn to adapt or be adaptive in regenerating Self-MAPs in alignment with external needs in a rapidly changing world. SOAR serves as a future-facing regenerative model.

Figure 11. SOAR can bridge across transition levels and stages of development

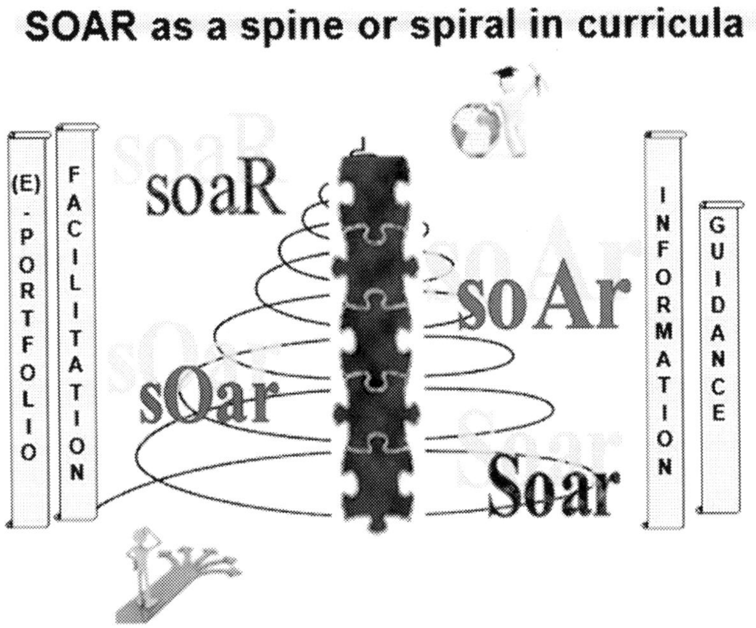

CONCLUSION

Returning to the statements at the start of this chapter, *SOARing to Success* requires and enables teachers to role model and develop their own response-ability while enabling all students to develop theirs, in the spirit of Appreciative Inquiry and relationship-building. It is possible and feasible to educate in compassionate response to intrinsic personal needs and wants which are universally similar: we all seek to live with a sense of purpose, connection, wellbeing and resilience in the pursuit of personal and collective goals. Despite disciplinary and technical demands, teachers are in a powerful position to accommodate human psychological and social needs in teaching styles and environments and develop all students 'from the inside out'. This type of interconnected, intrinsic, and positive empowerment is essential for personal agency in developing response-able transferable and transformative behavioural competencies aligned with sustainable employability, sustainable development, general wellbeing and fulfilling lives.

Humanity is at a crossroads where decisions made today will impact people and planet for better or worse. Real success for teachers lies in developing the whole person for a whole life, empowering each student to construct a personal pathway from education to sustainable employability and the co-creation of sustainable global futures. Along this pathway behavioural competencies will need to be further developed and applied response-ably as and when personal and external circumstances change in the broader life-career context. It is more important than ever to use the principles of response-able and responsive education to empower students. SOAR offers potential power to achieve this, but that power only takes effect when teachers implement its methodology and evaluate its outcomes. Teachers can add value to themselves, their curriculum and teaching styles and, in turn, enable students to add value to themselves, to the communities that nurture them, to the occupations they enter, and to the world at large.

On a broader scale and scope, the systemic approach of the SOAR model offers powerful potential beyond its use by individual teachers to design and deliver specific modules or programs. It can be the organizing paradigm at a strategic level for institutions, faculties, academic departments as well as individual practitioners to form a collaborative community of practice across disciplines and subject areas. This would require new coordinated top-down policies and bottom-up praxis, drawing upon the synergies between disciplinary knowledge, personal, social, academic and career development, encompassing employability and sustainability outcomes. The SOAR model, with its transdisciplinary, integrated, innovative and regenerative methodology can empower staff to work across disciplines, departments and services, for mutual benefit and collective change, and deliver multiple agendas in a more holistic joined up and systematic way. Since this is a transformative and effective way to address the multiple concerns and needs of teachers and students alike, under one umbrella, can HEIs afford not to do this?

ACKNOWLEDGMENT

The author wishes to thank her former academic and careers service colleagues, students and employers, who helped in various ways to shape the concepts and practical methodology of 'the SOAR model' over several years. Special thanks to staff at the University of Bedfordshire: Mark Atlay for his leadership support; Rob Carman and Tricia Smart for piloting SOAR units of study and action research in their courses. Student comments quoted in this chapter are extracted from the written assessments on these courses, with permission.

The University of Bedfordshire provided freedom, opportunity and support for the development and evaluation of SOAR-framed modules and projects in all subject fields. Much of this would not have been possible without a Centre of Excellence in Teaching and Learning (CETL), award, funded by the Higher Education Funding Council for England (HEFCE). The money was made available for enhancement projects from 2005 – 2010, during which SOAR became an essential integral component of all degree programmes within the University's revised curriculum at whole-institution level.

The Higher Education Academy, UK (now Advance HE) deserves special mention for awarding a funded National Teaching Fellowship to the author, Arti Kumar. This enabled her to further develop SOAR, disseminate it widely, write for publication and make an extensive contribution in higher education.

REFERENCES

Advance, H. E. (2011). *The UK Professional Standards Framework (PSF) for Teaching and Supporting Learning in Higher Education*. Advance HE. Available at: www.advance-he.ac.uk/guidance/teaching-and-learning/ukpsf

AGCAS. (2009). *At the Assessment Centre*. Sheffield, UK: Association of Graduate Careers Advisory Services. Available at: www.agcas.org.uk/Knowledge-Centre/a752384c-02f5-434c-b8e1-802b151652ab

Biggs, J. (2014). Constructive alignment in university teaching. *HERDSA Review of Higher Education*, *1*, 5–22.

Biggs, J., & Tang, C. (2011). *Teaching for Quality Learning at University*. McGraw-Hill/Society for Research into Higher Education / Open University Press.

Cooperrider, D. L., & Srivastva, S. (1987). Appreciative Inquiry. *Research in Organizational Change and Development*, *1*, 129–169.

Covey, S. (2004). The Seven Habits of Highly Effective People. Free Press. (Original publication 1989)

Gallup. (2017). *How millennials want to work and live*. Gallup. https://www.gallup.com/workplace/238073/millennials-work-live.aspx

Gallup. (2019). *Forging pathways to meaningful work – The role of Higher Education*. https://www.gallup.com/education/248222/gallup-bates-purposeful-work-2019.aspx

García-Crespo, F. J., Fernández-Alonso, R., & Muñiz, J. (2021). Academic resilience in European countries: The role of teachers, families, and student profiles. *PLoS One*, *16*(7), e0253409. Advance online publication. doi:10.1371/journal.pone.0253409 PMID:34214094

Hawkins, P. (1999). The Art of Building Windmills: Career Tactics for the 21st Century. Graduate into Employment Unit, University of Liverpool.

Hudzik, J. K. (2011). Comprehensive Internationalization: From Concept to Action. NAFSA. doi:10.100710734-013-9696-7

Jackson, D. (2014). Factors influencing job attainment in recent Bachelor graduates: Evidence from Australia. Higher Education, 68, 135–153. doi:10.100710734-013-9696-7

Jarvis, P. (2002). *Career Management Paradigm Shift: Prosperity for Citizens, Windfall for Governments*. National Life/Work Centre.

Kumar, A. (2009). 'Using Assessment Centre Approaches to Improve Students' Learning. In C. Nygaard & C. Holtham (Eds.), *Understanding Learning centred Higher Education*. Copenhagen Business School.

Kumar, A. (2013). SOARing to Success: Employability Development from the inside out. In T. Bilham (Ed.), *For the Love of Learning: Innovations from Outstanding University Teachers* (pp. 221–227). Palgrave Macmillan. doi:10.1007/978-1-137-33430-5_32

Kumar, A. (2015). *Enabling All Learners to SOAR for Employability: An Inclusive, Integrative Pedagogy*. Advance HE. www.advance-he.ac.uk/knowledge-hub/enabling-all-learners-soar-employability-inclusive-integrative-pedagogy

Kumar, A. (2022) *Personal, Social Academic and Career Development in Higher Education – SOARing to Success*. Routledge Taylor & Francis. www.routledge.com/9780367648053 (Original publication 2007)

McMahon, M., Patton, W., & Tatham, P. (2003). *Managing Life, Learning and Work in the 21st Century*. Miles Morgan Australia.

Papatheodorou, T., & Moyles, J. R. (Eds.). (2009). *Learning Together in the Early Years - Exploring Relational Pedagogy*. Routledge.

PattonI. (2014). *Embedding sustainability in universities*. https://www.universityworldnews.com/post.php?story=20140513111222724

Patton, W., & McMahon, M. (1999). *Career development and systems theory: A new relationship*. Thomson Brooks/Cole Publishing Co.

Porritt, J. (2013). *The World We Made: Alex McKay's story from 2050*. Phaidon.

Reddan, G., & Rauchle, M. (2012). Student Perceptions of the Value of Career Development Learning to a Work-Integrated Learning Course in Exercise Science. *Australian Journal of Career Development*, *21*(1), 38–48. doi:10.1177/103841621202100106

Reddan, G., & Rauchle, M. (2017). Combining quality work-integrated learning and career development learning through the use of the SOAR model to enhance employability. *Asia-Pacific Journal of Cooperative Education, Special Issue*, *18*(2), 129–139.

Watts, A. (2008). Review: 'Personal, Academic and Career Development in Higher Education: SOARing to Success'. *British Journal of Guidance & Counselling*, *36*(3).

Watts, A. G. (1999). *Reshaping Career Development for the 21st Century*. Centre for Guidance Studies, University of Derby.

Watts, A. G., & Hawthorn, R. (1992). 'Careers Education and the Curriculum in Higher Education'. *NICEC Project Report*. Careers Research and Advisory Centre.

Wolf, A., & Kolb, D. A. (1980). Career development, personal growth, and experimental learning. In J. W. Springer (Ed.), *Issues in Career and Human Resource Development*. American Society for Training and Development.

ENDNOTES

[1] Main publication: Kumar, A (2nd edition 2022) *Personal, Social, Academic and Career Development in Higher Education – SOARing to Success* London & New York: Routledge Taylor & Francis London & New York
Companion website with digital resources: www.routledge.com/9780367648053

[2] This phrase is attributed to Jonathan Porritt. His book, *The World We Made* reveals how it is possible to reach a genuinely sustainable world by 2050. It describes the key events, technological breakthroughs and lifestyle revolutions that will transform our planet.

[3] Kumar, A (2007; 2022) *Personal, Social Academic and Career Development in Higher Education – SOARing to Success* London & New York: Routledge Taylor & Francis London & New York

[4] Kumar, A (2015) 'Enabling all learners to SOAR for employability: an inclusive, integrative pedagogy' *Innovative pedagogies series* York, UK: Higher Education Academy
https://www.advance-he.ac.uk/knowledge-hub/enabling-all-lear
ners-soar-employability-inclusive-integrative-pedagogy

[5] All student comments are quoted here with permission, as they are extracted from students' written evaluations, as part of a formal action research project undertaken at the University of Bedfordshire (2007-13)

[6] Hudzik introduces the emerging imperative of a broader scope and scale of internationalization, which can be the organizing paradigm for institutions as a whole, academic departments, or professional programs.

[7] published in the ***Pearson School Report***

[8] Iain Patton is CEO of the Environmental Association for Universities and Colleges (EAUC),

[9] Dr Emily Beaumont is President of Enterprise Teachers UK (EEUK). The citation above is taken from the abstract for her presentation at the 2022 conference: Solving Wicked Problems: How to embed enterprise, entrepreneurship and sustainability *education for excellent graduate employability outcomes*

[10] Ban Ki-moon (UN Secretary-General 2007-2016) as quoted in Red Sea Economic Development: https://www.redseasearch.com/sectors/economic-development/

[11] 'Begin with the end in mind' is the second of Stephen Covey's *7 Habits of Highly Effective People*

[12] Based on the work of Peter Hawkins in *The Art of Building Windmills* and used with his permission.

[13] Cooperrider, D. L. and Srivastva, S. (1987) 'Appreciative Inquiry'. *Research in Organizational Change and Development*, 1: 129–69.

Chapter 3
Responsive and Responsible Learning in the Malaysian Education System:
A Game Changer

Sheela Jayabala Krishnan Jayabalan
Universiti Teknologi MARA, Malaysia

EXECUTIVE SUMMARY

Responsive and responsible learning connects the learner to the content. It is grounded in the teacher's understanding of the subjects taught and connects with each student to not only comprehend the subject but also apply the knowledge to real-life situations. Responsive and responsible teaching should help students build on prior learning to develop skills, mold attitudes, and cultivate independent learning. The pedagogies of teaching, therefore, should be attuned to a student-centered learning approach instead of teacher-centered, which is the practice in most educational institutions around the world including Malaysia. However, the process of teaching should start with early childhood education. Only then can the effectiveness of nurturing students to be independent learners and thinkers, which is the foundation of responsive and responsible learning, be achieved. This chapter, therefore, discusses the weaknesses of the current teaching and learning approaches (pedagogies) practiced in Malaysia and the reasons why a change is desirable (i.e., a game changer).

INTRODUCTION

Education is significant to any nation's social, political, and economic development. Therefore, effective teaching becomes paramount to guiding and assisting children progressing from one level to another in a sociable interactive environment and being independent learners (Béteille, T. & Evans, D., 2021). Effectiveness does not mean passing with excellence or getting good grades during the evaluation processes, but it should be to bring out the best in students holistically (Turdieva N.S., 2021). This starts right from when a child begins schooling, as the Malay proverb states, "Melentur rebung biarlah

DOI: 10.4018/978-1-6684-6076-4.ch003

daripada rebungnya," meaning that you can only bend the bamboo while it is s still a shoot. Therefore, if a child is to be molded to be a responsive and responsible learner, the process should start from the time they are enrolled in early childhood education and not just when they pursue their studies to the tertiary level at higher education institutions. Moreover, the effectiveness of responsive learning rests in perceiving education in a holistic manner. One of the leaders of the holistic education movement, Ron Miller (1997), stated that holistic teaching does not refer to a specific methodology (Miller, 1997). Instead, it should be viewed as a collection of fundamental assumptions and values that can be seen in various ways. Therefore, responsive and responsible learning with a holistic approach should generate students capable of handling and adapting to any situation.

The author presupposes that the current design of the education system is more akin to one size fits all, as the significance of education was to cater to the industrial revolution. The industrial revolution necessitated skilled human capital. Thus, the education system was interconnected with the needs of the industrial revolution. The needs of the industry were attained through an effective education system that leveraged the workforce to respond to the many facets of the industrial revolution. Therefore, the education system during the Industrial Revolution was based on the factory model of education, i.e., the one size fits all model, a curriculum to train and teach mass numbers to generate factory workers. The belief was that children were solely prepped and groomed to learn essential skills required to become competent factory workers. Students, therefore, were not grouped based on their abilities and needs but rather on their chronological age and industry demands. Alvin Toffler (1974), who criticized the "Industrial Era School" in his book, stated that "Mass education was the ingenious machine constructed by industrialism to produce the kind of adults it needed." As industrial needs became competitive and advanced, education that turned agrarian human capital into skilled factory workers was not sufficient, especially with the progress of science and technology. Science and technology require cognition for ideas and innovation. A revamp in the education system was necessitated. The focal point or emphasis of education was to prepare an individual for work to suit the many phases and evolution of the industrial revolution and to invent and innovate. Though the current education system still caters to the needs of the industry market, the need for an education system to equip a child to be an independent learner or thinker is gaining superiority. The emphasis, however, is on intellectual intelligence, a knowledge base that stresses the cognitive domain. The Malaysia Education Blueprint 2013-2025 also emphasizes the cognitive domain;

"Every student needs to develop skills of inquiry and learn how to continue acquiring knowledge throughout their lives, to be able to connect different pieces of knowledge and to create new knowledge. These higher-order thinking skills and the ability to innovate are especially critical in a rapidly evolving technological world. Every student needs to master a range of critical cognitive skills:

- Creative Thinking and Innovation: the ability to innovate, generate new possibilities, and create new ideas or knowledge;
- Critical Thinking and Reasoning: the ability to analyze information, anticipate problems, and approach issues critically, logically, inductively, and deductively in order to find solutions and ultimately make decisions; and
- Learning Capacity: the ability to independently drive one's learning, coupled with the appreciation of the value of lifelong learning." Lifelong learning, however, is stated to require more improvement.

The cognitive domain (Bloom, 1956) involves knowledge and the development of intellectual skills. This includes the recall or recognition of specific facts, procedural patterns, and concepts that serve in the development of intellectual abilities and skills. The view of philanthropist Swami Vivekananda, as cited by S.A.Bhat(2021) in his article, stated that the philosophy of education should not be a mere accumulation of information but instead a comprehensive training for life. To Swami Vivekananda: "Education is not the amount of information that is put into your brain and runs riot there undigested, all your life" as stated by Shanti (2019) in her article. Education, for Swami Vivekananda, is a process by which character is formed, the strength of the mind is increased, and intellect is sharpened to assist a person in standing on one's own feet, inferring the affective domain. The affective domain (Krathwohl, Bloom, Masia, 1973) includes how we deal emotionally, such as feelings, values, appreciation, enthusiasm, motivations, and attitudes. Therefore, education should not only be about building intellectual capital and self-development, i.e., self-learning, but also about strengthening emotional intelligence. Studies indicate that the affective and cognitive domains are needed to mold students' capabilities and competencies (Nor Asniza Ishak & Hazri Jamil, 2020). The study carried out by Nor Azniza & Hazri Jamil investigated pedagogical practices amongst Malaysian teachers in secondary schools, which consist of: (i) teaching plans/design of teaching; (ii) strategy of teaching; and (iii) evaluation of teaching, found that,

"The main finding of this study is that secondary school teachers' pedagogy practices improve students' intellectual through various techniques and teaching approaches which are influenced by demography factors among teachers, including years of experience and the subject taught. Creativity, innovation, and the affective aspect of teachers are important elements in carrying out specific teaching pedagogy practices to improve students' intellectual capital. This study's main finding is to show the role of teachers in planning, implementing, and evaluating effective teaching to engage students in learning actively, i.e., through activities, discussions, asking questions, providing opinions, and solving problems using higher-order thinking skills. Teachers also need to be open-minded and provide opportunities for students to submit ideas/insights to encourage them to expand their thinking scope and thus think intellectually."

It was interesting to note in the research conducted by Nor Asniza Ishak & Hazri Jamil (2020) that the initiatives undertaken by the teachers to get a response from the students were effective. For example, in the interviews, using set induction skills to teach was an effective tool for gaining the students' interest. Set induction refers to using a thought-provoking statement, interesting fact, or an audio-visual stimulus at the beginning of a lecture to gain students' attention and give an overview of the lecture topic. Set induction was used as one of the tools because it was deemed an effective method by the teacher to get a response from the students. The study also indicated that teachers' concern about the student's level of understanding might vary, prompting them to try different teaching methods to draw the students' attention to learning. However, it was left to the teacher's initiative to undertake the appropriate pedagogy of teaching based on a student's needs and competency. Private school teachers with a smaller number of students may be able to adopt this approach, but it may not be feasible in national schools as the number of students are large. The same presupposition can be drawn between public and private institutions. Teaching pedagogies that cater to individualized needs should be made possible during preschool because the number of students are small. Teachers can assess the different needs of the students and teach them accordingly, which is responsive learning.

The significance of responsive learning has been amplified by Tomlinson (2013). Tomlinson accentuates the need for differentiated learning through responsive learning because different students have different needs. Differentiated learning caters to individualized needs, the learning strengths, and the weaknesses of the school children. Differentiated instruction is attempted to address the needs of multiple groups of students in a heterogeneous setting. It is an approach to teaching where teachers proactively modify the curriculum, teaching methods, resources, and learning activities to address students' diverse needs in a classroom (Tomlinson, 2013). While heterogeneous instruction is attractive because it addresses equity of opportunity for a broad range of learners, mixed-ability classrooms are likely to fall short of their promise unless teachers are equipped to address the varied learners' needs. In such settings, equality of opportunity becomes a reality only when students receive instruction suited to their varied readiness levels, interests, and learning preferences, thus enabling them to maximize the opportunity for growth (McLaughlin & Talbert, 1993). Teachers must be equipped to address a wide range of talents and experiences to meet various needs. This is easier said than done because actualizing in practice is more challenging than articulating in theory. For example, to individualize teaching students in a classroom that come from diverse cultures and backgrounds, different levels of learning capabilities such as slow learners or fast learners, different characters such as extroverts or introverts, or personal issues such as identity crisis, broken family, different demographic location such as urban and rural would require much time to prepare.

Nonetheless, the demands of progression call for a change in the teaching pedagogies that cater to the industrial and educational revolutions. An environment that encourages teachers and students to use their cognitive skills in the classroom should be created. Teachers and students need to undergo a process of change that involves learning new strategies and developing their roles, examining their strength and commitment, and experiencing a variety of feelings of doubt and despair before reaching a feeling of satisfaction, such as responsive and responsible learning. This chapter therefore discusses (i) teaching and learning approaches and pedagogies practiced in Malaysia; (ii) deliberates the reasons why a change is desirable, i.e., a game changer; and (iii) discourses that responsive and responsible learning should be the way forward to enhance the education system in Malaysia.

THE CURRENT EDUCATION SYSTEM

The teaching of Science, Technology, Engineering, and Mathematics (STEM) is to be improved further and reinforced under the 12th Malaysia Plan 2021-2025, the National Education System. The infrastructures of schools and institutions are to be upgraded. TVET (Technical and Vocational Education and Training) will be revamped, and a flexible higher education system will be created. The National Education System aims to address current issues, restart and rejuvenate socioeconomic development for long-term sustainability and prosperity, and enhance the nation's competitiveness to become a more resilient and sustainable player on the world stage. Many of the strategies drawn up in the 12th Malaysia Plan are in response to the challenging situation brought about by the COVID-19 pandemic. The COVID-19 pandemic has caused a spike in unemployment and affected how people work, and businesses operate. These societal changes necessitate the realignment of the labor market, education, and training landscape.

Since human capital is a crucial driver of economic growth and socioeconomic development, the measures taken should be to develop a capable, skilled, flexible, and relevant workforce, i.e., intellectual capital. The focus now for the education sector is to;

- improve the quality of education;
- transform technical and vocational education and training (TVET);
- strengthen lifelong learning (LLL);

- increase the efficiency of training people to meet industry demands.

To implement the plans of the National Educational System, efforts must be made to improve the quality of education to enhance labor productivity. There is no doubt that high-quality education produces a high-caliber talent pool with high industrial skills and people who are highly adaptable. However, the education system needs to be revamped from time to time to meet the changing skills required by industries and embrace new evolving technologies. The quality of education should be improved in Malaysia. Apart from curriculum review, the subjects taught in schools and universities should also be reviewed. The teaching pedagogies/approaches to achieve quality education are pertinent. Research suggests that it is up to the teachers' and lecturers' creativity in indulging and experimenting the varies pedagogies to connect and relate the subjects taught to the students to achieve the learning outcomes. Research carried out, however, indicates that school teachers practice the conventional method of teaching, such as rote teaching, which is teacher-centered (Grapragasem et al., 2014). Does rote teaching, which is teacher-centered, conform to the theories of education? 'Educational theory' is an overarching term that describes a collection of theories that explain the application, interpretation, and purpose of learning and education. Personal and environmental experiences inhibit and enhance learning experiences that enrich world views and knowledge. Learning theories develop hypotheses that describe how this process takes place. The central concepts and theories of learning include behaviorist theories, cognitive psychology, constructivism, social constructivism, experiential learning, multiple intelligence, situated learning theory, and community of practice. Both curriculum and learning ought to conform to the many theories of education which are (Suzanne et al., 2006);

i. behaviorist theories: Learning is based on systematically feeding knowledge into students with positive feedback from teachers and the educational institution. If students' do an excellent job, they are awarded the due recognition.
ii. cognitive psychology: In cognitive psychology, learning is understood as acquiring knowledge: the learner is an information processor who absorbs information, undertakes cognitive operations, and stocks it in memory.
iii. constructivism: Constructivism states that learners construct meaning only through active engagement with the world (such as experiments or real-world problem solving).
iv. social constructivism: This theory incorporates some of the tacit tenets of peer pressure. Specifically, students observe other students and model their behavior accordingly. Sometimes it is to emulate peers; other times; it is to distinguish themselves from peers. Harnessing the power of this theory involves getting students' attention, focusing on how students can retain information, identifying when it is appropriate to reproduce a previous behavior, and determining students' motivation
v. experiential learning: There are plenty of clichés and parables about teaching someone something by doing it. Experiential learning became an official learning theory, not until the early 1980s. This approach emphasizes both are learning about something and experiencing it so that students can apply knowledge in real-world situations.
vi. multiple intelligence: This theory states that each person has different way of learning and using intelligence in their daily lives.

And

Responsive and Responsible Learning in the Malaysian Education System

vii. situated learning theory and community of practice: Situated learning is a theory that explains an individual's acquisition of professional skills and includes research on apprenticeship into how legitimate peripheral participation leads to membership in a community of practice.

Inferences drawn from these theories are; that students should not be treated as empty vessels, blank slates, or passive observers. There is more to learning than just imparting knowledge, and education should keep pace with progression. The lacunae in the education system in Malaysia were glaring during the Covid-19 pandemic. The movement control order (MCO) during the covid-19 pandemic in Malaysia resulted in the education system being in a state of anomaly. Accessibility to education became a significant obstacle as children could not attend school. Eventually, when the online platform was utilized to teach, the many learning theories seemed redundant. For example, programmes that require experiential learning could not be carried out. Hands-on approaches suffered a setback. It was a learning process for primary school children, let alone preschool children, to adapt to online teaching and learning. At the tertiary level, top management had to decide on the suitable mode of assessments, issues on plagiarism, and grades for formative and summative assessments had to be revamped. At the students' end, since face-to-face teaching shifted to an online teaching method, accessibility to Wi-Fi and internet connections became an issue. At the tertiary level, students complained that the home environment was not suited for studying.

Teachers and academicians were grappling with the new norm of teaching and learning. Students suffered from stress and tension because they could not self-study, as online learning required them to be independent learners. Teachers and academicians suffered the same as they had to retailor teaching approaches suited to online mode of imparting knowledge. The MCO duration demarcated the weakness in the Malaysian education system. It reflected that the education system in Malaysia needs to be equipped for online learning. It also reflected that students were unprepared and unable to cope with independent learning. The genuine fear that the educational gaps will widen further needs to be addressed in practical ways. One means of harnessing independent learning but taking a holistic approach should be responsive and responsible learning.

RESPONSIVE AND RESPONSIBLE LEARNING

Charney, R.S. (1992), co-founder of responsive learning, wrote a book on "Teaching Children to Care: Management in the Responsive Classroom." The book amplifies that responsive teaching results from a strong focus on students as individuals and emphasizes the students' social, emotional, physical, and cognitive development. The book also emphasizes the role of the teacher, who ought to be given autonomy to connect with the students to relate to what has been taught instead of being confined to the mainstream curriculum and conventional teacher-centered pedagogies. Research has shown that reluctant students progress academically when they experience responsive teaching. Case studies have documented the importance of "responsive teaching" characterized by ongoing personal support, candid feedback, and dialogue regarding academic and personal choices (Robertson et al., 2015).

Responsive learning is student-centered. This approach emphasizes the social and emotional learning approach to teaching and discipline. It is research and evidence-based practices designed to create safe, joyful, and engaging classroom and school communities for students and teachers. Schools and teachers that adopt the 'Responsive Classroom' approach focus on (1) creating optimal learning conditions for students to develop the academic, social, and emotional skills needed for success during school and after school and (2) building positive school and classroom communities where students learn, behave, hope, and set to achieve goals. In responsive learning, building intrinsic motivation that leads to the development of self-control and self-regulation is given prominence. External motivators such as the promise of rewards or the threat of punishment to shape behavior are discouraged. Schools using this approach have experienced increased teacher effectiveness, higher student achievement, and improved school climate in the United States of America. Several studies, including a large-scale randomized, controlled trial recently completed by researchers at the University of Virginia, have found that teachers' use of Responsive Classroom practices is associated with growth in student academic achievement and social skills. The recent study also showed responsive teaching pedagogies to be equally beneficial for students from all socioeconomic backgrounds. This research also indicated that children who struggle with school, such as juvenile delinquency, showed improved attitudes and excelled academically (Horsh et al., 2002). Charney (1991) states in her book that responsive classroom is about inculcating ethical ideals in students, i.e., developing the desire and interest in students to learn. Teachers were also motivated and enjoyed teaching under responsive learning. Responsive learning focuses on the following:

- Engaging Academics: Effective teaching requires that teachers know how to offer academic lessons, assignments, and activities that are active and interactive, appropriately challenging, purposeful, and connected to students' interests.
- Effective Management: Effective teaching is possible only in well-managed classrooms and schools. In such classrooms, teachers establish and teach behavior expectations, manage the schedule, and organize physical spaces in ways that enable students to work with autonomy and focus.
- Positive Community: Effective teaching requires a classroom and school where every child feels safe, valued, and fully included in the learning community; where teacher and students share a common purpose along with regular routines and traditions that form a comforting underpinning for their days; and where a sense of joy envelops hard work.
- Developmental Awareness: Effective teaching results when teachers have knowledge of child development and use that knowledge, along with regular observations of students, to create a developmentally appropriate environment for learning.

Apart from teaching and learning methodology, educational policies, and professional standards, assessments are pertinent to support, monitor, and report on student learning. Educational research confirms assessment-based teaching as a potentially effective educational strategy to improve student achievement (Black & Wiliam, 1998). Therefore, assessment is part of the education process. However, the most visible assessments are summative in schools and higher educational institutions. Summative assessments are used to measure what students have learned at the end of a programme or subject, to promote students, to ensure they have met required standards on the way to earning certification for school completion or tertiary education completion or to enter certain occupations, or as a method for selecting students for entry into further education. Between formative and summative assessment, formative assessment seems more suited for responsive learning. Research findings suggest that,

"Formative work involves new ways to enhance feedback between those taught and the teacher, which require new modes of pedagogy and significant changes in classroom practice. Underlying the various approaches are assumptions about what makes for effective learning, particularly that students have to

be actively involved. For assessment to function formatively, the results have to be used to adjust teaching and learning, so a significant aspect of any programme will be the ways in which teachers do this." (Black & Wiliam, 1998).

Therefore, teachers using formative assessment approaches and techniques are better prepared to meet diverse students' needs. Furthermore, through formative assessment, differentiation and adaptation of teaching will raise levels of student achievement and achieve more significant equity of student outcomes. Students will better grasp what is being taught to them. The current assessment method practiced in schools in Malaysia and higher educational institutions is exam-oriented. Students are taught based on the syllabus of a subject to prepare them for a summative examination at the end of a semester in a school or university. Most of the time, teachers and lecturers alike are in a hurry to complete the syllabus to prepare students for the summative assessment. On the other hand, students have no choice but to grasp the lessons taught to prepare themselves for the exams. This approach leaves little or no time to appreciate or reflect on what has been taught, which is why formative assessment is better suited for a responsive learning approach. For example, a subject with ten topics will be better taught and learned if some assessment is assigned after teaching every topic to test the students understanding and appreciation of the subject taught.

Furthermore, in a globally networked community, society is assumed to be knowledge-based because knowledge is easily accessible. The current generation is familiar with the Internet of things and Big Data. Apprehending evaluation should be attuned to the development of science and technology that is formative-based.

The following features should be present in an excellent formative assessment tool namely:

1. It should be goal-oriented and based on what is taught daily. An excellent formative assessment is precise, tangible, and measurable since it is intended to assist students in performing well and appreciating what is being taught. The student should be able to reflect their own performance.
2. Formative assessment tools must concentrate on higher-order thinking abilities to reason, rationalize, invent and innovate. It should not be to apply and justify, but also to resonate is equally essential.
3. The assessments should keep students responsible for their results. The student's performance will be used as a guide to assist the student in understanding and appreciating the subject taught. The assessment should be a tool to better themselves and project themselves for further development.
4. Good formative assessment tools should be coherent and cognizant of accommodating the student's needs, understanding, background, and surrounding environment. A holistic approach should be undertaken.
5. The assessment should excite, stimulate, motivate, and draw the student to participate and assimilate what has been taught.
6. Learning should be without any form of fear and students should be expected to make mistakes. Most importantly the students who lag in their studies should be given the opportunity to learn from their mistakes instead of being penalised for it.

Adapting Responsive Learning in Malaysia and Suggestions for Reform

The education system and curriculum in Malaysia adopt the conventional method, which is teacher-centered, as research findings by Radzali, U. S., Mohd-Yusof, K., & Phang, F. A. (2018) indicated for the engineering discipline. Lau, H. (2020) stated in his article that students fared better if the teaching pedagogy was student-centered, specifically in teaching economics. In adapting to responsive and responsible learning in Malaysia, a paradigm shift is needed for effective learning. Learning should be student-centered. Pedagogies of teaching methods ought to be creative and cognitively stimulating, such as application of set-induction activities. Self-induction activities require a learning process where the teacher is required to devise innovative and creative activities that arouse the student's attention (Ikramina, A. F. (2020). The set-induction activities aim to facilitate communication and promote learning possibilities among students.

Apart from teaching pedagogies, the subjects taught also play an important role in effective, responsive, and responsible learning. Instead of emphasizing teaching standard subjects such as maths, science, and languages, other subjects that should be taught to students should be considered, such as the law, the environment, world history or politics. Current subjects taught in school are very much based on industry needs. A robust change is necessary to apply responsive and responsible learning, which should be a game-changer in Malaysian education. As mentioned at the beginning of the chapter, the implementation of responsive and responsible should start at preschool. For example, in the author's view of being an academician and a law teacher, children should be exposed to the importance of law as value-based education. Once enrolled in primary education, values taught should be differentiated to a conduct that is considered wrong. At the secondary level, the connection between law and conducts that is wrong in the eyes of the law should be introduced. The importance of law should be taught. Education systems that uphold and promote respect for the rule of law, in adherence with international human rights and fundamental freedoms, teach the students basic fundamental rights (UNESCO, 2019). Primary and secondary education is meant to provide children with the tools necessary to be productive adults in the real world or rather to cater to the needs of industrial revolutions. Education emphasizes gaining academic knowledge and analytical skills by learning science, math, literature, and history. Social skills and moral values are cultivated by religious or co-curriculum activities teaching children the difference between doing good and bad. Educating the young about the basic needs of the industry and nurturing good moral values in school are deemed sufficient. However, educating children to be law-abiding citizens is not given the due significance in the school curriculum, even though children are told to be law-abiding citizens.

Rightfully, legal education should start from school. Children should be taught the role of law, the machinery of law, and the types of law so that they are nurtured to be law-abiding citizens. Only then ignorance of the law can be of no excuse. Furthermore, knowing how judges think and decide cases and how legislators cooperate to create laws will equip students to participate productively in the political and legal process, which will be the outcome of responsive and responsible learning. Children and teenagers will learn how to apply a general rule to a situation and how to think about how laws ought to be applied. Moreover, education that adheres to the principles of the rule of law can help develop learners' ability to critically understand essential elements of accountability, equality, and fairness (UNESCO, 2019). Through responsive learning and teaching, applying set-induction activities in the form of role-playing, storytelling, and audio-visuals would allow students to appreciate and understand the significance of law apart from drawing their attention and interest in law. Consequently, in a globally networked society, the psychomotor domain should be cultivated with the cognitive and affective domains for effective, responsive learning.

By the time a student enrolls in the law programme, the appreciation and significance of law would have been captured. Promoting the rule of law through education also helps learners acquire the knowledge, skills, values, and attitudes they need to contribute constructively to society. It allows them to positively shape public institutions and policies, encouraging non-violent and peaceful avenues of civic engagement. Teachers are vital in developing students' knowledge, attitude, and skills to constructively and responsibly engage in society, uphold the principle of justice and help build effective, accountable, and inclusive institutions. The subjects taught matter to responsive and responsible learning. Responsive and responsible learning is not only about teachers paying attention to the needs of the students, teachers' autonomy, and aligning teaching pedagogies to the child's best interest. It also involves the subjects taught that should be suited to the current era. Are the subjects taught in the schools in Malaysia thought-provoking and pertinent to evolution? Even more so in the current era of Big Data and AI. These are the matters that ought to be considered in implementing responsive and responsible learning.

CONCLUSION

Changing evolution in education calls for a change in teaching and learning methodologies. Holding on to traditional methodologies that are not effective will only be detrimental to the future generation. Children will become bored, and education will be perceived as a mere paper qualification. More so, it will also be detrimental to the nation's social, political, and economic development. As Woodie Thomas (2016) said,

"As educators, parents, or anyone that works with children, we must first learn to love children. Then teach them knowledge, including respect for others who may look or think differently than they do. We must never frighten, force, or intimidate our children into submission. We must teach them personal discipline and other tools to govern themselves. Finally, we must teach them the ability to read, write and do arithmetic and how to understand and apply that knowledge to function independently in a free democratic society."

Therefore, a meaningful educational process is warranted, such as responsive and responsible learning that addresses the students' traditional academic learning needs and, most importantly, the educational process that includes an educational learning plan to address the needs of the student as a whole which includes any learning disability, learning disorders, social, cultural, behavioral, emotional, physical, mental health, nutritional health, family problems or any other learning issues that impact the student's ability to learn. The teachers must also be equipped to materialize responsive and responsible learning through systemized training. To realise and achieve the objectives of responsive and responsible learning, therefore, requires due consideration of the teaching pedagogies, assessment and evaluation methods, subjects, creativity, and autonomy of the educators and the curriculum as a whole which will be a game-changer in the Malaysian education system.

REFERENCES

Allen, K., & Friedman, B. (2010). Affective Learning: A Taxonomy for Teaching Social Work Values. *Journal of Social Work Values and Ethics*.

Béteille, T., & Evans, D. (2021). *Successful Teachers, Successful Students: Recruiting and Supporting Society's Most Crucial Profession*. World Bank. Retrieved from https://policycommons.net/artifacts/2445925/successful-teachers-successful-students/3467666/

Bhat, S. (2021). *An Evaluative Study of Educational Philosophy of Swami Vivekananda*. doi:10.31426/ijamsr.2021.4.7.4511

Black, P., & Wiliam, D. (1998). 'Assessment and Classroom Learning, Assessment in Education: Principles. *Policy & Practice, 5*, 1.

Bloom, B. (1956). *Taxonomy of Educational Objectives. Book I: Cognitive Domain*. David Mckay.

Charney, R. S. (1993). Teaching children to care: Management in the responsive classroom. Northeast Foundation for Children.

DeLuca, C., LaPointe-McEwan, D., & Luhanga, U. (2016). Approaches to Classroom Assessment Inventory: A New Instrument to Support Teacher Assessment Literacy. *Educational Assessment, 21*(4), 248–266. Advance online publication. doi:10.1080/10627197.2016.1236677

Grapragasem, S., Krishnan, A., & Mansor, A. (2014). Current Trends in Malaysian Higher Education and the Effect on Education Policy and Practice: An Overview. *International Journal of Higher Education, 3*(1). Advance online publication. doi:10.5430/ijhe.v3n1p85

Horsch, P., Chen, J.-Q., & Wagner, S. (2002). The Responsive Classroom Approach. *Education and Urban Society, 34*(3), 365–383. doi:10.1177/0013124502034003006

Ikramina, A. F. (2020). Teachers'set Induction And Closure In Efl Young Learners Classroom. *Eeal Journal, 3*(3), 226–231.

Ishak, N. A., & Jamil, H. (2020). Pedagogies towards enhancing students' intellectual capital in Malaysian secondary schools. *Asia Pacific Journal of Educators and Education, 35*(2), 57–76. doi:10.21315/apjee2020.35.2.4

Jayabalan, S. (2017). Teaching Law: The Learner in the Driver's Seat. In *Student-Driven Learning Strategies for the 21st Century Classroom*. IGI Global. . doi:10.4018/978-1-5225-1689-7

Lau, H. (2020). Comparing the Effectiveness of Student-Centred Learning (SCL) Over Teacher-Centred Learning (TCL) of Economic Subjects in a Private University in Sarawak. *International Journal of Innovation, Creativity, and Change, 10*(10), 147–160.

McLaughlin, M., & Talbert, J. (1993). *Contexts That Matter for Teaching and Learning: Strategic Opportunities*. Academic Press.

Miller, R. (1997). *What are schools for? Holistic education in American culture* (3rd ed.). Holistic Education Press.

Radzali, U. S., Mohd-Yusof, K., & Phang, F. A. (2018). Changing the conception of teaching from teacher-centered to student-centered learning among engineering lecturers. *Global Journal of Engineering Education, 20*(2), 120–126.

Robertson, A. D., Atkins, L. J., Levin, D. M., & Richards, J. (2015). What is responsive teaching? In *Responsive teaching in science and mathematics* (pp. 1–35). Routledge. doi:10.4324/9781315689302

Shanti, S. (2019). Swami Vivekananda's Perspective on Education. *JETIR, 6*(5). Retrieved from http://www.jetir.org

Strahan, D. (2008). Successful Teachers Develop Academic Momentum with Reluctant Students. *Middle School Journal, 39*(5), 4–12.

Thomas, W. (2016, August 1). The Education Revolution. Academic Press.

Toffler, A. (1974). *Learning for tomorrow: The role of the future in education.* Vintage Books.

Tomlinson, C. A., & Moon, T. R. (2013). *Assessment and Student Success in a Differentiated Classroom.* Association for Supervision and Curriculum Development.

Turdieva, N. S. (2021). Didactic conditions for the formation of attitudes toward education as a value among primary school pupils. *Middle European Scientific Bulletin, 10.* Retrieved from http://cejsr.academicjournal.io/index.php/journal/article/view/368

UNESCO & UNODC. (2019). *Strengthening the Rule of Law through Education: A Guide for Policymakers.* Author.

Wilson, S. M., & Peterson, P. L. (2006). *Theories of Learning and Teaching: What Do They Mean for Educators?* Working Paper.

Chapter 4
Meaningful Learning Didactic Strategies in Higher Education

José G. Vargas-Hernández
https://orcid.org/0000-0003-0938-4197
Posgraduate and Research Department, Tecnológico Mario Molina Unidad Zapopan, Mexico

Omar C. Vargas-González
https://orcid.org/0000-0002-6089-956X
Tecnológico Nacional de México, Ciudad Guzmán, Mexico

Selene Castañeda-Burciaga
https://orcid.org/0000-0002-2436-308X
Universidad Politécnica de Zacatecas, Mexico

Adlet D. Kariyev
https://orcid.org/0000-0002-7789-9080
Kazakh National Women's Teacher Training University, Kazakhstan

EXECUTIVE SUMMARY

This work aims to analyze and explain the didactic strategies used to achieve meaningful learning. It begins under the assumption that if meaningful learning is created and students are given freedom and confidence, they can find their own answers and develop their knowledge both in the classroom and in practical life. The method used is the analytical-descriptive one of the reviews of the literature of the main authors who have given rise to this approach, its elements, and the didactic strategies used. It is concluded that the design and implementation of didactic strategies focused on meaningful learning with the application of active didactic methodologies and strategies in meaningful learning processes depending on the context in which it takes place obtains better results in the training of professionals.

DOI: 10.4018/978-1-6684-6076-4.ch004

INTRODUCTION

Changes in the historical evolutionary process of education are relevant factors that influence the economic, social, political, and environmental development of peoples. In the evolution of educational models, the constant is the characterization of the need to give meaning to values and attitudes that guide the generation and development of ideas, projects, strategies, and programs that allow the reproduction and preservation of the material and social conditions that they facilitate the contemplation and incorporation of the human being to his concrete reality from a comprehensive perspective of inclusive and meaningful learning.

However, the dynamic forms and processes of learning have undergone transformations over time at the service of human development (Apodaca-Orozco, et al. 2017), which, in turn, have led to significant advances in learning, attributing shared responsibilities for the achievement of goals based on the self-care of people and with a clear trend of protagonist recognition of the beneficiaries of these processes (Lillo, 2014). The foregoing has caused that the rote learning of disciplinary concepts with traditional approaches has been exceeded by the expectations that students have, and the demands posed by economic, labor, social, political, cultural reality, etc.

Likewise, the methodological approaches that support the didactic strategies applied in learning have always been under the traditional approaches to teaching as absolute models in university systems, which, to be implemented, repress culture, language, history, traditions, customs, and practices of peoples. These types of learning have not been significant because there is no correspondence with the cultural traits of the peoples (Arnold & Yapita, 2000).

On the other hand, over time, the development of higher education has been perfected in all fields of knowledge, but in health, with the implementation of curricular reforms based on pedagogy and sciences related to education that they are necessary and indispensable to face the paradigms. For example, in meaningful learning different paradigms are presented, since the teacher goes from being the person in charge and protagonist of the students' learning to the one who plans and organizes their process in the form of self-regulation so that the students choose and decide their behavior as promoters. and architects of their own learning (Garrote, et al. 2016). Therefore, through essential changes in study plans and programs, progress is made in achieving curricular flexibility, towards meaningful learning with the incorporation of new ethical values and modern technologies (Vergara, Travieso & Crespo, 2014).

Thus, the different pedagogical and didactic models are relevant to the extent that they promote a vision in which the student is considered the center of active and meaningful learning (Espejo, 2016). In this regard, there are several models of meaningful learning that use creative learning and that define all forms of learning methods that involve students in meaningful teaching-learning processes (Bonwell & Eison, 1991).

In accordance with the above, it is necessary to guarantee significant learning with the results of the experiences that students have and that, in turn, requires their motivations, interests and actions as a subject with its own content, where there is a permanent relationship. with the content of the previous knowledge and the link with the new knowledge of their environment; connected with local problems and global trends, in such a way that opportunities and solutions to problems are identified (Beck, et al. 2015). Recognizing that, part of the meaningful learning experiences is the participation of students in discursive and disciplinary activities instead of being only receptive (Almulla, 2020).

Over the past two decades we have heard an historically unprecedented volume of talk about and praise of democracy, and many governmental, non-governmental, and international organizations have been engaged in democracy promotion. Democracy is a subject that crosses the boundaries in political science, and within my own field of political theory there has been a major revival of democratic theory.

In political theory, argument about "democracy" is usually now qualified by one of an array of adjectives, which include cosmopolitan, agonistic, republican, and monitory. But the new form that has been by far the most successful is deliberative democracy. By 2007 John Dryzek could write that "deliberative democracy now constitutes the most active area of political theory in its entirety (not just democratic theory)." Not only is there an extremely large and rapidly growing literature, both theoretical and empirical, on deliberative democracy, but its influence has spread far outside universities (Pateman, 2012).

However, it can be said that there are few studies focused on strengthening teacher training processes, to improve teaching-learning processes through the design and implementation of didactic strategies in environments focused on meaningful learning.

In this work, the objective of which is to analyze and explain the didactic strategies used to achieve meaningful learning, first a conceptualization is carried out and then the elements or components are analyzed and finally a detailed analysis is made in the delimitation and design of the didactic strategies that are implemented for the achievement of the best results in meaningful learning.

CONCEPTUALIZATION

Meaningful learning is a strategy for the implementation of teaching-learning processes, based on the reality of practice that promotes student autonomy to achieve maximum results. A quality education implies prioritizing the understanding and use of new learning content based on the reality of the context (Galdames, et al. 2011). Likewise, the knowledge and experiences that are identified and related to community activities, such as actions, images and the use of objects that help to develop meanings and concepts, contribute to generating significant learning (Julca, 2000).

Meaningful learning is defined as the non-arbitrary substantive incorporation of new concepts, propositions, and knowledge into the non-arbitrary frame of reference of cognitive structure. That is, meaningful learning goes beyond the scope of cognition, due to the contextualization supported by the possibilities of sharing meaning. While the design of meaningful learning has as a specific framework the significance of learning with the creation of cognitive-constructivist conceptual activities based on students' contextual problems and using the environment as a learning resource (Suyatno, 2009). Therefore, the significant learning process implies that the student understands the meanings of the new learning contents, connecting with the new concepts and propositions, expanding, reorganizing, and rebuilding the existing cognitive structure (Ausubel, 1963; Ausubel et al., 1978).

It is necessary to mention that automatic learning differs from significant learning because it only involves memorization by repetition without recognition of meaning, and it contributes little to modifying the cognitive structure of students who have diverse backgrounds of prior knowledge, in quality and quantity to do. associations between old and new knowledge, giving rise to the appearance of various levels of meaningful learning (Novak, 1993).

For its part, the learning assimilation theory defines meaningful learning as the substantive incorporation of new knowledge or propositions into the hierarchical frame of reference of cognitive structure (Ausubel, 1963; Ausubel et al., 1978). The student's learning must be a significant assimilation, with potentially significant materials and contents, with logical meanings relevant to the cognitive structure and, where the main objective is to have the intention to learn significantly.

According to the above, meaningful learning is described as learning that has the purpose of building knowledge based on students' experiences, feelings, and interactions with other students (Scott & Friesen, 2013). It should be noted that deep meaningful learning is an elevated level of thinking and development that is conducted through intellectual participation in questioning, critical thinking, problem solving and metacognitive skills that are oriented to the construction of meanings through patterns of recognition and association of concepts (Mystakidis, 2021).

The concept of significant learning is polysemic and is inserted in the sociocultural reality and with a perspective of the future proposed by the same society. This conception of significant learning is related to the educational practices of the teaching-learning processes that have migrated from approaches focused on the transmission of disciplinary theoretical knowledge to more dynamic practices, where the student adopts a more autonomous role of significant learning. The construction of meaningful learning is the hallmark of higher education achieved through a sustained critical discourse (Ausbel, 1961), linked to teaching methods that result in the ability to identify and analyze the structure to connect existing concepts with new ones. (Jonassen, 2003; Mystakidis, et al. 2019).

Significant learning is achieved with theoretical-practical aspects that can be conducted simultaneously. Therefore, meaningful learning provides skills to be creative and innovative; Likewise, students have access to knowledge, skills, and attitudes to solve problems. In this same sense, for teachers, understanding meaningful learning is valuable to apply it to all levels of education.

So, for learning to be meaningful, the content to be studied is assimilated and related to previously acquired knowledge, therefore, it is a process that is associated with added information in relevant concepts contained in the cognitive structure and connects them to produce understanding of the environment. Therefore, students must understand the situation to solve the problem in a way that is meaningful to them (Ausubel, 1978; Sriraman, 2010).

Theoretical Foundation of Significant Learning

It is recognized that the theory and epistemology of meaningful learning is humanistic constructivism. The concept of meaningful learning has a greater integration with constructivism as a combination of the psychology of human learning and the epistemology of knowledge production (Novak, 1990; Mintzes & Wandersee, 2000). Cognitive learning theory is the basis for developing meaningful learning as a process for the acquisition of new meanings, assuming a set of tools potentially for meaningful learning tasks (Ausubel, 1978).

Similarly, it is identified that the concept of meaningful learning is consistent with constructivism, according to which students build their knowledge with their experiences, establishing significant connections between new experiences and content already acquired. Constructivism is a theoretical current that considers knowledge as an active process of transformation of the human being that is integrated into their own knowledge structures (Aznar, 1992; Carretero, 1993; Gómes and Gargallo, 1993) in an emotional-affective and semantic way. that give meaning to learning.

Therefore, students learn significantly when they relate new knowledge to existing ones. For meaningful learning to occur, new concepts must be integrated into the existing knowledge structure, connecting existing concepts with new knowledge (Fletcher & Chróinín, 2021; Bao, & Koenig, 2019). It is a process of relating added information to concepts already contained in the cognitive structure (Dahar, 2011).

As a theory, meaningful learning accommodates the demand for teaching-learning processes achieved through the application of knowledge in authentic contexts. Meaningful learning is related to contextual learning supported by problems and situations. For meaningful learning to occur, it is necessary to relate learning to the problems of the context. Students need to understand the situation to solve the problem in such a way that it is meaningful learning (Sriraman, 2010).

Therefore, having activities, creativity and innovation are relevant factors to create meaningful learning outcomes. On the other hand, inclusive concepts are entities of the cognitive structure that allow meaningful learning with new elements that form categories through reality representation systems that integrate knowledge into the subject's structure (Ausubel, 1968). In accordance with what was previously indicated, the model of human cognitive architecture based on the theory of the cognitive load of instruction is identified in an intrinsic, extrinsic, and pertinent way of the elements of interactive information and the time required for meaningful learning (Romero Juárez, 2020).

The notion that emphasizes the cognitive processes by which students incorporate knowledge into their existing knowledge structures is meaningful learning, regardless of the context that is conducted, cognitive, socio-constructivist and socio-cultural learning theories differ in the types of meanings of learning. emerging context. The cognitive approach emphasizes the existence of a cognitive structure in which the student learns, which means that meaningful learning emerges in the context of what he already knows, so teachers need to prepare the environment in a way that offers relationships to the pre-existing cognitive structures that are used as anchors to deliver new content in the cognitive structure (Ausubel, 1968).

Regarding the above, the contributions of Ausubel stand out, who developed the theory of cognitive psychology as a branch of psychology to include scientific studies of mental symptoms in the acquisition of knowledge, that is, in the way in which beings humans obtain knowledge, the way in which new information is assimilated and assumes that knowledge is the result of human construction. For this reason, if students relate the information with the knowledge they already have, they obtain significant learning that has more advantages than rote learning. Thus, learning can range from rote learning to meaningful learning in which information is delivered to learners to identify, select, and learn outcomes (Novak & Gowin, 2006).

However, socio-constructivist approaches emphasize social interaction, communication, and collaboration to create meaningful learning contexts (Roelofs & Terwel, 1999; Roelofs et al. 2003). Whereas sociocultural approaches define social learning as the participation of students in social practices (Van Oers, 1998), rather than in contexts focused on specific problem-solving tasks, but on participation in social practices (Volman & Ten Dam, 2015). It should be noted that there is no homogeneous and uniform approach to teaching and learning that has been nourished by complementary theories and their applications, which support the promotion of academic and social skills that contribute to meaningful learning, such as the development of cooperation. and social communication (Sharan, 2015).

ELEMENTS OF MEANINGFUL LEARNING

The promotion of inclusive education throughout the academic community must be done from the participation of significant learning, close to the comprehensive quality approaches of the educational system that values society as a right in relation to people and the type of society that is established. wants to achieve (UNESCO and OREALC, 2007). Inclusive education requires a conceptual redefinition of the creation and development of common learning spaces delimited by special conditions under teaching and evaluation models of significant learning, from humanistic perspectives that respond to the sociocultural historical complexity to train quality students, capable of developing all their human potential, which remains and culminates in their training (Rosano, 2007).

Among the elements of the construction of an inclusive education with significant learning is the awareness of the actors directly involved in the teaching-learning processes, teachers, and students, who perform the substantive functions of teaching, research and validated socioeconomic projection. by the results (Arizabaleta et al., 2016).

Meaningful Learning in The Student

Meaningful learning for millennials is a process that adds experiences through their content problems in their environments that make students understand and relate to the content. According to Gowin (1990), the process is significant when there is interaction between students, educators and the content that allows understanding of learning by sharing meanings. Meaningful learning is the interaction of students, educators, and content with innovative concepts and without eliminating scientific values (Moreira, 2011). Meaningful learning prepares millennials to respond appropriately to the competition of the information age.

In this same order of ideas, Hanani (2020) explores learning that provides students with the training of creative, critical, and innovative thinking skills and that can be achieved through various methods, such as active learning, collaborative learning, learning cooperative, problem-based learning, etc. Therefore, meaningful teaching-learning processes encourage students to compare the new knowledge they acquire with previously acquired ones, and support students in building personal knowledge structures (Wang et al., 2014). The quality and quantity of the learner's prior knowledge allow for diverse types of associations with added content, leading to various levels of meaningful learning (Wang, et al. 2020).

It should be noted that the concept of meaningful learning varies among students who can understand what is learned in everyday experiences, so teachers use different contexts such as activation, connection with reality and the creation of intercultural contexts to apply the concepts. learning content in school. Teachers have different concepts of meaningful learning that can be inspired by education aligned with theoretical notions to create contexts and environments, setting goals for their students, although their practices are not always clearly linked to concepts and theories, so that it is not possible to find consistent patterns.

However, cultural, and social assumptions about the nature of responsible learning imply that students authentically participate in the activities of the teaching-learning process (Hammer et al., 2012). The assumption that learning takes place in meaningful learning environments considers that students' motivation and understanding is shared by different theoretical approaches to meaningful learning (Loyens & Gijbels 2008; Mayer, 2004; Wardekker et al. 2012). Meaningful learning is created under the assumption that if students are given freedom and confidence, they can find their own answers and develop their knowledge, both in the classroom and in practical life.

As has been said, meaningful learning allows solving the challenges of the environment with the recognition of a new world order by the new generations that demand quality education and pedagogical innovation, training spaces, didactics, curricular contents, evaluation, training teacher etc (Vincent-Lancrin et al., 2019).

Likewise, meaningful learning takes place in recognized contexts to create learning environments in which students can interact (Van Oers, 1998; Lui & Bonner, 2016; Verschafel & Greer, 2013). Practices such as dialogue, collaboration, independent work, and experiential learning support meaningful learning (Polman, et al. 2021). Collaborative processing promotes meaningful learning because the student understands the meaning of each concept and discovers their similarities, dependencies, and contrasts.

This new model aims for the student to be competent with the abilities to face current demands with the acquisition of significant knowledge according to the different contexts in which they will have their professional development. The use of capacities based on multiple intelligences with an axiological approach contributes to the development of meaningful learning. It should also be mentioned that the perceived individual capacities to organize and execute the courses of action required to obtain significant learning represent a construct of motivation to achieve different forms of performance (Bandura, 1986, p. 391).

The role of teachers in Meaningful Learning

Meaningful learning is a characteristic of education (Oostdam et al. 2007), but little is known about what teachers do to achieve it in their students, how they interpret it and establish it based on their personal points of view. It is also reflected in the educational concept that the teacher has, who creates meaningful learning environments in accordance with his pedagogical concept and philosophy, with which the context is developed to create meaningful learning environments.

It must be recognized that the concept of meaningful learning has different meanings in practice. In relation to the teaching-learning processes, this goes beyond the mere application of knowledge and practice within a context that gives meaning to students. However, there is not full knowledge about the practices that teachers conduct in their process of generating meaningful learning for students. Because teachers have different perceptions of what meaningful learning is, based on different theoretical-conceptual notions and pedagogical practices that they contribute and with varied objectives depending on what students understand they should learn by creating an intercurricular context.

It should be added that teachers have new roles as facilitators, advisors, and administrators rather than teachers. The teacher is conceived as a learner in the process of his own formation with the support of historical-cultural components and contents that are essential to promote meaningful learning. Whose purpose is to create and maintain learning environments that involve students in meaningful learning activities that have social presence, learning presence and cognitive presence as components (Valverde-Berrocoso, et al. 2020; Arbaugh, 2013; Thomas, et al., 2017; Shea & Bidjerano, 2009; Joo, et al., 2011; Joksimovic, et al., 2014; Shea & Bidjerano, 2012; Kozan & Caskurlu, 2018; Rubin, et al., 2013; Kim, et al. 2011; Zhan & Mei, 2013; Borup, et al. 2012; Ke, 2010).

Teachers who offer meaningful learning experiences to their students consider their design to be constructive, active, intentional, cooperative, authentic, and relational (Howland, et al. 2011; Mystakidis, 2019). Meaningful learning requires tasks linked to authentic experiences; it is cooperative and relational because it occurs naturally in communities of knowledge construction, emotionally involving students in designs that link theory and practice with experiences in which teachers and students express themselves (Kostiainen et al. 2018).

The teacher is responsible for the development of his class, the maker of pedagogical knowledge and his own teaching practice; their professional academic training should promote critical, reflective, and innovative teaching-learning processes for meaningful student learning (Araujo & Campos, 2006). Greater involvement in reflecting on the relationships between knowledge concepts increases the generation of significant learning (Nesbit & Adesope, 2013).

Likewise, the responsibility of the complex functions of the teacher requires more than the simple transmission of information, the use of affective and cognitive processes that contribute to the meaningful learning of the students. The teacher must have the ability to integrate technology, pedagogy, and disciplinary content, to build knowledge and facilitate meaningful learning. These activities contribute to self-assessment processes to identify the appropriation of new knowledge and changes in skills as evaluation strategies of the significant teaching-learning process, to improve (Del Campo, 2000; Delgado & Oliver, 2010).

In the classes, the teachers put into practice active and participatory methodologies so that the students reflect and use the knowledge learned as subjects that generate knowledge through meaningful learning. Thus, the variables that most influence the generation of significant knowledge are the role of the teacher and the practical activities.

In the same way, it is recognized that the cultural identity of the teacher in her community is inherent, because she is the mediator between the knowledge, knowledge, traditions, and customs that are integrated with the new knowledge to generate significant and quality learning. Cultures have a large amount of knowledge, knowledge, experiences and practices on certain trades and topics that can be used in socio-intercultural teaching-learning processes for the development of community identity and meaningful learning. Therefore, the committed teacher is always up to date with new knowledge in all fields of human knowledge.

In accordance with the above, the role of the teacher is to adapt the teaching-learning processes to the educational profile of the students to enhance their will and action in the generation of significant learning. In the significant teaching-learning process, the teacher ceases to be the protagonist and responsible according to the behavioral theory to become the planner and organizer of the work of his students, whom he must motivate in their interest in the subject. The teacher enables meaningful learning in his students by producing relationships between previous organizers that, as cognitive bridges, establish inclusive concepts and new materials organized so that relationships with prior knowledge and what must be learned are produced.

DIDACTIC STRATEGIES FOR SIGNIFICANT LEARNING

Meaningful learning uses processes of organization, elaboration and introduces critical concepts and principles of the content. Learning experiences that use pre-structured thinking skills have been associated with deep understanding of content and long-term retention of meaningful learning (Kay & Kibbl, 2016). On the other hand, transformative learning implies the construction of learning processes through significant, inclusive, and democratic interaction and active participation in the construction of significant knowledge processes that facilitate positive attitudes and skills. The meaningful learning process is facilitated by collaborative, interactive, investigative, and high-level thinking activities (Tsimane & Downing, 2019).

In the same way, operational and differentiated educational planning allows extrapolating in different dimensions the performance of didactic activities with significant learning proposed in the study program with the vision of turning them into innovative, creative, and fair actors. Selecting the subject by coupling the contents to the socioeconomic context and establishing the learning objectives of knowledge, attitudes, skills, and abilities that are to be developed are necessary elements for a more meaningful learning. The essential elements for the meaningful learning of a specific subject are its multidimensional reality, its historical-cultural background, its socioeconomic environment, its characteristics, approaches, values, principles, material, and didactic strategies, etc.

However, teachers introduce learning strategies in accordance with the instructional objectives for the achievement of significant learning. The participation and interventions of teachers in the activities of the teaching-learning process through didactic strategies should be aimed at achieving meaningful learning. Therefore, the meaningful learning approach requires a teacher who, beyond the traditional approach, uses the most proactive, creative, and innovative teaching strategies, ethically committed in his or her guiding action, who assumes changes in the environment, understands reality and visualizes the challenges of the opportunities. In this way, the implementation of innovative didactic strategies that transform pedagogical and didactic practices aimed at the construction of significant learning becomes relevant.

In line with the above, different didactic strategies can be used to increase the quality of the teaching-learning processes with meaningful results. The didactic material to be used in the strategies of a significant teaching-learning process must motivate considering the learning styles, the aesthetics of the design, the style, and the purpose of the communication (Morales-Ceballos, 2020). On the other hand, the contents of the subjects that students consider complex require, in addition to mastering the subject, the training of teachers in educational strategies that aim to promote significant learning to transmit knowledge effectively.

DIDACTIC STRATEGIES FOR MEANINGFUL LEARNING

The design of didactic strategies of virtual education with tools of the blended learning (b-learning) modality, allow strengthening significant learning, with the support of active learning methods in training close to the reality of practice and with an increase in the student autonomy. Virtual education with the use of information and communication technologies facilitates the use of tools in the educational process that favor the development of significant learning (Guerrero Castañeda, et al. 2019). It should be noted that information and communication technologies as part of a didactic strategy have a positive impact on significant teaching-learning processes, where the more ICTs are used in learning, the better the learning results of the students. students (Al-Ansi et al. 2019).

Likewise, the development of skills and knowledge of didactic strategies to be implemented through information and communication technologies through communication platforms is essential for students to achieve meaningful learning (Flores et al. 2020). Likewise, interactive learning activities (Wu et al. 2017), as didactic strategies, contribute to improving significant teaching-learning processes with the development of skills through the creation of online learning communities from home and with the practice of authentic tasks in face-to-face sessions, focus groups, presentations, and with direct questions to the online instructor.

On the other hand, interaction in collective works as a didactic strategy between equals facilitates the construction and natural acquisition of knowledge, abilities and skills that lead to significant learning. The blended and blended learning model is a strategy that provides students with opportunities that help them achieve deeper and more complex levels of meaningful learning (Patrick & Sturgis 2015; Şentürk, 2021).

Therefore, the acquisition of methodologies and didactics for the creation of e-learning and b-learning strategies facilitate the generation of virtual learning modalities that allow metacognition and meaningful learning. In the same way, the use of augmented reality and neurodidactics as recreational tools allow the design and optimization of the use of didactic strategies for significant learning processes through cerebral and sensory stimulation of emotions and imagination, which affect the meaningful learning from a motivating perspective.

Similarly, significant learning environments, reception and discovery, and individual differences influence prior knowledge about learning effectiveness. The environment integrates discovery learning to encourage active participation in meaningful learning. Using a meaningful learning environment framework using a machine-guided ontology, Wang et al. (2017) developed a visualization support system that helps the ebook user to identify and understand the concepts and relate them to their cognitive structure, which results in a better environment to receive meaningful learning.

Likewise, the development of skills in foreign languages in the so-called flipped classroom stands out, where the group of students who work with the platform, including learning strategies, contribute to the achievement of cognitive learning results, who achieve more significant learning in grammar, speaking, reading, and writing. Similarly, Kostaris, et al. (2017) have revealed that meaningful learning in the flipped classroom contributes to greater involvement and motivation in information and communication.

Therefore, self-regulated meaningful learning strategies affect the performance of abilities, skills, and abilities in favor of the groups that work in the inverted room model (Öztürk & Çakıroğlu, 2021). In contrast, other research results show that students have learning difficulties to achieve meaning in computer courses taught under the flipped classroom strategy compared to traditional methods, due to time constraints and quick anger (Cabi, 2018).

It is important to point out that the results of the research are not conclusive in terms of improving the meaningful learning of the students, in such a way that it allows them greater knowledge and autonomy in their professional training, although it was shown that in virtual education one learns as much or more than in traditional education. In virtual learning, students do not always have previous experience, but it is more effective than with traditional learning. The achievement of significant learning depends on the student's experience in the use of virtuality after conducting training activities in any type of technological tool.

In short, the correct use of technological tools and knowledge of active methodologies allow the construction and consolidation of significant learning, such as problem-based learning, the flipped classroom and case studies, among other methodologies. However, it is necessary for teachers to demonstrate a broad conceptual proficiency in the flipped classroom, its implementation process in the classroom, accompanying students in the various stages of the teaching-learning process, considering that the student is the protagonist of the educational model.

Meaningful Learning Environments

Meaningful learning environments relate students' needs and interests to their learning and make their experience worthwhile beyond school (Newman et al. 1996; Roelofs & Terwel 1999; Van Oers, 2009). Reception and discovery learning are two diverse types of meaningful learning environments (Ausubel et al., 1978; Novak & Cañas, 2008). In the receiving learning environment, relationships are explicitly provided in the map for transmission to the learner, while in the discovery learning environment, relationships between knowledge and learner autonomy are identified (Ausubel et al., 1978). To foster meaningful learning, cognitive maps and connections help students organize and structure their own frames of reference (Novak & Cañas, 2008).

In the meaningful learning environment, students are provided with concept maps, knowledge, and knowledge topics so that they can associate content elements, definitions, and explanations of knowledge with the structure provided (Chu et al., 2011; Novak & Cañas, 2008; Lee & Segev, 2012; O'Donnell et al., 2002; Wang et al. 2020). Concept maps are an effective learning tool, and because they provide an additional resource to make them meaningful, they allow feedback to students and offer a means to assess meaningful learning performance (Baliga et al. 2021; Daley & Torre, 2010).

For its part, active participation prevents the erosion of curiosity and willingness to explore, as in the case of the meaningful reception learning environment, which also serves as an assessment tool that encourages the construction of learning using meaningful learning strategies. The extensive connections made between learning tasks, instruction, and assessment feedback help students achieve meaningful learning. Likewise, connective feedback helps students navigate through blended learning and connects new learning tasks and different instructional modules that help make sense of assessment results (Wang, et al. 2021). It should be noted that self-assessment judgments on self-efficacy in teaching-learning processes must be realistic to demonstrate significant changes in learning after instruction (Graham, et al. 2005).

In the same way, the knowledge of a wide vocabulary by teachers and students facilitates the understanding of readings, teaching materials, classroom communications and promotes meaningful learning (Pun & Jin, 2021). The experience that results from the need to learn to revise academic work provides the opportunity for teachers and students about the characteristics of effective writing as meaningful instructional learning (Chen, et al. 2021; MacArthur, 2015, 2018). Proficiency in the language used in the teaching-learning processes is essential to conduct oneself in academic activities and achieve superior performance in meaningful learning, and cognitive differences should be considered based on individual characteristics and differences, such as gender. (Zhang & Mi, 2010; Chen et al. 2019).

Now, motivation and learning attitude are two factors to consider creating meaningful learning. Making learning meaningful improves students' motivation to learn. Meaningful learning improves student motivation and performance (Loyens & Gijbels 2008; Van Rijk et al. 2017). Evaluative judgments of self-efficacy, such as the ability to perform a function, demonstrate significant changes in learning and self-efficacy after instruction. Pedagogical and didactic interventions that are more connected to the individual needs of students are more likely to achieve better performance in meaningful learning.

CONCLUSION

Traditional teacher-centered and rote learning styles can only be replaced by meaningful learning that focuses more on student engagement. Likewise, the application of methodologies and active didactic strategies that manage to start significant learning processes according to the context in which it is developed, achieve better results in the training of professionals. It is in this sense that no didactic method and strategy is adequate for all contexts. For example, case studies in which students analyze specific situations presented to arrive at an experiential conceptualization and find effective solutions, allows the content and learning to be more meaningful.

Significant learning is comprehensive learning, which relates through knowledge construction schemes, sequences the use of previous learning to cause the significant generation of knowledge. For a significant learning, the conditions must be given that the curricular contents of the study's lead to a significant learning based on psycho-pedagogical bases and that the student has an interest and an attitude of motivation for the attitudes, abilities, skills, competences, and capacities of the subject. that learns the fulfillment of the acquisition of significant learning corresponds to the development of abilities and skills of analysis and synthesis.

On the other hand, the results of academic performance as indicators of significant learning achieved by students in virtual environments are favorable, although they are not always optimal due to multiple factors. Being that the generation of significant teaching-learning processes is subject to the complexity of the subject and the design of the virtual didactic strategy. So, the advantages of the meaningful learning design are that it eliminates the tendency towards passive learning because students organize their learning activities, it improves collaboration in the group, working together to stimulate the ability to think and the ability to understand the content.

Likewise, the results of research on the impact of information and communication technologies on meaningful learning are not entirely conclusive, although it has been shown that, in virtual learning, although students do not have experiences and knowledge previous ones, achieve greater effectiveness than with the traditional learning system. Recognizing that the student's previous experience and knowledge about the use of virtual education is related to their significant learning.

Now involved in the more recent context, this paper focuses on new insights into the challenges facing the academic environment as all teaching and learning activities moved online. Since online education implies a different approach, related to the creation of new learning environments that combine digital technologies and adapt the most recent findings in psychology, it is useful to ask what professional roles and core practices need to be reconsidered. And how can university professors facilitate cooperative learning, build positive relationships and an emotionally safe online learning environment? Based on the authors' personal knowledge, empirical observations, and practice, this paper illustrates some examples of online learning design activities that respond to current stresses, changes, and student expectations and needs emerging (Airasian & Walsh, 1997).

Finally, questions are opened to conduct future lines of research on the cognitive abilities of recovery, understanding, analysis and application of knowledge that must be applied for each specific competence and to evaluate the profile of the teacher in the achievement of significant learning. In future research on meaningful learning, the conceptualization must consider the diversity of practices with which teachers try to create environments.

REFERENCES

Airasian, P. W., & Walsh, M. E. (1997). Constructivist cautions. *Phi Delta Kappan*, *78*, 444–449. https://www.ncbi.nlm.nih.gov/pmc/articles/PMC8448099/

Al-Ansi, A., Suprayogo, I. & Abidin, M. (2019). *Impact of Information and Communication Technology (ICT) on Different Settings of Learning Process in Developing Countries*. doi:10.5923/j.scit.20190902.01

Almulla, M. A. (2020). The Effectiveness of the Project-Based Learning (PBL) Approach as a Way to Engage Students in Learning. *SAGE Open*, *10*(3). Advance online publication. doi:10.1177/2158244020938702

Apodaca-Orozco, G. U. G., Ortega-Pipper, L. P., Verdugo-Blanco, L. E., & Reyes-Barribas, L. E. (2017). Modelos educativos: Un reto para la educación en salud. *Ra Ximhai*, *13*(2), 77–86. doi:10.35197/rx.13.02.2017.06.gg

Araujo, M. & Campos, M. (2006). La praxis pedagógica en la educación física y los estilos de enseñanza predominantes en los docentes de educación básica. *Revista EDUCARE-UPEL-IPB-Segunda Nueva Etapa 2.0, 10*(3).

Arbaugh, J. B. (2013). Does academic discipline moderate CoI-course outcomes relationships in online MBA courses? *Internet High. Educ, 2013*(17), 16–28. doi:10.1016/j.iheduc.2012.10.002

Arizabaleta, S. L., & Ochoa, A. F. (2016). Hacia una educación superior inclusiva en Colombia. *Pedagogía y saberes*, (45), 41-52.

Arnold, D. Y., & Yapita, J. D. (2000). *El rincón de las cabezas: Luchas textuales, educación y Tierras en los Andes*. Instituto de Lengua y Cultura aymara IICA.

Ausubel, D. (1961). In Defense of Verbal Learning. *Educational Theory, 11*(1), 15–25. doi:10.1111/j.1741-5446.1961.tb00038.x

Ausubel, D. (1963). *The psychology of meaningful verbal learning*. Grune & Stratton.

Ausubel, D. (1968). *Educational psychology. A cognitive view*. Holt Rinehart and Winston.

Ausubel, D. (1978). *Educational Psychology: A Cognitive View*. Holt, Rinehart and Winston.

Ausubel, D., Novak, J., & Hanesian, H. (1978). *Educational psychology: A cognitive view*. Holt, Rinehart & Winston.

Aznar, P. (1992). *Constructivismo y educación*. Tirant lo Blanch.

Baliga, S. S., Walvekar, P. R., & Mahantshetti, G. J. (2021). Concept map as a teaching and learning tool for medical students. *Journal of Education and Health Promotion, 10*(1), 35. doi:10.4103/jehp.jehp_146_20 PMID:33688544

Bandura, A. (1986). *Social Foundations of Thought and Action: A Social Cognitive Theory*. Prentice Hall.

Bao, L., & Koenig, K. (2019). Physics education research for 21st century learning. *Discip Interdscip Sci Educ Res, 1*(1), 2. Advance online publication. doi:10.118643031-019-0007-8

Beck, E., Sollbrekke, T., Sutphen, M., & Fremstad, E. (2015). When mere knowledge is not enough: The potential of building as self-determination, co-determination, and solidarity. *Higher Education Research & Development, 34*(3), 445–457. doi:10.1080/07294360.2014.973373

Bonwell, C. C., & Eison, J. A. (1991). Active Learning: Creating Excitement in the Classroom. *ASHE-ERIC Higher Education Report, 1*(1), 16–17.

Borup, J., West, R. E., & Graham, C. R. (2012). Improving online social presence through asynchronous video. *Internet High. Educ., 2012*(15), 195–203. doi:10.1016/j.iheduc.2011.11.001

Cabi, E. (2018). The impact of the flipped classroom model on students' academic achievement. *International Review of Research in Open and Distance Learning, 19*(3), 203–221. doi:10.19173/irrodl.v19i3.3482

Carretero, M. (1993). *Constructivismo y educación*. Luis Vives.

Chen, J., Zhang, L. J., Wang, X., & Zhang, T. (2021). Impacts of Self-Regulated Strategy Development-Based Revision Instruction on English-as-a-Foreign-Language Students' Self-Efficacy for Text Revision: A Mixed-Methods Study. Journal. *Frontiers in Psychology, 12*, 2609. https://www.frontiersin.org/article/10.3389/fpsyg.2021.670100

Chen, M. P., Wang, L. C., Zou, D., Lin, S. Y., & Xie, H. R. (2019). Effects of caption and gender on junior high students' EFL learning from iMap-enhanced contextualized learning. *Computers & Education, 140*(103602). Advance online publication. doi:10.1016/j.compedu.2019.103602

Chu, K. K., Lee, C. I., & Tsai, R. S. (2011). Ontology technology to assist learners' navigation in the concept map learning system. *Expert Systems with Applications, 38*(9), 11293–11299. doi:10.1016/j.eswa.2011.02.178

Dahar, R. W. (2011). *Teori belajar dan pembelajaran*. Erlangga.

Daley, B. J., & Torre, D. M. (2010). Concept maps in medical education: An analytical literature review. *Medical Education, 2010*(44), 440–448. doi:10.1111/j.1365-2923.2010.03628.x PMID:20374475

Del Campo, S. (2000). *Análisis del manejo de la autoevaluación de los alumnos por parte de los profesores que imparten cursos transferidos con el nuevo modelo de rediseño creado en la misión del ITESM para el año 2005 en el campus Cd. Juárez* [Tesis de maestría]. Instituto Tecnológico y de Estudios Superiores de Monterrey. https://repositorio.tec.mx/bitstream/handle/11285/628762/EGE00000007633.pdf?sequence=1

Delgado, A. M., & Oliver, R. (2010). Interacción entre la evaluación continua y la autoevaluación formativa: La potenciación del aprendizaje autónomo. *Revista de Docencia Universitaria, 4*, 2-13. https://revistas.um.es/redu/article/view/92581

Espejo, R. M. (2016). ¿Pedagogía activa o métodos activos? El caso del aprendizaje activo en la universidad. *Revista Digital de Investigación en Docencia Universitaria, 10*(1), 16. doi:10.19083/ridu.10.456

Fletcher, T., & Chróinín, D. N. (2021). Pedagogical principles that support the prioritisation of meaningful experiences in physical education: Conceptual and practical considerations. *Physical Education and Sport Pedagogy, 27*(5), 455–466. doi:10.1080/17408989.2021.1884672

Flores, G., De Alba, R., & Caicedo, E. (2020). Recomendaciones básicas de competencias docentes para la modalidad no escolarizada en tiempos de la pandemia. *Humanidades, Tecnología y Ciencia, del instituto Politécnico Nacional, 22*(25). http://revistaelectronica-ipn.org/ResourcesFiles/Contenido/23/HUMANIDADES_23_000877.pdf

Galdames, V., Walqui, A., & Gustafson, B. (2011). *Enseñanza de la lengua indígena como Lengua Materna*. PROEIB Andes.

Garrote, D., Garrote, C., & Jiménez Fernández, S. (2016). Factores Influyentes en Motivación y Estrategias de Aprendizaje en los Alumnos de Grado. *REICE. Revista Electrónica Iberoamericana sobre Calidad, Eficacia y Cambio en Educación, 14*(2). Advance online publication. doi:10.15366/reice2016.14.2.002

Gómes, C., & Gargallo, B. (1993). Las bases de una concepción constructivista de la educación. Implicaciones pedagógicas. In *Construcción humana y procesos de estructuración: propuestas de intervención pedagógica* (pp. 35–65). Quiles Artes Gráficas.

Gowin, D. B. (1990). *Educating* (2nd ed.). Cornell University Press.

Graham, S., Harris, K. R., & Mason, L. (2005). Improving the writing performance, knowledge, and self-efficacy of struggling young writers: The effects of self-regulated strategy development. *Contemporary Educational Psychology, 30*(2), 207–241. doi:10.1016/j.cedpsych.2004.08.001

Guerrero Castañeda, A., Rojas Morales, C., & Villafañe Aguilar, C. (2019). Impacto de la Educación Virtual en Carreras de Pregrado del Área de Ciencias de la Salud. Una Mirada de las Tecnologías Frente a la Educación [Trabajo de Grado presentado como requisito parcial para optar al título de: Especialización en Docencia Universitaria Línea de Investigación]. Monografía Universidad Cooperativa de Colombia Facultad de Educación Especialización en docencia universitaria.

Hammer, D., Goldberg, F., & Fargason, S. (2012). Responsive teaching and the beginnings of energy in a third-grade classroom. *Review of Science, Mathematics, and ICT Education, 6*(1), 51–72.

Hanani, N. (2020). Meaningful Learning Reconstruction for Millennial: Facing competition in the information technology era. *IOP Conference Series. Earth and Environmental Science, 469*(1). doi:10.1088/1755-1315/469/1/012107

Howland, J. L., Jonassen, D. H., & Marra, R. M. (2011). *Meaningful Learning with Technology* (4th ed.). Pearson.

Joksimovic, S., Gasevic, D., Kovanovic, V., Adesope, O., & Hatala, M. (2014). Psychological characteristics in cognitive presence of communities of inquiry: A linguistic analysis of online discussions. *Internet High. Educ, 2014*(22), 1–10. doi:10.1016/j.iheduc.2014.03.001

Jonassen, D. (2003). *Learning to Solve Problems with Technology: A Constructivist Perspective* (2nd ed.). Merrill.

Joo, Y. J., Lim, K. Y., & Kim, E. K. (2011). Online university students' satisfaction and persistence: Examining perceived level of presence, usefulness and ease of use as predictors in a structural model. *Computers & Education, 2011*(57), 1654–1664. doi:10.1016/j.compedu.2011.02.008

Julca, F. (2000). *Uso de las lenguas quechua y castellano en la escuela urbana: un estudio de caso* [Tesis de maestría]. Universidad Mayor de San Simón. http://bvirtual.proeibandes.org/bvirtual/docs/tesis/proeib/Tesis_Felix_Julca.pd

Kay, D., & Kibbl, J. (2016). Learning theories 101: Application to everyday teaching and scholarship. *Advances in Physiology Education, 40*(1), 17–25. doi:10.1152/advan.00132.2015 PMID:26847253

Ke, F. (2010). Examining online teaching, cognitive, and social presence for adult students. *Computers & Education, 2010*(55), 808–820. doi:10.1016/j.compedu.2010.03.013

Kim, J., Kwon, Y., & Cho, D. (2011). Investigating factors that influence social presence and learning outcomes in distance higher education. *Computers & Education, 2011*(57), 1512–1520. doi:10.1016/j.compedu.2011.02.005

Kostaris, C., Sergis, S., Sampson, D. G., Giannakos, M. N., & Pelliccione, L. (2017). Investigating the potential of the flipped classroom model in K-12 ICT teaching and learning: An action research study. *Journal of Educational Technology & Society, 20*(1), 261–273.

Kostiainen, E., Ukskoski, T., Ruohotie-Lyhty, M., Kauppinen, M., Kainulainen, J., & Mäkinen, T. (2018). Meaningful learning in teacher education. *Teaching and Teacher Education, 2018*(71), 66–77. doi:10.1016/j.tate.2017.12.009

Kozan, K., & Caskurlu, S. (2018). On the Nth presence for the Community of Inquiry framework. *Computers & Education, 2018*(122), 104–118. doi:10.1016/j.compedu.2018.03.010

Lee, J. H., & Segev, A. (2012). Knowledge maps for e-learning. *Computers & Education, 59*(2), 353–364. doi:10.1016/j.compedu.2012.01.017

Lillo, V. (2014). Salud y Educación: Dos Vocaciones Al Servicio De Los Derechos Humanos. *Revista Médica Clínica Las Condes, 25*(2), 357–362. doi:10.1016/S0716-8640(14)70047-1

Loyens, S., & Gijbels, D. (2008). Understanding the efects of constructivist learning environments: Introducing a multi-directional approach. *Instructional Science, 36*(5-6), 351–357. doi:10.100711251-008-9059-4

Lui, A. M., & Bonner, S. M. (2016). Preservice and inservice teachers' knowledge, beliefs, and instructional planning in primary school mathematics. *Teaching and Teacher Education, 56*, 1–13. doi:10.1016/j.tate.2016.01.015

MacArthur, C. A. (2015). Instruction in evaluation and revision. In C. A. MacArthur, S. Graham, & J. Fitzgerald (Eds.), *Handbook of Writing Research* (pp. 272–287). Guilford Publications.

MacArthur, C. A. (2018). Evaluation and revision. In S. Graham, C. A. Charles, M. Hebert, & J. Fitzgerald (Eds.), *Best Practices in Writing Instruction* (pp. 287–308). Guilford Publications.

Mayer, R. E. (2004). Should there be a three-strikes rule against pure discovery learning? *The American Psychologist, 59*(1), 14–19. doi:10.1037/0003-066X.59.1.14 PMID:14736316

Mintzes, J., & Wandersee, J. (2000). Reforma e Inovação no Ensino da Ciência: uma visão construtivista. In Ensinando Ciência para a compreensão – uma visão construtivista. Plátano Edições Técnicas.

Morales-Cevallos, M. B. (2020). Trends in Educational Research about e-Learning: A Systematic Literature Review (2009–2018). *Sustainability, 2020*(12), 5153. doi:10.3390u12125153

Moreira, M. A. (2011). Why Concepts, Why Meaningful Learning, Why Collaborative Activities and Why Concept Maps? *Aprendizagem Significativa em Revista/Meaningful Learning Review, 6*(3), 5.

Mystakidis, S. (2019). Motivation Enhanced Deep and Meaningful Learning with Social Virtual Reality. University of Jyväskylä.

Mystakidis, S. (2021). Deep Meaningful Learning. *Encyclopedia, 2021*(1), 988–997. doi:10.3390/encyclopedia1030075

Mystakidis, S., Berki, E., & Valtanen, J. (2019). The Patras Blended Strategy Model for Deep and Meaningful Learning in Quality Life-Long Distance Education. *Electron. J. e-Learning, 17*, 66–78.

Nesbit, J. C., & Adesope, O. O. (2013). Concept maps for learning: Theory, research, and design. In G. Schraw, M. T. McCrudden, & D. Robinson (Eds.), *Current perspectives on cognition, learning, and instruction. Learning through visual displays* (pp. 303–328). Information Age Publishers.

Newman, F. M., Marks, H. M., & Gamoran, A. (1996). Authentic pedagogy and student performance. *American Journal of Education, 104*(4), 280–312. doi:10.1086/444136

Novak, J. (1990). Human Construtivism: A Unification of Psychological and Epistemological Phenomena in Meaning Making. *Dalam Fourth North American Conference on Personal Construct Psychology,* 15.

Novak, J., & Gowin, D. (2006). *Learning How to Learn.* Cambridge University Press.

Novak, J. D. (1993). A view on the current status of Ausubel's assimilation theory of learning. In *Proceedings of the Third International Seminar on Misconceptions and Educational Strategies in Science and Mathematics.* Misconceptions Trust.

Novak, J. D., & Cañas, A. J. (2008). *The theory underlying concept maps and how to construct them.* Technical report IHMC CmapTools 2006-01 Rev 01-2008.

O'Donnell, A. M., Dansereau, D. F., & Hall, R. H. (2002). Knowledge maps as scaffolds for cognitive processing. *Educational Psychology Review, 14*(1), 71–86. doi:10.1023/A:1013132527007

Oostdam, R. J., Peetsma, T. T. D., & Blok, H. (2007). *Het nieuwe leren in basisonderwijs en voortgezet onderwijs nader beschouwd* [New learning in primary and secondary education reconsidered]. SCO-Kohnstamm Instituut.

Öztürk, M., & Çakıroğlu, Ü. (2021). Flipped learning design in EFL classrooms: Implementing self-regulated learning strategies to develop language skills. *Smart Learn. Environ., 8*(1), 2. doi:10.118640561-021-00146-x

Patrick, S., & Sturgis, C. (2015). *Maximizing competency education and blended learning: Insights from experts.* iNACOL

Polman, J., Hornstra, L., & Volman, M. (2021). The meaning of meaningful learning in mathematics in upper-primary education. *Learning Environments Research, 24*(3), 469–486. doi:10.100710984-020-09337-8

Pun, J., & Jin, X. (2021). Student challenges and learning strategies at Hong Kong EMI universities. *PLoS One, 16*(5), e0251564. doi:10.1371/journal.pone.0251564 PMID:33961675

Roelofs, E., & Terwel, J. (1999). Constructivism and authentic pedagogy: State of the art and recent developments in the Dutch national curriculum in secondary education. *Journal of Curriculum Studies, 31*(2), 201–227. doi:10.1080/002202799183232

Roelofs, E., Visser, J., & Terwel, J. (2003). Preferences for various learning environments: Teachers' and parents' perceptions. *Learning Environments Research, 6*(1), 77–110. doi:10.1023/A:1022915910198

Romero Juárez, M. G. (2020). *Enseñanza de programación de estructuras de datos aplicando estrategias didácticas basadas en la teoría de carga cognitiva* [Tesis de maestría en informática y tecnologías computacionales]. Universidad Autónoma de Aguascalientes. Centro de Ciencias Básicas. http://hdl.handle.net/11317/1857

Rosano, S. (2007). *La cultura de la diversidad y la educación inclusiva.* http://benu.edu.mx/wp-content/uploads/2015/03/La_cultura_de_la_diversidad_y_la_educacion_inclusiva.pdf

Rubin, B., Fernandes, R., & Avgerinou, M. D. (2013). The effects of technology on the Community of Inquiry and satisfaction with online courses. *Internet High. Educ*, *2013*(17), 48–57. doi:10.1016/j.iheduc.2012.09.006

Scott, D., & Friesen, S. (2013). Inquiry-Based Learning: A Review of the Research Literature. *Alberta Education*, *1*, 1–29.

Şentürk, C. (2021). Effects of the blended learning model on preservice teachers' academic achievements and twenty-first century skills. *Education and Information Technologies*, *26*(1), 35–48. doi:10.100710639-020-10340-y PMID:33020691

Sharan, Y. (2015). *Meaningful Learning in the Co-operative Classroom. Education 3-13: International Journal of Primary, Elementary and Early Years Education, 43(1), 83-94.*

Shea, P., & Bidjerano, T. (2009). Community of inquiry as a theoretical framework to foster "epistemic engagement" and "cognitive presence" in online education. *Computers & Education*, *2009*(52), 543–553. doi:10.1016/j.compedu.2008.10.007

Shea, P., & Bidjerano, T. (2012). Learning presence as a moderator in the community of inquiry model. *Computers & Education*, *2012*(59), 316–326. doi:10.1016/j.compedu.2012.01.011

Sriraman, B. (2010). *Theories of Mathematics Education*. Springer-Verlag Berlin Heidelberg. doi:10.1007/978-3-642-00742-2

Suyatno. (2009). *Menjelajah Pembelajaran Inovatif.* Bumi Aksara.

Thomas, R. A., West, R. E., & Borup, J. (2017). An analysis of instructor social presence in online text and asynchronous video feedback comments. *Internet and Higher Education*, *2017*(33), 61–73. doi:10.1016/j.iheduc.2017.01.003

Tsimane, T. A. & Downing, C. (2019). Transformative learning in nursing education: A concept analysis. *International Journal of Nursing Sciences, 7*(1), 91-98. doi:10.1016/j.ijnss.2019.12.006

UNESCO/OREALC. (2007). El derecho de una educación de calidad para todos en América Latina y el Caribe. *Revista Electrónica Iberoamericana sobre Calidad, Eficacia y Cambio en Educación*, *5*(3), 1–21.

Valverde-Berrocoso, J., Garrido-Arroyo, M. C., Burgos-Videla, C., & Morales-Cevallos, M. B. (2020). Trends in Educational Research about e-Learning: A Systematic Literature Review (2009–2018). *Sustainability*, *2020*(12), 5153. doi:10.3390u12125153

Van Oers, B. (1998). From context to contextualizing. *Learning and Instruction*, *8*(6), 473–488. doi:10.1016/S0959-4752(98)00031-0

Van Oers, B. (2009). Developmental education: Improving participation in cultural practices. In M. Fleer, M. Hedegaard, & J. Tudge (Eds.), *Childhood studies and the impact of globalization: Policies and practices at global and local levels* (pp. 213–229). Routledge.

Van Rijk, Y., Volman, M., de Haan, D., & Van Oers, B. (2017). Maximizing meaning: Creating a learning environment for reading comprehension of informative texts from a Vygotskian perspective. *Learning Environments Research*, *20*(1), 77–98. doi:10.100710984-016-9218-5

Vergara, I., Travieso, N., & Crespo, M. (2014). Dinámica del proceso enseñanza-aprendizaje de la Química en tecnología de la salud. *Educación Médica Superior*, 28(2), 272–281.

Verschafel, L., & Greer, B. (2013). Mathematics education. In J. M. Spector, M. D. Merrill, J. Elen, & M. J. Bishop (Eds.), *Handbook of research on educational communications and technology* (pp. 553–563). Springer. doi:10.1007/978-1-4614-3185-5_43

Vincent-Lancrin, S., Urgel, J., Kar, S., & Jacotin, G. (2019). *Measuring Innovation in Education 2019: What Has Changed in the Classroom? Educational Research and Innovation*. Paris: OECD Publishing. https://www.oecd-ilibrar

Volman, M., & Ten Dam, G. (2015). Critical thinking for educated citizenship. In M. Davies & R. Barnett (Eds.), *The Palgrave handbook of critical thinking in higher education* (pp. 593–603). Palgrave Macmillan. doi:10.1057/9781137378057_35

Wang, H., Tlili, A., Lehman, J. D., Lu, H., & Huang, R. (2021). Investigating feedback implemented by instructors to support online competency-based learning (CBL): A multiple case study. *Int J Educ Technol High Educ*, 18(1), 5. doi:10.118641239-021-00241-6

Wang, J., Mendori, T., & Xiong, J. (2014). A language learning support system using course-centered ontology and its evaluation. *Computer Education*, 78, 278–293. doi:10.1016/j.compedu.2014.06.009

Wang, J., Ogata, H., & Shimada, A. (2017). A meaningful discovery learning environment for e-book learners. *IEEE Global Engineering Education Conference*, 1158–1165. 10.1109/EDUCON.2017.7942995

Wang, J., Shimada, A., Oi, M., Ogata, H., & Tabata, Y. (2020). Development and evaluation of a visualization system to support meaningful e-book learning. *Interactive Learning Environments*, 1–18. Advance online publication. doi:10.1080/10494820.2020.1813178

Wardekker, W., Boersma, A., Ten Dam, G., & Volman, M. (2012). Motivation for school learning: Enhancing the meaningfulness of learning in communities of learners. In M. Hedegaard, A. Edwards, & M. Fleer (Eds.), *Motives in children's development: Cultural–historical approaches* (pp. 153–170). Cambridge University Press.

Wu, W. C. V., Hsieh, J. S. C., & Yang, J. C. (2017). Creating an online learning community in a flipped classroom to enhance EFL learners' oral proficiency. *Journal of Educational Technology & Society*, 20(2), 142–157.

Zhan, Z., & Mei, H. (2013). Academic self-concept and social presence in face-to-face and online learning: Perceptions and effects on students' learning achievement and satisfaction across environments. *Computers & Education*, 2013(69), 131–138. doi:10.1016/j.compedu.2013.07.002

Zhang, Y., & Mi, Y. (2010, September). Another look at the language difficulties of international students. *Journal of Studies in International Education*, 14(4), 371–388. doi:10.1177/1028315309336031

Chapter 5
Humanistic Teaching During the Pandemic:
Education Beyond the Lesson

Nadia Ainuddin Dahlan
Universiti Teknologi MARA, Malaysia

Melissa Malik
Universiti Teknologi MARA, Malaysia

Khadijah Said Hashim
Universiti Teknologi MARA, Malaysia

Fatin Aliana Mohd Radzi
Universiti Teknologi MARA, Malaysia

Farhana Wan Yunus
Universiti Teknologi MARA, Malaysia

EXECUTIVE SUMMARY

During the COVID-19 crisis, teaching and learning activities were largely conducted online through open and distance learning (ODL). As a result, educators and students lacked the personal warmth and emotional support usually found in face-to-face classes, which affected the quality of the teaching and learning process. Therefore, what could educators do to facilitate the teaching and learning process during the pandemic? This chapter features narratives on humanistic practices in teaching that were carried out during the pandemic by five university lecturers. The narratives shed light on how they embedded humanistic elements in either one or several of these aspects of teaching: delivery, content, consultation, and assessment. Their pedagogical approaches indicate that education is not a rigid domain, but it can be extended beyond the four walls of the classroom and executed from the sincere heart.

DOI: 10.4018/978-1-6684-6076-4.ch005

INTRODUCTION

The recent global pandemic saw countries across the world take great strides in making education as accessible as possible to students during lockdowns. These include embracing change and managing expectations, involving all levels of education – from preschool to university.

Many universities, though familiar with online learning and may have already conducted some of their courses through blended learning, still faced huge challenges when they needed to go fully online. Besides grappling with the need to quickly upskill themselves in using online learning platforms and technology whilst working from home, educators also needed to be mindful of the challenges that their students were facing and how this new learning environment had impacted them as well. Learning during the pandemic meant that students missed out not only on face-to-face physical contact with their lecturers and peers, but more importantly, the emotional support that came with such personal interactions. Some students, too, faced financial constraints and health issues brought about by the pandemic, which further affected their academic performance.

Humanistic views on education recognize that students' motivation in learning is related to their emotional well-being and that educators should endeavor to create a caring and supportive classroom environment (Hanley, Winter & Burrel, 2019; Schneider, Pierson & Bugental, 2014; Khateb, Sarem & Hamidi, 2013). Supporting students emotionally should therefore be an important part of day-to-day teaching practice, what more in times of crisis as the pandemic. In view of this, educators had to seriously reflect on the desired student outcomes of their courses and manage their expectations of what could realistically be expected from their students. In the local context of Malaysia, online learning is often interchangeably referred to as Open and Distance Learning (ODL). Thus, how did ODL during the pandemic affect students' overall learning experience? And most importantly, how could educators responsibly facilitate students' learning and other educational processes during this time?

This chapter features narratives on humanistic practices in teaching that were carried out during the pandemic by five university lecturers. The narratives shed light on how they embedded this in either one or several of these aspects of teaching - delivery, content, consultation and assessment.

A narrative inquiry method was implemented in gathering these narratives for its nature in "revealing unique perspectives and deeper understanding of a situation" (Padgett, 2012). It is an effective method in disclosing the lived experiences and voice of the individuals involved. The authors then coded and grouped these lived experiences into several themes and subthemes which were done inductively based on the individual narratives. To ensure the trustworthiness of these narratives (Lincoln and Guba, 1985), peer debriefing, thick descriptions and member checks were utilized.

HUMANISTIC LEARNING THEORY

Humanistic psychology, developed by Maslow around the 1950s and expanded later on by Rogers, as well as Bugental among others, emerged as a prominent theory in education towards the 1960s (Schneider et al., 2014). It, then, spread extensively in the 1970s (Untari, 2016). Unlike behaviorism and psychoanalysis, the two more prominent learning theories that directly preceded it, which tended to focus on only specific aspects of students as learners, humanistic learning theory regarded them as holistic learners or, in other words, as 'whole' human beings. Behaviorism reduced humans to organisms that 'learned' desired behaviors through shaping and conditioning by manipulation of their external environments.

Meanwhile, psychoanalysis proposed almost the opposite, adopting a biological deterministic view of humans. Maslow, however, sought to understand human beings from a different, more positive lens, taking into consideration learners as multi-faceted human beings, complex and unique (Hare, 2019; Johnson, 2014; Schneider et al., 2014).

At the core of modern humanistic learning theory is Maslow's idea of hierarchy of needs. It considers learners' motivation towards personal growth and ultimately, self-actualization which is contingent upon the fulfilment of their more basic needs. Most importantly as well, human beings were perceived to be inherently good and possess free will. This implied that humans have a natural desire to better themselves. They can be self-directed to achieve their goals and realize their potential, provided that their fundamental needs are considered and met. Human beings are therefore, both extrinsically and intrinsically motivated.

The humanistic view further emphasizes the importance of taking into consideration all aspects that make human beings 'whole', especially the affective aspect. When students feel supported emotionally by their teachers and peers, they are more likely to be motivated to learn. It is also important to note that motivation can fluctuate within individuals and differ from one individual to another as their contexts and realities are unique. Therefore, educators should try to understand the underlying causes for students' motivation rather than resort to punitive measures. In fact, students have an innate desire to learn, according to humanists. Thus, educators should encourage and facilitate learning through a number of ways such as by making learning more meaningful to students (relevant to their interests, lives, realities, contexts), provide a safe, threat-free environment (both physically and emotionally), allow students some degree of autonomy in deciding what they want to learn and how they prefer to go about it, encourage students to engage in self-evaluation (reflect on their own progress based on the standards that they have set for themselves) and help students form positive peer relations, to name a few (Untari, 2016; Hare, 2019).

It is also perhaps worth mentioning that an idea of similar vein, known as pedagogy of care, proposed by Noddings in the 1980s as 'ethic of care' (Mutch & Peung, 2021), has gained attention in recent years in line with the rise of blended learning and ODL. It shares some similarity with humanistic learning theory as it highlights the 'human' aspect of learning, calling for 'care and connectedness' in schools. This is achieved by teachers exhibiting care to students, considering students' needs when planning for instruction (emotional needs included) and forming positive relationships between teachers and students (Owusu-Ansah & Kyei-Blankson, 2016). It would seem then that when non-traditional classrooms take effect, it leads to not only physical, but also emotional disconnection experienced by both educators and students. Henceforth, these must be addressed in order for effective and meaningful learning to take place.

NARRATIVE 1

Emotion-Checking and Storying as Tools for Students' Engagement in an ODL Classroom

Thank you for always asking how we feel in each class. (Zul, 2020)

Reading this feedback from Zul in the last class brought tears to my eyes. Zul, a final year student, was in my class for the Professional Development course. Although content-wise, this course is not as challenging as other theoretical courses, like other ODL classes, encouraging student participation is still a challenge (Ag-Ahmad, 2020). To make matters worse, having online classes also brought a different type of anxiety as academics and learners must unlearn and relearn new ways in conducting classes (Chiu, 2022). Many learners do not possess the ability to succeed in unfamiliar learning environments, as well as staying motivated and engaged during online classes (UNESCO, 2020). This frustration has led me to find a way to at least make my students enjoy being in my class. I started searching for ways to respond to cabin fever and pandemic anxiety that I feel many of my students are suffering from during the COVID-19 lockdown. Like most of my students, I suffered from them too. Thus, one of the proactive measures I had taken was to check on the students' emotions before starting the class. We took a few minutes, prior to the lectures, to listen to each other's stories.

Storying is defined as a space in which individuals feel safe to share feelings, emotions, stories and events that occur in co-constructing relationships and knowledge (San Pedro, Kinloch, 2017). The storying in my class always starts with us expressing our emotions. When I first started doing this, many of them were confused about what was going on. Well, new methods definitely need some time to get used to. Besides, it is not our culture to express ourselves in front of others. The idea of doing this derived from my time studying in the United States in which one of the instructors for one of the courses I took, always began her class by opening a space for us to share our feelings, home news and questions to discuss if we had any. Being a person who rarely expresses emotions in public, it took me almost two weeks to muster up the courage of expressing myself and sharing my story. So, I figure my students must be in a similar situation.

I began my first day of storying by asking the students "How do you feel today?". Of course the usual "fine, thank you" were the answers. "Today we are going to try something new. Let us start by switching on our cameras and saying hi to each other." After a few minutes, I continued, "Alright, today we are going to try something new. We will start our class by sharing our home news today. It can be about what makes you happy at home today or what makes you tired or sad. Let's use this platform to tell our stories". I waited for five minutes for someone to volunteer. As there was none, I ended up sharing my stories and feelings instead. At the end of the class, I informed the students that we would be doing the same exercise in the next class and for them to be ready.

The same incident occurred in the next class. I ended up telling my story again. The third time I did this, I decided to conduct a poll on the students' feelings via Doodle. I identified one student to tell the reason for her happiness. "Fifi (pseudonym), can you share with us what makes you happy today?" "Well Dr., it is because my mother has been discharged from the hospital," she answered. Her remark then triggered a conversation on COVID-19 at home and how this pandemic had led to stress for staying home too long. That morning we spent about 15 minutes talking about it. The students began sharing news about the people around them. Those who were infected, close contacts and their anxiety of getting the disease.

That was how we ended up storying by first expressing our emotions before describing the events occurring in our lives for approximately 15 minutes every time before our classes began. We would get to listen to many stories on how happy, sad, nervous or tired everyone was of having to play various roles at home. I would share my story in which I too could not commit entirely to being an educator, but also mother, wife, chef, housekeeper and the list goes on. The students, too, would reflect on their lives of also playing multiple roles at home: student, son, daughter, sibling and caretaker in which all these contributed to their pandemic anxiety. This lasted throughout the entire semester. In the last class, they expressed how at ease they felt when attending my classes. How my classes actually provided them with the space to express their feelings, talk to each other and share news/stories, as well as get to know each other better. That last day of class, I left crying with happiness.

Why Are Emotion-Checking and Storying Such Powerful Tools?

Many studies (Anastasakis, Triantafyllou, & Petridis, 2021; Ag-Ahmad, 2020; Chakraborty, Mittal, Gupta, Yadav, & Arora, 2021) on online learning reported emotional and social connections with the students as the main barriers to having a successful class. In a physical classroom, we get to interact naturally with our students, meet with them face-to-face and respond directly to their questions; accompanied with our body language, facial expressions, intonation of our voice and many other forms of non-verbal communication. Students get to experience all these in real time. We get to also have effortless social-emotional interactions with them. All these are really quite impossible to achieve by staring at the screen.

According to Cavanagh (2016), emotions play a crucial role in students' engagement during online learning. Emotions provide a direct link between one's motivation and focus in class. Students have shown to be more engaged if their feelings are validated in class. The feeling of happiness and ease also contribute to better comprehension and better engagement. As human beings, we cannot deny the fact that emotions affect our actions, thus contributing indirectly to academic success (Trettenero, 2020). Online classes, without the physical presence of other human beings, can create a daunting feeling of loneliness, anxiety, anger, frustration and boredom (Marchand & Gutierraz, 2012). Hence, the way to encourage students' engagement and participation remotely is by catering to their emotions (Cavanagh, 2016; Darby, 2020; Eyler, 2018) because emotions move us as human beings.

Glasser (1986), through choice theory, explains that opening up one's emotion requires a space where the person feels safe and accepted in a particular situation. Thus, this is where storying takes place. San Pedro and Kinloch (2017), in their Projects in Humanization (PiH) studies, revealed using storying as a powerful tool in discovering participants' feelings and experiences. Storying involves a process where individuals are given the freedom to share their emotions and any stories they want to tell. However, for participants to be able to come to the stage of storying, researchers need to create a space where respondents are emotionally positive and feel unthreatened in any way.

Applying these concepts is not easy for me. It takes many hours of coaxing and many hours of opening up my feelings to my students. This process is important to establish trust so that they feel comfortable to share theirs and later contribute to the process of storying. Sharing our feelings is something that is quite alien in our culture. In doing this, I am also showing my students that I too have my own battles to fight. Perhaps, it is the vulnerability that I have showed that made my students feel more comfortable to share their stories. However, this experience taught me that catering to emotions is crucial in creating a space where storying can occur. Without positive emotions, students will not feel engaged. Without engagement, they may not attend the online class (by sitting in front of the screen, not just to park their names on screen). Without attending, storying will not occur. Thus, emotion-checking should occur first before storying and before lessons start.

NARRATIVE 2

Consultation: Helping Each Other Rise Up, The Best We Can

Let's face it. We all need help. No matter how clever you are, how rich you are, how important you are, you still need help from someone, somewhere. That someone can be your partner, your colleague, your family member or a complete stranger. The issue might be very small or so big, but you still hope help will come your way. A scientist might call a plumber to help with his kitchen sink because he cannot handle it alone! A surgeon needs other doctors and nurses around during a critical surgery. A housewife needs help with ironing mountains of clothes, so she hired a maid. The point is: we all need help from others in order to complete our goals.

As an educator, I give out help and consultations when needed, most of the time to my students. Nevertheless, I find myself seeking for help and advice all the time too (probably more than the consultations I gave out to others). This is because I cannot survive in academia alone. I consult other educators, the admin staff, the Ministry of Education and my students as well. Consultations in a teaching and learning setting usually occur in two directions. The first one is when you as an educator gives out consultations to others and the second one is when you as an educator receive consultations from others. During the COVID-19 pandemic, I feel that consultations (both giving and receiving) have doubled or even tripled. Realization then hit me: we need extra help in accomplishing our goals!

Student Learning

Giving Consultations - Of course as an educator, my first priority in giving out consultations would be to my students. Other people in the university would come second. During the COVID-19 pandemic lockdown, my students had many concerns and worries. They texted me enquiring about how to go about doing the classes, what kind of devices would be suitable to use (some did not have a laptop, so they had to use their phones) and how long would the class take because they did not have unlimited internet data and so on. Teaching students from multiple backgrounds is not easy. Some can afford devices with ease while others struggle to purchase Internet data. When the Prime Minister announced about the lockdown that we were going to have, all of the students were instructed to return to their hometowns. No one was allowed to stay on campus. Problems arose. Students said they did not have Internet coverage at their hometowns, they had multiple roles at home, they had to share laptops and computers with their siblings who were also home for the lockdown and many more issues. Well, classes must go on. So, I had to come up with ways on how best to help these students. Helping students learn should be any educators' utmost priority.

So, I told my students that we could have less than one hour of online class while the rest of the class time, we could do offline activities and continue chatting in our WhatsApp group (an application on smartphones). By not having a long online class, the students could save up on their Internet data. I also recorded all my online classes so that the students who lost their connection during the online classes or missed the classes for whatever reason would be able to replay the recordings in their own free time. At this point in time, I was not strict about attendance and I understood if they could not attend the classes. I had a student who would sit in the car every time he had classes. This is because he lived in a small house where there was little privacy. I also had a student who climbed up a tree just to get a 4G bar on his phone. Having a recorded class would be easier for the students rather than having the classroom live. I also made it a point to ask them about their day and wellbeing every time we had class just to make them feel less tense from the COVID-19 stress. This is because some of the students and their families were affected with the virus. We would pray together in the class for our affected friends and family. The students appreciated this act and, when the semester ended, they thanked me for looking out for them. Apart from that, I also made myself available whenever the students needed consultations on their assignments or projects. We would set up a video call if they wanted to or I would answer their questions on text. Both group and individual consultations were welcomed. Some students needed extra help in their projects so I would help them develop ideas. I also showed them samples of their seniors' work, but I warned them that the samples might not be the best and thus they had to strive to do better. The sample assignment would act as a guideline for the students so that they could have a general idea on how to go about doing the assigned work. It was not easy for them to be on their own at home to figure things out with limited resources. So, every help counts. Other kinds of consultations include giving feedback to students regarding their work, whether individual or group feedback. My students valued feedback from educators because it made them feel "on track and relieved," as Sarah (pseudonym) put it. I also set up a support group for the students because they complained that they had difficulties studying alone. By having a support group online where they could study together and consult each other academically, mentally, emotionally and spiritually, the online learning journey was not so lonely anymore. I would also extend the assignment submission date. Having to work from home, I understood how we all needed extra help and extra time in finishing a certain task. Therefore, I allowed my students to submit their work whenever they were ready to do so, but within a certain timeframe. This is because I also needed time to read, mark and key-in their grades into the university's system. At the end of the semester, several students texted me and wrote, "Thank you for working so hard for us." That sentence left me shocked. I did not know I was working hard. I did not feel like I was working hard enough, but my students saw through me. I felt appreciated. I replied to them, "We helped each other work hard, ok?" and to that, they replied back, "Ok, deal!" and I smiled:).

Receiving Consultations - Like I said, consultation is a two-way communication. I get consultations from my students too, especially on developing ideas for my writing, research projects and creative learning. In my online classes, I would sometimes ask them, "How would you teach today's topic? Can you think of ways to make it creative and interesting?" The students enjoyed brainstorming ideas and they came out with lots of fun ways on how the lesson could be fun and better. Their input gave me ideas in improving my teaching and research. In addition to that, I like getting feedback about my classes. I do not want to just teach the students. I want to be able to make an impact on their lives. Usually, at the end of the semester, I will ask the students to give feedback on my classes. Sometimes, we do this live via an online platform and other times we do it by texting in the Whatsapp group and online form. The feedback questions include: How did you feel in my class? Did you understand the topics discussed? Did you enjoy the class? Was it interesting? Was it boring? Can you suggest ways on how I can improve my classes for future students? According to Piccinin, Cristi and McCoy (2006), getting feedback on your teaching is very important as it can make an impact on teaching improvement and changes in student ratings. In 2021, I was acknowledged by the university for getting a high mark in students' rating. *Thank you students for your kind feedback. I would not have done it without all of you.*

Positivity Helps

The COVID-19 pandemic has left a huge impact on the world. Nonetheless, not everything caused by the pandemic has been negative. The pandemic has given us a new life experience in teaching and learning. We are forced to reach out to people by using the technologies available. Consultations can be done fully online now, something that we probably did not think about during pre-COVID-19. This way, we save a lot of time and money. We may be saving carbon footprints too by limiting our trips from one place to another. In the end, we have to keep doing our best to help each other. Virus or no virus, we must rise up!

NARRATIVE 3

Care Pedagogy: The Stories of a Human Teacher

Classroom teaching has been a great sharing platform with the students, for both content knowledge and skills. In fact, the excitement of sharing beyond formal lessons is even higher because students feel welcomed, appreciated and engaged.

I look forward coming to your class Dr K, although I know this course is not an easy one. You never fail to relate the subject with real life situations including daily activities and in fact the future. (Student 1)

We share stories, we learn, we laugh and we enjoy. (Student 2)

In every class, you put in the effort to engage with everyone. You made time to ask us personally after the class too. I feel acknowledged and appreciated. (Student 3)

These are the responses from the students when I asked them to write individual reflections at the end of the semester. I remember going through the feedback from them which really made my day. Positive responses and feedback are so powerful and critical indicators for teachers. They help teachers like me to improve and enhance pedagogical skills, motivate and sustain teaching. Admittedly, having face-to-face and physical interactions, acknowledging responses and giving immediate feedback are among meaningful activities that help enrich my personal substance and experiences as an educator and mentor. Most importantly, they function as positive reinforcement and source of motivation.

However, the pandemic has impacted my educational routine and teaching excitement following the school closure and transition to remote learning. The evidence of online teaching and digital education have contributed to teaching hesitation, learning anxiety and emotional fluctuations which basically accompanied my personal journey as a pandemic educator. Initially, when online learning which is locally referred as Open and Distance Learning (ODL) was first implemented to replace the physical mode of learning, I was clueless and in fact it was like the 'emergency stage' for me. Most of the time, I was skeptical about the students' acceptance of and responses on ODL. Honestly, I was confused with all the new platforms, applications and online teaching requirements, including documentations and weekly reports. Consequently, I started feeling mentally and emotionally exhausted. I remember being physically fatigued almost every day, especially at the very beginning of the stage, due to the struggles in understanding the new situation and demands, as well as adjusting to this new norm of teaching.

At the very beginning of ODL, I kept looking at my computer screen questioning myself not only about my teaching, but I was more concerned about how the students would cope and deal with this. Until now, I keep thinking about my students' overall acceptance and adaptation to online learning. Fortunately, I believe that my realization of adjusting to pandemic teaching is because of my personal knowledge and experiences and most importantly my purpose of teaching. I begin to realize and scrutinize all these limitations and challenges. I started seeking ways and strategies to respond to the crisis, including having an emotional chat with my small circle of trusts, establishing strong and significant support system, learning about new technology to reduce my digital divide, and setting a new yet more realistic goals and expectations towards student learning and achievement, as well as joining professional development courses.

Why is it important for a teacher like me to adapt to pandemic teaching? And how can my adjustment impact my perspective on teaching and my motivation? What would be the implications to the students and their learning? These are some of the core questions that guide me to refer and revisit the humanistic approaches in learning that can benefit both students and teacher-educators. The following narratives include stories of humanistic approach as a responsive teaching, particularly the care pedagogy.

Care Pedagogy: Care before Content

Let me tell you this. Many of us think that when we care about someone, we can simply tell them we care for them. Care is not just simply saying …. *Hey, I care about you.* Or asking your students this question, *How are you feeling today?* The pedagogy of care is more than that and it goes beyond asking students' current situation. Let us explore this narrative.

I was looking at the attendance when I found out one of the students in my class did not attend the linked classroom. I was told by the class representative that Ahmed (pseudonym) had to leave the class because his mother and younger sister were involved in an accident. Sadly, Ahmed lost his mother in the accident. His sister was on a life support machine for a few months before the doctors had to stop it due to poor progress. It was at the end of the semester when students were required to submit their individual research proposals. I managed to speak to Ahmed asking about his well-being, acknowledging his situations and giving him the best emotional support that I could offer to help him cope. In a series of phone conversations, he shared his difficulties in coping, his sadness and how much he missed his late mother and sister. Despite the challenges he had encountered, Ahmed managed to submit all of his assignments on time. Honestly, I did not expect this from him because he was experiencing a moment of grief and bereavement. These are some of Ahmed's reflections on my class and my teaching.

In the moments of loss of my late mother, she pushed aside her hectic schedule, making time to call me, coax me down and listen to my story of loss. For so many reasons, I am moved by the act. Massive thanks for the thousandth time, Dr, for the knowledge, time, words of wisdom that really shape us learners who see honestly in learning, learners who always thrive for better. (Ahmed, 2022)

Ahmed's story is a piece of evidence of how learning experiences can be so broad, personalized and meaningful. Society must realize that education is more than developing students' ability and potentials. It must also value students' emotions and feelings. Consequently, the role of teachers is not only confined to ensuring students' academic achievement and talent development are fulfilled.

In addition, the emphasis of care pedagogy is to highlight the importance of looking at students' emotional aspects and establishing relationships before teaching formal lessons to students. Burke and Larmar (2020) believe that as a dominant pedagogical approach in higher education, online learning may have deleterious impacts on students' engagement and connection, which ultimately can lead to isolation and disempowerment. Therefore, to connect and foster a positive engagement within the student life cycle during an online learning is critical, that is, by primarily establishing care and relationships.

I have been consistent about doing this *care before content* since the first time I started my career in teaching back in 2006. I remember how much I valued relationships before and after class with my students, which consequently promoted the joy of learning. I believe the joy of learning is an intrinsic motivation resulting from good rapport and positive relationships with students. Additionally, Damon (2006) and Bronk (2011) argued that meaningful engagement is a critical experience when students deeply understand the relevance of learning, as well as the existence of a support system and positive relationships. These are some of the pieces of evidence to show how a caring teacher can help maximize learning by considering emotional engagement and connection with students in the first place.

Personal Pandemic Initiatives (PPI): Sizing up Assessment

The linked lectures and classrooms have resulted in revealing of the student's limitations and challenges in attending, engaging and focusing on ODL mode. In other words, from my experiences of conducting online classes, I have validated and observed similar patterns of students' participation and engagement. Apparently, less than 20% of my students would share and open their camera, as well as participate. Therefore, I introduced and applied a strategy which I called the personal pandemic initiatives (PPI) primarily to encourage students to share with me privately prior to the lesson, if they encountered any issue of joining the online class. I gave students the options to text, email or call, in whichever method they felt comfortable and convenient to reach me. Throughout the pandemic, I received many students' instant messages and calls sharing about their struggles, hesitations and challenges with ODL, including family and financial issues. All of these have impacted students' motivation to learn and distracted their focus in the class.

As an educator, my role has expanded and changed. In fact, it is beyond teaching. I believe listening to students and helping them cope are part of my roles and responsibilities, as well. In return, I personally feel relieved because at least I could give them assurance that they are not alone in facing all the challenges, and to convince them that there are ways to handle the issues.

Majority of teacher-educators now agree that our present focus is to highlight on helping students to continue their learning amidst the pandemic. Hence, the direction of my teaching has shifted beyond formal lessons, conducting assessments and merely finishing the syllabus to care pedagogy which emphasizes on caring for students' psychological well-being, motivation and emotional state before the lesson takes place. Rosadah et al. (2018) highlighted the critical component in teaching. A teacher must be able to listen, show concern and affection in order to ensure students' adaptation to any circumstances and situation, which is also known as resilience.

Personalized Schedule of Consultation (PSC): We Respond to Them instead of Correct Them

Some students felt lost, both in motivation and focus, when attending online classes. Some of them opened up to me and admitted that the intensity of stress during online classes was increasing and resulted in a feeling of anxiety. This was particularly related to completing assignments and assessments. It worried them so much because the physical, face-to-face consultation was not available for them during the remote learning. In response to their worries and complaints, I decided to schedule an adaptive strategy which I named as personalized schedule of consultation (PSC). In a class of 40 students, I promoted PSC, in which a group of five to six students attended the session. The positive thing about doing this was students were more willing to open and share their camera. Henceforth, we felt close and connected with each other. Furthermore, students started to discuss their concerns and learning issues. I found that having this small circle had a positive impact on students' learning and more importantly their lives and coping capability. This was again to make sure that all of the students experience the presence of emotional engagement before cognitive engagement. This approach and strategy is supported by the

Dynamic Holistic Individual Potential Development Framework which emphasizes that students can develop holistically if society provides care and consistent support for their learning (Rosadah et al, 2018). Therefore, as human teachers, our role is to respond to them instead of correcting them. In other words, listening and caring before teaching and learning.

NARRATIVE 4

Flexi Scaffolding: A Teacher's Tool to Sustain Students' Engagement and Motivation during COVID-19 Pandemic

Madam, I find this challenging and to be honest... I am clueless on what to do for this task. I have watched the class recording, but I still cannot fully comprehend the task. Could you please explain it to me, step-by-step? (Imran, 2022)

I am certain that many teachers out there have encountered a similar situation, specifically in online teaching during the COVID-19 pandemic. Before the pandemic hit us, it would be a lot easier to explain to students in class while they were attempting tasks. In addition, they had classmates sitting together with them in class or after class, who could also assist the process of completing the tasks. However, when students are in an internet-based (online) class, and communication is heavily facilitated by technology, there is a chance that some of them may lose their motivation to complete tasks. Not to mention, if they suddenly lost connection in the middle of the teacher's explanation regarding an important step in the class, this could later cause potential misunderstandings and learning gaps. Each student is a unique individual with a different personality, background knowledge and learning pace (Ellis, 2015). These make it even more challenging when delivering course content through ODL. In addition, most Asian students are shy and not brave or critical enough to voice out their opinions or concerns in class unless being repeatedly probed and encouraged. Some of the students even feel that asking questions during class may take a portion of the class time and therefore prefer to wait until the class is over. This is because they are also overly concerned about their peers' opinion about them.

Imran (pseudonym) was one of my students who experienced difficulties when writing his speech outline. He had some workable ideas, but had trouble expressing and organizing them in words using a specific speech outline template that had been earlier provided. Thus, he personally contacted me to have a one-to-one coaching session in order to complete the assigned task. Nevertheless, Imran was not alone. There were many other students who were just like him, and they all voiced the same concern, i.e., inability to fully gauge the demands of a task. As I am teaching a language class, I also find it difficult to provide support to students during this pandemic. We have to resort to online meetings and repetitive actions of giving explanations and assurance to students. These acts of support are provided beyond classroom hours and included different approaches to cater to different types of learners. However, these supports were not one-sided. This is because in my attempts to provide support to students, I would probe and ask guiding questions that would force them to also think of the solutions to the task they had been assigned with. Providing support to students in well-rounded interactions is known as scaffolding, which is in-line with Vygotsky's social constructivist theory and Zone of Proximal Development (Nguyen, 2022). Nguyen (2022) reviewed a number of scaffolding strategies that teachers can utilize in online teaching. He stated that instructors must consider a number of factors, such as initiating and familiarizing students with the online platform used, concerns about class-size and multiple ZPDs due to differences among learners and their linguistic proficiency. By taking into consideration the above factors, I implemented two kinds of support to engage my students in learning.

Personalized Coaching

The first one is personalized coaching where I met my students individually through *Google Meet* or *Zoom* without their peers. It was deliberately conducted that way so that they felt more comfortable to talk and discuss the problems they encountered with the task. Another reason for personalized coaching is because ZPD for each learner is different from another and therefore, the consultation was tailored specifically for the student.

Below is an excerpt taken from my discussion with Imran that centers around his attempt to identify a specific speech topic. As the speech was a short one (7 minutes), the topic must be specific enough for the student to clearly elaborate the main ideas within the stipulated time.

Imran: Madam, I am confused about how I should narrow down my speech topic. I wanted to talk about how people can improve their overall life.

Me: Okay, are you referring to people's well-being?

Imran: Sort of. Like how they can be happier, live a quality life, hmm.. I mean how can they combat their anxiety... you know... Nowadays, many people are suffering with anxiety...

Me: Okay, perhaps you might want to look at specific strategies to overcome anxiety.

From the discussion above, I helped Imran to narrow down a very broad topic of well-being improvement to something that he would actually want to highlight in his speech (in this case, strategies to combat anxiety) and the topic that he had chosen was within his own capabilities. In addition, he already had some background knowledge of the topic. This could increase originality in the work that he would produce and simultaneously drive him to complete the task.

Peer Support Through Collaborative Tasks

The second scaffolding strategy that I employed is by utilizing peer support in collaborative tasks during a synchronous session. Nguyen (2022) mentioned that teachers must first familiarize themselves with the platform before using it with the students and demonstrate to their students how to use the platform. This is also known as 'technical scaffolding'. So, I would definitely explore the new platform first before introducing it to my students. I also communicated with students in Telegram groups to give them a heads-up about what to expect in the next lesson.

For this collaborative activity, I made full use of Google Jamboard and shared the link with the students as editors. This was conducted in a language class where they were required to practice the grammar rules that they had learnt. I gave them the instruction and demonstrated the steps before putting them in groups. Prior to this, I also identified a group leader for each group from a list of more capable students so that these leaders could also provide support to their peers. Each group was given a similar task with similar requirements, which was to develop a paragraph based on a series of words provided. As an instructor, I monitored each group closely, probing them from time-to-time to ensure that they were on the right track. After all groups completed the task, I would first ask them to check the paragraphs they had written by giving them a checklist of what to look for – spelling errors, capitalization and punctuation. This small activity became a second task that allowed them to learn from one another before I provided the finalized feedback. This collaboration enabled the students to engage with their peers and promoted more interactions among themselves despite not being able to meet face-to-face.

In conclusion, I discovered that online scaffolding involves a lot of effort from the teachers. The principles of scaffolding may be similar to the ones implemented in a physical classroom, but adaptations are required, especially in the incorporation of technology and dealing with students' emotional needs without meeting them face-to-face, which proves to be more challenging. Therefore, teachers have to be flexible in choosing the scaffolding strategies they wish to employ based on their students' needs. In addition to this, teachers also must be warier of how they phrase their instructions and be more generous in providing praises (when necessary) and emotional support which includes giving assurance, encouragement and words of advice. This is because the students are not able to meet their peers physically, when they need it even more to consolidate their learning.

On the last day of the semester, I received a Google Jamboard loaded with kind words that expressed my students' gratitude and sincere wishes. They were thankful to be able to finally complete the course successfully via ODL. The fact that they survived ODL is a mark to remember in their academic journey. As an educator, I felt honored and relieved that I had tried my best to facilitate my students' learning regardless of our internal and external constraints.

NARRATIVE 5

Having Good Faith: Accommodating Students in Online Assessments

Before the pandemic, I honestly have never imagined conducting classes fully online, much less assessing students entirely through virtual means. While I knew a handful of colleagues who were already integrating technology into their assessments through blended learning, it still remained at that point, a matter of choice for many of us. Nevertheless, when the pandemic hit, there was no other option, *but* to get on board. I had to really step out of my comfort zone, overcome any hesitations and embrace the new normal, as I was sure many other educators did as well. And in doing so, I realized that it was not only challenging for me, but also for my students.

As a result of the Movement Control Order (MCO) that was imposed across Malaysia at the time, students and educators alike were in neither the most conducive physical environment nor optimal frame of mind for teaching and learning. The feeling was quite overwhelming in the beginning and personally, I doubted whether learning really could continue *'as usual'*. In particular, I was worried about how assessment would be impacted during this time as it bore significant implications for both teachers and students. Assessment is intrinsic to teaching and learning, providing on-going feedback for informing instruction and improving learning as it takes place (formative assessment), as well as describing students' achievement (summative assessment) upon which significant decisions regarding educational policies, programs and future employment are made (Djoub, 2018; Archer, 2017; Popham, 2006).

As mentioned earlier, many students faced challenges in online learning - ranging from technical issues such as internet connection problems, financial issues like lack of funds for purchasing internet data (financial issues), to being distracted by the home environment and being afflicted by COVID-19 (personal and health issues) - thereby inadvertently affecting their learning in class. In light of these circumstances, how well then could we expect students to *'perform'* in their assessments? How would the assessment process accurately reflect student learning in these times? How could we fairly assess students entirely online?

Thus, universities had to reconsider and make adjustments to their assessments as most assessments were previously designed to take place mainly in the physical classroom. This was not an easy task. In the process of doing so, educators needed to also be mindful of issues like validity. It was necessary to consider not only the challenges students were facing, but also that the restructured assessments should still align with and fulfill the intended course learning outcomes. At our faculty, traditional assessments such as face-to-face final examinations were replaced with other forms of assessments such as online tests, article reviews and video presentations, where appropriate. However, even with the adjustments made in assessment methods, I found that it was important to also adjust my expectations with regards to what students could realistically achieve in their circumstances.

Personal Anecdotes on Accommodating Student Assessments

Madam, can I get the form early, because I am on work and I am break now *teary eyed emoji*"...I'll submit by 1 a.m. ok. (Syah, 2022)

This was part of a text I received as I was about to administer an online test during the pandemic. One of my students texted to inform me that he would be taking my online class test in between his breaks at work. My first thought was "Oh no!". This student was definitely not in the best environment for taking a test. Would he be able to do well? Would he be too distracted? To make matters worse, the test was being conducted at night, so it was reasonable to expect that he would be pretty exhausted from working all day. It was not uncommon for students to be working during the pandemic, sometimes out of necessity to support themselves and even their families who might have suffered financial hardships due to COVID-19. This was the reality that I had little control over. And so, the only thing I could do for him was to accommodate his request. He informed me that he would finish his work shift at midnight and would turn in his test within the next hour. However, what was more of a concern for me at that point was his safety and well-being. I told him not to worry about the time. I did not want him traveling too late in the night or rushing to get home just to answer the test and so, I did not pressure him to stick within the stipulated time. What was more important was that he got home safely and that he took the time needed to answer the test the best he could.

In another instance, one of my students said:

I'm sorry for the late submission madam, my laptop been hang a little... I do appreciate if you would understand, but it's your judgment on me. I surely accept it. (Haris, 2002)

A student informed me that he experienced some problems with his laptop which would delay the submission of his test. It had been three semesters into the pandemic and I really could not recall how many times that something similar had happened each time I would give a test since online learning began. Problems with devices, problems with internet connectivity and even problems with electricity supply (which I came to know was common in the East Malaysian states). The list of problems just seemed to repeat itself each semester. I honestly felt quite frustrated at first because we hardly faced any problems when administering face-to-face tests, so this took some time to get used to. Sometimes, I also had my doubts initially. Were these cases genuine? However, when I confided my worries to my colleagues, they shared that they too had similar experiences with their students and we came to the conclusion that the fair thing to do was to give students the benefit of the doubt. These issues were unavoidable when using technology and neither my students nor I could do much about them. With that mindset, I actually felt so much less stressed and became more flexible in extending submission times for tests and assignments too. I needed to learn to trust my students and have some faith in them. After all, in line with 21st century teaching and learning, students should be accountable for their learning, too, which includes taking ownership of their assessments. In the face-to-face setting of pre-COVID-19 times, I would normally be quite strict about meeting submission deadlines etc. and had deducted marks for late turn-ins. However, the pandemic forced me to rethink my approach. In fact, one conversation I had with a colleague teaching the same course really left an impact on me when she said that she did not believe in penalizing her students for turning in late work. If students deserved less marks, it should be because the work they produced failed to meet the expected standards. That was truly an *aha* moment for me. It got me thinking, what were my priorities in assessment, especially given the limitations that students faced during the pandemic? What kind of inference about students did I hope to make through my assessments? Shouldn't educators provide students with the opportunity to produce their best work in order to make a more accurate interpretation of student mastery? Yes!

The last anecdote I would like to share is about providing consultations to students on their on-going assessments. There is a course that I teach which requires students to construct test items as the major assignment. Although we have gone through the assignment guidelines, uploaded our lectures on the do's and don'ts of item writing, how items should correlate to the table of specifications etc. onto Google Classroom, yet students often need further guidance to really carry out the assignment as intended. So, for this particular assignment, I would really maximize the full three hours of our virtual class for one-to-one group consultations and made myself available outside of work hours too, through WhatsApp, to go over any enquiries that they might have later on. Sometimes, no matter how detailed you think you have laid it out for them, students may not understand the assignment until you go through those details with them step-by-step, and it somehow "clicks" for them. Giving personalized feedback is so important. It is not just about the end result. The process of getting there is as important and becomes a valuable learning point for both my students and I.

Lessons Learned

Pre-pandemic, I conducted tests, assigned and guided students in their assessments mainly through direct face-to-face consultations and had them submit hardcopy work. I had little knowledge of how to use the various online platforms and integrate technology in my teaching and assessments. Now I can say that I am quite comfortable with it and can use it with relative ease. That is perhaps one of the upsides of the pandemic for me. Thus, an important fact to remember post-pandemic is that when it comes to virtual assessments – we have done it! Now, we have the actual experience of assessing students virtually and therefore, we are at a better position than before to know what works for us and our students.

Moving forward, what I am taking from this pandemic teaching experience is that I need to remember that students as human beings, who in the process of learning, require a 'human touch'. Empathy, compassion and providing emotional support are things I hope to integrate into the teaching and learning process which includes assessment. There should be more flexibility in assessing students in the future, as and when it is appropriate, duly considering my future students' genuine circumstances and needs. I need to acknowledge that different students face different circumstances and limitations. Thus, educators need to show more empathy and consideration for the unique context of the students. There should be room for flexibility when it is warranted. Part of facilitating learning is also to assist the process of assessment. I would also like to continue encouraging online consultations well after the pandemic passes as it saves a lot of time and energy compared to physical face-to-face sessions. In fact, it may be more practical and could actually encourage students to consult us more regularly leading to better monitoring and guidance of their assignments and progress. In the end, when it comes to teaching and learning, as well as assessment, we need to ask ourselves what is important for us and our students. What are the outcomes that we hope to achieve? Sometimes, those outcomes are not contained in the course outline and cannot be expressed in terms of typical tangible learning outcomes or standards. If through teaching, I am able to not only help increase my students' knowledge and skills, but also and more importantly, have any kind of positive impact on their self-development as human beings, then I shall indeed be quite happy.

CONCLUSION

This chapter attempts to present humanistic teaching efforts conducted by educators during the pandemic. This is conveyed through the educators' heartfelt narratives that delve on the challenges of navigating teaching and learning via ODL during the times of pandemic and how they responded to the various situations that emerged due to the absence of physical contact which we used to take for granted in conventional classrooms. Despite the waves of challenges encountered, these educators remained steadfast in their efforts to ensure learning still continues which were motivated by strong will and dedication to their profession.

The narratives above shared several common themes that educators worldwide are facing. The themes include the need to place empathy and kindness while engaging with students during and outside class hours, the open-mindedness and non-judgmental attitude when responding to students' personal issues (financial, family and health) and the willingness to go the extra mile – learning new technologies to support online learning, preparing new learning activities that can be conducted through online learning, putting in extra time and energy to consult and scaffold students, etc. while navigating the teaching and learning process beyond the four walls of a traditional classroom.

The narratives have shown that the educators have unanimously displayed the essence of humanistic practices in teaching that is embedded through instructional delivery, assessment adaptations and the effort to emotionally connect with the students despite the odds encountered. The students were not the only party that was struggling, but the educators too were facing their own battles. In the earlier phase of the pandemic, when everyone was under lockdowns, educators had to juggle their roles and responsibilities as an educator, mother, wife, daughter, sibling, friend, caretaker and many more. However, from the narratives above, it can be observed that the efforts put in by the educators were commendable, sincere and heartfelt. They willingly took the extra initiative to ensure a meaningful learning process still prevailed. The process was also conducted beautifully and it managed to nurture the hearts and minds of these students, taught them to face their fears and never give up when faced with challenges.

Teaching and learning is not merely imparting knowledge and skills but also a process to nurture students to be better individuals who are physically, emotionally, intellectually and spiritually balanced. To conclude, the pandemic has taught valuable lessons to both students and educators that the art of teaching and learning does not only involve theories and techniques, but also warm and sincere hearts which reflect the qualities that we must possess as human beings.

REFERENCES

Ag-Ahmad, N. (2020). Open and Distance Learning (ODL): Preferences, issues and challenges amidst Covid-19 Pandemic. *Creative Practices in Language Learning and Teaching, 8*(2), 1-14.

Anastasakis, M., Triantafyllou, G., & Petridis, K. (2021). *Undergraduates' barriers to online learning during the pandemic in Greece.* Tech Know Learn. doi:10.100710758-021-09584-5

Archer, E. (2017). The assessment purpose triangle: Balancing the purposes of educational assessment. *Front. Educ., 2*(41), 41. Advance online publication. doi:10.3389/feduc.2017.00041

Burke, K., & Larmar, S. (2021). Acknowledging another face in the virtual crowd: Reimagining the online experience in higher education through an online pedagogy of care. *Journal of Further and Higher Education, 45*(5), 601–615. doi:10.1080/0309877X.2020.1804536

Cavanagh, S. R. (2016). *The spark of online learning: energizing the college classroom with the science of emotion.* West Virginia University Press.

Chakraborty, P., Mittal, P., Gupta, M. S., Yadav, S., & Arora, A. (2021). Opinion of students on online education during the COVID-19 pandemic. *Human Behavior and Emerging Technologies, 3*(3), 357–365. doi:10.1002/hbe2.240

Chiu, T. (2022). Applying the self-determination theory (SDT) to explain student engagement in online learning during the COVID-19 pandemic. *Journal of Research on Technology in Education, 54*(1), S14–S30. doi:10.1080/15391523.2021.1891998

Darby, F. (2020). *Emotions in online teaching: A powerful tool for helping online students engage, persist, and succeed.* https://www.facultyfocus.com/articles/online-education/online-student-engagement/emotions-in-online-teaching-a-powerful-tool-for-helping-online-students-engage-persist-and-succeed/

Djoub, Z. (2018). *Assessment for learning: Key principles and strategies.* Edulearn2change. https://edulearn2change.com/article-assessment-for-learning-key-principles-strategies/

Ellis, R. (2015). *Understanding second language acquisition* (2nd ed.). Oxford University Press.

Eyler, J. R. (2018). *How humans learn: The science and stories behind effective college teaching.* West Virginia University Press.

Glasser, W. (1998). *Choice theory in the classroom.* HarperCollins Publishers.

Hanley, T., Winter, L. A., & Burrel, K. (2019). Supporting emotional well-being in schools in the context of austerity: An ecologically informed humanistic perspective. *The British Journal of Educational Psychology*, *90*(1), 1–18. doi:10.1111/bjep.12275 PMID:30912121

Hare, C. (2019). *An introduction to humanistic learning theory.* Age of Awareness. https://medium.com/age-of-awareness/an-introduction-to-humanistic-learning-theory-1489cdde6359

Johnson, A. P. (2014). *Educational psychology: Theories of learning and human development.* National Science Press. www.nsspress.com

Khatib, M., Sarem, S. N., & Hamidi, H. (2013). Humanistic education: Concerns, implications and applications. *Journal of Language Teaching and Research*, *4*(1), 45–51. doi:10.4304/jltr.4.1.45-51

Lincoln, Y. S., Guba, E. G., & Pilotta, J. J. (1985). Naturalistic inquiry. *Sage (Atlanta, Ga.)*, *9*(4), 438–439. Advance online publication. doi:10.1016/0147-1767(85)90062-8

Marchand, G. C., & Gutierrez, A. P. (2012). The role of emotion in the learning process: Comparisons between online and face-to-face learning settings. *The Internet and Higher Education*, *15*(3), 150–160. doi:10.1016/j.iheduc.2011.10.001

McLeod, S. A. (2018, May 21). *Maslow's hierarchy of needs.* https://www.simplypsychology.org/maslow.html

Mutch, C., & Peung, S. (2021). 'Maslow before Bloom': Implementing a caring pedagogy during Covid-19. *New Zealand Journal of Teachers' Work*, *18*(2), 69–90. doi:10.24135/teacherswork.v18i2.334

Nguyen, Q. N. (2022). Teachers' scaffolding strategies in internet-based ELT classes. *Teaching English as a Second Language Electronic Journal*, *26*(1). doi:10.55593/ej.25101a1

Owusu-Ansah, A., & Kyei-Blankson, L. (2016). Going back to the basics: Demonstrating care, connectedness, and a pedagogy of relationship in education. *World Journal of Education*, *6*(3). Advance online publication. doi:10.5430/wje.v6n3p1

Padgett, D. (2012). *Qualitative and mixed methods in public health.* SAGE. Retrieved from http://ezproxy.deakin.edu.au/login?url=http://search.ebscohost.com/login.aspx?direct=true&db=cat00097a&AN=deakin.b3657335&authtype=sso&custid=deakin&site=eds-live&scope=site

Piccinin, S., Cristi, C., & McCoy, M. (2006). The impact of individual consultation on student ratings of teaching. *The International Journal for Academic Development*, *4*(2), 78–88. doi:10.1080/1360144990040202

Popham, W. J. (2006, October 10-13). *Defining and enhancing formative assessment* [Paper presentation]. Annual Large-Scale Assessment Conference, Council of Chief State School Officers, San Francisco, CA, United States.

San Pedro, T., & Kinloch, V. (2017). Toward Projects in Humanization: Research on Co-Creating and Sustaining Dialogic Relationships. *American Educational Research Journal*, *54*(1), 373S–394S. doi:10.3102/0002831216671210

Schneider, K. J., Pierson, J. F., & Bugental, J. F. T. (2014). *The Handbook of Humanistic Psychology: Theory, Research, and Practice* (2nd ed.). SAGE Publications Inc.

Trettenero, S. (2020). *Human beings are emotional creatures.* Psychreg. https://www.psychreg.org/human-beings-are-emotional-creatures/

UNESCO. (2020). *Education: From disruption to recovery.* UNESCO. https://en.unesco.org/covid19/educationresponse

Untari, L. (2016, January-June). An epistemological review on humanistic education theory. *Leksema, 1*(1), 59–72. Advance online publication. doi:10.22515/ljbs.v1i1.26

What is humanistic learning theory in education? (2020, July 21). Teaching & Education. Western Governors' University. https://www.wgu.edu/blog/what-humanistic-learning-theory-education2007.html#close

KEY TERMS AND DEFINITIONS

Care Pedagogy: The emphasis on connection (human connection, feelings, and relationship) before content delivery and assessment.

Flexi Scaffolding: Any form of support or assistance from the instructor and peers in a flexible and interactional learning environment to promote student engagement.

Humanistic Learning Theory: A learning theory founded by Abraham Maslow that emphasizes the need to consider all aspects of the learner as a 'whole' human being, particularly the affective domain, so that they may reach their full potentials.

Motivation: The drive for someone to pursue a particular task.

Online Assessments: Assessments that are conducted and administered entirely through virtual means including providing feedback and consultation.

Pandemic Teaching: Teaching and learning that occurred during the pandemic which requires a pedagogical approach that is more adaptive and flexible in nature.

Storying: A space in which individuals feel safe to share feelings, emotions, stories, and events that occur in co-constructing relationships and knowledge.

Chapter 6
Creating a Responsive and Responsible Learning Environment:
Bookopolis@UiTM Malaysia

Norshiha Saidin
https://orcid.org/0000-0002-6290-5118
Universiti Teknologi MARA, Malaysia

Nur Hidayah Md Yazid
Universiti Teknologi MARA, Malaysia

Sakinatul Ain Jelani
Universiti Teknologi MARA, Malaysia

Leele Susana Jamian
Universiti Teknologi MARA, Malaysia

EXECUTIVE SUMMARY

New ideas about learning spaces offer a significant opportunity for higher education to transform learning. The creation of a reading-friendly space and a book exchange program, 'Bookopolis', offered UiTM Foundation Centre an opportunity to encourage active learning and create a responsive learning environment. 'Bookopolis' fulfilled the reading needs of the students in an economic and innovative way. Creativity and necessity provided the impetus to transform a non-functional space into an accessible and exciting area for reading and discussions. A flexible system of self-check in and out inculcates the values of trust and integrity, thus heightening a sense of responsibility. The redesigned learning space optimizes the current learning theory to support and extend students' learning environment. This chapter shares the journey and experience in creating a responsive learning space, encouraging a reading culture and literacy skills in a demanding one-year foundation program.

DOI: 10.4018/978-1-6684-6076-4.ch006

INTRODUCTION

"I love borrowing the books from Bookopolis because there's such a wide variety of books available and we are also not restricted to a set timeframe to borrow the books. And the space provided at Bookopolis itself has helped me and my friends a lot because we see that we can have group discussions and we can have revisions at the space. By having better facilities, we see that it would greatly help us to have a more comfortable study period."

- Asasi TESL Student, Female, 18 years old

"Bookopolis is Your Space"

Effective learning occurs when learners take the initiative and are proactive in taking charge of their own learning. This includes seeking for external sources and personalising their learning goals. Responsive learners are capable of organising their own learning, applying new knowledge to wider contexts, overcoming challenges, and are open to growth and change. Furthermore, they possess self-confidence and awareness, an eagerness to learn, are able to use a variety of learning strategies, and are aware of their own learning preferences, interests, and talents (Rawson, 2000; Giese, 2006; Fredriksson and Hoskins, 2007; Hofmann, 2008, as cited in Tekkol and Demirel, 2018).

Bookopolis@UiTM Malaysia was conceived with the aim of improving the learning environment in the new campus. Realizing that there were limited resources and books on the new campus and the dire need to encourage self – directed and responsive learning, the Asasi TESL department initiated the creation of the learning space in 2015. We were a new campus housing nearly 4000 students, the library had just been set up and the number of books were dismal. Bright young minds in an environment with limited books and restricted Internet connectivity. Bookopolis began modestly with little money and with used books donated by lecturers and friends. Soon after its launch, Bookopolis became more than just a place to read, borrow and donate books, it became a popular space for discussions, poetry recitations, public speaking, busking and many other students-initiated activities. Truly achieving its aim of extending the students learning environment.

SETTING UP THE SPACE

In response to the ever-changing requirements of behaviour and learning needs among Generation Z and the networked society, the idea of learning spaces and the ways it accelerates their participation and activates thoughts of knowledge and outlook have been and should always be reconceptualized (Evans & Kersh, 2014). Additionally, living in a Covid-19 pandemic and subsequently endemic situations, the instructors have been pushed to tweak the curriculum to ensure that students become responsive and responsible learners since it has not been easy to meet face-to-face. A group of lecturers initiated this intervention project as we wished to extend the learning experience beyond the confines of the classroom, and create a space that promoted collaboration, rather than isolation of learners, providing mobility and flexibility in grouping.

Responding to the generation of volatile, uncertain learners, we felt the need to create a student-centric space. Bookopolis' is unlike the library in several aspects, firstly it is the transformation of a non – functional space of about 4mx5m, located on the ground floor of the academic main building. The location is such that students will have to walk past the area on their way to classes, and since its part of the lobby there are no confining walls. Secondly, Bookopolis gives students 24 hours access and employs a flexible self- check in system for borrowing and returning books. We removed the gatekeepers and empowered the students. Thirdly, accessibility and informality of learning for the millennials is an important concern, and Bookopolis is designed to appeal to that. Students can lounge on beanbags or stretch out on the floor, they can talk, help each other, play the guitar, eat and drink. Mobility and flexibility to change arrangement in learning spaces is encouraged thus promoting student choice and ownership. Finally, Bookopolis offered an alternative learning space, welcoming yet personalized, and encourages self -directed and self -regulated learning. We wanted to cultivate a reading community, where it was cool to be seen with a book. Thus, the introduction of the tagline" Bookopolis is your space". And the selection of the name aims to add to its appeal to the young crowd.

Bookopolis: Polis is an ancient Greek word for city/state/society. Bookopolis is a center of books created for people who wants to be surrounded by books.

Bookopolis's Main Educational Objectives

- Individualize learning environment
- Provide accessible learning resources in an open learning environment
- Create a learning environment that is welcoming and engaging
- Encourage self-directed and responsive learning
- Expand BOOKOPOLIS to more communities and a wider population

Basic Rules at Bookopolis

- **Donate**
    - Collect any used books you'd like to donate.
    - Send your books to Bookopolis and place them on the shelves.
    - Or swap your preloved book with something new at Bookopolis.
- **Borrow**
    - Write your name in the logbook.
        - When you're done kindly return the book and recommend it to someone else.
        - Should you love the book and would like to keep it, please send in your preloved book instead to replace.

LEARNING SPACES

The architectural practice of 'classroom-as-container' is a prevalent dialogue in educational research. According to Leander, Phillips & Taylor (2010), this discussion acts as an 'imagined geography' of education, including the time and place educators should expect learning to take place. Over the past decade awareness in the reconsideration of learning spaces has progressively driven strategic investment in educational infrastructure of universities worldwide.

The Ministerial Council on Education Employment Training and Youth Affairs (2008) stated that learning is now no longer expected to happen in confined classrooms but rather in a stretched geography of accessible, flexible, 21st century learning spaces. In other words, students are no longer believed to be passive receivers of knowledge but encouraged to actively formulate knowledge.

In moving away from the traditionally rigid classrooms, students are encouraged to be in active learning spaces where they can openly discuss in groups, with books available within arm's reach such as at Bookopolis. Talbert & Mor-Avi (2019) mentioned that the active learning space can augment the practice of active learning and strengthen its positive effects in learners from young children through tertiary level students. Evidently, open learning spaces like Bookopolis are relevant to students of any age range.

Likewise, Newton and Gan (2012) indicated that students work in a way that brings together learning across disciplines instead of having one subject-specific instructor in a single classroom. This argument is supported by Mulcahy (2015) who specified that 21st century learning spaces foster the growth of collaborative learning, personalized learning and self-directed learning, skills that are crucial at the tertiary level.

Self-Directed Learning

There is adequate research that supports the importance of self-directed learning among university students. Certainly, a rigid teaching arrangement may fulfill the course requirements but a cooperative learning surrounding, in which the student identifies as being self-governing, adaptable and most vitally, non-threatening ensures higher success (Robotham,1995). Robotham further expounded the benefits of an open learning space, it improves self-motivation and self-discipline, encourage students' flexibility in setting objectives and better awareness of how they learn and their strengths and weaknesses. Numerous employers would also vouch that self-direction is a vital component of adult learning in the workplace. Self-directed learning approaches have appeared as an organization's effective responses to the intricate demands of the shifting nature of work (Ellinger, 2004). Instructors unwilling to let go of traditional approaches, wanting to control students' learning strategies and not promoting independence will slow down the development of workplace skills.

Independent learning and curiosity are expedient skills for successful learning. The learning process occurs in a more andragogic approach, more transformative-dialogical interaction patterns, more thematic-inspirational material or teaching material, and more varied-motivational media and techniques (Sucipto, Ihsan & Wiyono, 2019). A learning space like Bookopolis is able to ignite curiosity as it provides books of various genres and promotes collaboration, rather than isolation. Naturally, the students will develop independent and self-directed learning to further study their topic of interest.

Responsive and Responsible Learning

Creating an open space for learning such as Bookopolis has also trained students to become responsive and responsible learners. Previous studies have highlighted how responsive and responsible learning should be included in the curriculum. Moore (2015) proposed one characteristic that should be inserted in the curriculum which is to ensure that education—learning—is both relevant (to society and to the learner) and entertaining. As Bookopolis is a liberal space open to all students and faculty members, it promotes collaboration and cooperation, removing the normal pressures and dynamics of the classroom. We hope this allow students to take a more purposeful and thought-out ethical stance regarding interests and issues that are global rather than local or national (Moore, 2015). Indirectly, both responsive and responsible learning skills will set in.

In some cases, students who are struggling in literacy acquisition could be identified as having extreme shortfalls in the mechanics of the reading process and, having been placed in this way, might then be engrossed in remedial programmes constructed from a bottom-up standpoint only (Wearmouth, 2004). This could prove problematic if the tasks and activities produced within these remedial programmes become so concentrated on mechanics and so disintegrated and decontextualised that the social and meaning-making qualities of literacy activities are damaged or obliterated (Glynn et al, 2006). However, the students who are struggling with literacy acquisition will not have to go through the pressure as Bookopolis does not focus on mechanics and is not fragmented and decontextualised.

Fuller & Rivera (2021) hypothesized that using a culturally responsive approach boost engagement and learning gains. A culturally responsive approach allows students to begin learning from their own place of understanding that concentrates on students' lived experiences. Books, as we know it, provide vast resources on culture and society and we of cultural and society information from around the world that they can relate to or learn from, with the combination of the way they have been living their life. Therefore, with this blend of this approach and resources, students and the community can engage and learn something from each other without the need of rigid evaluation.

STUDENTS' FEEDBACK

What Did the Students Think?

When Bookopolis was launched in 2016, there were 3928 students on campus. After a year, students' feedback was obtained. Data was collected via two methods, a log book and an online survey. Book loans and returns were recorded in the log book from December 2016 until October 2017. An online survey was disseminated to gather students' perceptions and satisfaction level. We also invited students to share recommendations for future improvement. The survey yielded data from 256 Asasi students, 90 (35.2%) are TESL students, 84 (32.8%) are Science students, 56 (21.9%) from Law and 26 (10.2%) from Engineering.

As a learning space, 59.2% of students rated Bookopolis as excellent. 80% of the students agreed with the tagline "Bookopolis is your space" and gave very positive comments regarding the accessibility and flexibility of the resources. 58.8% said that they have borrowed or read the books in 'Bookopolis' and would read at least one book per semester. 7% of the students read one book a week. 91.7% responded that they liked the self-service system when borrowing and returning books. The students liked the convenience as they can access 'Bookopolis' at any time. They could use the space for discussions and collaborative work and need not seek permission from any gatekeepers. They appreciated the flexible policy and the trust given to them.

Some of the comments are as below:

- *Convenient to borrow. Like, sometimes we don't have enough time to read some books.*
- *Because there's no time limit when you borrow the books there and you can return it anytime.*

Creating a Responsive and Responsible Learning Environment

- *Because I can return the book whenever I want to.*
- *Because it's more convenient in terms of borrowing books at any time that I want because of the self- service system.*
- *It feels much more like the students' space.*
- *It's a simple system and self -explanatory.*
- *It teaches the students to be responsible, once you borrow, you have full responsibility on the book.*
- *Because I can borrow books anytime I want and I can send it back anytime. Means that I have a lot of time to read those books.*
- *It's all about trust. The system shows that the authority understands very much students' lack of time to read. They also trust the students will be responsible for the book they borrow. The kindness of the system will subtly discipline students to not take the Bookopolis for granted–they will send back the books once they've finished read them.*
- *We don't have to wait for the librarians to borrow it.*
- *There's no time limit for me to read the book I borrowed so I don't have to pay any late fees unlike borrowing from a library.*
- *It encourages people to read because there's no hassle. People can just grab a book when needed, especially since everyone passes Bookopolis every day.*
- *It gives freedom for the readers to read the books without worrying about when to return it, and they can borrow as many books as they can.*

Access to Other Activities Besides Reading

'Bookopolis' created a space for students to not only read, but provided a platform for other activities. 77.3% said that they used the space for to complete assignments and studying, conduct club activities, hold class discussions and others. This shows how functional 'Bookopolis' is for students, providing them an alternative venue for active learning. In short, 'Bookopolis' encourages group interaction and collaborative learning, thus allowing these millennial students to be independent and self- motivated. This finding is supported by research of Cheaney et al. (2005) and Asyari et al. (2016) who contend that group discussions generate many advantages such as instigating students' critical thinking, decision making and problem-solving abilities, exercising to deduce and induce as well as consolidating lifelong learning. Figure 1 shows the types of activities that students participated in or organised at Bookopolis.

Usefulness and Benefits Gained from The Space: Bookopolis

As shown in Figure 2, there were many useful or interesting aspects of Bookopolis to students. The most cited aspect of 'Bookopolis' was the 24-hour access to books. Students' feedback also revealed that they think the space is useful as it provides unrestricted borrowing policy (62.9%) and a platform to read more books (45.6%). Other aspects of how useful the space for students include the availability of interesting books (44.8%) and as a medium to improve their language proficiency.

When asked what had they gained from Bookopolis, more than half of the students (62%) responded that Bookopolis had helped improve their general knowledge. Other benefits included literary appreciation and improvement in reading and language skills. Generation Z learners are also drawn to community-based learning (CBL) for various reasons, such as being able to negotiate and work in groups. These 21st century students prefer to learn beyond something different, useful and outside the classroom or lecture hall (Holdsworth and Quinn, 2010). Figure 3 displays all the areas that improved students' performance after using Bookopolis.

Figure 1. Types of activities students participated/organised at Bookopolis

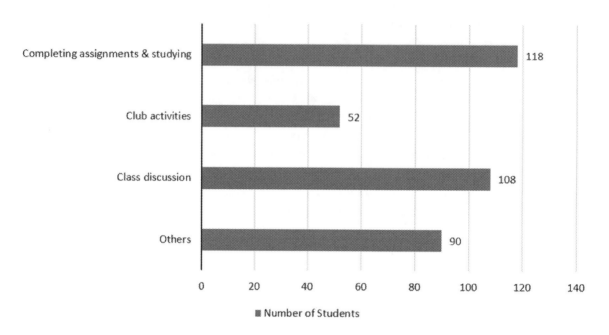

Figure 2. Aspects of Bookopolis that were most useful or interesting to students

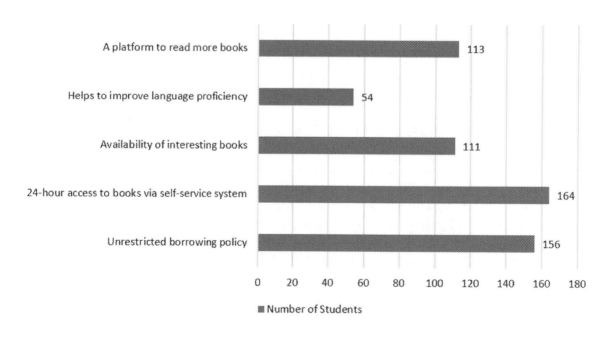

Creating a Responsive and Responsible Learning Environment

Figure 3. Areas that improved students' performance after utilizing Bookopolis

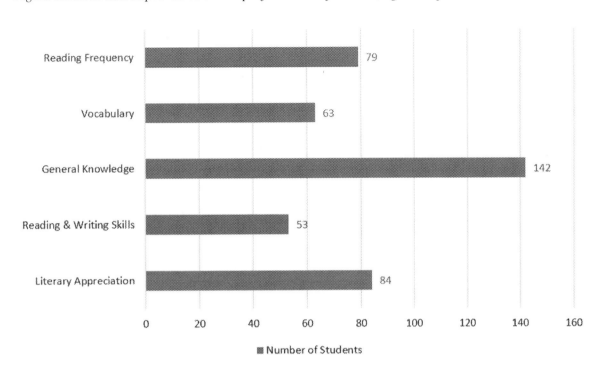

RECOMMENDATIONS FOR THE LEARNING SPACE: BOOKOPOLIS

Students were asked to give recommendations to help improve the space and there were many interesting ones. Top of the list were suggestions to increase the size of the space to accommodate more students.

"Enlarge the space, sometimes there are just too many bookworms in one place, the space given is just not enough to hold that many people."

"Definitely bigger space, and as a member of the book club I'd like to suggest a fan as we have our weekly meetings there hehe."

"Put more books at Bookopolis and maybe we can have a bigger space."

"Please make it larger because sometimes the place is filled with lots of students & there aren't much space to sit."

There were also suggestions to place a fan in the area and add more books.

"Add fans at this place, because this place is kinda hot sometimes:)"

"Extend the space a bit to the back and a fan would be highly appreciated:)"

"Add more books (latest and interesting) with more genre, so there will be many people use the Bookopolis service."

CONCLUSION

This project has demonstrated the importance of creating new learning spaces and places within institutions of higher learning. Students who enjoy reading benefit from the diverse reading materials and need not spend their hard-earned allowance on purchasing books. Those with reading anxiety benefits from being in a learning space that is flexible and informal. An alternative space like this provides a welcoming and dynamic environment that empower learners and encourages collaboration. A valuable outcome with regard to education policy is that Universities should set up conditions to facilitate new learning and the creation of new spaces that are flexible and student-driven.

REFERENCES

Ellinger, A. D. (2004). The concept of self-directed learning and its implications for human resource development. *Advances in Developing Human Resources*, 6(2), 158–177. doi:10.1177/1523422304263327

Evans, K., & Kersh, N. (2014). Training and workplace learning. In K. Kraiger, J. Passmore, N. R. Santos, & S. Malvezzi (Eds.), *The Wiley-Blackwell handbook of the psychology of training, development and performance improvement* (pp. 50–67). Wiley. doi:10.1002/9781118736982.ch4

Fuller, K. S., & Rivera, C. T. (2021). A Culturally Responsive Curricular Revision to Improve Engagement and Learning in an Undergraduate Microbiology Lab Course. *Frontiers in Microbiology*, *2021*, 577852. Advance online publication. doi:10.3389/fmicb.2020.577852 PMID:33519726

Glynn, T., Wearmouth, J., & Berryman, M. (2006). *Supporting students with literacy difficulties: A responsive approach*. Open University Press/McGraw Hill.

Holdsworth, C., & Quinn, J. (2010). Student volunteering in English higher education. *Studies in Higher Education*, 35(1), 113–127. doi:10.1080/03075070903019856

Leander, K. M., Phillips, N. C., & Taylor, K. H. (2010). The changing social spaces of learning: Mapping new mobilities. *Review of Research in Education*, *34*(1), 329–394. doi:10.3102/0091732X09358129

Ministerial Council on Education Employment Training and Youth Affairs. (2008). Learning spaces framework: Learning in an online world. Author.

Moore, A. (2015). *Understanding the school curriculum: Theory, politics and principles*. Routledge.

Mulcahy, D. (2015). Re/assembling spaces of learning in Victorian government schools: Policy enactments, pedagogic encounters and micropolitics. *Discourse (Abingdon)*, *36*(4), 500–514. doi:10.1080/01596306.2014.978616

Newton, C., & Gan, L. (2012). Revolution or missed opportunity. *Architecture Australia*, *101*(1), 74–78.

Robotham, D. (1995). Self-directed learning: The ultimate learning style? *Journal of European Industrial Training, 19*(7), 3–7. doi:10.1108/03090599510092918

Sucipto, S., Ihsan, M. I., & Wiyono, B. B. (2019). Fostering Curiosity to Form Self-Directed Learning Traditions. *SAR Journal*. http://www.sarjournal.com/content/22/SARJournalJune2019_61_67.pdf

Talbert, R., & Mor-Avi, A. (2019). A space for learning: An analysis of research on active learning spaces. *Heliyon, 5*(12). doi:10.1016/j.heliyon.2019.e02967

Tekkol, İ. A., & Demirel, M. (2018). An investigation of self-directed learning skills of undergraduate students. *Frontiers in Psychology, 23*(9), 2324. doi:10.3389/fpsyg.2018.02324 PMID:30532727

Section 2
Pedagogy and Strategies in Responsive and Responsible Learning

Chapter 7
Collaborative Pedagogy for Global Learners:
Adaptive Teaching for Borderless Learning

Malai Zeiti Sheikh Abdul Hamid
Universiti Teknologi Brunei, Brunei

Khadijah Said Hashim
Universiti Teknologi MARA, Malaysia

Kriscentti Exzur P. Barcelona
Lourdes College Inc., Cagayan de Oro City, Philippines

Rene II Mediana Babiera
University of the Immaculate Conception, Philippines

EXECUTIVE SUMMARY

Collaborative pedagogy is one of the teaching approaches that focuses on students' engagement and teamwork in classroom activities to develop critical skill sets such as socio-emotional skills, intercultural communication skills, leadership skills, and problem-solving skills. This study explores students' experiences and reflections on collaborative pedagogy. The objectives of this study are to (1) identity the challenges of online learning, (2) uncover students' insights on collaborative learning, (3) explore significance of collaborative learning, and (4) examine implementation of collaborative pedagogy. This study employed a qualitative design involving 11 college/university students from three different ASEAN countries: Philippines (n=6), Brunei (n=2), and Malaysia (n=2). The primary findings revealed themes including lack of focus and social isolation as the main challenges faced by students. The implication of this study is crucial to optimise learning through the practice of collaborative pedagogy.

DOI: 10.4018/978-1-6684-6076-4.ch007

INTRODUCTION

Since the start of the COVID19 pandemic that hit the world at unprecedented rates, students and educators alike have been very unprepared with the effects of the pandemic on teaching and learning. When the pandemic outbreak first reached countries globally in 2020, many ASEAN countries were affected with the highest number of COVID19 infected cases being recorded in countries such as Indonesia and Singapore. Among the ASEAN countries, Laos is the least affected country, apart from Brunei with zero active cases, while Cambodia has only three active cases (Hamid, 2020). Other countries including Laos, Cambodia, Brunei, Malaysia, Thailand, and Vietnam that have reported more than 90% recovery rate throughout the pandemic (Hamid et al., 2022; Hamid & Karri, 2021).

During the COVID-19 pandemic, two groups in the education sector that are most affected and faced various challenges are students and the teaching community including professors and instructors (Beser et al., 2020; Martin et al., 2017). One of the main challenges faced is the sudden transition from face-to-face learning to online learning. Online learning is admittedly not new to all of us. However, the implementation of remote learning and the enforcement of total lockdown during the COVID19 pandemic has shifted physical face to face mode to move drastically to online mode to nearly all educational activities and in teaching and learning. Consequently, this creates multitude of issues for those in the education sectors, as the main `clients' and stakeholders' , particularly students who are the most affected and encounter various challenges with online learning (Dung, 2022; Li & Che, 2022).

After the pandemic two years on, students are now exposed to online learning as one of the consequences of the COVID19 pandemic. Now, with the recent development in technology, this has allowed both students and the teaching community to use blended approaches for learning, which include a combination of online and face to face learning. As a consequence, collaborative learning has turned into a common familiar practice for those who are involved in the teaching and learning process.

Collaborative pedagogy is viewed as an approach in teaching that emphasises on active engagement, group participation and networking with others, while collaborative learning allow learners to develop connections and understanding (Bravo et al., 2018; Cotterill, 2015; Laal & Laal, 2012; Scager et al., 2016). Through collaborative learning, students from diverse backgrounds including global learners can work together to achieve mutual and multiple goals in learning (Falcione, et. al, 2019).

Throughout the times of pre and post pandemic, global learners have learned new and adapted to unfamiliar territories. Global learners are defined as learners who have drawn their knowledge of the world from various sources, and able to distinguish fact from non-fact, and have developed strong critical skills and open to new ideas and concepts due to their personal experiences and encounters from the ways of the world. These learners, therefore are learners who have become responsive and adaptive in their existing practices, roles and responsibilities in order to suit respective needs and demands. Global learners have also become more familiar and accustomed to different modes of learning virtually, which is in fact both borderless and limitless, for as long as they have access to technology and are connected to cyberspace. It is thus imperative that the adaptation or adaptive strategies should assist global learners to find new ways of facing any types of challenges and obstacles. However, there is no `one-size fit all' practice that can be used to ensure that teaching and learning remain suitable and relevant for global learners. On this premise, this paper aims to discuss and compare the interaction of several themes based on Vygotsky's social learning theory to include three related themes: collaborative pedagogy, collaborative learning and borderless learning for global learners.

Research Objectives

The aim of this study is to highlight the importance of collaborative pedagogy for teachers and educators by uncovering students' experiences and their reflections on collaborative learning in physical class and online learning platforms. The findings in this study can shed some light for teachers and educators to review their current teaching practices by suggesting ways to equip them with a dynamic collaborative pedagogy as a response to the current educational crisis. In other words, this study will offer different perspectives for teacher-educators and to propose collaborative activities that could be beneficial for students for use beyond physical learning and face to face activities.

The purpose of this study is to examine the students' experiences and reflections on collaborative pedagogy and its learning activities. This paper has four main objectives:

i. to identity the challenges of online learning during pandemic;
ii. to uncover students' insights on collaborative learning;
iii. to explore the significance of collaborative learning; and
iv. to examine the implementation of collaborative pedagogy during pandemic and beyond.

More specifically, this paper sought to find answers to the following research questions:

(RQ1) What are the challenges faced by the students during the pandemic?
(RQ2) What are the common insights shared by students on collaborative learning?
(RQ3) What is the significance of collaborative learning?
(RQ4) What strategies have been implemented on collaborative pedagogy during pandemic and beyond?

Problem Statement

The issues and challenges of online learning during the recent pandemic are diverse, ranging from minor to more serious ones. The interdependence is often related to various human-related issues and advancement of technology. Some of the human issues and challenges can stem from global learners' inability to cope and adjust with the rigorous new demands of technology including technical and internet connection (slow and not connecting, out of control), online requirements and lack of guidance and support systems, among others. More importantly, these issues could lead learners to experience serious mental health problems and negative psychological well-being including feeling stress and feeling of loneliness, overly fatigued physically, mentally and emotionally, experiencing anxiety and lack of motivation in learning (Besser et, al., 2022; Faisal & Ali, 2022; Hamid, 2020; Hamid et al., 2022; Hamid & Karri, 2021; Suci & Chaeruman, 2022; Zimmermann, et al., 2021).

Some of these issues and challenges on online learning can thus be reduced and minimised through the practice of collaborative pedagogy and collaborative learning. Most learners often encounter difficulty in staying focused and to maintain attention in learning due to the relentless distractions during online learning. Some advantages of collaborative approach include giving students opportunities to gain new knowledge (Bravo et al., 2018), to function as motivation and support system through creating learning relationships (Cotterril, 2015). Learning can take place through various disciplines (Donaldson et al., 2017; Laal & Ghodsi, 2012; Sahota et al., 2016; Zhang & Cui, 2018) and may lead to increase in exam performance (Duret et al., 2018). In terms of engagement, collaborative learning can also be viewed to contribute in assisting with engagement among learners in two ways, (i) meaningful engagement and (ii) level of engagement (intensity). Through collaborative learning, the experience can also enhance students' purpose, focus and attention, which in turn will contribute to positive academic achievements (Said Hashim et al., 2018).

Collaborative pedagogy is not a new method of teaching and has been commonly used in physical and face-to-face classrooms. Collaborative approach, however, is less common particularly when conducted through online platforms, as this approach tends to cause more hesitation for many teacher-educators and students alike. The latter requires time, appropriate skills and knowledge to ensure that the outcome of online experiences through collaborative learning is positive and highly encouraging. This study intends to explore the significance of collaborative learning and identify the implementation of collaborative pedagogy which can be a useful guide for teacher-educators, teacher-candidates and students as global learners.

LITERATURE REVIEW

Collaborative pedagogy is one of the teaching approaches which focuses on the importance of students' engagement, and participation through teamwork in various classroom activities, learning tasks or projects. In other words, students are taught to interact, discuss, and exchange views in order to broaden their perspectives and to create meaningful experiences. This kind of practice will in turn help students to develop critical skills sets such as socioemotional skills, intercultural communication skills, leadership skills, and problem solving skills.

Students have faced various challenges during online learning since the COVID19 pandemic, which has brought about both positive and negative impacts (Aristovnik et al., 2020; Ali et al., 2020). On the positive note, some students are completely reliant on their ability to become very focused during their online meetings and classes as a consequence of the physical social isolation. Students are `forced' to work on their own in a virtual space, so inadvertently, this means that there is much need for effective and enhanced writing skills through the exchanging of replies and ideas, particularly for forum discussions and channels. This method for global learners has become crucial as one of the main modes of communication, and in particular for shy or reluctant learners. The public display of posts online will engage students to become active and continuously reflect on their course materials through feedback with their teachers or tutors (Robinson & Hullinger, 2008).

Through online learning platforms, students are able to learn at their own pace (both synchronised and asynchronous learning) with this type of student-centred approach. Collaborative learning is arguably one of the best learning approaches for global learners. This is more so in the event that face to face learning sessions were challenging and not feasible, as reflected during the COVID19 pandemic. On the other hand, there are expectations that through online sessions, students have also become self independent global learners, self motivated and self disciplined (Kemp & Grieve, 2014). There is also an increased need for students to use different learning strategies such as note-taking, information seeking and attention focusing strategies (Adam et al., 2017).

In collaborative learning, the use of online learning becomes more prominent and is a useful tool for offering student support among their peers and teachers. Collaborative learning requires students to be engaged with peer interaction to develop conceptual connections and alternative methods of understanding (Laal & Laal, 2012). It can also be viewed that there is expectation for learners to work with each other to achieve a shared goal, which results in the product or learning experiences that goes beyond individual contribution (Falcione et al., 2019).

Collaborative learning assessment is also applicable and relevant at higher education and the construct and consequential validity of assessment methods in collaborating work can vary widely within and across cohorts (Meijer et al., 2022). In higher education, various challenges are inevitable for online learning as most students struggle and will require the use of certain strategies to support their learning (Yeung & Yau, 2022).

Since the pandemic, online learning has been transformed into a bolder and more relevant learning avenue, which has been accepted more positively among students. Student learning experiences have been transformed from the single or one way learning, in which students previously learn on their own into collaborative learning, in which students currently learn with peers and instructors (Smart & Cappel, 2006). Other research that focused on constructivist-based pedagogies have also pointed out on the ways that students are having more interaction with one another and through collaboration, has allowed the global learners to become more effective and simulate the face-to-face-learning environment on online platforms (Arasaratnam-Smith & Northcote, 2017; Ruey, 2010).

Current changes in education have also created an atmosphere which is no longer limited to solo activities for these global learners. There are now more benefits of active learning with maximum opportunities for students to share their ideas and thoughts that lead to meaningful experiences in collaborative pedagogy. In relation to student engagement, they are involved more directly in active learning as collaborative learning is one of the ways for students to work together with their peers, despite their diverse backgrounds. In addition, through collaborative pedagogy, students can easily connect with one another, hence improving their own knowledge (Bravo et al., 2018). The students also become independent learners and can build better relationships (Cotterill, 2015) among their peers. Furthermore, the learning process can be shared across various disciplines (Donaldson et al., 2017; Jackson et al., 2018). In addition, with the advancement in digital learning tools such as Google Docs, Microsoft Teams, and the multitude of learning management systems, this further allow the global learners to have effective collaborative experiences and ask their peers for help if they are stuck, thus improving their knowledge on different content areas (Chu & Kennedy, 2011, Davies 2014).

Collaborative active learning has turned into a more well-established pedagogical approach that offers student autonomy, positive interdependence (Scager et al., 2016) and opportunities to regulate their own behaviour. In addition, it is one of the educational approaches that can foster active learning through student engagement. Collaboration creates an effective learning environment that enhances relationships (Cotterill, 2015) or increases efficiency in exam performance (Duret et al., 2018). In other examples, online lectures, WebCT communication tools and video case studies have been used by students to develop their reflective skills to enable working with diverse communities (Cooner, 2010).

Collaborative learning also enhances the communication and exchange of information and ideas among peers through group bonding or cohesion. It sets the background for global learners to establish critical arguments in order to build group and individual success (Kolikant & Pallack, 2015). Another benefit of collaborative learning is that it builds further understanding as communication becomes more effective when shared understanding is developed among learners (Balasooriya et al., 2020).

Theoretical Framework

The idea of collaborative pedagogy and collaborative learning have stemmed from Vygotsky's Social Learning Theory (1978). The approach of social constructivists is to emphasise collaboration with others in order to produce knowledge and understanding (Gauvin, 2016; Santrock, 2018). In other words, this approach actively engages learners to process and synthesise information by working together in a team and involves key elements of assistance and guidance, which is a concept that has been popularly known as Scaffolding and Zone of Proximal Development (Vygotsky, 1978).

In the current study, the researchers will validate the importance and usability of this theory through an exploration of the four research objectives posed earlier. The findings will show the relevance of the Vgotskian theory that could be adapted and applied in both physical (face-to-face) and online classrooms. In addition, the discussion on application of the theoretical framework is intended to support the findings of the study and will be indicative of the dynamic part of the theory. This paper will also offer creative ideas and lend opportunities for innovations to be conducted in the teachings among teacher-educators across all sectors.

Conceptual Framework

The conceptual framework in this study has been derived from Vygotsky's Social Learning Theory. Three variables have been identified to establish the conceptual framework, namely, collaborative pedagogy, adaptive teaching and borderless learning. The following diagram illustrates the conceptual framework to further guide the current study and used to achieve the research objectives.

Figure 1. Conceptual Framework on Collaborative Pedagogy

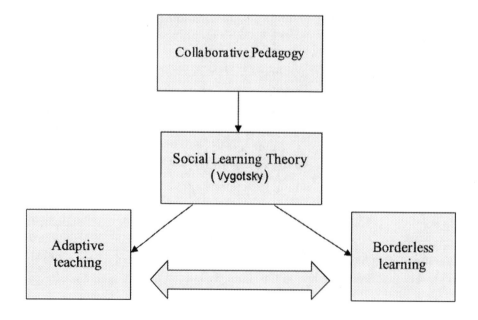

Collaborative Pedagogy for Global Learners

The new education landscape has shifted as a result of the COVID19 pandemic. As shown in the theoretical framework in Figure 1, it illustrates how the classroom routine and climate has now changed due to the adaptation and adoption of online and digital pedagogy. However, not all practices are new; instead previous experiences of student learning can be adapted and enhanced further through the use of technology (or adaptive teaching).

The theoretical framework works on the premise that adaptive teaching, particularly in collaborative pedagogy, will be able to help to create a learning space to offer opportunities for students to become more effective global learners in an educational setting that permits borderless learning. Using Vygotsky's Social Learning Theory, there is much emphasis on the importance of providing assistance and support systems by working together to maximise learning (collaborative learning). In collaborative pedagogy, knowledge imparted will empower students to have confidence to exchange their views and expertise and to assist one another, and this is turn will facilitate the process of learning. When there are collaborative learning experiences, there is likely to be student engagement. The practice of collaborative pedagogy and collaborative learning also needs to be adapted to match the characteristics of global learners, who are of diverse backgrounds and abilities.

Adaptive teaching will require innovative thinking, creative pedagogy and positive attitudes, which can be combined with eclectic theories as point of reference. Furthermore, the dynamic of the Zone of Proximal Development (ZPD) as highlighted in Vygotsky's Social Learning Theory is now applicable to go beyond the classroom and has turned into borderless learning, which can happen anytime, anywhere and through educational tools that are within the disposal of the students. It is collaborative learning that connects both adaptive teaching and borderless learning, and forms an integral part of collaborative pedagogy, stemming from Vygotsky's Social Learning Theory. This theoretical framework is referred to describe some of the views and experiences of global learners in the study.

RESEARCH METHODOLOGY

For the purpose of this study, a qualitative method was employed to uncover and explore the nature of collaborative pedagogy which emphasises on the students' learning experiences and their reflections, rather than quantitative method. Creswell (2011) implied that a case study is a product of inquiry where the researcher(s) explores a bounded system or a case. In this study, data has been collected from college and/university students from three different countries and of similar ages between 18 to 25 years old (n = 11).

It is the intention of this study to be an explanatory case study, which is carried out to describe a phenomenon based on an existing theory and to describe some of the cause and effect of a phenomenon that has already happened (Chua, 2020). This research has been based on the framework that will explore collaborative pedagogy through online learning experiences, through the application of Vygotsky's theory of Scaffolding and Zone of Proximal Development (ZPD).

Sample

A total number of 11 college/university students (n =11) participated in the online interview conducted and were recorded by the researchers using Google Meet and Zoom Meeting platforms. In particular, the participants comprise a total number of 6 students from Philippines, 2 students from Brunei, and another 2 from Malaysia.

The non-random sampling procedure has been used through purposive sampling in which the informants (participants) were purposely selected by the researchers based on similar characteristics and experiences as mentioned in the research objectives. Common factors among the respondents are similar-age range of students who must have experiences with (i) online learning and participated in (ii) collaborative activities during online learning. Chua (2020) stated that purposive sampling is a process whereby a group of subjects has been chosen as respondents because they have certain characteristics as a requirement in the intended research objectives.

Focus Group Discussion and Research Ethics

For the study, a semi structured interview method was employed and was purposely conducted online. This method offers participants more flexibility and the freedom to voice out their opinions about the issue discussed. It is noted that the interview questions have been developed based on the research objectives. Discussions with the participants are closely guided by the interview protocol. The protocol was first developed, and this was later followed with obtaining consent that was communicated to each participant, prior to the interview. All participants are aware that information and data collected from them will only be used for the purpose of the study and their identities will be kept confidential. After participants' consent was obtained to participate in the study, the next process was carried out.

The group interviews with participants were conducted at a later stage, known as the focus group discussion (FGD). Chua (2020) claimed that this method is useful to gather information on a specific issue from a group of respondents, through the sharing, exchanging and discussion of ideas in order to achieve research objectives. Through the focus group discussion, any phenomenon will be easily identified and the sharing of information by respondents will provide insights of which were not easily obtained through quantitative data collection.

Thematic Analysis

After all responses have been submitted from participants, each reflection was coded by team members using thematic analysis (Clarke & Braun, 2017). The thematic analysis involved a few steps which included identification of themes, examination and interpretation of data.

Using an open-coding approach, the data was analysed by the team members (researchers) and codes were then used to organise the information into meaningful chunks and later identified into smaller collections of themes or sub categories. After the first analysis was completed, significant statements related to the research objectives were identified as findings of the data. These statements were later grouped together according to similar meanings and ideas identified. From the responses, there were common attributes which were found among the participants, who are global learners from different ethnic backgrounds but representing their respective institutions and countries around the three Asian regions. To ensure rigour to the whole process of collecting and analysing the data, the study employed

Collaborative Pedagogy for Global Learners

several other strategies to enhance reliability and validity. Among the processes included keeping a record of audit trail, utilising data triangulation, employing members check and peers check.

FINDINGS

Several numbers of emerging themes have been identified and were systematically grouped into significant categories, and this guided research objectives and questions (**RQ1 - RQ4**). From the findings, it was interesting to note there was some general overlap in responses made by respondents, in relation to different research questions. To recap, the following were research questions posed earlier:

(RQ1) What are the challenges faced by the students during the pandemic?
(RQ2) What are the common insights shared by students on collaborative learning?
(RQ3) What is the significance of collaborative learning?
(RQ4) What strategies have been implemented on collaborative pedagogy during pandemic and beyond?

The first research objective (**RO1**) focused on issues and challenges of online learning which were faced by the students, and provided answers for, **RQ1 `What are the challenges faced by the students during the pandemic?'**. There were at least 17 emerging themes identified. The sub categories identified included (i) lack of focus ii) source of motivation and (ii) social isolation.

The following excerpts are some of the examples of the categories that reflected the issues and challenges of online learning during the COVID19 pandemic for **RQ1.**

1) **Lack of focus**

In my own opinion the main challenge that is faced by the students during online learning is distraction. Some of this distraction includes the environment at home. With the existing form of online learning, it is evident that it is quite difficult for us to separate school and home. (Participant PH, lines 1-6)

2) **Social Isolation**

Social isolation was a serious challenge for me. As compared to life before the pandemic, learning was fun, exciting, because I was surrounded by friends, and I could meet my teachers/ lecturers for consultations after class. (Participant MY, lines 8-12)

From Research Question 1 (**RQ1**), `**What are the challenges faced by the students during the pandemic?'**, responses showed that researcher participants reported that their learners faced lack of focus due to distraction at home with online learning and social isolation (Aristovnik et al., 2020; Ali et al., 2020). These two challenges have been discussed extensively in previous work earlier as the most common challenges faced by global learners from the onset of the COVID19 pandemic.

The second research objective (**RO2**), investigated on insights that the respondents shared about their students' learning experiences and opinions about collaborative learning, through the **RQ2**, `**What are the common insights shared by students on collaborative learning?'**. A total of 3 categories were identified from 21 emerging themes. The categories identified as (i) source of motivation (ii) learning different cultures and perspectives, and (iii) relationships, networking and linkages.

The following excerpts reflect significant categories that reflected issues and challenges of online learning during the COVID19 pandemic for **RQ2.**

3) **Source of motivation**

By having friends to discuss with, sharing ideas and thoughts to complete lessons and its tasks it made me more positive and motivated. (Participant MY, lines 5-8)

I prefer working together in a group as it is less stressful when it comes to completing a task alone and the feeling of winning/completing a task in a group feels much more rewarding especially for the less able ones. (Participant BR, lines 1-5).

4) **Learning different cultures and perspectives**

Working together in a group also lets pupils learn from their friends as different pupils have different answers and perspectives so they can learn new things from one another. (Participant BR, lines 11-15)

It teaches me more than teamwork but accepting differences and trying out to reach mutual agreement (Participant MY, Lines 10-12)

5) **Relationship, linkages and networking**

It offers opportunities for new friendships, relationships, linkages, and networking too. (Participant MY, lines 10-12)

From Research Question 2 (**RQ2**), the insights shared by participants revealed how collaborative learning can be a source of motivation for students. There is a preference to work together (collaboratively) than alone not only reduces but viewed positively and motivating. The responses reflect that group work/teamwork and building relationships and networking are traits and characteristics of collaborative learning, while acceptance and coming into an agreement with differences is another important characteristic of collaborative learning. These responses are very similar to the issues raised on the positive aspects of collaborative learning, which included student engagement and enhancement of relationships (Cotterill, 2015), efficacy in exam performance (Duret *et al.*, 2018) and the ability to work with diverse communities (Cooner, 2010) and for building effective communication among learners (Balasooriya et al., 2020).

The third research objective (RO3) investigated insights in which respondents shared about their students' learning experiences and opinions about collaborative learning, through the **RQ3**, `What is the significance of collaborative learning?'.

As outlined in Research Question 3 (**RQ3**), `What is the significance of collaborative learning?', the participants' responses corresponded to some insights shared by participants that focused on the need to work with others through collaborative learning. More importantly, as described in the approach of social constructivists, it is emphasised that collaboration with others will lead to producing

Collaborative Pedagogy for Global Learners

knowledge and understanding (Gauvin, 2016; Santrock, 2018). In this study, as global learners, one of the key aspects of collaborative pedagogy is to be actively engaging with one another, to process and synthesise information which can be achieved by working together in a team and involves key elements of assistance and guidance. This fits in with the theoretical framework of the study, using Vgotsky' Scaffolding and Zone of Proximal Development (1978), in which adaptive teaching and borderless learning are both elements that are key to maintaining collaborative learning, through collaborative pedagogy in light of the technological changes.

In terms of relationship, linkages and networking and source of motivation, the participants have shared some of the insights that have previously discussed which highlighted the source of motivation, developing social skills, diversity in learning/ global learning and (promotion of better understanding in learning. The ability to work with diverse communities (Cooner, 2010) and building effective communication among learners (Balasooriya et al., 2020) have lend support to maintain relationships, linkages and networking which is easily obtained through communication by collaborating with other globalised learners, particularly by learning with peers and lecturers/ academicians through feedback with their teachers or tutors (Robinson & Hullinger, 2008). As outlined in Research Question 3 earlier, in terms of source of motivation, the participants relayed that discussing ideas, sharing thoughts and working in groups is less stressful and much preferred that working alone. With collaborative learning, students are often engaged with peer interaction to develop conceptual connections and alternative methods of understanding (Laal & Laal, 2012), able to achieve a shared goal, which results in the product or learning experiences that goes beyond individual contribution (Falcione et al., 2019). More importantly at higher education, collaborative learning assessment is applicable and relevant across cohorts (Meijer et al., 2022) and some strategies can be used to support their learning (Yeung & Yau, 2022).

For Research Question, **RQ4**, `What strategies have been implemented on collaborative pedagogy during pandemic and beyond?' there were at least 4 categories that were found from 22 emerging themes to cover the following sub themes:

6) **Diversity in Learning/ Global learning**

It is essential in terms of building a diverse community without any hints of judgments from one another. (Participant PH, lines 11-12)

Working together in a group also lets pupils learn from their friends as different pupils have different answers and perspectives so they can learn new things from one another. (Participant BR, lines 11-15)

7) **Multiple sources, creativity and platform**

Series of webinars, seminars, talks, web lecturers and other online activities are part of Collaborative pedagogy and its manifestations. (Participant MY, Lines 7-9)

This pedagogy can be implemented using either video conferencing or any LMS platforms widely available online provided pupils have enough access to technological devices equipped with stable data/ wifi connections during the online learning. Back to normal classroom setting, pupils should be exposed to this collaborative learning as early as it can to normalise learning through working together so that they are familiar with this learning approach. (Participant BR, lines 1-9)

8) **Integrated curriculum and extracurricular**

In this time of the pandemic, I believe that we can utilise collaborative pedagogy by implementing it in our studies and even extracurricular activities such as webinars and workshops. (Participant PH, lines 1-4)

9) **Flexible and adaptive learning**

I was initially thought it had to be done face to face and onsite. Now, thanks to the pandemic. We have to learn to adapt to new things including teaching and learning. CL now can be done virtual; in fact it has now become the trend to have frequent meetings, discussion, programs, online lecturers, or linked classrooms by inviting participants, audiences, speakers, and panels from all around the globe. (Participant MY, lines 1-9)

The four sub themes above 6) to 9) are related to Research Question 4 (RQ4) and have provided answers for what strategies have been implemented on collaborative pedagogy.

It was found in this study that there were at least 22 emerging themes with several categories identified which covered from flexible and adaptive learning, to integrated curriculum and extracurricular that were raised by participants in the current study.

With collaborative learning during online sessions, students have also become self independent global learners, self motivated and self disciplined (Kemp & Grieve, 2014) and have led to different learning strategies such as note-taking, information seeking and attention focusing strategies (Adam, et. al., 2017). This is essential in order to keep up with the new changes that have been made to curriculum as a consequence of the COVID19 pandemic. It is noted that collaborative learning will also allow learners to be engaged with one another through peer interactions in order to develop conceptual connections and to find alternative methods of understanding (Laal & Laal, 2012) and in order to achieve a shared goal (Falcione et al., 2019).

DISCUSSION AND CONCLUSION

Various collaborative experiences were shared by different students at four different colleges/universities. Analysis revealed nine emerging themes: familiarity with collaborative learning, relationships, benefits, motivations, and design and process. Upon analysis of these themes, nine discrete patterns emerged:

(a) Lack of focus and motivation,
(b) Social isolation,
(c) Learning different cultures and perspectives,
(d) Relationship, linkages and networking,
(e) Source of motivation,
(f) Diversity in learning/global learning.
(g) Multiple sources,
(h) Creativity and platform.

Collaborative Pedagogy for Global Learners

(i) Integrated curriculum and extracurricular. and

(j) Flexible and adaptive learning.

As stated in the above findings, there were 9 emerging themes that were found to be significant among all respondents. The 9 emerging themes will be used to find answers to the four research questions posed in this study. The following themes were found to be relevant and important sources of information for the study.

In order to achieve successful collaborative learning, it is important that students be allowed to be highly involved in the collaborative activities to allow them the freedom to speak out and share their personal learning experiences or own encounter and the roles they play in the collaboration. Teachers and educators need to be more aware of the importance of preparing and designing appropriate collaborating activities that match and suit students' own learning experience.

The following research questions will now be addressed:

RQ1: What are the challenges faced by the students during the pandemic?

Based on the responses shared by the students, out of the 9 emerging themes, respondents in the study found that they lack focus and motivation, social isolation as the two main challenges faced. These challenges are to be as expected and it is not uncommon, which started at the onset of during the pandemic. There is a lack of support when students cannot come to regular face to face physical classes and instead, they need to embark on the non face to face learning experience and revert to online learning, which may seem contrived and difficult. The most common problems faced by students are due to technical problems, lack of infrastructural support, connectivity, among others. More importantly, the students will have to rely on various sources for learning, and to each other for support to help them in becoming an independent learner online. Students also need to reach out and communicate regularly with their peers or teachers/instructors because outline learning makes them feel the impact of social isolation, as expressed by some students in this research.

Social isolation is thus a common consequence that is faced by global learners during online learning. The online learning environment itself also is likely to cause more negative effects than positive ones with detrimental impact on students' physical and mental health. This is inevitable when students are constantly having to revert to using electronic/digital communication devices for their learning. Common side effects include fatigue, eyestrain, mental boredom of facing the computer daily, and even the monotonous routine of attending classes online for each day with no real human contact. Most students also prefer to switch off their camera due to shyness or to unreadiness to be seen online by others.

The respondents in this study have also stated that distractions at home are common during the pandemic, so online learning is not necessarily conducive for them. Staying at home is not the best way to learn due to the distractions from the home environment such as noise or consistent interaction with members of the family during the online classes. At school environments, there is little to no distraction so students stay focussed in the class and that tasks and assignments are delegated accordingly in a timely manner. Students have become disciplined to the school rules and regulations and tend to abide by the rules. Overall, at home, such strict adherence to a highly regulated practice for learning is difficult for students who face distractions such as noisy environments, connectivity or other home practices or rituals which are highly unavoidable.

RQ2: What are the common insights shared by students on collaborative learning?

Out of the 9 emerging themes, respondents in the study found that in terms of collaborative learning, students described certain areas that were familiar with this type of learning experience. When students gave their insights on what collaborative learning meant to them, learning different cultures and perspectives, relationship, linkages and networking and source of motivation were the most common insights. These showed that in the students' viewpoint, collaborative learning and working with another person and learning together have allowed them to build and have better relationships and that they are capable of strengthening their networking skills through collaboration.

With regular and consistent good connection which is a requirement to connect for online learning, students have been able to meet their friends, and learn quickly with their friends, peers, teachers, tutors as there is no physical distance as a barrier and students can do this in collaborative learning online. In other words, without face to face or being physical in the classroom, students may work with others (including teachers/ tutors or other students), not just within the same country but also from international countries. Through online learning platforms, communication and the exchange of information becomes highly accessible and within reach at their fingertips at any time by navigating through digital devices, or learning platforms such as smartphones, laptop.

Furthermore, with collaborative learning, students have the chance to strengthen their networking and that diversity in learning/global learning which provides the impetus for students to share their ideas without any judgement or bias when students are treated as equally as a learner online. In addition, online learning has become the most common form of source of motivation for students who are not deprived of an education during the COVID19 pandemic when most schools were forced to shut down or close. Thus, online learning unites everyone in cyberspace and that no one will be left out from obtaining an education. This further enhanced learning together in which collaboration became the best way to support each other, particularly during the COVID19 pandemic which made it impossible for anyone to meet physically for fear of being infected.

RQ3: What is the significance of collaborative learning?

The respondents in the study found that collaborative learning is a source of motivation and leads to diversity in Learning/Global learning. In terms of diversity in learning/global learning, this has been possible through collaborative learning, which is significant in a virtual environment. It is also a source of motivation for students as one of the emerging themes found. It is to be expected that through online learning and collaborative learning, this allows students to be able to communicate constantly with each other, their friends, peers, tutors, teachers and others as the online platform provides the perfect avenue to speak to other people globally regardless of location and where they come from. Students connect with each other as a global learner and citizen and make sense of what they learn with the ease of technology.

Furthermore, online learning has become one of the best practices for obtaining an education when physical meets are hard or impossible, and regardless of distance or which country they come from, every learner is treated equally and with respect. Connection is mainly done through online learning platforms and that meetings can be conducted easily and regularly at any time with other people globally. Online learning is thus very convenient, saves travel time, and does not require money or other external support except regular connection online.

Collaborative Pedagogy for Global Learners

RQ4: What strategies have been implemented on collaborative pedagogy during pandemic and beyond?

In the case of collaborative pedagogy that were used during the pandemic and beyond, the students described that an integrated curriculum and extracurricular and flexible and adaptive learning were the most common emerging themes. In addition, the use of multiple sources, creativity and platform were also found to be most supportive for their learning. These strategies have been identified by the students in this study.

In order to achieve successful collaborative learning, it is important that students be allowed to be highly involved in the collaborative activities as this allows the freedom for them to speak out and share their personal learning experiences or own encounters. Teachers and educators need to be more aware of the importance of preparing and designing appropriate collaborating activities that match and suit students' own learning experience (customized learning). The use of an integrated curriculum and extracurricular and flexible and adaptive learning becomes vital to allow learners to become successful and creative methods will impart useful knowledge to cope with the various challenges faced since the COVI9 pandemic outbreak. Post pandemic, similar strategies that worked to enhance their learning must be continued for students to enhance collaborative experiences. Overall, students in this study expressed that having strategies which incorporate an integrated curriculum and extracurricular and the use of flexible and adaptive learning were the most common practices, while at the same time, the use of multiple sources, creativity and platform were felt to be the best way to enhance collaborative learning.

The above discussion has shown that nine discrete patterns have emerged which included: (a) Lack of focus and motivation, (b) social Isolation, (c) Learning different cultures and perspectives, (d) Relationship, linkages and networking, (e) Source of motivation (f) Diversity in Learning/Global learning (f) Multiple sources, (g) creativity and platform (h) Integrated curriculum and extracurricular and (i) Flexible and adaptive learning. Among these themes, there is strong support as expressed by the students in the study that collaborative pedagogy through collaborative learning activities have been viewed as beneficial to students. Since online learning has become a predominant learning tool after COVID19 pandemic, most global learners have now been exposed to various learning strategies that promote the inherent need to be able to work with others. Learning different cultures and perspectives, and building relationships through linkages and networks has also enhanced collaboration and as a source of motivation. Social isolation was one of the main challenges faced by global learners, yet through the use of creativity and integrated curriculum and flexible and adaptive learning, these students could learn better collaboratively.

In conclusion, the outbreak of COVID-19 has given opportunity for students to revisit and examine essential conditions for online learning to take place during the pandemic and that any previous experiences have paved ways for global learners to venture into creative and critical ways of thinking, and for coping with new challenges (including technological ones). It is through collaborative learning, strategies and activities, combined with collaborative pedagogy that could play a major factor for assisting global learners to supporting learning from each other, with their peers and teachers even after the COVID19 pandemic.

In this paper, the emerging themes also lend support for the theoretical framework that has been proposed earlier in this study. Through collaborative learning, it can be used to actively engage learners to process and synthesise information by working together in a team, with assistance and guidance (Vygotsky, 1978) and with the inclusion with two other components, borderless learning and adaptive teachings.

REFERENCES

Adam, N. L., Alzahri, F. B., Cik Soh, S., Abu Bakar, N., & Mohamad Kamal, N. A. (2017). Self-regulated learning and online learning: A systematic review. In H. Badioze Zaman, P. Robinson, A. F. Smeaton, T. K. Shih, S. Velastin, T. Terutoshi, A. Jaafar, & N. Mohamad Ali (Eds.), *Advances in visual informatics* (pp. 143–154). Springer International Publishing. doi:10.1007/978-3-319-70010-6_14

Ali, A., Siddiqui, A. A., Arshad, M. S., Iqbal, F., & Arif, T. B. (2022, June). Effects of COVID-19 pandemic and lockdown on lifestyle and mental health of students: A retrospective study from Karachi, Pakistan. *Annales Médico-Psychologiques*, *180*(6), S29–S37. doi:10.1016/j.amp.2021.02.004 PMID:33612842

Arasaratnam-Smith, L. A., & Northcote, M. (2017). Community in online higher education: Challenges and opportunities. *Electronic Journal of e-Learning, 15*(2), 188–198.

Aristovnik, A., Keržič, D., Ravšelj, D., Tomaževič, N., & Umek, L. (2020). Impacts of the COVID-19 pandemic on life of higher education students: A global perspective. *Sustainability*, *12*(20), 8438. doi:10.3390u12208438

Besser, A., Flett, G. L., & Zeigler-Hill, V. (2022). Adaptability to a sudden transition to online learning during the COVID-19 pandemic: Understanding the challenges for students. *Scholarship of Teaching and Learning in Psychology, 8*(2), 85. doi:10.1037/stl0000198

Chua, Y. P. (2022). *Mastering Research Methods*. McGraw-Hill Education.

Creswell, J. W. (2011). Controversies in mixed methods research. The Sage Handbook of Qualitative Research, 4(1), 269-284.

Dung, N. T. (2022). Challenges of Online Learning and Some Recommendations for University Students in Vietnam. *Journal of Algebraic Statistics, 13*(2), 350-358. https://publishoa.com

Faisal, F. A., & Ali, M. M. (2022). Cabaran Pembelajaran Atas Talian Di Rumah: Tinjauan Ibu Bapa Murid Berkeperluan Khas Bermasalah Pembelajaran [Challenges Of Online Learning At Home: A Survey Of Parents Of Students With Special Needs With Learning Disabilities]. *International Journal of Advanced Research in Islamic Studies and Education, 2*(1), 129–141.

Falcione, S., Campbell, E., McCollum, B., Chamberlain, J., Macias, M., Morsch, L., & Pinder, C. (2019). Emergence of Different Perspectives of Success in Collaborative Learning. *The Canadian Journal for the Scholarship of Teaching and Learning, 10*(2), n2. doi:10.5206/cjsotl-rcacea.2019.2.8227

Hamid, M. Z. B. S. A., & Karri, R. R. (2021). Overview of Preventive Measures and Good Governance Policies to Mitigate the COVID-19 Outbreak Curve in Brunei. In I. Linkov, J. M. Keenan, & B. D. Trump (Eds.), COVID-19: Systemic Risk and Resilience. Risk, Systems and Decisions. Springer. https://doi.org/10.1007/978-3-030-71587-8_8.

Hamid, M. Z. B. S. A., Karri, R. R., & Karri, Y. (2022). Status quo of outbreak and control of COVID19 in the Southeast Asian Nations during the first phase: A case study of sustainable cities and communities. In COVID-19 and the Sustainable Development Goals. Elsevier.

Hamid. (2020). An Analysis of the success in suppressing COVID-19 cases in Brunei Darussalam. *International Journal of Advanced Research, 8*(6), 718-725.

Kemp, N., & Grieve, R. (2014). Face-to-face or face-to-screen? Undergraduates' opinions and test performance in classroom vs. online learning. *Frontiers in Psychology, 5*, 1278. doi:10.3389/fpsyg.2014.01278 PMID:25429276

Laal, M., & Laal, M. (2012). Collaborative learning: What is it? *Procedia: Social and Behavioral Sciences, 31*, 491–495. doi:10.1016/j.sbspro.2011.12.092

Li, J., & Che, W. (2022). Challenges and coping strategies of online learning for college students in the context of COVID-19: A survey of Chinese universities. *Sustainable Cities and Society, 83*, 103958. doi:10.1016/j.scs.2022.103958 PMID:35620298

Martin, F., Ahlgrim-Delzell, L., & Budhrani, K. (2017). Systematic review of two decades (1995 to 2014) of research on synchronous online learning. *American Journal of Distance Education, 31*, 3–19. .1264807 doi:10.1080/08923647.2017

Meijer, H., Brouwer, J., Hoekstra, R., & Strijbos, J. W. (2022). Exploring Construct and Consequential Validity of Collaborative Learning Assessment in Higher Education. *Small Group Research*. Advance online publication. doi:10.1177/10464964221095545

Olt, P. A. (2018). Virtually there: Distant freshmen blended in classes through synchronous online education. *Innovative Higher Education, 43*, 381–395. https://dx.doi.org/10.1007/s10755-018-9437-z

Robinson, C., & Hullinger, H. (2008). New benchmarks in higher education: Student engagement in online learning. *Journal of Education for Business, 84*, 101–109. .84.2.101-109. doi:10.3200/JOEB

Ruey, S. (2010). A case study of constructivist instructional strategies for adult online learning. *British Journal of Educational Technology, 41*(5), 706–720.

Said Hashim, K., Abdul Majid, R., & Alias, A. (2018). Gender and Ability Differences on the Profile of Purpose in Life among Adolescents. *Journal of Advance Research in Dynamical & Control Systems, 10*(12).

Santrock, J. W. (2018). *Educational Psychology* (6th ed.). McGraw-Hill Education.

Smart, K. L., & Cappel, J. J. (2006). Students' perceptions of online learning: A comparative study. *Journal of Information Technology Education, 5*(1), 201–219.

Suci, W., Muslim, S., & Chaeruman, U. A. (2022). Use of Social Media for Collaborative Learning in Online Learning: A Literature Review. *Al-Ishlah: Jurnal Pendidikan, 14*(3), 3075-3086. DOI: doi:10.35445/alishlah.v14i3.833

Vygotsky, L. S. (1978). *Mind in Society: the Development of Higher Psychological Processes*. Harvard University Press.

Yeung, M. W., & Yau, A. H. (2022). A thematic analysis of higher education students' perceptions of online learning in Hong Kong under COVID-19: Challenges, strategies and support. *Education and Information Technologies, 27*(1), 181–208. https://doi.org/10.1007/s10639-021-10656-3

Chapter 8
Engaging Responsive and Responsible Learning Through Collaborative Teaching in the STEM Classroom

Mawarni Mohamed
https://orcid.org/0000-0003-0978-1301
Univeristi Teknologi MARA, Malaysia

Nor Syazwani Mohd Rasid
Universiti Teknologi MARA, Malaysia

Norezan Ibrahim
Universiti Teknologi MARA, Malaysia

Padmanabhan Seshaiyer
George Mason University, USA

EXECUTIVE SUMMARY

This chapter explores how the elements of responsive and responsible learning were adopted in the first STEM education classroom through collaborative teaching with external experts in a public university in Malaysia. The objectives for the introduction of the course were to enable students to apply the knowledge of mathematical and pedagogical aspects in the teaching of science and mathematics to solve problems in a scientific and systematic manner and to demonstrate the ability to seek new knowledge independently. Three class projects involving collaborators fulfilled 8 weeks of lectures. These included Training of Trainers (ToT), Green Energy Project – Solar Panel and the University Centre for Innovative Delivery and Learning Development (CIDL) focused on Internet of Things (IoT) content. Collaborative teaching in the STEM education classroom has successfully served the specific technical requirements of industry using the design-thinking framework into the university classroom setting.

DOI: 10.4018/978-1-6684-6076-4.ch008

Engaging Responsive and Responsible Learning Through Collaborative Teaching in the STEM Classroom

INTRODUCTION

Along with the need to address global challenges in the 21st century, there is even a greater need for an integrated STEM (Science, Technology, Engineering, and Mathematics) education with the aim of preparing students to be competitive and ready for a workforce with deep technical and personal skills. STEM Education helps to improve critical thinking skills and help students to become creative problem solvers. STEM Education also helps to empower students with the skills to succeed and adapt to this increasingly changing in technological world. It also helps to enhance 21st Century skills through building a strong foundation in the skills of collaboration, critical thinking, communication, creativity, inquiry skills, critical analysis, teamwork and collaboration, initiative, and digital literacy in which they can apply to solve real-world challenges grounded in science, technology, engineering, and math (STEM Education) content. Thus, STEM subjects are effective means to produce competitive graduates for better global competitiveness in the 21st century ((Aydın-Günbatar, Öztay, & Ekiz-Kıran, 2021); (Seshaiyer, 2021)).

An important strategy for improving STEM education is to intentionally include various types of learning strategies, this may include responsive and responsible learning, inquiry-based learning, experiential learning, project-based learning, and challenge-based learning along with the creation of high-quality, integrated instruction and materials, as well as the placement of problems associated with grand challenges of society at the centre of study. One framework that motivates the need to employ STEM solutions to face societal challenges is the Sustainable Development Goals (SDG 2030[1]) adopted by United Nations Member States in 2015. These goals provide a shared blueprint for peace and prosperity for people and the planet, and the 17 Sustainable Development Goals (SDGs) provide a framework for important global challenges including ending poverty, improving health and education, reduce inequality, spur economic growth, tackling climate change and more ((Jamali, Ale Ebrahim, & Jamali, 2022); (Seshaiyer & McNeely, 2020)). We believe STEM education is a promising educational framework to help address these international goals.

STEM Education has been recently introduced to students majoring in Science and Mathematics at the Faculty of Education, Universiti Teknologi MARA (UiTM), a higher learning institution in Selangor with a first batch commence in September 2021. The objectives for the introduction of this course were to enable students to apply the knowledge of Mathematical and pedagogical aspects in the teaching of science and mathematics, to solve problems in a scientific and systematic manner and to demonstrate the ability to seek new knowledge independently, as students as well as future educators. An integrated STEM Education will also help to provide new frameworks for upskilling the mathematics education workforce (Seshaiyer, 2021).

One of the reasons for STEM Education being introduced in the curriculum was due to the low number of students' enrolment in the science stream in Malaysia, which later can give impact to the future of science and STEM education in Malaysia. STEM has been implemented in schools beginning 2017, it's aimed to produce students with science literacy (Ramli & Talib, 2017). Since the aim of STEM Education is to produce STEM literate students who can apply and integrate STEM concepts into the solutions, accordingly, be creative, innovative, and inventive in line with the skills needed in 21st century and Industrial Revolution 4.0, therefore, STEM Education was an added value subject and should be taught in a more interesting way. Due to this, the Science and Mathematics Departments at the Faculty of Education, UiTM decided to collaborate with three different agencies within their area of specialization to give lectures and to assist students with hands-on group projects. This chapter seeks to explore how likely are the elements of responsive and responsible learning were adopted in STEM Education classroom through collaborative teaching with external experts. This phenomenological study examines the outcomes from the implementation of a STEM education course that was taught collaboratively and the course consisted of project-based collaborative teaching practices and assessment methods taught using a human-centred approach. Along with studying the impact on responsive and responsible student learning, this work also hoped to gain insights into the impact of collaborative teaching with STEM education reforms on teacher education practices in preparing the next generation of teachers in Malaysia.

MODELS AND METHODS

STEM Education course was conducted within the 14 weeks of classes, with three projects involving collaborators fulfilled 8 weeks of lectures and projects. The earlier weeks were handled by Science and Mathematics lecturers who introduced the lesson, provided the background and nature of the course, assignments, and project work. The lecturers covered the topics on *Introduction to Integrated STEM Education* (Definition, purpose of integrating Science, Technology, Engineering and Mathematics disciplines in Teaching & Learning, career-related, framework and theories in STEM Education) and *Strategies in Integrated STEM Education* which covers the approaches, implementation method, activities, and assessment for learning. Subsequently, the collaboration began under the topic of *Designing Integrated STEM Instruction and Instructional Materials*. Specifically, the collaboration with industry was to fulfil the second learning outcome for STEM Education, to ensure strong students' engagement in STEM activities. This course learning outcome (CLO) is mapped to the program learning outcome (PLO) which is to enable learners to solve problems in a scientific and systematic manner in the teaching of mathematics and science.

The STEM education approach employed in this work includes a new 4C framework that connects ***contexts*** to evaluation of the student ***competencies*** (See figure 1). As such, we wanted the learning process to start by getting insights into the local ***context*** that is evaluating the problems of each the three collaborators were presenting. The goal was then to develop an integrated ***content*** that connects all areas of STEM and teach it collaboratively with pedagogically sound ***concepts***. This should help students to develop lifelong 21st century ***competencies*** including critical thinking, creativity, collaboration, and communication. Figure 1 presents a holistic framework which helps to engage students to not only be able to represent, understand and solve real-world problems but also in being able to make data-driven decision making (Seshaiyer, 2021). Similar frameworks have been employed for enhancing STE(A)M competencies for educators (Spyropoulou & Kamaes, 2021). Such frameworks have become even more important with the advent of the COVID-19 pandemic which has resulted in a major shift in the higher education landscape. With COVID-19 itself as a "context", higher education had to migrate to virtual learning through which "content" was delivered with new pedagogical "concepts" that dependent on the use of virtual tools innovatively. This has not only transform teachers pedagogical practices to make innovations in their own instruction, but also led to new understanding of whether students are able to cope with such sudden transitions in learning from the perspective of lifelong learning "competencies".

Figure 1. A holistic STEM education framework: From Contexts to Competencies (Seshaiyer, 2021)

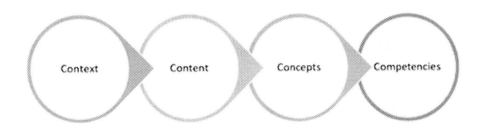

The holistic STEM approach employed in this work was motivated by integrating a Design-Thinking framework (Brown, 2008) that involves five steps including Empathize, Define, Ideate, Prototype, and Test which we integrated with a STEM education framework. Specifically, for each of the projects, a needs-assessment (***empathy***) was conducted first by discussing with the collaborators. Then a problem statement was identified (***define***) which was followed by potential solution methodologies (***ideate***). Once the most feasible idea was selected, a working model was created (***prototype***) and then finally evaluated (***test***). This process helps to create knowledge through an iterative and innovative learning approach by applying experience, reflection, critical thinking, and taking actions. The design thinking process therefore allows the opportunity for students (and teachers) to have dispositions that embraces experimentation, accepts failure and leverages it for redesign, persists through setbacks to reiterate for better solutions (Suh, et. al., 2014).

The first step of design thinking is to empathize and identify needs assessments. For this, several meetings were scheduled with potential collaborators before the semester started to identify potential contexts within Malaysia. Lecturers together with collaborators discussed the course content and the expected projects to be delivered and assisted by them. The cost for any materials needed were also discussed and finalised. The involvement started in week 3 under the topic *Designing Integrated STEM instruction and instructional materials.*

The first collaborator was Sasbadi Learning Solutions. Sasbadi Learning Solutions was established in 2005 and is specialized in promoting hands-on learning through effective educational tools and dynamic learning platforms. The company works closely with the global brand LEGO® Education. Being the organizer of Malaysia's largest annual robotics competition, Sasbadi Learning Solutions is capable of nurturing skills needed in STEM education. This included Training of Trainers (ToT) given by Sasbadi to the lecturers in the department. This project relates to SDG-4 (Quality Education) which aims to *"Ensure inclusive and equitable quality education and promote lifelong learning opportunities for all"*. It is relatable because as a champion in STEM education and to promote skills needed in the 21st century environment, Sasbadi provides quality products and trainings across all ages to establish interest in STEM, robotics and pedagogy.

The second integrative project delivered was on Green Energy Project – Solar Panel. The collaborator was from Zull Design Autotronic. The theoretical online learning and project based-learning approach enabled students to receive input on research and advancement related to green energy. They were introduced to solar power system, basics of solar power capstone and the growth of photovoltaic markets and its infrastructure, as well as PV module and array circuit (*see Table in the Appendix*). By the end of this module students should be able to explain the fundamental knowledge underlying their project.

Students should also be able to explain their incomplete project if happened, so they are able to analyze and evaluate their end products, thus promote critical thinking and problem solving. In this case, their solar boats. This project relates to SDG-7 (Affordable and Clean Energy) which aims to *"Ensure access to affordable, reliable, sustainable and modern energy for all."*

The third collaborator was from the University Centre for Innovative Delivery and Learning Development (CIDL) and the content focused on the Internet of Things (IoT). Students learned about Arduino (an open-source electronics platform based on easy-to-use hardware and software) together with ESP32 (series of low-cost, low-power system on a chip microcontrollers). They also experienced a series of task that required them to apply the knowledge they have learned in first part of the workshop with the supervision of the expert. This project on IoT has the potential to address some of the most acute human, economic and environmental needs which can also directly contribute to achieving the targets in the Sustainable Development Goals (López-Vargas, A., Fuentes, M., & Vivar, M. (2020)). The main function of the centre is to spearhead innovation in delivery and learning in line with the latest technological advances. It is also to ensure the successful and sustainable adoption of creative and innovative technologies in delivery and learning at UiTM. Thus, the collaboration is in line with SDG-9 on Industry, Innovation and Infrastructure which aims to *"build resilient infrastructure, promote inclusive and sustainable industrialization and foster innovation"*. It helps on promoting sustainable scientific research and bridging digital divide to foster innovation and significantly increase access to information and communication technology, and access to the internets.

Besides that, the students were required to complete two hands-on STEM projects. The purpose of these STEM projects was to expose the students to the actual situation while completing the project. This was to encourage learners to anticipate and define potential problems that arise, to ideate feasible solutions by taking essential aspects and to test through an evaluation process that can be done to achieve the objectives of the project. At the end of the project, the students produced a prototype product integrated with STEM elements, for instance, a smart dustbin.

The evaluation of the STEM projects emphasized on two vital skills in teaching and learning STEM which are problem solving and scientific skills. These skills were measured throughout the process of completing the STEM projects. For problem solving skills, the students were evaluated in terms of identification of ideas, analysis of information, and decision making. Meanwhile, for scientific skills, they were assessed based on Engineering Design Process (EDP). The EDP included the conceptualization (ability to understand a situation and relate with the science or mathematical concepts/theories/laws), integration of knowledge (ability to integrate the science or mathematics concepts/theories/laws in innovating a product), creation (ability to develop new ideas/innovate the product), evaluation (testing the product), creation of solutions (ability to suggest/solve problems arising from the product testing). See Figure 2.

After the completion of the course, all students were given a set of questionnaires that required them to provide their personal learning outcome and expectancy beliefs, as well as responsive and responsible learners expectancy based on the projects that they have accomplished through the experts' collaborations while having the classes via online learning.

However, due to the pandemic and SOP imposed by the government, classes were conducted online. Therefore, students learned from video demonstrations and online lectures and discussions. Throughout the learning process, the experts who collaborated in assisting with the specific group projects were guided by lecturers as facilitators.

Figure 2. STEM-themed teaching process based on EDP

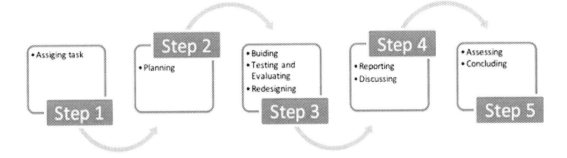

BENEFITS OF COLLABORATIVE TEACHING

Collaborative learning or sometimes referred to as cooperative learning can take several forms based on the pedagogical approach and the contexts of learning employed. In collaborative learning approaches such as problem-based learning and inquiry-based learning, students solve problems, design artifacts, or engage in inquiry in small groups ((Seshaiyer, 2021), (Suh et. al., 2014)). Group work and collaboration during the problem-solving process are encouraged as they help students to engage with the learning materials and develop deep disciplinary understanding. Pedagogical approaches may also focus on how students should be grouped and rewarded and emphasized conditions to ensure productive modes of collaborative engagements (Johnson & Johnson, 2009).

One of the implications of this work was to understand the impact of collaborative teaching with STEM education reforms on teacher education practices in preparing the next generation of teachers in Malaysia. Often collaborative teaching is coordinated with experts from various domains coming together to engage students in a holistic and integrated learning. The uniqueness of this work is the extension of collaborative teaching approaches with industries or external experts that was established to benefit the STEM classrooms. Specifically, these experts brought the much-needed industrial experience that can then be integrated with successful pedagogical practices to make the learning more practical and meaningful. Collaborative teaching also offers an extra pair of eyes and ears for supervision, extra knowledge and expertise, and different viewpoints on topics. It helps educators incorporate different life experiences and adding depth to the curriculum. It even helps with time-management when two educators or more split the workload for projects. However, the biggest benefit of collaborative teaching aimed for the students. It offers more hands to ensure the achievement of goals in the curriculum and that students get the help they need to achieve regardless of their gender, previous knowledge, or level of STEM education.

RESPONSIVE AND RESPONSIBLE LEARNING OUTCOMES

Collaborative teaching allows all future STEM teachers to have a direct consultation with the experts throughout the project. The consultation could develop responsive and responsible beliefs among prospective teachers. Hence, a questionnaire was distributed to the students once the two projects were completed to see the values of the collaborative teaching approach implemented in this course. The questionnaire focused on the students' responsive and responsible learning outcomes.

This section presents the analysis of the findings related to the students' level of responsive and responsible beliefs. It starts with the demographics background, then the responsive and responsible beliefs items on STEM Education from the students' perspectives.

Demographic Background

Table 1 shows the distribution of respondents according to their gender and programs. It depicts 53 female students and only 8 male students were involved in this survey. 31 students came from the mathematics program, 21 students from the Biology program, 5 students from the Chemistry, and 4 students from the Physics program. In total, there were 61 students from four programs taking the course for the first time.

Table 1. Distribution of Respondents according to Gender and Program

Program	Gender Female	Gender Male	Total
Biology	19	2	21
Chemistry	5	0	5
Mathematics	26	5	31
Physics	3	1	4
Total	53	8	61

Table 2 shows the level of STEM knowledge before they attended workshops in SME543 course across all programs. It shows most of the students (70.5%) are beginner-level in STEM knowledge. While 10 out of 61 students (16.4%) have zero knowledge of STEM. Only 8 (13.1%) of the students have an intermediate level of STEM knowledge.

Table 2. STEM knowledge before they attended workshops in the SME543 course

Level	Frequency	Percent (%)
None	10	16.4
Beginner	43	70.5
Intermediate	8	13.1
Total	61	100.0

Responsive and Responsible Beliefs

This section presents the descriptive statistics of the students' responsive and responsible beliefs through collaborative teaching in learning STEM education.

Table 3. Descriptive statistics of Responsive and Responsible Beliefs

No.	Responsive and Responsible Beliefs	Mean	Std. Deviation
1	You managed to remain focus and present during the hands-on activities (Mindful)	4.08	0.76
2	You were able to use your life learning experiences to make meaning of materials introduced in the class projects (Seamless Learning)	4.02	0.74
3	You were actively engaged with the course material through discussions, problem solving, and other methods used in the classroom (Active)	4.11	0.73
4	You can maintain and prolong the knowledge and skills from the learning until successful accomplishment of performance or project work (sustaining learning).	4.02	0.72
5	You believe in your ability to find and use available resources to solve problems and achieve goals in completing your STEM projects.	4.02	0.72
6	The course has helped you to improve your motivation toward active learning.	4.25	0.75
	overall	4.08	0.74

Based on Table 3, the overall mean of the responsive and responsible beliefs is 4.08 (SD = 0.74). It showed that the students agreed that learning through collaboration could increase their responsive and responsible beliefs in learning STEM. The students rated items 2, 4, and 5 with a mean score of 4.02 (SD = 0.72, 0.73, and 0.74 respectively). Item 2 and 4 showed that students can have seamless learning and sustain the knowledge after attending this course. The students also rated the highest level of agreement of 4.25 (SD = 0.75) for item 6, which indicates that the students were feeling motivated to learn actively by joining this course.

Table 4a. below shows the descriptive statistics of the students' responsive and responsible beliefs based on courses

Program	N	Mean	Std. Deviation
Physics	4	4.083	0.319
Chemistry	5	3.833	0.553
Biology	21	3.984	0.693
Mathematics	31	4.188	0.579
Total	61	4.082	0.606

Table 4b. below shows the descriptive statistics of the students' responsive and responsible beliefs based on gender

Gender	N	Mean	Std. Deviation
Male	8	4.188	0.710
Female	53	4.066	0.595

By referring to Table 4a, the Chemistry students' mean score is the lowest (M = 3.833, SD = 0.553). It shows that students majoring in Mathematics rated the highest responsive and responsible beliefs in learning STEM through collaboration (M = 4.188, SD = 0.579). Table 4b shows the mean scores of male students (M = 4.188, SD = 0.710) is slightly higher than the female (M = 4.066, SD = 0.595) students on their responsive and responsible beliefs.

Hence, to determine the significant difference in the mean score of responsive and responsible beliefs among gender, an independent sample t-test was conducted.

Table 5. Independent Samples T-Test

	Levene's Test for Equality of Variances		t-test for Equality of Means						
	F	Sig.	t	df	Sig. (2-tailed)	Mean Difference	Std. Error Difference	95% Confidence Interval of the Difference	
								Lower	Upper
Equal variances assumed	0.198	0.658	0.525	59	0.601	0.12146	0.23126	-0.34128	0.58421

Then, One Way ANOVA was conducted to measure the significant difference of the mean scores of students' responsive and responsible beliefs between four programs.

Table 6. One-way ANOVA test

	Sum of Squares	Df	Mean Square	F	Sig.
Between Groups	.860	3	.287	.771	.515
Within Groups	21.175	57	.371		
Total	22.035	60			

There is no significant difference in the mean score of students' responsive and responsible beliefs among the four programs (F = 0.771, p-value >0.05).

Table 7. Correlation between Students STEM knowledge and Their Responsive and Responsible Beliefs

	STEM knowledge before attended workshops in SME543 course	Responsive and Responsible beliefs
Correlation Coefficient	1.000	.309*
Sig. (2-tailed)		.015
N	61	61
*. Correlation is significant at the 0.05 level (2-tailed).		

Table 7 shows that there is a significant correlation between students' STEM knowledge before attended workshops in SME543 course with collaborative partners with their responsive and responsible beliefs after attending SME543 course (r = 0.309, p-value < 0.05). However, the strength of the correlation is low with correlation coefficient $r^2 = 0.095$, hence only 9.5% of the students' STEM knowledge influences their responsive and responsible beliefs.

Statistically, the students believed that STEM Education has enabled them to use their life learning experiences into context to make meaning of learning tasks more meaningful in the class projects. This is the context of seamless learning of being responsive learners. Seamless learning context, for instance, are distinguishing a design paradigm within the broader domain of learning and instructional design and exemplifying the organizational change of interweaving formal and non-formal learning, and to label specific learning scenarios (Hambrock et al., 2020). In view to this, some examples of the students' responses are given in Table 8 below:

Table 8. Students' Responses on Seamless Learning

Collaborators	Examples of responses
SASBADI Learning Solutions	"Creating something to ease work such as a robot to help chores". "Create teaching aids via mathematical software".
Green Energy Project-Solar Panel	"I don't have any pool or basin (container) for my solar boat, so I used half manual washing machine". "I used my previous knowledge about factors affecting the boat speed". "Solar project is one of the examples that I can apply in real-life situation". "I used more batteries that can provide higher voltage for the lighting of the lamp. Like solar panel, the more solar panels you use, the faster the speed of the boat can be achieved". "I can build a solar car to play with my cousins (cost effective)". "I transformed solar energy into electrical source or energy". "I used life learning experience to make the boat balance and move faster". "The application of solar can be used for science project to make the class become more interesting and attractive". "On the solar boat project, we managed to overcome and understand the situation where and why it can function well".
CIDL- IoT	"I can create many great projects". "I completed the last project related to the flash on and off (of a light) from life-experiences. Our group did a sensor for detecting parcel in which I think it gives benefits to people". "Make an automated trash bin". "Smart dustbin using sensor".

Being responsible learners mean students are also being resourceful. STEM Education projects encouraged students to explore and experiment and provide them with opportunities to use resources and solve problems, as part of being independent learners. Some examples of their responses are given in Table 9 below:

Table 9. Students' Responses on being Responsible Learners

Collaborators	Examples of responses
SASBADI Learning Solutions	"Using Minecraft in teaching and learning session".
Green Energy Project-Solar Panel	"I can manage to find resources from a lot of platforms to complete the project". "I used recyclable items to create the project". "When conducting solar boats, the motor of the boats went slow, and I found an alternative by replacing the motor". "Circuit choice to switch between battery cells and solar power. I also believed that I could use electronic tools to stabilize the solar power source". "I'm using all the resources that I can obtain from home like plastic bottle for the body parts and polystyrene to balance the boat for the project".
CIDL- IoT	"When my IoT project was not successful, I asked my cousin for more knowledge about it since he took engineering course. I tried to apply what he explained in my project". "The actual component that I need for my project is a sensor to detect human presence or motion (infrared sensor). However, the kit that we bought only provided us with simple and basic sensor. Thus, my team changed the actual idea, to use ldr sensor". "I can invent a product to detect the dryness of my wet shoes whenever I feel lazy to check it outside home". "I did a project on a smart door detector for IoT project. So, I did some research on it and I did it well". "I applied critical thinking to do Arduino projects". "I applied critical thinking to excel in Arduino projects". "I created an automated trash bin cover that can automatically open when it senses the motion from our hand using microcontroller from Arduino projects".

CONCLUSION

The first STEM education classroom for Science and Mathematics students at the faculty was successfully conducted through open distance learning (ODL). Students may have encountered some challenges in adjusting to handling, cooperating, organizing, and demonstrating their projects online, but with the presence and assistance from lecturers as facilitators during the collaborative teachings from the selected industries, there was engaging, and active learnings encountered. Students can adopt with the teaching approaches; they enjoyed the process and are more focused and able to exhibit curiosity by asking questions through interesting and motivating class projects and activities. Questions and answers during the project presentations usually receive immediate responses from facilitators thus encourage attentive and responsive learning environment.

The scheme of work was successfully delivered and assessments from the collaborative teachings indicated high cognitive involvement from all students regardless of majoring and gender. In response to the responsive and responsible beliefs, the students were mindful during the hands-on activities. Which means they stayed focus and present during lectures from the industry practitioners. Creative approaches and hands-on learning activities in the collaborative classroom have encouraged deep listening and reflections through clear pedagogical approach and serve the purpose towards achieving the course learning outcomes.

In the aspect of seamless learning, the students were able to apply life learning experiences through problem solving skills in the class projects. For example, they explored different devices in their learning to determine how they move between technologies and the support their required for the class project completion, which means they were able to bring real life issues into the classroom. Other than that, active learning was further developed through various methods used in the classrooms since they were 'learning by doing'. This was further maintained and prolonged through the accomplishment of the first project and the next (sustaining learning).

The overall methodology of design-thinking process helped students to gain new skills and competencies for lifelong learning. The students' comments revealed how the design of the course allowed them to take risks and expressed their individual thinking through the project planning. Their comments also seemed to indicate that they were allowed to be creative in their thinking and this new skill set would influence the way they approach future projects.

Collaboration plays a major role in interdisciplinary activities among Science, Technology, Engineering & Mathematics (STEM) disciplines and act as the vehicles for sharing responsibility and combining knowledge, creativity, and experience of others. To expedite collaboration in program development is commentative to provide a strong educational foundation to all learners in STEM education (Haruna, 2015).

To sum up, responsive and responsible learning were achieved among the undergraduate students through collaborative teaching in STEM education classroom and has successfully served the specific technical requirements of industry and specialisms within the STEM field into the classroom in the university.

REFERENCES

Aydın-Günbatar, S., Öztay, E. S., & Ekiz-Kıran, B. (2021). Examination of pre-service chemistry teachers' STEM conceptions through an integrated STEM course. *Turkish Journal of Education*, 251-273.

Brown, T. (2008). Design Thinking: Harvard Business Review. *Academia (Caracas)*.

Hambrock, H., Villiers, F. d., Rusman, E., MacCallum, K., & Arrifin, S. A. (2020). *Seamless Learning in Higher Education: Perspectives of International Educators on its Curriculum and Implementation Potentia*. PRESSBOOK. Retrieved from https://pressbooks.pub/seamlesslearning/

Haruna, & Ibrahim, U. (2015). The Need for an Effective Collaboration Across Science, Technology, Engineering & Mathematics (STEM) Fields for a Meaningful Technological Development in Nigeria. *Journal of Education and Practice*, 6(25), 16-21.

Jamali, S. M., Ale Ebrahim, N., & Jamali, F. (2022). The role of STEM Education in improving the quality of education: A bibliometric study. *International Journal of Technology and Design Education*, 1–22. doi:10.100710798-022-09762-1

Johnson, D. W., & Johnson, R. T. (2009). An Educational Psychology Success Story: Social Interdependence Theory and Cooperative Learning. *Educational Researcher*, 38(5), 365–379. doi:10.3102/0013189X09339057

López-Vargas, A., Fuentes, M., & Vivar, M. (2020). Challenges and opportunities of the internet of things for global development to achieve the united nations sustainable development goals. *IEEE Access: Practical Innovations, Open Solutions*, 8, 37202–37213. doi:10.1109/ACCESS.2020.2975472

Ramli, N. F., & Talib, O. (2017). Can education institution implement STEM? From Malaysian teachers' view. *International Journal of Academic Research in Business & Social Sciences, 7*(3), 721–732. doi:10.6007/IJARBSS/v7-i3/2772

Seshaiyer, P. (2021). Novel frameworks for upskilling the mathematics education workforce. In *Mathematics Education for Sustainable Economic Growth and Job Creation* (pp. 90–107). Routledge. doi:10.4324/9781003048558-8

Seshaiyer, P., & McNeely, C. L. (2020). Challenges and Opportunities From COVID-19 for Global Sustainable Development. *World Medical & Health Policy, 12*(4), 443–453. doi:10.1002/wmh3.380 PMID:33362943

Spyropoulou, N., & Kameas, A. (2021). A holistic framework of STE(A)M educators competences. *13th annual International Conference of Education, Research and Innovation*, 504-514.

Suh, J., Seshaiyer, P., Lee, K. H., Peixoto, N., Suh, D., & Lee, Y. (2014, October). Critical learning experiences for Korean engineering students to promote creativity and innovation. In 2014 IEEE Frontiers in Education Conference (FIE) Proceedings (pp. 1-6). IEEE. doi:10.1109/FIE.2014.7044438

ENDNOTE

[1] https://sdgs.un.org/goals

APPENDIX

Table 10. Lesson Design for Engaging Stem Activities (Renewable Energy -Solar Photovoltaic)

WEEK	ACTIVITIES	LECT	CONTENT	EQUIPMENT/ MATERIALS COST	IMPLEMENTATION/ACTIVITIES	LEARNING OUTCOME
1	HANDS-ON SESSION 1 SOLAR ENERGY BASIC SYSTEM OVERVIEW	1. Key Opinion Leader 2. Lecturer (Nominate)	1. Introduction to solar power systems 2. Determining energy needs and sizing a PV system 3. The growth of photovoltaic markets 4. Infrastructure of Photovoltaics 5. Basics of Solar Power Capstone	1. Personal Computer 2. Individual I Basic Training Set inclusive of : Solar Mini Cells, LED, Bulbs, Micro Fan, Wire) (RM 55.00) (Min 50 orders) 3. Trainer Fees inclusive of Course Module RM 500 / Hour (Min 3 hours per session)	1. INSTRUCTOR ONLINE MODE 2. VIDEOS 3. READINGS 4. STEP-BY-STEP HANDS-ON GUIDE 5. QUIZZES	By the end of this module you should be able to comprehend and understanding of electrical power and energy, be able to calculate the energy needs of a site as well as energy production potential for a PV system at a given location under optimal conditions.
2	HANDS-ON SESSION 2 SOLAR ENERGY SYSTEM DESIGN	1. Key Opinion Leader 2. Lecturer (Nominate)	1. Following solar energy from source to panel 2. PV module and array circuits 3. PV sizing and output under different conditions 4. Grid-tie PV System design under real world conditions		1. INSTRUCTOR ONLINE MODE 2. VIDEOS 3. READINGS 4. STEP-BY-STEP HANDS-ON GUIDE 5. QUIZZES	By the end of this module you should be able to incorporate and perform system design calculations.
3	HANDS ON SESSION 3 SOLAR ENERGY AND ELECTRICAL SYSTEM DESIGN	1. Key Opinion Leader 2. Lecturer (Nominate)	1. Analyze advantages and disadvantages of various PV systems 2. Evaluate PV system requirements 3. Identify key PV design considerations and planning tools		1. INSTRUCTOR ONLINE MODE 2. VIDEOS 3. READINGS 4. STEP-BY-STEP HANDS-ON GUIDE 5. QUIZZES	By the end of this module you should be able to demonstrate about system sizing considerations and calculations
4	HANDS-ON SESSION 4 COURSE CAPSTONE PROJECT BRIEFING, PREPARATION, CONSULTATION	1. Key Opinion Leader 2. Lecturer (Nominate)	The capstone project will evaluate the level of culminating advanced cognitive skills from integrative STEM's experience, 1. Explain the desired outcome and integrate the scientific reasoning with mathematical logic to support your justification. 2. Scores are based on the level of demystification ability and not bound to the project completion	**Final Project :** 1. Group Projects of 10 per group 2. Project . Presentation: UiTM lecturers to bring along volunteers with age range from 12 to 15 years old during project presentation	You will need to design a PV system using commercially available components for the usage of households and calculate it's output under site specific conditions	By the end of this module you should be able to explain the end result expected from the project built, For workable project you have to explain the fundamental knowledge underlying your project. For incomplete project you have to explain your analysis and evaluation to support your result

Chapter 9
Creativity and the Self:
A Higher Educational Praxis for Responsive Learning

Mohd Hafnidzam Adzmi
Universiti Teknologi MARA, Malaysia

Zainuddin Ibrahim
Universiti Teknologi MARA, Malaysia

Suriati Saidan
Universiti Teknologi MARA, Malaysia

EXECUTIVE SUMMARY

This chapter conceptualizes the approach to nurturing creativity in higher education. The chapter begins by describing the creative self based on personality theories discussed in the creativity research literature. This chapter then engages in the discussion of the contradiction between the concept of the creative self and some aspects of the current educational policies in Malaysia, in particular the implementation of outcome-based education (OBE) as outlined by the Malaysian Qualifications Agency (MQA). This chapter ends with the discussion of proposing the activity theory as a framework for creative education.

INTRODUCTION

The ability to be creative is crucial for the future. The way that creativity is now understood sets it apart from the idea of intelligence. Therefore, rather than emphasizing the kind of concrete information that is typically found in the natural sciences like engineering, biology, and mathematics, education that attempts to cultivate creative talents should instead focus on developing ideational skills. Consequently, the goal of this chapter is to conceive a responsive learning environment that uniquely serves educational institutions that aims to encourage creativity.

DOI: 10.4018/978-1-6684-6076-4.ch009

Creativity and the Self

The fact that students and their educational environments work together to nurture creative skillsets highlights the significance of conceiving creativity in a way that is consistent with present educational policies. It is possible to gain insights into a theoretical understanding and suggestive implementation strategies that, in turn, can be the praxis of a responsive learning environment that emphasizes creativity by conceptualizing creative education within these two extremes: 1) the individual or self, and 2) the current educational policies.

What is Creativity?

The definition of creativity and the various perspectives on it should be discussed first. The definition of creativity is the production of something new and appropriate (Runco & Jaeger, 2012). From the extremity of business and innovation to the preservation of cultures, it is advantageous to society. Additionally, creativity is a crucial component of learning since it helps pupils come up with fresh approaches to issues.

Nowadays, creativity research has its own field. Before the field was founded, many people conjectured about the special talents of some people in invention and creation. The study by Guilford, in which he suggests divergent thinking as a thought process related with ideation, is one of the cornerstones of creativity research (Guilford, 1956). He makes the case that concepts, and ideas can have literal or symbolic manifestations. Guilford's seminal study was able to spark interest in the study of creativity by contrasting its reliance on ideas with other mental functions such as intelligence.

Fulfilment is one of the main issues in studies on creativity. This query can shed light on what distinguishes creative people from others. Understanding creativity is crucial in a setting where intelligence is valued so that its development can be examined objectively, and any misunderstandings may be avoided. The relationship between intellect and creativity is still up for question, as data from studies on The Threshold Theory suggests that there is no correlation between creativity and intelligence for IQ scores above 120 (Runco & Albert, 1986; Weiss et al., 2020). Furthermore, by defining creativity within the context of the individual, creative curriculums can avoid applying educational theories that is unrelated.

Currently, creativity research is a discipline with well-defined sub-interests. Researchers have claimed that research on creativity should be considered from two perspectives to comprehend why some people are more creative than others. One perspective of creativity, *the Big-C and Small-C* of creativity is proposed (Simonton, 2017). The *Big-C* is used to characterize eminent individuals who are experts in a certain field, which led to the notion that creativity is contextual. *Small-C* on the other end address everyday problems. Another perspective according to Rhodes, creativity may be perceived from four different aspects, known as the "4-Ps of creativity". These aspects include, namely, 1) the process of thinking, or simply *Process*, 2) the impact on the surroundings, or *Press*, 3) the results of creative endeavors, or *Products*, and 4) the viewpoint of the individual, or *Personality* (Rhodes, 1961). This demonstrates that creativity is a rich body of knowledge that can answer a variety of requirements and queries. The primary goal of this chapter, according to the authors, is to address creativity in the context of the self (*personality*) and its responsive learning concepts in higher education.

HIGHER EDUCATIONAL POLICIES IN MALAYSIA

In the 1990s, Malaysia's educational policies were focused on developing human capital to deal with the rising urbanization, industrialization, and globalization of the world. Since most creative disciplines require some level of technical proficiency, the call for the expansion of technical education (Lee, 1997) implies the need for creativity. The interpretation of education is currently exacerbated by new economic theories and concepts such as the *fourth industrial revolution* (4IR), the *knowledge-based* economy, and others. While there are several interpretations, most have either emphasized or implied the value of creativity. This is evident as both private and public higher education institutions frequently promote themselves as a location that fosters creativity because it is regarded as a skill for the future (Pettinger et. al, 2018). We can all agree that innovation is crucial for society. Despite the focus on innovation, the National Educational Blueprint does not emphasize or, at the very least, clearly identify the value of creativity (MOHE, 2015). This demonstrates the lack of conceptualization and planned implementation of cultivating creative talents.

To guarantee that high-quality education is provided, higher education institutions must also adhere to certain norms or criteria. By the end of 2005, the Malaysian Qualifications Agency (MQA) had been set up to monitor the standardization of academic institutions' degree-awarding practices. Implementing outcome-based education, also known as OBE, is one of its strategies (Karim & Yin, 2013). Its adoption is thought to help teachers create curriculum, assessment, assignments, and methodologies. OBE presupposes that learning occurs when efforts are focused on a clearly defined objective or outcomes (Spady, 1994). As a strategy for putting education into practice, learning depends on the creative self's compatibility with OBE. And knowing the characteristics of the creative self can therefore show whether or not there is a clear understanding of the educational praxis of creativity. This chapter's subsequent subsection will go over this connection.

CREATIVITY AND THE SELF

The self is a notion related to an individual, according to this chapter. The self is one of the theories relating to creativity, and it refers to a person or individual and how they present themselves in the outside world. Because of this, theories of creativity that are most closely related to personality are appropriate for the consideration of this chapter. Thus, this subsection discusses on several personality qualities that address the creative person or self.

One of the primary research areas of creativity study is creativity and personality, as was mentioned in the previous subsection. This is the case because creative people exhibit a typical personality feature. These characteristics, according to some, are what motivates a person to be creative. The *Big Five Personality* trait of *openness to new experiences* is where creativity and its mediator, *intrinsic motives*, are associated (Feist, 2010). This suggests that creative people seek new challenges as it inspires fresh ideas or viewpoints. As new experiences develop, new information must be processed, which results in new outlook of the world. There are many examples of people who are appreciative of things outside of their field of expertise, especially among eminent people. Albert Einstein, for instance, who is often cited as the epitome of the genius, is open to experiences outside of his primary field of expertise. His interest in playing the violin and his appreciation of poetry are indications of his love of the arts. Moreover, his whimsical depictions in popular media, which were unusual for his period demonstrate his openness to new experiences. To put it another way, a creative person is willing to attempt new things and is open to doing so. Therefore, creative people thrive in an environment where ideas may be openly shared and traded.

Creativity and the Self

In addition to being receptive to new experiences, creative people are resourceful or approach their ideas with a sense of self-efficacy. To put it another way, a highly creative individual has faith in their capacity to do tasks. A survey of the literature shows that *self-efficacy* is closely related to the individual part of creativity, which lends credence to this (Haase et al., 2018). The relevance of motivation in creativity may be related to the important role that self-efficacy plays. According to researchers, *motivation* is a factor in creativity and is one of the elements of creative cognition (Runco & Chand, 1995). This relationship may lean more toward intrinsic than extrinsic incentives (Amabile, 1983). A person's desire and willingness to create artefacts or solutions might be influenced by their own internal benefits, such as learning new abilities, disproving critics, or taking on new tasks. On the other hand, it gives them confidence in their own capacity to identify issues and find answers. It may also be connected to the openness factor because mystery, ambiguity, and the potential for new issues frequently inspire fresh solutions. It might be that self-efficacy expresses motivation, or vice versa.

Aside from their openness, self-efficacy, and motivational qualities, which characterize their personal identities, creatives are also notable for their *nonconformist* or contrarian outlook (Beghetto, 2017). Finding new ideas is considered in relation to non-conformity or contrarianism. Creatives must, to some extent, identify alternatives in their pursuit of novel ideas by thinking in opposition to the conventional wisdom. This is because adhering to widely held thoughts or opinions entails accepting pre-made concepts, which are unauthentic or unoriginal. This does not imply, though, that being on the other end of the spectrum necessarily results in what is sought, as meeting appropriateness or usability standards necessitates approval by the ecosystem to which they belong. For instance, a creative might have figured out a unique solution to societal issues, but for such solutions to be implemented and developed further, they must be appropriate for the people who are experiencing those issues. As a result, in certain ways, creatives must adhere to certain practical realities. This implies that artists must balance their degree of contrarian opinions by meeting other people's needs. This demonstrates that being in the opposite position is equally important. To sum up this section of the chapter, the notion of creativity and the self requires that a person exhibit traits such as *self-efficacy*, *intrinsic motivation*, and a *contrarian* perspective. The second half of the chapter will go through how these personal requirements fit within Malaysia's higher education system.

The Concept of Outcome and the Creative-Self

The creative self has been defined thus far in this chapter as those who are open to new experiences, have a feeling of self-efficacy, have strong intrinsic motives, and have a contrarian perspective. We must first develop the concept of its practice in the educational landscape to conceptualize the praxis of the creative self in higher education. As a result, an education that fosters the creative self must be able to:

- Permit pupils to sense and encounter novel things
- Permit pupils to self-evaluate their efficacy by doing what they feel capable of
- Create compelling challenges to support intrinsic motives
- flexible goals or objectives that allow contrarian outlook

We can now decide whether the existing higher education landscape is enough or suited for nurturing creativity based on the characteristics that have been provided.

The MQA have established a standardized framework on which curriculums are developed, as was mentioned in the previous subsection. The primary concept used is the implementation of learning outcomes (LO) to direct teaching, learning, and subsequent evaluation strategies. LO is described as *"statements about what students should know, comprehend, and be able to accomplish upon successfully completing a period of study, which often lead to a qualification or part of a qualification"* in accordance with official MQA guidelines (Malaysian Qualifications Agency, 2021, p. 13). According to the previously stated argument, using learning outcomes required teachers to set a target that students had to follow. It indicates that students must comply with the duties at hand. This is inherently at odds with the creative personality. The instructors' predetermined goals are not always in line with what the students truly want. Students may therefore disagree with the intended results because creativity is motivated by internal forces that are formed by individual worldviews. Additionally, whereas results may provide a pathway for the development of technical skills (if the skill is expressed clearly), intrinsic incentives may result in an awareness of the need for other abilities. As a result, this may result in challenges that are not emotive in nature and leverage the learning experience towards achieving extrinsic rewards (such as performing activities for the sake of grades). The sense of accomplishment or *catharsis* that characterizes an accomplishment in creative efforts is hindered by the absence of emotive components like intrinsic motivation. In other words, the task should be enjoyable for the pupils rather than solely for compliance. Moreover, a hallmark of an autotelic activity that completes the optimal experience of creativity or flow is the feeling of enjoying something for its own sake (Csikszentmihalyi, 2013, p. 113).

As of instructors, they become the knowledge's gatekeeper when outcomes are put into practice. This is because, before learning happens, the instructors set 'targets' that represent knowledge. However, creativity strives for originality. In the creative arts fields for instance, creating something new and original is what the students should strive for as originality and newness is what defined creativity (Runco & Jaeger, 2012). Outcomes present an ideal state, which are often consists of prior knowledge and therefore, not new. From the perspective of creative learning, something new in its essence should be beyond anyone's comprehension other than that of the student. This led to the suggestions that creativity requires an element of surprise. This tendency for humans to be in awe on new things is one of the reasons why some academics link creativity with a sense of surprise (Simonton, 2017). In some sense, a new creation is also comparable to discovering new information. However, finding new knowledge is undermined by outcomes that are objectively predetermined. As McKernan puts it, educators *"should aim at motivating students to seek the information that none now hold, rather than mastering fields already known"*(McKernan, 2010). This repeats the criticism of objective-based training as detrimental to creative learning. The pupils need to have a space to think creatively, thus it's crucial that it is constantly provided. Additionally, learning outcomes are rigid by nature, or much worse if they are applied strictly, can prevent the overall growth of creativity.

In addition, as previously mentioned, outcomes suggest what the student *should do* rather than *what they think they can do*. What the students truly wanted to undertake is hindered by Learning Outcomes (LO). In other words, because goals are established, students have little input in what they desire and therefore undemocratic (McKernan, 2010). A creative activity is driven by intrinsic motivation and their sense of self-efficacy, as was previously discussed in this chapter. Prioritizing goals over these may cause student to divert from the path that they believe in and lose confidence in their own abilities. Coupled with the stress of meeting deadlines for assignments and projects causes more uncertainty since external variables rather than internal demands gradually becomes the primary focus of the learning experience.

Creativity and the Self

LO is a requirement that must be met at the macro level, such as the level of the curriculum. Although specific learning outcomes or objectives (LO) can be modified quickly, each curriculum includes a higher and generic outcome that cannot be changed. This implied that pupils must accomplish the same goal on an abstract level. As a result, instructors or curriculum developers may be forced to use the same ideas and techniques that are streamlined to achieve efficiency to meet standards. This is perhaps sensible in terms of upholding standards. However, as previous discussion shows, the same cannot be said in terms of creative learning.

Standards are concerning as it considers previous method that is successful to be implemented. Therefore, in the long run, the learning experience becomes repetitive and disallow the students to *feel and experience new things*. Although standards can be achieved, the same cannot be said to achieve creativity. In general, this shows that current standards do not emphasize creativity. Current guidelines by MQA are based on the latest higher education policy which did not explicitly mention creativity at all. This is despite the importance of innovation which is mentioned twelve times in contrast to creativity which should be mentioned more extensively (MOHE, 2015). As creativity precedes innovation, this is rather ironic.

From Content to Activity

The previous paragraph did not object OBE as a general educational framework. However, it did present some of the potential challenges that the creative self would encounter in its application. What is known is that knowledge serves as the foundation for outcomes or aims. Conceptual and technical knowledge are frequently used in creative fields, and it is because of these two types of information that an artefact can be created (Runco & Chand, 1995). Knowledge shapes ideas, while technical expertise enables ideas to materialize. Additionally, creativity has a particular historicity, which denotes a process in which it necessitates the creative self to participate in the creative process within a specific period leading to completion (Dasgupta, 2019). This suggests that activities are preferable to planned declarative content for nurturing the creative self.

A curriculum that focus on activities allows the creative self to participate and become active in their environment. Their interaction with the world can become the medium in which ideas or new knowledge is constructed. Instead of conforming to outcomes, students interact with the world and assimilate what they see and accommodate to the context they desired (Piaget, 2001). Therefore, learning becomes constructive which is in line to creative fields as constructive thinking is suggested as one of the elements that is ideal to the creative education such as in the fields of creative design (Cross, 1982).

By allowing students to interact with the world, learning becomes pragmatic. This meant that a sense of discovery can be instilled to the students if they are interacting with the environment that they are situated in. Taking what they see outside and use it to explore and learn in schools is a progressive approach, which is suitable especially in an era where technology constantly evolve, with new approaches and techniques are often introduced and made available. Moreover, the internet technology of today allows more interaction with the world. This allows students to improve their knowledge either conceptually or technically, which in turn aids the creative development.

Conceptual and technical knowledge is important to the creative process, and so does the context of the endeavor (Runco & Chand, 1995). The innovation industry welcomes students who can work in teams. This is the context or role that should be introduced early on or across the curriculum. This highlights the importance of activity instead of content. For instance, gaining new information in teams through discussion, dialogue, and critique is more relevant than relying on information from instructors that is mediated through LOs. Moreover, working in teams allow different types of activities which enables various ways to interact with the world. This provides a learning context that allows experimentation. Therefore, it is important for students to understand their personality or how they themselves behave or act in real life situations so that they understand their future roles. Hopefully, students or the creative self ultimately does not only contribute to his own well-being and those close to them, but also to the community.

The learning experience of a creative self is multidimensional. This is because, activities are motivated by various factors. Producing creative artefacts is complex. Immediately, it looks as if only the creative self and the creation are the only elements of the creative activity. However, other factors such as the *tools* that mediate the project, certain *rules* that provide context or purpose, the group or *community* that they belong to and how the effort is communicated between team members plays an important role in the success of the activity. This means that an activity is an amalgam of several systems. The relationship between these systems is the founding blocks of *Activity Theory* (Engeström & Glaveănu, 2012). In short, the theory is an interplay between the elements of a *subject* or person, an *objective* or outcome, *tools*, *rules* or customs, *community* and roles or *divisions of labor*.

A creative self, while on the way to learn and develop his creative skills must experience the real-life situation. Hence, it must involve a group of individuals (or *community*), with relevant and appropriate *tools*, *rules* and customs to govern the project that includes inputs as concepts for the project, his *role* in the team and how his activity contributes to the whole development project. These elements enable the environment which underlies the creative activity. In completing the project these elements contribute to one another and thus provides a holistic representation of knowledge that is relevant and significant as it is attained according to real-life situation.

For instance, if the aim of the project was to produce games for kids, and the student aspires to become a programmer, it will orient the student to find or understand new rules of a programming language in accordance of gameplay for kids, consider the tools or types of programming language that fits the project — which provides a meaningful role in the group —, and finally discuss his role within the group to form specific tasks in order to achieve outcomes and objectives. The change of objectives such as the change of game genre, will again reorient the elements and subsequently all the elements in his activity. As tasks are negotiated, with certain technologies and tools, with certain set of rules, individuals in the groups will go through a learning process that is *situational*. This ensure that learning will not succumb to repetitive actions which can shape a ritualistic strategy among the students and therefore antithetical to the creative self that strives for the experience of new things, the sense of self-efficacy, affective challenges, and flexible objectives. This framework is illustrated in Figure 1 below.

CONCLUSION

This chapter concludes that Activity Theory should be promoted and can be considered as a framework to understand creative activities and how it can be observed in educational settings. The theory, since it is based on activity instead of outcome, can represent a complete view of the real-world situation that the students can relate to. Moreover, since skills and knowledge are acquired in real life, so does the development of the self. A focus on the creative activity instead on strict learning outcomes encourage students to confront real life situation, balanced between learning new skills and the required freedom for creative fulfillment.

Creativity and the Self

Figure 1. The Activity Theory in game development for kids

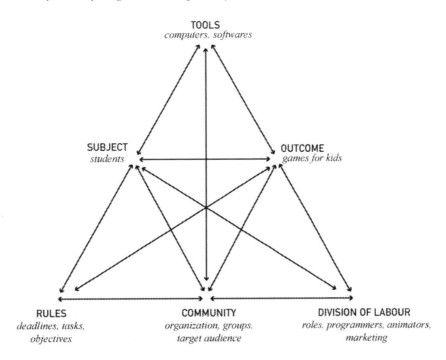

For teachers, Activity Theory can expose the continuity — or praxis— between learning theories and how it is practiced in the real world and thus allow greater understanding of student development and achievement. This meant that learning and teaching is responsive as students are viewed not from an isolated point of view, but instead, they are viewed in a larger context that includes his community and the environment that they dwell in. In practice, it allows the creative activity to be observed and therefore aids in class preparation or evaluation strategies.

Educational concepts, either it pertains to learning, teaching, or evaluating is plenty. This chapter does not intend to cram more theoretical approaches to an already curriculum standards that are at times convoluted. However, as creativity is a unique trait, the theory can provide an alternative to existing practice especially for creative teaching, learning, and nurturing in higher education. Finally, this chapter recommends the study of Activity Theory in creative education to further enhance the literature, opens new avenues for debates and increase efforts in human development that benefits the self and society.

REFERENCES

Amabile, T. M. (1983). Motivation and Creativity: Effects of Motivational Orientation on Creative Writers. *Journal of Personality and Social Psychology, 48*(2), 393–399. doi:10.1037/0022-3514.48.2.393

Beghetto, R. A. (2017). Creativity and Conformity: A Paradoxical Relationship. In J. A. Plucker (Ed.), *Creativity & Innovation* (pp. 267–275). Prufrock Press Inc.

Cross, N. (1982). Designerly Ways of Knowing. *Design Studies*, *3*(4), 221–227. doi:10.1016/0142-694X(82)90040-0

Csikszentmihalyi, M. (2013). *Creativity: the psychology of discovery and invention*. Harper Perennial Modern Classics.

Dasgupta, S. (2019). *A Cognitive Historical Approach to Creativity*. Routledge. doi:10.4324/9780429032363

Engeström, Y., & Glaveănu, V. (2012). On Third Generation Activity Theory: Interview with Yrjö Engeström. *Europe's Journal of Psychology*, *8*(4), 515–518. doi:10.5964/ejop.v8i4.555

Feist, G. J. (2010). The Function of Personality in Creativity. In J. C. Kaufman & R. J. Sternberg (Eds.), *The Cambridge Handbook of Creativity* (pp. 113–130). Cambridge University Press. doi:10.1017/CBO9780511763205.009

Guilford, J. P. (1956). The Structure of Intellect. *Psychological Bulletin*, *53*(4), 267–293. doi:10.1037/h0040755 PMID:13336196

Haase, J., Hoff, E. V., Hanel, P., & Innes-Ker, A. (2018). A Meta-Analysis of the Relation between Creative Self-Efficacy and Different Creativity Measurements. *Creativity Research Journal*, *30*(1), 1–16. doi:10.1080/10400419.2018.1411436

Karim, N. A., & Yin, K. Y. (2013). Outcome-based Education: An Approach for Teaching and Learning Development. *Journal of Research. Policy & Practice of Teachers and Teachers Education*, *3*(1), 26–35.

Lee, M. N. (1997). Education and the State: Malaysia After the NEP. *Asia Pacific Journal of Education*, *17*(1), 27–40. doi:10.1080/02188799708547741

Malaysian Qualifications Agency. (2021). *Malaysian Qualifications Framework (MQF)* (2nd ed.). Retrieved 10 9, 2022, from Malaysian Qualifications Agency: https://www.mqa.gov.my/pv4/document/mqf/2021/MQF%20Ed%202%2002102019%20updated%2017022021.pdf

McKernan, J. (2010). A Critique of Instructional. *Education Inquiry*, *1*(1), 57–67. doi:10.3402/edui.v1i1.21929

MOHE. (2015). *Malaysia Education Blueprint, 2015-2025 (Higher Education)*. Retrieved 10 September, 2022, from Kementerian Pengajian Tinggi: https://www.mohe.gov.my/muat-turun/penerbitan-jurnal-dan-laporan/pppm-2015-2025-pt/102-malaysia-education-blueprint-2015-2025-higher-education/file

Pettinger, L., Forkert, K., & Goffey, A. (2018). The Promises of Creative Industry Higher Education: An Analysis of University Prospectuses in Malaysia. *International Journal of Cultural Policy*, *24*(4), 466–484. doi:10.1080/10286632.2016.1223644

Piaget, J. (2001). *The Psychology of Intelligence* (M. Piercy & D. E. Berlyne, Trans.). Routledge Classics.

Rhodes, M. (1961). An Analysis of Creativity. *Phi Delta Kappan*, *42*(7), 305–310.

Runco, M. A., & Albert, R. S. (1986). The Threshold Theory Regarding Creativity and Intelligence: An Empirical Test With Gifted and Nongifted Children. *The Creative Child and Adult Quarterly*, *11*(4), 212–218.

Runco, M. A., & Chand, I. (1995). Cognition and Creativity. *Educational Psychology Review*, *7*(3), 243–267. doi:10.1007/BF02213373

Runco, M. A., & Jaeger, G. J. (2012). The Standard Definition of Creativity. *Creativity Research Journal*, *24*(1), 92–96. doi:10.1080/10400419.2012.650092

Simonton, D. K. (2017). Big-C Versus Little-c Creativity: Definition, Implications, and Inherent Educational Contradictions. In R. Beghetto & B. Sriraman (Eds.), *Creative Contradictions in Education. Creativity Theory and Action in Education* (Vol. 1, pp. 3–19). Springer. doi:10.1007/978-3-319-21924-0_1

Simonton, D. K. (2017). Domain-general Creativity: On Generating Original, Useful, and Surprising Combinations. In J. C. Kaufman, V. P. Glăveanu, & J. Baer (Eds.), The Cambridge Handbook of Creativity Across Domains (pp. 41-60). Cambridge University Press.

Spady, W. G. (1994). *Outcome-Based Education: Critical Issues and Answers*. American Association of School Administrators.

Weiss, S., Steger, D., Schroeders, U., & Wilhelm, O. (2020). A Reappraisal of the Threshold Hypothesis of Creativity and Intelligence. *Journal of Intelligence*, *8*(4), 38. doi:10.3390/jintelligence8040038 PMID:33187389

Chapter 10
Songs in the Key of Life:
Cultivating the Student qua Artist to Empower Authentic Becoming

Daniel Christopher Blackshields
https://orcid.org/0000-0001-7046-5629
University College Cork, Ireland

EXECUTIVE SUMMARY

Twenty-first century uncertainties privilege creative action. Creativity is an emergent property of dynamic relationships between individuals and their environment. Adopting a structured uncertainty curriculum design embodying the student qua artist and classroom qua creative recording studio, students experience actionable uncertainty. Such experiences foster intrapersonal insights. Giving expression to emerging self-concepts cultivates students' authentic voices, nurturing investment in care for who they are, who they are endeavouring to become, and to perceive their potentiality as they transition from university.

STRANGE DAYS HAVE FOUND US: NURTURING CARE FOR AN UNCERTAIN WORLD

*If there is a dark within and without
And there is a light. Don't let it go out*
"Song for Someone" (U2, 2014, track 4).

The world is increasingly interwoven with uncertainty manifesting in ruptures such as resurgent nationalism, increasing inequality, alienation, environmental foreboding, dissolving trust in institutions and post Covid 19 ambiguities (Beghetto, 2016; 2020). These are postnormal times "…[an] inbetween period where old orthodoxies are dying, new ones not yet emerged, and nothing really makes sense" (Sardar, 2010, p. 435). To effectively navigate postnormality, uncertainty must be welcomed as an "…animating force, [opening up] new states of awareness, new possibilities for thought and action…" (Beghetto, 2020, p.2). Supporting future change ready graduates requires nurturing students' care for ideas, others

DOI: 10.4018/978-1-6684-6076-4.ch010

Songs in the Key of Life

and critically, themselves (Dall' Alba, 2012). Encouraging students' authenticity stimulates agency that *there is a light* to effectively navigate uncertainty. For curricula to support students' effective transition from university a question arises:

Can Curricula Be Designed So Students Experience Creatively Navigating Uncertainty?

This chapter outlines a curriculum experiment: *Graduate Assessment Centre Simulations* (GACS hereafter) spanning the *Transition to Professional Life* module suite (TPL hereafter) in the *BA (Hons) Economics (through Transformational Learning)* (BAECN hereafter) programme, University College Cork. These classroom activities and assessment (called *performances)[1]* nurture students' investment in their ability, motivation, and willingness to invite *actionable uncertainty* (Beghetto, 2020). Encouraging students' engagement with who they are, concomitantly invites the excavation of ingrained psychological obstacles to who they are becoming. Through intrapersonal insights, Kaufmann & Beghetto's *mini-c creativity* (2007), students (individually and collaboratively) may "progress to interpersonally judged novel and meaningful contributions" (Beghetto & Kaufman, 2007, p. 59).

This chapter's prolegomenon highlights salient aspects of U2's recording process prefacing GACS's metaphorical frame. The significance of explicitly integrating students' epistemological and ontological development is outlined. The experiment's underpinning *Structured Uncertainty* design and student *qua* artist/classroom *qua* creative recording studio as performative metaphors are then considered. Specific GACS designs and students' reflective expressions unfolding from their experiences are then detailed.

ACROBAT: A MUSICIAL PROLEGOMENON

And you can dream
So dream out loud
And you can find
Your own way out
"Acrobat" (U2,1991, track 11).

During a 1989 concert Bono (U2's singer) announced "...we have to go away and dream it all up again" (cited in Leonard, 2021, section 1, para 2) foreshadowing U2's creative musical shift first expressed in 1991's *Achtung Baby*. Creativity is an emergent property of dynamic relationships between actor(s) and their cultural and material world (Glăveanu, 2013). Employing Glăveanu's *Five A's Framework of Creativity* (2013), the recording *(action)* of *Achtung Baby* *(artifact)* illustrates creativity as a dialogue between *actor(s)* (U2), perceived *affordances* and *audience* (others assisting, contributing, critiquing or using an artifact (including actor(s) as their own audience)).

To arrive at *Achtung Baby*'s creative plateau U2 had to *let go* their artistic certainties and *let come* uncertainty. U2 were facilitated through this liminality by Brian Eno (producer as *audience*) "[my role was] to come in and erase anything that sounded too much like U2" (cited in Leonard, 2021, section 3, para 2). Eno's role designing generative spaces was pivotal. Features such as his *Oblique Strategy cards* (aphorisms and gnomic suggestions e.g., *'Honour the error as a hidden intention'*; *'Trust in the you of now'* (Marshall, 2013)) provoked U2's presence within uncertainty through which their creative action emerged.

The uncertainties manifest in recording *Achtung Baby* generated doubt and conflict as U2's creative intentions encountered deep-rooted fears. Adam Clayton (bassist) reflected:

...it was something we had to go through to realise what we were trying to get to was not something you could find physically outside of ourselves...there was no magic to it...we actually had to put the work in, and figure out the ideas... (cited in Dombal, 2011, para 7).

Significantly, Eno sought to harness these anxieties to energise U2. They were experiencing an *event* (Žižek, 2014) as *how* they perceived and engaged musically evolved. Whilst destabilising, guided exploration of their anxieties enabled perspective making necessary for U2 to take the *beautiful risks* (Beghetto, 2021) of creative action.

U2's creativity evolved from ethical conversations (conversations grounded in humility, modesty, accountability, and imagination (Sardar, 2010) with Eno (particularly), pervading musical affordances (e.g., alternative, and industrial rock, electronica) and their artistic identities. Sustaining presence within Eno's designed uncertainty, U2 invited themselves to *"dream out loud"*. Through ability, motivation, and willingness to invest in their creative resources (Sternberg, 2006) U2 revealed unperceived and unexploited musical affordances to *"find their own way out."* As Bono later mused "[creating] the sound of four men chopping down *The Joshua Tree"* (cited in Lee, 2020, para 3).

Next a rationale for modelling curricula design form characteristics that nurture creative action is posited.

SMASHING A ROOM FULL OF MIRRORS: AN ONTOLOGICAL TURN IN EDUCATION

I hear voices, ridiculous voices
Out in the slipstream
Let's go, let's go overground
Take your head out of the mud baby
"Zooropa" U2 (1993, Track 1).

As postnormality signifies no well-worn graduate path a holistic appreciation of demands on graduates is required. The dimensions of the *Center for Curriculum Redesign*'s 21st century pedagogical design is noteworthy:

Knowledge: *What we know and understand (Traditional, Modern, Interdisciplinarity, Thematic).*
Skills: *How we use what we know (Creativity, Critical thinking, Communication, Collaboration).*
Character: *How we behave and engage in the world (Mindfulness, Curiosity, Courage, Resilience, Ethics, Leadership).*
Meta-Learning: *How we reflect and adapt (Metacognition, Growth mindset).*
(Horvathova, 2019, p.42-49).

These dimensions forefront engagement with students *qua* human beings, integrating *what* they know, *how* they act (epistemological (knowledge/skill)) with *who* they are (ontological (character/meta-learning)). Integrating epistemological and ontological development transcends traditional competency acquirement. It is reflective of Martin Heidegger's concept of *Being*:

Your being is who you are, and who you are involves and suffuses how you feel, how you act, how you are disposed, how you talk, with whom you congregate…it is embodied in the stands we take, the way we lead our lives…Our being is expressed through how we operate in the world, our attitudes, our worldview and therefore how we relate to others and things (Blatter, 2006, p. 38 cited in Vu & Dall Alba, 2014, p. 3).

Relationality is central to Heideggerian *Being*. Individuals are formed by their actions, who they interact with (audiences (proximal and distil)), affordances perceived, and institutions acted through (Vu & Dall Alba, 2014). Ways of *Being* are both *authentic* and *inauthentic*. Humans default *Being* is acting habitually unquestioningly. This inauthentic way of *Being* is necessary to effectively engage with everyday activities. However, it is a *fallen* way of *Being* when humans totally conform "…pursuing the possibilities of anyone and consequently have the experiences of anyone's rather than their own experiences" (Steiner & Reisinger (2006, p. 4 cited in Vu & Dall Alba, 2014, p.6). To be *fallen* is to *"…live in a room full of mirrors, [where] all I could see was me"* (Hendrix, 1971, track 4) negating personal creativity. To accept *authenticity's* call is to care for ideas, others, and oneself, taking responsibility for who one is. This requires ability, motivation, and willingness to look at what was previously unquestioned, dwelling within *events* to, as exemplified by Jimi Hendrix, *"…take my spirit and … smash my mirrors"* creating an authentic way of *Being*.

Nurturing students' authenticity entails "get[ting them] in touch with their own thinking and practice…" (Hiley, 2006 p. 564) to discover "reference points to a truth of their own" (Hiley, 2006, p. 566). Moving students "… away from the 'dot's points [of disciplinarian content] to a more 'vital' language and voice" (Hiley 2006, p. 565) invites the *"…ridiculous voices"* of personal creativity encouraging students to "…take [their] head out of the mud [of habituality] …."

Achtung Baby's recording cautions that authenticity's call is fraught with anxiety when the 'I' is thrown into crisis. A psychological immunity system protects against such anxiety seeking to avoid confronting emotionally threatening issues and fears risking the *Self* (Kegan & Lahey, 2009). Whilst such immunity protects, its assumptions (often rooted in unexamined beliefs) dissuade the emergence of one's authentic voice. For educators to cultivate students' creativity they must, modelling Eno, design spaces such that anxieties are perceived as precious resources (Bochman & Kroth, 2010) for intrapersonal insights. Whilst destabilising, if uncertainty is perceived as actionable, students may be energised to arrive at "novel and personally meaningful interpretations of experiences, actions and events" (Kaufman & Beghetto, 2009, p.3).

Next the integration of structured uncertainty design principles and creative performative metaphors pertinent for curricula to embody actionable uncertainty are outlined.

UNCERTAINTY CAN BE A GUIDING LIGHT: RE-IMAGINING CURRICULA

You can't return to where you never left
"Cedarwood Road" (U2, 2014, track 8).

The TPL module suite (three 10-credit modules (48 contact hours annually)) within the BAECN degree[2] is co-delivered by the author, UCC Career Services and business community collaborators. Characterised as a *deep dive learning journey* (inspired by Scharmer's Theory-U (2009)) to employability, TPL integrates students' epistemological and ontological development, scaffolding self-concept experimentation.

Figure 1. TPL – A deep dive learning journey to employability
Source: Author

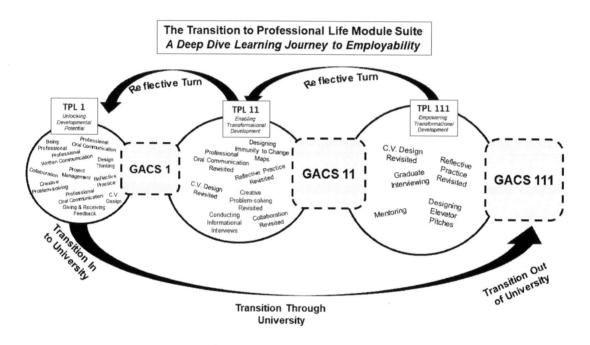

Each TPL module (see figure 1) sequentially and with increasing challenge facilitates students' developmental journeys from awareness of potential to empowering their transition through and ultimately from university to the professional world. TPL1's (year 1) thoroughline seeks to *unlock developmental potential*. Student-centred performances (focused on collaboration, communication, creative problem-solving, C.V. design, design thinking, feedback, project management, reflective practice culminating in GACS 1) cultivate students' intentional learning capacity. TPL 11 (year 2) leveraging from TPL 1 engages students in increasingly developmentally challenging experiences. Its throughline seeks to *enable transformational development*. Performances (conducting employer informational interviews, C.V. design, designing Immunity to Change Maps culminating in GACS 11) foster students' deeper reflexivity. As students commence their transition from university TPL 111's thoroughline seeks to *empower transformational development*. Performances (C.V. design, designing elevator pitches, graduate interviewing, peer mentoring culminating in GACS 111) invite students to integrate their experiences to reflect on possibilities integral to them as they transition from university.[3]

The three GACS support students' future-readiness by simulating *Graduate Assessment Centres*. Assessment Centres, increasingly significant in graduate recruitment, acclimatise applicants to organisational demands and assess potential 'fit' between organisation and applicant. Typical activities include psychometric tests, group case study/discussion exercises, interviews, role plays and presentations. The nature of assessment centres and their activities have various degrees of uncertainty through which recruiters assess candidate's competencies and capacities to problem-solve, create, and communicate in frequently collaborative contexts.

A question for the author was how to holistically prepare students for graduate recruitment engagement. Traditionally educators seek to remove uncertainty from classroom activities and assessment by embedding predictability into how the following core curriculum design questions are addressed:

What ... is the task to be accomplished?
How... is the task to be accomplished?
Outcomes...what is the expected result of engaging with the task?
Criteria... what are the guidelines, rules, supports etc that determine success?
(Beghetto, 2020, p. 4).

Removing uncertainties from curricula privileges reproductive learning (Montuori, 2006). This is learning denoted as competence acquisition, retention, and reproduction. Students (and educators) are incentivised to think and act to meet pre-determined expectations thus encouraging the conformity of inauthentic ways of *Being*. The creative modes of thinking and action required in Assessment Centres (a microcosm of the professional world) requires students *qua* graduates to sustain presence in uncertainty, disrupt expectations, experiment with affordances, cultivating the humility, modesty, accountability, and imagination necessary for authenticity. This denotes learning as creative inquiry (Montuori, 2006) where students, through curricula, engage in a recursive exploration into their ways of *Being-in-the-world*. For the GACS to authentically prepare students for Assessment Centre engagement they needed to be designed as Archimedean points for students to consciously experiment with their knowledge, skill, and self-concepts.

For GACS design the author addressed the four core curriculum design questions through the lens of Beghetto's *Structured Uncertainty* principles (2019, 2020, 2021). These principles task curriculum designers with intentionally blending pre-determined learning tasks and activities with to-be determined aspects. Pre-determined aspects of *What, How, Outcome* and *Criteria* provide structure to an experience for students so that they are neither under nor over-whelmed. The to-be determined aspects embed tasks and activities with degrees of uncertainty as the resolution of these aspects are not determined in advance by facilitators. The magnitude of possibility for students' creative expressions is in part, dependent on the extent to which the educator privileges to-be determined aspects in learning activities. Curriculum designers can alter the complexity of the activity by the extent to which students must identify their own task (*What*) and/or their own ways of engaging with a task (*How*), and/or their own artifacts demonstrating successful accomplishment of a task (*Outcomes*) and/or their own identification of what successful accomplishment of a task might look like (*Criteria*). The effective blending of pre-determined and to-be determined aspects will enable students to experience uncertainty but ensure that their experiences are perceived as actionable.

To implement a structured uncertainty design the author considered the significance of how educators' language classroom activities and assessment. Metaphors are "…pervasive in everyday life, …[how] we both think and act, is fundamentally metaphorical in nature" (Lakoff & Johnson, 1980, p.3). Metaphor choice (conscious and unconscious) define and can redefine our experience and actions.[4] A deeply embedded metaphor governing curricula's frame of reference is akin to a "regimented factory" (Montuori, 1996, p. 57). Its organisational characteristics tend to be talked and crucially, thought about and acted upon in terms of the inputs-outputs of a highly controlled social organisation whose characteristics are underpinned by predictability and the management of uncertainty. This manifests in the predominance of segmented and fragmented disciplinary silos, pre-determined learning outcomes, focusing on rigidly defined and delivered content and assessment (Montuori, 1996) and students as passive consumers of said content. The author sought to move both students and facilitators psychologically and performatively from engagement with classroom activities and assessment embedded in such creatively and consequently ontologically restrictive metaphors.

To nurture students' authentic voices the performative metaphors underlining GACS designs represent Collingwood's *artist proper*. For Collingwood artists seek to *express* an emotion individualising the representation of experience (1938). Challenging and supporting students *qua* artists when engaged in learning activities encourages insights and expressions of the uniqueness and peculiarities of their emotions, thoughts, expectations, beliefs, and values nurturing their authentic voices.

The author modelled the student *qua* artist for participants through an exposition on song writing (*action*) and song lyrics (*artifact*). Selected lyrics from U2's *Songs of Innocence* album (2014) (illustrated throughout this chapter) are explored as artifacts of the *artist proper*. This album resonates with students (mostly Irish) as expressions of experiences in Irish cultural and historical contexts. To scaffold students *qua artists* the GACS performances are designed to embody the classroom *qua* creative recording studio. Drawing on the *5 A's Framework of Creativity, Structured Uncertainty principles* and U2's experience recording *Achtung Baby* students are re-cast from passive knowledge consumer to *actor* (artist) and educators from experts (*actors*) to facilitators (*audience*). In this design the educator's primary responsibility is cultivating actionable uncertain learning spaces through a deliberate blending of pre-determined and to-be determined design dimensions in classroom activities and assessment. To foster the ethical conversations necessary for creative action, facilitators purposely immerse themselves in the students' world. Facilitators are present and patient, recognising anxieties, inviting students to let go certainties, let come evolving uncertainty and to take to *beautiful risks*.

SONGS IN THE KEY OF LIFE: CURRICULA AS EVENTS

Time is a train
Makes the future the past
Leaves you standing in the station
Your face pressed up against the glass
"Zoo Station" (U2, 1991, track 1)

GACS 1, 11 and 111 are the culminating performances for TPL 1,2 and 3 respectively. In 2021-22 each GACS took place in semester 2. 29 students (8 females) participated in GACS 1; 32 students (6 females) participated in GACS 11 and 36 students (14 females) participated in GACS 111. The primary aim of the following case studies is an experiential understanding of student experiences inhabiting uncertainty and its impact on their self-concepts represented in their reflective expressions. Following close thematic reading of students' expressions, the author curated evocative student voices (F for female; M for male) of prominent evolving themes interwoven with lyrics from *Song of Innocence*, into reflective 'songs'.

The following case studies on GACS 1, 11, 111 offer readers a vicarious experience of each simulations' design, students' experiences, and the author's interpretations to support their own naturalistic generalisations (Stake, 1995) about this experiment's potential significance for their own curriculum design.

GACS 1: *Smashing Mirrors* to Unlock Potential

GACS 1 (Blackshields, 2022a) is TPL1's 3-hour on campus performance simulated assessment centre's group activities.

Figure 2. Graduate Assessment Centre Simulation 1
Source: Author

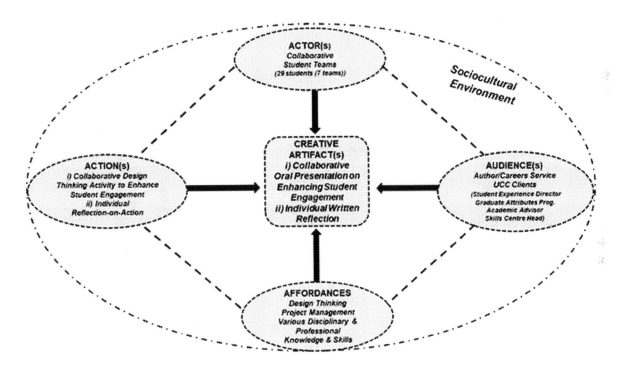

Students were allocated by the author into 7 diversely profiled teams (6 teams of four and 1 team of five) enabling students' reflections on their ability, motivation, and willingness to engage in ethical conversations. The performance theme was:

Design a Big Idea to improve the quantity and quality of Student Engagement with their programme of study in UCC in 2022-2023

This open-ended, future-oriented theme was chosen given its increasing significance in higher education post pandemic and its familiarity to students. The clients (*audience*) were UCC's Director of Student Experience, Academic Advisor for the Graduate Attributes Programme and Head of the Skills

Centre. The author's 10-minute introduction outlining research on student engagement formed part of the pre-determined *affordances*. Teams could use any disciplinary knowledge and skills perceived relevant. Discretionary behaviour was encouraged with teams invited to explore any aspect of student engagement they considered significant.

The expected *artifact* was a four-minute oral team presentation for their clients (recorded in the presence of all teams and facilitators) that would:

i. State their student engagement focus.
ii. Outline their Big Idea.
iii. Outline why their Big Idea matters in terms of the challenge considered.
iv. Outline what advice they would give UCC to enact their Big Idea.

This design, inspired by the *Big Think* https://bigthink.com/, kept pre-determined aspects of *How* and *Outcomes* to a minimum giving teams discretion shaping their artifacts.

Teams had 15 minutes to collectively review their brief. They were encouraged to use *Bohmian Dialogue* (see Blackshields, 2014). This invited them to *think together* (suspending judgement, avoiding self-censorship, building on ideas), encouraging ethical conversation. A parallel aim was that students generate evidence on their ability, motivation, and willingness to *think together* recognising when they are *thinking alone* (defending positions, withholding information, feeling vulnerable, losing respect, avoiding hurt). Facilitators observed teams' interactions for feedback purposes but did not intervene, letting teams' collaborative atmosphere naturally evolve.

Following a 10-minute question and answer session where facilitators encouraged teams to inhabit uncertainty and provoked individual and collaborative creative potentiality, teams had 20 minutes to develop a *'project design template'* using project management principles. Rather than working directly on the activity, potentially narrowing focus, this required detachment, stepping back, and 'jamming' together to scope out their task. This encouraged the evolution of communities of practice, evolving mutual understanding, perspective making and experimentation. There followed a 10-minute question and answer session, where facilitators sought to provoke maximal possibilities inviting teams to:

i. Develop Point of View statements
   _____ needs to_____ because _____
   [audience] [audience need] [insight]
ii. Generate wishes using statements such as:
    I wish….
    What I really need to do is…
    In my dreams I would…
iii. Play a game where the objective is to come up with the wildest idea. Take some of these ideas and for the key concepts within these, asking how else these could be achieved.

Inspired by Eno's *Oblique Strategy Cards* these sought to disrupt students' expectations, encourage conversation and experimentation.

Teams worked on their *Big Idea* for 60 minutes. Facilitators observed emerging conversations, remaining vigilant to indicators of doubt, anxiety, and conflict, asking teams to think aloud and where necessary, provoking teams drawn to premature closure. Teams were advised with 20 minutes left to

Songs in the Key of Life

consider how they were going to communicate their *Big Idea*. Each team then presented, facilitators giving feedback on teams' ideas, presentations, and collaborative ethic.

To be a potential *event,* students were asked to compose individual reflections (1500-2000 words) on their experiences. Designed by the author, the reflection's structure encouraged perspective making on collaborative traits (personal responsibility (self-reliance, presence, preparedness, organisation, supportiveness) and contribution (participation, adaptability, reciprocity, open-mindedness, mediation) along two dimensions:

i. *Temporality* – connecting students' present actions to their history, aspirations and expectations.
ii. *Sociality* – connecting students' actions to their relationships with audiences (proximal and distil).

The following guidelines structured reflections:

Step 1: Describe a critical incident for you relating to your performance as a 'Collaborative Agent' (What?).

Describe your role in the incident. What were your actions, interactions, reactions? What were the outcomes/consequences? How did others react? What were your thoughts and feelings?

These prompts scaffold students to individualise representations of their experiences and recognise the relationality of their ways of *Being*.

Step 2: Reflecting on the critical incident (So What?)

Why do you view this incident as critical for you (why is this an 'event')? Why do you think you thought and felt as you did (your assumptions/beliefs)? What were the origins of your thoughts and feelings?

These prompts invite students to explore how their actions unfolded from their assumptions, beliefs, values, and self-concept. This encouraged exploration of possible incongruencies between students' *being* and who they wish to *become,* potentially revealing anxieties manifesting in immunities to change.

Step 3: Prospective Reflection (Now What?)

What has this incident helped you to understand about YOU?

What developmental goals have unfolded for you. Outline an experiment to achieve these goals.

These prompts invite students to care for their *Being* and *Becoming*, taking responsibility for their developmental needs.

A thoroughline in students' reflective expressions was their recognition of immunities to change. The following 'song' captures the author's representation of students' excavation of significant psychological obstacles to their potential leaving their development *"standing in the station"*.

Standing in a Station of My Own Design

You think it's easier to put your finger on the trouble
When the trouble is you
And you think it's easier to know your own tricks
Well, it's the hardest thing you'll ever do
"The Troubles" (U2, 2014, track 11)

I remembered vividly feeling my face flush red…
… I was overwhelmed…
…Thinking to myself…
…No one else had embarrassed themselves as much as I had…
…My immediate reaction was annoyance and defensiveness…
…I was irritated with my teammates …
In reality,
I was simply annoyed with myself
After some time,
I began to realise that…

(F4)

At the dawn you thought would never come
But it did
Like it always does
"California (There Is No End to Love)" (U2, 2014, track 3)

…Presenting in front of everyone
My control over my anxiety disappeared
… I kept my eyes glued pretty much to the paper in my hands
…My feet were…rooted to the spot
…If it was not for those reasons
I would have fainted or started crying

(M12)

…I have created a stigma for myself and public speaking
I made myself far more nervous than I should be
…I am an overthinker
I tend to think the worst in most situations…
…I doubt myself…
…Drill the worst into my mind

(F3)

Something in your eyes
Took a thousand years to get here
"Iris (Hold Me Close)" (U2, 2014, track 5)

Songs in the Key of Life

This feeling of rejection resonated with me…
…Almost felt like I was five years old again…
…No one was allowing me join their games in the playground
This is where my strong dislike of rejection began…

(F1)

Somebody stepped inside your soul
Little by little they robbed and stole,
Till someone else was in control

"The Troubles" (U2, 2014, track 11)

This [mortification] … I have always suffered with
…It may have stemmed from when my first class teacher…
Made me stand up in front of all of my classmates…
…Play the thin whistle on my own
…She thought I was not practicing…
Wanted to teach me a lesson
Truthfully I was just not very good
No matter how much I practiced
This was a huge blow to my confidence…
…It still haunts me to this day

(F8)

I didn't call you
A risk can scare a thought away

"California (There Is No End to Love)" (U2, 2014, track 3)

I …sometimes find it hard to articulate what is going on in my head
I think a little too hard about how people will react to my ideas
…How they possibly will not like them…
…These internal questions sometimes mean …I say to myself
Maybe its easier not to say anything at all…
Then people can't think this of me, or that of me…

(M5)

I am a perfectionist…
…Punish[…] myself for minor errors
…My dignity has been shattered before
I don't seem to allow myself to make any mistakes
…Take out my rage on other people
Because I am so annoyed with myself

(F4)

You can't return to where you never left

"Cedarwood Road" (U2, 2014, track 8)

155

...I should be braver
Life will knock you back many times
But its only these knocks that make you stronger
... I may need to come out of my comfort zone
Nothing ever grows in a comfort zone

(M5)

The potential for creative action is contextually embedded. Students must navigate their past, expectations, interrelationships, and their sense of *Self* to invite and nurture personal and collaborative insights. Students' reflections reveal that challenges to creative inquiry unfolded from their self-concepts. The most powerful themes were students' anxiety, guilt, and doubt in the communicative act with each other and formally presenting. The most prominent expressions were *"stress"; "anxiety"* (F2); *"nervous"; "daunting"; "anxiety"* (F3); *"ashamed"; "anxious"; "overwhelmed"; "embarrassed"; "humiliate myself"; "rage"* (F4); *"embarrassed"; "afraid"; "mortified"; "shock"* (F8); *"daunting"; "full of nerves"; "pressure"* (M4); *"fell into a bit of a shell"; "fear"* (M11); *"anxiety attack"* (M12).

Students' actions, whilst working within their teams and presenting, emerged from self-concepts they sought to protect or deny. The communicative act was not perceived as solely being about the 'it' of the activity or an epistemological challenge but as embedded in social relationships between the 'I' and 'thou', implicating the student *qua* human. Personal and collaborative creativity depends on the levels of freedom humans allow themselves to be open to others, alternatives and communicating ideas. Students recognised difficulties letting themselves go. F4 expressed *"I am a perfectionist who punishes myself for minor errors"*. She *"depis[ed] the feeling of being incorrect"*. There were strong competing commitments to avoid being hurt and feeling vulnerable. F4 *"...didn't want to humiliate [her]self anymore"*. This sense of vulnerability manifested physically for some *"...my stomach turned as I ... knew everyone would be watching me"; "I can almost feel the blood rushing through my veins "* (F8); *"...I would have fainted or started crying"* (M12); *"vividly feeling my face flush red"* (F4). Students recognised that these competing commitments, these *"internal questions"* (M5) led to self-censorship *"I felt cautious...I didn't want to say something stupid...."; "holding back my own views...fear that my idea might not be accurate"* (F6).

Students acknowledged the influence of distil audiences on their present attitudes, worldviews and how they related to others and themselves, *"that somebody stepped inside [their] souls"*. This is apparent in psychological resonances from a primary school teacher's 'punishment' and childhood playground experiences of two females. Their sense of *"rejection"* (F1) and *"embarrassment"* (F8) respectively, being emotional apertures through which they now acted *"...it still haunts me to this day"* (F8).

Competing commitments create powerful psychological immunities from the *"stigma"* (F3) to avoid hurt, loss of respect and vulnerability. This led to strategies of withholding information *"I rarely shared ideas and only listened to ideas like mine"* (F6); *sometimes ...I say to myself maybe its easier not to say anything at all as then people can't think this of me, or that of me...* (M5) and defence *"take out my rage on other people"; "...attempting to shield myself...by almost pretending it did not happen"* (F4). What is clear from students' voices is that ' *"faces [can be] pressed up against the glass"* of their own potential as they struggle to let go of certainties about themselves.

Whilst psychologically difficult, giving expression to these anxieties is important to unlock potential. Students acknowledged the impact of these emotions on their actions, but also a willingness to get out of their own way. As F1 stated *"...I am now willing to explore my dislike of rejection"* and M5's aspiration to invite uncertainty *"...I may need to come out of my comfort zone. Nothing ever grows in a comfort zone"*.

The privilege of hearing their voices reminds educators that students filter curriculum through deep-seated, albeit often invisible or unconscious, self-concepts. These ontological filters can be significant barriers to student engagement. Educators must have horticultural patience (Kegan & Lahey, 2009) to support students to get out of their own ways to hear the *"ridiculous voices"* of personal creativity. Cognisant of this, GACS 1 while a developmental plateau for TPL 1, vibrates in GACS11's design to which we now turn.

GACS 11: *Moving Cross the Borders of My Secret Life* to Embrace Potentiality

GACS 11 (Blackshields, 2022b) was a blend of on campus and on-line performances. As with GACS 1, it simulates Assessment Centres' 'group case study activity' encouraging students to revisit their previous experiences, observing their development since TPL1. Complexity was increased as clients were eight business community collaborators. To encourage increasing reflexivity students were invited to consider their GACS 1 experiences of the characteristics of effective collaboration and then self-allocate into 8 teams of four.

Figure 3. Graduate Assessment Centre Simulation 2
Source: Author

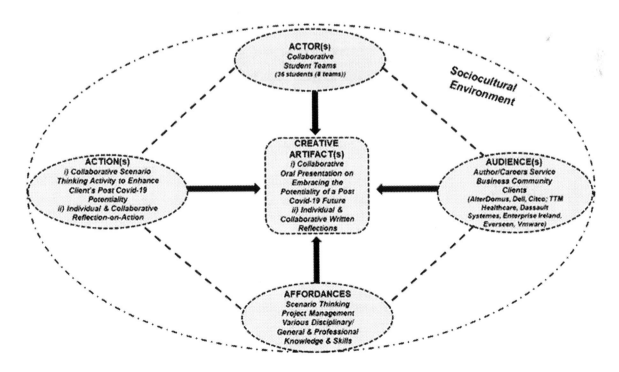

A series of four guided performances were designed, in part, from facilitators and this cohort's GACS1 reflections. Guided performance 1 focused on creative problem-solving. Facilitators, led by Career Services, explored De Bono's *Six Thinking Hats* as a tool through which collaborative creativity could be harnessed. Guided performance 2 focused on deepening students' collaborative engagement. Facilitators considered how communication impacts teams' capacity to *think together*. The author led an exploration of *Kantor's Four Player Communication Model* through an exposition of a recording session from *The Beatles' Let It Be* album, exploring how band members' communicative acts had corrosive impacts on their creativity (Blackshields, 2021). Guided performance 3, led by Career Services, revisited the principles and practice of oral presentation, highlighting online presentation's subtleties. Guided performance 4, jointly led by Career Services and the author, re-visited C.V. design.

The performance's theme was *Embracing the Potentiality of a Post Covid-19 Future.* The author explored how organisations creatively embrace uncertainty and that GACS 11's learning goal was for students to authentically engage with this challenge. Through a series of conversations with our clients (AlterDomus; Dell; Citco; TTM Healthcare; Dassault Systemes; Enterprise Ireland; Everseen and VMware) four prominent foci emerged:

i.   The Transforming Post Covid-19 Consumer.
ii. The Post Covid-19 Employee and the Evolution of Workspaces.
iii. Sustainability for Business Resilience for a Post Covid-19 World.
iv. The Place of Higher Education for the Post Covid-19 World of Work.

As per *structured uncertainty* principles, pre-determined design elements were kept to a minimum, fostering optimal learning stimulus for creative inquiry. Facilitators met the eight teams on campus, outlining clients' foci of interest and possible dimensions (but not restricted to) that they could explore. Teams were challenged to identify a dimension which they believed would have significance for their client. For example, the *Dassault Systèmes* team were advised to:

i. Identify a dimension of your choice pertaining to the Post Covid-19 Employee and the Evolution of Workspaces that you believe would have significance for Dassault Systèmes.
    Possible dimensions may include (but not restricted to):
    a) The drive towards gender equality and diversity.
    b) The increasing importance of employee well-being.
    c) Supporting accelerating skills and flexibility in an uncertain world.
ii. Outline your insight(s) into what Dassault Systèmes should explore to ensure that it can actively engage with the Post Covid-19 world of work.

The expected *artifact* was a 15-minute presentation (via Microsoft Teams) to their client. This presentation's broad structure was:

i. Long Fuse, Big Bang Issues
    Explain the focus of your case study by setting out:
        i) The issue driving your research.
        ii) The motivation for the research from the client's perspective.

iii) Your key message for your client.
iv) A roadmap of your presentation.

ii. Breathing In-Enriching Views & Challenging Consensus
Set out what you found out and what it means:
i) The What you have found out – outline the most significant evidence/ideas/opinions.
ii) The So What about what you have found out – outline your interpretations on the significance for your client.

iii. From Foresight to Insight – Your Big Idea
Summarise the main argument of your case study by setting out:
i) Overall significant conclusion(s) for your audience.
ii) The Now what about what you have found out – your recommendations for your audience.
iii) The Careful Now – briefly outline any research limitations and implementation difficulties you perceive your audience should be aware of.
iv) Restate what you believe is the relevance of your case study for your audience about the Post-Covid-19 world.

This structure, inspired by scenario analysis (Schwartz, 1991, Blackshields, 2014), emphasised the open-ended, future-oriented nature of the activity, keeping pre-determined aspects of *How* and *Outcomes* to a minimum, giving each team maximal discretion.

Teams were also required to develop a portfolio for their clients including:

i. An Executive Summary.
ii. Presentation slides.
iii. Team member's C.V.s
iv. Resources of interest to clients.

Facilitators collated and shared on TPL 11'as *Canvas* site research and consultancy insights on the broad theme and foci to form part of the activity's pre-determined *affordances*. As with GACS 1, students were invited to use disciplinary knowledge and skills they deemed relevant.

Over three weeks, teams were allocated a minimum of three private full dress-rehearsals (approximately 45-60 minutes each). Rehearsals and feedback were recorded. The primary responsibilities of facilitators (Career Services and the author acting as proxy clients), was to enable perspective making, respond to ideas, provoke individual and collaborative creativity, and explore doubts, anxieties, and conflicts. To encourage teams to hang out together and 'jam' with facilitators, rehearsals took place on campus. The first rehearsal focused on preliminary ideas and foundational presentation competencies. For the other rehearsals, teams (and one facilitator) met on campus to present together in one room on Microsoft Teams (other facilitators watching online). Where deemed necessary facilitators requested further rehearsals for specific teams.

Presentations to clients occurred over four sessions (90 minutes each) on two separate days. Presenting teams and facilitators met on campus, clients on Microsoft Teams. Two teams presenting in each session with the business community collaborators giving feedback on teams' content and communication. Presentations and feedback were recorded.

To nurture shared learning students were invited to reflect individually and collaboratively on their experiences by developing a 3000-word reflective memorandum with two themes:

i. Theme 1: Your Collective Transformative Learning Experience
Use the traits of collaboration to describe your experience, using this data to collaboratively reflect on your learning as a team.
- *Identify and reflect on what worked in terms of collaborating effectively.*
- *Identify and reflect on what needs improvement for effective collaboration.*
- *Summarise the key learning for you as a team. What is the relevance of this experience for your future collective development?*

ii. Theme 2: Your Individual Transformative Learning Experience
Given the traits of collaboration consider:
- *How did your experience of collaborating and your performance as a collaborating agent match or divert from your expectations? Your worry box?*
- What are the specific areas of strength and development highlighted for you as a collaborating agent? How do you think you can enhance your strengths and engage with these development areas?

Students were invited to use the author's collaboration rubric, *De Bono's Six Thinking Hats* and *Kantor's Four Player Communication Model* as reflective prompts.

As with their TPL1 peers, *communication* was a dominant theme in these reflections. However, there was a noticeable shift in students' expressions of their thoughts and emotions. Repeated exposure, in a scaffolded way, to communicative acts enabled students detach themselves from their thoughts and feelings, observe them, take perspective, and critically examine them. The language of anxiety still resonates, but now interlaced with the language of resilience, tolerance and a growth mindset. Students are *"moving cross the border of [their] secret life"* (Cohen & Robinson, 2001) closing the gap between who they are and who they are endeavouring to be.

The Bittersweet Crack that Lets Light In

I was shaking from a storm in me
Haunted by the spectors that we had to see
"The Miracle (of Joey Ramone)" (U2, 2014, track 1)

I am a person ...very afraid of expressing myself
...Speaking in front of a real company
...I would call intimidating

F1

I was challenged
...Academically and emotionally
I was apprehensive

F2

Songs in the Key of Life

> *We come from an ancient place*
> *Beyond what we can see*
> *We've come to colonise your night*
> *And steal your poetry*
>   "This is Where You Can Reach Me Now" (U2, 2014, track 10)

Such fears went along with the phobia of public speaking
This fear was attending
All the times I had to present in front of the lecturers

          M9

In the past
This would have been difficult for me
…I would have struggled
With not inputting my opinions
…The issue …was always
I wouldn't listen to others

          M5

… [I] needed to overcome
…The psychological barrier
Of being brave enough
To express our ideas

          F1

I woke up at the moment when the miracle occurred
Heard a song that made some sense out of the world
Everything I ever lost now has been returned
The most beautiful sound I ever heard
     "The Miracle (of Joey Ramone)" (U2, 2014, track 1)

I can see how far I have come
…It is now a matter of developing my confidence …
…To prevent myself from getting inside my own head …
…Holding myself back

          F3

I managed to go beyond my expectation
…This assessment has helped me grow
I found myself stronger than what I was expecting

          M9

In hindsight, I now realise
…Lack of direction was simply freedom
…The freedom to choose our own course…
It allowed us to be
Responsible and trusted

          F2

If I open my eyes
You disappear
"Raised by Wolves" (U2, 2014, track 7)

...That I was present at the presentation
...Though I was scared to present
"Not being a coward and run-away"
I was told that I was bold
For staying and facing my fears
Instead of letting it control me
...I am happy about it

F6

I think in the past
I went into these efforts
Hoping not to mess it ...
But now I know
..Getting something wrong is part of the experience
I look at getting something wrong more like a learning experience now
Rather than feeling embarrassed by it

M4

She said free yourself to be yourself
If only you could see yourself
"Iris (Hold Me Close)" (U2, 2014, track 5)

...Looking back...
I can see how these 'challenges' actually helped ...
...I was motivated, encouraged, ... forced to be innovative
Sometimes, being outside of my comfort zone is a bittersweet thing

F2

Students had a growing self-awareness of the significance of their self-concepts on their potential. The 'I' was still 'thrown' into crisis in their expectations and initial communicative acts. This atmosphere of crisis was heightened (as expected) given clients' perceived significance for students (representing employers). One female was initially *"very afraid"* finding the performance *"intimidating"* (F1). Another found the thought of presenting *"quite daunting"; "something I detest'"*, always *"...a fear of mine"* (F3). Others felt *"apprehensive"* (F2); *"scared"* (F6). M9 spoke of his persistent *"phobia"* with presenting while others *"struggled"* (M3 and M5). One male recognised how his initial communicative acts reflected his habitual defensiveness restricting himself to *"...hoping not to mess it up for my team..."* (M4).

Despite the fraught nature of students' expectations, there was, concomitantly, an evolving motivation and willingness to look at what was previously looked through. Students acknowledged but also challenged their habitual ways of *Being*, to *"smash [their] mirrors"*. One male, whilst acknowledging his *"phobia"* of public speaking, *"...managed to go beyond [his] expectations"*, consequently *"...this assessment...helped [him] to grow"* (M9). Turning full circle on himself he recognised that *"I found myself stronger than what I was expecting"* energising a commitment to self-development *"...by doing*

Songs in the Key of Life

further similar projects I could enhance and eventually overcome this fear". One female acknowledged her vulnerability when communicating but also her willingness to accept the call to care for her ideas and herself to *"overcome the psychological barrier of being brave enough to express... ideas"* to *"face [the audience] with courage"* (F1).

Overcoming the vulnerability of *thinking together* was significant for one team collectively acknowledging that they needed to *"learn to trust both ourselves and the team"* creating a *"safe space to share ideas and opinions"*. This virtue of trust encouraged ethical conversations *"allow[ing] them to grow as a group"*. M4 recognised that he restricted his own potential *vis-a-vis* his unwillingness to suspend judgement and accept criticism constructively. He acknowledged his development through this performance recognising that *"getting something wrong is part of the experience"*. He articulates a developing growth mindset *"I look at getting something wrong more like a learning experience now...rather than feeling embarrassed by it"*.

The significance of inhabiting uncertainty for one female empowered her to see her own growth from her initial fears to *"see how far [she had] come"*, committing to combatting self-imposed censorship *"... developing my confidence...to prevent myself from getting inside my own head ... holding myself back"* (F3). Taking the *beautiful risk* of *thinking together* was apparent for one male. Whereas historically M6 acknowledged he *"...wouldn't listen to others"*, by letting himself go he *"...learned a lot by taking on what everyone had to say"*. Similarly, the significance of the activity's open-endedness became apparent for F2 acknowledging that she found the to-be determined dimension of GACS11 challenging cognitively and emotionally. She struggled with the *"lack of direction"*, concerned whether she was *"...delivering... correct information...answering ...questions correctly"*. However, reflecting on her experiences these questions began to dissolve, her expression signifying her evolving transcendental horizon *"I now realise the lack direction was simply freedom"*. She recognised the growth potential of actionable uncertainty empowering her and her team *"...to be responsible and trusted...engage with our creative side"*.

Interestingly, F2's expression also acknowledges 'loss' as one 'leaves' a way of being. She recognised that she learned about herself whilst outside her comfort zone, but this was *"bittersweet"*. This sense of regret is not unusual as one's self-concept changes. Facilitator vigilance is necessary to both acknowledge this sense of loss of *Being* but nurture students to continue to let come this *Becoming*.

The resilience required to inhabit liminality was apparent for one female acknowledging her own strength that despite *"stuttering ....and shaking while talking"* she remained *"present"*. She was *"not a coward and run-away"* (F6). Facilitators' sensitivity to students is apparent in her acknowledgement *"I was told that I was bold for staying and facing my fears instead of letting it control me"*. Her use of the word *"it"* is noteworthy signifying looking *at* as opposed to *through* an experience. For her this is the achievement *"I am happy about it"*. There is a privilege to being invited to hear students compose new expressions about their self-concepts. For an educator this is unapologetically *"the most beautiful sound I ever heard"*.

These reflections represent students inviting authenticity's call, beginning to take responsibility for their development. In the movement of students' language, we 'see' the movement of their inner selves (Hiley, 2006). Students begin to perceive uncertainty as an *"animating force"* and take *"beautiful risks"*. From restrictive self-concept expressions; *"very afraid"*; *"intimidating"*; *"apprehensive"*; *"fear"*; *"scared"* to expressions of potential and hope; *"brave"*; *"confidence"*; *"bold"* *"motivated"*; *"encouraged"* students begin to embody a more dynamic sense of self and recognise that *"there is a crack in everything, that's how the light gets in"* (Cohen, 1992, track 5). The third GACS, to which we now turn, increased the performance's complexity further.

Songs in the Key of Life

GACS 111: *Can't You Hear Me Knocking?*
Empowering Transformative Learning

GACS 111's overarching goal was for students to draw on their experiences in TPL1 and 11 and gain further experience of actionable uncertainty by exposure to a more diverse array of assessment centre activities (interviews, ice breakers, psychometric testing, role playing as well as group activities). GACS 111 was a three-part performance held over three sessions (on campus and online).

Figure 4. Graduate Assessment Centre Simulation 3
Source: Author

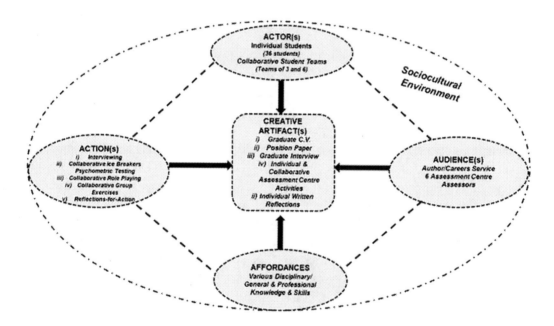

In part 1 students role-played applying for a graduate position as a Research Assistant in the Department of Economics, UCC. Students submitted a targeted CV to match the position's essential attributes. The author assessed these C.V.s giving feedback on whether and why students would have been shortlisted. Students had one week to prepare for an online interview (20 minutes duration on Microsoft Teams). Students were advised that the interview would be competence-based but also explore disciplinarian expertise. With the latter in mind, students developed a 500-word position paper on a topic (decided by the author) based on (then) current issues. Topics in 2021-2022 included: *The Energy Crisis Means that the World Needs to Park Long Term Environmental Strategies – Yes or No?; The OECD Corporation Tax Deal – The Death Rattle for Economic Policy?* This position paper (submitted 24 hours prior to interview) formed part of the activity's *affordances*. Students were given an *Interview Guide* (Blackshields, 2022c) enabling them to appreciate an interviewer's (as *audience*) perspective. Students were expected to conduct themselves as they would for a graduate interview. Interviews and feedback were recorded. Students were assessed on first impressions, professional competencies, the position paper (topic understanding, ability to address challenging questions), attitude, communication, manner, motivation, organisation, and preparation.

Part 2 was a 4-hour on campus Assessment Centre designed to simulate the diverse activities of an Assessment Centre day. Firstly, students participated in an Ice Breaker group activity *'The Space Survival Exercise'* https://www.psychologicalscience.org/observer/nasa-exercise (regularly used in Assessment Centres). Given its novel, open ended nature, it enables students to warm up to the collaborative and creative nature of the activities. Students were then introduced to and individually completed sample psychometric tests. Thereafter, there was a general discussion on these tests and preparation for them. Students were then randomly allocated into three person teams for a 10-minute role play exercise. They were given information about their role, the organisation, and the scenario. We chose an 'upset customer' scenario (frequently used in Assessment Centres (see https://www.tidio.com/blog/customer-service-scenarios/ for examples). Students rotated roles as customer, organisation representative and observer. Facilitators observed without intervening. This activity's goal was for students to reflectively experience the nature of professional communication. Students were given feedback on their negotiation, persuasion, and broad interpersonal skills. Part 2 concluded with a shared reflection on students' learning with facilitators exploring students' articulated doubts and anxieties.

Part 3 was a 4-hour, online Assessment Centre (on Microsoft Teams). Facilitators from Career Services and the author explored the nature of online Assessment Centres, their similarities and distinctions *vis-a-vis* on-site centres. Facilitators outlined what assessors look for from candidates in group activities to support conscious perspective making. Students were randomly allocated into 6 six person teams and relocated to a virtual breakout room. Here they met their assessor and were given their group activity brief. Permission was given to use a specific organisation's Assessment Centre group activity (on the proviso of confidentiality). Teams had 10 minutes to review the activity. Then they could ask clarification questions. Thereafter, assessors turned off their video and sound and teams had 25 minutes to discuss their scenario, agreeing on a common response to the issues. Teams then gave a 10-minute presentation to their assessor. Throughout the activity, assessors observed teams' ability to plan effectively, communicate clearly, share ideas, influence others, and work effectively to deliver task objectives. Following their presentation, the assessor gave feedback and teams engaged in a 30-minute collective reflection using a series of prompts focusing on: i) broad learning themes (e.g., *how did you feel during the activity? What challenges did you face? What surprised you the most? What lessons have you learned?*) and; ii) more targeted prompts on communication, problem-solving, and collaboration. Teams and facilitators then returned to the class Microsoft Teams room for a shared reflection.

Cognisant that students were on the cusp of transitioning from university GACS 111's individual reflection (1500-2000 words) invited students to become consciously aware of the possibilities open and integral to them. Leveraging from Patti Dobrowolski's visualisation tool *Picturing Your Future Self* http://pattidobrowolski.com/ students were asked to:

i) *Visualise your current way of being*

What is your current state? Think of your thoughts and feelings about your scholarly, professional, and personal development. What do you value about your current state and what do you think/ feel you would like to change.

ii)   *Visualise your desired new reality*

Give yourself the best-case scenario and ask yourself: By September 2022 – what is your desired way of being?

In your visualisation you can draw, sketch, doodle, use images to create a picture of your current state and desired new reality. In your written reflection summarise how your visualisation represents your current way of being and who you endeavour to become.

iii)   *Visualise your Way Forward Roadmap set out how you believe you can bridge the gap between your current way of being and your desired way of being.*

Identify three transformative steps for you. In your reflection summarise your steps and why you feel these are transformative for you.

Several significant themes were revealed in students' reflections. Students experienced their imminent transition from university as ontologically destabilising. Nevertheless, they sought to marry their anxieties with a motivation and willingness to take responsibility for self-care and to seek authenticity. There was an associated willingness to invite uncertainty recognising its necessity as an animating force. Whereas the 'I' and 'thou' relationship was privileged in GACS 1 and 11 reflections, there was a noticeable shift in GACS 111 reflections towards examining the nature, tone, and intensity of how they communicated with themselves. There was a perceptible expressiveness with students evoking personally meaningful figurative language as they sought to articulate and evolve their self-concept. Relatedly, the process of reflective writing itself was perceived as a method of inquiry with students reporting self-discoveries as they wrote. Curating evocative fragments of students' voices, a 'song' of taking responsibility to "… free [themselves] to be [themselves]" as they invite themselves to "see [themselves]" is clear.

Moving Cross the Borders to Hope and Possibility

The world is spinning fast tonight
You can hurt yourself tryin' to hold on
To what you used to be
I'm so glad the past is all gone

"Volcano" (U2, 2014, track 6)

I was self-sabotaging…
…Telling myself
… I do not care……If I do not succeed…
…It was a way of shifting the blame away from myself
…Onto something outside myself
It felt like someone had turned the volume down in my life…
I was hiding my struggle …neglecting it…
I felt like an imposter in my own skin…
A new chapter is awaiting me

Songs in the Key of Life

> *I am running down a corridor*
> *...There is a door at the end*
> *I know if I opened that door*
> *...Light will shine through*
> *My future is bright...*
> *Caring about myself*
> *Will give the world what is best of me*
> *Instead of what is left of me*
>
> (F9)
>
> *You no longer got a hold on me*
> *You're no longer in control of me*
> *I am*
>
> "Lucifer's Hands" (U2, 2014, track 12)
>
> *I no longer fear the judgement of others*
> *I have grown confident in my ability to learn and to share*
> *...[I] have learned to communicate with myself*
> *... Recognising my capabilities*
> *Understanding my capacities*
> *...Trusting my competencies*
> *I am no longer the person I was ...*
> *I am ready for change ...*
> *Any nerves I may feel*
> *...Cannot withstand my desire of [sic] new experiences*
> *I can continue to expand as a person*
> *...The fig tree of opportunities in my life can continue [sic] grow*
>
> (F2)
>
> *I normally play down my accomplishments*
> *...Act as though I'm just being humble*
> *I don't ...feel like I'm being humble*
> *I'm just feeling discomfort in ever showing confidence*
> *...I want to hide and shrink back out of sight*
> *I want to have released myself*
> *From a stagnant way of life*
> *...Be more willing to take risks*
> *... A sort of leap of faith*
> *...I'm willing to take the jump*
>
> (M10)
>
> *I can be my own worst enemy*
> *...Questioning my abilities*
> *...I wonder if I like to tell myself*
> *I can't do something*
> *Even before trying*
> *Almost like a cop out*

Songs in the Key of Life

...*If I put my everything into it and fail*
It would hurt a lot more
I hope to find excitement in the unknown rather than fear
"Just keep swimming, just keep swimming"
...*I am doing everything I can*
...*Keep calm*
...*Keep going*
If you hear a voice within you say
"you cannot paint, then by all means paint
and that voice will be silenced"
...*It's okay not to have everything figured out*
Take every opportunity

(F8)

This is where you can reach me now
"This is Where You Can Reach Me Now" (U2, 2014, track 10)

...*Nothing scares me more*
Than the uncertainty that currently clouds my future
...*Caused me a huge deal of stress, tears, and sleepless nights*
I have come to the realisation
That its totally okay
...*I really believe that I can do it*
For anyone to believe in me
I must first believe in myself
...*A greater faith in myself*
Will allow me to expose myself to things I am not familiar with
Maybe even enjoy it
While on a journey to self-discovery
I want to explore all the options which present themselves to me
...*The more opportunities I explore*
The more I will come
To know myself

(F4)

These are all questions
I had not asked myself for some time
I have gotten quite good at sweeping certain things under the "rug"
...*Not taking full responsibility for what is going on in my life*
...*I should take a seat and evaluate how my week has gone*
What do I have to do?
How am I feeling
About what's to come in my week?

(M3)

...*I am going through an overwhelming phase*
...*Not knowing who I am or what I want*

Songs in the Key of Life

What should be feelings of excitement for the future
…Recently turned to feelings
Of hopelessness,
Inadequacy
…Maybe even dread
Of what lies ahead of me
Inside, I feel dull, grey and mundane
I want to nourish my soul
…Follow dreams …personal to me
After writing this
I actually feel a lot more positive and motivated
Than I did …about my future
…that in itself makes this reflection worthwhile
I am excited for what is to come
…That I have the power to control how my life goes …
Is spectacular!

(F6)

I have realised …writing this reflection,
…I go too long without checking in with myself
How is … doing?
How is my current state?
If there is a dark
Within and without
And there is a light
Don't let it go out

"Song for Someone" (U2, 2014, track 4)

I remind myself
…I am not useless
…Try to remember the growth mindset
But being in what might be described
As a "moment of perceivable uselessness"
Is somewhat painful …
Regardless of everything
I do have hope throughout it all
…What has underlined this whole reflection is hope
At first it might have looked quite dark
but then hope came in
…The whole thing started to change in tone
I have hope
And that is very real
I will go forward in hope
…See where this takes me

(M14)

The ontological challenge of transitioning from university is visceral throughout these reflections. F4 acknowledged that *"nothing scares [her] more than the uncertainty that clouds [her] future"* culminating in *"...stress, tears, and sleepless nights"*. Words employed by students to represent their *being* included *"overwhelming"* (F1); (F4); (F6); (M3); (M6), *"scary"* (F3); (M11), *"pressure"* (F3); (M2), *"fear"* (F5); (F9); (M1); (M11), *"anxious"* (F7); (M2); (M5); (M9), *"unnerving"* (M5), and *"distraught"* (M12). Students acknowledged the damaging nature of these negative emotions on their self-concepts and potentiality. F9 recognised she was *"self-sabotaging"* and she felt *"someone had turned the volume down in [her] life"*. F6 felt *"dull, grey and mundane"*, M2 felt *"stuck behind an imaginary wall, unable to break it down"*, whilst M10 struggled to *"show pride"*, *"feeling ashamed"*. M12 conceded that *"...when I consider where I am in life it can seem quite sad"*. M14 described contemplation of his self-concept as *"somewhat painful"*.

Nevertheless, for the *"...dark, within and without"* permeating these reflections *"...there is a light"*. Students were not content to 'merely' surface and acknowledge their anxieties. They sought to take responsibility for transforming their self-concepts. They recognised the dynamic nature of their *Being* and that how they language their sense of self can re-sound their voice of self-doubt to more dynamic ways of *Being*. F10 realised *"...how much I have grown"* and that hers was a more active self-concept *"...I am still growing"*. M9 recognised that his potential evolves through the stories he tells himself *"...altering my mindset into believing that I am deserving..."*. M10 sought to *"release himself from a stagnant way of life..."*, whilst M14 recognised that *"I need to be easier on myself and give myself a bit of credit.... ditch the negatively,... look at the positives,..."*. F9 powerfully represented the significance of self-care as she aspired to *"...give [her] soul a rest...replacing ...negative thoughts with positive ones...find validation from within"*. She recognised the implication of re-sounding her voice for her way of *Being-in-the-world "caring about myself will give the world the best of me instead of what is left of me"*. There is movement in the language these students used to express their self-concepts. Through such dynamism, students began *"move cross the borders of their secret [lives]",* looking at as opposed to through their self-concepts, surfacing and challenging deep-seated immunities.

A growing willingness to see uncertainty as a gateway through which students might 'discover' their authentic selves was apparent. F1 recognised that *"...to further grow as an individual...I am choosing to take some risks"*, therefore she *"welcome[s] the uncertainty of the future"*. M10 was ready to take *"a sort of leap of faith. I'm willing to take the jump"*. F8 hoped to *"...find excitement in the unknown rather than fear"* and it was *"...the potentiality within this uncertainty that excites [her]"*. F4 wanted *"to explore all the options which present themselves to me... "* appreciating that *"...the more opportunities I explore, the more I will come to know myself"*. One female declared that she *"...values authenticity and doing what I feel is right for me..."* (F5), while F6 was *"...excited for what is the come...the fact that I have the power to control how my life goes from here on in is spectacular!"* Hope resonates behind these words, vibrating with her use of an exclamation mark to express her emotion's intensity.

Students' confidence in their evolving voice through how they expressed their thoughts and feelings was apparent. More so than TPL1 and 11 participants these reflections' poetic sensibility embody the student *qua* artist. Students used figurative language to express their experiences in personally authentic ways. They employed personally meaningful aphorisms such as one female consciously using lines from *Finding Nemo "just keep swimming, just keep swimming"* (F8) and later a quote she attributed to Van Gogh *"if you hear a voice within you say you cannot paint then by all means paint and that voice will be silenced"*. F2 intentionally evoked the growing 'fig tree' metaphor from Sylvia Plath's *'The Bell Jar'* to symbolise possibility. F9 personified her self-doubt as a *"parasite"* that was *"consuming more*

Songs in the Key of Life

and more of myself, feeding on my self-esteem, my self-worth, my self-efficacy". Through such figurative language she recognised that she *"…felt like an imposter in [her] own skin"*. She further employed metaphor to visualise her release from self-doubt *"running down a corridor … there is a door…I know that if I opened that door, the light would shine through"*. M2 employed the metaphor of a *"wall"* he was stuck behind symbolising his anxiety but then redefined this "wall" is an *"imaginary barrier"* lessening its perceived solidity and his commitment to *"breaking down that barrier"*. Students' urge to represent their own stories through language expressing their 'truths' breathes life into their reflections moving them away from abstractions that cut them off from their experiences creating space for self-discovery.

Significantly, some students acknowledged that the reflective writing process led to (as opposed to documented) self-discoveries. For F1 *"[t]his reflection has allowed me to take a step back and welcome the uncertainty of the future"*. M3 realised *"from just writing this reflection …that I go too long without checking in on myself"* and F6 believed that through expressing she *"…felt a lot more positive and motivated…that in itself makes this reflection worthwhile"*. Through expression students surfaced their *unknown knowns,* giving themselves permission to let go of potentially debilitating certainties and let come who they are endeavouring to become. Cultivating spaces where students experience actionable uncertainty empowers their recognition of when they meet developmental impasses to take perspective and invest in their motivation and willingness to seek out new possibilities. The music behind the words used by one male to express his evolving way of *Being-in-the-world*.

…What has underlined this whole reflection is hope
At first it might have looked quite dark
but then hope came in
…The whole thing started to change in tone
I have hope
And that is very real
I will go forward in hope
…See where this takes me

pulsates with hope and potentiality.

DREAM OUT LOUD

She's gonna dream up
The world she wants to live in
She's gonna dream out loud
"Zooropa" (U2, 1993, track 1)

As students transition from university, they increasingly meet existentialist challenges. To successful navigate 21st century's uncertainties require sustained investment in resources (ability, motivation, and willingness) to self-actualise. Students' development must be rooted in ethical conversations with others and within themselves. They must nurture care about ideas, others, and themselves to accept authenticity's call. This is an ontological challenge wherein *unknown knowns* are revealed. These *unknown knowns,* pregnant with our sense of *Self*, are fraught with anxieties. As documented in this chapter's curated 'songs', to care about *Being* and *Becoming* invites the excavation of deep-rooted psychological immunities.

Educators can create safe spaces for students to explore their *Being, Becoming* and psychological immunities through a conscious movement in how we talk about, think about, and embody curriculum design. To design curricula privileging creativity educators must shift from the deeply embedded 'regimented factory' metaphor manifesting in classrooms seeking to eliminate uncertainty to a metaphor inviting uncertainty into the fabric of our teaching and student learning.

This chapter's intention is to assist readers developing naturalistic generalisations about curriculum design. It offers a vicarious experience into the design, enactment, assessment, and outcomes of performances consciously enabling students' dwelling in uncertainty, cultivating optimal learning stimulus, and embodying the assumption that all humans have creative capacities. To do so, the author outlined the movement in figurative language used to converse, think about and act as curriculum designers. Designing the curriculum to embody the student *qua* artist and classroom *qua* creative recording studio enables students experience actionable uncertainty. Modelling the dynamic relationships between actor, audience, affordance, action, and artifact through the experiences of artists such as U2 supports a paradigmatic shift to a forward-looking curriculum.

Dwelling in uncertainty is psychologically difficult. However, unless educators cultivate spaces where the *"Joshua Tree"* of students' deep-seated psychological immunities can be surfaced, explored and *"chopped down"* then, notwithstanding epistemological development, ontologically they may possess neither the motivation nor willingness to nurture or invest in the *"ridiculous voices"* of intra and interpersonal creativity. The significance of a pedagogy that nurtures student's care for their way of *Being* is illustrated by the heartfully expression of one female *"caring about myself will give the world the best of me instead of what is left of me."* Postnormality needs students *qua* graduates to give the best of themselves.

Educators must have the courage to let go of their own certainties and let come the liminality of a structured uncertainty curriculum. Educators must model the teacher *qua* artist inviting uncertainty into how they talk, think, and enact curricula. Scaffolding students' holistic development and cultivating expressions of their dynamic biographies, educators encourage them to compose 'songs' in the key of their own lives. We invite them to *"dream out loud"*.

ACKNOWLEDGMENT

Sincere thanks to UCC Career Services; especially Mary McCarthy, Ruth MacConaill and Aileen Waterman and our business community sponsors without whom the ability to dream out loud would be muted, to U2 and other artists who, through their creative actions and artifacts, inspired leaps into a forward-looking curriculum and to our students, without whose trust, resilience, and courage to invite authenticity's *'ridiculous voice'* this experiment would remain a design.

REFERENCES

Beghetto, R. A. (2016). Creative openings in the social interactions of teaching. *Creativity. Theories Research-Applications*, *3*(2), 261–273. doi:10.1515/ctra-2016-0017

Beghetto, R. A. (2019). Structured uncertainty: How creativity thrives under constraints and uncertainty. In C. A. Mullen (Ed.), Creativity under duress in education? (Vol. 3, pp. 27–40). Springer Nature.

Beghetto, R. A. (2020). Uncertainty. In V.P. Glăveanu (Ed.), The Palgrave encyclopaedia of the possible (pp. 1-7). Palgrave Macmillian.

Beghetto, R. A. (2021). There is no creativity without uncertainty: Dubito ergo creo. *Journal of Creativity, 31*, 1–5. doi:10.1016/j.yjoc.2021.100005

Beghetto, R. A., & Kaufman, J. (2007). The genesis of creative greatness: Mini-c and the expert performance approach. *High Ability Studies, 18*(1), 59–61. doi:10.1080/13598130701350668

Blackshields, D. (2010). Making connections for mindful inquiry: using reflective journals to scaffold an autobiographical approach to learning in economics. In B. Higgs, S. Kilcommins, & T. Ryan (Eds.), *Making connections: Intentional teaching for integrative learning* (pp. 45–64). NAIRTL.

Blackshields, D. (2014). Yes, and... cultivating the art of conversation through improvisational classroom experiences. In *Integrative learning: International research and practice* (pp. 68–82). Routledge. doi:10.4324/9781315884769

Blackshields, D. (2016). Encountering the 'unknown knowns': Scaffolding contemplative reading to cultivate a creative inquiry disposition in 21st century undergraduate economics students. In N. Alias & J. Luaran (Eds.), Student driven Learning in the 21st Century (pp. 217-238). IGI Global.

Blackshields, D. (2019). Songs in the key of life: Designing a deep dive learning journey to employability. *Guidance Matters,* (3), 42-49.

Blackshields, D. (2021, December 12). *Within you, without you: The imperative to cultivate the creative promise of thinking together* [Powerpoint slides]. UCC, Cork, Ireland.

Blackshields, D. (2022a, April 8). *Provocating competence to provoke strategic conversations* [course document]. UCC, Cork, Ireland.

Blackshields, D. (2022b, February 3). *Embracing the potentiality of a post-covid 19 future* [course document]. UCC, Cork, Ireland.

Blackshields, D. (2022c, October 25). *Research assistant: Interview guide* [course document]. UCC, Cork, Ireland.

Blackshields, D., & McCarthy, M. (2013). The game is afoot – playing the sleuth in creative problems solving performances by business economics students. In *Innovative business school teaching: Engaging the millennial generation* (pp. 109–127). Routledge.

Bockman, D. J., & Kroth, M. (2010). Immunity to transformational learning and change. *The Learning Organization, 17*(4), 328–342. doi:10.1108/09696471011043090

Cohen, L. (1992). Anthem [Recorded by L. Cohen]. On *The future* [CD]. Columbia.

Cohen, L., & Robinson, S. (2001). In my secret life [Recorded by L. Cohen]. On Ten new songs [CD]. Columbia.

Collingwood, R. G. (1938). *The principles of art*. Oxford University Press.

Dall'Alba, G. (2012). Re-imagining the university: Developing a capacity to care. In R. Barnett (Ed.), *The future university: Ideas and possibilities* (pp. 112–122). Routledge.

Dombal, R. (2011, November 9). Achtung baby (super deluxe edition). *Pitchfork*. Retrieved from https://pitchfork.com/reviews/albums/16022-achtung-baby-super-deluxe-edition/

Glăveanu, V. P. (2013). Rewriting the language of creativity: The five A's framework. *Review of General Psychology, 17*(1), 69–81. doi:10.1037/a0029528

Hendrix, J. (1971). Room Full of Mirrors [Recorded by J. Hendrix]. On *Rainbow bridge* [CD]. Reprise.

Hiley, T. J. (2006). Finding one's voice: The poetry of reflective practice. *Management Decision, 44*(4), 561–574. doi:10.1108/00251740610663081

Horvathova, M. (2019). *Study on employability skills in the ib diploma programme and career-related programme curricula*. Center for Curriculum Redesign. Retrieved from https://www.ibo.org/globalassets/publications/ib-research/employability-skills-full-report.pdf

Kaufmann, J. C., & Beghetto, R. A. (2009). Beyond big and little: The four c model of creativity. *Review of General Psychology, 13*(1), 1–12. doi:10.1037/a0013688

Kavanagh, E., & O'Kane, A. (2014). Developing the self in economics: The role of developmental space in an integrated undergraduate education. In *Integrative learning: International research and practice* (pp. 130–142). Routledge.

Kegan, R., & Lahey, L. (2009). *Immunity to change*. Harvard Business Press.

Lakoff, G., & Johnson, M. (1980). *Metaphors we live by*. University of Chicago Press.

Lee, P. (2020, November 9). *Achtung baby: A second listen*. Hooks and Harmony. Retrieved from https://hooksandharmony.com/achtung-baby-a-second-listen/

Leonard, M. (2021, April 14). *The genius of...Achtung baby by U2*. Guitar.com. Retrieved from https://guitar.com/review/album/the-genius-of-achtung-baby-by-u2/

Marshall, C. (2013, July 2). Jump start your creative process with Brian Eno's "oblique strategies" deck of cards (1975). *Open Culture*. Retrieved from https://www.openculture.com/2013/07/jump_start_your_creative_process_with_brian_eno_oblique_strategies.html

Montuori, A. (1996). The art of transformation: Jazz as a metaphor for education. *History of Education Review, 9*(4), 57–62.

Montuori, A. (2006). The quest for a new education: From oppositional identities to creative inquiry. *ReVision, 28*(3), 4–20. doi:10.3200/REVN.28.3.4-20

Sardar, Z. (2010). Welcome to postnormal times. *Futures, 42*(5), 435–444. doi:10.1016/j.futures.2009.11.028

Scharmer, C. O. (2009). *Theory U: Leading from the future as it emerges*. The Society for Organizational Learning.

Schwartz, P. (1991). *The art of the long view*. Doubleday.

Stake, R. (1995). *The art of case study research*. SAGE Publications.

Sternberg, R. (2006). The nature of creativity. *Creativity Research Journal, 18*(1), 87–98. doi:10.120715326934crj1801_10

The Doors. (1967). Strange Days [Recorded by The Doors]. On Strange days [CD]. Elektra.

U2. (1991). Acrobat [Recorded by U2]. On Achtung baby [CD]. Island.

U2. (1993). Zooropa [Recorded by U2] On Zooropa [CD]. Island.

U2. (2014). California (There is no End to Love); Cedarwood Road; Every Breaking Wave; Iris (Hold Me Close); Lucifer's Hands; Song for Someone; The Troubles; The Miracle (of Joey Ramone); This is Where you Can Reach Me Now; Raised by Wolves; Volcano [Recorded by U2]. On Songs of innocence [CD]. Island.

Vu, T., & Dall'Alba, G. (2014). Authentic assessment for student learning: An ontological conceptualisation. *Educational Philosophy and Theory, 46*(7), 778–791. doi:10.1080/00131857.2013.795110

Wiske, M. S. (1998). *Teaching for understanding: Linking research with practice*. Jossey-Bass Publishers.

Žižek, S. (2014). *Event*. Penguin Books.

KEY TERMS AND DEFINITIONS

Actionable Uncertainty: A sense of doubt in human experience motivating new ways of thinking and acting.

Authenticity: Living life in a way that one becomes all that they can become.

Being: Who you are, expressed through your attitudes, worldviews, how you act, relate to others and the world.

Creativity: A sociocultural phenomena where the interactions between an actor(s) and their cultural and material environment leads to novel and useful artifacts.

Ethical Conversation: Conversation underpinned by the virtues of humility, modesty, and accountability.

Expression: Representing an experience in a way that seeks to embody the uniqueness and peculiarity of the experience.

Immunity to Change: A psychological system that seeks to avoid engaging with change that is emotionally threatening.

Postnormality: A period categorised by uncertainty caused by environmental complexity, chaos, and contradictions.

Structured Uncertainty: Intentionally designing uncertainty into a learning experience.

Žižekian Event: A change in the way a human perceives and acts in the world.

ENDNOTES

[1] *Performances* derives from the *Teaching for Understanding* framework. See (Wiske, 1998; Blackshields & McCarthy, 2012) on designing pedagogy as *performances of understanding*.

[2] See Kavanagh & Kane (2014) on the design of the BAECN.

[3] See Blackshields (2019) on the design of the TPL modules.

[4] Blackshields has experimented with visual arts (2010); detective fiction (2013); jazz (2014) and poetry (2016)) as performative metaphors for curriculum design.

Chapter 11
Cultivating and Nurturing an Empathy-Ready Mindset Through Value-Based Innovation

Serit Banyan
Taylor's University, Malaysia

Zaim Azizi Bin Abu Bakar
Taylor's University, Malaysia

Fadhilah Raihan Binti Lokman
Taylor's University, Malaysia

EXECUTIVE SUMMARY

The Social Innovation Project focuses on developing and implementing innovative solutions to impact students and the community positively. In this module, students are engaged in an interdisciplinary and collaborative setting to identify opportunities in today's global and local environments that create and capture values. The project-based learning activities for this module emphasize situated learning, which deals with authentic and unique real-world issues. Students will be involved in collaborative decision-making and problem-solving as they have to discuss, consult, collaborate, and solve the problem to provide services or create a product for the desired community. After taking this module, students are able to enhance their creativity and instill values, such as leadership, teamwork, communication, and interpersonal skills, among students through the completion of the group's project.

DOI: 10.4018/978-1-6684-6076-4.ch011

BACKGROUND OF THE PROJECT

As part of the graduating criteria, all local and international students pursuing degree programs in both public and private universities in Malaysia must complete a set of General Studies or *Mata Pelajaran Umum* (MPU) modules, including the MPU4. These MPU modules have been developed to inculcate value-based education embedded with affective, cognitive, and psychomotor domains in higher learning. The MPU4 modules are designed to complement the MPU1, MPU2, and MPU3 modules, which focus on philosophy, knowledge, skills, values, patriotism, and citizenship values.

Under MPU4 modules, universities are offering modules that allow students to become participative by being involved physically and directly with the outside community, such as community service modules and co-curricular modules, intending to produce students capable of utilizing their social and interpersonal skills. At Taylor's University, the MPU4 Community Service Initiatives was initially offered and designed to help foster a sense of care and concern among students for their community, environment, and the world at large through service experiences and the opportunity to apply their skills and knowledge in real-life situations.

Challenges of Students in Learning MPU4 Module

Several significant learning challenges were observed during the implementation of the MPU4 Community Service Initiatives in the past years. Firstly, there is a lack of emphasis on empathy among students when performing the social service activity through the Community Service Initiatives module. Based on students' course evaluations, most students were primarily motivated by task completion rather than attempting to comprehend the viewpoints and genuine needs of the community. This has left students unable to respond to the issue appropriately or avoid misinterpreting what the community is trying to say. This similar observation of behaviour was also seen in the lecturers. According to Gerdes and Segal (2011), empathetic values are essential for individuals who perform social work because they improve the effectiveness of the activity and lead to better outcomes. With students and lecturers merely motivated by the need to finish tasks, the social service given to the community may not reflect a high level of quality. Without learning what the community genuinely needs, the students created their assumptions to give a certain social service activity based on a simple observation of the neighbourhood area.

Secondly, because the community's true needs are not being met, it has been discovered that the community services provided have very little impact on the community. For example, suppose a certain neighborhood area is discovered to be filthy and littered. In that case, performing a clean-up project session in that community area is a typical social service activity. Such services are not sustainable because the same area will eventually require another cleaning session if the community's failure to keep the neighbourhood area clean is not addressed. While it benefits the community in the short term, the outcome of clean-up services can lead to failure due to resource fatigue and the need for labour to do the same thing over and over again, resulting in a lack of sustainability. Partnerships between the institution and the community must be mutually beneficial for a project to succeed to provide more substantial, useful, and sustainable contributions to the community.

Thirdly, the MPU4 Community Service Initiative module lacks a proper teaching and learning strategy, which limits students' learning opportunities. Despite working on a community-based project, it has been found that students' motivation to learn the module was poor and the experience was described as insignificant. Therefore, having no proper teaching and learning approaches has inhibited the students

Cultivating and Nurturing an Empathy-Ready Mindset Through Value-Based Innovation

from reaching their full potential. In the Community Service Initiatives module, students were required to make their analysis of a variety of problems. Although the exercise may have enhanced the students' analytical thinking skills, there is no proper guidance to scaffold the student's learning and to analyze more effectively. As a result, students are more likely to feel demotivated, which can lead to poor outcomes (Han et. al., 2019). On top of that, Martin and Bolliger (2018) emphasized the importance of an engaged learning environment, particularly in an online learning environment, because it increases students' attention and focus, creates meaningful learning experiences, fosters higher levels of student achievement, and inspires students to exercise higher-level critical thinking abilities.

High Impact Educational Practices (HIEPs)

The said challenges have prompted the development of the MPU4 Social Innovation Project at Taylor's University in 2019. While addressing the challenges, this development is also aligned with the direction set by the Ministry of Education of Malaysia to incorporate High Impact Education Practices that meet 21st-century teaching and learning (Kementerian Pengajian Tinggi Malaysia, 2016).

On August 16, 2018, the Malaysian Ministry of Education (KPM) implemented a new policy, High Impact Educational Practices (HIEPs), in managing MPU1 to MPU4 category modules at higher education institutions utilizing the following framework: HIEP1: human cultural and physical knowledge; HIEP2: intellectual and practical skills; HIEP3: integrated and applied to learn; HIEP4: personal and social responsibility and active participation. Yusoff and Ali (2018), interactive and connected high-impact educational methods can boost student involvement in behaviour, emotions, and cognition. Abdullah et al. (2019) add that HIEPs are a teaching and learning strategy and technique that is particularly advantageous to student involvement and effective learning for students from diverse backgrounds. Thus, HIEPs can be described as a high-impact educational technique that involves students from varied backgrounds in effective teaching and learning sessions.

Taylor's University MPU4 Social Innovation Projects employ the HIEP3 framework, emphasizing personal and social responsibility and active participation. This is consistent with the module learning outcomes of the module, which are to propose a comprehensive solution to issues to capitalize on opportunities presented in contemporary real-world settings that encapsulate social and ethical values in MLO 1 and to execute a project on social innovation for a variety of disciplines that benefits users and society in MLO 2. The module is also employing the technique provided by HIEPs, which incorporates Collaborative Assignments and Projects (CAS) Methods by implementation such as case studies, learning problem-based (PBL), social experiments, visits, scientific and field studies, and Service/Community Based Learning (SBL) - such as solving community and NGO concerns and difficulties, aiding the homeless, charity work in orphanages, homes for the elderly, hospitals, and other charities.

As stated by the Ministry, the following attributes of HIEPs make them appropriate for MPU delivery: -

1. Knowledge about Culture and the Physical and Real World, which focuses on the student involvement in examining the broad, intricate and contemporary issues;
2. Intellectual and Practical Skills across the curriculum through handling challenging projects or cases and the use of standards performance-based assessment;
3. Personal and Social Responsibility involvement through active participation in a diverse community full of real-world challenges; and

4. Integrated and Applied Learning are highlighted through the use of knowledge and skills, as well as the attributes of responsibility, in the solution of complex issues and new situations

INTRODUCTION TO SOCIAL INNOVATION PROJECT

Social Innovation Project is a module that introduces 'social innovation' that focuses on developing and implementing innovative solutions to impact the community positively. Social innovation can take many forms to benefit users and society, including technology, product or prototypes, and social programs with multidisciplinary projects. In this module, students are engaged in an interdisciplinary and collaborative setting to identify opportunities in today's global and local settings that create and capture values based on United Nations Sustainable Development Goals (UN SDG).

Project-based learning is a student-centred form of instruction based on three constructivist principles: learning is context-specific, learners are actively involved in the learning process, and they achieve their goals through social interactions and the sharing of knowledge and understanding (Cocco, 2006). Students work on a project o – from a week up to a semester that engages them in solving a real-world problem or answering a complex question. They demonstrate their knowledge and skills by creating prototypes or presentations for real audiences.

On the other hand, situated learning involves students in cooperative activities where they are challenged to use their critical thinking and kinesthetic abilities. These activities should be applicable and transferable to students' homes, communities, and workplaces (Stein, 1998). While immersed in the experience, students reflect on previously held knowledge and challenge other students' assumptions. Meanwhile, in collaborative learning, students participate in small-group activities in which they share their knowledge and expertise. In these student-driven activities, the teacher usually acts as a facilitator

The project-based learning activities for this module emphasize situated learning and apprenticeship learning which deals with real-world issues. Collaborative decision-making and problem-solving are necessary as the teams will have to discuss, consult, collaborate and problem-solve to provide services or create a product. This module is conducted 100% online in Taylor's University's Learning Management System, which is developed on Moodle platform. Through a systematic design thinking process, students are required to propose and produce a sustainable and enterprising project that can be used for creating social values and innovation. Furthermore, students are also engaged in collaborative decision-making, and problem-solving processes as the teams will have to generate new and better ideas to solve the problem together before filtering and narrowing it down into the best, most practical innovation.

On top of utilizing MOOC as an asynchronous teaching and learning platform, SIP coaches use synchronous teaching online tools such as Microsoft Teams, Zoom and MIRO to facilitate weekly lectures and tutorials. Students then document their project activities using Project Management Document and reflect on their learning journey and experience using Gibbs Reflective Cycles. Prototypes that serve as potential solutions to various UNSDG community problems are presented and exhibited in various platforms such as Facebook, Taylor's INNOFEST and Me.Reka website, which may attract real collaboration with investors and industry partners. Implementing this module will open more possibilities for value-based education that promotes empathy, creativity and innovation to extend its impact on real communities.

TEACHING AND LEARNING STRATEGIES

The MPU4 Social Innovation Project modules employ an integrated pedagogical framework which comprised of project-based learning, situated learning, and cross-disciplinary collaborative learning to provide a more effective learning environment for students. These various learning methods can enrich students' learning because they allow students to understand the subject thoroughly and help them apply that learning in their daily lives outside of the classroom. Furthermore, this also ensures that students are more likely to be exposed to methods that fit their preferred individualized learning style, improving their learning ability.

Through project-based learning with an emphasis on situated learning, the Social Innovation project module adopts design thinking, focusing on empathizing with the community to uncover their real needs. This is in contrast to the Community Service Initiatives module, which provides no proper teaching and learning approach to address community problems and does not include the community anywhere while developing the solution. Incorporating UNSDGs into project-based learning raises students' knowledge of the problems and challenges affecting their local communities and the global community. The unique and authentic nature of the project conducted by each group Project-based learning optimizes learning efficiency by empowering students to use and expand their knowledge. This greatly enhances their critical thinking abilities since students must pitch ideas and deliver potential solutions at the end of the semester.

Furthermore, this module incorporates cross-disciplinary collaborative learning using a projec-based learning approach. Numerous studies in various fields have called for greater cross-disciplinary collaboration in tackling the world's ever-increasingly complicated challenges. Students work together in groups to determine what they need to learn to address an issue. Students must form groups of at least three different schools from the start of the semester, resulting in collaborative learning with a multi-disciplinary background. The collaborative learning in this module does not confine itself to a single discipline's perspective on how to look at problems and solve them. Rather, it includes at least three different major perspectives from other disciplines. This is highly reinforced by Gooch et al. (2015)'s analysis, which shows that multidisciplinary approaches provide a unique opportunity to create an impact on various levels while also introducing a rich range of sustainable outputs beyond commercialization. Hence, this new MPU 4 Social Innovation Project module incorporates value-based education, creating a strong online learning environment that enhances students' ability to empathize and develop innovative solutions to impact the community positively.

Integrated Elements in Teaching the SIP Module

I. *Design Thinking*

Design Thinking is a repetitive process in which people strive to understand the end users (community), redefine challenges, and build novel solutions that can be prototyped and tested. Design thinking is a fundamental problem-solving method to improve products or services. It aids in analyzing an issue's features and identifying more ambiguous or peripheral factors that contribute to the conditions of a problem. A study by Liedtka and Ogilvie (2011) has observed that the principles and assumptions of design thinking constitute a significant—and valuable—challenge to the analytical methodologies at the heart of business education today. This out-of-the-box thinking is now taught at world-class institutions and encouraged at all levels of business.

Design thinking is a five-stage process that includes the following steps: 1-Empathize, 2-Define, 3-Ideate, 4-Prototype, and 5-Test. Students in this Social Innovation Project module are taught to instil principles such as empathy with the end user or community to uncover insights that are often difficult to describe or articulate. Patnaik and Mortensen (2009) express that a crucial component in today's design thinking ideas is the importance of empathy, a topic almost entirely absent from prior design theories. The first stage of the Design Thinking process, Empathize, is a mechanism for understanding and sharing the users' sentiments to encourage deep user comprehension and find deep user insights and requirements. Empathy is utilized to obtain a larger perspective of the community's life to identify profound user insights and requirements. Field observations and in-depth interview sessions can be utilized to emphasize the importance of the community.

The Define phase is the second stage in the Design Thinking process. It entails gathering data from the empathy stage to define the difficulties and obstacles. Students can build an actionable design issue statement or Point of View that inspires the generation of ideas to address it by employing methods for synthesizing raw data into a meaningful and useable body of knowledge. This stage has two goals: to develop a deep understanding of the end users/community and the design space and, based on that understanding, to develop an actionable problem statement which is the point of view. The point of view should be a guiding statement that focuses on individual users and insights and requirements discovered during the empathy mode. It is essential to the design process because it directly explains the problem that learners are attempting to solve. Without a well-defined issue statement, it is difficult to determine what the learners are striving. Besides that, a persona must be created simultaneously in the process. Persona development is the process of humanizing the end user by giving them a voice and making them come to life. Personas are fictitious characters created to imitate end users with similar behaviours, patterns, motives, and ambitions. Persona development will represent the community's end users throughout the design process, from brainstorming solutions to constructing the ideal user experience journey.

The third stage Design Thinking process is Ideation. During this stage of design thinking, students are prepared to generate ideas, where students and teams elevate and celebrate the power of possibility. It is the transition from identifying a particular question or problem to generating a wide variety of potential answers and solutions. The goal of Ideation is to generate a large number of ideas. These ideas may inspire newer, better ones, allowing the team to narrow down to the best, most practical, and most innovative ones. Students will generate as many ideas as they can. While some of these ideas will be developed into potential solutions to the design problem, others will be vetted and discarded. Eventually, the primary aim of the ideation session is to uncover and explore new angles and avenues—to think beyond the box. The ideation phase must be a "judgment-free zone" for invention and creativity. Some tools or strategies can be used to generate ideas, such as group brainstorming approaches, analogous inspiration, and SCAMPER techniques (Substitute, Combine, Adapt, Modify/Magnify, Purpose, Eliminate/Minimize and Rearrange/Reverse). Group brainstorming is the most utilized tool for complex problem solving because it allows for more in-depth development of ideas.

The fourth stage of the Design Thinking process is prototyping. Prototyping in design thinking serves to promote real-world experimentation in service of learning rather than to exhibit, persuade, or sell; these prototypes serve as "playgrounds" rather than "dress rehearsals," as per described by Schrage (1999). The prototypes will be built on everything the students have done thus far, interviewing end users, developing end-user problem statements, and brainstorming potential solutions. This is an experimental phase in which the goal is to find the best potential solution to each of the challenges highlighted in the previous three stages. This phase is a method of making ideas and concepts more concrete and visual than textual

Cultivating and Nurturing an Empathy-Ready Mindset Through Value-Based Innovation

ideas. A prototype is a scaled-down product; it is a simulation or sample version that allows students to test their ideas and designs before investing time and money in building the product.

Finally, the final stage of the Design Thinking process, the Test process, requires students to present their prototypes to end users/community for feedback. At this point, students will know whether their prototypes suit users' needs. Any positive and constructive criticism is encouraged to learn the issues and enhance students' future prototypes. Because the design thinking approach is non-linear and iterative, students can continuously examine, question, and refine their product or process by returning to any stage and working on the product until the output fulfils the users' needs.

II. *United Nations Sustainable Development Goals*

The Social Innovation Project module uses the United Nations 17 Sustainable Development Goals to aid coaches and students in selecting themes based on their interests and enthusiasm. Coaches and students must choose one of the 17 UNSDGs listed below to engage in discussions about the difficulties and challenges that real communities confront. The following are the 17 lists and goals that will be chosen as the group's theme:

Figure 1. United Nations Sustainable Development Goals. Source: https://sdgs.un.org/goals

The Social Innovation Project provides learning flexibility through topic selection. Coaches and students can choose any UNSDG topic and work on projects that will give relevant learning experiences throughout the 14-week semester.

183

III. *Gibbs Reflective Cycle*

The Gibbs Reflective Cycle, developed by Graham Gibbs in 1988, was designed to provide a framework for learning from experiences. It is one of the most common theoretical frameworks that encourage people to reflect on what they experienced during a certain circumstance or incident. This strategy allows people to pay greater attention. It assesses the good and bad effects of an event by making people aware of their actions and recognizing the areas that need to be improved based on their own experiences.

The cycle is extremely useful for thinking thoroughly about a certain scenario. By reflecting on those experiences, people become conscious of their behaviours and can change or adjust their behaviour. Gibb's reflecting cycle was originally designed for Rolfe's nursing-like reflection paradigm. Gibb's reflecting cycle has the virtue of simplicity and straightforwardness. It has only three main questions to be answered and may be used to refine reflective thinking: - *What? So What? and Now What?* The model was developed initially for nursing and care education but has become broader in its subsequent applications, not least because of the clarity of the model and its ease of use (Rolfe, 2001).

However, this has gained popularity across a wide range of fields and is widely used as a major model of reflective practice. Because of its cyclical character, it is said to lend itself especially well to repeated experiences, allowing you to learn, plan, and analyze things that went well or poorly. Choo et al. (2018) researched patterns of reflective practice in written journals. The findings indicated that Gibbs is an excellent model for reflective practice when keeping a journal.

The Social Innovation Project uses the Gibbs Reflective Cycle, in which students are given a reflection template and a list of questions at the start of the semester to scaffold their reflective activity. This method documents the students' experiences working on the project. After finishing their project, students turn in their reflections. Six steps are included in the Gibbs Reflective Cycle. Each phase encourages participation in and reflection on a particular learning experience. The six steps of the Gibbs Reflective Cycle are listed below:

Step 1- Description

The first stage of reflection requires students to describe the situation, experience, action, or even minute facts without concluding too early. The student's objective at this phase is to ascertain what transpired in a weekly review. Students can make the following inquiries to comprehend the circumstance better. Some examples of the queries are: *What happened; When and where did it happen; Who was present; What did you and the other people do; What was the situation's outcome; and Why were you there?*

Step 2- Feelings

In this stage, discussing what students were thinking and feeling during the situation is pivotal. Students must avoid making any emotional comments during this time. To assess this, students can use these questions:- *What were you feeling during the situation?; What were you feeling before and after the situation?; What do you think other people were feeling about the situation?; What do you think other people feel about the situation now?; What were you thinking during the situation?; and What do you think about the situation now?*

Step 3- Evaluation

This third step of the cycle is known as evaluation, where students assess their experience positively or negatively on the situation. This is the stage where students must be objective and comprehend what worked and did not. To assess this, students can use these questions:- *What was good and bad about the experience?; What went well?; What didn't go so well?; and What did you and other people contribute to the situation (positively or negatively)?*

Step 4- Analysis

This stage determines the lesson the students have acquired from the event, situation, or activity. Based on previous experience, students can think to perform well if a similar kind of situation arises in the future. The analysis is usually conducted along with the evaluation. To assess this, students can use these questions: *Why did things go well?; Why didn't it go well?; What sense can I make of the situation?; What knowledge – my own or others (for example, academic literature) can help me understand the situation?*

Step 5- Conclusion

This is the stage when students are required to look back and reflect during the 14-week semester. Students must imagine what else could be done for the project. The information gathered while concluding can bring huge significance to becoming a better person. It can help prevent unwanted things from happening in the future. To assess this, students can use these questions:

What did I learn from this situation? How could this have been a more positive situation for everyone involved?; What skills do I need to develop for me to handle a situation like this better?; What else could I have done?

Step 6- Action Plan

The last step is called the action plan. Students describe how they will deal with similar situations in the future and how to do better next time. This is an exceptional step to make changes and develop a plan to do things differently. To assess this, students can use this questions:-*If I had to do the same thing again, what would I do differently?; How will I develop the required skills I need?; and How can I make sure that I can act differently next time?*

IMPLEMENTATION OF THE PROJECT

The Social Innovation Project is being implemented over 14 weeks. During the 14-week implementation period, there are four major phases which are Introduction to the module (Week 1 – Week 2), The Proposal (Week 3 – Week 6), The final product and exhibition (Week 7 – Week 13) and Individual reflection (Week 14).

Introduction to the Module (Week 1 – Week 2)

The semester begins with a module briefing on the first day of class, which all students and coaches must attend. The briefing session is held online via ZOOM and FB live to accommodate the many students taking the MPU4 module each semester. Students are exposed UNSDGs and Design Thinking during the briefing session, in addition to being briefed on module information and assessments. At the end of the briefing session, students will select a theme for the SIP project based on their interests, with the list of themes determined by the coaches based on their expertise. Examples of themes are included sustainable tourism that promotes local culture or products, mental health issues among students, infrastructure and education for Orang Asli children, and efforts to develop affordable and sustainable urban transportation systems. The theme may or may not address only one UNSDG, and the theme may address multiple UNSDGs.

Students are assigned to their respective classes in the second week based on the theme they chose in the first week. Students in each class must form a to conduct their project where the students' group must consist of a cross-disciplinary group of at least three different disciplines. Each group is then given a Project Management Document to monitor the progress of their work. This document contains a list of all the steps structured based on the design thinking process that must be taken to complete the project, and all group members are given access to edit and contribute to it.

The Proposal (Week 3 – Week 6)

Students must go through three stages of design thinking to prepare for writing the proposal: empathy, definition, and ideating.

In the first stage of design thinking, which is empathy, students are trained and required to conduct interviews and observations to gain insight and understanding of the end user's needs. Therefore, the students have to identify their end users and approach them to collaborate to conduct their project. Rather than making assumptions about what the community needs, observing the community in its natural environment and engaging with them through interviews allows the students to empathize with the community better. To perform this, students must first comprehend the challenge and develop interview questions on the community's motivations and frustrations concerning the issue. A clearer context will emerge if students consult on the project with entities such as NGOs or government agencies, which they are encouraged to do. Empathize is a mechanism that allows students to understand and share the users' emotions to foster deep user understanding and connect with how they feel about their problems and circumstances.

Based on the accumulation of information and insights obtained from the interview and observation, students must interpret the information and insights obtained from the interview and observation and work on the next step in the design thinking process, which is to define the insight. The define stage necessitates a thorough understanding of the end user's requirements by synthesizing and analyzing the information gathered during the empathy stage to produce a meaningful problem statement or point of view that inspires the generation of ideas to solve it in the subsequent stage. This problem statement must be actionable for students to carry out the ideation process in a goal-oriented manner.

Following the formulation of the problem statement, students will engage in the idea generation process to generate as many ideas as possible to address the problem statement. This process is carried out without any attempt to judge or evaluate them to allow students to "think outside the box" and generate as many alternative ways of viewing the problem. The purpose of this stage of Ideation is to go for quantity by generating a vast number of ideas that might stimulate newer and better ideas before filtering them down to the best, most practical, and innovative solutions. To accommodate this process, MIRO is utilized as an online platform for students to collaborate and brainstorm their ideas, bringing different perspectives and uncovering the unexpected areas of innovation possible.

After completing the three stages of design thinking, all groups will submit a proposal containing potential solutions to the challenges or problems they are working on. Students must determine the values of the solutions presented to the targeted audience and identify the needs being addressed. Students must present multiple solutions to their respective coaches and end users. However, the proposed idea may not be the final one because students will need to prototype and test the ideas before turning them into the final product.

The Final Product and Exhibition (Week 7 – Week 13)

To find out if the proposed concept of ideas works, students must undertake the other two stages of the experimental phase in design thinking: prototype and Test. At the end of this phase, groups will present and exhibit their final product.

Prototyping is the stage of the design thinking process that occurs after students have narrowed down their ideas to the best solutions. It is a simulation or sample version of a real and finished product used for testing before the final product is launched and mass-produced. The primary purpose of prototyping is to transform an abstract concept into a sample form that is tangible enough to elicit a response from the intended users. Students have the flexibility of making a prototype in low or high fidelity. Although a high-fidelity prototype is more accurate and closer to the final product, low-fidelity is more practical for students because it is less expensive and takes less time to build. It is important because students will be permitted to fail quickly and fix problems immediately. Students can use the prototype to evaluate the design, identify its strengths, and address design defects without investing too much time or money.

Students will test each prototype to evaluate if the ideas solve the problem discovered during the empathy stage. Each group will test its prototype by getting feedback from coaches, end users, experts, and peers. It is a crucial step since it allows students to evaluate the product or service with real users and gain insights into how they will utilize it. Even though testing is the final stage of design thinking, the process is iterative. Students can always go back to any earlier stages of design thinking for alterations and refine ideas and concepts. The Test involves collecting user input on the prototypes built and acquiring a deeper understanding of the users. The execution of this stage assists students in improving their prototypes and may even result in the production of novel ideas to tackle the problem. The students will execute and present the final product using the concept that appears to be the best based on input from end users during the prototype and testing phases.

The project concludes with the final product presentation, which is the best possible outcome of all stages of design thinking. All groups then showcase and pitch their ideas on the Taylor's University Social Innovation Project Facebook page, which is open to the public. In addition, selected products and concepts will be featured on Taylor's INNOFEST page, which is an end-of-semester innovation festival displaying projects performed by undergraduate students from various programs at the university.

Individual Reflection (Week 14)

Following the completion of the group project, each student must write an individual reflection using the Gibbs Reflective Cycle model of reflective writing in describing and reflecting on their ability to be self-aware and self-regulate emotions while dealing with challenges and opportunities during project execution while fostering a stable and harmonious relationship for productive teamwork. Self-reflection is essential since it is the key to self-awareness. More crucially, it allows you to gauge the fulfilment of the module's third learning outcome, which is to demonstrate resilience and adaptability in dealing with disruptions and opportunities through reflective writing. This must be substantiated by evidence of their development throughout the module.

Role of SIP Coaches

The roles of SIP Coaches as stated in Table 1 below:

Table 1. The Roles of SIP Coaches

Week	Learning Activities	Role of Coaches
1	Module briefing	1. Conduct module briefing through ZOOM and FB Live. 2. Explain to students module information, assessments, MIRO and theme selection.
2	Group formation	1. Conduct lectures via ZOOM/TEAMS. 2. Guide students to form a group of 6 with a minimum of 3 programs.
3	Design Thinking: Empathy	1. Help students learn a deep understanding of the problems and realities of the community they are designing. 2. Help students learn how to develop empathy process in design thinking. 3. Help students conduct interview sessions with the community they want to help or work. 4. Help students to work collaboratively using MIRO.
4	Design Thinking: Define	1. Help students to learn and understand the process of defining in design thinking. 2. Help students analyze and synthesize information gathered through an interview session. 3. Help students create a point of view (POV) based on the information from synthesizing and analyzing information. 4. Help students find the problems faced by the community.
5	Design Thinking: Ideate	1. Help students learn the process of ideating in design thinking. 2. Help students generate a large number of ideas based on the ideation process. 3. Help students to do the idea generation process through brainstorming, sketching and the worst possible ideas. 4. Help students do the concept development process where they develop the idea of the product they want to produce. 5. Help students choose the best solution to solve the community's problem.
6	Presentation of proposal	1. Conduct a session of proposal presentation where students will present their proposal to the lecturer and community based on empathy, define, and ideate processes. 2. Help students to receive constructive feedback on their idea of their product design thinking.
7	Design Thinking: Prototype & Test	1. Monitor students' progress in building their sample version of the final product, which is used for testing before launching the product. 2. Give constructive feedback on students' prototypes of the product.
8-12	Implementation of project	1. Mentoring students to prepare their final product after building students' prototypes.
13	Presentation and Exhibition	1. Conduct a presentation session for students to present their final product by showing how they created and developed their product and explaining the functions and strengths of their product. 2. Help students to exhibit their product online via the FB page Taylor's University Social Innovation Project by sharing their 3 – 5 minutes video pitching.
14	Submission of Individual Reflection	1. Marking students' reflections based on Gibbs' Reflective Learning Cycle.
15	Submission of Project Management Document	1. Marking students' Project Management Documents

IMPACTS ON STUDENTS' LEARNING EXPERIENCE AND PERFORMANCE

Learners' marks for all assessment components are very high, and all scores are evenly good for all, reflecting the fulfilment of all MLOs. See Figure 2.

Figure 2. Students' results for the August 2021 semesters

	A	A-	B+	B	B-	C+	C	D+	D	D-	F	WD	IN	F(W)	AU	P(V)	P	TOTAL
SABD	78	16	2	2	0	1	0	0	0	0	0	0	0	0	0	0	0	99
SBS	57	10	3	0	0	0	1	0	0	0	0	0	0	0	0	0	0	71
SCE	31	9	2	0	1	0	0	0	0	0	0	0	0	0	0	0	0	43
SFSG	25	6	1	0	0	0	0	0	0	0	1	0	0	0	0	0	0	33
SHTE	98	17	9	2	0	0	0	0	0	0	0	0	0	0	0	0	0	126
SLAS	57	8	7	0	1	0	0	0	0	0	2	0	0	0	0	0	0	75
SoAF	107	22	7	1	3	0	0	0	0	0	3	0	0	0	0	0	0	143
SoC	103	10	1	4	4	2	0	0	0	0	2	0	0	0	0	0	0	126
SoCIT	108	22	8	4	0	0	0	0	0	1	1	0	0	0	0	0	0	144
SoE	18	2	3	1	1	0	0	0	0	0	1	0	0	0	0	0	0	26
SoEd	19	7	3	0	0	0	0	0	0	0	1	0	0	0	0	0	0	30
SoM	47	2	2	1	1	1	0	0	0	0	0	0	0	0	0	0	0	54
SoMM	154	28	7	4	1	0	0	0	0	0	2	0	0	0	0	0	0	196
TDS	64	9	6	3	1	1	0	0	0	0	1	0	0	0	0	0	0	85
TLS	85	16	2	1	0	1	0	0	0	0	0	0	0	0	0	0	0	105
TOTAL	1051	184	63	23	13	6	1	0	0	1	14	0	0	0	0	0	0	1356

Students' Feedbacks

Based on students' reflections, this module impacted their learning experience in three areas, namely cognitive, affective and psychomotor

Cognitive:

Learners demonstrated a deep understanding of the community's genuine needs by working on potential solutions to various UNSDGs issues. They also demonstrated the ability to evaluate and synthesize the various perspectives expressed by other members on the same topic to find the best solution. The testing phase allows learners to evaluate the prototypes before producing the best and most effective solution. Because of the unique nature of this project, learners gained expertise in an authentic context that the learners experienced.

These are some of the examples of what students in their reflections:

- *Pick your members wisely & being able to be creative, and ability to experience different topics aside from your main course studies.*
- *how we've been taught to think out of the box and can help the society become a better one.*
- *I have learn that gender inequality is a serious problem in workplace and we have found out some innovation solution to help*
- *The real world issues and knowledge which identified and learned from class and the NGO organization (Rise Against Hunger)*
- *The new knowledge and fun gained when getting to know more about the NGOs and also during the creation of the product*

- *The concepts that were not known to me before this module, such as Gibbs' Reflective Cycle and The Design Thinking Process.*
- *the ideation part where we have to think outside the box for the creative thinking process*
- *I got to work with a company that cares about zero hunger, so from them, i can actually understand the concept and how we should end zero hunger.*
- *I have learned how to create a basic prototype of an application and also I have the opportunity to practice my presentation skills through the presentations.*
- *I learned that empathy is actually very important than I thought before. We need to implement empathy in our daily life.*
- *I get to understand the actual problem that the public is facing and had created solutions that is useful to the public.*
- *The fact that it deals with the SDG's was interesting as i learnt a lot about sustainability.*

Affective:

Empathy allowed learners to define the problem statement from a more human-centric perspective, gain insight into the problem that it sets out to resolve, help to understand the requirements of the user or community, and deliver a more customized solution. Learners internalized values upon listening to various perspectives and are able to make sense of things that are going on around them. When learners communicate effectively and show empathy when interacting with others, they work well in a team and cultivate and nurture networks.

These are some of the examples of what students in their reflections:

- *always appreciate to the inventors who make our life more convenient and comfortable because inventing an item is not that easy*
- *I loved seeing how people from the same class can produce ideas surrounding the same topic and it being completely different, which is very unique in my opinion.*
- *Inventing an item is not easy, and we tend to take things lightly at times and forget that it takes more than a single mind to invent or innovate an idea.*
- *the point that this module is set to let the youths implement their responsibilities as a world citizens in the society besides just academics.*
- *Adaptability is very important in entrepreneurship. Ideas, prototypes and businesses have to be always receptive to change and adapt to different environments to be able to thrive and succeed*
- *The character building I have learnt throughout which will help me be a efficient team member*
- *Collaborating with others has allowed me to realize my potential and to think out of the box. What I believe is the correct or best solution may not necessarily be what certain people view as what is indispensable to them*
- *The empathy part was my favorite because it made me appreciate areas I hadn't covered before and improved my ability to empathize.*
- *Social Innovation Project provided platform for collaborative learning when students communicates effectively with others, shows empathy when interacting with others, Works well in a team, and cultivates and nurtures networks*
- *I think it was the experience I gained in the group task, which brought me a whole new experience. It was a very meaningful session and I think the process of teamwork in group tasks will help me a lot in the future.*

- *It provides a chance for me to collaborate with others that come from different majors.*
- *It allowed me to work with other students from different schools, which was really insightful and fun as we had different ways of thinking, and brought different ideas and skills to the table.*

Psychomotor:

Learners developed new behavioural patterns to adapt and coordinate by working collaboratively with learners from other disciplines. Learners harnessed observing skills by going to the field, communication skills by interviewing the community and immersing in the community real problems/issues. Learners must define and brainstorm ideas and assemble/create/construct prototypes to solve the community problems/issues. Learners coordinate and build low-fidelity prototypes according to the UNSDG selected themes of apps, awareness, policy, and 2D and 3D models.

These are some of the examples of what students in their reflections:

- *how it challenged me in my presentation skills*
- *Working with people from other schools and degrees*
- *doing the project with my group members*
- *It can bring our final product to the reality*
- *treating everyone equally and with respect*
- *The interaction with the community outside of taylors*
- *Improved a lot in my thinking skills and communication skills*
- *Innovating a product using our own idea.*
- *Being innovative & building connections with other people*
- *Getting things done in a short amount of time. And how we as a team work together to solve a problem when making the prototype*
- *Challenging myself to create a product that is useful for my target audience*
- *It's important not to panic, and to manage your time well for this project.*
- *brainstorming with my teammates about the final idea*
- *How to manage time, be attentive and empathetic, communicate with each other*
- *Being self-independent on the work given and having the problem-solving skills*
- *The most valuable lesson from this module was that careful planning is important for any projects, and learned about how to plan the projects more detailed*
- *hands- on experience, not being spoon-fed, everything from planning to Ideation to the final result all up to us and our thinking*
- *The most valuable lesson from this module was that careful planning is important for any projects, and learned about how to plan the projects more detailed*
- *brainstorming with my teammates about the final idea, manage time, Being innovative & building connections with other people, hands- on experience, Working with people from other schools, The interaction with the community outside of taylors, careful planning is important for any projects, and learned about how to plan the projects more detailed, hands- on experience, not being spoon-fed, everything from planning to Ideation to the final result all up to us and our thinking*

Survey

A survey was conducted at the end of the August 2021 semester to identify students' acceptance of the implementation of the Social Innovation Project module at the institutional level. Overall, 306 students answered the survey that was distributed to students using google Forms. The demographics of the respondents are shown in Table 2.

Table 2. Demographic of Respondents (N=306)

Demographic		Percentage (%)	Frequency
Nationality			
	Malaysian	63.1	193
	Non-Malaysian	36.9	113
Age			
	18-19 years	24.5	75
	20-21 years	61.8	189
	22-23 years	10.8	33
	24 years and above	2.9	9
Gender			
	Female	63.7	195
	Male	36.3	111
School			
	Taylor's Business School	32.0	98
	School of Hospitality, Tourism and Events	20.6	63
	School of Computer Science and Engineering	7.8	24
	School of Education	6.5	20
	School of Pharmacy	5.6	17
	School of Biosciences	5.2	16
	School of Food Studies and Gastronomy	4.2	13
	Taylor's Law School	3.9	12
	School of Liberal Arts and Sciences	3.9	12
	School of Media and Communication	3.9	12
	School of Architecture, Building And Design	2.6	8
	The Design School	2.0	6
	School of Medicine	1.0	3
	Taylor's College	0.7	2

Based on the data from the survey (Table 3), students agreed that Social Innovation Project had achieved its module learning outcome 1 (MLO1). The Majority of students said that Social Innovation Project developed their ability to design solutions, conceptualize and present ideas, provide constructive critiques, think critically, and improve students problem-solving skills.

Table 3. Students' Acceptance on Module Learning Outcome 1

Indicators		Agree	Mean (of 6 scales)
MLO1: Propose a comprehensive solution to issues to capitalize on the opportunities presented in contemporary real world setting, that encapsulate social and ethical values.	U4 SIP developed my ability to propose comprehensive solutions to real-world issues	83.00%	4.62
	U4 SIP helped me to conceptualize my ideas	83.00%	4.71
	U4 SIP helped me to present my ideas	86.40%	4.74
	U4 SIP developed my ability to provide constructive critiques to others	84.30%	4.62
	U4 SIP improved my problem-solving skills	85.10%	4.70
	U4 SIP developed my ability to think critically about the subject	86.60%	4.71

Students agreed that Social Innovation Project achieved module learning outcome 2 (MLO2). Table 4 below illustrates this agreement. The Majority of students agreed Social Innovation Project developed their ability to execute a project, transform ideas, and offer the solution and a sense of accomplishment upon completing my assessments.

Table 4. Students' Acceptance on Module Learning Outcome 2

Indicators		Agree	Mean (of 6 scales)
MLO2: Execute a project on social innovation for a multitude of disciplines that benefits users and society	U4 SIP developed my ability to execute a project that benefits users and society	85.10%	4.66
	U4 SIP helped me to transform ideas into prototype	87.90%	4.79
	U4 SIP developed my ability to offer a solution which provides value	87.10%	4.77
	I feel a sense of accomplishment upon completion of my assessments	88.10%	4.88

Students agreed that Social Innovation Project achieved module learning outcome 3 (MLO3). The Majority of students agreed Social Innovation Project developed their ability to stay resilient and adaptable to any disruptions and opportunities that arise. Refer Table 5 below.

Table 5. Students' Acceptance on Module Learning Outcome 3

Indicators		Agree		Mean (of 6 scales)
MLO3: Demonstrate resilience and adaptability in handling disruptions and opportunities through reflective writing	U4 SIP developed my ability to stay resilient and adaptable to any disruptions and opportunities that arise	86.20%		4.71

Based on the data from the survey, students agreed that Social Innovation Project has broken down the barriers among disciplines. Table 6 shows that majority of students agreed that Social Innovation Project developed their ability to interact and practice collaboration with students from other programs, helped students manage conflicts, and students are happy working in their group.

Table 6. Students' Acceptances on How the SIP Enhance Students' Learning

Indicators	Agree	Mean (of 6 scales)
U4 SIP developed my ability to interact with students from different schools/programs	88.40%	4.85
U4 SIP allowed me to practice collaborative	88.10%	4.84
U4 SIP helped me to manage conflicts among group members	84.30%	4.69
I am happy working with my group members in completing group projects.	82.80%	4.69

Social Innovation Project also benefited students in other aspects such as helping students to understand design thinking concepts, understand others, apply theory to practice and synthesize knowledge. In addition, majority of students agreed that the SIP module gave them a deeper insight into the topics and the output from the SIP module help them to progress in their studies. This is illustrated in Table 7.

Table 7. Students' Acceptances on the Benefits of SIP Module

Indicators	Agree	Mean (of 6 scales)
U4 SIP helped me understand design thinking concepts more clearly	81.50%	4.63
U4 SIP developed my ability to empathize with others	89.70%	4.78
U4 SIP helped me to understand the insights into human nature	86.60%	4.70
U4 SIP helped me to identify real problems/issues affecting the society	89.20%	4.81
U4 SIP developed my ability to apply theory to practice	84.10%	4.63
U4 SIP provided the opportunity to practice the skills required in the class	85.10%	4.68
U4 SIP allowed me to synthesize fundamental knowledge and skills	84.50%	4.65
U4 SIP gave me a deeper insight into the topics	84.70%	4.64
I believe the output from this module will help me to progress in my degree journey	82.10%	4.60

Majority of students are satisfied with the implementation of the Social Innovation Project, such as grouping, module briefing, the usage of module site, the using of MIRO and the using of class platforms such as TEAMS and ZOOM. Table 8 also shows that the students are also satisfied with the course contents, such as module synopsis, module information, and assignment.

Table 8. Students' Acceptances on the Implementation of PEP Module

Indicators	Agree	Mean (of 6 scales)
Choosing the class and SDG theme using Google form was easy	87.30%	4.72
The module briefing was well-delivered by all speakers	81.50%	4.44
Forming a group in class was easy	80.00%	4.44
Can access TiMes and retrieve the information/documentation easily	84.90%	4.66
The MIRO platform has helped me to work collaboratively with my group members	75.40%	4.48
Using MIRO, TEAMS/ Zoom and other multiple online platforms simultaneously is positive my attention and learning progress	78.90%	4.45
The use of TEAMS/ ZOOM platforms is practical for this module	81.90%	4.59
The module synopsis accurately reflected the content of the module	84.10%	4.63
Expectations were clearly outlined in the Module Information (MI)	81.30%	4.54
The assignments and lectures usefully complemented each other	78.90%	4.52
The module was organized in a way that helped me understand the underlying design thinking concepts	78.20%	4.51
Social Innovation Project module provided a mixture of explanation and practice	79.30%	4.54
The module course content was effectively organized	78.90%	4.51
Lectures and tutorials contributed to my appreciation and understanding of the subject	79.70%	4.53
Module instructions (including assignments) were clear	75.60%	4.42
Social Innovation Project module was appropriate for the first-year degree student	75.60%	4.43

COMMERCIALIZATION POTENTIAL

In a study, Pellikka et al. (2021) found that the strong relationship between the value of knowledge and the commercialization process is critical since commercialization is the only way for the company to realize the value of the new knowledge-based idea and innovation. Final prototypes of Social Innovation Projects are displayed and shown on numerous platforms, such as Taylor's Social Innovation Project Facebook Page, Taylor's Innovest, and Impact4Change by Me.Reka website to attract actual collaboration with funders and industry partners.

According to Hall (2021), many students had sought to apply their innovations inside their university and, in so doing, found navigating bureaucracy and knowing "whom to talk to" to be the biggest obstacles. Therefore, SIP projects have been supported by a few platforms that allow commercialization, especially with the help from Mere.ka, a social entrepreneurship business entity creating the Impact4change website for students to submit their ideas and prototype. Impact4Change is a collaboration of Me.Reka and Taylor's University provides students with a platform to solve real-world issues and develop 21st-century skills. Impact4Change connects students to industry players and gives access to resources through the Me.reka Makerspace. Taylor's Me.reka also has an in-house team of designers, builders, engineers and technology experts who will help students with diverse projects. Social Innovation Project products that have potential may receive an allocation of grants for the products to be developed and commercialized.

The same study by Hall (2021) also suggested partnered services, technology entrepreneurship, system add-ons and immersion as four strategies to overcome obstacles to make universities more innovative in their practices. Therefore, Taylor's University has implemented the two strategies by providing immersion exposure for the students by participating in Taylor's Innofest. Taylor's InnoFest is an end-of-semester innovation festival that showcases projects completed by undergraduate students at the university. This event aims to promote the university's spirit and culture of creativity and innovation by showcasing student works that spark debate, stimulate ideas, and foster collaboration. Projects with potential for spin-off are also identified during the festival, and these project teams are coached and allowed to pitch to investors.

SUMMARY

More than 3200 first-year degree students across programs and faculties have enrolled and benefited from the SIP module at Taylor's University since August 2020. Students have been able to meet the Module Learning Outcomes and address UN SDG issues to expand the value-based education that encourages empathy, creativity, and innovation in real-world communities. The Social Innovation Project (SIP) has shifted learners' perspectives on the university as more than just a place for academics but also a beneficial ground to launch new initiatives through a journey of invention and innovation. This module is also aligned with the direction set by the Ministry of Education to incorporate High Impact Education Practices which meet the needs of 21st-century teaching and learning.

REFERENCES

Abdullah, S., Alias, N. A., Elias @ Mayah, A., & Jusoh, C. R. (2019) *Buku panduan amalan pendidikan berimpak tinggi (High-Impact Educational Practices-HIEPs) dalam matapelajaran pengajian umum.* Jabatan Pendidikan Tinggi, Wilayah Persekutuan Putrajaya.

Choo, Y. B., Abdullah, T., & Nawi, A. M. (2018). Learning to teach: Patterns of reflective practice in a written journal. *LSP International Journal, 5*(2). Advance online publication. doi:10.11113/lspi.v5n2.80

Cocco, S. (2006). *Student leadership development: The contribution of project-based learning* [Unpublished Master's thesis]. Royal Roads University, Victoria, BC. https://www.collectionscanada.gc.ca/obj/thesescanada/vol2/002/MR17869.PDF?oclc_number=271429340

Gerdes, K. E., & Segal, E. (2011). Importance of empathy for social work practice: Integrating new science. *Social Work, 56*(2), 141–148. doi:10.1093w/56.2.141 PMID:21553577

Gibbs, G. (1988). *Learning by doing: A guide to teaching and learning methods.* Further Education Unit.

Gooch, D., Vasalou, A., & Benton, L. (2015, July). Exploring the use of a gamification platform to support students with dyslexia. In *2015 6th international conference on information, intelligence, systems and applications (IISA)* (pp. 1-6). IEEE. 10.1109/IISA.2015.7388001

Hall, R. (2021). Students as Partners in University Innovation and Entrepreneurship. *Education + Training, 63*(7–8), 1114–1137. doi:10.1108/ET-01-2021-0003

Kementerian Pendidikan Tinggi. (2016). *Buku Garis Panduan Matapelajaran Pengajian Umum (MPU) Edisi Ke-2.* Kementerian Pendidikan Tinggi.

Kirschner, P. A. (2001). Using integrated electronic environments for collaborative teaching/learning. *Learning and Instruction, 10*, 1–9. doi:10.1016/S0959-4752(00)00021-9

Liedtka, J., & Ogilvie, T. (2011). *Designing for Growth: A design thinking tool kit for managers*. Columbia Business Press.

Martin, F., & Bolliger, D. U. (2018). Engagement matters: Student perceptions on the importance of engagement strategies in the online learning environment. *Online Learning, 22*(1), 205–222. doi:10.24059/olj.v22i1.1092

Patnaik, C., & Mortensen, P. (2009). *Wired to care: How companies prosper when they create widespread empathy*. FT Press.

Pellikka, J., Ruuskanen, J., & Suazo de Kontro, P. R. (2021). Fostering commercialization of innovation and student entrepreneurship in innovation ecosystems: The case of the Business Center of North Savo in Finland. *Revista Nacional de Administración, 12*(1), e3556. Advance online publication. doi:10.22458/rna.v12i1.3556

Rolfe, G. (2002). Reflective practice: Where now? *Nurse Education in Practice, 2*(1), 21–29. doi:10.1054/nepr.2002.0047 PMID:19036272

Schrage, M. (1999). *Serious play: How the world's best companies simulate to innovate*. Harvard Business Press.

Stein, D. (1998). *Situated learning in adult education* . ERIC Clearinghouse on Adult, Career, and Vocational Education, Center on Education and Training for Employment, College of Education, the Ohio State University. http://www.edpsycinteractive.org/files/sitadlted.html

Yusoff, A. N. M., & Ali, N. (2018). Kaedah MOOC (Massive Open Online Course) dalam Pengajaran dan Pembelajaran Tamadun Islam dan Tamadun Asia (TITAS), Hubungan Etnik (HE), Kenegaraan dan Pengajian Islam Alaf 21 di Universiti Awam dan Swasta. In *Proceeding of INSIGHT 2018 1st International Conference on Religion, Social Sciences and Technological Education, Universiti Sains Islam Malaysia* (pp. 18-19). Academic Press.

Chapter 12
The Determinants of Potential Volunteering Among Moroccan Students:
An Empirical Analysis

Jabrane Amaghouss
Faculty of Law, Economics, and Social Sciences, Cadi Ayyad University, Morocco

Aomar Ibourk
Faculty of Law, Economics, and Social Sciences, Cadi Ayyad University, Morocco

EXECUTIVE SUMMARY

The aim of this chapter is to measure the potential for volunteering and to analyze and understand the determinants of participation in volunteering. The data comes from a survey of students enrolled at two open-access institutions of the Cadi Ayyad University in Morocco. Using Tobit model, which combines both continuous and discrete variables, the results show a high potential supply of volunteering compared to the supply actually realized and a high potential supply of female students compared to that of male students. The potential volunteering supply comes much more from students from a low socio-economic status as measured by the level of education of the parents. Student members of associations are predisposed to perform voluntary tasks, and this offer increases with seniority in the association. Age is positively correlated with the potential supply of volunteering. The motivational framework can strengthen the potential supply of volunteering.

INTRODUCTION

Volunteering is an unpaid activity or service for the benefit of society other than parents and members of the same household (International Labour Organisation (ILO), 2021). The benefits of volunteering are identified at two complementary levels: at the level of the well-being of society and the level of the well-being of the person himself (Plagnol and Huppert (2010), Stukas et al., (2016)). In relation to

DOI: 10.4018/978-1-6684-6076-4.ch012

societal aspects, volunteering contributes to the increase of social solidarity and the creation of wealth (Stukas et al., 2016)). Participation in voluntary activities could have positive effects on young people themselves. Indeed, volunteering allows the acquisition of a number of skills that can be transferred to the workplace. It strengthens team spirit (Schiff, 1990), raises awareness of responsibility (Andreoni 1990; Degli Antoni 2009), facilitates communication, has a positive impact on earnings (Mantovan et al., 2020), expands the network of the individual (Lin et al. 1998; Musick and Wilson 2003) while increasing the likelihood of their employability (Prouteau and Wolff, 2006) and breaking monotony (Cook and Burchell, 2018).

At the psychological level, being a volunteer helps to protect psychological health through mental simulation (Piliavin and Siegel, 2007; Choi and Boham, 2007) contributes to stress reduction (Kim and Pai 2010), and combats depression (Krause, 1987; Yeung et al., 2018). In addition to that, Fiorillo and Nappo (2020) argue that volunteering can encourage a state of emotional trust. According to these authors, volunteers are seen as altruists by others and gain social recognition.

Although volunteering is practiced by several socio-professional categories, the participation of young people in volunteering activities gives rise to wide debate (Vaillancourt, 1994; ILO, 2011). These two works show that individuals become more and more inclined to volunteer with age.

Compared to the Moroccan text, the country can derive benefits through the involvement of young people in volunteer activities. Two factors will favor this opportunity. First, on the demand side, we are witnessing a spectacular development of the Moroccan associative fabric. Indeed, through its proximity to citizens and its concern to meet the needs of the vulnerable population, the associative world has become an essential component of the economic and social life of the country. Statistical data concerning associations in Morocco are limited. They are neither always published nor regularly updated (CSEFRS, 2017). According to the High Commission for Planning (2011), the number of associations was estimated at almost 45000 in 2007. Recent data suggests that their number is 130000 in 2015 (CSEF, 2017). This rapid expansion is explained by the political openness of the early 1990s and the launch of the National Initiative for Human Development (INDH) in 2005.

The work of the associative fabric is essentially based on the mobilization of volunteers whose number reached in 2007 more than 352000 people. Converted in terms of hours, this represents nearly 96 million hours of work or the equivalent of 56524 full-time jobs[1]. The availability of volunteers, necessary for the associative fabric, constitutes one of the problems of its development. More than half of the associations say they find it difficult to mobilize volunteers or to convince those already involved to continue to work within them.

Then, on the supply side, the expansion of higher education in Morocco has contributed to the increase in student numbers. Recent data from the supervisory ministry affirms that for the academic year 2019/2020, the number of students enrolled in universities reached 913713, of which 788930 are enrolled in open access establishments, i.e. 86.34%.

Although there are no official statistics, the share of young people in the total number of volunteers remains low compared to the potential they have. In other words, a distinction must be made between actual volunteering and potential volunteering. An analysis of the factors that can trigger potential volunteering is necessary.

The objective of this paper is first to measure the potential for volunteering among Moroccan students, then to analyze and understand the determinants of participation in volunteering. The data comes from a survey of students enrolled at two open-access institutions of the Cadi Ayyad University of Marrakech in Morocco: The Faculty of Law, Economics, and Social Sciences (FLESS) and the Faculty of Arts and Humanities (FAH). These two institutions account for almost two-thirds of the university's total enrollment.

The paper is structured as follows: the second section provides a literature review on the main determinants of participation in volunteering activities. The third section describes the methodology followed and the data sources. The fourth section will analyze the results obtained. The fifth concludes.

LITERATURE REVIEW

The objective of this section is, first, to review the definition of the notion of volunteering. Then, we draw up a review of the literature in relation to the determinants of participation in volunteering activities.

Review of The Definition of Volunteering

It is important to make a distinction between volunteer and volunteer. Although the two concepts are similar, however, nuances exist. The common feature between the two concepts is the free acceptance of putting at the service of the other part of these financial, physical, moral, or intellectual assets at the service of the other. The main distinction is compensation. Indeed, the volunteer can ask for a counterpart of the work accomplished. On the other hand, the volunteer acts free of charge and without remuneration.

The first definitions of volunteering date back to the early 1990s. Indeed, Bjarne (1992) points out that volunteering is an unpaid activity provided for the benefit of non-profit institutions. For the Estonian Ministry of the Interior (2006), volunteering is an unpaid voluntary commitment in terms of time, energy, or skills. Volunteers help other people or undertake activities primarily in the public interest and for the benefit of society. Family support activities are not counted as voluntary work. For Statistics Canada (2003), a volunteer is an individual who provides an unpaid service for the benefit of a charity or other non-profit organization. This concerns unpaid aid provided to schools, religious institutions, sports associations, or community associations. The National Center for Social Research and the Institute for Volunteering Research (2007) state that volunteering is any unpaid work done that has positive impacts on a person, group of people (including parents), on the environment. Furthermore, the US Bureau of Labor Statistics (2008) considers volunteers as individuals who have provided unpaid work through or for an organization. More recently, Boucher (2010) considers volunteering as any unpaid activity performed voluntarily by a person for the benefit of others or for the benefit of a cause that does not seek profit.

In its 2011 report, the ILO suggests a synthetic definition of volunteering according to which volunteering is defined as any unpaid activity or service for the benefit of society other than parents and members of the same household (ILO, 2011).

Determinants of Volunteering

The literature review made it possible to offer several theoretical and empirical models on the determinants of volunteering. From a theoretical point of view, Prouteau (2002) made a distinction between microeconomic models and macroeconomic models that explain the involvement of individuals in volunteering behavior. While macroeconomic models focus on economic aggregates that can influence the supply of volunteering, microeconomic models focus on individual behaviors to explain volunteering.

For microeconomic models, Prouteau (2002) proposed a cross-sectional reading of the main determinants of volunteering. Thus, he distinguishes, first, the model of public goods, in which the desire to increase the public good motivates contributors to make charitable donations that only make sense if it increases the supply of the good public (Hillman, 2003; Handy and Mook, 2011), then it deals with models of public consumption motivated by altruism and utility satisfaction by giving (Maki and Snyder 2017). Then, he identified the model of impure altruism which is nothing other than a synthesis of the first two models. The last model is based on the acquisition of new skills (human capital function) and new experiences (signal function) that are useful in the labor market.

In his paper, Carson (1993) emphasizes the role played by social factors such as gender, race, and culture. In this context, Kaplan and Hayes (1993) argue that women have more credibility in volunteer work than men. Vaillancourt's (1994) analysis reveals that Canadian men are less likely to volunteer than women, even controlling for other factors. The author argues that this result likely reflects gender differences in the allocation of time and the organization of non-market activities. The other factors considered by the author also have an impact, the extent of which varies according to sex.

In a study conducted in the United States, Musick et al. (2000) show that white Americans volunteer more than Americans. Their study also showed that black American volunteers are more influenced by church attendance than whites. Additionally, the authors find that socioeconomic differences have a lesser impact on black volunteerism. These results reflect the prominent role that religious beliefs play in the lives of black Americans.

In addition to race, culture, and gender, the literature review looked at another form of capital, namely human and social capital. These two forms of capital are essential factors in triggering volunteering (Bryant et al., 2003). Already the theory of human capital (Becker, 1993) considers age, education, skills, and experience as determinants of employee productivity.

Social capital, on the other hand, refers to the social networks and connections that people establish between them allowing them to access social markets (Denton et al., 2006). According to Janoski et al. (1998), social capital includes past social experiences and marital status. Single people and divorced people have fewer social connections than married people (Bryant et al., 2003). The explanation put forward by these authors is that married people share each other's social networks. Empirically, many studies have confirmed the positive impact of human and social capital on the probability of undertaking volunteer activities (Musick et al., 2000. Miller et al., 2005).

The relational motivations of the person also play a role. Prouteau and Wolff (2006) insist on the person's relational motivations. People agree to volunteer in order to meet other people and make friends which is seen as gratification in themselves. This determinant is part of the social integration theory literature that states that individuals improve psychologically, emotionally, and physically when they see themselves as an integrated and recognized part of society (Fiorillo et al. Nappo, 2020).

Geographical factors are also considered as elements that can explain volunteering behavior. Indeed, studies show that people from rural areas are more willing to get involved in volunteering than people from urban areas (Hughes, 2019). This result can be explained by the fact that people living in rural areas are more "religious" than people living in urban areas. Vaillancourt (1994) has already found similar results. He points out that volunteering is more marked in the Canadian Prairies (the Canadian Prairies are a large region of areas, one of the largest agricultural regions in the world).

Rutherford and Woolvin (2013) find identical results. In their report, they show that rates of formal volunteering are higher in rural Scotland than in urban areas. The importance of volunteering is particularly important in rural areas because of its role in bridging the gaps between services provided and service needs.

While most studies have focused on a single category of volunteering, namely actual and actually done volunteering (either in a formal or informal setting), potential volunteering has received little attention in the theoretical literature. and empirical. By potential volunteering, we mean the theoretical disposition of a person to carry out voluntary work, all other things being equal. The choice of studying potential volunteering is justified when the loss of private earnings and the loss of social earnings are enormous.

Some individuals are willing to invest in voluntary activities but cannot convert this desire into concrete action in the presence of a number of factors. The objective of this paper is to analyze the determinants behind volunteering by making a distinction between actual volunteering and potential volunteering.

METHODOLOGY, MODEL SPECIFICATION, AND DATA

Methodology

To be able to analyze the determinants of potential and effective volunteering, we conducted a survey of students enrolled at Cadi Ayyad University in Marrakech. We opted for two types of analysis: a descriptive analysis and a confirmatory analysis.

Descriptive analysis

The purpose of the descriptive analysis is, first, to know the characteristics of the study sample as well as to give a measure of the two types of volunteering.

Confirmatory analysis

The confirmatory analysis aims to measure the impact of the variables of interest on potential volunteering and actual volunteering (dependent variable). In this analysis, the use of econometric techniques is essential. As reported in the literature review, the level of involvement in volunteering is affected by several explanatory variables (independent variables).

The model is written as follows:

Model Specification

The volunteer supply variable is continuous and can only be observed over a certain defined time interval. The number of hours is between 0 and 18, which challenges the linearity assumption. Therefore, the ordinary least squares method is not relevant for the estimation, (Cadoret, 2004). We are in the case of a censored qualitative variable (the absence cannot be negative) which is estimated using a Tobit method which combines both a continuous part and a discrete part, linked to the point of censorship.

The appropriate model is as follows: y^*_i given a latent variable distributed according to a normal law such that:

$$y_i^* \begin{cases} = \beta_1 + \beta_2 x_{2i} + \ldots + \beta_k x_{ki} + \xi_i = x_i'\beta + \xi_i \\ = E(y_i^*) + \xi_i \end{cases}$$

$$y_i^* \sim N(x_i'\beta, \sigma^2), \text{ and } y_i = \begin{cases} 0 & si \quad y_i^* \leq 0 \\ y_i^* & si \quad y_i^* \succ 0 \end{cases}$$

The normal distribution and the maximum likelihood method are used to estimate the values of the parameters β_i.

Dependent Variables

We retain the definition of volunteering developed by Wilson (2000) according to which volunteering is any activity carried out freely and free of charge for the benefit of a cause, a person, or a group of people. Although volunteering has largely been treated as a distinction between 'formal' and 'informal' volunteering, this article distinguishes between two types of dependent variables: actual volunteering and potential volunteering. Actual volunteering is defined as volunteering actually performed. Potential volunteerism is defined as a person's willingness to engage in volunteer activity. We use the number of volunteer hours per week as a measure of the dependent variable.

Independent Variables

In this paper, we have retained four blocks of variables likely to explain volunteering behavior: individual variables (sex, age, place of residence, discipline of study, enrollment cycle), variables of the family context (father's level of education, mother's level of education, father's profession, mother's profession), variables related to the perception and experience in associative work (association member, perceptions on associations, sector of involvement, duration of associative experience) and variables linked to the source of motivation (culture, credibility of the associative world, the incentive framework, and training).

Given the technique used, each variable is identified through modalities. The interpretation of the results is done in relation to a reference modality. All the variables, modalities as well as the reference modalities are reported in the following table:

Data

The data comes from a 2018 survey of students enrolled in two institutions belonging to Cadi Ayyad University: The Faculty of Law, Economic, and Social Sciences and the Faculty of Arts and Humanities. The total workforce of these two establishments represents almost two thirds of the total workforce enrolled at the Cadi Ayyad University located in Marrakech. The survey is based on the distribution of a questionnaire. We opted for two types of questions: closed questions and open questions. The first category consists of offering the respondent a choice of previously defined answers. The second category aims to let the interviewee answer the question freely.

1897 questionnaires were distributed to students, of which 1698 are enrolled in the bachelor's cycle, and the rest (199 students) are enrolled in the master's cycle. The choice of these percentages reflects the enrollment structure in the university. We used the technique of probability sampling according to which each student has the same chance of being selected. Despite our insistence, some questions remain unanswered. However, the share of missing values remains very low in the constructed database.

Table 1. List of variables, modalities, and reference modalities

Variable blocks	Variables	Terms	Reference modality
Individual factors	Your faculty	Economic Law	Economic law
		Letters and Human Sciences	
	Study level	Bachelor	Bachelor
		Master	
	Registration semester	Semester 2	Semester 2
		Semester 4	
		Semester 6	
		Semester 8	
	Sex	Male	Male
	Age	18-21	18-21
		22-25	
		26 and over	
	Place of residence	Urban	Urban
		Rural	
Family factors	Father's level of education	No	No
		Primary	
		Secondary	
		Superior	
	The education level of the mother	No	No
		Primary	
		Secondary	
		Superior	
	Fathers profession	agric_artisant_commercant	agric_artisant_commercant
		liberal profession	
		civil servant	
		others	
	mother's activity	Nope	inactive
		active	

continues on following page

Table 1. Continued

Variable blocks	Variables	Terms	Reference modality
Perceptions and experience of associative work	Are you a member of an association	Nope	Nope
		Yes	
	What do you think of community work	Not Useful	Not useful
		useful	
	The investment sector	no	no
		development	
		culture	
		Human rights	
		environment	
		culture	
	Duration of integration of the associative world	no	no
		More than 5 years	
		less than 5 years old	
motivations	Non-integration of volunteering into culture	Yes	Yes
		Nope	
	Lack of credibility of the associative world	Yes	Yes
		Nope	
	The lack of an incentive framework	Yes	Yes
		Nope	
	Training shortcomings	Yes	Yes
		Nope	

RESULTS AND DISCUSSION

In the first paragraph, we present the results of the descriptive analysis. The second paragraph will be devoted to the presentation of the analytical results.

Descriptive Statistics

Socioeconomic Variables

The breakdown by gender of our sample reveals near equality between the two sexes. In terms of enrollment, almost three quarters (73%) of students are enrolled in the Faculty of Law, Economics, and Social Sciences. Those enrolled in the Master's cycle represent 10.49% while those enrolled in the Bachelor's cycle represent 89.5%. The age pyramid of respondents shows that the 18-21 age group contains just over 61% of the sample. A third of the interviewees are between 22 and 25 years old. 5% of students are over 25 years old. By area of residence, students from urban areas make up 64.44% of our sample, while those enrolled from rural areas represent **35.56%**.

Table 2. Characteristics of the sample

	Variables	Modality	Workforce	Percentage
Sample characteristics	Sex	Male	961	50.79
		Feminine	931	49.21
		total	1892	100
	Establishment	FSJES	1401	73.85
		FLSH	496	26.15
		total	1897	100
	Level	Bachelor	1698	89.51
		Master	199	10.49
		total	1897	100
	Sector	Economy	700	36.92
		Straight	530	27.95
		letters	666	35.13
		total	1896	100
	Age	18-21 years old	1167	61.65
		22-25 years old	633	33.44
		25 years and over	93	4.91
		total	1893	100
	Place of residence	Urban	1214	64.44
		Rural	670	35.56
		total	1884	100

Compared to family social capital, the survey data suggests that students have different family social capital. By family social capital we mean the level of education of the parents and their professions. Thus, 59.5% of the respondents come from fathers with at most a primary level education (23.55% having no school level and 25.95% have the primary level), 27.6% of the fathers of respondents have secondary level, 22.9% have higher level. Regarding the schooling of the mother, 72.6% of the mothers of the respondents have at most the primary level (49.87% have no school level and 22.73% have primary level). Only 11.1% of students whose mothers have a higher level. These data make it possible to identify two observations: The weakness of the family social capital of students in terms of schooling and inequalities in terms of access to the education system in favor of fathers.

As expected, parents' level of education affects the nature of their occupation. Thus, the majority of students come from fathers who have no profession or who exercise trades requiring little human capital (agriculture, trade, crafts, and some liberal professions). In addition, almost 80% of mothers are housewives. This result is largely explained by the low level of their education.

In regards to membership in social institutions, just under two-thirds of students say they do not belong to social organizations. Only one in five students is a member of an association. Participation in the activities of other social organizations is very low (political party 2%, Club 6.58%, youth center 3.68%, etc.). All in all, we can say that our young students are weakly involved in the activities of social organizations, which reduces their offer of volunteering, given that this type of organization relies on the participation of volunteers.

Table 3. Characteristics of the sample (continued)

Variables		Modality	Father		Mother	
			Workforce	%	Workforce	%
family social capital	Level of education	No	441	23.55	939	49.87
		Primary	486	25.95	428	22.73
		Secondary	517	27.6	307	16.3
		Superior	429	22.9	209	11.1
		total	1873	100	1883	100
	Occupation	No	251	15.33	1449	81.54
		Agriculture	190	11.61	47	2.64
		Craft	125	7.64	49	2.76
		Trader	291	17.78	33	1.86
		Liberal profession	175	10.69	38	2.14
		Public sector employee	350	21.38	99	5.57
		Private sector employee	255	15.58	62	3.49
		total	1637	100	1777	100

Table 4. Characteristics of the sample according to the social institution to which they belong

	Modality	Dad	
		Workforce	%
Member of social institution	No	1161	64.72
	Association	392	21.85
	Political party	38	2.12
	Club	118	6.58
	Youth club	66	3.68
	House of associations	11	0.61
	Dar Al Mouwaten[2]	7	0.39
	Others	1	0.06
	Total	1794	100

Compared to the supply of volunteering, the results suggest that the current supply (actual volunteering) is low although the potential supply is considerable. Therefore, on average, each student currently offers 2.8 hours per week while the average potential offer is 4.92 hours.

The breakdown of current supply (effective volunteering) suggests that 70% of students devote between [0-2h] per week to volunteer work, 26.69% of respondents devote between [2h-10h], 1.36% devote between [10 am- 3 pm], and 1.86% of respondents spend more than 15 hours.

Compared to the field of voluntary activity, the results show that the development sector is of much greater interest to young people. They present almost half of the volunteer activities. The field of culture comes in third place with 16% of activities. Other activities interest young people but with low proportions: human rights, environment, health, and water, with rates of 8.75%, 7.58%, 4.71%, and 4.04% respectively.

Table 5. Volunteer offer

	Intervals	Current offer		Potential offer	
		Workforce	Percentage	Workforce	Percentage
Current offer and potential volunteer offer	**[0h-2h [**	**1055**	**70.05**	**806**	**48.06**
	[2h-10h [	402	26.69	642	38.28
	[10am-3pm [	21	1.39	81	4.83
	More than 3 p.m.	28	1.86	148	8.83
	total	1506	100	1677	100

Table 6. Characteristics of the sample according to the social institution to which they belong

Variables	Terms	Workforce	Percentage
	Education	147	24.75
	Development	145	24.41
	Culture	95	15.99
Areas in which the youth invests	Straight of man	52	8.75
	Water	24	4.04
	Environment	45	7.58
	Health	28	4.71
	Others	58	9.76
	Total	594	100

Regarding the source of motivation, the results show that almost 58% of respondents have no motivation regarding volunteer work. Only 12.22% say they are motivated by the defense of human values, 9.57% are motivated by promoting citizenship, and 8.09% get involved in activities thanks to their relational networks and their group spirit.

Table 7. Characteristics of the sample according to the social institution to which they belong

	Modality	Frequency	
		Effective	Percentage
	None	939	57.96
	Defending human values	198	12.22
	Citizenship	155	9.57
motivations	Relationship and group spirit	131	8.09
	Fighting against poverty	88	5.43
	Integrating the associative world	109	6.73
	Total	1620	100

At the end of these statistics, we identified the profiles of the students according to the two types of voluntary work studied.

- **The profile of the effective volunteer student is as follows:**

Among the individual characteristics, sex plays a limited role in determining volunteering with a slight propensity in favor of the male gender. Concerning the sector, it is revealed as a determining factor insofar as the most voluntary students are those enrolled in the sector of economics and Arab law in comparison with the other sectors; to this is added the residence in a rural environment which favors voluntary work. The other variables have the expected effect, namely age, level of education and level of education of the father and mother.

With regard to the social involvement variables, we see that the house of associations favors voluntary work the most among its members. Next come associations, political parties, youth centers, Dar Al Mouwaten and clubs, while non-adherence to any institution records the lowest rate.

- **The profile of the potential volunteer student is as follows:**

Among the individual characteristics, sex plays a limited role in determining volunteering with a slight propensity in favor of the male sex. Concerning the sector, it appears to be a determining factor insofar as the most voluntary students are those in the sector of Economics, Arabic Studies, and French Law in comparison with other sectors; to this is added the residence in a rural environment which favors voluntary work.

Other variables show a linear effect, such as age, which is positively related to volunteering, while the level of education of the father and mother is negatively related. For, the levels of study "bachelor" and "master" have a similar effect on potential volunteering.

With regard to the social involvement variables, we find that the associations most favor potential volunteering among their members, followed by the clubs; the house of associations and political parties. Then come the non-adherence to any institutions, the youth center and Dar Al Mouwaten.

Confirmatory Analysis

The analysis of the determinants of effective volunteering (model 1) shows that the impact of individual factors such as type of institution, the cycle of study, gender, and place of residence do not have a significant impact, compared to the terms of reference, on the level of potential volunteering. Only age is noted as a variable that can reinforce the level of participation in effective volunteering. Indeed, students enrolled in Semester 6 are more likely to carry out volunteering activities than those enrolled in Semester 2. This result is confirmed by the analysis of the age group: the age group 22-25 is more involved in actual volunteering than the younger age group. Thus, age reflects a certain maturity of the person which makes him more aware of the importance of volunteering.

The results of our estimations suggest that the variables of the family context are of little significance with respect to the determination of the level of effective volunteering. Indeed, only students who come from parents with a secondary level of education are significantly penalized compared to students who come from parents with a primary level of education.

Perceptions about association work and experiences in associations play a significant role in the expansion of volunteering. Although being a member of an association does not have a significant effect on the level of volunteering, positive perceptions of the usefulness of associations reinforce the probability of carrying out volunteering activities. Regarding the sector of intervention, the data from the survey confirm that all fields of action (development, culture, human rights, and the environment) promote the practice of volunteering. The survey data also suggests that, as expected, seniority in associations is a contributing factor to involvement in volunteer activities. In fact, the longer the duration of the association's integration, the greater the impact on the duration of effective volunteering.

Compared to motivational factors, the absence of an incentive framework significantly penalizes participation in effective volunteering activities. Similarly, the lack of training intended to improve the performance of volunteer activities reduces the level of involvement in these activities. In addition, the reasons for participating in effective volunteering activities, the most significant reasons are the defense of human values, the development of relationships, group spirit, and the fight against poverty.

Table 8. Estimation of models

	Variables	Terms	Model 1: Dependent variable: actual volunteering	Model 2: Dependent Variable: Potential Volunteering
Individual factors	Establishments	Arts and Humanities	0.302 (0.646)	6.308*** (0.676)
	Study cycle	Master	-6.616 (5.510)	-6.038 (7.546)
	Study semester	S4	0.00735 (0.578)	-3.639*** (0.636)
		S6	2.328*** (0.667)	2.291*** (0.806)
		S8	7.279 (5.503)	13.91* (7.540)
	Sex		0.296 (0.463)	1.133** (0.499)
	Age	22-25	1.354*** (0.507)	-0.678 (0.553)
		26 and over	1.486 (0.922)	-1.461 (1.107)
	Place of residence	Rural	0.487 (0.480)	0.671 (0.533)
Family background	Father's level of education	Primary	-0.878 (0.628)	0.298 (0.690)
		Secondary	-1.617** (0.672)	-1.871** (0.734)
		Superior	-0.468 (0.756)	-2.330*** (0.856)
	Mother's level of education	Primary	0.821 (0.599)	0.314 (0.643)
		Secondary	1.082 (0.668)	-0.327 (0.759)
		Superior	0.0645 (0.854)	-0.454 (0.959)
	Father's profession	liberal profession	-0.187 (0.827)	-1.043 (0.921)
		Public sector	1.078 (0.689)	-0.769 (0.767)
		Others	0.815 (0.540)	0.508 (0.579)
	Mother's profession	Active	-0.760 (0.621)	-0.541 (0.717)

continues on following page

Table 8. Continued

	Variables	Terms	Model 1: Dependent variable: actual volunteering	Model 2: Dependent Variable: Potential Volunteering
Perceptions and experience of associative work	Member	No	0.143 (0.477)	-2.339*** (0.565)
	usefulness of associative work	Useful	0.991** (0.498)	0.711 (0.558)
	Voluntary sector	Development	6.755*** (0.599)	7.794***(0.671)
		Culture	6.378*** (0.881)	7,338*** (1,015)
		Human rights	7.512*** (1.055)	9.544*** (0.834)
		Environment	6.127*** (1.194)	9.502*** (1.073)
		Culture	6.527*** (1.003)	7.301*** (0.965)
	The duration of integration of an association	More than 5 years	10.52*** (1.251)	11.15*** (1.173)
		Less than 5 years old	7.185*** (1.143)	7.605*** (0.982)
Motivation	Culture	No	-0.0558 (0.473)	0.266 (0.516)
	lack of credibility of the associative world	No	-0.202 (0.848)	-1.707* (0.959)
	Absence of the incentive framework	No	-2.725** (1.319)	-3.567** (1.423)
	Training shortcomings	No	-1.543*** (0.517)	-6.257*** (0.610)
	Involvement	Defending human values	3.133*** (0.687))	-0.262 (0.833)
		Citizenship	2.303*** (0.771)	-0.786 (0.933)
		Developing relationships and group spirit	2.413*** (0.795)	-1.556 (0.969)
		Fighting poverty	2.662*** (0.941)	0.302 (1.124)
		Integrating the associative world	5.207*** (0.815)	2.523** (0.982)
Constant			-16.13*** (1.406)	-10.34*** (1.266)
Comments			1869	1869

The estimation of model 2, in which the dependent variable is the potential for volunteering, made it possible to identify the following observations: compared to the individual factor, students enrolled in the Faculty of Letters and Human Sciences are more willing to provide volunteering activities than those enrolled in the faculty of legal, economic and social sciences, contrary to model 1 in which the type of establishment was not significant. Additionally, enrollment in higher semesters is likely to increase the potential supply of volunteering compared to students enrolled in the second semester. Unlike actual volunteering in which the gender of the student is not significant, female students are more willing to join volunteering activities than male students. Another interesting result is that potential volunteering seems to be lower among students who come from parents with secondary or higher education. Regarding the variables reflecting perceptions of associations, students who are members of associations are more willing to undertake volunteer activities. Regarding the other motivational variables, there are no major differences except that the lack of credibility in the associative world could negatively affect potential volunteering. Thus, the lack of an incentive framework and the lack of training also penalizes potential volunteering.

In the literature, several factors have been identified as determinants of volunteering. Already Payette and Vaillancourt (1986) analyze to what extent individual characteristics such as age, education, marital status, and occupation explain the choice of whether or not to volunteer. Their results suggest that people who have benefited directly or indirectly from volunteering do more than those who have not.

CONCLUSION

The objective of this paper is to analyze the determinants of volunteering by distinguishing between actual volunteering and potential volunteering. The first type of volunteering is measured by the number of hours actually worked per week. The second type of volunteering is measured by the number of hours per week for which students are predisposed to perform. Several results can be drawn from this paper.

The first result concerns the high potential supply of volunteering available to students compared to the supply realized. The second important result concerns the extent of the potential supply of female students compared to that of male students. The third result, the offer of potential volunteering comes much more from students from a low socioeconomic status as measured by the level of education of the parents. The fourth result concerns student members of associations who are predisposed to perform voluntary tasks and that this offer increases with seniority in the association. The fifth result concerns age, which is positively correlated with the potential supply of volunteering. The sixth result is related to the motivational framework that can strengthen the potential supply of volunteering. Indeed, greater credibility of associations, the establishment of an incentive framework, and training appear to be ingredients that can improve the offer of volunteering. This offer can, within the framework of the social and solidarity economy, contribute to the reduction of poverty.

Whatever the motivation for volunteering, it contributes to the socio-economic development of society. Thus, faced with the failure of economic development models, especially in developing countries, volunteering could constitute an alternative for public decision-makers to draw up development strategies based on increasing the rate of participation in volunteering, especially through the attraction of potential volunteers. In this context, the proliferation of associations can also be interpreted as a means of supplementing or even filling in the gaps in public action, especially in the field of services (Rutherford and Woolvin (2013).

In view of these results, we propose a range of actions that could improve the offer of volunteering in Morocco:

- We propose the creation and membership of networks for female volunteers for those who wish, the objective of which is to strengthen inter-woman volunteering.
- Awareness among young people, especially those from privileged backgrounds, of the importance of volunteering not only for themselves but also for society. This can be done through the facilitation of access to information, the creation of platforms for the attraction of volunteers as well as associations to facilitate communication between them. Reinforce associative marketing with students through the organization of volunteering awareness days at the university.
- Establishment of a legal framework for the status of volunteering to value the work of the volunteer and to determine the obligations and rights of each of the parties involved in a volunteering activity. For example, require the party engaging volunteers to purchase insurance to protect volunteers.

- Consideration of volunteer activities as criteria for access to university establishments, especially establishments with regulated access.
- Aware of its importance for young people, some countries require a minimum service of volunteering to obtain a high school or university diploma. For example, more than 93% of federal states in the United States require students to take educational training or complete a set number of hours of community service before graduating. A reconversion of this American experience is very promising for Morocco. Indeed, we propose the creation of "volunteer" modules which will be validated in the form of face-to-face training and the form of an internship in volunteer organizations for the obtaining of diplomas. The new higher education reform that Morocco is in the process of building is an opportunity to include this proposal in the new pedagogical model.

Other general recommendations resulting from this research can be addressed to the public authorities. Stimulate the spirit of volunteering from early childhood through the introduction into school programs of activities that encourage volunteering. Although a number of statistical offices, international organizations and researchers around the world have already developed surveys on volunteer activity, there is a dearth of data relating to volunteering in Morocco. Hence, the establishment of a methodology to guide Morocco in the generation of systematic and comparable data on volunteering.

The proposed actions can only be effective if they are apprehended in an integrated approach. Indeed, the new development model of Morocco that "The special commission on the development model" is in the process of elaborating on constitutes an opportunity for the implementation of these recommendations.

The limitations of this work concern two points. The first point concerns the failure to take into consideration psychological and emotional traits that belong to another disciplinary field that has its own methods (Kolm, 2000). This first limitation leads us to the second limitation that research methodologies have a significant effect on how individuals respond to volunteering surveys (Denton et al., 2006). Indeed, the response of the surveys may depend on the conditions of the survey, especially their psychological states.

In terms of perspective, to derive more from volunteering, actions must reach other categories of the population other than students. Thus, the unemployed, employees in the private sector, and doctors are invited to get involved in voluntary activities. The treatment of issues related to these categories will be the subject of future work.

REFERENCES

Andreoni, J. (1990). Impure altruism and donations to public goods: A theory of warm-glow giving. *Economic Journal (London), 100*(401), 464–477. doi:10.2307/2234133

Becker, G. S. (1993). Nobel lecture: The economic way of looking at behavior. *Journal of Political Economy, 101*(3), 385–409. doi:10.1086/261880

Bjarne, I. (1992). *Frivilligt Arbejde i idrætsforeninger*. DHL/Systime.

Boucher, A. (2010). Les usages politiques des politiques publiques et des enquêtes sociologiques. L'instrumentalisation d'une politique sportive départementale et de son évaluation. *Sciences sociales et sport, 3*, 157-192.

Bryant, W. K., Jeon-Slaughter, H., Kang, H., & Tax, A. (2003). Participation in philanthropic activities: Donating money and time. *Journal of Consumer Policy*, *26*(1), 43–73. doi:10.1023/A:1022626529603

Cadoret, I., Benjamin, C., Martin, F., Herrard, N., & Sandré, T. (2004). Économétrie appliquée: méthodes, applications, corrigés. De Boeck University.

Carson, E. D. (1993). On race, gender, culture, and research on the voluntary sector. *Nonprofit Management & Leadership*, *3*(3), 327–335. doi:10.1002/nml.4130030311

Choi, N. G., & Bohman, T. M. (2007). Predicting the changes in depressive symptomatology in later life: How much do changes in health status, marital and caregiving status, work and volunteering, and health-related behaviors contribute. *Journal of Aging and Health*, *19*(1), 152–177. doi:10.1177/0898264306297602 PMID:17215206

Cook, J., & Burchell, J. (2018). Bridging the gaps in employee volunteering: Why the third sector doesn't always win. *Nonprofit and Voluntary Sector Quarterly*, *47*(1), 165–184. doi:10.1177/0899764017734649

CSEFRS. (2017). Rapport sur l'éducation non formelle. Author.

Day, K. M., & Devlin, R. A. (1996). Volunteerism and crowding out: Canadian econometric evidence. *The Canadian Journal of Economics. Revue Canadienne d'Economique*, *29*(1), 37–53. doi:10.2307/136150

Degli Antoni, G. (2009). Intrinsic vs. extrinsic motivations to volunteer and social capital formation. *Kyklos*, *62*(3), 359–370. doi:10.1111/j.1467-6435.2009.00440.x

Denton, C. A., Fletcher, J. M., Anthony, J. L., & Francis, D. J. (2006). An evaluation of intensive intervention for students with persistent reading difficulties. *Journal of Learning Disabilities*, *39*(5), 447–466. doi:10.1177/00222194060390050601 PMID:17004676

Estonian Ministry of the Interior. (2006). *Civic initiative action plan 2007-2010/Development plan of voluntary action 2007 - 2010*. Author.

Fiorillo, D., & Nappo, N. (2020). Volunteering and self-perceived individual health: Cross-country evidence from nine European countries. *International Journal of Social Economics*.

Gérard-Varet, L. A., Kolm, S. C., & Mercier Ythier, J. (2000). *The Economics of Reciprocity, Giving and Altruism*. Palgrave Macmillan. doi:10.1007/978-1-349-62745-5

Handy, F., & Mook, L. (2011). Volunteering and volunteers: Benefit-cost analyses. *Research on Social Work Practice*, *21*(4), 412–420. doi:10.1177/1049731510386625

High Commission for Plan. (2007). *Summary Report National Survey of Non-Profit Institutions*. ISBL.

High Commission for Planning. (2011). Enquête Nationale sur les jeunes 2011. Author.

Hillman, A. L. (2003). *Public finance and public policy: responsibilities and limitations of government*. Cambridge University Press.

Hughes, P. (2019). The Churches' Role in Volunteering in Urban and Rural Contexts in Australia. *Rural Theology*, *17*(1), 18–29. doi:10.1080/14704994.2019.1585111

International Labour Office. (2011). *Global employment trends 2011: The challenge of a jobs recovery*. International Labour Office.

International Labour Organisation. (2021). *Volunteer work measurement guide*. ILO Department of Statistics.

Janoski, T. (1998). *Citizenship and civil society: A framework of rights and obligations in liberal, traditional, and social democratic regimes*. Cambridge University Press. doi:10.1017/CBO9781139174787

Kaplan, A. E., & Hayes, M. J. (1993). What we know about women as donors. *New Directions for Philanthropic Fundraising*, *1993*(2), 5–20. doi:10.1002/pf.41219930203

Kim, J., & Pai, M. (2010). Volunteering and trajectories of depression. *Journal of Aging and Health*, *22*(1), 84–105. doi:10.1177/0898264309351310 PMID:19920207

Kim, J., & Pai, M. (2010). Volunteering and Trajectories of Depression. *Journal of Aging and Health*, *22*(1), 84–105. doi:10.1177/0898264309351310 PMID:19920207

Kolm, S. C. (2000). Introduction: the economics of reciprocity, giving and altruism. In The economics of reciprocity, giving and altruism (pp. 1-44). Palgrave Macmillan. doi:10.1007/978-1-349-62745-5_1

Krause, N. (1987). Life stress, social support, and self-esteem in an elderly population. *Psychology and Aging*, *2*(4), 349–356. doi:10.1037/0882-7974.2.4.349 PMID:3268227

Lin, Fu, & Hsung. (1998). Position Generator: A Measurement for Social Capital. In *Social Networks and Social Capital*. Duke University.

Maki, A., & Snyder, M. (2017). Investigating similarities and differences between volunteer behaviors: Development of a volunteer interest typology. *Nonprofit and Voluntary Sector Quarterly*, *46*(1), 5–28. doi:10.1177/0899764015619703

Mantovan, N., Wilson, J., & Sauer, R. M. (2020). The economic benefits of volunteering and social class. *Social Science Research*, *85*, 102368. doi:10.1016/j.ssresearch.2019.102368 PMID:31789200

Miller, K. D., Schleien, S. J., Brooke, P., Frisoli, A. M., & Brooks, W. T. (2005). Community for all: The therapeutic recreation practitioner's role in inclusive volunteering. *Therapeutic Recreation Journal*, *39*(1), 18–31.

Musick, M. A., & Wilson, J. (2003). Volunteering and depression: The role of psychological and social resources in different age groups. *Social Science & Medicine*, *56*(2), 259–269. doi:10.1016/S0277-9536(02)00025-4 PMID:12473312

Musick, M. A., Wilson, J., & Bynum, W. B. Jr. (2000). Race and formal volunteering: The differential effects of class and religion. *Social Forces*, *78*(4), 1539–1570. doi:10.2307/3006184

National Centre for Social Research and the Institute for Volunteering Research. (2007). *Helping out: A national survey of volunteering and charitable giving*. Prepared for the UK Cabinet Office.

Périer, F. (2005). *Study on volunteering and volunteering in Morocco*. UNDP Rabat.

Piliavin, J. A., & Siegl, E. (2007). Health benefits of volunteering in the Wisconsin longitudinal study. *Journal of Health and Social Behavior*, *48*(4), 450–464. doi:10.1177/002214650704800408 PMID:18198690

Plagnol, A. C., & Huppert, F. A. (2010). Happy to help? Exploring the factors associated with variations in rates of volunteering across Europe. *Social Indicators Research*, *97*(2), 157–176. doi:10.100711205-009-9494-x

Prouteau, L. (2002). Le bénévolat sous le regard des économistes. *Revue Française des Affaires Sociales*, (4), 117–134.

Prouteau, L., & Wolff, F. C. (2006). Does volunteer work pay off in the labor market? *Journal of Socio-Economics*, *35*(6), 992–1013.

Rutherford, A., & Woolvin, M. (2013). *Volunteering and public service reform in rural Scotland*. SRUC Rural Policy Centre.

Schiff, J. (1990). *Charitable Giving and Government Policy. An Economic Analysis*. Greenwood Press.

Statistics Canada. (2003). *Cornerstones of Community: Highlights from the National Survey of Nonprofit and Voluntary Organizations, 2003*. Author.

Stukas, A. A., Hoye, R., Nicholson, M., Brown, K. M., & Aisbett, L. (2016). Motivations to volunteer and their associations with volunteers' well-being. *Nonprofit and Voluntary Sector Quarterly*, *45*(1), 112–132.

Tousignant, J. (2001). *Gifts of time, gifts of money: An econometric analysis of the determinants of Quebec behavior in 1997* [Unpublished Master dissertation]. Université de Montréal, Montréal, Canada.

UNDP. (2005). Human Development Report 2005: International cooperation at a crossroads: Aid, trade and security in an unequal world. UNDP.

US Bureau of Labor Statistics. (2008). *May 2008 national industry-specific occupational employment and wage estimates*. https://www.bls.gov/oes/current/oessrci.htm

Vaillancourt, F. (1994). To volunteer or not: Canada, 1987. *The Canadian Journal of Economics. Revue Canadienne d'Economique*, *27*(4), 813–826.

Vaillancourt, F., & Payette, M. (1986). The supply of volunteer work: The case of Canada. *Journal of Voluntary Action Research*, *15*(4), 45–56.

Wilson, J. (2000). Volunteering. *Annual Review of Sociology*, *26*, 215–240.

Yeung, J. W., Zhang, Z., & Kim, T. Y. (2018). Volunteering and health benefits in general adults: Cumulative effects and forms. *BMC Public Health*, *18*(1), 1–8.

ENDNOTES

[1] KINGDOM OF MOROCCO HIGH COMMISSIONER FOR PLANNING *Summary Report* Survey National with Non-Profit Institutions (ISBL) (Fiscal year 2007)

[2] A local social institution to meet the needs of the population

Chapter 13
Mathematics Preservice Teachers' Responsiveness in Microteaching Using 21st Century Skills

Teoh Sian Hoon
Universiti Teknologi MARA, Malaysia

Priyadarshini Muthukrishnan
https://orcid.org/0000-0003-1545-0963
HELP University, Malaysia

Geetha Subramaniam
SEGi University, Malaysia

Nor Azah Mohd Rathi
Universiti Teknologi MARA, Malaysia

Nurshamshida Md Shamsudin
https://orcid.org/0000-0002-3940-4040
Universiti Teknologi MARA, Malaysia

Koo Ah Choo
https://orcid.org/0000-0002-1706-1796
Multimedia University, Malaysia

EXECUTIVE SUMMARY

The development of 21st century abilities necessitates satisfying students' needs. Preservice teachers may find it difficult to meet the criteria. Responsive teaching needs to take precedence to effectively meet student needs. As a result, it is essential to consider how preservice teachers view this issue. This chapter first sets to highlight some of the issues preservice teachers face during microteaching in a mathematics classroom. Next, it looks at possible ways to promote responsiveness by using 21st century skills. It further discusses some solutions, suggestions, and recommendations based on the highlighted issues. Specifically, this chapter aims to identify ways for preservice teachers to contribute to teaching mathematics in a more creative way based on their responsiveness in microteaching. Finally, input is provided to educators on how to meet the output of responsive teaching by applying classroom microteaching strategies.

DOI: 10.4018/978-1-6684-6076-4.ch013

INTRODUCTION

Responsiveness in teaching is a skill that should be made more common for preservice teachers (PSTs). Responsive teaching can be defined as deliberate instruction which prioritises the needs of their students (Burns & Botzakis, 2016). Responsive teaching centralises students' thinking / ideas, elicits and notices students' ideas, listens to their ideas, and uses those ideas to inform adjustment to teachings and even to the curriculum (Gouvea & Appleby, 2022). The instructional goal of responsive teaching is to get the students immersed in the material or content which is being taught. The science, technology, engineering, and mathematics (STEM) education in the twenty-first-century era has necessitated a great deal of feedbacks and responsiveness from preservice teachers. STEM education serves as the foundation for science and technological advancement.

Classroom discussions are commonly engaged in mathematical facts or information only. However, responsive teaching has the potential of engaging discussions to achieve higher levels of intellectuality for both teachers and students such as mathematical reasoning, asking or probing questions, providing justifications, and revoicing students' thinking. Responsive teaching is applicable in mathematics classrooms since it simply means, making students think in the foreground of STEM learning (Gouvea & Appleby, 2022), and making it more common in STEM classes.

Preparing PSTs for microteaching that helps them to gain active and responsive teaching experience, ought to be all-rounded, considering not just the thinking aspect, but also the supportive environment (namely the classroom) for optimum learning. Hence, when preparing lesson plans, PSTs should consider the whole aspect of learning support for students which includes contents, curriculum, pedagogy, environment, and infrastructure.

Objectives of the Chapter

The current chapter focuses mainly on the discussions of mathematics teaching amongst PSTs. The main objective of this chapter is to discuss some key features of responsive teaching by employing thematic analysis in the context of microteaching in mathematics classroom. The chapter also highlights some of the gaps in responsive teaching among preservice teachers in a case study during microteaching in a mathematics classroom. Next, it looks at possible ways to promote responsiveness by using 21st century skills. It further discusses some solutions, suggestions, and recommendations.

RESPONSIVE TEACHING IN TWENTY-FIRST-CENTURY MATHEMATICS EDUCATION

There is a growing demand to strengthen teacher training programmes to adapt in embracing the changing scenario of twenty-first-century education. In this regard, skill development in teacher preparation is a cornerstone for overcoming the current educational challenges (Alahmad et al., 2021; O'Sullivan & Dallas, 2010). Responsive teaching should be made more common in STEM education (Gouvea & Appleby, 2022) in the 21st century education.

The report "21st Century Knowledge and Skills in educator preparation" by Grenhill (2010) calls for educators to incorporate the four Cs of the 21st Century skills into their teaching and learning processes. The 4Cs of the 21st century skills are critical thinking and problem solving, communication, collaboration and creativity, and innovation. These skills are the requirements for creating responsive and active classrooms. Alongside this, the National Council of Teachers of Mathematics (NCTM) (2000) recommends five mathematical process standards for applying mathematical knowledge: problem-solving, reasoning and proof, communication, connections, and representation. A comparison of NCTM process standards and 21st century 4Cs reveals concordance and agreements in the skills that lay a foundation for preparing teacher trainees for 21st century classrooms.

Primarily, mathematics teaching should focus on incorporating critical thinking, problem-solving, and reasoning skills, which involves investigating mathematical conjecture, developing and evaluating mathematical arguments and proofs. Besides, collaboration skills in the 21st century skills resonate with the NCTM process standards "communication" which recommends the use of concise mathematical language for effective communication, presenting mathematical ideas, and communicating coherently with peers, students, and others. These collaboration skills represent the ability to build relationships to work as a team while the NCTM process standards "connections" represent the ability to relate and understand the interconnections within mathematical ideas, apply mathematics outside the context, and able to build concepts and ideas.

Creativity in the 21st century skills is similar in its aspects to the process standard "representation" which involves creating models and representations of mathematical ideas, interpreting physical, social, and mathematical phenomena, and applying mathematical approaches to solving problems. Therefore, it is crucial that mathematics PSTs develop the 4Cs and they are professionally competent to utilise those skills in teaching mathematics. Moreover, this could be achieved only if PSTs receive training in 4Cs during their teacher preparation programmes which subsequently encourage them to employ 21st century skills while designing and delivering their lessons. Furthermore, mathematics teaching skills necessitate the ability to represent mathematical terms and concepts in simpler visual experiences, provide mathematical reasons and procedures, and relate with real-life examples. Besides, teachers should have a grasp of their students' understanding and the causes of mathematical errors to provide remedial lessons.

However, there are concerns about the lack of mathematical teaching skills among PSTs such as problem posing, lack of mathematical content knowledge, mathematical literacy and innovative pedagogical practices (Crespo, 2003; Desfitri, 2018, Jarrah, 2020). Iksan et al. (2014) whom supported by Murtafiah and Lukitasari (2019) added that lack of self-confidence and weak grasp in mathematics content eventually were the main concerns among the PSTs.

These challenges could be overcome if teacher educators explicitly utilise the model 21st century teaching approaches in the preparation of teacher trainees. Furthermore, PSTs' earlier learning experience may impact their disposition, beliefs, and practices toward incorporating 21st century skills in teaching. One of the pressing challenges in mathematics teaching is unpacking the complexities of mathematical knowledge and delivering it in a responsive manner. In this regard, it demands PSTs to develop their professional competencies in conceptual knowledge, procedural fluency, mathematical communication, pedagogical knowledge, and digital skills. Besides, PSTs need to understand the difference between knowing and teaching mathematics.

Knowing mathematics represents sound mathematical knowledge and skills in applying, verifying, and confirming mathematical problems, and enabling a person to claim knowledge. Teaching mathematics requires deploying 21st century skills, embracing appropriate instructional tactics and pedagogical approaches to unfold abstract and complex mathematical knowledge into a simpler form that enables learners to construct their knowledge.

In summary, the responsiveness of PSTs in adapting to 21st century challenges and building their professional competencies is crucial.

RESPONSIVE TEACHING, STEM EDUCATION AND MICROTEACHING

STEM Education Challenge

Recently, the Ministry of Science, Technology and Innovation (MOSTI) in Malaysia launched MOSTI's five technology roadmaps (MOSTI, 2022) which are in alignment with the 10-10 Malaysian Science, Technology, Innovation and Economy (MySTIE) Framework by the Academy of Sciences Malaysia (2020).

The five roadmaps are:

a. Electricity and Electronics Roadmap: Technology Development 2021-2030
b. National Blockchain Technology Roadmap 2021-2025
c. Artificial Intelligence Roadmap 2021-2025
d. National Advanced Materials Roadmap 2021-2030
e. National Robotics Roadmap 2021-2030.

These roadmaps outline plans for innovation and technology developments in the country. The quality of delivery of STEM education must be aligned with nurturing more talents to support technology developments. Nevertheless, there seems to be a declining interest in STEM education, which is a cause for concern in Malaysia (Mohtar et al., 2019; Ali et al., 2021). There is also a shortage of skilled employees in STEM stream due to the lack of abilities to cope with the workforce demands (Ali et al., 2021). According to a recent survey by the Department of Statistics, one of the most alarming findings revealed that many SPM school leavers reported their disinterest in pursuing STEM studies but were more interested to become YouTubers or social-media influencers (Mutalib, 2022). Though these striking findings was reported in 2019, the findings predicted a similar percentage to be expected for 2020 and 2021 (Mutalib, 2022). Therefore, it is important to attend to the growing concerns on the decline of mathematical and science pursuits among school leavers. Therefore, PSTs must be aware of their obligations in addressing the workforce demands and the learning experiences of students. In this context, they need to be trained on how to act responsively to develop scientific attitude and mathematic thinking among students.

Teaching effectiveness necessitates a high level of creativity to attract interest and improve learning. The types of creativity are various, from creative arts and craft creation to the fostering of creative solutions or products as needed (Rahimi & Shute, 2021). Teachers' creativity can be sourced from teaching and learning theories. Teachers should be well-versed in teaching and learning theories prior to any educational advancement (Plucker et al., 2004). A rigid way of teaching can be a hindrance to creativity. Rahimi and Shute (2021) proposed numerous strategies and techniques such as analogy making, brainstorming, the SCAMPER method, etc. for enhancing student's creativity PSTs' practicum requires feedback from many perspectives on knowledge content and pedagogical approach, including their creative abilities in teaching. Viewing through the lens of learning theories such as cognitivism and constructivism, some sound pedagogical approaches can be explored, in this case, the responsive teaching approach.

Responsive Practises in Microteaching

Recent research on PSTs' microteaching practices, shows preservice teachers gained confidence under a new practice of the teaching model via online learning (Nasar & Kaleka, 2020). Nonetheless, the COVID-19 barriers have prompted all instructors to put forth a significant amount of effort and innovation in utilising any available resources that will help to contribute to the education field. Despite research that investigated PTSs' confidence in teaching (Grant & Ferguson, 2021), questions about how they maintain that confidence remain unresolved. Flexibility is necessary, especially given the current state of educational transmission. For example, the abrupt shift in teaching platforms from physical to online has created numerous hurdles among teachers. Teachers' ingenuity in adjusting their teaching, including a concentration on responsive teaching, is critical to addressing all unforeseen changes. Kartal and Cinar (2022) specifically emphasised the need of observing PTSs' technology pedagogical content mastery in mathematics education. While using technology to teach mathematics is crucial, it also relies on teachers' creativity in demonstrating responses to any creative instruction. In today's teaching, teachers' responsibility in carrying out their duties is seen as a crucial influence. They need to think about what they are teaching (Aghakhani, 2022). As a result, it is critical to look at PSTs' abilities to be responsible educators by proving their ability to apply responsive practices in microteaching.

Microteaching vs. Teaching in Schools

As PSTs are new to the field of education, they face numerous hurdles which call for more directions. Even if they are exposed to learning philosophy and theories, the transfer of knowledge to practice such as applying different methods of teaching is challenging. Hence, PSTs' experiences as teachers should be monitored. More practical experience can be done through the sharing of ideas in microteaching and enriching ideas and experiences through responsive teaching in the real classroom environments.

Most mathematical issues are solved using rule-based reasoning procedures. Teachers are encouraged to use effective teaching strategies to raise students' cognitive levels to build formal operational logic and creativity (Park et al., 2006)). As a result, developing cognitive skills in logical reasoning is viewed as critical among university students. In addition, the 21st century skills framework emphasises logical reasoning as a vital talent for the development of critical thinking. Even though formalised procedures with mathematical logic are used in logical reasoning, the use of social elements may improve practice. As a result, their ability to use logical reasoning in the workplace needs to be strengthened. Preservice mathematics teachers are exploring this environment. It may provide a good environment for them to develop their teaching skills. Nevertheless, they are expected to be doing more than learning the teaching skills when they are in the field of teaching.

Social Constructivism and Responsive Teaching

PSTs have sound knowledge on the pedagogical theories and its implications in teaching. such as the use of behaviourism, cognitivism, and constructivism. These major theories are presented in Figure 1. As various ideas are regarded for unique needs and requirements, the presentation of the sequence of theories should not be viewed separately. When observing shifting behaviour among students in a classroom, the practices of behaviourism are focused. Cognitivism, on the other hand, is thought to enable learners to connect to any new knowledge with the existing knowledge. This is because it assesses the learners' cognitive activities, and it may help them improve long-term memory. PSTs are also introduced to constructivism, which focuses on ways to create opportunities for students to discover, explore, and apply ideas that will help them learn more effectively.

Responsive teaching, according to Burns and Botzakis (2016), is deliberate instruction which prioritises the needs of the students. The aim of this instructional mode is to get the students immersed in the material which is being taught. Therefore, teachers must be adaptable and able to engage students in providing them with more possibilities. As an alternative, Au (1998) argues that constructivism should be used to organise peer work groups in a responsive manner. Microteaching takes place in a university classroom in front of their classmates and with their friends who are posing as students, they are not actually teaching students in a real classroom setting. It may be difficult for PSTs to conduct microteaching while focusing on responsive teaching. As a result, they need to comprehend the influence of constructivism on education in delivering responsive instruction.

Figure 1 illustrates how constructivism plays a role in responsive teaching based on the understanding of behaviourism and cognitivism. In a typical university course on pedagogical methods or methods of teaching mathematics, PSTs conduct microteaching based on a prepared lesson plan. The lesson plan structures the content of the lesson and provides a strategy for a teaching scenario. PSTs microteaching demonstrates knowledge, skills and attitudes that are expected to be transmitted to the targeted individuals (acting students) which places emphasis on the transfer of learning to real settings at schools. Microteaching is viewed as a recursive process of assimilation and accommodation of learning and teaching experiences, whereby teaching skill development is interpreted by assigning it to existing internal representations or schema (Wagoner, 2013).

The method in the written work may also highlight the practicality of behaviorism by focusing on some feedbacks on the student's answers. It may be difficult for the PSTs to present constructivism in their lesson plan since social constructivism involves entities of social factors such as immediate response according to students' feedbacks and reaction. In social constructivism, promoting 21st century skills are highly dependent on PSTs' efforts. They need to focus on providing students with opportunities to discover, explore and apply ideas that will satisfy learning objectives. On the other hand, the target students must be active in building understanding to make sense of the world. The understanding that is based on knowledge, must necessarily be grounded in the social values, standards, societies, language, and culture by which the learner acquires an understanding of the world. It is also to be developed socially in the classroom via open communication between instructor and student and by peer interactions in common exploration activities.

AN EXPLORATORY APPROACH IN UNDERSTANDING THE RESPONSIVENESS IN MATHEMATICS MICROTEACHING

Microteaching is essentially a training platform for preparing PSTs to adapt to the real classroom settings. Hence, it is important to observe how PSTs act responsively during microteaching. Microteaching a mathematics lesson is challenging for PSTs as illustrated in the above figure. In the context of microteaching, it is imperative that PSTs actively interact with the learning environment in constructing their knowledge, skills and attitudes towards a responsive mathematics teaching. This study is novel, since there is a dearth of study related to responsiveness in microteaching. In addition, this study seeks to find connections between responsive teaching and microteaching, drawing on the act of responsive-

Figure 1. Constructivism in Micro-Teaching

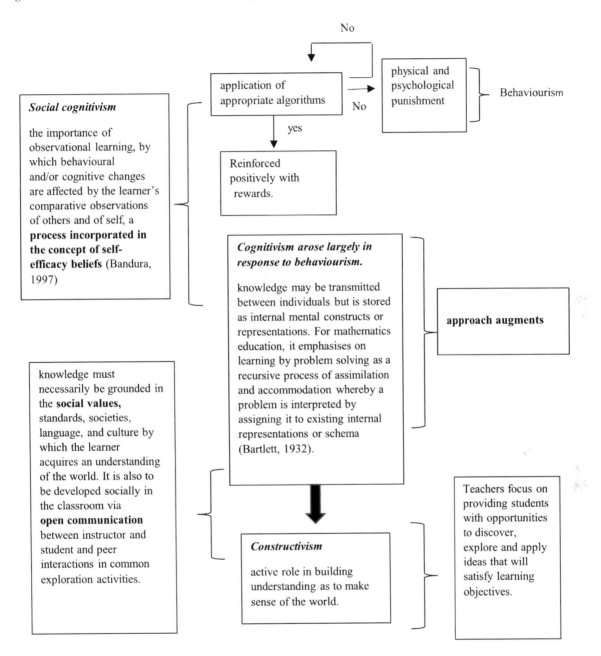

ness exhibited by PSTs while preparing lesson plans for microteaching and demonstrating microteaching. Therefore, this study employed an exploratory case-study approach that could be considered as a preliminary attempt in exploring the attributes of responsiveness in microteaching. The rationale for considering an exploratory case study design is because the study was set out to explore the experiences of PSTs in microteaching and the data collected served as a point of interest in gaining an understanding of the attributes that underpin responsive teaching. In addition, this case study is a prelude in drawing a framework for responsive microteaching (Yin, 1994). The authors caution the reader that this chapter is a preliminary attempt to comprehend responsiveness in microteaching and that the research data utilised for analysis implicitly demonstrates the underlying acts of responsiveness in microteaching.

In the current study, a total of thirty-four Mathematics PSTs studying in an undergraduate teacher training programme from a public university in Malaysia were involved. Each PST engaged in a 20-minute microteaching session as part of their training in a course on Mathematics Teaching. The aim of microteaching sessions was two folds: to enhance mathematics teaching skills and to understand responsive micro-teaching. In order to elicit responsiveness in PSTs, the instructor provided an active learning environment through constructive feedback and discussions followed by allowing PSTs to relook at their lesson planning and delivery for improvements. The instructor provided both, individual and collective feedback to help PSTs to rewrite lesson plans. Therefore, PSTs completed two versions of lesson plans, one before and one after revision. In addition, they were permitted to request guidance from the teacher at least once throughout the 20-minute session. The data utilised for the study were the lesson plans, reflection notes of PSTs, and observation notes by the course instructor.

The microteaching sessions were assessed using a rubric that encompasses delivery of the mathematics curriculum, content, inquiry, humanities, and language, the PSTs took turns participating in microteaching. After the micro-teaching session, the PSTs submitted one page of reflective writing about their experiences. The reflections as well as the initial and the revised lesson plans were the first-hand evidence to understand the responsiveness in micro-teaching. The responses were analysed using thematic analysis to identify the emerging themes on responsive microteaching. The themes provide a guide on ways for PSTs to engage in responsive teaching.

Responsive Teaching in Microteaching

Based on the PSTs' reflections of their microteaching experiences, it was found that they had put a lot of effort into listening closely to their "students" (acting school students') ideas and questions. Overall, they were pleased with their performance and proud of their versatility in assisting students' comprehension. They were trying to adapt the classroom activities within their lessons while working towards learning objectives as identified before the teaching. The reflection has brought out their practice of responsive teaching as an instructional approach centred on listening closely to students' ideas. Their ability to do so was also due to their consistent effort in lesson plan preparation which contributed significantly to microteaching. Jaber et al. (2019) also shared that responsive teaching, which focuses on students' centred ideas required teachers' planning. Thus, responsive teaching in a mathematics classroom comes from a well-planned lesson. Hence, this case study provides a coherent situation of classroom microteaching in response to responsive teaching.

Inquiry-based Learning for Responsive Teaching

Analysis of the PSTs' reflection journals revealed that they used a systematic approach in inquiry-based instructions to engage students. They began the class with a set of pre-determined questions to tap students' motivation and engagement. However, they failed to explicitly display their questioning skills during the development of conceptual knowledge and procedural skills in teaching mathematics. Most of their questioning was at the beginning or at the closure of the lesson, whereas instructions during the mathematical conceptual development were predominantly delivered as teacher-led instructions. Given the promising impacts and widespread recognition of the use of inquiry-based learning in mathematics teaching, the majority of the PSTs considered having inquiry-based instructions in their lesson plans. However, it remains challenging for them to deliver inquiry-based instructions as they faced several constraints in constructing questions that stimulate rigorous mathematical thinking and questions that integrate mathematical concepts and real-world applications of the concepts. Further, PSTs admitted that rigorous questioning skills are crucial for mathematics inquiry.

Moreover, a few PSTs acknowledged that their lack of conceptual and in-depth grasp of mathematical conceptual knowledge were significant barriers in setting up an inquiry-based instruction. While the primary function of inquiry is to seek an answer to the question, the nature of questions varies in its form. Questions could be open or closed-ended; the locus of control is either teacher-centred or student-centred; and the magnitude could be simple or full (Richardson & Liang, 2008). Analysis of the students' questioning skills revealed that most questions posed were fundamental, simple, closed, and teacher centred.

In practice, responsive teaching is a process where firstly teachers attempt to recognise and listen to students' thinking, stimulate ideas, followed by checking for misconceptions, and finally use those misconceptions and ideas to adjust to the trajectory of teaching (Robertson et al., 2016). There were a few opportunities for students to engage in divergent and creative thinking. This could be attributed to one of the limitations of microteaching sessions, which is restricted to 10-20 minutes per session, which might be a concern among PSTs in demonstrating in-depth inquiry-based instructions. Moreover, conducting microteaching in a simulated classroom or peer observation setting limits the possibilities of teacher-student interactions, therefore directing PSTs to deliver teacher-centred structured instructions while claiming it to be inquiry-based instruction.

Inquiry is the process of finding answers to questions through exploration, observation, and experimentation (Richardson and Liang,2008). In addition, the notion of inquiry is amorphous and does not advocate a prescriptive approach to instructions, and it is also intangible (Wu & Krajcik, 2006). Consequently, inquiry-based instruction lacks a predetermined systematic method. Similarly, in a responsive teaching classroom, teachers may face a key dilemma in efforts to be responsive to students' contributions. Thus, teachers must be very knowledgeable to make the connections with students' discussions to draw meaningful interpretations and conclusions. Thus, teachers should be aware of handling students' unstructured and independent thoughts that are categorised as divergent thinking (Guilford, 1950).

Mathematics Communication for Responsive Teaching

In Mathematics teaching, PSTs are expected to communicate the mathematics content precisely in microteaching presentations. The proficiency of PSTs' in using accurate and precise mathematical language could potentially reduce misconceptions in mathematics classrooms, subsequently resulting in reducing the occurrence of mathematical errors in students' mathematical computations (Hilt et al., 2008).

According to the current case study, a few PSTs faced challenges in precisely communicating mathematical languages. Specifically, the majority of PSTs had made deliberate attempts to explain mathematical symbols, terms, operations, labelling units, measurements, processes, and steps in calculations, using appropriate formula and calculations. However, a few of them acknowledged that they faced challenges in demonstrating precise mathematical language in communication. A few examples from their reflections are: *"too fast in instructions"*, *"However, there are some parts that I need to improvise in the future such as giving more detail explanation during the demonstration"*, *"better demonstration, explain more detail and focus more on student-centred teaching style"*, *"Wrong term used when teaching (Instead of use identify/write, I use the word "guess" which is totally a wrong term for existing formula)", "What I can improve here is I can adjust my language in order to make the teaching clear".*

The NCTM (2000) recommends that teachers need to focus their mathematics instructions in achieving five process standards: mathematical communication, mathematical reasoning, mathematical problem solving, mathematical connections, and mathematical representations. Furthermore, to achieve the process standards, it is crucial that teachers communicate precisely (Smith & Cotton, 1980). Additionally, precision in mathematics teaching is a relatively new concept that applies to communication, computation and measurements (Cheng, 2017). Aleksandrov (1956) asserted the importance of precision in mathematics classrooms since it is one of mathematics' unique attributes. In a similar notion, Fitzsimmons and Thompson (2022) pointed out that imprecision can result in mathematical misconceptions and misunderstandings in students.

This study calls for teacher educators to improve PSTs' precision in mathematics communication. This could be achieved by allowing PSTs to observe classes of experienced teachers (Cheng, 2017). Alternatively, a guided practice that involves collaborative efforts of teacher educators and expert teachers in observing the microteaching sessions could be beneficial. Furthermore, recorded video sessions of expert teachers' classes could be insightful to PSTs (Li et al., 2011). Thus far, microteaching session is conducted at the trainees' institutions under the guidance of teacher educator, while the mentor teachers at school primarily supervise the internship. To bridge the gap between training and practice, collaborative efforts: teacher training institutions - student teacher-mentoring teachers is beneficial in shaping prospective teachers' teaching competencies. Teacher education institutions could appoint subject experts who could be mentor teachers to observe microteaching and offer teaching skills clinics and guided support to PSTs.

Dealing with Mathematics Teaching Anxiety in Responsive Teaching

In the current study, one of the major issues to be addressed is mathematics teaching anxiety among the PSTs, which concurred with several other findings of past studies. Notably, a few PSTs displayed a high level of mathematical anxiety when they lacked conceptual grasp of the teaching content but had a high level of procedural knowledge. Moreover, research evidence indicated that a high level of procedural knowledge does not warrant the absence of mathematics anxiety in order to improve teaching performance (Brady & Bowd, 2005; Uusimaki & Nason, 2004).

Another key finding from the PSTs' reflections was that a few PSTs encountered challenges during induction set of the lesson, especially in delivering the lesson as planned. Nonetheless, they persevered and improved their lesson flow as they progressed in micro-teaching. According to Brady and Bowd (2005), there is a strong relationship between mathematics learning and teaching of PSTs. One of the probable reasons for developing mathematics teaching anxiety stems from PST's early mathematics learning experiences, as early as primary school (Brady & Bowd, 2005). Such early learning experiences that did not foster conceptual development in mathematics understanding will eventually undermine the level of confidence in mathematics teaching skills, resulting in a low level of teaching performance when assessed (Brady & Bowd, 2005; Trujillo & Hadfield, 1999). Despite the impracticality of reversing prior learning experiences, teacher training institutions should promote meaningful mathematics instructions and pedagogical approaches while preparing PSTs for 21st century teaching.

Using Visualisation in Responsive Teaching

Visualisation in mathematics teaching is a powerful tool for transforming complex and abstract concepts into mental imagery for better conceptual development. Visualisation reduces cognitive load and aids in advancing conceptual grasp, by simplifying the complexity of the multitude of abstract concepts (Rösken & Rolka, 2006; Zimmermann & Cunningham, 1991). Presmeg (1986) categorised visual images into five different types: concrete imagery, which is the use of pictures to understand how everyday objects are constructed; pattern imagery, which explores visual-spatial relationships, visual imagery of formulae, which involves writing the formulae on the whiteboard or notebooks and allowing students to attend to details of the formulae or image to enhance memory, inaesthetic imagery which involves muscles and tactile movements, and dynamic imagery which are active images.

In the current study, a few PSTs recognised the benefits of visualisation techniques in their teaching highlighting their responsiveness in micro-teaching. While there are a variety of ways to create visualisations, PSTs primarily leveraged the affordances of digital technology, using applications such as GeoGebra in their teaching and demonstrated a limited use of analogue forms of visualisation, such as mental imagery, concept maps, diagrams, pictures, and 2D images mental imagery on papers or whiteboards. Importantly, the purpose of visualisation is to allow learners to reflect on the creation of mental images and consolidate their new understandings. PSTs have a limited time during micro-teaching to demonstrate complex concepts using the visualisation technique. Though PSTs are convinced with their teaching methods using visualisation, it is crucial that PSTs enhance their competency in the usage of different forms of visualisation techniques.

Responsive Teaching Framework in Mathematics Microteaching

As a preliminary attempt to understand responsive teaching in mathematics microteaching, the current case-study has outlined the significance of the features that embed responsive microteaching practises. In light of the findings, the study delineates a framework for a responsive microteaching in mathematics as shown in Figure 2. The framework depicts six key aspects that could be regarded as measures of responsiveness in mathematics micro-teaching.

In mathematics microteaching, preservice teachers need to use appropriate pedagogical approaches. The case study revealed that the PSTs focused on applying inquiry-based learning while interacting with the students. Responsive teaching skills used to respond to the students were inquiry-based approach, mahemtical language & communication and visualization, but they dealt with anxiety during the process. Their effort of applying responsive teaching need to be comprehensive by consciously acting responsively to the abundance of learning opportunities available in a microteaching setting.

CHALLENGES AND OPPORTUNITIES IN A MATHEMATICS MICROTEACHING CLASS

Using the SWOT analysis, the PSTs' abilities can be categorised into challenges or opportunities. The major challenge the PSTs faced was putting responsive teaching into practice.

Figure 2. A Framework for a Responsive Micro-teaching in Mathematics

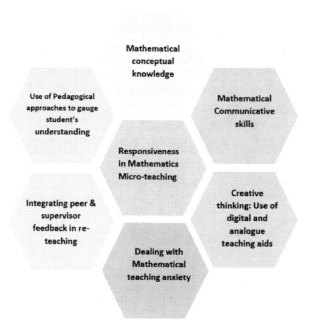

This is despite the enthusiasm of many teachers, academics, preservice teachers, and other stakeholders for the teaching paradigm that responsive teaching embodies. The case study shows that responsive teaching in a mathematics classroom can be effective with a well-planned lesson.

In fact, the research highlights a variety of challenges that PSTs faced when attempting to implement responsive classroom education. Levin (2008), for instance, highlights the importance of teachers' accountabilities in dealing with teaching and learning tasks, especially in managing students' thinking.

One challenge faced was during induction set of the lesson, especially in delivering the lesson as planned. This could be possibly due to mathematics teaching anxiety which stems from PST's early mathematics learning experiences. Secondly, the emphasis of PSTs is on the accuracy of students' thinking rather than the content of their work. Hence, teachers may focus on the degree to which they pay attention to and respond to students' ideas, as well as the position teachers adopt toward what students are saying, which are often the two aspects along which responsive teaching is typically defined. Since assessing for accuracy as opposed to deriving meaning, it is suggested that descriptions of the development of responsive teaching should also be considered on the disciplinary importance of the practices that instructors see and address in students' thinking.

The final major challenge is PSTs used visualisation techniques in their teaching, however there is a need for PSTs to enhance the competency in the usage of different forms of visualisation within a limited time during micro-teaching to demonstrate complex concepts using the visualisation technique.

In terms of opportunities, it is well established that responsive teaching, which bases instruction on the content of students' thoughts, is particularly beneficial for student learning (Carpenter et al. 1989; Franke et al. 2009; Pierson 2008). Nevertheless, there are challenges to promote students' thinking. Research is demonstrating more and more instructional strategies that support student learning, especially in science and mathematics, depending on interacting with students' thinking (Dyer & Sherin, 2016).

To debunk this instructional strategy and encourage instructors in implementing responsive teaching techniques, a greater knowledge of responsive teaching is required.

Through case studies and in-depth assessments of discourse practices, research on responsive teaching in mathematics and science classes has started to define what responsive teaching looks like (e.g., Pierson 2008). Even though exemplary responsive practices focus on students' thinking, there are arguments on ways to practise it effectively. In addition, PSTs may need more sharing and discoveries on how to practise it. Thus, accessing PSTs' thoughts may provide guidance to the deployment of responsive practices, however it has not been made available by this research. By examining the cognitive components of responsive teaching, or the ways in which instructors make sense of students' ideas as they participate in responsive teaching, PSTs will be provided opportunities to fill this gap in their knowledge.

PROPOSED SOLUTIONS AND RECOMMENDATIONS

In the 21st century, teaching mathematics needs a more creative, hands-on and student-centred approach that centralises instructional teaching. Responsive teaching is an approach to instruction that centralises student thinking which foregrounds students' ideas.

Firstly, given the widespread adoption of the twenty-first-century skills framework, logical reasoning is emphasised as a vital talent for the development of critical thinking. PSTs should be encouraged to inculcate logical thinking in the classroom and one effective way will be to use real-life examples for students to easily relate to a problem. This will inspire student engagement as per the constructivism theory which focuses on students' discovery, exploration and applying ideas.

Secondly, cognitivism in a mathematics class is best manifested in problem-solving. PSTs should adopt more student-centred approaches such as cooperative learning, collaborative learning, and inquiry-based learning which enhance problem-solving skills. Besides, it enables students to expound on new ideas which stimulate their minds.

Thirdly, visualisation using technological tools should not be over-emphasised, as most times, it is used to demonstrate and explain concepts only. Rather, it will be more important for PSTs to design and orchestra the use of technology in a more creative and engaging way to inspire the thought process and bring the students to the next level.

Fourthly, bridging the gap between training and practice should be part of the pre-service teaching programme whereby PSTs need to review recorded or virtual sessions of experienced teachers conducting a class. To improve PSTs' precision in mathematics communication, they need to observe classes of experienced teachers. This will allow the PSTs to get practical insights into an effective and good classroom setting.

Finally, PSTs should also not exclude the nurturing aspect where responsive teachers need to attend and respond to students in all of their humanity and take into account the broader socio-political narratives that influence teaching. An ecosystem that is humanistic which includes friendly and positive attitudes will enhance both the teacher-student experience and the social behaviours in the class.

Figure 3 summarises the solutions and recommendations. Specific training and practice are necessary for PSTs since technological advanced development is compelling PSTs to equip with 21st-century skills in multiple aspects such as visualization and logical thinking. The focus on communication should also be emphasised on how to create student-centred approaches and respond to students.

Figure 3. Summary of the Solutions

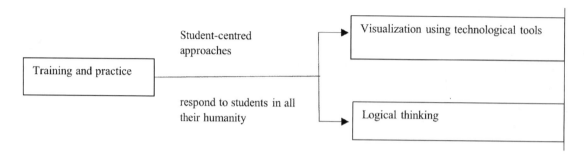

CONCLUSION

Referring to the outcomes of the case study as described in "An exploratory approach in understanding the responsiveness in mathematics microteaching," a consensus regarding the necessity for PSTs to elicit, pay attention to, and adapt their instruction in response to the content (rather than just the correctness or incorrectness) of students' ideas is extremely essential. The attention is described as crucial efforts in mathematics and science teacher education and professional development. These "responsive teaching" approaches, which shall collectively be referred to as "noticing, attending, and reacting to student thought," (Hammer, Goldberg, & Fargason, 2012, p. 54) are central to developing programmes of study on ambitious teaching (e.g., Lampert et al., 2013) and correlate with deeper student learning. Nevertheless, how to get students' attention, drive to deep thinking, and connect students' thinking to the content become the major problem in the practices.

This chapter embarked on highlighting some of the issues with PSTs' microteaching in a mathematics classroom regarding responsiveness. As nurturing and positive school climate are important for PSTs' performance, it will be necessary to further review studies. Responsive teaching in a non-STEM class should be conducted and compared to a mathematics class.

REFERENCES

Academy of Sciences Malaysia. (2020). *10-10 Malaysian Science, Technology, Innovation and Economy (MySTIE) Framework: Trailblazing the way for prosperity, societal well-being & global competitiveness*. Academy of Sciences Malaysia. www.akademisains.gov.my/10-10-mystie

Aghakhani, S. (2022). *Developing reflective practice among teachers of mathematics: A case study of four teachers* [Doctoral dissertation]. University of Toronto.

Alahmad, A., Stamenkovska, T., & Gyori, J. (2021). Preparing Pre-service Teachers for 21st Century Skills Education: A Teacher Education Model. *GiLE Journal of Skills Development*, *1*(1), 67–86. doi:10.52398/gjsd.2021.v1.i1.pp67-86

Aleksandrov, A. D. (1956). *Mathematics, its essence, methods and role*. USSR Academy of Sciences.

Ali, G., Jaaffar, A. R., & Ali, J. (2021). STEM Education in Malaysia: Fulfilling SMEs' Expectation. *Modeling Economic Growth in Contemporary Malaysia*, (February), 43–57. doi:10.1108/978-1-80043-806-420211005

Au, K. H. (1998). Social constructivism and the school literacy learning of students of diverse backgrounds. *Journal of Literacy Research*, *30*(2), 297–319. doi:10.1080/10862969809548000

Bastable, E., McIntosh, K., Falcon, S. F., & Meng, P. (2022). Exploring educators' commitment to racial equity in school discipline practice: A qualitative study of critical incidents. *Journal of Educational & Psychological Consultation*, *32*(2), 125–155. doi:10.1080/10474412.2021.1889194

Borup, J., & Stevens, M. (2016). Parents' perceptions of teacher support at a cyber charter high school. *Journal of Online Learning Research*, *2*(3), 227–246. https://files.eric.ed.gov/fulltext/EJ1148409.pdf

Brady, P., & Bowd, A. (2005). Mathematics anxiety, prior experience and confidence to teach mathematics among pre-service education students. *Teachers and Teaching*, *11*(1), 37–46.

Burns, L. D., & Botzakis, S. (2016). *Teach on purpose! Responsive teaching for student success*. Teachers College Press.

Carpenter, T. P., Fennema, E., Peterson, P. L., Chiang, C. P., & Loef, M. (1989). Using knowledge of children's mathematics thinking in classroom teaching: An experimental study. *American Educational Research Journal*, *26*(4), 499–531. https://doi.org/10.3102/00028312026004499

Cheng, J. (2017). Learning to attend to precision: The impact of micro-teaching guided by expert secondary mathematics teachers on pre-service teachers' teaching practice. *ZDM Mathematics Education*, *49*(2), 279–289. doi:10.100711858-017-0839-7

Cotter, R., Kiser, S., Rasmussen, J., & Vemu, S. (2022). Supporting biology education research at community colleges: Implementing and adapting evidence-based practices. *New Directions for Community Colleges*, *2022*(199), 201–213.

Crespo, S. (2003). Learning to pose mathematical problems: Exploring changes in preservice teachers' practices. *Educational Studies in Mathematics*, *52*, 243–270.

Desfitri, R. (2018). Pre-service teachers' challenges in presenting mathematical problems. *Journal of Physics: Conference Series*, *948*(1), 012035.

Dewsbury, B., & Brame, C. J. (2019). Inclusive teaching. *CBE Life Sciences Education*, *18*(2), fe2.

Dyer, E. B., & Sherin, M. G. (2016). Instructional reasoning about interpretations of student thinking that supports responsive teaching in secondary mathematics. *ZDM*, *48*(1), 69–82.

Fitzsimmons, C. J., & Thompson, C. A. (2022). Developmental differences in monitoring accuracy and cue use when estimating whole-number and fraction magnitudes. *Cognitive Development*, *61*, 101148. https://doi.org/10.1016/j.cogdev.2021.101148

Gouvea, J., & Appleby, L. (2022). Expanding Research on Responsive Teaching. *CBE Life Sciences Education*, *21*(2), 1–3. https://doi.org/10.1187/cbe.22-03-0064

Grant, M., & Ferguson, S. (2021). Virtual microteaching, simulation technology & curricula: A recipe for improving prospective elementary mathematics teachers' confidence and preparedness. *Journal of Technology and Teacher Education, 29*(2), 137–164. https://www.learntechlib.org/primary/p/218262/

Greenhill, V. (2010). 21st Century Knowledge and Skills in Educator preparation. *Partnership for 21st Century Skills.*

Guilford, J. P. (1950). Creativity. *The American Psychologist, 5*(9), 444–454. https://doi.org/10.1037/h0063487

Hammer, D., Goldberg, F., & Fargason, S. (2012). Responsive teaching and the beginnings of energy in a third grade classroom. *Review of Science, Mathematics and ICT Education, 6*(1), 51-72.

Hill, H. C., Blunk, M. L., Charalambous, C. Y., Lewis, J. M., Phelps, G. C., Sleep, L., & Ball, D. L. (2008). Mathematical knowledge for teaching and the mathematical quality of instruction: An exploratory study. *Cognition and Instruction, 26*(4), 430–511.

Iksan, Z. H., Zakaria, E., & Daud, M. (2014). Model of lesson study approach during micro teaching. *International Education Studies, 7*(13), 253–260. https://doi.org/10.5539/ies.v7n13p253

Jaber, L., Herbster, C., & Truett, J. (2019). Responsive Teaching. *Science and Children, 57*(2), 85–89. https://orcid.org/0000-0003-1523-3889

Jarrah, A. M. (2020). The challenges faced by pre-service mathematics teachers during their teaching practice in the UAE: Implications for teacher education programs. *International Journal of Learning. Teaching and Educational Research, 19*(7), 23–34.

Kartal, B., & Çınar, C. (2022). Preservice mathematics teachers' TPACK development when they are teaching polygons with geogebra. *International Journal of Mathematical Education in Science and Technology*, 1-33. doi:10.1080/0020739X.2022.2052197

Killpack, T. L., & Melón, L. C. (2016). Toward inclusive STEM classrooms: What personal role do faculty play? *CBE Life Sciences Education, 15*(3), es3.

Lampert, M., Franke, M. L., Kazemi, E., Ghousseini, H., Turrou, A. C., Beasley, H., ... Crowe, K. (2013). Keeping it complex: Using rehearsals to support novice teacher learning of ambitious teaching. *Journal of Teacher Education, 64*(3), 226–243.

Leong, Y., Cheng, L., & Toh, W. (2021). Teaching students to apply formula using instructional materials: a case of a Singapore teacher's practice. *Math Ed Res J., 33*, 89–111. doi:10.1007/s13394-019-00290-1

Levin, B. (2010). Leadership for evidence-informed education. *School Leadership and Management, 30*(4), 303-315. https://doi/abs/ doi:10.1080/13632434.2010.497483

Li, Y., Huang, R., & Yang, Y. (2011). Characterizing expert teaching in school mathematics in China: A prototype of expertise in teaching mathematics. In Y. Li & G. Kaiser (Eds.), *Expertise in mathematics instruction: An international perspective* (pp. 167–195). Springer.

McKown, C., & Weinstein, R. S. (2008). Teacher expectations, classroom context, and the achievement gap. *Journal of School Psychology, 46*(3), 235–261. https://doi.org/10.1016/j.jsp.2007.06.001

Min, M., Lee, H., Hodge, C., & Croxton, N. (2022). What empowers teachers to become social justice-oriented change agents? Influential factors on teacher agency toward culturally responsive teaching. *Education and Urban Society*, *54*(5), 560–584.

Moreau, C. S., Darby, A. M., Demery, A. J. C., Arcila Hernández, L. M., & Meaders, C. L. (2022). A framework for educating and empowering students by teaching about history and consequences of bias in STEM. *Pathogens and Disease, 80*(1), ftac006.

MOSTI. (2022). *Pelan hala tuju teknologi diperkenalkan bagi menjadikah Malaysia negara pembangun teknologi teknologi*. YouTube. https://www.youtube.com/watch?v=v5TPh-lEizk

Mother, L. E., Halim, L., Rahman, N. A., Maat, S. M., Iksan, Z. H., & Osman, K. (2019). A model of interest in STEM careers among secondary school students. *Journal of Baltic Science Education*, *18*(3), 404–416.

Murtafiah, W., & Lukitasari, M. (2019). Developing Pedagogical Content Knowledge of Mathematics Pre-Service Teacher through Microteaching Lesson Study. *Online Submission*, *13*(2), 201–218.

Mutalib, H. (2022). *72.1% lepasan SPM tidak sambung belajar*. Utusan Malaysia. https://www.utusan.com.my/nasional/2022/07/72-1-lepasan-spm-tidak-sambung-belajar/

Nasar, A., & Kaleka, M. B. U. (2020). The effect of distance learning with Learner Center Micro Teaching Model On student' teaching confidence and teaching skills. *Jurnal Ilmu Pendidik. Fisika*, *5*(3), 159-168. https://journal.stkipsingkawang.ac.id/index.php/JIPF

National Council of Teachers of Mathematics (NCTM). (2000). *Principles and standards for school mathematics*. NCTM.

NCTM. (2000). *Principles and Standards for School Mathematics*. NCTM.

O'Leary, E. S., Shapiro, C., Toma, S., Sayson, H. W., Levis-Fitzgerald, M., Johnson, T., & Sork, V. L. (2020). Creating inclusive classrooms by engaging STEM faculty in culturally responsive teaching workshops. *International Journal of STEM education*, *7*(1), 1-15.

O'Sullivan, M. K., & Dallas, K. B. (2010). A collaborative approach to implementing 21st century skills in a high school senior research class. *Education Libraries*, *33*(1), 3–9.

Park, S., Lee, S., Oliver, J. S., & Cramond, B. (2006). Changes in Korean science teachers' perceptions of creativity and science teaching after participating in an overseas professional development program. *Journal of Science Teacher Education, 17*, 37–64. doi:10.1007=s10972-006-9009-4

Pierson, J. L. (2008). *The relationship between patterns of classroom discourse and mathematics learning*. The University of Texas at Austin.

Plucker, J. A., Beghetto, R. A., & Dow, G. T. (2004). Why isn't creativity more important to educational psychologists? Potential, pitfalls, and future directions in creativity research. *Educational Psychologist, 39*, 83–96. doi: 10.1207=s15326985ep3902_1

Prater, M. A., & Devereaux, T. H. (2009). Culturally responsive training of teacher educators. *Action in Teacher Education*, *31*(3), 19–27. https://doi.org/10.1080/01626620.2022.2058641

Presmeg, N. C. (1986). Visualization in high school mathematics. *For the Learning of Mathematics*, *6*(3), 42–46.

Rahimi, S., & Shute, V. J. (2021). First inspire, then instruct to improve students' creativity. *Computers & Education*, *174*(January), 104312. https://doi.org/10.1016/j.compedu.2021.104312

Ramsey, L. R., Betz, D. E., & Sekaquaptewa, D. (2013). The effects of an academic environment intervention on science identification among women in STEM. *Social Psychology of Education*, *16*(3), 377–397. https://doi.org/10.1007/s11218-013-9218-6

Rayner, V., Pitsolantis, N., & Osana, H. (2009). Mathematics anxiety in preservice teachers: Its relationship to their conceptual and procedural knowledge of fractions. *Mathematics Education Research Journal*, *21*(3), 60–85.

Richardson, G. M., & Liang, L. L. (2008). The use of inquiry in the development of preservice teacher efficacy in mathematics and science. *Journal of Elementary Science Education*, *20*(1), 1–16.

Rissanen, I., Kuusisto, E., Hanhimäki, E., & Tirri, K. (2018). The implications of teachers' implicit theories for moral education: A case study from Finland. *Journal of Moral Education*, *47*(1), 63–77. https://doi.org/10.1080/03057240.2017.1350149

Robertson, A. D., Scherr, R. E., & Hammer, D. (2016). *Responsive teaching in Science and Mathematics*. Routledge.

Rösken, B., & Rolka, K. (2006, July). A picture is worth a 1000 words–the role of visualization in mathematics learning. In *Proceedings 30th conference of the International Group for the Psychology of mathematics education* (Vol. 4, pp. 457-464). Charles University.

Smith, L., & Cotten, M. (1980). Effect of lesson vagueness and discontinuity on student achievement and attitude. *Journal of Educational Psychology*, *72*, 670–675.

Spencer, S. J., Logel, C., & Davies, P. G. (2016). Stereotype threat. *Annual Review of Psychology*, *67*(1), 415–437. https://doi.org/10.1146/annurev-psych-073115-103235

Trujillo, K. M., & Hadfield, O. D. (1999). Tracing the roots of mathematics anxiety through in-depth interviews with preservice teachers. *College Student Journal*, *33*(2), 219–232.

Uusimaki, L., & Nason, R. (2004). Causes underlying pre-service teachers' negative beliefs and anxieties about mathematics. In M. J. Høines & A. B. Fuglestad (Eds.), *Proceedings of the 28th conference of the International Group for the Psychology of Mathematics Education* (Vol. 4, pp. 369-376). Bergen University.

Villegas, A. M., & Lucas, T. (2002). Preparing culturally responsive teachers: Rethinking the curriculum. *Journal of Teacher Education*, *53*(1), 20–32. https://doi.org/10.1177%2F0022487102053001002

Wagoner, B. (2013). Bartlett's concept of schema in reconstruction. *Theory & Psychology, 23*(5), 553-575. doi:https://doi.org/10.1177/09593543500166

Wu, H., & Krajcik, J. S. (2006). Inscriptional practices in two inquiry-based classrooms: A case study of seventh graders' use of data tables and graphs. *Journal of Research in Science Teaching*, *43*(1), 63–95.

Yin, R. (1994). *Case study research: Design and methods* (2nd ed.). Sage Publishing.

Zimmermann, W., & Cunningham, S. (1991). Editor's introduction: What is mathematical visualization. In W. Zimmermann & S. Cunningham (Eds.), *Visualization in Teaching and Learning Mathematics* (pp. 1–8). Mathematical Association of America.

Chapter 14
Responsive and Responsible Preservice Teacher Reflective Thinking Towards Chemistry for Life

Canan Koçak Altundağ
Hacettepe University, Turkey

EXECUTIVE SUMMARY

This study aims to determine the relationship between preservice teachers' responsive and responsible learning skills attained in their university education along with their reflective thinking tendencies. The participants of this research were preservice teachers from the Education Faculty at Hacettepe University. Data were collected through the reflective thinking scale, and metaphors of preservice teachers about chemistry of daily life were collected through a diagram prepared according to the lotus flower technique. Both qualitative content analysis and statistical analysis were employed. It was found that most of the preservice teachers have basic reflective thinking at least at the intermediate level (habitual action, understanding, reflection, and critical reflection). This research also illustrates the need for practices such as responsive teaching and differentiated instructional practices. However, the limited studies on responsive and responsible learning poses a significant problem for chemistry education.

INTRODUCTION

Responsible learning has been one of the most popular concepts studied in the field of education in recent years. Responsible learning skills of individuals could or could not be improved within various processes during education at home or at school (Boyd, Mykula & Choi 2020). Therefore, teachers play a great role in developing the responsible learning skills of students (Boyd, 2016). Teachers are the leading actors within the education system as they play the crucial role in developing of a country, training qualified manpower, providing welfare and social peace in the society, socializing individuals as parts of

DOI: 10.4018/978-1-6684-6076-4.ch014

the community and transferring the social culture and values to younger generations (Villegas & Lucas, 2007). Teacher competence, as well as being extremely essential in education in a country, is the most prominent factor affecting the quality of education (Prater & Devereaux, 2009). In order to improve the level of teacher competence, which is an inevitable element of effective and qualified education, the construction of views and behaviors regarding teaching profession within the pre-service education is of great importance (Villegas & Lucas, 2002). Today, teachers are required to have better skills than transferring the content or attaining skills to students (Brookfield, 2015). According to the constructivist theory, each individual should be encouraged to participate actively in the learning process and be responsible from his/her own learning. This highlights the importance of teacher roles in Responsive and Responsible Learning Environment (Martin & Strom, 2016; Smith, et.al.2016). It is assumed that preservice teachers' have attained various personal responsive and responsible in chemistry education as a result of their communication or interaction with teachers with different characteristics or through their informal observations during their school years. Therefore, revealing and analyzing these perceptions attained by the preservice teachers has great importance. Studies have shown that the pragmatic philosophy matches with the innovativeness within teacher training process while reflective thinking as an important aspect of teaching is highly emphasized (Calderhead, 1989; Goodman, 1984; Kocak & Onen, 2011; LaBoskey, 1993). Definitions on reflective thinking involve style of thinking using a knowledge structure supportive of any thought, knowledge and reaching their expected outcomes in an effective, coherent, and careful way (Dewey, 1991; reported by: Unver, 2003; Semerci, 2007). Additionally, reflective thinking is known to have essential effects in education. Training programs, which improve reflective thinking contribute positively to preservice teachers' planning, application and evaluation processes as well as improving their reflective thinking skills (Kocak & Onen, 2012; Lim, et al., 2003; Norton, 1994; Schweiker et.al, 2003).

Today, the individuals are expected to produce knowledge rather than consume it. The individual that is accepted by the modern world is the one, who apprehends the knowledge learnt and participates effectively in the process of evaluating and commenting on it rather than being guided and shaped. The nature of knowledge and learning sets the basis of the constructivist learning, which has recently been appreciated (Brooks & Brooks, 1993). In this respect, students need to associate the concept they have learned to daily life in order to structure it in a meaningful way (Bernard & Mendez 2020; Demirdağ vd., 2010; İngenç & Aytekin, 2010; Koray et.al., 2007; Önder & Beşoluk, 2010; Özmen, 2003; Özmen & Yıldırım, 2005; Özsevgeç & Ürey, 2010). When the studies conducted to closen everyday life and science are examined, it can be seen that there are many interesting learning-teaching activities designed with items frequently used in daily life (Heimann & Müller, 2007; Kempke, & Flint 2021; Nashan et al, 2007; Sommerfeld, 2008; Vries et al., 2006). For instance, Ducci (2005) who contends that using everyday items as materials in chemistry classes would increase student motivation towards chemistry classes, has used kitchen items (lemons, jellybeans, raspberries) as indicators in student classes, and he achieved successful results. Likewise, Worn et al (1998) in chemistry classes they designed, managed to decompose bitter chocolate without using complex chemistry analysis procedures but just simple chemistry knowledge and acetone as chemical (Oil: 26%, Sugar: 48%, and Cocoa: %24). The experiment, which can easily be done in class, is designed so as to improve students' motivation and interest in chemistry courses.

Designing everyday-life-based chemistry classes is not limited to this. Moreover, there are fun and equally scientific chemistry classes where such everyday items as vitamin pills (Vries, 2002), pastilles, pills (Mönich et al., 2006), coke (Schunk et al., 2008), carbonate (Schmidt et al, 2002), jellybeans (Lemke,

1997), potatoes (Jentsch, 1996), soap (Martin, 1997), and other detergents (Rossow & Flint, 2007) are used. The common trait of these chemistry classes is that they enable students to apply their chemistry knowledge to everyday life, because every day-life based learning and teaching activities should not only be entertaining but they should also meet the targeted learning and direct students towards everyday life (Bulte et al., 2006).

Metaphors

According to Lakoff and Johnson (1980), abstract facts can be concreted and become more understandable thanks to the metaphors. When associated with texts, metaphors or everyday experiences that students are familiar with, a chemistry symbol becomes more meaningful for students, because in order for students to learn new things, it is necessary for them to believe that these new things have a correspondence to everyday life. As metaphors consist of various words, discrimination and analyze aren't become a matter for the researchers.

To describe the unknown, we must resort to concepts that we know and understand. That is the essence of a metaphor… an unusual juxtaposition of the familiar with the unfamiliar (MacCormac, 1990). A metaphor does not just represent an actual event or an actual relationship between events. It may use representations. But its purpose is to recommend how to think about events relative to one another. It is a proposal to give meanings to events which, in isolation, have no inherent meaning at all (Belth, 1993). In this regard, metaphors play an important role in understanding preservice teachers' attitudes towards the theories they choose to embrace or reject and provide a frame of reference for understanding the philosophical orientations, roles and practices of teachers. A review of the research literature also reveals that there are numerous metaphors for assessing the concept of "chemistry", each one providing different information and calling for different responses (Koçak & Yücel, 2008).

Metaphors, which enrich the language when used in daily speech and could be used for educational purposes, also have limitations. As metaphors affect individuals' meaning construction processes (Wulf & Dudis, 2005; Yalçın, 2012), they could cater for limited meanings. They could sometimes reflect only a single aspect of a complex situation (Perry & Cooper, 2001) and cause misunderstandings. Additionally, meanings related to concepts may intersect and create unexpected complexities (Arslan & Bayrakçı, 2006; Tyson, 1995). Therefore, different methods and techniques could be used in studies using metaphors. For this reason, this study made use of the Lotus Flower Technique to determine preservice teachers' perceptions about "chemistry" as a technique different from the techniques used when working with metaphors (Kocak, 2013). It is assumed that preservice teachers' have attained various personal attitudes towards the concept of "chemistry" as a result of their communication or interaction with teachers with different characteristics or through their informal observations during their school years. Therefore, revealing and analyzing these perceptions attained by the preservice teachers towards the concept of "chemistry" has great importance.

The Aim of Study

Determining reflective thinking skills of current teachers and preservice teachers and developing these skills are essential for the provision of effective chemistry education. The study is conducted with a purpose that reflects the theoretical framework it is based on and with a method, which will serve to this purpose (Keeves, 1998). Findings are interpreted within the scope of this purpose. It focused on how the concepts of responsive and responsible learning are translated into practice by the preservice teachers, learning on chemistry education. It is very important to analyze characteristics of preservice teachers as important actors in training new generations, along with their reflective thinking and responsive and responsible learning skills. Therefore, this study aims to determine the relationship between preservice teachers' responsive and responsible learning skills attained in their university education along with their reflective thinking tendencies.

METHOD

The aim of this study is to analyze the effects of responsive and responsible learning on preservice teachers' reflective thinking for chemistry classes and their perceptions towards everyday life chemistry. The sampling of this study consists of 65 preservice teachers studying at Hacettepe University, Faculty of Education. Data were collected through Reflective Thinking Scale, and the Lotus Flower Technique. Reflective Thinking Scale was developed by Kember et.al. (2000) and was adapted into Turkish by Basol et.al. (2013).

How to Design a Responsive and Responsible Learning in Chemistry Education: Step 1: Preliminary Research

In this study, special chemistry courses were designed. Before developing courses, it is needed to determine preservice teachers' perception about "chemistry". Because it is assumed that preservice teachers' have attained various personal attitudes towards the concept of "chemistry" as a result of their communication or interaction with teachers with different characteristics or through their informal observations during their school years. Therefore, revealing and analyzing these perceptions attained by the preservice teachers towards the concept of "chemistry" has great importance.

The Description of the Preliminary Method

In this preliminary research chemistry concept was interpreted with the help of the ideas and images revealed through metaphors. Metaphors of preservice teachers about chemistry of daily life were collected through a diagram prepared according to the Lotus Flower Technique. The lotus blossom technique developed by Yasuo Matsumura helps to figure out technique, schematic and essential topics.

This is a two-dimensional research study where qualitative and quantitative research methods are used together. Qualitative research methods were made use of in the study to support the picture displaying the preservice teachers' states, reveal the conflicting points as well as providing data reliability. In other words, to determine the effects of learning activities designed according to the responsive and responsible learning on preservice teachers' reflective thinking, this study involved alternative assessment techniques.

In lotus blossom technique preservice teachers, are asked to fill in the leaves of the lotus flower leaves. The preservice teachers were given 40 minutes to list their metaphor images. The basic data source of this study is the response papers of the preservice teachers in their own handwritings. There is no demographic information taken from preservice teachers that give evidence about themselves (name, surname, number, class etc.). They can surely and freely express their opinions by this way.

Lotus Flower technique helps thinking on schematic and important topic, all components of Chemistry concept are placed in the middle of the diagram. Preservice teachers are expected to think about the Chemistry as a whole. Additionally, the lotus flower leaves surrounding the diagram are placed boxes, in which metaphors related to components are to be written. Preservice teachers are asked to create a maximum of 8 metaphors and write them separately in the boxes surrounding the concepts. Therefore, preservice teachers could create 72 different metaphors related to Chemistry.

Figure 1. Lotus Flower Technique

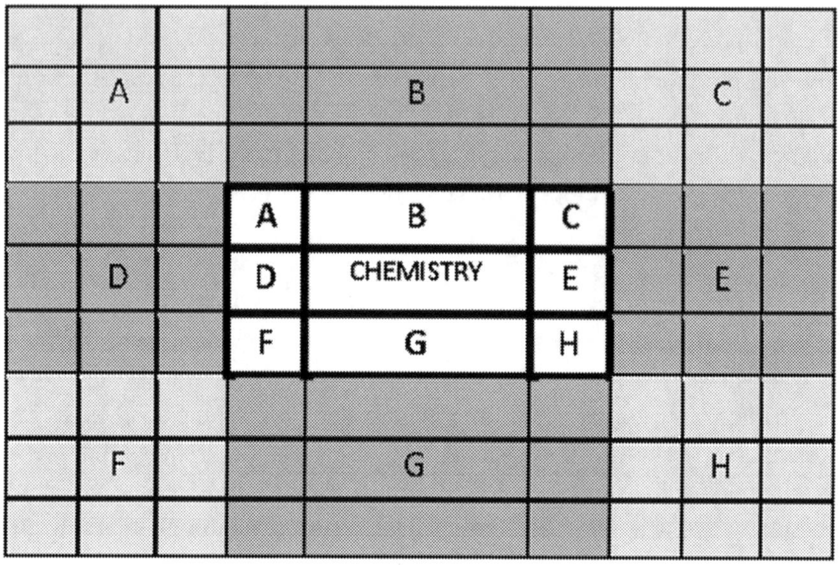

It was investigated whether the preservice teachers expressed a certain metaphor significantly and the metaphors were listed separately. All metaphors were analyzed in terms of their similarities to and differences from the other metaphors. The papers that involved weakly structured metaphorical images were eliminated in order to avoid incoherence. The remaining metaphors were listed under 8 categories in order to construct the metaphorical image that represents them well. In order to check whether the metaphors listed under imaginary categories represented these categories, expertise was requested. Therefore, the validity of the data analysis process and comments of this study was tried to be obtained.

The Description of the Preliminary Results

In this phase, the determined imaginary categories were compared. Within this scope, the answers to the following questions were sought:

1) What are the metaphors that the preservice teachers could think of for the concept of "chemistry"?
2) In terms of their common characteristics, what conceptual categories could these metaphors be listed under?

The analysis concluded with the categorization of metaphors obtained under categories according to their common characteristics. The 8 imaginary categories and the main metaphors they represented are listed below:

A: Acid B: Base C: Atom D: Reactions E: Element / Compound F: Alcohols G: Substance H: Bonds

In this study, components are categorized separately to determine the metaphorical images that preservice teachers had for "chemistry". After the 3754 metaphors were defined and 8 imaginary categories to represent these metaphors were developed, the number of metaphors and its percentage were calculated for each category. Some of the boxes, which are drawn by the preservice teachers, can be seen in Figure 2.

Figure 2. Lotus Flower Boxes

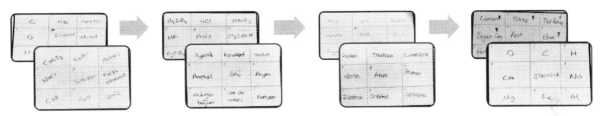

Following the completion of 3754 metaphors and developing the imaginary categories consist of these metaphors, they are presented to take expert ideas for the reliability and validity study for the categories. These categories are completed by taking expert ideas and after 15 days the affirmation meeting about their metaphorical images is held with 30 individuals selected from the participants. Categories, metaphorical images collected under these categories, meanings and interpretations determined in the research are shared with the participants. These two questions whether the information providing the data of the categories are provisional or periodic and whether metaphorical images are correctly understood and collected under the right categories by the participants are addressed to the participants.

The descriptive statistics was administered in order to test whether these metaphors altered according to categories of these preservice teachers' and the results were analyzed. Table 1 displays these categories and the number of metaphors listed under these categories.

Table 1. The categories and the descriptive statistics value of metaphors

Metaphors	A	B	C	D	E	F	G	H	Total
Total	477	472	466	464	476	466	466	467	3754
%	12.7	12.5	12.4	12.3	12.6	12.4	12.4	12.4	100

As Table 1 displays, the images of preservice teachers at 8 imaginary categories. According to the number of metaphors the preservice teachers' regarding the concept of "chemistry" do not indicate a significant difference (A: 477, B: 472, C, F and G: 466, D: 464, E: 476 H: 467). The category defined as "A: Acid" was determined to represent the most preferred metaphors for all preservice teachers (A: 477). The category defined as "D: Reactions" was determined to represent the least preferred metaphors for all preservice teachers (D: 464). This study aimed to determine preservice teachers' perception about "chemistry" through metaphors. In this respect, components of chemistry were categorized separately to determine metaphorical images of preservice teachers about chemistry of daily life.

Table 2. Metaphorical images of preservice teachers about chemistry of daily life

Categories	Metaphorical perceptions of the daily life chemistry		Metaphorical perceptions of the general chemistry	
	n	%	n	%
A	86	18	391	85
B	69	15	403	85
C	0	0	466	100
D	64	13	400	87
E	6	1.2	470	98.8
F	18	4	448	96
G	10	2	456	98
H	0	0	467	100
Total	247		3040	
%	19		81	

As a result, it appears that, the images of the preservice teachers' of regarding the metaphorical perceptions of the chemistry of daily life and general chemistry are significantly different from each other. Table 2 shows that metaphorical perceptions of preservice teachers for chemistry of daily life are mainly listed under the metaphorical perceptions of the general chemistry concept. Among the 3754 metaphors expressed by preservice teachers for chemistry of daily life, 81% related chemistry with general chemistry, while 19% related it with daily life chemistry concept. Also "H: Bonds" category was involved the metaphors of only general chemistry concepts.

Findings of this study clearly indicated that Lotus Flower Technique enabled the expression of metaphors by preservice teachers hers on "chemistry", being an effective data collection tool in revealing, understanding, and explaining a concept together with its components. Data obtained allowed preservice teachers to reflect their opinions on the components of chemistry through metaphorical images. Through construction of metaphorical categories and analysis of metaphorical images on chemistry, preservice teachers were enabled to understand the schemes they created in their minds on chemistry and restructure them when necessary.

How to Design a Responsive and Responsible Learning in Chemistry Education: Step 2: Outcomes and Content Overview

In this step, special chemistry courses were designed. The courses encompass cases on responsive and responsible learning in teacher education. The purpose of the courses; preservice teachers, the importance of chemistry for life and the use of life is to be knowledgeable, about the area.

Responsibility Through Content Setting:

- The importance and purpose of chemistry for life
- Home, school, and the surrounding chemical events that occur
- Application areas in different parts of the chemistry of life
- Chemistry of the materials produced to facilitate the life

Responsibility in Learning Outcomes:

- Preservice teachers will have information about the importance of chemistry for life and the intended use.
- Preservice teachers will examine areas of chemistry in various fields of life.
- Preservice teachers with examples the importance of chemistry in our lives to learn and practice skills to win.
- Preservice teachers will examine cooperation between life and chemistry.

The courses enter teachers the content of chemistry classes to preservice teachers' according to the importance and purpose of chemistry for life principles in an applied manner.

Figure 3. Teacher and Student Responsibility

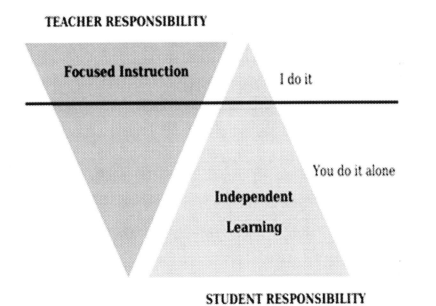

The course was carried out by researcher. The chemistry courses should be deliberated to perpetuate and generate both responsive and responsible learning. Therefore, this step should be to include aspects of a responsive and responsible learning environment and lifelong, connected learning.

Table 3. Focused Instruction

COURSE OUTLINE WEEKLY Focused Instruction: I do it	Week 1: The importance and purpose of chemistry for life
	Week 2: Elements and Compounds We Use in Everyday Life
	Week 3: Acids and Bases We Use in Everyday Life
	Week 4: Chemistry in school, stationery supplies
	Week 5: Cleaning chemicals and surfactants
	Week 6: Alcohol Uses in Daily Life
	Week 7: Water and life
	Week 8: Common materials
	Week 9: Paint chemistry and cosmetic chemistry
	Week 10: Chemistry for health, medicines

During the ten weeks of the course, preservice teachers focused on sensitive and responsible learning in chemistry education. The aim of these courses was to enrich the life by imparting chemical literacy much needed in introducing the basic usefulness of chemistry in everyday life and to inculcate and disseminate responsive and responsible learning in chemistry education to preservice teachers.

Table 4. Responsibility in Learning activites

Some Examples of Responsibility in Learning Activities: You do it alone	How to Make Vinegar at Home
	Natural Ink Making
	How To Make Soap at Home
	Make your Own Natural Skin Cream

How to Design a Responsive and Responsible Learning in Chemistry Education: Step 3: Application Stage

According to Kembera et al (2008) " Many courses cite goals related to promoting reflective thinking or developing the ability to reflect on practice. Where courses aim to promote reflective practice, If the level of reflective thinking is evaluated, the goal will be achieved. "The origins of the concept of reflective thinking are normally attributed to Dewey (1933), who wrote of it as a thought process that education should strive to cultivate (Kembera et al, 2008).

Figure 4. Responsive teaching in chemistry education

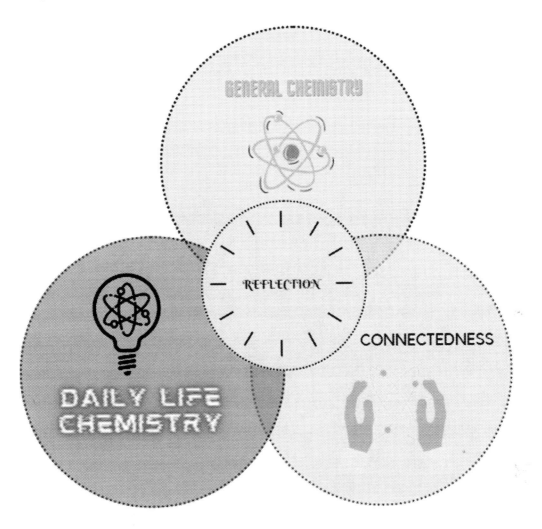

How to Design a Responsive and Responsible Learning in Chemistry Education: Step 4: Findings

The research is limited to the reflective thinking tendencies of the 65 preservice teachers at Hacettepe University, which is located in the capital of Turkey, Ankara. The number of samplings in the study was not changed. Preservice teachers responded to the statements in the reflective thinking scale sincerely.

The study sought the answer to the question how the reflective thinking of preservice teachers towards the special chemistry courses could be classified:

- "How could the tendencies of preservice teachers towards the reflective thinking be classified?
- Could reflective thinking scale serve as a guiding tool or a performance evaluator by tethe classification of the thinking in different dimensions?"

The ideas of the items that formed the scale indicate and classify the reflective thinking of preservice teachers towards the course. Moreover, the role of the scale, which was reevaluated through classification, was investigated in terms of serving as a guiding tool and a performance evaluator. A classification of four dimensions was created. The levels of reflection can be translated into grades, if necessary, in which case a form of criterion-based assessment is used. The most obvious grading scheme is (Kember, McKay, Sinclair & Frances Wong, 2008):

- Critical Reflection
- Reflection
- Understanding
- Non-reflective

As a result of the study, the existing 16 items were classified as the four dimensions as "Habitual Action, Understanding, Reflection, and Critical Reflection". Descriptive statistics regarding the average of the scale carried out within the scope of the analysis on reflective thinking of preservice teachers have been summarized in Table 5.

Table 5. The descriptive statistics of the Reflective Thinking Scale

	Minimum	Maximum	Mean	Sd	Skewness	Kurtosis
Habitual Action	1.50	4.50	3.25	.681	-.572	-.145
Understanding	2.50	5.00	3.67	.487	-.108	.988
Reflection	2.75	5.00	4.12	.453	-.174	.376
Critical Reflection	2.25	5.00	3.87	.521	-.293	.455
Reflective Thinking	3.00	4.75	3.73	.330	.508	.520

When the kurtosis skewness values are examined, it is seen that the data are distributed normally (Tabachnick & Fidell, 2013). To observe whether there are multivariate normality and extreme values, the mean and the trimmed mean were compared, and if these two mean values were very different from each other, the Q–Q plot was first checked to specify the outliers. In these data set when means compared to 5% trimmed means a few outliers were observed and Mahalanobis distance value was examined. In the data file, outliers whose Mahalanobis distance is above the critical value are excluded from the data set. In graphical methods, the distribution of scores is presented visually, where an its position on the line is determined (McKillup, 2012). In order to control the values, firstly, the normal Q-Q plot and the trend-free Q-Q plot were examined. The results of the graphical method are shown in Figure 5.

Based on the normal Q-Q plot and the trend-free Q-Q plot the distribution is found to be normal. In other words, the data show normal distribution according to graphical methods. When findings are examined before doing statistical analyses, parametric hypothesis are applied as it's found that numerical data is in normal distribution.

In this section of the research in order to evaluate the preservice teachers' reflective thinking in the concept of dimensions, they get from reflective thinking analyzed by One-Sample Test.

In the light of the findings, it's examined in each dimension whether there are meaningful differences.

Figure 5. Normality Assumption Regarding Reflective Thinking Scale Graphical Methods

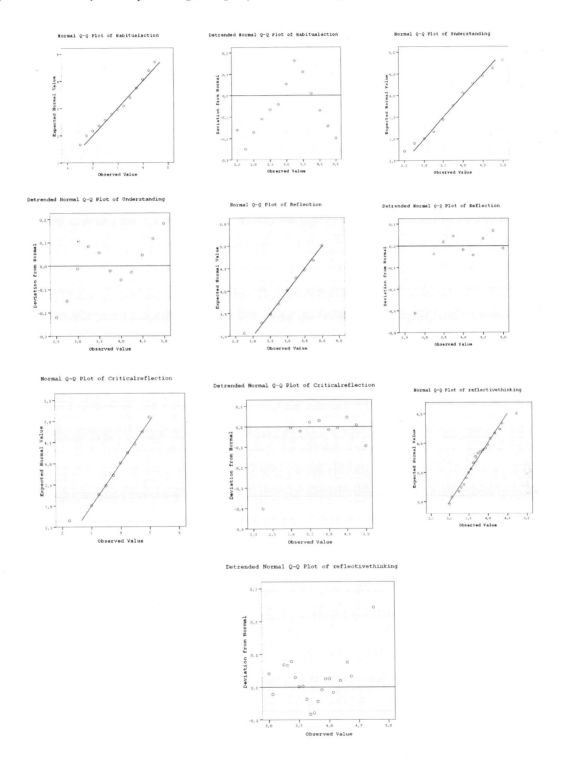

Table 6. The One-Sample Statistics Results of the Reflective Thinking Scale

	N	Mean	Sd	Std. Error Mean
Habitual Action	65	3.25	.681	.084
Understanding	65	3.67	.487	.060
Reflection	65	4.12	.453	.056
Critical Reflection	65	3.87	.521	.064

When the table is investigated. the reflective thinking value dimensions of preservice teachers are as follows: Reflection (Mean: 4.12). Critical reflection (Mean: 3.87). Understanding (Mean: 3.67). and Habitual action (Mean: 3.25). It appears that preservice teacher's place importance on Reflection and Critical reflection at most. The preservice teachers One-Sample Test results are summarized in Table 2.

Table 7. The analysis between the sub-factors

	t	df	Sig. (2-tailed)	Mean
Habitual Action	38.525	64	.000	3.25
Understanding	60.798	64	.000	3.67
Reflection	73.361	64	.000	4.12
Critical Reflection	59.903	64	.000	3.87

Seen that (Table 7) there are statistically meaningful differences among preservice teachers. At the end of the research process, it's found that most of the preservice teachers have basic reflective thinking at least mediate level and when analyzed according to the four dimensions as Habitual Action, Understanding, Reflection, and Critical Reflection.

RESULTS AND DISCUSSION

This study aims to determine the relationship between preservice teachers' responsive and responsible learning skills attained in their university education along with their reflective thinking tendencies. The special courses were designed on responsive and responsible learning in chemistry education. It is assumed that preservice teachers have attained various personal attitudes towards the concept of "chemistry" as a result of their communication or interaction with teachers with different characteristics or through their informal observations during their school years. Therefore, revealing and analyzing these perceptions attained by the preservice teachers towards the concept of "chemistry" has great importance before the lessons are designed. The first preliminary study during the preparation of chemistry courses process was to examine preservice teachers' perception about "chemistry" through metaphors.

Metaphor means catching the essence of experience and is an active process which helps us to understand our own world and the others. Metaphors are personal symbols for an indefinable attitude and don't need to limit verbal expressions. In fact, metaphor is a presentation of an individual's own output depends on his imagination as a part of the environment. In other words, metaphor is an individual expression of what he says, sees, hears, feels and does as imagine (Lawley &Tompkins. 2000; Önen & Koçak, 2011). According to Lakoff and Johnson (1980) who break new ground in this field, metaphor is a poetic instrument for many people that becomes more beautiful with imagination. Rather than using ordinary language metaphor is an extraordinary expression of a matter. From these points of views, the perceptions of preservice teachers about the chemistry of daily life analyzed with metaphorical images.

Metaphors play a crucial role in gaining insights into more complex concepts and provide important ways of comprehending people's personal experiences (Miller, 1987). According to Zhua and Chen (2022) "Metaphors act as powerful cognitive framework in understanding preservice teachers' professional identities." The use of metaphor as a powerful research tool in the field of teaching and teacher education is well documented in the research literature. A review of the current research literature reveals that teachers often make use of metaphorical expressions when they talk about their profession. Their beliefs and their daily teaching practices (Ben-Peretz et al.,2003; Carroll & Eifler, 2002; Carter, 1990; Collins & Green, 1990; Guerrero & Villamil, 2002; Inbar,1996; Marchall, 1990a; Martinez et al., 2001; Oxford et al., 1998; Tobin, 1990; Wallace, 2001; Weade & Ernst, 1990; Yung,2001). Therefore, this study aimed to determine preservice teachers' perception about "chemistry" through metaphors. Metaphors allow educators to explain things by comparing two things. Emphasizing the similarities between two things or replacing one thing with another. The purpose of this study was to determine the metaphorical perceptions of preservice teachers' "Chemistry" concepts. The chemistry concept was interpreted with the help of the ideas and images revealed through metaphors. With the help of these metaphors, the certain imaginative categories, and statements of preservice teachers about the chemistry of daily life. Research on metaphors included studies where participants were expected to indicate a single metaphor and express the metaphor at the same statement with the reason of its. In these studies, it is an obligation to focus on a single metaphor, which leads the sampling group to express. Metaphors of preservice teachers about chemistry of daily life were collected through a diagram prepared according to the Lotus Flower Technique.

In this technique preservice teachers, are asked to fill in the leaves of the lotus flower leaves. Perceptions of preservice teachers towards chemistry metaphor are analyzed separately through the metaphors written in the lotus flower leaves. The analysis concluded with the categorization of 8 metaphors obtained under categories according to their common characteristics. Findings of this study clearly indicated that Lotus Flower Technique enabled the expression of metaphors by preservice teachers on "chemistry", being an effective data collection tool in revealing, understanding, and explaining a concept together with its components. Although the number of participants in the study was 65, the leaves of the lotus flower were observed to contain 3754 metaphors for chemistry. This conclusion allows for more number of data than the number of participants in the sampling group. In this study, it appears that, the images of the preservice teachers' metaphorical perceptions the chemistry of daily life and general chemistry are significantly different from each other. The findings show that metaphorical perceptions of preservice teachers for chemistry are mainly listed under the metaphorical perceptions of the general chemistry concept. Among the 3754 metaphors expressed by preservice teachers for chemistry, 81% related chemistry with general chemistry, while 19% related it with daily life chemistry concept. This is thought to be caused by the nature of chemistry as a science, types of courses in which it is taught, the appreciation levels of preservice teachers' or the differences of their ways of thinking (Alkan & Yücel, 2019).

Student separating real life and chemistry lessons at school causes students to develop useless information systems related to chemistry (Osborne & Freyberg, 1985). Providing students with useful information that they can use in their daily lives can make them aware of the relationship between chemistry and daily life, and this can cause them to prefer using their chemistry knowledge in interpreting the phenomena they encounter in their daily lives (Busker & Flint, 2022; Georgiou & Sharma, 2012; Kim, Yoon, Ji & Song, 2012). As Yob (2003) puts it, a "metaphor is employed when one wants to explore and understand something esoteric, abstract, novel, or highly speculative". Recently, Boostrom (1998) has pointed out that "to use a metaphor (for teaching) is not a way of doing teaching; it is (rather) a way of talking about teaching. A metaphor is a compressed imaginative expression of a perspective". Findings of this study clearly indicated that Lotus Flower Technique enabled preservice teachers to express their metaphors on "chemistry" and is an effective data collection tool in revealing, understanding, and explaining a concept together with its components. The obtained data allowed preservice teachers to reflect their opinions on the components of chemistry through metaphorical images. Through construction of metaphorical categories and analysis of metaphorical images on chemistry, preservice teachers were enabled to understand the schemes they created in their minds on chemistry and restructure them when necessary. Metaphors are able to change conceptual systems and the perspectives of individuals towards the world. Therefore, this study catered for the introduction of metaphorical images, which bring new perspectives to preservice teachers about chemistry of daily life.

In this study, the effects of the designed chemistry courses on reflective thinking, sensitive and responsible learning, and daily life chemistry perceptions of preservice teachers in chemistry education were examined. In the study, 10 special chemistry courses were designed. The courses encompass cases on responsive and responsible learning in teacher education. During the ten course, preservice teachers will focus on responsive and responsible learning. The aim of these courses is to enrich the life by imparting chemical literacy much needed in introducing the basic usefulness of chemistry in everyday life and to inculcate and disseminate responsive and responsible learning in chemistry education to preservice teachers. At the end of the research process, it's found that most of the preservice teachers have basic reflective thinking at least mediate level and when analyzed according to the four dimensions as Habitual Action, Understanding, Reflection, and Critical Reflection. It has been revealed in the studies conducted that students are unable to apply scientific knowledge they have acquired to real-life situations. The reason of this is presenting the information to the students with mainly other methods and techniques apart from traditional methods. This is not surprising, because in traditional approaches, it is highly unlikely for students to be able to apply knowledge to everyday life and responsive learning in chemistry education (Wu, 2003). Although students may sometimes find associations between everyday life and the knowledge, they acquire in learning environments based on traditional learning, this association cannot go beyond mere association because students cannot fully adapt their knowledge to everyday life (Gilbert, 2011). Therefore, it's very important to support the topics with easy and clear experiments (Helfensteller & Flint 2022). According to Pilot and Bulte (2006), comparing the results of traditional chemistry education and everyday-life based chemistry education is possible only to some extent because it is not possible to compare the learning outcomes and objectives of these two methods. When compared, it is revealed that every day-life based education programs have a better way of promoting students' interest, motivation, and success (Wu, 2003; Gilbert,2006).

The literature contains varied studies, which obtained findings that are supportive of the research result. In the study conducted by Zhua and Chen (2022), preservice teachers' reflections and metaphorical professional identities were examined. This study confirms that metaphors act as powerful cognitive frameworks in gaining in-depth insights into preservice teachers' dynamic and evolving professional identities in learning-to-teach settings. Implications for facilitating preservice teachers' metaphorical professional identity (trans)formation and reflection in the teaching practicum context are discussed. The study by Broza et al. (2021) focuses on the challenge of promoting important mathematical discourse among preservice teachers. The study was conducted as part of an academic course that accompanies their practical training. Twenty-three math pre-service teachers' learning process was examined as a result of using an analytical model designed for discourse protocols' analysis. Findings revealed that an active and dynamic process occurred, modifying teacher practice and developing critical reflective thinking among preservice teachers. Reflective thinking is a thinking activity marked by the appearance of confusion and efforts to overcome it through planned steps based on knowledge, experience, and problem-solving skills. Reflective thinkers involve specific skills to identify problems, examine, evaluate, formulate problems, and draw conclusions (Kholid, et.al, 2021). Based on another result, reflective thinking provides an opportunity for the students to improve their weakness. When they get some difficulties and find some mistakes or some misconceptions related to their answer, they will correct it and try to interpret it to obtain logical answer (Agustan, et.al, (2017). Goodell (2000) and Ville (2010) stated that one of goals of the educational personnel and institutions creates a prospective teacher who is responsible and capable reflective thinking. Preservice teachers should engage in activities promoting reflection and reflective thinking early on in their teacher education preparation programs so that they can make sense of the studied theoretical content during their coursework (Rieger, et. al. 2013). New research is expected to emerge in the area of 21st century pedagogy, psychology of the learner and educational experience. This research provides a complete analysis of research-based instructional practices that teachers can use to improve teaching and learning. Instructional practices such as responsive teaching and differentiated instructional practices are all discussed in detail. The limitedness of studies on Responsive and Responsible Learning poses a significant problem for chemistry education. Resources necessary for the solution of this problem should be examined and then applied to our case. Following the studies realized in the world and adding new studies to these would contribute immensely to the responsive and responsible learning. Thus, it is highly important to carry out future studies.

REFERENCES

Acar, B., & Yaman, M. (2011). The effects of context-based learning on students' levels of knowledge and interest. *Hacettepe University Journal of Education, 40,* 1–10.

Agustan, S., Juniati, D., & Siswono, T. Y. E. (2017). Reflective thinking in solving an algebra problem: A case study of field independent-prospective teacher. *Journal of Physics: Conference Series, 893*(1), 012002. doi:10.1088/1742-6596/893/1/012002

Akpınar, İ. A., & Özkan, E. (2010). *Kimya dersi çözünürlük konusunda 5E modeline uygun etkinlikler geliştirme [Develop appropriate activities to 5 models in chemistry resolution].* Paper presented at IX. National Science and Mathematics Education Congress, Izmir, Turkey.

Alkan, F., & Yücel, A. S. (2019). Investigation of epistemological beliefs and creativity fostering behaviours of prospective teachers' in terms of various variables. *Journal of Educational Studies Trends and Practices, 9,* 212–226.

Andrée, M. (2003). *Everyday-life in the science classroom: A study on ways of using and referring to everyday-life.* Paper presented at the ESERA Conference, Noordwijkerhout, The Netherlands.

Arslan, M. Ö., & Bayrakçı, M. (2006). Metaforik düşünme ve öğrenme yaklaşımının eğitimöğretim açısından incelenmesi. *Millî Eğitim, 171*, 100.

Ayas, A. (1995). Fen bilimlerinde program geliştirme ve uygulama teknikleri üzerine bir çalışma: İki çağdaş yaklaşımın değerlendirilmesi. [A study on curriculum development and application techniques: Evaluation of two modern approaches]. *Hacettepe University Journal of Education, 11*, 149–155.

Barker, V., & Millar, R. (1999). Students' reasoning about basic chemical reactions: What changes occur during a context-based post-16 chemistry course? *International Journal of Science Education, 21*(6), 645–665. doi:10.1080/095006999290499

Barker, V., & Millar, R. (2000). Students' reasoning about basic chemical thermodynamics and chemical bonding: What changes occur during a context - based post-16 chemistry course? *International Journal of Science Education, 22*(11), 1171–1200. doi:10.1080/09500690050166742

Başol, G., & Evin-Gencel, İ. (2013). Yansıtıcı Düşünme Düzeyini Belirleme Ölçeği: Geçerlik ve güvenirlik çalışması [Reflective thinking level determination scale: valitidy and reliability study]. *Kuram ve Uygulamada Eğitim Bilimleri [Educational sciences in theory and practice], 13*(2), 929–946.

Becker, H. J. (1983). Eine empirische untersuchung zur beliebtheit von chemieunterricht. [An empirical investigation on the popularity of chemistry teaching]. *Chimica Didactica, 2*, 97–123.

Belth, M. (1993). *Metaphor and thinking*. University Press.

Ben-Peretz, M., Mendelson, N., & Kron, F. W. (2003). How teachers in different educational contexts view their roles. *Teaching and Teacher Education, 19*(2), 277–290. doi:10.1016/S0742-051X(02)00100-2

Bennett, J., & Lubben, F. (2006). Context-based chemistry: The Salters approach. *International Journal of Science Education, 28*(9), 999–1015. doi:10.1080/09500690600702496

Bennett, J., Lubben, F., & Hogarth, S. (2006). Bringing science to life: A synthesis of the research evidence on the effects of context-based and sts approaches to science teaching. *Science Education, 91*(3), 347–370. doi:10.1002ce.20186

Bernard, P., & Mendez, J. (2020). Low-Cost 3D-Printed Polarimeter. *Journal of Chemical Education, 97*(4), 1162–1166. doi:10.1021/acs.jchemed.9b01083

Böcher, J. (2005). *Halogenverbindungen im alltag. [Halogen compounds in everyday life]* CHIDS. http://www.chids.de/dachs/expvortr/ 719Halogenverbindungen_Boecher.pdf .

Boostrom, R. (1998). Safe spaces: Reflections on an educational metaphor. *Journal of Curriculum Studies, 30*(4), 397–408. doi:10.1080/002202798183549

Boyd, M., Mykula, V., & Choi, Y. (2020). Responsive and responsible teacher telling: An across time examination of classroom talk during whole group writing workshop minilessons. *Research Papers in Education, 35*(5), 574–602. doi:10.1080/02671522.2019.1601761

Boyd, M. P. (2016). Calling for Response-Ability in Our Classrooms. *Language Arts, 93*(3), 226–233.

Brookfield, S. D. (2015). *The skillful teacher: On technique, trust, and responsiveness in the classroom*. John Wiley & Sons.

Broza, O., Lifshitz, A., & Atzmon, S. (2022). Exploring a Model to Develop Critical Reflective Thought Among Elementary School Math Preservice Teachers. *Journal of Education, 202*(4), 406–415. doi:10.1177/0022057421998336

Busker, M., & Flint, A. (2022). Neue Zugänge zu chemischen Reaktionen: Das Basiskonzept des Chemieunterrichts [New approaches to chemical reactions: the basic concept of chemistry teaching]. *Unterricht Chemie, 2022*(190), 2–5.

Carroll, J. B., & Eifler, K. E. (2002). Servant, master, double-edged sword: Metaphors teachers use to discuss technology. *Journal of Technology and Teacher Education, 10*, 235–246.

Carter, K. (1990). Meaning and metaphor: Case knowledge in teaching. *Theory into Practice, 29*(2), 109–115. doi:10.1080/00405849009543440

Collins, E. C., & Gren, J. L. (1990). Metaphors: The construction of a perspective. *Theory into Practice, 29*(2), 71–77. doi:10.1080/00405849009543435

Georgiou, H., & Sharma, M. D. (2012). University students' understanding of thermal physics in everyday contexts. *International Journal of Science and Mathematics Education, 10*(5), 1119–1142. doi:10.100710763-011-9320-1

Goodell, J. (2000). Learning to teach Mathematics for understanding: The role of reflection J. Math. *Teacher Education and Development, 2*, 48–60.

Guerrero, M. C. M., & Villamil, O. S. (2002). Metaphorical conceptualizations of ESL teaching and learning. *Language Teaching Research, 6*(2), 95–120. doi:10.1191/1362168802lr101oa

Helfensteller, R., & Flint, A. (2022). POLARIO–A simple low-cost-polarimeter for the chemistry lesson. *CHEMKON*.

Inbar, D. (1996). The free educational prison: Metaphors and images. *Educational Research, 28*(1), 77–92. doi:10.1080/0013188960380106

Kember, D., Leung, D. Y. P., Jones, A., Loke, A. Y., McKay, J., Sinclair, K., Tse, H., Webb, C., Yuet Wong, F. K., Wong, M., & Yeung, E. (2000). Development of a questionnaire to measure the level of reflective thinking. *Assessment & Evaluation in Higher Education, 25*(4), 381–395. doi:10.1080/713611442

Kember, D., McKay, J., Sinclair, K., & Frances, Y. W. (2008). A four-category scheme for coding and assessing the level of reflection in written work. *Assessment & Evaluation in Higher Education, 33*(4), 369–379. doi:10.1080/02602930701293355

Kempke, T., & Flint, A. (2021). The introduction of the particle concept in inclusive chemistry lessons based on the concept of "Chemistry for Life". *CHEMKON, 28*, 1–5. doi:10.1002/ckon.202100049

Kholid, M. N., Telasih, S., Pradana, L. N., & Maharani, S. (2021). Reflective thinking of mathematics prospective teachers' for problem solving. [). IOP Publishing.]. *Journal of Physics: Conference Series, 1783*(1), 012102. doi:10.1088/1742-6596/1783/1/012102

Kim, M., Yoon, H., Ji, Y. R., & Song, J. (2012). The dynamics of learning science in everyday contexts: A case study of everyday science class in Korea. *International Journal of Science and Mathematics Education*, *10*(1), 71–97. doi:10.100710763-011-9278-z

Koçak, C. (2013). Metaphorical perceptions of teacher candidates towards the school concept: Lotus flower model. [MIJE]. *Mevlana International Journal of Education*, *3*(4), 43–56. doi:10.13054/mije.13.61.3.4

MacCormac, E. (1990). *A cognitive theory of metaphor*. MIT Press.

MacCormac, E. (1990). *A cognitive theory of metaphor*. MIT Press.

Marshall, H. H. (1990). Beyond the workplace metaphor: The classroom as a learning setting. *Theory into Practice*, *29*, 94–101.

Martin, A. D., & Strom, K. J. (2016). Toward a linguistically responsive teacher identity: An empirical review of the literature. *International Multilingual Research Journal*, *10*, 239–253.

Martinez, M. A., Sauleda, N., & Huber, G. L. (2001). Metaphors as blueprints of thinking about teaching and learning. *Teaching and Teacher Education*, *17*, 965–977.

Miller, S. (1987). Some comments on the utility of metaphors for educational theory and practice. *Educational Theory*, *37*, 219–227.

Osborne, M., & Freyberg, P. (1985). *Learning in science: Implications of children's knowledge*. Heinemann.

Oxford, R. L., Tomlinson, S., Barcelos, A., Harrington, C., Lavine, R. Z., Saleh, A., & Longhini, A. (1998). Clashing metaphors about classroom teachers: Toward a systematic typology for the language teaching field. *System*, *26*, 3–50.

Perry, C., & Cooper, M. (2001). Metaphors are good mirrors: Reflecting on change for teacher educators. *Reflective Practice*, *2*, 41–52.

Prater, M. A., & Devereaux, T. H. (2009). Culturally responsive training of teacher educators. *Action in Teacher Education*, *31*(3), 19–27.

Rieger, A., Radcliffe, B. J., & Doepker, G. M. (2013). Practices for developing reflective thinking skills among teachers. *Kappa Delta Pi Record*, *49*(4), 184–189.

Smith, K., Gamlem, S. M., Sandal, A. K., & Engelsen, K. S. (2016). Educating for the future: A conceptual framework of responsive pedagogy. *Cogent Education*, *3*(1).

Tobin, K. (1990). Changing metaphors and beliefs: A master switch for teaching? *Theory into Practice*, *29*, 122–127.

Tyson, P. A. (1995). *The metaphor of students as mathematicians: issue and implications* [Unpulished Doctorial Thesis, Stanford University].

Ville, P. A. (2010). Mentoring reflective thinking practice in pre-service teachers: A reconstructions through the voices of australian science teachers. *Journal of College Teaching and Learning*, *7*(9).

Villegas, A. M., & Lucas, T. (2002). Preparing culturally responsive teachers: Rethinking the curriculum. *Journal of Teacher Education*, *53*(1), 20–32.

Villegas, A. M., & Lucas, T. (2007). The culturally responsive teacher. *Educational Leadership, 64*(6), 28.

Wallace, S. (2001). Guardian angels and teachers from hell: Using metaphor as a measure of schools' experiences and expectations of General National Vocational Qualifications. *International Journal of Qualitative Studies in Education: QSE, 14,* 727–739.

Weade, R., & Ernst, G. (1990). Pictures of life in classrooms, and the search for metaphors to frame them. *Theory into Practice, 29,* 133–140.

Wulf, A., & Dudis, P. (2005). Body partitioning in ASL metaphorical blends. *Sign Language Studies, 5*(3), 317–332.

Yalçın, M. (2011). İlköğretim okullarında okul müdürüne ilişkin metaforik algılar [Metaphorical perceptions of the school principal in primary schools] [Master's Thesis, Gaziosmanpaşa Üniversitesi].

Yob, I. M. (2003). Thinking constructively with metaphors. *Studies in Philosophy and Education, 22,* 127–138.

Yücel, A.S. & Koçak, C. (2008, September). *The mental images of preservice teachers related to teacher concept: forming imaginary metaphor groups.* The Current Trends in Chemical Curricula, Praque.

Yung, B. H. W. (2001). Examiner, policeman or students' companion: Teachers' perceptions of their role in an assessment reform. *Educational Review, 53,* 251–260.

Zhu, G., & Chen, M. (2022). Positioning preservice teachers' reflections and I-positions in the context of teaching practicum: A dialogical-self theory approach. *Teaching and Teacher Education, 117,* 103734.

Chapter 15
Multiple-Multimodal Skills Through Responsive and Responsible Learning:
Audiovisual Media Communications Classifications

Constantinos Nicolaou
https://orcid.org/0000-0002-6737-1653
Aristotle University of Thessaloniki, Greece

EXECUTIVE SUMMARY

This chapter investigates and highlights the multiple-multimodal skills from and through literature review that can be acquired in the educational path using audiovisual media technologies and audiovisual content (henceforth, audiovisual media communications) through technology-enhanced learning perspective. Specifically, an attempt is made to present how audiovisual media communications help both learners and educators to achieve these multiple-multimodal skills under the lens of responsive and responsible learning. The chapter also presents and comments indicative ways in which audiovisual media communications can be used in technology-supported learning environments to support teaching, professional learning, and effective educator-learner communication. Nowadays society is highly visualized and requires all of us, in addition to being receptive to the continual use of audiovisual media communications, to somehow maintain a positive outlook for every emerging cutting-edge innovation, and to possess a plethora of skills in order to survive in this digital technological world.

INTRODUCTION

The current society in which we live in is highly technologically visualized and requires, in addition to the continued use of audiovisual media and communication technologies (audiovisual media technologies from here on), to be receptive and to maintain a positive perspective on any emerging innovation

DOI: 10.4018/978-1-6684-6076-4.ch015

(Dimoulas et al., 2019, 2014; Matsiola et al., 2015; Nicolaou, 2021a; Sarridis & Nicolaou, 2015). Admittedly, the use and adoption of audiovisual media technologies and audiovisual content (henceforth, audiovisual media communications) are omnipresent in our daily lives due to digital technological advancements. Audiovisual media technology is defined as electronic and technological media/medium possessing both sonic or audio media and visual components (Matsiola et al., 2019; Yeromin, 2020). Audiovisual content, on the other hand, encloses any combination of sound or audio media and/or visual image/picture/photograph (photo/s from here on) with or without filmic/visual texts or even non-linear multimedia and/or hypermedia (Dimoulas et al., 2015; Kalliris et al., 2019, 2014; Kotsakis et al., 2014; Podara et al., 2021).

As already researched and stated in the literature, the use of audio content in the framework of teaching or even learning procedure (henceforth, teaching–learning procedure) is of paramount importance (Nicolaou et al., 2021b), since it can significantly increase oral communication. Particularly, it (a) creates feelings, affects and emotions; as well as (b) activates memory and nostalgia (Nicolaou, 2022c, p. 237). On the other hand, the employment of electronic recording of moving photos (i.e., video content) in the didactic process with responsive and responsible learning provides motivation, repetition, and imitation of activities, thus helping for the development of *receptive skills* and *oral productive skills* or the acquisition of *psychomotor skills* through repeated observation and practice or even through numerous interactive teaching activities (cf. Burton, 2022; Kanellopoulou & Ginnakoulopoulos, 2021; Nicolaou, 2022c, Nicolaou et al., 2019). Additionally, if the use of appropriate Quality of Experience and Learning (QoE/QoL) metrics are considered, the learning outcomes will also be even greater (Kalliris et al., 2014, 2011; Kotsakis et al., 2014).

It is a fact that Audiovisual Media Communications (AMCs) are mostly integrated into education in conjunction with communication features and modern trends, approaches and learning methodology in teaching frameworks. Educators who employ them in teaching frameworks achieve Technology-Enhanced Learning (TEL) in-class or remote teaching (Gordon & Brayshaw, 2014; Matsiola et al., 2019; Nicolaou, 2022a, 2021b). Similarly, they can impart a range of different skills to their learners through their use inside and outside the conventional or online classroom (Chakravarti & Stevenson, 2021; Lorenzo-Lledó et al., 2022; Nicolaou et al., 2021b). This impartation seems to be best achieved through the educational methods of responsive and responsible learning. Although there is an abundance of books or book chapters and/or academic articles in journals about these two educational methods, they have not received the attention they deserve as audiovisual technology-supported educational methods. In the same context, due to the digital technological world that we live in, it is more than ever necessary to consider these methods in relation to both the challenges and the affordances provided by modern and educational merging digital trends and cutting-edge technological communication tools. Overall, digital technological advancements have also brought about a digital transformation in education at all educational levels and disciplines (including adult education and afterschool programs), while AMCs are now an integral part of many curricula (Foutsitzi, 2022; Matsiola et al., 2019; Nicolaou & Kalliris, 2020; Nicolaou et al., 2022; Palioura & Dimoulas, 2022). Likewise, multiple ways of getting educated and modern approaches to traditional teaching methodologies and methods in education have emerged to provide or even develop a range of additional numeracy skills to *pre-existing skills* (e.g., acquired experience and knowledge, background knowledge, etc.) (Nicolaou et al., 2019).

The research purpose of this chapter is to highlight these numerous skills that can be applied (a) primarily through teaching activities implemented to foster responsive and responsible learning; or even (b) within an educational framework in complex technological and digital socio-cultural environments.

Notably, the chapter emphasizes the employment of AMCs in the context of educational process to support teaching, professional learning, and effective communication between educators and (adult) learners (18 years-old and older) through familiar paradigms. Therefore, beyond higher education, the chapter focuses on adult education as well. So, to recap, in other words, an attempt is made to demonstrate the employment of cutting-edge AMCs and the way they help 21st century learners and educators acquire so-called *multiple-multimodal skills* under the lens of responsive and responsible learning. Arguably, today's adult learners (18 years-old and older) who are now at various and different educational levels and stages seem to "*approach information in diverse and innovative ways, and therefore, learning environments should adapt to their existing skills, needs, and prior knowledge in order to be effective*" (Nicolaou et al., 2019, p. 2). Furthermore, through theory and practice, the correct use of AMCs that educators may employ in TEL is also presented. The concept of TEL provides an excellent paradigm for the conceptualizing and classifying of AMCs, and their potential for adoption into education (Nicolaou et al., 2019). Summing up, this chapter will deal with issues of the effective integration of Information and Communications Technologies (ICTs) into education utilizing audio and video content (audiovisual content from here on), aiming at quality, effective and responsive–responsible teaching as well as sustainable education and learning for all.

Undoubtedly because of the complexity of the above issues involved, this chapter follows a bibliographical approach. Specifically, the chapter is a kind of literature case study (cf. Griffith & Laframboise, 1998), and the literature review process was generated through an online library technology-enhanced research method, applying the methods of finding information on the Internet and evaluating information (Nicolaou, 2022b, 2021d). Meanwhile, through this process, the chapter provides a rich, useful, and beneficial bibliography and historical evidence which can be used as a source for further study. Besides, the latent goal of this chapter is to become an important guide, that can serve as a helpful reference of audiovisual media technologies as cutting-edge audiovisual educational communication tools (i.e., ICT-tools and/or ICT-devices) that create and develop *multiple-multimodal skills* in the framework of an effective regular formal or informal, hybrid, distance and/or in-person as well as online teaching and learning. For this reason, the contribution of the presented paradigms is straightforward. Also, this chapter can be considered an exploration of the impact of AMCs in TEL, thus contributing to the current debate of using them within the educational process in the literature, as well as to enhanced stimulating educational engagement, retention, and critical thinking.

In conclusion, this chapter is also part of a broader ongoing cross-cultural research project, regarding the employment of AMCs in adult education and higher education in Greece and Cyprus in the light of media studies and broadcast journalism. More precisely, the cross-cultural research project began in 2016 and explores the multidisciplinary field that incorporates media, audiovisual content, and education (MACE) among generational cohorts with adult members (18 years-old and older), both as educators and as adult learners. Finally, the remainder of the chapter is organized into three parts in which, as mentioned above, characteristic paradigms are listed to assist potential educators and readers: (a) the first part reflects a brief literature review from diverse set of studies under the theme of the wider employment of AMCs in education, thus laying the groundwork for the theoretical background of this chapter; subsequently, (b) the second part presents the *multiple-multimodal skills* that can be acquired based on the theoretical background through discussion; while (c) the last part outlines a summary and presents the final conclusions and suggestions.

THEORETICAL BACKGROUND FROM AND THROUGH LITERATURE REVIEW: ADVANTAGES, BENEFITS, AND CLASSIFICATIONS

Recent research and literature reviews have indicated that the use of AMCs is an important factor in achieving TEL acquiring numerous skills (Bergdahl, et al., 2020; Dias, 2009; Frolova et al., 2020; Gordon & Brayshaw, 2014; Matsiola et al., 2019; Nicolaou et al., 2021b, 2019). Contemporary AMCs are mainly used from and through a verbal or visual mental model (see also Mayer, 2014) and can be useful in responsive and responsible learning in multiple ways (cf. Abrams, 2021; Balasubramanian et al., 2014), offering the potential to influence learning outcomes and transform the didactic process (Frolova et al., 2020; Martyushev et al., 2021; Nicolaou et al., 2019). More concretely, they are specifically employed to access, analyze, evaluate, create, and disseminate visual literacy in digital media through alternative educational approaches (Nicolaou, 2022c, p. 238). Characteristic paradigms are the serious games (cf. Katsaounidou et al., 2019; Gounaridou et al., 2021) or the various interactive online games (e.g., the free online interactive game-based learning software application *Kahoot!*) for game-based learning, aimed at enhancing *thinking skills* (e.g., analysis, interpretation, inference, explanation, self-regulation, open-mindedness, problem-solving, etc.) and *literacy skills* (e.g., alphabetic principle, phonological awareness, word recognition, vocabulary, structural analysis, etc.) in delivering content (such as television content through streaming) from and through online use, information-seeking, and web-based audiovisual media applications (see also Abrams, 2021; Brayshaw et al., 2019; Ernawati, et al., 2021; Kanellopoulou & Giannakoulopoulos, 2021; Mahzan et al., 2019; Middleton et al., 2020; Nicolaou, 2021b; Platz et al., 2021). Additionally, they are also used to assimilate and implement any advanced abilities and *competence skills* (such as collaboration, critical thinking, creativity, etc.) (Farrington et al. 2012; Nicolaou et al. 2019). Extending the above, they are also employed to achieve proper and constructive (verbal and non-verbal) communication in order to acquire *human communication skills* (e.g., listening, straight talking, stress management, emotion control, etc.) (cf. Hargie, 2006; Martyushev et al., 2021; Nicolaou, 2020; Tugtekin & Koc, 2020), for the learners and for the educator too.

Looking back, the blackboard (1841), motion picture (1940), the radio (1920), and television (TV from here on) (1957) in their time were considered cutting-edge and innovative ICT-tools or ICT-devices (ICT-mediums from here on) (Nicolaou, 2022a), while in our time any communication devices, applications or even services from and through the Internet after the official birth of the Internet on January 1, 1983 (cf. Nicolaou, 2022a, 2021a, 2011a, 2011b; Nicolaou & Kalliris, 2020; Sarridis & Nicolaou, 2015). Undoubtedly, nowadays, contemporary ICT-mediums are considered to be the ones developed in the new streamlined digital era such as (a) what we call today "social medias" (SMs from here on); (b) the Internet applications and services; (c) the new media; and (d) the mobile technologies (Matsiola, 2008; Nicolaou et al., 2021b; Nicolaou & Kalliris, 2020; Nicolaou, 2022a); that have made a significant contribution to the field of education as TEL mainly from 2006 onwards (see also Nicolaou et al., 2019; Sarridis & Nicolaou, 2015). In order to better decipher these contemporary ICT-mediums:

1. SMs are considered the following, for example,
    a. online social networks; OSNs, social networking sites; SNSs, social media, and platforms (e.g., *LinkedIn*, *Facebook*, *Twitter*, etc.);
    b. audiovisual platforms (e.g., *YouTube*, *DailyMotion*, *Vimeo*, *Netflix*, etc.);

c. audiovisual platforms with interactivity (e.g., *YouTube*, *Netflix*, *Twitch*, etc.) as content-hosting or even video-sharing websites that can be moved into the software as a service (SaaS) model (e.g., a video posted on *YouTube* to transport you to the *Netflix*);
   d. sound platforms (e.g., *Mixcloud*, *SoundCloud*, *Spotify*, etc.) as music or even other various audio media content streaming and media services;
   e. photo or even video sharing social networking services (e.g., *Pinterest*, *Instagram*, *Flickr*, *TikTok*, etc.);
   f. interactive websites or even weblogs/blogs or microblogs (e.g., interactive documentary, etc.);
   g. hypermedia authoring/storytelling platforms;
   h. online communication applications and services (e.g., multimedia messaging apps/social messaging/social chat, such as *Skype*, *Viber*, *Facebook Messenger*, *WhatsApp*, *Snapchat*, etc.);
   i. social networking website for scientists and academics as databases for the search and export of information and sources (e.g., *ResearchGate.net*, *Academia.edu*, etc.), and so on;
2. Internet applications and services are considered the following, for example,
   a. electronic mail (or e-mailing or e-mail or email or mail) (email/s from here on) (e.g., *Gmail* by Google, *Microsoft Outlook*, etc.) and electronic mailing lists (e.g., *Google Groups*, *Yahoo! Groups*, etc.);
   b. web browsers (e.g., *Google Chrome*, *Mozilla Firefox*, *Microsoft Edge*, etc.);
   c. web search engines (e.g., *Google*, *Yahoo!*, *Microsoft Bing*, etc.) or specialized web search engines (also known as internet-based academic engines such as *Google Scholar* by Google, and *Microsoft Academic* by Microsoft Research which was shut down on December 31, 2021);
   d. Internet Relay Chats (IRCs) (e.g., *mIRC*, *XChat*, etc.);
   e. file hosting services (e.g., *Dropbox*, *Mega*, *Google Drive*, *4shared*, *Microsoft OneDrive*, etc.);
   f. online bibliographic databases (e.g., *ERIC*, *PubMed*, *Scopus*, *Web of Science*, etc.);
   g. online web presentation software tools (e.g., *Prezi*, *Google Slides*, *PowerPoint Online*, *Keynote*, *LinkedIn SlideShare*, etc.);
   h. online survey administration software tools (e.g., *Google Forms*, *SurveryMonkey*, *Survs.com*, *Microsoft Forms*, etc.);
   i. online learning management systems (OLMSs) (e.g., *Blackboard*, *WebCT*, *Moodle*, as well as *Wikis* or blogs, etc.);
   j. online game-based learning platforms (e.g., *Kahoot!*, *Edufiq*, *Gametize*, *GoSkills*, etc.);
   k. business communication platforms (e.g., *Zoom Video Communications*; *Zoom*, *Microsoft Teams*, *Skype for Business*, *Webex* by Cisco; *WebEx*, etc.), and so on;
3. new media (e.g., news portal, Internet radio/TV or web-radio/TV, multimedia portals media-service providers as subscription video on-demand over-the-top streaming—such as *Netflix*, *Amazon Prime Video*, *HBO Max*, *Apple TV+*, *Disney+*, and so on—etc.); and finally
4. mobile technologies are generally considered to be two-way communication and computing devices with information technology that rely primarily on the wireless technology of wireless devices or internet-enabled devices (such as, for examples, personal computers; PCs, laptops, tablets, personal digital assistants; PDAs, mobile phones, smart phones, smart watched, and other electronic devices, etc., as well as information technology integration equipment), and are typically characterized as devices that go where the user goes. (cf. Dimoulas et al., 2019, 2015, 2014; Giomelakis et al., 2019; Newby et al., 2019; Matsiola, 2008; Matsiola et al., 2015; Nicolaou, 2022a, 2021a, 2021d, 2011a, 2011b, 2023; Podara et al., 2021; Sarridis & Nicolaou, 2015)

Figure 1. The timeline of ICTs evolution

Overall, at this point it should be mentioned that today the Internet as ICTs is considered the culmination of the field of communication as an information container (Kholdarvovna, 2021; Nicolaou et al., 2021b; Nicolaou, 2022a). Similarly, it provides access to *comprehensive multimedia communication* (Nicolaou 2011b, p. 43) to humans as *active online users* from and through the Internet and SNs with multimodal content and materials as well as digital copies (i.e., online and offline texts, photo, audio media in the form of sound recordings, certain sounds, music/songs, music investments, sound effects; sfx, etc., as well as in the combined format with video or even other visual content, e.g., aminations, etc.) (Dimoulas et al., 2015; Matsiola et al., 2015; Nicolaou, 2021a; Nicolaou & Karypidou, 2021; Sarridis & Nicolaou, 2015). Characteristic paradigms are the media websites with TV content or even the (modern) Internet forums (e.g., torrent community portals/forums) that add an additive value through the contributions of online users, which may continue to influence public opinion for a long time to come (Nicolaou, 2021a; Nicolaou & Karypidou, 2021).

Research has consistently shown that the effectiveness of using AMCs can be further enhanced by implementing a plethora of theoretical frameworks, such as Roger's theory of diffusion of innovation (Rogers, 2003), von Glasersfeld's theory of constructive learning (or the theory of constructivism) (von Glasersfeld, 1985), Knowles's theories of andragogy (Knowles, 1989) and self-directed learning (Knowles, 1975), Vygotsky's theory of social constructivism (Vygotsky, 1978), Dewey's theories of democracy (Dewey, 1916) and education as well as experiential learning (Dewey, 1938), or even Michelson's theory of experiential learning (Michelson, 1996). Additionally, modern theoretical approaches to teaching methodologies suggest audiovisual technology-supported teaching methodologies, such as *differentiated teaching* and *interdisciplinary teaching* for the purpose of effective teaching and educational effectiveness (Nicolaou et al., 2019; Nicolaou, 2022a, 2019a, 2019b, 2017, 2015). Recent research studies of cross-cultural research project MACE have shown that differentiated teaching using AMCs in adult learners (18 years-old and older) has been successful (a) in non-distance/regular formal or informal education, teaching and learning with participants from higher, professional, or vocational, and adult educations (cf. Nicolaou et al., 2021a, 2021b; Nicolaou & Kalliris, 2021, 2020; Nicolaou, 2020); as well as (b) in online teaching and learning with participants from adult education (cf. Nicolaou, 2021b).

Admittedly, since we live in a digital technological world and in a new streamlined digital era where technology is changing rapidly, education should be continuous and always focused on learning to learn as well as lifelong adult learning (Nicolaou, 2022a; Nicolaou et al., 2021b). Undoubtedly, education is a broad field and if any technology is properly applied in the context of learning, both intellectual capacity and beneficial creativity can be achieved (Nicolaou et al., 2019). Overall, the correct use of cutting-edge AMCs in the educational path with responsive and responsible learning has proven to offer generously a plethora of *multiple-multimodal skills* for both 21st century learners and educators. As a final conclusion, it could be said that there will always be room for further improvement with the aim of effective teaching and multimodal learning effectiveness from and through TEL, as long as we do not forget it.

MULTIPLE-MULTIMODAL SKILLS: FROM THEORY TO PRACTICE

Undoubtedly the pedagogical value of the use and implementation of ICTs as audiovisual educational communication tools or even as educational techniques is already a carefully guarded secret throughout time, both inside and outside the classroom in the context of educational process (e.g., through the curriculum, textbook-centered materials, implementation of a lesson plan, etc.) (cf. Dhamija & Dhamija, 2020; Foutsitzi, 2022; Khvilon & Patru, 2004; Lorenzo-Lledó et al., 2022; Nicolaou et al., 2022; Papastergiou & Solomonidou, 2005). The literature and studies in recent years (Budiarto, 2020; Frolova et al., 2020; Lee et al., 2021; Matsiola et al., 2019; Nicolaou et al., 2021b, 2019; Pavla et al., 2015; Ryabova et al., 2018; Sumamol, 2019) have also highlighted that this pedagogical value of using ICTs is owed to the fact that learners have (a) now cultivated as new entrants to a field; and (b) the ability and the capacity to evaluate, assess and adapt a suitable audiovisual educational communication tool or even medium. It might be that due to the statement mentioned, educators began to look for practical teaching activities as well as alternative or new, more modern pedagogical approaches (such as, for example, 2C-2I-1R—*Constructivist, Collaborative, Integrative, Reflective* and *Inquiry Based Learning*) and educational techniques (e.g., theatrical performance, etc.) to integrate ICTs into teaching–learning procedures in the 21st century (cf. Franada, 2018; Nicolaou et al., 2019; Nicolaou, 2021c, 2021e; Veglis & Avraam, 2001). This leads to the conclusion that each cutting-edge audiovisual educational communication tool now has its own pedagogical values in a certain and specific technology-supported learning environment and helps learners develop *contemporary novice skills* (e.g., *digital narrative writing skills*, etc.) (see also Budiarto, 2020; Frolova et al., 2020; Nicolaou et al., 2021b; Riyanti et al., 2021; Sumamol, 2019). Likewise, at the same time, it may require educators to possess specific *technical skills* or even *engineering skills* and *digital media technology skills* (e.g., online research abilities, digital critical analysis, linking diverse types and sources of information, reformulating retrieved data, etc.), in addition to *pedagogical skills* (e.g., lesson planning, classroom management, etc.) and *basic ICT-skills* (such as *computer skills, screen navigation skills, website navigation skills, search skills*, etc.) for its use, execution, and application (see also Matsiola et al., 2019; Nicolaou et al., 2021b, 2019; Thanavathi, 2021).

Despite what we already know about the influence of these modern pedagogical approaches and ICT-supported educational techniques (such as, for example, *distancing*), the most recent literature has also shown that their effectiveness is determined by the educational needs of the learners themselves (Frolova et al., 2020; Nicolaou et al., 2019; Nicolaou, 2022a). Similarly, the right choice of the most appropriate ICTs as audiovisual educational communication tool or medium (Nicolaou et al., 2019; Nicolaou, 2022a). On the other hand, it is a fact that ICTs also contribute to the enhancement of the learning experience of learners, the development of positive values and the acquisition of specific skills, such as *social handling skills* (e.g., humility. empathy, compassion, decisiveness, creativity, etc.) and *production skills* (e.g., attention to detail, critical thinking, computer-aided technology, etc.) (Hashim et al., 2019; Koehler & Mishra, 2005; Law et al., 2011; Nicolaou et al., 2021b, 2019; Røkenes & Krumsvik, 2014). In the same context, they also help to (a) acquire *human communication skills* or even *life skills* (e.g., problem solving, critical thinking, *effective communication skills*, decision-making, creative thinking, *interpersonal relationship skills, self-awareness building skills*, empathy, coping with stress and emotions, etc.) (cf. Hargie, 2006; Hashim et al., 2019; Nicolaou, 2020, 2014; Nicolaou & Kalliris, 2021; Tugtekin & Koc, 2020); and (b) develop positive and healthy relationships between their educator and learners (e.g., through SMs such as online communication applications and services, etc.) (cf. Baytiyeh, 2021; Nicolaou, 2022a, 2021c, 2021e). Hence, this leads to the conclusion that *human communication skills*, *life skills* and *social handling skills* or even *production skills* from and through ICTs are authentically a lot more than just *basic technical skills* (e.g., software proficiency, data analysis, etc.) (see also Matsiola et al., 2022, 2019; Nicolaou et al., 2021b).

Currently, in the new streamlined digital era in which we live, the contribution of AMCs is characterized as necessary and the most suitable for use in the didactic process with responsive and responsible learning. A characteristic paradigm is the various electronic and interactive audiovisual media (i.e., e-Audio Visual) as e-Learning material of a course that are used as an alternative aid within the classroom, to bring more media elements and visualization as well as enhance the learners' learning experience, focusing more on audio and visual content (cf. Kalliris et al., 2014; Nugraini et al., 2009; Palioura & Dimoulas, 2022; Patahuddin et al., 2022). In this sense, a multimedia-enriched e-learning can be considered to represent a very demanding case of mediated communication, making mediated learning a very suitable case-study for the analysis and investigation of various audiovisual communication issues, including emotional aspects (Kalliris et al., 2014, 2011; Kotsakis et al., 2014). Other typical and promising paradigms are (a) machine-assisted learning in highly interdisciplinary media fields (Chatzara et al., 2019); (b) the employment of SMs (such as OSNs, SNSs, audiovisual platforms, etc.) or other innovative collaborative, community-driven technologies, and ICT-mediums as educational resources; or even (c) when conventional or distant learning utilizes audiovisual content or streaming videos via SMs (usually through audiovisual platforms with or without interactivity) to distribution and broadcast lectures (cf. Kalliris et al., 2014; Martyushev et al., 2021; Nicolaou et al., 2021b; Quinn-Allan, 2010; Tomyuk et al., 2019). Generally, when AMCs are used effectively for teaching in a wide variety of fields, learner achievement increases, responsive and responsible learning in a subject is significantly enhanced, and learners acquire a range of skills, abilities, and capacities (cf. Frolova et al., 2020; Nicolaou et al., 2021b, 2019; Quinn-Allan, 2010).

According to the literature (Al-Maatouk et al., 2020; Domunco, 2011; Kefala, 2021; Martyushev et al., 2021; Perifanou et al., 2021; Quinn-Allan, 2010), the employment of SMs in the context of educational process is usually applied for purposes and ways of communication, giving learners the appropriate *human communication skills* and *digital skills* (e.g., communicating via SMs, researching information online, handling sensitive information, etc.). Admittedly, SMs as social-media learning tools enable learners not only to discover and read, but also to create, share, discuss and modify the learning content created in the teaching–learning procedure, thereby gaining integrated *social media skills* (e.g., *analytical skills*, *friendship skills*, etc.) (see also Kourti et al., 2018; Kordoutis & Kourti, 2016; Novakovich et al., 2017; Fenwick, 2016). Likewise, the development of *social media skills* allows learners to participate in meaningful discussions, and more precisely in the framework of relationship building and control (Quinn-Allan, 2010). In particular, they "*allow learners to participate in formal (e.g., study of course material) and informal (e.g., look for useful information everywhere) learning conditions. Moreover, learners can find other people with a similar way of thinking and exchange knowledge in an informal way (e.g., exchange of their educational experiences) for educational purposes*" (Nicolaou et al., 2019, p. 6). On the one hand, this is due to the easy and free access to the benefits and advantages they offer, making them particularly popular and immediately well-known (Matsiola et al., 2015; Nicolaou, 2021a; Nicolaou & Karypidou, 2021; Sarridis & Nicolaou, 2015). SMs have already been in our daily lives for years, and over time the way we communicate our rounds has apparently changed due to their now *"offering user-based customization and promoting more-friendly game-like communication"* (Matsiola et al., 2015, p. 199). By extending the above in the education sector, the use of SMs in the didactic process with responsive and responsible learning as a social-media learning tool nowadays can also be characterized as crucial. Obviously, not because they are fashionable or due to the current circumstances (e.g., due the effects of a pandemic)—such as in the case of (a) the telecommunication application *Skype* from Microsoft during the first wave of the COVID-19 pandemic or even (b) *"podcasts and vodcasts, which have been in the spotlight for more than a decade and have gained popularity in the educational environment"* (Nicolaou et al., 2021b, p. 159) in the last couple of years, due to the pandemic again—but because of their uniqueness and that their adoption as social-media learning tools is leading to the provision of a sustainable education with TEL for all. To summarize, through their utilization, learners are empowered to create discussions and to make the exchange and sharing of information and knowledge faster and easier (cf. Nicolaou, 2022a, 2021c, 2021e). Lastly, it can be said that the integration of SMs into the educational path with responsive and responsible learning can contribute to the creation of progressive, interactive, effective, and modern technology-supported learning environments with several perspectives, if they are used sparingly (cf. Kefala, 2021; Martyushev et al., 2021; Novakovich et al., 2017; Quinn, 2018; Quinn-Allan, 2010; Tomyuk et al., 2019).

Regarding the utilization of Internet applications and services, it seems to be highly valued by the learners in a traditional face-to-face teaching–learning procedure or even a distance learning course (Kalliris et al., 2014), especially if they are employed through mobile technologies (cf. Psomadaki et al., 2022; Nicolaou, 2021b). Although mobile technologies are mostly used for cellular communication purposes, they are perhaps the fastest growing cutting-edge technologies available nowadays and enable us to leverage multimedia content with rich multimedia experience in our daily lives (cf. Dimoulas et al., 2014; Psomadaki et al., 2022; Sidiropoulos et al., 2019). It is a fact that mobile technologies can enhance teaching–learning experiences and offer enormous potential to transform education, if used by educators in an appropriate way to keep pace with the respective socio-cultural framework of teaching–learning procedure with responsive and responsible learning (cf. Ernawati et al., 2021; Sani & Adiansha, 2021). Additionally, over time, the employment of Internet applications and services as a contemporary audiovisual educational communication tool for TEL seems to have become significantly entrenched in every aspect of educational life (Ernawati et al., 2021; Naismith et al., 2004; Veglis & Avraam, 2001). Indicatively, the various websites or portals as web-based educational platforms in the form of OLMSs that are usually created from the educators, offer the learners everything they need in one place (cf. Aris et al., 2020; Chang & Wang, 2021; Martyushev et al., 2021; Kalliris et al., 2014; Matsiola et al., 2019; Nicolaou et al., 2019; Werth & Werth, 2011). This facilitates the management of courses, additional digital materials, and resources through a user-friendly interface environment (cf. Aris et al., 2020; Martyushev et al., 2021; Matsiola et al., 2019; Ngubane-Mokiwa & Khoza, 2021; Nicolaou et al., 2019; Werth & Werth, 2011), while also helping to develop the curriculum as well as to acquire a variety of *teaching skills* (such as communication, project management, problem-solving, creativity, patience, etc.) for the professional development of the educators themselves (Chang & Wang, 2021; Martyushev et al., 2021). Furthermore, communication through online meetings and chat with the educator and other learners that takes place via them, is always accessible (even through mobile technologies), which can lead to increased learner engagement and improved learning outcomes across the entire ability range (cf. Crowder et al., 2019; Nicolaou et al., 2019; Werth & Werth, 2011). Finally, the educator along with the learners can also participate in IRCs or even online discussion groups or newsgroups (i.e., Internet form or message board—such as *Google Groups* and *Yahoo! Groups*), ask questions, discuss issues, and share experiences with each other or even with other online users from and through the Internet and mobile technologies (cf. Calvo et al., 2014; Newby et al., 2019; Nicolaou et al., 2019).

New media, in recent years, have begun to dramatically influence a human's values, expectations, and interests, creating new trends, attitudes, and stereotypes (Florescu, 2014; Nicolaou, 2021b; Podara et al., 2022, 2021, 2019). Likewise, they created new forms of TV viewing, modern usage patterns, and new types of streaming content in the entertainment space (cf. Podara et al., 2022, 2021, 2019). Also, new media nowadays are mainly used for digital and online production practices through digital and mobile media (i.e., mobile technologies) which are ubiquitous in our daily lives (see also Nicolaou & Karypidou, 2021; Matsiola et al., 2015; Matsiola, 2008; Hashem et al., 2017). Their use in the context of educational process contributes mostly to media education and digital visual literacy, creating modern learning opportunities, but also shaping learners with different educational needs (Matsiola et al., 2019; Nicolaou et al., 2022; Nicolaou & Kalliris, 2020). Moreover, as cutting-edge audiovisual educational communication tools, new media are not the purpose, but they are there to help in the framework of the teaching–learning procedure as a catalyst or inhibitor of information and new, more modern knowledge. On the one hand, in this context, educators must necessarily possess specific or even or a plethora of *combined skills* and self-regulative abilities which they will pass on to the learners in the light of *media skills*. More precisely, the co-compromise and co-exchange skills among educators and learners are *Journalists' ICTs skills* (i.e., *basic skills, web publishing skills, web 2.0 skills, webcasting skills, mobile skills*, etc.), *data journalism skills, growing media skills* and *cognitive skills* (cf. Nicolaou, 2022a; Nicolaou et al., 2021b; Sidiropoulos et al., 2019).

In recapitulating, all the aforementioned leads to the conclusion that maximizing learners' involvement in the educational journey through AMCs can create motivation and stimulation of new *perceptual skills* (e.g., *digital skills* or digital competence, such as *digital literacy skills, media literacy skills*, etc.) or even development of *pre-existing skills* (e.g., *soft skills*, such as *persuasive communication skills*, versatility, critical thinking, *emotional intelligence skills*, etc.) through upskilling and reskilling as well as self-regulative abilities over time (cf. Anthonysamy et al., 2020; Antoniadou et al., 2021; González-Salamanca et al., 2020; Livingstone et al., 2021; Makri & Vlachopoulos, 2019; Martyushev et al., 2021; Nicolaou, 2020, 2014; Nusrat & Sultana, 2019; Rao, 2018). The same framework applies of course to educators as well. Additionally, utilizing AMCs through TEL can provide more opportunities, challenges and social benefits that will lead to improved and enhanced learning outcomes (Cheng et al., 2021; Nicolaou et al., 2019; Quinn, 2018). Similarly, the interaction and interplay with AMCs that we already use in our daily lives can provide them with extended learning from a different perspective or even better learned material and/or their proper use (Matsiola et al., 2019; Nicolaou et al., 2019). In the same context, the learner–learner interaction or enjoyment which will help in a timely manner in exchanging experiences and gaining access to best teaching practices is also achieved (cf. Nagy, 2018; Turan & Cetintas, 2020; Saeed et al., 2018; Frisen & Kuskis, 2013), offering educational effectiveness in TEL (cf. Frolova et al., 2019; Nicolaou et al., 2021b). The essence is that the correct use of AMCs in the educational path with responsive and responsible learning has proven to offer generously a plethora of *multiple-multimodal skills* for both 21st century learners and educators.

CONCLUSION, SUGGESTIONS, AND EPILOGUE

AMCs mentioned above can be unrestricted in the context of educational process from all educational levels and disciplines (including adult education and afterschool programs). Notably, they can be used either as audiovisual educational communication tools by educators to impart knowledge through the stimulation of the senses, as a vivid teaching and technology-supported learning environment is created, or as audiovisual educational communication tools by learners to use related concepts to or acquire a plethora of skills—*multiple-multimodal skills*. Besides, it is a fact that *"any type of technologically mediated environment must be customized to the learners' needs, and all parameters should be taken into account so that training will never end and will be evidently lifelong as new educational fields will always come to light"* (Nicolaou et al., 2019, p. 9). On the other hand, the correct choice of any AMCs in the framework of teaching–learning procedure with responsive and responsible learning to create numerous skills for the acquisition of *multiple-multimodal skills*, is a challenge and at the same time not an easy task for the educators, resulting in a constant huge risk of unnecessary and superficial application and use of them (cf. Nicolaou et al., 2022, 2019). First of all, the educators themselves, as mentioned, must already have *specific skills* and abilities in ICTs (i.e., *technical skills* or even *engineering skills* and *digital media technology skills*) as well as other various *authentic skills* (e.g., *human communication skills*, *life skills*, *social handling skills*, etc.) in order to be able to effectively cope with the modern requirements of their profession (see also Antoniadou, 2020; Antoniadou & Quinlan, 2022, 2020; Matsiola et al., 2019; Ngah et al., 2019; Nicolaou, 2022a, 2021c, 2021e; Thanavathi, 2021; Pekrum, 2019; Sueb et al., 2020). To summarize, nowadays a multimodal educator is required to possess *"imagination, charisma, uniqueness, nervousness, patience, and perseverance"* (Nicolaou & Kalliris, 2020, p. 987) to strengthen the curriculum, to support school material, to effectively integrate AMCs into a lesson plan for educational effectiveness, and so on.

Admittedly, the youngest (adult) learners that are now at the various educational stages seem to approach information in different and innovative pathways, while using cutting-edge mobile technologies or even other various electronic or smart devices (i.e., audiovisual media technologies) in different multifaceted ways and practices (such as, for example, creation of multimedia content, e.g., podcasts, vodcasts or videos, etc., from and through SMs) (cf. Podara et al., 2022, 2019; Aslanidou & Menexes, 2008; Podara & Kalliris, 2022). Similarly, their personality also seems to be related to the most important precedents of the actual use, adoption, and adaptation of technology (Manolika et al., 2021), resulting in them being characterized as *technological learners*. This concludes that educational techniques therefore need to be adapted while AMCs as audiovisual educational communication tools need to be chosen based on the existing needs of learners in order to be effective. Additionally, research studies have shown that learners (a) learn more and better when watching audiovisual content (Galatsopoulou et al., 2022; Matsiola et al., 2022; Nicolaou, 2021b; Nicolaou & Kalliris, 2020) or listening to sound or audio media content (Matsiola et al., 2019; Nicolaou et al., 2021a, 2021b); (b) can handle more than one screen simultaneously; and (c) prefer interactivity (see also Nicolaou & Karypidou, 2021; Podara et al., 2022, 2019). Specifically, recent research has confirmed the use of contemporary AMCs in higher education teaching reflects the above perspective of learners and can ensure long-term success (Matsiola et al., 2022). All these lead to the conclusion that one-way teaching or not using AMCs in the teaching–learning procedure, can make learners less interested in it. Furthermore, given the *multimedia skills* of modern learners, educators have the opportunity to add value to their curricula by implementing the aforementioned theoretical frameworks and leveraging learners' willingness to hone their numerous skills.

Over time, there are vigorous and ever-increasing ongoing technological developments and unexpected conditions (such as, for example, the COVID-19 pandemic) which have brought about and will continue to bring about newly introduced changes in this digital technological world. Undoubtedly, we currently live in a borderless world dominated by SMs and multimedia portals media-service providers due to the new streamlined digital era, creating new behaviors, forms of TV viewing, usage patterns, and audiovisual consumption habits (cf. Matsiola et al., 2015; Nicolaou, 2022c, 2022d, 2021a, 2021b; Podara et al., 2022, 2019; Podara & Kalliris, 2022); where educators must take them seriously. Additionally, there has been a significant increase in the number of immigrants, migrants, and transmigrators around the world (cf. Shutaleva et al., 2022), while on the other hand we are threatened by health threats, climate changes, conspiracy theories and fake news, and so on (cf. Lamprou et al., 2021; Katsaounidou & Dimoulas, 2019; Kefalaki & Karanicolas, 2020; Shutaleva et al., 2021). Also, in the future, utilization of data mining from and through AMCs will be able to further help in providing an educational experience for the learners by setting up a responsive–responsible learning environment and structuring the effectiveness of learning as well as the development of additional abilities (see also Cerratto Pargman et al., 2021; Podara et al., 2021; Veglis et al., 2022). Finally, from now on, we will all have to acquire *multiple-multimodal skills* to cope with this (un)real and virtual (digital) world through a fair, quality, and sustainable education, and TEL for all, because skills are built and not born.

ACKNOWLEDGMENT

I would like to acknowledge the valuable contribution of Maria Matsiola, for pointing out important comments and carefully proofreading and correcting the English language in this chapter. I am also particularly grateful to Paschalia Poppi, Eliza Stylianou Fatta, Giolanta-Alexia Stoits, and Kiki Katsafiloudi who participated in the proposed procedures and strategies for rendering culture-specific concepts when writing the initial draft of the chapter. Additionally, I thank George Kalliris for believing in me and overseeing the cross-cultural research project MACE. Furthermore, I would like to thank the anonymous reviewers as well as the handling editors for the valuable comments and suggestions that helped me to improve this chapter. Moreover, I would like to thank the book editors, Nor Aziah Alias, Sharipah Ruzaina Syed-Aris, and Hamimah Hashim, as well as all those who believed in my work. Finally, this chapter is dedicated to those young adults who are in their 30s and have suddenly developed an autoimmune diabetes (e.g., MODY—Maturity Onset Diabetes of the Young or LADA—Latent Autoimmune Diabetes in Adults) due to thyroid or autoimmune thyroid disorder (e.g., Hashimoto's disease) and/or because they have experienced or continue to experience some type of depression or anxiety and/or stress or even post-traumatic stress disorder (PTSD) after a traumatic experience and/or loss of a loved one.

REFERENCES

Abrams, S. S. (2021). Game-Informed Cooperative Assessments and Socially Responsible Learning in Public School Math Classes. In M. Harvey & R. Marlatt (Eds.), *Esports Research and Its Integration in Education* (pp. 168–184). IGI Global. doi:10.4018/978-1-7998-7069-2.ch010

Al-Maatouk, Q., Othman, M. S., Alsayed, A. O., Al-Rahmi, A. M., Abuhassna, H., & Al-Rahmi, W. M. (2020). Applying Communication Theory to Structure and Evaluate the Social Media Platforms in Academia. [IJATCSE]. *International Journal of Advanced Trends in Computer Science and Engineering*, *9*(2), 1505–1517. doi:10.30534/ijatcse/2020/92922020

Anthonysamy, L., Koo, A. C., & Hew, S. H. (2020). Self-regulated learning strategies in higher education: Fostering digital literacy for sustainable lifelong learning. *Education and Information Technologies*, *25*(4), 2393–2414. doi:10.100710639-020-10201-8

Antoniadou, M. (2020). From euphoria to letting go: experiences of cross-cultural adaptation of international academics in UK higher education. In M. Antoniadou & M. Crowder (Eds.), *Modern Day Challenges in Academia: Time for a Change* (pp. 82–98). Edward Elgar Publishing. doi:10.4337/9781788119191.00014

Antoniadou, M., Crowder, M., & Andreakos, G. (2021). Emotional Intelligence in Engineering Management Education: The Missing Priority. In D. Ktoridou (Ed.), *Cases on Engineering Management Education in Practice* (pp. 92–104). IGI Global. doi:10.4018/978-1-7998-4063-3.ch005

Antoniadou, M., & Quinlan, K. M. (2020). Thriving on challenges: How immigrant academics regulate emotional experiences during acculturation. *Studies in Higher Education*, *45*(1), 71–85. doi:10.1080/03075079.2018.1512567

Antoniadou, M., & Quinlan, K. M. (2022). Holding true or caving in? Academics' Values, Emotions, and Behaviors in Response to Higher Education Reforms. *Higher Education Policy*, *35*(2), 522–541. doi:10.105741307-021-00225-1

Aris, S. R. S., Salleh, M. F. M., & Ismail, M. H. (2020). Guided Cooperative Flipped Classroom Approach in Learning Molecular Orbital Theory. *International Journal of Academic Research in Business & Social Sciences*, *10*(14), 200–212. doi:10.6007/IJARBSS/v10-i14/7689

Aslanidou, S., & Menexes, G. (2008). Youth and the Internet: Uses and practices in the home. *Computers & Education*, *51*(3), 1375–1391. doi:10.1016/j.compedu.2007.12.003

Balasubramanian, K., Jaykumar, V., & Fukey, L. N. (2014). A study on "Student preference towards the use of Edmodo as a learning platform to create responsible learning environment". *Procedia: Social and Behavioral Sciences*, *144*, 416–422. doi:10.1016/j.sbspro.2014.07.311

Baytiyeh, H. (2021). Social Media Tools for Educational Sustainability in Conflict-Affected Regions. *Education Sciences*, *11*(11), 662. doi:10.3390/educsci11110662

Bergdahl, N., Nouri, J., & Fors, U. (2020). Disengagement, engagement and digital skills in technology-enhanced learning. *Education and Information Technologies*, *25*(2), 957–983. doi:10.100710639-019-09998-w

Brayshaw, M., Gordon, N. A., & Grey, S. (2019). Smart, Social, Flexible and Fun: Escaping the Flatlands of Virtual Learning Environments. In K. Arai, R. Bhatia, & S. Kapoor (Eds.), *Intelligent Computing. CompCom 2019. Advances in Intelligent Systems and Computing* (Vol. 998, pp. 1047–1060). Springer. doi:10.1007/978-3-030-22868-2_70

Budiarto, M. K. (2020). Identification of students' needs for multimedia development in craft and entrepreneurial topic: Information technology-assisted learning. *COUNS-EDU: The International Journal of Counseling and Education*, 5(4), 153–162. doi:10.23916/0020200525740

Burton, R. (2022). Nursing Students Perceptions of Using YouTube to Teach Psychomotor Skills: A Comparative Pilot Study. *SAGE Open Nursing*, 8. doi:10.1177/23779608221117385 PMID:35923914

Calvo, R., Arbiol, A., & Iglesias, A. (2014). Are all chats suitable for learning purposes? A study of the required characteristics. *Procedia Computer Science*, 27, 251–260. doi:10.1016/j.procs.2014.02.028

Cerratto Pargman, T., McGrath, C., Viberg, O., Kitto, K., Knight, S., & Ferguson, R. (2021). Responsible learning analytics: creating just, ethical, and caring. In *Companion Proceedings 11th International Conference on Learning Analytics & Knowledge (LAK21)*.

Chang, C.-C., & Wang, Y.-H. (2021). Using Phenomenological Methodology with Thematic Analysis to Examine and Reflect on Commonalities of Instructors' Experiences in MOOCs. *Education Sciences*, 11(5), 203. doi:10.3390/educsci11050203

Chatzara, E., Kotsakis, R., Tsipas, N., Vrysis, L., & Dimoulas, C. (2019). Machine-Assisted Learning in Highly-Interdisciplinary Media Fields: A Multimedia Guide on Modern Art. *Education Sciences*, 9(3), 198. doi:10.3390/educsci9030198

Cheng, M.-M., Lacaste, A. V., Saranza, C., & Chuang, H.-H. (2021). Culturally Responsive Teaching in Technology-Supported Learning Environments in Marine Education for Sustainable Development. *Sustainability*, 13(24), 13922. doi:10.3390u132413922

Crowder, M., Antoniadou, M., & Stewart, J. (2019). To BlikBook or not to BlikBook: Exploring student engagement of an online discussion platform. *Innovations in Education and Teaching International*, 56(3), 295–306. doi:10.1080/14703297.2018.1502091

Dewey, J. (1916). *Democracy and education: an introduction to the philosophy of education*. The Free Press.

Dewey, J. (1938). Experience & Education. *Touchstone (Nashville, Tenn.)*.

Dhamija, A., & Dhamija, D. (2020). Impact of Innovative and Interactive Instructional Strategies on Student Classroom Participation. In M. Montebello (Ed.), Handbook of Research on Digital Learning (pp. 20–37). IGI Global. doi:10.4018/978-1-5225-9304-1.ch002

Dias, A. (2009). Technology Enhanced Learning and Augmented Reality: An Application on Multimedia Interactive Books. *International Business & Economics Review*, 1(1), 69–79.

Dimoulas, C., Veglis, A., & Kalliris, G. (2014). Application of Mobile Cloud-Based Technologies in News Reporting: Current Trends and Future Perspectives. In J. Rodrigues, K. Lin, & J. Lloret (Eds.), *Mobile Networks and Cloud Computing Convergence for Progressive Services and Applications* (pp. 320–343). IGI Global. doi:10.4018/978-1-4666-4781-7.ch017

Dimoulas, C., Veglis, A., & Kalliris, G. (2015). Audiovisual Hypermedia in the Semantic Web. In M. Khosrow-Pour, D.B.A. (Ed.), Encyclopedia of Information Science and Technology, Third Edition (pp. 7594–7604). IGI Global.

Dimoulas, C. A., Veglis, A. A., & Kalliris, G. (2019). Semantically Enhanced Authoring of Shared Media. In M. Khosrow-Pour, D.B.A. (Ed.), Advanced Methodologies and Technologies in Media and Communications (pp. 277–289). IGI Global. doi:10.4018/978-1-5225-7601-3.ch022

Domunco, C. F. (2011). Social media and the social (re)construction of the educational reality. *Journal of Educational Sciences & Psychology*, *1*(2).

Ernawati, R., Rahman, F. F., Khoiroh, M. S., Rahmah, F. D., Sulistiawan, J., & Moslehpour, M. (2021). The Effectiveness of Web-Based Audiovisual Media Applications in Monitoring Children's Growth to Prevent Stunting. *Advances in Decision Sciences*, *25*(3), 1–11.

Farrington, C. A., Roderick, M., Allensworth, E., Nagaoka, J., Keyes, T. S., Johnson, D. W., & Beechum, N. O. (2012). *Teaching Adolescents to Become Learners. the Role of Noncognitive Factors in Shaping School Performance: A Critical Literature Review*. University of Chicago Consortium on Chicago School Research.

Fenwick, T. (2016). Social media, professionalism and higher education: A sociomaterial consideration. *Studies in Higher Education*, *41*(4), 664–677. doi:10.1080/03075079.2014.942275

Florescu, O. (2014). Positive and Negative Influences of the Mass Media upon Education. *Procedia: Social and Behavioral Sciences*, *149*, 349–353. doi:10.1016/j.sbspro.2014.08.271

Foutsitzi, A. (2022). Images in Educational Textbooks and Educational Audiovisual Media. *European Journal of Language and Literature*, *8*(2), 26–32.

Franada, J. M. (2018). 2C-2I-1R Pedagogical Approaches in Teaching Technology and Livelihood Education Exploratory Courses and the Academic Performance of Grade 8 Students in the Division of Lipa. *Ascendens Asia Journal of Multidisciplinary Research Abstracts*, *2*(6).

Frisen, N., & Kuskis, A. (2013). Modes of Interaction. In M. G. Moore (Ed.), *Handbook of Distance Education* (pp. 351–371). Routledge. doi:10.4324/9780203803738.ch22

Frolova, E. V., Rogach, O. V., & Ryabova, T. M. (2020). Digitalization of Education in Modern Scientific Discourse: New Trends and Risks Analysis. *European Journal of Contemporary Education*, *9*(2), 313–336.

Frolova, E. V., Ryabova, T. M., & Rogach, O. V. (2019). Digital Technologies in Education: Problems and Prospects for "Moscow Electronic School" Project Implementation. *European Journal of Contemporary Education*, *8*(4), 779–789.

Galatsopoulou, F., Kenterelidou, C., Kotsakis, R., & Matsiola, M. (2022). Examining Students' Perceptions towards Video-Based and Video-Assisted Active Learning Scenarios in Journalism and Communication Courses. *Education Sciences*, *12*(2), 74. doi:10.3390/educsci12020074

Giomelakis, D., Karypidou, C., & Veglis, A. (2019). SEO inside Newsrooms: Reports from the Field. *Future Internet*, *11*(12), 261. doi:10.3390/fi11120261

González-Salamanca, J. C., Agudelo, O. L., & Salinas, J. (2020). Key Competences, Education for Sustainable Development and Strategies for the Development of 21st Century Skills. A Systematic Literature Review. *Sustainability*, *12*(24), 10366. doi:10.3390u122410366

Gordon, N., & Brayshaw, M. (2014). Technology-Enhanced Learning in Higher Education: Tribes and Territories. In V. Zuzevičiūtė, E. Butrimė, D. Vitkutė-Adžgauskienė, V. Vladimirovich Fomin, & K. Kikis-Papadakis (Eds.), *E-Learning as a Socio-Cultural System: A Multidimensional Analysis* (pp. 224–236). IGI Global. doi:10.4018/978-1-4666-6154-7.ch013

Gounaridou, A., Siamtanidou, E., & Dimoulas, C. (2021). A Serious Game for Mediated Education on Traffic Behavior and Safety Awareness. *Education Sciences*, *11*(3), 127. doi:10.3390/educsci11030127

Griffith, P. L., & Laframboise, K. L. (1998). Literature case studies: Case method and reader response come together in teacher education. *Journal of Adolescent & Adult Literacy*, *41*(5), 364–375.

Hargie, O. (2006). *The Handbook of Communication Skills* (3rd ed.). Routledge. doi:10.4324/9780203007037

Hashem, M. E., Hashem, J., & Hashem, P. (2017). Role of new media in education and corporate communication: Trends and prospects in a middle Eastern context. In M., Friedrichsen, Y. Kamalipour (Eds.), Digital Transformation in Journalism and News Media: Media Management, Media Convergence and Globalization (pp. 443–466). Media Business and Innovation. Springer.

Hashim, A. M., Aris, S. R. S., & Chan, Y. F. (2019). Promoting empathy using design thinking in project-based learning and as a classroom culture. *Asian Journal of University Education*, *15*(3), 14–23. doi:10.24191/ajue.v15i3.7817

Kalliris, G., Dimoulas, C., Veglis, A., & Matsiola, M. (2011). Investigating quality of experience and learning (QoE & QoL) of audiovisual content broadcasting to learners over IP networks. *IEEE Symposium on Computers and Communications (ISCC 2011)*, 836-841. 10.1109/ISCC.2011.5983946

Kalliris, G., Dimoulas, C. A., & Matsiola, M. (2019). Media Management, Sound Editing and Mixing. In M. Filimowicz (Ed.), *Foundations in Sound Design for Linear Media: A Multidisciplinary Approach* (pp. 82–112). Routledge. doi:10.4324/9781315106335-3

Kalliris, G., Matsiola, M., Dimoulas, C., & Veglis, A. (2014). Emotional Aspects and Quality of Experience for Multifactor Evaluation of Audiovisual Content. [IJMSTR]. *International Journal of Monitoring and Surveillance Technologies Research*, *2*(4), 40–61. doi:10.4018/IJMSTR.2014100103

Kanellopoulou, C., & Giannakoulopoulos, A. (2021). Internet-Assisted Language Teaching: The Internet as a Tool for Personalised Language Exploration. *Creative Education*, *12*(03), 625–646. doi:10.4236/ce.2021.123043

Katsaounidou, A., Vrysis, L., Kotsakis, R., Dimoulas, C., & Veglis, A. (2019). MAthE the Game: A Serious Game for Education and Training in News Verification. *Education Sciences*, *9*(2), 155. doi:10.3390/educsci9020155

Katsaounidou, A. N., & Dimoulas, C. A. (2019). Integrating content authentication support in media services. In M. Khosrow-Pour, D.B.A. (Ed.), Advanced Methodologies and Technologies in Digital Marketing and Entrepreneurship (pp. 395–408). IGI Global. doi:10.4018/978-1-5225-7766-9.ch031

Kefala, A. (2021). Social Media Effects and Self-Harm Behaviors Among Young People: Theoretical and Methodological Challenges. *Journal of Education. Innovation and Communication*, *3*(2), 13–25.

Kefalaki, M., & Karanicolas, S. (2020). Communication's rough navigations: 'fake'news in a time of a global crisis. *Journal of Applied Learning and Teaching*, *3*(1), 29–41.

Kholdarvovna, T. M. (2021). The Role Of Information And Communication Technologies In The Global Environment. *The American Journal of Social Science and Education Innovations*, *3*(1), 564–570. doi:10.37547/tajssei/Volume03Issue01-99

Khvilon, E., & Patru, M. (2004). *Technologies de L'Information ET de la Communication en éDucation: Un Programme D'Enseignement ET un Cadre Pour la Formation Continue Des Enseignants* [Information and Communication Technologies in Education: A Curriculum AND Framework for Continuing Teacher Education.]. UNESCO.

Knowles, M. S. (1975). *Self-Directed Learning: A Guide for Learners and teachers*. Association Press.

Knowles, M. S. (1989). *The Making of an Adult Educator: An Autobiographical Journey*. Jossey-Bass.

Koehler, M. J., & Mishra, P. (2005). What Happens When Teachers Design Educational Technology? The Development of Technological Pedagogical Content Knowledge. *Journal of Educational Computing Research*, *32*(2), 131–152. doi:10.2190/0EW7-01WB-BKHL-QDYV

Kordoutis, P., & Kourti, E. (2016). Digital Friendship on Facebook and Analog Friendship Skills. In *Proceedings of the European Conference on Social Media Research*, Caen, France 2016 (pp. 109–115).

Kotsakis, R., Dimoulas, C., Kalliris, G., & Veglis, A. (2014). Emotional Prediction and Content Profile Estimation in Evaluating Audiovisual Mediated Communication. [IJMSTR]. *International Journal of Monitoring and Surveillance Technologies Research*, *2*(4), 62–80. doi:10.4018/IJMSTR.2014100104

Kourti, E., Kordoutis, P., & Anna, M. (2018). Social perception of Facebook friendship among Greek students. *Psychology: The Journal of the Hellenic Psychological Society*, *23*(2), 53–68. doi:10.12681/psy_hps.22603

Lamprou, E., Antonopoulos, N., Anomeritou, I., & Apostolou, C. (2021). Characteristics of Fake News and Misinformation in Greece: The Rise of New Crowdsourcing-Based Journalistic Fact-Checking Models. *Journalism and Media*, *2*(3), 417–439. doi:10.3390/journalmedia2030025

Law, N., Yuen, A., & Fox, R. (2011). *Educational Innovations Beyond Technology: Nurturing Leadership and Establishing Learning Organizations*. Springer. doi:10.1007/978-0-387-71148-5

Lee, L., Liang, W.-J., & Sun, F.-C. (2021). The Impact of Integrating Musical and Image Technology upon the Level of Learning Engagement of Pre-School Children. *Education Sciences*, *11*(12), 788. doi:10.3390/educsci11120788

Livingstone, S., Mascheroni, G., & Stoilova, M. (2021). The outcomes of gaining digital skills for young people's lives and wellbeing: A systematic evidence review. *New Media & Society*. Advance online publication. doi:10.1177/14614448211043189

Lorenzo-Lledó, A., Lledó, A., Lorenzo, G., & Gilabert-Cerdá, A. (2022). Outside Training of Spanish University Students of Education for the Didactic Application of Cinema: Formal, Non-Formal, and Informal Perspectives. *Education Sciences*, *12*(1), 38. doi:10.3390/educsci12010038

Mahzan, M. S. W., Alias, N. A., & Abdullah, N. (2019). Infusing Engagement into Digital Game-based Learning Design for Orang Asli Learners. In Improving Educational Quality Toward International Standard (ICED-QA 2018) (pp. 178–184). SCITEPRESS.

Makri, A., & Vlachopoulos, D. (2019). Professional development for school leaders: A focus on soft and digital skills. In L. G. Chova, A. L. Martínez, & I. C. Torres (Eds.), *Proceedings of EDULEARN19 Conference,* (pp. 6200–6209). IATED Academy. 10.21125/edulearn.2019.1492

Manolika, M., Kotsakis, R., Matsiola, M., & Kalliris, G. (2021). Direct and Indirect Associations of Personality With Audiovisual Technology Acceptance Through General Self-Efficacy. *Psychological Reports*, *125*(2), 1165–1185. doi:10.1177/0033294121997784 PMID:33632017

Martyushev, N., Shutaleva, A., Malushko, E., Nikonova, Z., & Savchenko, I. (2021). Online Communication Tools in Teaching Foreign Languages for Education Sustainability. *Sustainability*, *13*(19), 11127. doi:10.3390u131911127

Matsiola, M. (2008). *New Technological Tools in Contemporary Journalism: Study Concerning Their Utilization by the Greek Journalists Related to the Use of the Internet as a Mass Medium* [Unpublished Ph.D. Thesis, School of Journalism and Mass Communications, Aristotle University of Thessaloniki, Thessaloniki, Greece].

Matsiola, M., Dimoulas, C., Kalliris, G., & Veglis, A. A. (2015). Augmenting User Interaction Experience through Embedded Multimodal Media Agents in Social Networks. In J. Sahlin (Ed.), *Social Media and the Transformation of Interaction in Society* (pp. 188–209). IGI Global. doi:10.4018/978-1-4666-8556-7.ch010

Matsiola, M., Spiliopoulos, P., Kotsakis, R., Nicolaou, C., & Podara, A. (2019). Technology-Enhanced Learning in Audiovisual Education: The Case of Radio Journalism Course Design. *Education Sciences*, *9*(1), 62. doi:10.3390/educsci9010062

Matsiola, M., Spiliopoulos, P., & Tsigilis, N. (2022). Digital Storytelling in Sports Narrations: Employing Audiovisual Tools in Sport Journalism Higher Education Course. *Education Sciences*, *12*(1), 51. doi:10.3390/educsci12010051

Mayer, R. E. (2014). *The Cambridge Handbook of Multimedia Learning* (2nd ed.). Cambridge Handbooks in Psychology—Cambridge University Press. doi:10.1017/CBO9781139547369

Michelson, E. (1996). Usual suspects: Experience, reflection, and the (en)gendering of knowledge. *International Journal of Lifelong Education*, *15*(6), 438–454. doi:10.1080/0260137960150604

Middleton, N., Koliandri, I., Hadjigeorgiou, E., Karanikola, M., Kolokotroni, O., Christodoulides, V., Nicolaou, C., & Kouta, C. (2020). Mixed-method study on internet use and information seeking during transition to motherhood. *European Journal of Public Health*, *30*(Supplement_5), ckaa165.905.

Nagy, J. T. (2018). Evaluation of online video usage and learning satisfaction: An extension of the technology acceptance model. *The International Review of Research in Open and Distributed Learning*, *19*(1), 160–185. doi:10.19173/irrodl.v19i1.2886

Naismith, L., Lonsdale, P., Vavoula, G. N., & Sharples, M. (2004). *Mobile technologies and learning*. University of Leicester.

Newby, T. J., Stepich, D. A., Lehman, J. D., Russell, J. D., & Leftwich, A. T. (2019). *Educational Technology for Teaching and Learning* (4th ed.). Pearson Education.

Ngah, R., Junid, J., & Osman, C. A. (2019). The Links between Role of Educators, Self-Directed Learning, Constructivist Learning Environment and Entrepreneurial Endeavor: Technology Entrepreneurship Pedagogical Approach. *International Journal of Learning. Teaching and Educational Research*, *18*(11), 414–427. doi:10.26803/ijlter.18.11.25

Ngubane-Mokiwa, S. A., & Khoza, S. B. (2021). Using Community of Inquiry (CoI) to Facilitate the Design of a Holistic E-Learning Experience for Students with Visual Impairments. *Education Sciences*, *11*(4), 152. doi:10.3390/educsci11040152

Nicolaou, C. (2011a). *Public Relations and New Technologies* [Unpublished CIPR Professional PR Diploma Thesis, Chartered Institute of Public Relations, London, UK].

Nicolaou, C. (2015, June). *Modern trends in teaching methodology in adult education* [Paper presentation]. The 1st Panhellenic Scientific Conference on Lifelong Learning on Lifelong Learning and Modern Society: Local Government, Education and Work, Thessaloniki, Greece.

Nicolaou, C. (2017, June). *Modern theoretical approaches to adult education* [Paper presentation]. The 5th Student Excellence Conference 2017 of the Mediterranean College (Thessaloniki), Thessaloniki, Greece.

Nicolaou, C. (2019a, March). *Audiovisual media of mass media in the teaching methodology* [Paper presentation]. The 18th Pancyprian Scientific Conference of the Educational Group of Cyprus on REview of the Public School of Cyprus in a World of Constant Changes and Challenges, Limassol, Cyprus.

Nicolaou, C. (2019b). The use of audiovisual media in adult education. In *Proceedings of the 5th International Scientific Conference on Communication, Information, Awareness and Education in Late Modernity* (vol. A, pp. 155-163). Institute of Humanities and Social Sciences.

Nicolaou, C. (2020). Communication Skills through Audiovisual Media and Audiovisual Content. *ΣΚΕΨΥ*, *7*(1), 166–174.

Nicolaou, C. (2021a). Development of Business Through the Internet and Social Media: The Professional Use of Audiovisual Media Technologies Through Strategic Tactics and Practices. In H. El-Gohary, D. Edwards, & M. Ben Mimoun (Eds.), Handbook of Research on IoT, Digital Transformation, and the Future of Global Marketing (pp. 193–211). IGI Global.

Nicolaou, C. (2021b). Media Trends and Prospects in Educational Activities and Techniques for Online Learning and Teaching through Television Content: Technological and Digital Socio-Cultural Environment, Generations, and Audiovisual Media Communications in Education. *Education Sciences*, *11*(11), 685. doi:10.3390/educsci11110685

Nicolaou, C. (2021c, October). *Outlining the profile and professional identity of the Greek and Cypriot Adult Educators through a phenomenological approach in the era of the three dimensions* [Paper presentation]. The 4th Annual International Symposium of the International Network of Vignette and Anecdotes Research Symposium on "Learning as Experience: Phenomenological Approaches in Educational Research", Thessaloniki, Greece.

Nicolaou, C. (2021d). Qualitative methods research through the Internet Applications and Services: The contribution of audiovisuals media technology as technology-enhanced research. *International Research in Higher Education*, 6(1), 1. Advance online publication. doi:10.5430/irhe.v6n1p1

Nicolaou, C. (2021e, July). *The description of the profile and the professional identity of Greek and Cypriot Adult Educators in the era of the triptych dimension* [Paper presentation]. The 7th International Scientific Conference of the Institute of Humanities and Social Sciences, Heraklion, Crete, Greece.

Nicolaou, C. (2022a). Information and Communications Technologies Through Technology-Enhanced Learning in Adult Education: The Re-Approach of the Adult Educator and the Adult Learners. In C. Krishnan, F. Al-Harthy, & G. Singh (Eds.), *Technology Training for Educators From Past to Present* (pp. 73–94). IGI Global. doi:10.4018/978-1-6684-4083-4.ch004

Nicolaou, C. (2022b). Methodological Approaches utilizing Information and Communication Technologies (ICTs): Trends and Perspectives of Research Methods from and through the Internet. *Open Education: The Journal for Open and Distance Education and Educational Technology*, 18(1), 290–315.

Nicolaou, C. (2022c). The Secret Power of Digital Storytelling Methodology: Technology-Enhanced Learning Utilizing Audiovisual Educational Content. In J. DeHart (Ed.), *Enhancing Education Through Multidisciplinary Film Teaching Methodologies* (pp. 235–246). IGI Global. doi:10.4018/978-1-6684-5394-0.ch013

Nicolaou, C. (2023). Generations and Branded Content from and through the Internet and Social Media: Modern Communication Strategic Techniques and Practices for Brand Sustainability—The Greek Case Study of LACTA Chocolate. *Sustainability*, 15(1), 584. doi:10.3390/su15010584

Nicolaou, C., & Kalliris, G. (2020). Audiovisual Media Communications in Adult Education: The case of Cyprus and Greece of Adults as Adult Learners. *European Journal of Investigation in Health, Psychology and Education*, 10(4), 967–994. doi:10.3390/ejihpe10040069 PMID:34542430

Nicolaou, C., & Kalliris, G. (2021). The (Non-Verbal) Communication and the use of Audiovisual Media. In *Proceedings of the 6th International Scientific Conference on Communication, Information, Awareness and Education in Late Modernity* (vol. A, pp. 303–311). Institute of Humanities and Social Sciences.

Nicolaou, C., & Karypidou, C. (2021). Generations and Social Media: The case of Cyprus and Greece. In *Proceedings of the 7th International Scientific Conference* (vol. A, pp. 592–601). Institute of Humanities and Social Sciences.

Nicolaou, C., Matsiola, M., & Kalliris, G. (2019). Technology-Enhanced Learning and Teaching Methodologies through Audiovisual Media. *Education Sciences*, 9(3), 196. doi:10.3390/educsci9030196

Nicolaou, C., Matsiola, M., & Kalliris, G. (2022). The Challenge of an Interactive Audiovisual-Supported Lesson Plan: Information and Communications Technologies (ICTs) in Adult Education. *Education Sciences*, *12*(11), 836. doi:10.3390/educsci12110836

Nicolaou, C., Matsiola, M., Karypidou, C., Podara, A., Kotsakis, R., & Kalliris, G. (2021b). Medias Studies, Audiovisual Media Communications, and Generations: The case of budding journalists in radio courses in Greece. *Journalism and Media*, *2*(2), 155–192. doi:10.3390/journalmedia2020010

Nicolaou, C., Podara, A., & Karypidou, C. (2021a). Audiovisual media in education and Generation Z: Application of audiovisual media theory in education with an emphasis on radio. In *Proceedings of the 6th International Scientific Conference on Communication, Information, Awareness and Education in Late Modernity* (vol. A, pp. 294–302). Institute of Humanities and Social Sciences.

Nicolaou, C. A. (2011b). *Public Relations: Future and New Technologies* [Δημόσιες Σχέσεις: Μέλλον και Νέες Τεχνολογίες of Greek language] [Unpublished Bachelor's Thesis, University of Nicosia, Nicosia, Cyprus].

Nicolaou, C. A. (2014). Life Skills: The Importance of Non-Verbal Communication. In M. Tzekaki, M. Kanatsouli (Eds.), Panhellenic Conference with International Participation: Re-Reflections on Childhood (pp. 1544–1546). TEPAE, AUTh.

Novakovich, J., Miah, S., & Shaw, S. (2017). Designing curriculum to shape professional social media skills and identity in virtual communities of practice. *Computers & Education*, *104*, 65–90. doi:10.1016/j.compedu.2016.11.002

Nugraini, S. H., Choo, K. A., & Hin, H. S. (2009, November). *The proposed conceptual framework of e-audio visual biology for teaching and learning in Indonesia senior high schools* [Paper presentation]. CoSMEd 2009 Third International Conference, Penang, Malaysia.

Nusrat, M., & Sultana, N. (2019). Soft skills for sustainable employment of business graduates of Bangladesh. *Higher Education. Skills and Work-Based Learning*, *9*(3), 264–278. doi:10.1108/HESWBL-01-2018-0002

Palioura, M., & Dimoulas, C. (2022). Digital Storytelling in Education: A Transmedia Integration Approach for the Non-Developers. *Education Sciences*, *12*(8), 559. doi:10.3390/educsci12080559

Papastergiou, M., & Solomonidou, C. (2005). Gender issues in Internet access and favourite Internet activities among Greek high school pupils inside and outside school. *Computers & Education*, *44*(4), 377–393. doi:10.1016/j.compedu.2004.04.002

Patahuddin, P., Syawal, S., Esnara, C., & Abdullah, M. (2022). Characterizing the Ideal Audio-Visual Learning Content of Writing Course Learned in Distance. *Lingua Cultura, 16*(1).

Pavla, S., Hana, V., & Jan, V. (2015). Blended learning: Promising strategic alternative in higher education. *Procedia: Social and Behavioral Sciences*, *171*, 1245–1254. doi:10.1016/j.sbspro.2015.01.238

Pekrun, R. (2019). Inquiry on emotions in higher education: Progress and open problems. *Studies in Higher Education*, *44*(10), 1806–1811. doi:10.1080/03075079.2019.1665335

Perifanou, M., Tzafilkou, K., & Economides, A. A. (2021). The Role of Instagram, Facebook, and YouTube Frequency of Use in University Students' Digital Skills Components. *Education Sciences*, *11*(12), 766. doi:10.3390/educsci11120766

Platz, L., Jüttler, M., & Schumann, S. (2021). Game-Based Learning in Economics Education at Upper Secondary Level: The Impact of Game Mechanics and Reflection on Students' Financial Literacy. In C. Aprea & D. Ifenthaler (Eds.), *Game-based Learning Across the Disciplines* (pp. 25–42). Advances in Game-Based Learning. Springer. doi:10.1007/978-3-030-75142-5_2

Podara, A., Giomelakis, D., Nicolaou, C., Matsiola, M., & Kotsakis, R. (2021). Digital Storytelling in Cultural Heritage: Audience Engagement in the Interactive Documentary New Life. *Sustainability*, *13*(3), 1193. doi:10.3390u13031193

Podara, A., & Kalliris, G. (2022). How Digital Poverty Affects Television Viewing Habits. In N. E. Myridis (Ed.), *Poverty and Quality of Life in the Digital Era* (pp. 105–123). Springer. doi:10.1007/978-3-031-04711-4_5

Podara, A., Matsiola, M., Nicolaou, C., Maniou, T. A., & Kalliris, G. (2019, November). *Audiovisual consumption practices in post-crisis Greece: An empirical research approach to Generation Z* [Paper presentation]. *The International Conference on Filmic and Media Narratives of the Crisis: Contemporary Representations*, Athens, Greece.

Podara, A., Matsiola, M., Nicolaou, C., Maniou, T. A., & Kalliris, G. (2022). Transformation of television viewing practices in Greece: Generation Z and audio-visual content. *Journal of Digital Media & Policy*, *13*(2), 157–179. doi:10.1386/jdmp_00034_1

Psomadaki, O., Matsiola, M., Dimoulas, C. A., & Kalliris, G. M. (2022). The Significance of Digital Network Platforms to Enforce Musicians' Entrepreneurial Role: Assessing Musicians' Satisfaction in Using Mobile Applications. *Sustainability*, *14*(10), 5975. doi:10.3390u14105975

Quinn, K. (2018). Congnitive Effects of Social Media Use: A case Case of Older Adults. *Social Media + Society*, *4*(3). doi:10.1177/2056305118787203

Quinn-Allan, D. (2010). Public relations, education, and social media: Issues for professionalism in the digital age. *Asia Pacific Public Relations Journal*, *11*(1), 41–55.

Rao, M. S. (2018). Soft skills: Toward a sanctimonious discipline. *On the Horizon*, *26*(3), 215–224. doi:10.1108/OTH-06-2017-0034

Riyanti, A., Nurgiyantoro, B., & Suryaman, M. (2021, December). The Use of Cartoon Film Media in Narrative Writing Skills for Elementary School Students. In *2nd International Conference on Innovation in Education and Pedagogy (ICIEP 2020)* (pp. 22–27). Atlantis Press.

Rogers, E. M. (2003). *Diffusion of Innovations* (5th ed.). Free Press.

Røkenes, F. M., & Krumsvik, R. J. (2014). Development of student teachers' digital competence in teacher education - A Literature Review. *Nordic Journal of Digital Literacy*, *9*(4), 250–280. doi:10.18261/ISSN1891-943X-2014-04-03

Ryabova, T., Frolova, E., & Rogach, O. (2018). Interaction of educational process participants in network online-space: The trends of new media reality development. *Media Education (Mediaobrazovanie)*, *58*(3), 140–146.

Saeed, M. A., Ghazali, K., & Aljaberi, M. A. (2018). A review of previous studies on ESL/EFL learners' interactional feedback exchanges in face-to-face and computer-assisted peer review of writing. *International Journal of Educational Technology in Higher Education*, *15*(1), 6. doi:10.118641239-017-0084-8

Sani, K., & Adiansha, A. A. (2021). Smartphone: Bagaimana Pengaruh terhadap Motivasi Belajar Siswa Sekolah Dasar? [Smartphone: How does it influence elementary school students' learning motivation?]. *Jurnal Ilmiah Mandala Education, 7*(2).

Sarridis, I., & Nicolaou, C. (2015, December). *Social Media: (Correct) Professional Use* [Paper presentation]. The 2nd Student Conference of the Department of Applied Informatics—University of Macedonia on Modern Entrepreneurship & Informatics Technologies, Thessaloniki, Greece.

Shutaleva, A., Martyushev, N., Nikonova, Z., Savchenko, I., Bovkun, A., & Kerimov, A. (2021). Critical thinking in media sphere: Attitude of university teachers to fake news and its impact on the teaching. *Journal of Management Information and Decision Sciences*, *24*, 1–12.

Shutaleva, A., Martyushev, N., Starostin, A., Salgiriev, A., Vlasova, O., Grinek, A., Nikonova, Z., & Savchenko, I. (2022). Migration Potential of Students and Development of Human Capital. *Education Sciences*, *12*(5), 324. doi:10.3390/educsci12050324

Sidiropoulos, E., Vryzas, N., Vrysis, L., Avraam, E., & Dimoulas, C. (2019). Growing media skills and know-how in situ: Technology-enhanced practices and collaborative support in mobile news-reporting. *Education Sciences*, *9*(3), 173. doi:10.3390/educsci9030173

Sueb, R., Hashim, H., Hashim, K. S., & Izam, M. M. (2020). Excellent Teachers' Strategies in Managing Students' Misbehaviour in the Classroom. *Asian Journal of University Education*, *16*(1), 46–55. doi:10.24191/ajue.v16i1.8982

Sumamol, N. S. (2019). *Strategies for reflective teaching practices*. Laxmi Book Piblication.

Thanavathi, C. (2021). Teachers' Perception On Digital Media Technology. [TURCOMAT]. *Turkish Journal of Computer and Mathematics Education*, *12*(10), 6972–6975.

Tomyuk, O., Dyachkov, M., Shutaleva, A., Fayustov, A., & Leonenko, E. (2019). Social networks as an educational resource. In *SHS Web of Conferences (vol. 69*, p. 00105). EDP Sciences. 10.1051hsconf/20196900105

Tugtekin, E. B., & Koc, M. (2020). Understanding the relationship between new media literacy, communication skills, and democratic tendency: Model development and testing. *New Media & Society*, *22*(10), 1922–1941. doi:10.1177/1461444819887705

Turan, Z., & Cetintas, H. B. (2020). Investigating university students' adoption of video lessons. *Open Learning*, *35*(2), 122–139. doi:10.1080/02680513.2019.1691518

Veglis, A., & Avraam, E. (2001, July). Using the Web in supplementary teacher education. In *EUROCON'2001. International Conference on Trends in Communications. Technical Program, Proceedings* (Cat. No. 01EX439) (*Vol. 2*, pp. 274–277). IEEE. 10.1109/EURCON.2001.938112

Veglis, A., Saridou, T., Panagiotidis, K., Karypidou, C., & Kotenidis, E. (2022). Applications of Big Data in Media Organizations. *Social Sciences, 11*(9), 414. doi:10.3390ocsci11090414

von Glasersfeld, E. (1985). Reconstructing the concept of knowledge. *Archives de Psychologie, 53*(204), 91–101.

Vygotsky, L. (1978). *Mind in society: The development of higher psychological processes*. Harvard University Press.

Werth, E. P., & Werth, L. (2011). Effective training for millennial students. *Adult Learning, 22*(3), 12–19. doi:10.1177/1045159511022200302

Yeromin, M. B. (2021). *Universal Codes of Media in International Political Communications: Emerging Research and Opportunities*. IGI Global. doi:10.4018/978-1-7998-3808-1

KEY TERMS AND DEFINITIONS

Audiovisual Media Communications (AMCs): A term that includes all audiovisual media technologies (i.e., audiovisual media and communication technologies) and audiovisual content.

Digital Transformation: A term that includes and defines the ability to adopt new, fast, and often changing digital technology in various fields to solve various problems and improve the experiences of those involved.

Information and Communications Technologies (ICTs): A term which is defined as a diverse set of technological communication tools and resources used to transmit, store, create, share, or even exchange information in various fields and sciences.

Multiple-Multimodal Skills: A term that refers to the combination of two or different or even more related skills that someone can possess.

Skill: The ability to use one's knowledge effectively and easily in execution or even performance of any physical tasks.

Social Medias (SMs): An umbrella term that refers to a list of new modern digital technologies which are growing day by day due to continuous digital technological advancements.

Technology-Enhanced Learning (TEL): A term that cannot be easily defined while it is commonly used to describe the application of technology in teaching and learning, as well as technology-equipped classrooms.

Chapter 16
The Environmental Commitment of Moroccan Students:
Measures and Determinants – Case of Cadi Ayyad University

Jabrane Amaghouss
Faculty of Law, Economics, and Social Sciences, Cadi Ayyad University, Morocco

Younes Elguerch
Faculty of Law, Economics, and Social Sciences, Cadi Ayyad University, Morocco

EXECUTIVE SUMMARY

The aim of the chapter is to investigate the factors that motivate Moroccan students to engage in pro-environmental behavior. In this study, the authors tried, within the framework of the theory of the motivation towards protection, to measure the degree of the environmental commitment and to explain the pro-environmental behavior of the students of Cadi Ayyad University Marrakesh, the FLESS. In this case, the authors took a sample of 415 students on which they proceeded to an analysis of their pro-environmental behavior through structural equation modeling. The major findings of this study support the notion that students' pro-environmental conduct is positively influenced by their environmental attitudes. Additionally, the escalating severity of environmental issues motivates individuals to accept environmentally friendly behaviors. Given the significance of environmental attitudes, it is possible to raise the likelihood of pro-environmental activities among students by using strategies and incentives aimed at enhancing their environmental attitudes.

INTRODUCTION

Nowadays, learning is considered a national priority in Morocco. That's why the government has carried out several reforms to make higher education a locomotive of economic growth in the country. In addition to the pedagogical aspects, the reforms also tend to stimulate responsible behavior among students towards society. This responsibility encompasses economic, environmental, and societal dimensions.

DOI: 10.4018/978-1-6684-6076-4.ch016

The Environmental Commitment of Moroccan Students

It is in this perspective that this chapter fits to measure and evaluate the environmental commitment of students. This theme rhymes with the objectives of this book. The effectiveness of the human dimension depends on the profiles of citizens who must demonstrate certain qualities such as a sufficient degree of environmental awareness. In this regard, several studies have been carried out by scientists from several fields and disciplines, in an attempt to provide scientific knowledge on environmental behaviour (Borden, 1977). In this perspective, interest was in studies of environmental behaviour which was limited, in the mid-1960s, to the measurement of public concern about the quality of the environment (Li et al., 2019). Over time, it has gradually evolved into a desire to understand the elements that lead to the acceptance and implementation of pro-environmental practices. (Casaló and Escario, 2018). Indeed, several studies have been conducted to explain the environmental lifestyles of various social groups, namely farmers (Wang et al., 2018), students (Chen et al., 2017), consumers (Akbari et al., 2019) and workers (Latif et al., 2022). These studies have attempted to explain human behaviour on the basis of several theories relating to environmental psychology, of which the most widespread remain: the Theory of "Reasoned Action" (M Fishbein and Ajzen, 1980), the Theory of "Planned Behaviour" (Ajzen, 1991), the Norms Activation Model (Schwartz, 1977), the Value-Belief-Norm Model (P. Stern, 2000) and the Protective Motivation Theory (Rogers, 1975). Referring to the literature, protective motivation theory has already proven its effectiveness in explaining health-related behaviours. In addition, compared with the other theories mentioned above, it provides more predictors of human behavior as well as it can identify the elements that encourage individuals to adopt environmentally friendly behaviors (Bockarjova and Steg, 2014; Keshavarz and Karami, 2016) .The protection motivation theory goes beyond the analysis of the costs related to adaptive practices to the analysis of the benefits of the present behaviors, that are not very respectful of the environment, in order to arouse beyond the emotional variable (fear), the rational variable which is also decisive in the adoption of preventive behavior following a persuasive message (Bockarjova and Steg, 2014; Wang et al., 2019) . Then, "Protection motivation theory" regarding the costs and benefits of adopting a pro-environmental behaviour considers both existing behaviours and expectations of new sustainable acts. (Bockarjova and Steg, 2014). This makes it possible to simultaneously identify the barriers and the factors of acceptance of an environmental adaptive behaviour.

Morocco, like many other countries, is aware of the various problems to which it is exposed. This is why it is present in most of the summits organized in this perspective. As it continues to express its strong commitment to environmental protection under the enlightened leadership of His Majesty King Mohammed VI, with the aim of designing a development model which focuses on sustainable development. This model will then make it possible to deal with the degradation of its environment which endangers the health of the population and hinders the sustainability of its development.

Morocco, in this case, has adopted several strategies to move to a new model of sustainable human development in order to be able to meet ecological challenges. This model grants a central role to citizens, something that requires them to adopt a profile that meets the necessary conditions for the success of this transition. In addition, the current context manifested by the continued presence of non-environmentally friendly behaviours has only worsened the already critical situation. The responsibility for past and present environmental disrespect must surely fall on the shoulders of the students since they represent the community's youth and because they are tomorrow's decision-makers (Leeuw et al., 2015). Likewise, they represent the class of people endowed with the technical and specialized knowledge necessary to advance adequate keys to modify environmental behaviours (Vicente-Molina et al.,2018). Therefore, gaining scientific knowledge about what motivates pro-environmental behaviour is an area of great concern that prompts practical applications to advance a sustainable future (Shafiei and Maleksaeidi, 2020).

Therefore, the objective of this work is to give a clear vision on the environmental behaviour of the students of the Faculty of Law Economics and Social Sciences (FLESS), Cadi Ayyad University in Marrakech through the framework of the Protection Motivation Theory (PMT). To do this, a questionnaire that addresses the following issue is sent to a sample of students.

With a view to developing an ecological awareness among students, to what extent is this part of the population committed to the environment? And what are the determinants that encourage him to behave in a pro-environmental way?

Research Questions

- Are these students committed to the environment? if so, how can this commitment be measured?
- What are the methods of improvement and the factors that influence it?
- What is the impact of all the PMT constructs on pro-environmental behaviour?

The Working Hypotheses

In the context of responding to our problem, we have put forward seven hypotheses which will be subjected to the validity test at the level of the empirical study. These assumptions are as follows:

- **H$_1$**: Perceived gravity positively influences students' willingness to engage in pro-environmental behaviour.
- **H$_2$**: Students' desire to engage in pro-environmental behaviour is positively influenced by their perception of vulnerability.
- **H$_3$**: Students' aspirations to engage in pro-environmental behaviour are negatively influenced by rewards.
- **H$_4$**: Response-efficacy influences students' intentions to engage in pro-environmental behaviour in a positive way.
- **H$_5$**: Self-efficacy affects students' desire to engage in pro-environmental behaviour in a positive light.
- **H$_6$**: Response costs negatively affects students' aspiration to engage in pro-environmental behaviour.
- **H$_7$**: Environmental attitude positively affects pro-environmental behaviour.

In order to provide answers to the problematic at hand, a plan which is subdivided into three chapters will be adopted:

The first chapter is devoted to the analysis of commitment in terms of definition and importance, and its role as a pillar of sustainable development. In addition, the analysis of the environmental commitment of the students while putting the action on the determining elements of the commitment and the opportunities offered to the students with the aim of arousing their commitment.

The second chapter is dedicated to the analysis of the two variables used to measure the environmental commitment of students as they allow the extraction of factors and determinants that encourage students to engage in environmentally friendly behaviour.

The third chapter analyses the relationship between environmentally friendly behaviour and the set of PMT constructs with environmental attitude. This analysis is carried out through an empirical study. Therefore, this chapter will focus first on the presentation of the research methodology and then on the processing and analysis of data as well as the discussion of the results.

LITERATURE REVIEW

The commitment in environmental matters in order to succeed in the strategic challenges of sustainable development does not concern a specific part (Forget, 2011) despite the existence of several studies made by many economic actors which limit the importance of the commitment. environmental as an exclusive responsibility of companies of a certain size (Rubinstein, 2006). In fact, the current context manifested by continuous changes in the business world has led all companies, regardless of their size, to integrate the environment into their production policies in order to guarantee their sustainability (Forget, 2011). In addition, the current context has called on all actors, including citizens, to pool their efforts in order to achieve a successful transition to a new development model centred on the principles of sustainable development.

The Environmental Commitment of Students: Towards A New Paradigm

This section will be devoted to studying the process of environmental commitment of students and also the opportunities offered to these students in the context of stimulating their commitment.

In order to recognize students' attitudes toward the environment, it seems very interesting beforehand to study their relationship with the environment (Gravel and Pruneau, 2004). generally, humans in daily life, maintain several relationships with the physical world and the living beings that surround them. Hence, in what follows, the focus will be on the relationship of humans to the environment. Furthermore, the different elements that define this relationship will be highlighted.

Berryman (2002), who is passionate about studying the relationship of human beings to their environment through the process of developing human life, has highlighted the importance of direct experience in the development of the human relationship to the environment. He called for a review of teaching methods in environmental studies in order to " *learn to feel at home and at peace in a world where nature occupies an important place* " (Berryman, 2002, p. 217). After considerable research, this author was able to conclude that there are two main elements that must be the subject of in-depth research. These two elements are attachment to places and experiences in environmental matters. Moreover, he assures that the concept of place encompasses several important elements that are experiential and affective (Goyette, 2019). All of his questions revolve around how adults and young people will be able to live their experiences in nature.

"Here arises the whole problem of the place, meaning and approach of nature in society. What are the instrumental links between adults and the environment and how are young people exposed to and introduced to them? Into what concrete and symbolic universe are young people initiated? (Berryman, 2002, p. 217).

In fact, these questions relate to the relationship to the environment. But in a precise way they focus on the role of the experiences in nature in the process of developing our relationship with the environment. Therefore, it seems obvious to ask the question around the place occupied by the environment embodied by nature in the lives of adults and young people. According to Gravel and Pruneau (2004), this concept essentially brings us back to the notion of environmental sensitivity (Goyette, 2019). According to them, the key is to study the determinants of a feeling of attachment and concern for nature. Also like Berryman, several authors intend to define and understand the affective dimensions that allow the creation of an attachment to places. This, therefore, brings us back to the same question which states that when deciphering what stimulates the development of an environmental sensitivity among young people is managed, educational activities that promote attachment to places can certainly be developed (Carrus et al., 2014).

According to Gravel and Pruneau (2004), the development of attachment to places must call on positive experiences with nature. This study shows clearly the importance of creating intensive moments with nature and encouraging individuals to live quality experiences, in a way that builds attachment and stimulates the development of environmental sensitivity. (Goyette, 2019).

Moreover, Boutet, Samson and Bisaillon (2009) propose that the relationship to the environment is not limited to the simple individual experience of the environment. According to these authors, *"the group in which we evolve becomes just as important"* (Goyette, 2019, p. 9). This, then, shows the reason why they announced the concept of environmental citizenship. The latter takes its origin from the ecological concept citizenship of Dobson (2003). According to these authors, the notion of environmental sensitivity is based on the relationship of exchange between a human being and his living environment as it reflects the cosmopolitan and interdependent approach of modern society (Dobson, 2003). Indeed, it is mainly based on the lived experience manifested through life in society and the real experience of the natural environment (Dobson, 2003). For Boutet et al. (2009), the structure of this experience is based on two dimensions, namely solidarity towards others and responsibility for individual and collective actions taken to maintain the different life systems. According to this author, this new concept takes into account the different aspects of the life of the citizen, something that allows to better represent life in society. These authors affirm that " *environmental citizenship* " highlights the democratic aspects more than the economic aspects of the human relationship to the resources that surround it, while insisting more on the use of the relationship of collective participation than on the individual relationship of consumption. (Boutet et al., 2009). As a result, environmental citizenship remains essential for a proper approach to the relationship with the environment, since it makes it possible to take into account all the societal aspects of the individual relationship with the environment. For Dobson (2003), it would be essential to take care in order to stimulate the commitment of individuals through the implementation of an approach aimed at the development of their consciences so that they can understand that this commitment is mobilized for the contribution to the community values and attitudes. According to Dobson (2003), the current human-environment relationship necessitates a paradigm shift in order to adopt a multi-cultural vision of the human community. Environmental citizenship for (Dobson, 2007) requires that citizenship rights and responsibilities go beyond national borders. Indeed, our ecological footprint takes into account national and international resources and environments. Therefore, the author invites citizens to activate their moral commitments towards the human community.

Through this ecological view, we can conclude that the environment embodied by nature has no boundaries and that any inappropriate act not only hinders the local community, but indeed threatens the entire universe. Thence, Dobson's vision is based on the need to approach the relationship to the environment in a cosmopolitan way so that actions are taken by both citizens and communities. This idea brings us back to one of the conclusions of the Stockholm conference, which is the importance of *"think global and act local"* [1].

To conclude, because of the globalization of human activities, the relationship with the environment must be conducted from a cosmopolitan approach where the repercussions of our actions and our choices extend beyond our national limits to a planetary scale. This implies then, the ecological vision of nature so that the latter is not divided into compartments, but is emboded a whole. From the above, we have also seen the importance of developing the relationship with the environment through concrete and positive experiences in the natural environment in order to stimulate environmental sensitivity and thus rebuild a link with nature. Through continuing our reflection on how these experiences can be at the service of citizen engagement, it appears that they further develop their awareness and encourage them to adopt environmentally friendly behaviour.

The Design of Protective "Motivation Theory" To Interpret Pro-Environmental Behaviours

The Protective Motivation Theory has been employed frequently in studies on risky behaviours connected to health (Dang et al., 2012). Subsequently, its scope has been widened by the integration of several domains, such as the description of pro-environmental behaviours. As an example, TMP has been applied by Bubeck, Laudan, Aerts, Wouter, Botzen, and Thieken (2018) in order to study the attenuation action of flood-affected households along the Rhine in Germany. In terms of mitigation behaviour, this study indicated that threat assessment and coping, particularly reaction efficacy, are crucial factors (Bubeck et al., 2018). Furthermore, Keshavarz and Karami (2016) discovered reaction effectiveness, perceived severity, attempts to improve, perceived vulnerability, and self-efficacy as major dimensions of PMT to be significant predictors of pro-environmental behavior among Iranian farmers during drought crises. Moreover, a study by Christensen and Rainear (2017) that examined a sample of institutions in the northeastern United States provided data supporting PMT's effectiveness in predicting pro-environmental behavioral intentions. According to this study, perceived severity and susceptibility, response effectiveness and self-efficacy, and response costs all negatively predicted pro-environmental affective commitment. According to Bockarjova and Steg (2014), "PMT" is a useful model for describing pro-environmental behaviours. They discovered that the biggest obstacles to acquiring protective behaviour were the high and unjustifiable costs of doing so and the large advantages of the status quo non-protective behaviours. Additionally, a study by Janmaimool (2017) revealed that PMT may be a good fit for explaining persistent Western management behaviours among Bangkok office workers. Likewise, Kim, Jeong, and Hwang (2013) discovered that the intention of American and Korean students to engage in pro-environmental actions was predicted by PMT components as perceived severity, reaction efficacy, and self-efficacy towards climate change adaptation (Kim et al., 2013). Overall, Steg and Bockarjova (2014) noted that the PMT is useful especially for examining pro-environmental behaviour because: "it shows how several psychological processes and mechanisms can interact, reminds us that all these processes and mechanisms can contribute to misjudgment and inaction at the same time, and suggests multi-component programs that are likely to be effective in efforts to increase people's estimation of environmental threats and/or their actions in the face of them. to these threats" (Shafiei and Maleksaeidi, 2020, p. 3).

As shown below by the TMP (Figure 2), two cognitive processes are initiated in sequential order based on the sources of information. These two processes are the impact assessment relative to the perceived threat and the assessment of potential adaptation to address that threat. The threat intensity assessment process consists of an assessment of perceived severity and vulnerability, conducted by an individual (Boudreau, 1997).

This evaluation process may create an emotional state of fear in the person. With regard to the process of assessing potential adaptation to the threat, the latter has three elements. First, the person must make a judgment about the effectiveness of the recommended behavior as a means of dealing with the perceived threat. Second, he must verify that he is capable of adopting and maintaining that behavior. Finally, the person must highlight and evaluate all the obstacles that he is likely to encounter when adopting the recommended behavior (Boudreau, 1997).

RESEARCH METHODOLOGY

a) The epistemological position of our research:

Our research aims at gaining scientific knowledge about the factors that influence students' behavioural intentions. To do this, we made use of the theory of protective motivation because of their effectiveness in explaining behaviour. Also this theory offers more predictors of human behavior compared to other theories (Keshavarz and Karami, 2016). On the basis of this theory, we formulated hypotheses to finally test them. This process comes in harmony with **the positivist paradigm**. In addition, we started first from a theoretical reference and then compare it to reality in order to pass judgment on its relevance. Therefore, we opt for the **hypothetico-deductive approach.** Regarding the research method, we have chosen **the quantitative method** to answer our problematic because it is the method that leads to the formulation of hypotheses that will then be tested in order to obtain explanations or predictions. Also, it is the method that fits perfectly into the positivist paradigm.

b) Construction of the conceptual research model:

Our conceptual research model is based on protective motivation theory (Rogers, 1975). Several studies based on this theory have opted for a linear model that studies only the direct effects of concepts on protective motivation behavior through "linear regression analysis" (Almarshad, 2017; Rainear and Christensen; Janmaimool, 2017; Xiao et al., 2014). In addition, we added a new variable (environmental attitude) to improve the model and increase its predictive power.

In fact, our conception of the model was based firstly on both the conception of protective motivation theory and the work of Ajzen and Fishbein (1973, 1977) and secondly, on the basis of studies earlier such as (Shafiei and Maleksaeidi, 2020; Almarshad, 2017). On this basis, our research model is a structural equation model since it indicates relationships between latent variables. These are variables that are not likely to be measured directly but are measured through other observed variables.

Thus, we present our conceptual research model as follows:

Figure 1. Conceptual model of research established on AMOS software

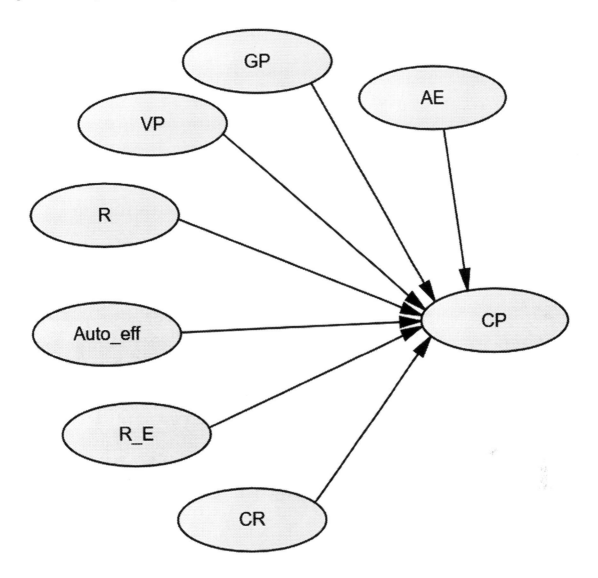

c) Operationalization of variables:

The present study, the topic of our research, is composed of eight variables, namely: pro-environmental behavior (**dependent variable**), environmental attitude (both **independent** from pro-environmental behavior and **dependent** on to the two variables: rewards and response costs). The rest are independent variables, namely: "Perceived vulnerability", "Perceived severity", Rewards", "Self-efficacy", "Response effectiveness" and "Response costs".

Table 1. Operationalization of variables

	Variables	Items	Codification
dependent	Pro-environmental behavior	The environment is among the criteria that determine my purchases.	a_CP
		I questioned my drinking habits.	b_CP
		The environment is the main reason that encourages me to question my consumption habits.	c_CP
		I try to save energy by turning off lights when I exit a room.	d_CP
		If I use a car, I carpool, i.e. I share this car with other passengers that I do not necessarily know.	e_CP
		I reduce my carbon footprint by using soft mobility (train, bike, public transport).	f_CP
		I help keep my neighborhood clean.	g_CP
		I take part in environmental conservation initiatives (tree planting, waste sorting and recycling).	h_CP
		I focus on spreading awareness about the environment.	i_CP
Independent	Environmental attitude	The perception of the future is worrying under the presence of environmental problems.	a_AE
		Environmental problems are mainly related to human activities.	b_AE
		Environmental issues are well taken into account in media and political discussions.	c_AE
		The interests of future generations are taken into account in the actions of political leaders.	d_AE
		The voice of young people is taken into account in media and political discussions on environmental topics.	e_AE
		Environmental issues are taken into account in the decisions of business leaders.	f_AE
		Compelling States, organizations and companies to respect the environment under pain of sanctions is a good solution.	g_AE
Independent	Perceived severity	Environmental pollution has become a serious threat to mankind.	a_GP
		The negative impacts of the depletion of natural resources are severe.	b_GP
		The thought of climate change scares me.	c_GP
		Environmental degradation is the main cause of the spread of disease.	d_GP
		Environmental issues are hampering the sustainability of our environment as well as that of future generations.	e_GP
Independent	Perceived vulnerability	Environmental pollution can affect me negatively.	a_VP
		I am sensitive to climate change's negative consequences.	b_VP
		Environmental degradation has a direct negative impact on me.	c_VP
		Environmental degradation is destroying our lives and those of future generations.	d_VP
Independent	Awards	I find it easier to spend time on personal pursuits than on environmental causes.	a_R
		In an effort to conserve energy, driving a private vehicle is more pleasant than taking public transportation.	b_R
		Integrating the preservation of the environment into my consumption habits costs me more money.	c_R
		The adoption of pro-environmental consumption habits deprives me of satisfying certain needs.	d_R

continues on following page

Table 1. Continued

	Variables	Items	Codification
Independent	Self-efficacy	I am aware of the daily precautions I can take to safeguard the environment.	a_Auto_eff
		If I try, I can tackle environmental issues.	b_Auto_eff
		I am capable of handling anything the environment throws at me.	c_Auto_eff
		I am secure in my capacity to deal with any challenges that may follow from widespread environmental issues, therefore I don't worry about them much.	d_Auto_eff
Independent	Response efficiency	Having an environmental ethic contributes to the reduction of environmental risks.	are
		My involvement in environmental aspects undoubtedly has a good effect on others' interest in and engagement in them.	b_RE
		I can minimize the possibility of environmental destruction by myself and others if I pay more attention to the environment.	c_RE
		If I manage to reduce environmental risks by adopting pro-environmental behaviors, I contribute to maintaining the sustainability of the environment for present and future generations.	d_RE
Independent	Response costs	The cost of taking action to mitigate environmental issues is too high.	a_CR
		Participating in environmental programs takes my time.	b_CR
		I find it challenging to adhere to environmental protection policies.	c_CR

Population and Sampling

All of the students in the various cycles are the study's target population in the FLESS in Marrakech. The sample size was estimated based on "**Cochran 's (1963) formula.**"

Data Collection Instrument

We adopted the quantitative method in order to answer our problem. So, the most appropriate tool to collect data in order to carry out our study is the questionnaire. The development of our questionnaire is based on a review of the literature on the predictors or factors influencing behavior as well as the theories that have the effect of modifying or promoting pro-environmental behavior among individuals. Therefore, our questionnaire was designed in the context of measuring the environmental attitude of students and determining the factors that impact it. It consists of 6 parts. In order to better take into account the variety of responses, we proceeded to categorize the responses on the basis of the fifth point "Likert scale" (from 1 to 5). This scale represents an appropriate psychometric tool for measuring attitudes among individuals. The degrees of the scale are manifested by the following response modalities: "Totally disagree" (code 1), "Disagree" (code 2), " No idea" (code 3", " agree " (code 4) and 'totally agree' (code 5).

In order to assess **the reliability of the questionnaire**, a study was made on the basis of 30 students from the Faculty of Legal, Economic and Social Sciences of Marrakech. This study has led to the calculations of "**Cronbach 's alpha**" coefficients of the variables.

PRESENTATION, ANALYSIS, AND INTERPRETATION OF RESULTS

Pro-Environmental Behavior of Students

In surveys based on a Likert -type scale, each question or item is ordered with a numerical answer which makes it easy to calculate the average by summing the numerical values of the answers and dividing them by the number of respondents. The average and standard deviation of the nine items used to gauge the behavior of the students who make up our sample are shown in table 16 below.

a) The average value of the items of the pro-environmental behavior of the students:

Table 16 shows that the average value of all items is greater than the average (above 3). This demonstrates that the students in this study are generally pro-environmental. The item " **I attempt to save power by turning off lights when I leave a room.** ", had the highest average score, namely an average equal to **4.42** with a difference of **0.732**, while the item " **If I use a car, I carpool, i.e. I share this car with other passengers that I do not necessarily know** " had the lowest average value is **3.02** with a standard deviation of **1.187**.

Table 2. Average pro-environmental behavior of students by indicator

	Statistics			
	NOT		Average	Std. Deviation
	Valid	missing		
The environment is among the criteria that determine my purchases	385	0	3.65	.917
I questioned my drinking habits	385	0	3.79	.943
The environment is the main reason that encourages me to question my consumption habits	385	0	3.75	1,041
I try to save energy by remembering to turn off the light when I leave a room	385	0	4.42	.732
If I use a car, I carpool, i.e. I share this car with other passengers that I do not necessarily know	385	0	3.02	1,187
I reduce my carbon footprint by using soft mobility (train, bike, public transport)	385	0	3.74	1,036
I help keep my neighborhood clean	385	0	4.26	.749
I take part in environmental protection initiatives (tree planting, waste sorting and recycling)	385	0	3.71	1,087
I collaborate in the process of disseminating environmental information.	385	0	3.54	1,194
Strongly disagree (1), Disagree (2), Don't know (3), Agree (4), Strongly agree (5).				

The Environmental Commitment of Moroccan Students

a) Confirmatory factor analysis:

The model of our research falls under the type of structural equation model because it represents the relations between latent variables. Also, the structural equation model has two models. The first is a measurement model, while the second is a structural model. The measurement model depicts the relations between the latent variables and the indicators (observed variables (Items)) used to quantify these latent variables. The structural model, on the other hand, reveals the connections between the latent variables. In addition, the confirmatory exploratory analysis is based on the same principle as the measurement model because it indicates the relationships between the latent variable and the indicators used to measure them.

In our case, the confirmatory factor analysis must be divided into two levels: a first-order analysis and a second-order analysis. These methods then differ from those of regression because they simultaneously allow the processing of estimates of several dependence relations. They also take into account measurement errors in the estimation process (Roussel et al, 2002). The resolution mechanism or process is based on the comparison of two matrix types, namely the matrix S of covariances and correlations of the observed variables and the matrix Σ of estimated covariances or correlations. The correct fit of the factor structure model to the data is verified if the elements of the two matrixes are close to each other. However, this analysis requires the prior verification of the conditions of use of the maximum likelihood method of which the most important hypothesis remains that of the normality of the multivariate distributions.

In our study, this condition is not verified since the **Mardia coefficient** (52.706) is greater than 1.96 as indicated in the following table:

Table 3. Normality assessment (Group number 1)

Variable	min	max	skew	cr.	kurtosis	cr.
d_Auto_eff	1,000	5,000	.600	3,871	-.791	-2.553
g_AE	1,000	5,000	-1.253	-8.088	.487	1,571
d_R	1,000	5,000	-.450	-2.905	-1.026	-3.311
d_VP	1,000	5,000	-1.846	-11.916	3,999	12,905
e_GP	1,000	5,000	-1.709	-11.034	2,991	9,655
a_VP	1,000	5,000	-1.888	-12.190	3,789	12,229
b_VP	1,000	5,000	-1.617	-10.436	3,450	11,135
c_VP	1,000	5,000	-1.310	-8.458	1,889	6,095
c_R	1,000	5,000	-.498	-3.218	-.915	-2.955
a_GP	1,000	5,000	-2.590	-16.718	6,919	22,331
b_GP	1,000	5,000	-2.114	-13.646	4,931	15,916
c_GP	1,000	5,000	-1.537	-9.921	2,410	7,777
a_AE	1,000	5,000	-1.329	-8.581	.652	2,104
b_AE	1,000	5,000	-1.913	-12.347	3,462	11,174
a_CR	1,000	5,000	-.080	-.515	-1.196	-3.860

continues on following page

Table 3. Continued

Variable	min	max	skew	cr.	kurtosis	cr.
b_CR	1,000	5,000	.189	1,218	-1.023	-3.303
are	1,000	5,000	-1.796	-11,594	3,555	11,475
b_RE	1,000	5,000	-1.471	-9.495	2,920	9,426
c_RE	1,000	5,000	-1.602	-10.342	3,328	10,742
d_RE	1,000	5,000	-1.822	-11,760	3,890	12,555
b_Auto_eff	1,000	5,000	-1.308	-8,440	1,504	4,855
c_Auto_eff	1,000	5,000	-.065	-.421	-1.135	-3.664
Multivariate					216,645	**52,706**

Figure 2. Measurement model

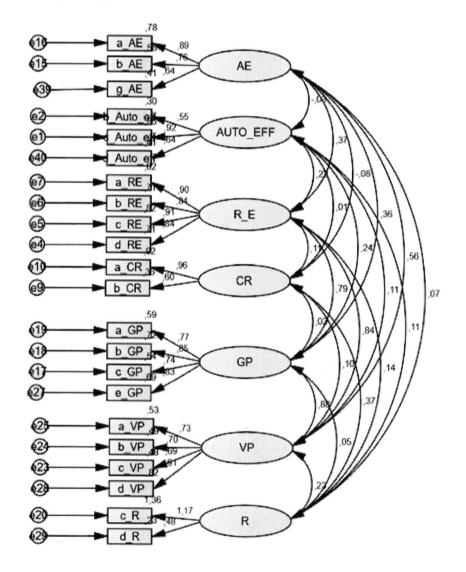

The Environmental Commitment of Moroccan Students

To overcome this problem, Byne (2001) suggests using the boostraptechnique. This technique represents a resampling procedure that allows the researcher to create multiple sub-samples based on the original sample (considered as the parent population).

- **First Order Confirmatory Factor Analysis:**

Table 4. Adjustment indices

Fit Index	Value
Modified Chi-square (CMIN/dl)	2, 325
Comparative Fit Index (CFI)	0.934
Normalized Fit Index (NFI)	0.900
Tucker Lewis Index (TLI)	0.911
SRMR	0.076
Root Mean Square Error of Approximation (RMSEA)	0.073

From the above table, we find that all of the fit indices of the measurement model are acceptable. Also, the means of the regression coefficients obtained by the **bootstrap technique** are significant at the 5% level and very close to the estimates of the original sample.

- **Second Order Confirmatory Factor Analysis:**

Table 5. Adjustment indices

Fit Index	Value
Modified Chi-square (CMIN/dl)	1,938
Comparative Fit Index (CFI)	0.952
Normalized Fit Index (NFI)	0.907
Tucker Lewis Index (TLI)	0.937
SRMR	0.060
Root Mean Square Error of Approximation (RMSEA)	0.061

We also find that all of the fit indices are acceptable.

b) Determinants of pro-environmental behaviors of students:

The figure below shows us the results of the SEM (structural equation model) on the determinants of the pro-environmental behavior of students. As shown in this figure, perceived seriousness has a statistically significant positive direct impact (b = .390, p = 0.031 < 0.05) on students' pro-environmental behavior. Also, the environmental attitude has a statistically significant positive direct effect (b =, 231, p = 0.009 < 0.05) on the pro-environmental behavior of the students. The cost of the response also has a statistically significant positive direct impact (b = .421, p = 0.01 < 0.05) on the "pro-environmental behaviour" of students. On the other hand, perceived vulnerability has a statistically insignificant negative impact (b = - .246, p = 0.239 > 0.05) on the pro-environmental behavior of students. In addition, there are indirect effects of three variables namely the effectiveness of the response and the cost of the

Figure 3. Results of second-order analysis

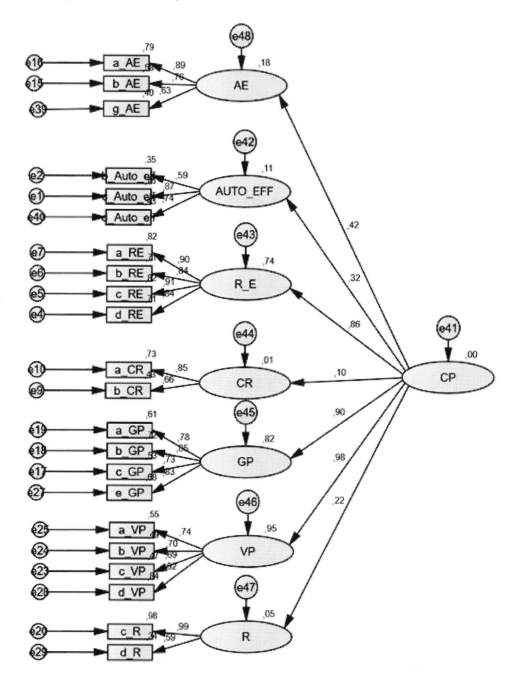

response and the perceived vulnerability. These three indirect effects are applied through the environmental attitude variable. For the indirect effect of response efficiency is negative and statistically significant (c = (-, 16×.231) = -0.036, p = 0.03 < 0.05), the second indirect effect applied by the response cost is also negative and statistically insignificant (c = (-, 12×.231) = -0.027, p = 0.279 > 0.05) and the third indirect effect applied by the perceived vulnerability is (c = (,690×,231) = 0.159, p = 0.009 < 0.05). We find that the cost of the response simultaneously has a direct and indirect effect on the pro-environmental behavior of students. This means that this variable has a total effect equal to the sum of the two effects, i.e. (0.421 + (-027) = 0.394 statistically significant (p = 0.01 < 0.05) Also, the same for the perceived vulnerability variable, the latter has a double effect, both direct and indirect, i.e. a total effect of (-0.246 + 0.159) = -0.087, but it is statistically insignificant (p = 0.646 > 0.05).

Table 6. Indicators selected for each variable after CFA

	Variables	Items	Codification
Independent	Environmental attitude	The perception of the future is worrying under the presence of environmental problems	a_AE
		Environmental problems are mainly related to human activities	b_AE
		Compelling States, organizations and companies to respect the environment under pain of sanctions is a good solution	g_AE
Independent	Perceivedseverity	The threat posed by environmental contamination to humanity is becoming increasingly real.	a_GP
		The negative impacts of the depletion of natural resources are severe	b_GP
		The thought of climate change scares me	c_GP
		Environmental issues are hampering the sustainability of our environment as well as that of future generations	e_GP
Independent	Perceivedvulnerability	Environmental pollution can affect me negatively	a_VP
		I am sensitive to climate change's negative consequences	b_VP
		Environmental degradation has a direct negative impact on me	c_VP
		Environmental degradation is destroying our lives and those of future generations	d_VP
Independent	Awards	Integrating the preservation of the environment into my consumption habits costs me more money	c_R
		The adoption of pro-environmental consumption habits deprives me of satisfying certain needs.	d_R
Independent	Self-efficacy	If I put in the effort, I can manage environmental challenges.	b_Auto_eff
		I am able to deal with anything the environment throws at me.	c_Auto_eff
		I am secure in my capacity to deal with any challenges that may follow from widespread environmental issues, therefore I don't worry about them much.	d_Auto_eff
Independent	Responseefficiency	Having an environmental ethic contributes to the reduction of environmental risks	Are
		The attention and participation of others are positively impacted by my commitment to environmental activities.	b_RE
		I can decrease the possibility of environmental destruction by myself and others if I pay more attention to the environment.	c_RE
		If I manage to reduce environmental risks by adopting pro-environmental behaviors, I contribute to maintaining the sustainability of the environment for present and future generations.	d_RE
Independent	Responsecosts	Carrying measures to address environmental issues is prohibitively expensive	a_CR
		Participating in environmental programs takes my time	b_CR

Final Research Model

Figure 4. Determinants of pro-environmental behavior of students Source: AMOS output

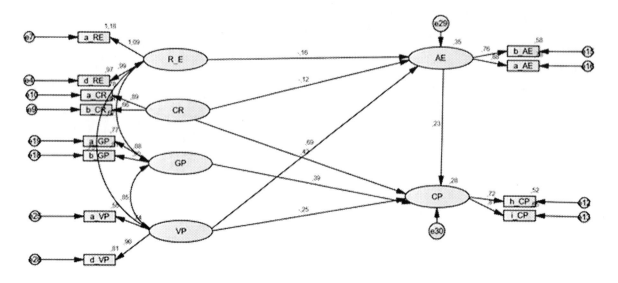

After describing the causal relationships resulting from our model, it is time to verify the certainty of all the initial hypotheses.

Reminders of Assumptions

- **H$_1$**: Perceived gravity positively influences students' willingness to engage in pro-environmental behavior.
- **H$_2$**: Students' desire to engage in pro-environmental behavior is positively influenced by their perception of vulnerability.
- **H$_3$**: Students' aspirations to engage in pro-environmental behavior are negatively influenced by rewards.
- **H$_4$**: Response-efficacy influences students' intentions to engage in pro-environmental behavior in a positive way.
- **H$_5$**: Self-efficacy affects students' desire to engage in pro-environmental behaviour in a positive light.
- **H$_6$**: Response costs negatively affect students' aspirations to engage in pro-environmental behavior.
- **H$_7$**: Environmental attitude positively affects pro-environmental behavior.

We start first by rejecting the two hypotheses H3 and H5 because the two variables object of these two hypotheses are abandoned at the level of the adjustment of the model. So, the two variables namely self-efficacy and rewards do not prove any causal relationship with pro-environmental behavior.

The Environmental Commitment of Moroccan Students

Table 7. Total Effects (Group number 1 - Default model). Source: AMOS Output

	GP	RC	D	VP	EA
PC	.473	.338	-.036	-.109	.199
GIS	.031	.010	.030	.646	.009

From the table above, we accept **hypothesis H1**, because perceived gravity applies a significant positive statistically effect on students' "pro-environmental" behavior. However, we reject **the H2 hypothesis** because the vulnerability applies a significant negative effect on the pro-environmental behavior of the students. We also reject **the H4 hypothesis** because response effectiveness has a negative and insignificant indirect effect on students' "pro-environmental behaviour". In addition, we also reject **the H6 hypothesis** because the cost of the response applies a significant positive effect on pro-environmental behavior. Finally, we accept **hypothesis H7** because environmental attitude has a significant positive effect on students' "pro-environmental" behavior.

Coefficient of Determination R^2

The coefficient of determination reflects the degree of explained variance of the endogenous variables by the exogenous variables introduced into our model. For our study, the coefficient of determination is equal to 28%. This means that our model explains only a modest part of the variance of pro-environmental behavior ($R^2 = 0.28$).

c) Discussion of results

The current context manifested by the increase in the severity of environmental problems as well as the persistence of non-respectful behavior towards the environment encourage all countries to enrol in a development process guided by an ecological vision reconciling economic, social and environmental requirements. In fact, any type of development requires the prior availability of human capital capable of carrying out the necessary directives. In other words, the success of this new development paradigm hinges on the quality of citizens. The latter has a central and indispensable role, something that makes it essential to encourage them to adopt pro-environmental behavior. To this end, it is very important to study the determinants of environmental behavior of citizens. We have chosen to focus our study on students because they represent the youth of the population who will be the decision-makers of tomorrow, as well as they have the knowledge and the means that enable them to put forward adequate solutions in favor of our environment. Indeed, based on a sample of students from the Faculty of Legal, Economic and Social Sciences in Marrakech, we make an empirical investigation. Our research model is based on the "Constructs of protection motivation" theory. In addition, in order to improve the predictive power of the TMP, we added another variable, namely the environmental attitude.

First, we quantified the average value of the items used to assess environmental behavior. Therefore, we found that, on average, students have above-average pro-environmental behavior. This shows that they have favourable behavior across all items. Then, we proceeded to a comparison of the pro-environmental behavior of the students according to the age, the gender, the status, the level of study, the specialty, the connection or not of the studies pursued with the environment, place of residence, family situation, and the level of education of the parents, whether or not they belong to environmental organisations. The findings show that there isn't a significant difference in students' pro-environmental behavior based on age, gender, status, level of study, connection or lack of connection of studies with the environment, family situation, father's level of education, and membership or absence of membership in environmental organizations. On the other hand, there is a statistically significant difference between the pro-environmental behavior of the students according to the specialty, the place of residence and the level of education of the mother. Therefore, we found that students majoring in law have higher pro-environmental behavior than economics students. Additionally, students from urban areas have a higher pro-environmental behavior than students from rural areas. Furthermore, students whose mother's level of education is below the baccalaureate have the highest pro-environmental behavior.

These results then agree with Shafiei 's study. A and Maleksaeidi. H, (2020), who confirm that there is no significant difference between the pro-environmental behaviors of students according to gender, marital status and level of study. However, our results contradict those of the study of Shafiei. A and Maleksaeidi. H, (2020), concerning the existence of a statistically significant difference between the pro-environmental behaviors of students according to the specialty, place of residence and the level of education of the mother.

In order to try to analyze the difference noted at the level of the specialty, we are going to use the pivot table between the specialty and the gender. As a result, we got the following table:

Table 8. Cross-tabulation of specialty and gender

Cross Tabulation				
			Gender	Total
			Man	Women	
Speciality	Economy	119	105	224
	Right	58	103	161
Total		177	208	385

According to this table, we find that students in Law specialty are mostly women with a frequency of 63.97%. Therefore, it may be that women have higher pro-environmental behavior than men, which is why we discovered that law students exhibit more pro-environmental conduct than do students of economics. We can also confirm this finding with a pivot table of pro-environmental behaviors, specialty (law) and gender.

Table 9. cross-tabulation of pro-environmental behavior, specialty and gender

Postponement						
Pro-environmentalbehavior						
Speciality	Gender	Average	NOT	Std. Deviation	F	Sig.
Right	Man	34.5172	58	5.00961	3,903	.049
	Women	34.5534	103	4.92040		
	Total	34.5404	161	4.93710		

From this table, we find that female law students have the highest pro-environmental behavior, which may show that they may be the source of the difference observed between pro-environmental behaviors according to the student's specialty.

Regarding the results of structural equation modeling about the determinants of pro-environmental behavior of students. We first dropped two variables, namely self-efficacy and rewards, in the context of improving the goodness-of-fit of our model. This contradicts the results obtained by Shafiei and Maleksaeidi (2020), the latter found the existence of a statistically significant causal association between these two factors and pro-environmental conduct, namely self-efficacy and rewards. In addition, we found that environmental attitude and perceived seriousness have a direct and statistically significant positive effect on pro-environmental behavior, which is consistent with our original research hypotheses. These findings are consistent with the results of the Shafieistudy and Maleksaeidi, (2020). On the other hand, the cost of the answer exerts a statistically significant direct positive effect on the behavior, something which contradicts the starting hypothesis and also contradicts the results of the Shafieistudy and Maleksaeidi (2020). Also, for the effectiveness of the response, the latter applies a statistically significant indirect negative effect and also the perceived vulnerability exerts a negative but not significant effect on the pro-environmental behavior. These findings are not consistent with the results of the Shafieistudy and Maleksaeidi (2020).

According to these findings, improving students' environmental attitude is synonymous with improving their pro-environmental behavior. In addition, increasing the degree of severity of environmental problems increases the tendency of students to adopt pro-environmental behaviors. In addition, we have findings that contradict the initial hypotheses, which is why these hypotheses were rejected. In addition, we found the existence of a significant correlation between perceived severity and response effectiveness and also between perceived severity and perceived vulnerability and also between vulnerability and response effectiveness. Indeed, this correlation is not a cause and effect relationship, but it is just a simple relationship. In contrast, the Shafieistudy and Maleksaeidi, (2020), revealed the existence of the causal relationships between rewards and response costs and between perceived severity and perceived vulnerability.

CONCLUSION

This research work focuses mainly on the measurement and determinants of student engagement in the Faculty of Legal, Economic and Social Sciences in Marrakech. So, this main objective is divided into two main sub-objectives. The first is that of measuring student engagement and the other represents the determinants of student engagement. By consulting the literature, we noticed two factors—environmental mindset and pro-environmental behavior—that can most effectively predict commitment. Regarding the determinants of commitment, we made use of the TMP because of their power to predict behavior. Indeed, TMP has already proven its effectiveness in explaining behaviors in the field of health as it can provide more predictors of behavior. It can also identify the elements that encourage individuals to adopt pro-environmental behaviors (Keshavarz & Karami, 2016).

The first chapter is devoted to the conceptual analysis of the environmental commitment of students while highlighting the importance of this commitment towards the environment as a pillar of sustainable development. Also, this chapter indicates the elements that determine the engagement of the students and the opportunities offered to the students within the framework of stimulating their engagement.

Regarding the second chapter, the latter is dedicated to the conceptual analysis of the variables chosen for the measurement of environmental commitment, namely the environmental attitude and the pro-environmental behavior. In addition, it highlights the determining factors and the sources of improvement of these two variables. Also, this chapter presents an overview of the theories that relate to behavior modification, and it also presents the basic theory of our research, namely the theory of motivation to protection.

After these two chapters, we have tried to make the link between the theoretical foundations (presented at the level of the two theoretical chapters) and the practices in the field. To do this, we opted for the positivist paradigm in order to test the hypotheses built on the basis of the TMP and previous studies. Also, we have chosen the hypothetico-deductive approach because we have a theoretical reference on which we want to pass judgment by confronting it with reality. We also chose the quantitative method to answer our problem because this method is perfectly in line with positivism, and it allows the formulation of hypotheses that will be tested later in order to obtain explanations and predictions. Indeed, the formulated hypotheses have led to the construction of a conceptual research model. The latter includes an endogenous latent variable, namely pro-environmental behavior, as well as seven independent latent variables, namely environmental attitude, perceived gravity, perceived vulnerability, rewards, self-efficacy, and response and the cost of the response. We started by testing the reliability of the questionnaire through a pilot study conducted on a sample of 30 students. The results gave "Cronbach 's alpha coefficients" of the variables vary from 0.608 to 0.926, something that shows the reliability of this questionnaire. Then, we began our analysis with a descriptive study aimed at exploring the characteristics of our sample (391 students). After that, we assessed the students' average pro-environmental behavior in light of the items that were used to gauge it, and we compared the students' pro-environmental behavior in light of age, gender, status, level of study, specialty, link or not of the studies pursued with the environment, place of residence, family situation, level of education of the parents, membership or not in environmental organizations. Then, we developed a confirmatory factor analysis in order to identify the representative items of each latent variable. Afterwards, we carried out an evaluation of the measurement model, namely the analysis of convergent validity and the analysis of discriminant validity. Subsequently, we proceeded to the test of the model in order to verify the indices of the goodness of fit of the model with the data collected. Finally, we proceeded to test the hypotheses by comparing them with reality.

Regarding the main results, we found that improving the environmental attitude positively affects the pro-environmental behavior of students. Also, the increase in the degree of seriousness of environmental problems promotes the adoption of pro-environmental behavior. In contrast to previous studies, we found that increasing response costs positively affect the adoption of pro-environmental behavior, and response effectiveness exerts a significant indirect effect on pro-environmental behavior. However, we found a non-significant causal relationship between perceived vulnerability and pro-environmental behavior. Thus, self-efficacy and rewards have no causal relationship with pro-environmental behavior.

Furthermore, we found the existence of significant correlations between perceived severity and response effectiveness, between perceived severity and perceived vulnerability, and also between vulnerability and response effectiveness. Indeed, this correlation is not a cause-and-effect relationship, but it is just a simple relationship.

Hinders on Theory and Application

Our analysis used TMP as a framework to analyze how students at the Faculty of Legal, Economic, and Social Sciences in Marrakech behaved in favor of the environment. In fact, 28% of the variance in pro-environmental behavior was explained by our research model. According to the results, environmental attitude and perceived seriousness have positive impact on pro-environmental behavior. Indeed, our results with respect to TMP only confirm the positive effect of perceived gravity on pro-environmental behavior. Furthermore, our findings show that including environmental attitude as a new construct in the TMP can improve its predictive power. Additionally, this study offers fresh insights and expertise to help planners and policymakers make informed choices with regard to the growth of pro-environmental behaviors among various social groups, particularly university students. According to the results, the environmental attitude is the crucial determinant of pro-environmental behavior which makes it necessary to adopt the measures in the framework of improving people's understanding of the need to protect the environment, the right to life for plants and animals, the impact of environmental degradation on individual health and social well-being, and the growing responsibility of different industries and businesses to observe environmental principles. In addition, given the significant impact of perceived seriousness in fostering the adoption of pro-environmental behavior, awareness of the severity of environmental problems through all types of media is also observed.

A Few Recommendations

In addition, we also found that the specialty, the place of residence and the level of education of the mother affect the pro-environmental behavior of the students. Therefore, it is essential in the first place to include modules relating to the importance of environmental protection in study programs at all levels. In addition, we must invest more in training programs on the education of women and put all the necessary measures to fight against dropping out of school and school abundance.

The Limits of the Work

This work has allowed us to extract some constructs that influence pro-environmental behavior. However, this study has some limitations. The first lies in the scarcity of documentation that deals with the same topic. The second limitation is at the level of data collection due to the length of the questionnaire and also the difficulty of understanding some of these concepts by students. The third limitation is the fact of not starting with an exploratory factorial study in order to choose suitable items because, in our study, we abandoned several items. The last limitation is manifested by the lack of sufficient information to readjust the sample according to the characteristics of the target population, namely the distribution of students according to gender, cycle of study and discipline.

Research Perspectives

Our study was carried out on a sample of 391 students, most of whom are under 25, which is a fairly narrow age range. So, it would be interesting to target a wider age group. In order to select the optimal measurement indicators for the latent variables covered by this theory, It is recommended that future researchers who use TMP as a framework for investigating pro-environmental behavior begin with an exploratory study. Moreover, the protection of the environment is the responsibility of several social groups. This makes it necessary to generalize this study to the different social groups in order to have knowledge of the factors that influence these behaviors. Furthermore, our study revealed that there is a significant difference in pro-environmental behavior between students from urban and rural backgrounds. Also, a significant difference in the pro-environmental behavior of the students according to the level of education of the mother has been observed. Therefore, it seems interesting that the results of our study examine the influence of both the place of residence and the level of education of the mother on the behavior of students. Let us take as an example the following question: to what extent does the place of residence influence pro-environmental behaviour?

REFERENCES

Ajzen, I. (1991). The theory of planned behavior. *Organizational Behavior and Human Decision Processes*, *50*(2), 179–211. doi:10.1016/0749-5978(91)90020-T

Akbari, M., Ardekani, Z. F., Pino, G., & Maleksaeidi, H. (2019). An extended model of Theory of Planned Behavior to investigate highly-educated Iranian consumers' intentions towards consuming genetically modified foods. *Journal of Cleaner Production*, *227*, 784–793. doi:10.1016/j.jclepro.2019.04.246

Almarshad, S. O. (2017). Adopting sustainable behavior in institutions of higher education: A study on intentions of decision makers in the MENA region. *European Journal of Sustainable Development*, *6*(2), 89–89. doi:10.14207/ejsd.2017.v6n2p89

Berryman, T. (2002). Éco-ontogenèse et éducation: les relations à l'environnement dans le développement humain et leur prise en compte en éducation relative à l'environnement durant la petite enfance, l'enfance et l'adolescence [Eco-ontogeny and education: relations to the environment in human development and their consideration in environmental education during infancy, childhoos, and adolescence]. *Open Edition Journals*.

Borden, R. J. (1977). One more look at social and environmental psychology: Away from the looking glass and into the future. *Personality and Social Psychology Bulletin*, *3*(3), 407–411. doi:10.1177/014616727700300309

Boudreau, I. (1997). *Attitude des adolescents et des jeunes adultes à l'égard de la pratique de comportements sécuritaires en planche à neige [Attitudes of adolescents and young adults toward practicing safe snowboarding behaviors]*. [Doctoral dissertation, Université du Québec à Trois-Rivières].

Bubeck, P., Wouter Botzen, W. J., Laudan, J., Aerts, J. C., & Thieken, A. H. (2018). Insights into flood-coping appraisals of protection motivation theory: Empirical evidence from Germany and France. *Risk Analysis*, *38*(6), 1239–1257. doi:10.1111/risa.12938 PMID:29148082

Carrus, G., Scopelliti, M., Fornara, F., Bonnes, M., & Bonaiuto, M. (2014). Place attachment, community identification, and pro-environmental engagement. *Place attachment: Advances in theory, methods and applications*, 156-162.

Casaló, L. V., & Escario, J. J. (2018). Heterogeneity in the association between environmental attitudes and pro-environmental behavior: A multilevel regression approach. *Journal of Cleaner Production, 175*, 155–163. doi:10.1016/j.jclepro.2017.11.237

Chen, F., Chen, H., Guo, D., & Long, R. (2017). Analysis of undesired environmental behavior among Chinese undergraduates. *Journal of Cleaner Production, 162*, 1239–1251. doi:10.1016/j.jclepro.2017.06.051

Dang, H., Li, E., & Bruwer, J. (2012). Understanding Climate Change Adaptive Behaviour of Farmers: An Integrated Conceptual Framework. *International Journal of Climate Change: Impacts & Responses, 3*(2), 255–272. doi:10.18848/1835-7156/CGP/v03i02/37106

De Leeuw, A., Valois, P., Ajzen, I., & Schmidt, P. (2015). Using the theory of planned behavior to identify key beliefs underlying pro-environmental behavior in high-school students: Implications for educational interventions. *Journal of Environmental Psychology, 42*, 128–138. doi:10.1016/j.jenvp.2015.03.005

Fishbein, M., & Ajzen, I. (1974). Attitudes towards objects as predictors of single and multiple behavioral criteria. *Psychological Review, 81*(1), 59–74. doi:10.1037/h0035872

Fishbein, M., Jaccard, J., Davidson, A. R., Ajzen, I., & Loken, B. (1980). Predicting and understanding family planning behaviors. In *Understanding attitudes and predicting social behavior*. Prentice Hall.

Forget, E. L. (2011). The town with no poverty: The health effects of a Canadian guaranteed annual income field experiment. *Canadian Public Policy, 37*(3), 283–305. doi:10.3138/cpp.37.3.283

Goyette, Y. (2019). *Le développement de la conscience écologique dans un cours d'éducation par l'aventure [The development of ecological awareness in an adventure education course]* (Doctoral dissertation, Université du Québec à Chicoutimi).

Gravel, H., & Pruneau, D. (2004). Une étude de la réceptivité à l'environnement chez les adolescents [A study of environmental responsiveness in adolescents]. *Revue de l'Université de Moncton, 35*(1), 165–187. doi:10.7202/008767ar

Janmaimool, P. (2017). Application of protection motivation theory to investigate sustainable waste management behaviors. *Sustainability, 9*(7), 1079. doi:10.3390u9071079

Keshavarz, M., & Karami, E. (2016). Farmers' pro-environmental behavior under drought: Application of protection motivation theory. *Journal of Arid Environments, 127*, 128–136. doi:10.1016/j.jaridenv.2015.11.010

Kim, S., Jeong, S. H., & Hwang, Y. (2013). Predictors of pro-environmental behaviors of American and Korean students: The application of the theory of reasoned action and protection motivation theory. *Science Communication, 35*(2), 168–188. doi:10.1177/1075547012441692

Latif, B., Ong, T. S., Meero, A., Abdul Rahman, A. A., & Ali, M. (2022). Employee-Perceived Corporate Social Responsibility (CSR) and Employee Pro-Environmental Behavior (PEB): The Moderating Role of CSR Skepticism and CSR Authenticity. *Sustainability, 14*(3), 1380. doi:10.3390u14031380

Rainear, A. M., & Christensen, J. L. (2017). Protection motivation theory as an explanatory framework for proenvironmental behavioral intentions. *Communication Research Reports, 34*(3), 239–248. doi:10.1080/08824096.2017.1286472

Rogers, R. W. (1983). Cognitive and psychological processes in fear appeals and attitude change: A revised theory of protection motivation. *Social psychophysiology: A sourcebook*, 153-176.

Rubinstein, M. (2006). Le développement de la responsabilité sociale de l'entreprise. Une analyse en termes d'isomorphisme institutionnel [The development of corporate social responsibility, an analysis in terms of institutional isomorphism]. *Revue d'Economie Industrielle*, (113), 83–105. doi:10.4000/rei.295

Schwartz, S. H. (1977). Normative influences on altruism. In Vol. 10, pp. 221–279). Advances in experimental social psychology. Academic Press.

Shafiei, A., & Maleksaeidi, H. (2020). Pro-environmental behavior of university students: Application of protection motivation theory. *Global Ecology and Conservation, 22*, e00908. doi:10.1016/j.gecco.2020.e00908

Steg, L., & Vlek, C. (2009). Encouraging pro-environmental behaviour: An integrative review and research agenda. *Journal of Environmental Psychology, 29*(3), 309–317. doi:10.1016/j.jenvp.2008.10.004

Vicente-Molina, M. A., Fernández-Sainz, A., & Izagirre-Olaizola, J. (2018). Does gender make a difference in pro-environmental behavior? The case of the Basque Country University students. *Journal of Cleaner Production, 176*, 89–98. doi:10.1016/j.jclepro.2017.12.079

Wang, Y., Liang, J., Yang, J., Ma, X., Li, X., Wu, J., Yang, G., Ren, G., & Feng, Y. (2019). Analysis of the environmental behavior of farmers for non-point source pollution control and management: An integration of the theory of planned behavior and the protection motivation theory. *Journal of Environmental Management, 237*, 15–23. doi:10.1016/j.jenvman.2019.02.070 PMID:30776770

Xiao, H., Li, S., Chen, X., Yu, B., Gao, M., Yan, H., & Okafor, C. N. (2014). Protection motivation theory in predicting intention to engage in protective behaviors against schistosomiasis among middle school students in rural China. *PLoS Neglected Tropical Diseases, 8*(10).

Chapter 17
Framing Responsive and Responsible Learning in Project-Based Assessment:
A Study on the Malaysian General Studies Subject

Aiedah Abdul Khalek
https://orcid.org/0000-0002-8219-2768
Monash University, Malaysia

EXECUTIVE SUMMARY

This chapter aims to reimagine learning and teaching general studies by embedding responsive and responsible learning elements in the project-based assessment. The author unfolds the educator's reflective experiences in carrying out the assessment and the student's experiences in completing the project. Data are collected through the educators' reflective journals and students' evaluations, including students' evaluation reports and qualitative feedback. The findings include a discussion on strategies and challenges in curating responsive and responsible learning in a project-based assessment, and how the project-based assessment creates an affective and effective learning environment. This study aspires to serve as evidence-based practice and reflections to develop responsive and responsible learning in the project-based assessment.

INTRODUCTION

General Studies in Malaysian Higher Education System

The Malaysian General Studies subjects aspire to contribute to nation-building by improving graduates' knowledge and soft skill in developing holistic human capital. In 1996, the Malaysian government implemented government-mandated subjects known as General Studies (previously known as Com-

DOI: 10.4018/978-1-6684-6076-4.ch017

pulsory Subjects), intending to improve students' soft skills and employability. Local and international undergraduate students who are enrolled in Malaysian higher education institutions are required to pass these subjects as a requirement for their graduation. The intention of offering these subjects aligned with the National Education Philosophy, which is to produce good citizens with balanced personality and identity that embrace the following characteristics:

i. Trusting and obeying God
ii. Knowledgeable
iii. Skilled
iv. Willing to contribute to society, religion, race, and country
v. Responsible to oneself, religion, race, society, and country.

The General Studies aim to curate general education that embeds aspects of knowledge that enhance communication skills and develop an appreciation of noble values, as well as general knowledge that transcends the boundaries of traditional disciplines such as philosophy, arts, and national language. The bigger vision of these subjects is to produce graduates with broad-minded, balanced, and holistic skills who can be competitive in modern society.

At the beginning of the implementation, there were five subjects introduced namely; Malaysian Studies, Islamic Studies, Moral Education, National Language A, and National Language B (for international students). In 2012, these subjects were replaced with the new General Studies subjects which are Malaysian Studies and Communicative Malay 2 for international students. Malaysian students are offered subjects namely Ethnic Relations, Islamic and Asian Civilization, and National Language A. The new subjects intend to align with the Ministry's National Higher Education Strategic Plan (NHESP) which seeks to strengthen nation-building by equipping graduates with both hard and soft skills, resulting in comprehensive human capital. (Yip & Burhanuddin, 2017).

The new subjects were embedded in a new General Studies structure which divides the General Studies subjects into four components (Ministry of Higher Education Malaysia, 2016);

U1: Appreciation of philosophy, values, and history
U2: Mastery of soft skills
U3: Expansion of knowledge about Malaysia, and
U4: Community service and co-curriculum.

In this new structure, students have to complete several credit hours in each component as a requirement for completing their degree. This regulation applies to all higher learning institutions regardless of homegrown institutions or foreign universities located in Malaysia.

Strategically, General Studies subjects were designed based on Malaysia's National Education Philosophy, Malaysia's Education Blueprint 2012–2025 (Higher Education), and High-Impact Educational Practices. These three strategies aspire to develop values, knowledge, as well as cognitive and social skills. The subjects emphasize nation-building, soft skills mastery and development, strengthening and increasing understanding of Malaysia, and utilizing soft skills in preparing students to meet problems in a real and competitive world in the future. (Yip and Burhanuddin, 2017). However, not all aspects are ideal when it comes to the implementation of the subjects at the ground level. There were some challenges that required improvement efforts to address the setback.

As previous research has shown the advantages of project-based assessment in learning and teaching include encouraging active learning among students (Carr et al., 2015), the researcher is interested to further discover whether project-based assessments improve the assessment practice and learning experiences in the General Studies subject. In addition, the researcher is also intrigued to unfold the responsible and responsive learning elements in the project-based assessment practice. Therefore, the study aims to unravel the impact of project-based learning on students' learning experience, particularly through the lens of responsible and responsive learning.

The following section discusses the challenges of learning and teaching General Studies and how the author used project-based assessments to enhance the assessment practice and students' learning experiences.

Challenges in Learning General Studies

Previous studies demonstrated that learning and teaching the General Studies subjects encountered some challenges that need to be addressed by the stakeholders in order to achieve the desired learning outcomes and meet the intended aspirations. The challenges come from students' perceptions about the subjects, teaching and learning practices, and institutional challenges in implementing higher learning education institutions.

Students, as the main stakeholders, are undoubtedly the main focus of learning. Students have diverse perceptions and opinions about learning the General Studies subjects (Awang et al., 2013). Some Malaysian students feel that the syllabus is a repetition of what they studied in school (Basir et al 2018). They feel that the content of the General Studies subjects is not relevant to their study and this leads to issues in learning the subjects efficiently. This is due to the fact that they view the subjects as not related to their degree and do not contribute to preparing them for a future career. (Nasir et al., 2019)

The second issue is learning and teaching strategies. The teaching approaches, in many institutions, are not favoured by the students (Idris et al., 2012). They comment that the General Studies subjects are taught in a similar style as the teaching of secondary school history, with a heavy emphasis on memorising and teacher-centered instruction. (Basir et al., 2018). The instructional methods are not suitable for the young generation's learning styles and preferences. The students reveal that some of the lecturers do not utilize technology to enhance their teaching. This might have also negatively affected the students' learning experiences and engagements (Yusof, 2019). The advancement of technologies should be effectively utilised to support students' learning and spark their interest in learning the subject. The data collected from 26 universities and higher educational institutions in Malaysia indicates that all the institutions provided a Learning Management System but only 77% of the lecturers utilise their Learning Management System. Technically, Malaysian higher learning institutions provide Learning Management Systems to support students' learning (Amin, 2012). In addition, some of the educational technologies are accessible at zero cost to enhance education. These resources could enhance students' learning experience if they are utilised effectively.

Endut et al. (2019) reveal that some of the institutions do not emphasise and support the teaching and learning of the General Studies subjects as much as they do for the other faculty subjects. The implementation of the General Studies subjects receives less attention and emphasis compared to the other degree subjects. Ibrahim (2018) gives an example that when selecting appropriate lecture periods and accommodating lecture spaces, the faculty frequently prioritises core subjects and sidelines the General Studies courses. The General Studies classes are scheduled during inconvenient times and in inconvenient lecture spaces. This setting may have an impact on lecturers' and students' motivation to learn the subjects. Furthermore, the lecturers have to manage a large number of students in a class, with a lack of financial assistance for organising teaching and learning activities that can impact students' learning experience. Learning environments are technically vital in influencing students' well-being, academic progress (Huang, 2012), and improved results and learning outcomes (Yee et al., 2018). Hence, the lack of institutional support in terms of facilities, finance, and a conducive learning environment might impede the implementation of the General Studies courses at higher education institutions.

Another important challenge in implementing a General Studies subject is to ensure appropriate and effective assessment. (Shaari et al., 2017; Yee & Baskaran 2017; Yaacob & Kassim, 2020). A pen-and-paper assessment, which is very examination-oriented and relies on memorising facts and points, seems not a preferable kind of assessment among students. This may have led to a lack of interest in learning General Studies subjects and developed a setback in learning (Endut et al. 2019; Rohana et al. 2020). Undoubtedly, assessment is one of the important aspects to look at if we want to develop high-impact practices as intended by the Ministry of Higher Education. Therefore, in this paper, the researcher implements a project-based assessment that embeds responsible and responsive learning elements, as an alternative to traditional assessment that creates a memorising human-machine among students to excel in the examination.

Hence, this paper analyses the impact of project-based assessment on responsible and responsive learning experiences among students. The following section provides narratives and analysis dependent on evidence-based and project-based assessments implemented previously in the General Studies classes. The next section, therefore, will unfold the project-based assessment from theoretical and practical perspectives.

ENHANCING THE ASSESSMENT THROUGH RESPONSIBLE AND RESPONSIVE LEARNING IN PROJECT-BASED ASSESSMENT

Project-Based Assessment

Project-based learning serves as an effective pedagogical method for enhancing the educational experience. In project-based learning, students act as active actors by engaging in repeated cycles of learning including synthesis, analysis, action, and reflection. It is a dynamic tool that could serve in two folds; as an active learning strategy and as an assessment tool to evaluate students' performance (Mioduser & Betzer, 2007).

Project-based learning as a learning strategy emphasises learning by doing and continuous learning engagement (Khalek, 2012). While as an assessment, it can be effectively translated into a project-based assessment that measures different aspects of learning, both cognitive and social skills. In project-based assessment, students must complete several learning activities and exercises, as well as develop ideas or outcomes based on the project information provided by the educators (Mioduser & Betzer, 2007).

The project-based assessment can be implemented in many forms, ranging from a single activity lasting a few weeks to a set of continuous activities that will be completed over the semester (Verner & Betzer, 2001, Ginestie, 2002). The marks are allocated based on the simplicity to the complexity of the assessment criteria. Project-based assessment technically is based on project-based learning activities

Framing Responsive and Responsible Learning in Project-Based Assessment

which are evaluated and graded. It has some distinctive characteristics that define the process, as listed by Mioduser and Betzer (2007);

1. A project-based assessment encompasses a series of processes that are driven by an authentic learning need or problem. The learning needs and problems derive students' motivation to learn and complete the project.
2. The project is creative, involving designing a solution, solving the problem, and creating innovations that are guided by predetermined criteria developed by educators. The guidelines must be clear and concise to guide students' learning.
3. The project demands a diverse set of skills related to a variety of tasks, including information retrieval, the recording of ideas, and the creation of physical or virtual models. Students normally utilise and develop a different set of knowledge and skills to complete the project.
4. The project requires collaborative work and cooperation among educators with students and students with their peers. It involves a lot of social interaction, communication skills, leadership, and teamwork.
5. Some of the projects entangle interaction outside the classroom, such as interacting with the community and industry.
6. The project-based assessment involves continuous assessment of each stage of learning. Each stage is connected to another stage to ensure the ongoing learning process corresponds to the outcome of the project. Each stage of learning is imperative, to assure the success of the project-based assessment.

The Implementation of Project-Based Assessment

Putting these criteria into a perspective, students must complete a set of activities, including identifying an issue, researching relevant resources, suggesting viable solutions to problems, implementing the solution, creating products, and evaluating the project outcome. The educator will play the role of facilitator of learning and guide the students. Students will play active roles and learn a variety of hard and soft skills relevant to their project in the process of completing it. These skills will prepare the students to work with others to accomplish a common goal in their future careers.

The project drives students' motivations to learn and participate actively in the learning process. (Mioduser & Betzer, 2007). In comparison to the traditional assessment, the project task involves a higher level of Bloom's taxonomy of learning, and cognitive and social skills but does not require a lot of memorisation of knowledge.

Project-based learning assessment is an educator-facilitated method of learning in which students are under the supervision of the educator (Bell, 2010). Therefore, the guidelines must be clear, concise, and comprehensive and will be able to guide students to learn independently.

The educators will analyse students' performance consistently and provide necessary and timely feedback to the students. Feedback would help students to reflect on their learning process and perform better in the next stage of the project. Project-based assessment is proven as one of the most promising methods for evaluating students' performance and the best pedagogical strategy for creating instructional materials (Mioduser & Betzer, 2007).

The Significance of Project-Based Assessment in Creating Responsive and Responsible Learning

Responsive and Responsible Behaviours in an Active Learning Sphere

Responsive and responsible learning exist as part of an active learning strategy. It gives autonomy to the students to take charge of their learning, construct knowledge and develop skills in the learning process. In project-based assessment, students need to participate in active learning activities. First, the author will explain the notion of active learning and how it is integrated with project-based learning which then is used as a part and parcel of the project-based assessment (Bonwell & Eison, 1991).

According to the National Survey of Student Engagement (NSSE) and the Australasian Survey of Student Engagement (AUSSE), active learning is described as students' participation to construct their knowledge. Students work with other students on projects, plan their work, and perform a presentation that involves asking questions or contributing to discussions (Coates, 2008). Furthermore, some of the projects require students to participate in a community, work with other students, discuss ideas in and outside the class, sharing knowledge with their peers (Carr et al., 2015).

Project-based learning encompasses active learning strategies which require students to actively participate in the learning process. This implies that the project-based assessment involves the active learning elements of "engaging students in doing things and thinking about what they are doing" (Bonwell & Eison, 1991).

Cognitive Development in Project-Based Assessment

Project-based assessment emphasises the development of cognitive skills rather than only the transmission of knowledge. It stimulates students' learning by doing, such as reading, talking, writing, planning, solving problems, creating solutions, and innovating. Most of the learning activities involve higher-order thinking and require active participation among students. The activities require students to create their knowledge, linking new ideas and experiences to current information and experiences to generate new or enhanced understanding.

This aligns with constructivist learning theory in developing knowledge in learning (Bransford et al., 1999). Students can either assimilate new knowledge into existing knowledge or alter the information to accommodate new knowledge that contradicts their existing knowledge. They are technically establishing connections between new knowledge and their present knowledge in active learning approaches. The process helps to broaden their cognitive capacities and knowledge. Educators will guide the students and allow them to address misunderstandings, build and rebuild new understanding and knowledge. Nevertheless, students are responsible for their own learning.

Mindfulness in Project-Based Assessment

Responsible learning necessitates students' mindfulness of the learning objectives and working on achieving them. Educators play an important role in creating a learning space that provides students with an opportunity to choose and engage in their learning experiences. Indeed, it is vital for educators and institutions to rethink their assessments, either they are set for the learning outcomes and for the benefit of students' cognitive and social knowledge, or they are only there to evaluate what is easier to measure.

For instance, multiple-choice and fill-in-the-blank questions are common in many educational institutions which may test some knowledge but may not be able to develop certain cognitive and human skills.

In contrast, project-based assessment integrates a seamless learning experience that connects individuals, allowing students to learn through individual and group efforts. Another important aspect of responsible learning is learning motivation. It is human nature that people will perform best when they have interest and motivation. This includes intrinsic and extrinsic motivations. Intrinsic motivation is powerful in deriving and sustaining learning. The desire to learn and achieve competence is fueled by one's interests. Learners acquire substantially higher-order learning results when the material is personally intriguing and relevant. Interests and passions acquired in a social setting are crucial aspects in connected learning. It helps to develop skills and dispositions for lifelong learning and making significant contributions to life and knowledge.

Connectedness in Learning

Being responsible learners, students are connected across time and situations, such as in-school vs outside school, formal vs informal learning, and physical world vs virtual/online. The consistency of learning experiences across diverse situations may involve multiple people and platforms of learning. The goal is to enable learners to study the knowledge that they are interested in. This allows them to effortlessly learn in multiple settings, such as formal and informal learning, and individual and social learning, and expand the social spaces in which they connect. Nevertheless, technology is crucial in facilitating the transition between these diverse places and platforms. Utilising technology would assist in diverse learning experiences in physical and virtual settings. (Looi et al., 2012)

In a context where learning is done responsibly, students are connected and actively pursue their learning objectives with the support of peers, educators, and people around them. It differs significantly from conventional education, which is founded on predetermined subjects, one-on-one training, and standardised testing. Research has shown that young people learn best when they actively participate in creating and resolving challenges that matter to them and when they are surrounded by peers who value and recognize their accomplishments. Traditional education practice seems less effective in engaging learners at different levels of education, such as middle school, high school, and college. This has to be changed to suit the characteristics of 21st-century learners (Looi. et al., 2012).

In addition, technology has made information accessible, for example, information on websites, social media, and interactive content are readily available to intensify out-of-school learning and a division between formal education and informal knowledge-seeking which is interest-driven ("What is connected learning?" 2020).

A culture of ongoing participation, self-expression, and active engagement that is knowledge-rich and socially significant is the ideal environment for responsible and connected learning, where learners actively participate, engage in discussion, negotiate ideas, receive and offer feedback ("What is connected learning?" 2020).

METHOD

Project-based Assessment in the Ethnic Relations Subject

This project-based assessment was implemented in the Ethnic Relations subject, one of the General Studies subjects offered to Malaysian students. In this project, students were required to perform a cultural presentation and submit a reflective report at the end of the project.

First, students would choose the topic that interests them on Malaysian cultures, ethnicities, and religions such as Malaysian costumes, ethnic food, cultures and ceremonies, arts and performance, traditional architecture/design, and ethnicity-based practices. They would have to propose their topic and outline their planning for the execution of the project. The lecturer would provide feedback based on the proposal to ensure the project is feasible and meets the learning outcomes. At the end of the project, students would present what they had learned about the chosen topic and write reflective reports on their learning experiences.

In this project-based assessment, the lecturer played a role of a facilitator and a mediator between knowledge and students. The lecturer is no longer a content and knowledge provider as students have to responsibly organise information and manage their learning from various resources, formal and informal settings such as expert interviews, community involvement, and searching for information from books and the internet.

The assessment aimed to develop responsive and responsible learning among the students. It is intended to give space to students to learn and master specific topics about Malaysian cultures that interest them. In addition, the project helped to develop soft skills in learning collaboratively, seeking knowledge in the field, and communicating the knowledge and skills in the classroom. For example, if the group wants to learn about the *"Sumazau"* dance, they will have to find information about the dance, watch the actual dance and learn how to dance from reliable sources. They would present their findings to the class and demonstrate the actual *"Sumazau"* dance to the classroom.

As the class accommodates typically more than 100 students in the lecture hall, their presentation would be a real cultural performance that normally would encourage full attendance and even attract students who were not enrolled in the Unit to attend the presentations.

Research Design

This is a practitioner inquiry research that adopts mixed methods data including survey and document analysis. The practitioner inquiry research aims for improving and understanding the adoption of educational theory to improve educational practices (Gutierez, 2019).

The researcher used the University Student Evaluation survey as the research instrument, consisting of 5 Likert scale items and open-ended questions. In addition, the researcher used the reflective journal to document the planning and implementation process particularly to record data and to provide the opportunity for reflection on the teaching and learning experience.

Data Collection and Analysis

The researcher collected and analysed the data through the lecturer's reflective journal, students' evaluations, and qualitative feedback. The lecturer documented a reflective journal to reflect on the implementation intentionally to improve the practice of the project-based assessment in her class. She also compiled and analyzed the data of the Student Evaluation quantitative report and the qualitative written feedback using thematic analysis.

The online surveys which include quantitative and qualitative questions were shared with all the students at the end of the semester but without any coercion to complete the survey. This survey which is anonymous does not collect personal identifiable information from the respondents, such as their name, email address, student number, and courses.

These three sources of data aim to provide data triangulation to understand and evaluate the assessment practice and to serve as a reflection for the project-based assessment. A total of 1989 students were involved in the project over the period of six semesters.

RESULT AND FINDINGS

Does Project-Based Assessment Improve Students Learning Experiences?

This section reveals the impact of project-based assessment through the lens of students who are the primary stakeholders in education. The author compares the students' evaluation data before and after the implementation of the project-based assessment. The project implementation started in Semester 1, 2017 until Semester 2, 2019.

Achieving Learning Outcomes

The first graph in Figure 1 shows a data comparison of student evaluation on the assessment that demonstrates the learning outcomes. The data shows the scores for this statement before the project implementation was 3.23 (Semester 1, 2015), 3.10 (semester 2, 2015), 3.5 (Semester 1, 2016), and 3.60 (Semester 2, 2016). The scores show an improvement in the first semester of the project implementation which indicated an increase to 3.70 (Semester 1, 2017), 3.83 (Semester 2, 2017), 3.85 (Semester 1, 2018), 3.85 (Semester 2, 2018), 3.99 (Semester 1, 2019), 4.21 (Semester 2, 2019).

Students' Learning Engagement

Secondly, figure 2 shows an improvement in students' engagement in learning the subject after the implementation of the project. The graph below shows a comparison of learning engagement. The data shows the scores for learning engagement before the project implementation were 3.49 (Semester 1, 2015), 3.18 (semester 2, 2015), 3.57 (Semester 1, 2016), and 3.57 (Semester 2, 2016). The scores show an improvement in the first semester of the project implementation with a record of 4.12 (Semester 1, 2017), 3.76 (Semester 2, 2017), 3.86 (Semester 1, 2018), 3.79 (Semester 2, 2018), 4.05 (Semester 1, 2019), 4.18 (Semester 2, 2019).

Figure 1. Comparison of student evaluation on the assessment that demonstrates the learning outcomes. (Student Evaluation of Teaching and Unit Report 2015-2019)

Figure 2. Comparison of student evaluation on learning engagement (Student Evaluation of Teaching and Unit Report 2015-2019)

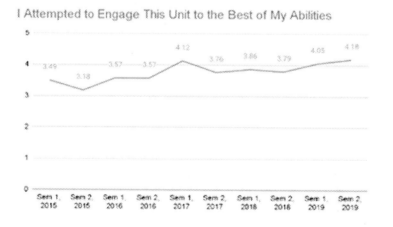

Overall Students' Satisfaction

Thirdly, figure 3 shows a comparison of the overall students' satisfaction with learning the subject. The data shows the overall students' satisfaction before the project implementation which were 3.49 (Semester 1, 2015), 3.18 (semester 2, 2015), 3.5 (Semester 1, 2016), and 3.49 (Semester 2, 2016). The scores show an improvement in the first semester of the project implementation which recorded 3.67 (Semester 1, 2017), and continuously improved to 3.83 (Semester 2, 2017), 3.84 (Semester 1, 2018), 3.8 (Semester 2, 2018), 4.0 (Semester 1, 2019), 4.17 (Semester 2, 2019).

Figure 3. Comparison of student overall satisfaction (Student Evaluation of Teaching and Unit Report 2015-2019)

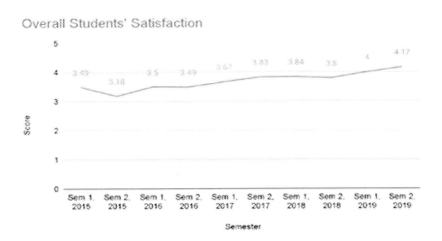

These findings demonstrate that since the implementation of the project-based assessment, students' learning has improved specifically in aspects related to learning outcomes, learning engagement, and overall learning satisfaction.

Unfolding Responsive Learning Experiences

This project-based assessment, as indicated earlier, has given learning autonomy to students to choose topics related to the subject syllabus and learning outcomes. This practice allows students to choose the topic that is linked to and contributes to the degree that they are enrolled in. For example, medical degree students would choose topics related to the traditional belief in medicine and treatment in different ethnicities in Malaysia. Hence, this opens a possibility of mindful learning as students would be aware of their existing knowledge and interest, and discover what they need to learn to enhance their knowledge and skills. Another example is students who study a food science degree would choose food as their topic and integrate multidisciplinary aspects of knowledge, such as Malaysian food culture and food science elements that they learned in the subjects that they are majoring in.

This project opens up opportunities to develop learning autonomy and learning responsibilities among students. Learning autonomy and responsibility have long been seen as essential components in supporting effective learning. A student must feel comfortable taking responsibility for their learning if they want to be self-directed learners (Kohns & Ponton, 2006). Students as self-directed learners must have a sense of responsibility for their learning to ensure effective learning occurs in the education system (Guglielmino, 1977).

The project, indeed, is a manifestation of self-directed learning that extends students' responsibilities in learning. In this project, students had to find information about the topic from multiple resources, including interviewing people with knowledge of the chosen topic. Some students went to different cultural associations and communities to learn deeper about the chosen topic. They were more connected to real life and developed various communication skills when they explored and sought information about the topic. Nevertheless, they embrace active and agile learning experiences.

This project stands on the basis that 'spoon feeding' in learning, especially at the tertiary level, is a thing of the past. It does not contribute much to the generation of new knowledge and social skills among students in the modern world. The project lends itself to multiple knowledge acquisition theories. It involves empiricism as students acquire knowledge through observation and experience about the chosen topic. In addition, the social aspect of the project involves constructivism, including the active and social problem-solving approach, which enhances student learning and thinking. On the other hand, the lecturer serves as a facilitator who provides guidance, moderates the learning process, and facilitates the development of students' soft skills.

Another aspect that was observed by the author was the impact of seamless learning, where students learn from various resources and people in society. Seamless learning constitutes two elements which are bridging the traditional learning dichotomies of formal and informal learning settings and developing a stronger connection between formal learning and informal learning experience among students. Students would take advantage of learning resources that exist both inside and outside of the classroom and use their life experiences to make meaning of the content introduced in classes (Wong & Looi, 2011)

In the project, some of the students learned about the background of ethnic dances, the history, and the culture of the dances. Some even went as far as taking the initiative to learn the dance movements and presented the dance in the final presentation. Furthermore, students actively engaged with their peers and the lecturer during the presentation to review and discourse on the topics covered.

One of the students commented:

The group presentation: there was a lot of fun in preparing for it, and I learned much about other cultures and their different celebrations, traditions, and activities.

Many students experienced a significant learning engagement and connection with their group mates in a meaningful way. Another student commented;

The group presentations held in Week 9 and Week 10 enabled my friends and I to strengthen friendship bonds among one another. It also enlightened my friend and I on the topic we presented on. I was certain that this is the Unit that we had the most amount of fun with, especially throughout the time we spent with one another. In addition, this Unit also pushed us to think creatively.

However, this does not mean collaborative learning is free from any challenges. The group work could turn problematic if the group members did not give full cooperation and could not reach an agreement in their discussion. For example, allowing 8-10 students in a group could be quite challenging as it requires multiple aspects in managing people's differences. Despite the challenges, a larger group collaboration allows students to learn leadership and team management skills which are important for their future careers. A student commented that working in a smaller group is preferable as a big group requires more commitment to managing people in a group. This feedback was important for the improvement of the project-based assessment implementation.

Analysis of Responsible Learning Experiences

The project provides space for sustaining students' learning. Students would learn consistently from week 1 to week 10 (weeks 11 and 12 are the presentation weeks). They submitted the proposal in week 3 which helps them to plan and structure their learning flow and plan the execution of the project successfully.

The lecturer plays an important role to provide continuous feedback to the students to guide their learning. Continuous feedback is crucial in project-based assessments as it supports continuous and sustained learning. In a common academic setting, many assessments take place after students have completed learning the subject, such as an assessment that is conducted at the end of the semester. Students will receive feedback after the assessments are over. However, research has shown that when the educator provides immediate feedback for the assessments, they are more effective as educational tools (U.S Department of Education, 2017).

The lecturer felt that timely feedback can easily be practised in project-based assessment as the educator has the opportunity to provide timely and continuous feedback at different stages of learning to engage students and enhance their learning. Even though students might sometimes face interruptions in their learning, probably due to an extended period of the project, they would always have a chance to rectify and reflect on their learning, with and without the lecturer's interference. Creating a learning support system at length is important for students to be able to maintain their learning pace and cope with challenges while completing the group project.

This project-based assessment demonstrates that students would learn independently in a project-based assessment and would go the extra mile if they are interested in the topic. Providing flexibility in choosing the topic around the prescribed syllabus would provide more opportunities for students to learn what they are interested in. Many students commented that the project was interesting and fun to work on. This reflects that learning should not only be focusing on the learning outcome but also on the learning process that motivates them to learn in a positive environment.

Students used the words 'fun' and 'interesting' to describe their learning experiences. For example, students commented;

The group assignment was interesting and fun to do.

The presentations allowed us to immerse ourselves in the objective of the unit, which is to appreciate the difference of ethnicity.

Furthermore, the project-based assessment taught students to be resourceful in finding information from the right resources and expressing their opinions in groups during the collaborations. A student commented;

The collaborative learning by the lecturer gives students (an) opportunity to engage with the topics and to voice out opinions and suggestions.

Another student also commented:

The presentation, I did a lot of research on and gained a lot of information from the research.

The findings demonstrate a constructivist-based technique that lays a special emphasis on the importance of social interaction and collaboration in active learning approaches. The sociocultural theory of development indicates that learning occurs when learners solve challenges and problems with guidance from educators and collaborations with peers (Vygotsky 1978). The theory emphasizes active learning techniques to focus on group work and leveraging peer-peer interaction in constructing knowledge and skills.

The lecturer observed that the project developed students to be agentic, where they initiate actions of their own volition that drive their learning, based on self-chosen learning goals that they set at the beginning of the project, specifically when they draft the proposal.

IMPLICATION AND RECOMMENDATIONS

The implementation of the project-based assessment in this study shows a significant increase in achievement of learning outcomes, learning engagement, and overall student satisfaction. The data demonstrates a significant improvement in the learning experience, a positive change in attitude, and enhanced social skills and motivation to learn the subject. However, there are a few aspects that require improvement to enhance the project-based assessment practice.

The author suggests an ongoing evaluation of the project implementation, in which marks will be granted not only for the end product (in this case the presentation and the reflective report) but for the learning process and experiences, such as the proposal submission and the experiential learning experiences.

Secondly, the author also recommends paying more attention to collaborative work as managing a group is a challenging task for some students particularly learning in a large group of students. Providing guidelines for managing teams and collaboration would help students to manage their group dynamics. The guidelines could serve as general references that suit different group dynamics. For example, guidelines for managing uncooperative members and the implications of it. Peer assessment is one of the strategies that involve group members' evaluation. Since most of the work was completed independently in groups without the lecturer's observation, it is fair to give a part of autonomy to the students to assess their group members and participate in grading the group members.

Last but not least, getting the students' feedback to improve their practice is also crucial. In this project, the author suggests reducing the reflective report pages as it seems too much workload for the students since students spent a lot of their time in the experiential learning experience; searching for information from various sources of information, engaging with other stakeholders in communities, and preparing for the presentation.

CONCLUSION

In a nutshell, project-based assessment is a promising assessment tool that supports holistic education. The effectiveness of project-based assessment in enhancing learning experiences is demonstrated in this study and has also improved responsible and responsive learning among students in the General Studies subject. However, the educator needs to constantly review the practice, understand the cultural considerations and get constructive feedback from the stakeholders as a reflective process to improve the practice. Learning by doing, indeed, increases responsible and responsive learning among students and leads to a positive learning experience and engagement.

REFERENCES

Khalek, A. K. (2012). Exploring the use of project-based learning on students' engagement at Taylors' University, Malaysia. *Jurnal BITARA UPSI, 5,* 17–29.

American Association of School Administrators. (2010). *2011 district excellence award for digital learning.* AASA. http://www.aasa.org/uploadedFiles/Programs_and_Events/Awards_and_Scholarships/Technology_Award/2011_Technology_Award/2011_Technology_Award2011_ AASA_LS_App_procedure_082410.pdf

Awang, M. M., Ahmad, A. R., Bakar, N. A. A., Ghani, S. A., Yunus, A. N. M., Ibrahim, M. A. H., & Rahman, M. J. A. (2013). Students' attitudes and their academic performance in nationhood education. *International Education Studies, 6,* 21–28.

Basir, S.N.M., & Bakar, M. Z. A., Hassan, Junainor., & Hassan, H. (2018). Persepsi terhadap penawaran Mata Pelajaran Umum Hubungan Etnik dalam meningkatkan kefahaman patriotisme di Universiti Malaysia Perlis. [Perception of the offering of the General Subject of Ethnic Relations in improving the understanding of patriotism at Universiti Malaysia Perlis]. *Journal of Human Development and Communication, 7,* 143–154.

Bell, S. (2010). Project-Based Learning for the 21st Century: Skills for the Future. *The Clearing House: A Journal of Educational Strategies, Issues and Ideas, 83*(2), 39–43. doi:10.1080/00098650903505415

Bonwell, C. C., & Eison, J. A. (1991). Active learning: creating excitement in the classroom. *ASH#-ERIC Higher Education Report No. 1.* The George Washington University.

Bransford, J. D., Brown, A. L., & Cocking, R. R. (Eds.). (1999). *How people learn: Brain, mind, experience, and school.* National Academy Press.

Carr, R., Palmer, S., & Hagel, P. (2015). Active learning: The importance of developing a comprehensive measure. *Active Learning in Higher Education, 16*(3), 173–186. doi:10.1177/1469787415589529

Coates, H. B. (2008). *Australasian Survey of Student Engagement.* Institution Report.

Embi, M. A., Hamat, A., & Sulaiman, A. (2012). The Use of Learning Management Systems Among Malaysian University Lecturers. *International Journal of Learning, 18*(4), 61–70. doi:10.18848/1447-9494/CGP/v18i04/47554

Endut, N. A., Amin, R., Mohamad, A. N., & Din, H. A. M. (2019). Impak Mata Pelajaran Umum dari kaca mata Kolej Universiti Islam Antarabangsa Selangor (KUIS) [Impact of general sucjects from the eyes of Selangor international Islamic university college (KUIS)]. *e-Bangi, 16*(2) 1-18.

Ginestie, J. (2002). The industrial project method in French industry and in French schools. *International Journal of Technology and Design Education, 12*(2), 99–122. doi:10.1023/A:1015213511549

Guglielmino, L. M. (1977). *Development of the self-directed learning readiness scale* [Unpublished doctoral dissertation, The University of Georgia, Athens, Georgia].

Gutierez, S. B. (2019). Teacher-practitioner research inquiry and sense making of their reflections on scaffolded collaborative lesson planning experience. *Asia Pacific Science Education, 5*(1), 1–15. doi:10.118641029-019-0043-x

Hed, N. M., Hussin, N. I., Yaacob, N. H., & Boyman, S. N. (2020). The impacts of the nationhood course on students' political engagement in Malaysia: A Comparative analysis. *Journal of Critical Reviews, 7*, 877–883.

Huang, S. Y. L. (2012). Learning environments at higher education institutions: Relationships with academic aspirations and satisfaction. *Learning Environments Research, 15*(3), 363–378. doi:10.100710984-012-9114-6

Husain, F. C., & Kadir, F. A. (2012). Contribution of the Islamic and Asia Civilization (TITAS) towards Holistic Formation of Students. *Journal of Al-Tamaddun, 7*, 15–35. .

Ibrahim, R. (2018). 'Ethnic Relations' Course for National Integration among Malaysian Universities' Students: Some Reflections. *JATLaC Journal, 12*, 4–14.

Idris, F., Yaacob, M., & Taha, M. (2012). Teaching and learning methods of ethnic relations course: Interactive or destructive? *Procedia: Social and Behavioral Sciences, 59*, 105–109. doi:10.1016/j.sbspro.2012.09.252

Jonathan, W. K., & Michael, K. Ponton. (2006). Understanding Responsibility: A Self-Directed Learning Application Of The Triangle Model Of Responsibility. *New Horizons in Adult Education and Human Resource Development, 16*, 16–27.

Ku Samsu, K. H., Adnan, Z. H., Ismail, M. M., Lee, Y. F., Ab Majid, A., & Razak, Ab. R. R. (2017). Kaedah menangani kebosanan mahasiswa terhadap subjek Kenegaraan Malaysia. [Methods of dealing with the boredom of students on the subject of Malaysia Nationality. In Persidangan Antarabangsa Sains Sosial & Kemanusiaan Kali ke-2 PASAK2017, Kolej Universiti Islam Selangor.

Looi, C. K., So, H. J., Chen, W., Zhang, B., Wong, L. H., & Seow, P. (2012). Seamless learning. In: Seel N.M. (eds) Encyclopaedia of the Sciences of Learning. Springer.

Ministry of Higher Education Malaysia. (2016). *Guidelines of General Studies*.

Mioduser, D., & Betzer, N. (2008). The contribution of Project-based-learning to high-achievers' acquisition of technological knowledge and skills. *International Journal of Technology and Design Education, 18*(1), 59–77. doi:10.100710798-006-9010-4

Nasir, M. F. M., Ridzuan, M. I. M., Hock, A. T. Y., Pei, O. S., Jamaludin, A. L., Hamidi, N. H. A., & Maswan, N. A. M. (2019). Keberkesanan subjek Matapelajaran Umum (MPU) dalam memperkasa Bahasa Melayu: Satu tinjauan awal. [The effectiveness of General Subjects (MPU) in strengthening the Malay language: A preliminary survey] *International Journal of Education. Psychology and Counselling, 4*, 85–96.

VandenBos, G., Knapp, S., & Doe, J. (2001). Role of reference elements in the selection of resources by psychology undergraduates. *Journal of Bibliographic research.* http://jbr.org/articles.html

National Writing Project. (n.d.). *National Writing Project, What Is Connected Learning?* National Writing Project. https://lead.nwp.org/knowledgebase/what-is-connected-learning/

Reimagining the Role of Technology in Education (2017). *National Education Technology Plan Update January 2017.* U.S. Department Of Education http://tech.ed.gov

Rohana, N. A. M., Hashim, S. N. I., Hamid, N. A. P., Rameli, M. F., & Mohamed, N. (2020). Pelaksanaan subject Hubungan Etnik tanpa peperiksaan akhir di UiTM cawangan Melaka. [Implementation of Ethnic Relations subject without final exam at UiTM Melaka branch]. *E-Journal of Islamic Thought and Understanding, 1,* 18–34.

Shaari, S. S., Besar, J. A., & Jali, M. F. M. (2017). Analisis keberkesanan subjek Hubungan Etnik sebagai pencetus literasi politik: Kajian ke atas mahasiswa. [Analysis of the effectiveness of the Ethnic Relations subject as a trigger for political literacy: A study on undergraduates] *e-Bangi, 14,* 26-33.

Verner, I., & Betzer, N. (2001). Machine control – a design and technology discipline in Israel's senior high schools. *International Journal of Technology and Design Education, 11*(3), 263–272. doi:10.1023/A:1011256612709

Vygotsky, L. S. (1978). *Mind in society.* Harvard University Press.

Wong, L. H., & Looi, C. K. (2011). What seams do we remove in mobile-assisted seamless learning? A critical review of the literature. *Computers & Education, 57*(4), 2364–2381. doi:10.1016/j.compedu.2011.06.007

Yaacob, N. H., & Kassim, F. (2020). Inovasi terhadap pengajaran dan pembelajaran bagi penerapan kemahiran insaniah dalam mata kuliah Tamadun Islam Dan Asia (TITAS) di Universiti Malaya Kuala Lumpur Malaysia. [Innovation in teaching and learning for the application of soft skills in Islamic and Asian Civilizations (TITAS) subjects at Universiti Malaya Kuala Lumpur Malaysia]. *Jurnal Pendidikan Ilmu Pengetahuan Sosial Indonesia, 7*(1), 1–21. doi:10.21831/jipsindo.v7i1.30844

Yee, T. Y., & Baskaran, V. (2017). The effectiveness of encouraging learning among the Gen Z students. In Farrah Dina Yusop · Amira Firdaus (Ed.), Alternative assessments in Malaysian higher education voices from the field (pp. 259-268). Springer Nature.

Wong, Y. L., & Siu, K. W. M. (2018). The curriculum development and project-based assessment of design education in Singapore and Hong Kong secondary schools. In V. X. Wang (Ed.), *Handbook of research on program development and assessment methodologies in K-20 education* (1st ed., pp. 220–243). IGI Global., doi:10.4018/978-1-5225-3132-6.ch011

Yip, N. M., & Burhanuddin, I. H. (2017, August). Matapelajaran Umum peneraju transformasi pendidikan holistik, [General subjects leading the transformation of holistic education] In N*ational Pre-University Seminar 2017 (NpreUS2017),* Kolej Universiti Islam Antarabangsa Selangor.

Yee, C. P., Yean, T. S., & Yi, A. K. J. (2018). verifying international students' satisfaction framework for the development of MISS-Model in Malaysia. *Pertanika Journal of Social Science & Humanities*, 26, 1–17.

Yusoff, A. N. M., & Ali, N. (2018, April). Penerapan model kolaboratif e-learning dalam kursus TITAS MOOC dan aplikasinya dalam platform Open Learning versi 02. [Application of the e-learning collaborative model in the TITAS MOOC course and its application in the Open Learning platform version 02.] In *e-Prosiding Persidangan Antarabangsa Sains Sosial dan Kemanusiaan 2018*. Kolej Universiti Islam Selangor. .

KEY TERMS AND DEFINITIONS

General Studies: A mandatory subject offered in Malaysian Higher Learning Institutions.

Project-Based Assessment: an assessment approach in which educators assess students' performance by assessing students' projects.

Project-Based Learning: is a learning method in which students learn by actively engaging in meaningful projects.

Seamless Learning: Students learn from various resources and people in society.

Chapter 18
Assessment Strategies in Empowering Self-Regulated Learning in Higher Education:
A Systematic Review

Zuraimi Zakaria
Universiti Teknologi MARA, Malaysia

Adibah Abdul Latif
Universiti Teknologi Malaysia, Malaysia

EXECUTIVE SUMMARY

Self-regulated learning (SRL) is essential to higher education. An increasing body of knowledge has attested to the significance of assessment activities in promoting SRL strategies. However, the influence of assessment practices on SRL in higher education is considered a neglected research area. Aimed to fill this gap, this paper presents a systematic review of six peer-reviewed articles focusing on the effective employment of assessment strategies to promote SRL. Five key features of the compelling interplay between assessment activities and SRL strategies were noted in the review: feedback-driven, discussion-focused, specific assessment designs that provide continuous SRL opportunities, and learning contexts that influence motivation and purpose, with educators' assessment competency as a pre-requisite for successful implementation.

INTRODUCTION

Many of the skills associated with self-regulated learning (SRL) were synonymous with the essential skills required in higher education (Liacuna & Mason, 2022; Steh & Saric, 2020). Goal setting, learning monitoring and ownership, constant reflection and evaluation are some of the skills critical in higher education context (Hawe, Dixon & Hamilton, 2021). A considerable research attention has been given to the role of specific assessment strategies in promoting SRL (Broadbent, Sharman, Panadero & Fuller-

DOI: 10.4018/978-1-6684-6076-4.ch018

Tyszkiewicz, 2021; Weldmeskel & Michael, 2016). A myriad of assessment methods, such as peer and self-assessments, reflective journals and process-based assessments (Fraile, Izquierdo, Iglesias & Zamorano-Sande, 2020; Hawe & Dixon, 2016; Weldmeskel & Michael, 2016) have been increasingly valued for their potentials in propelling SRL (Hawe & Dixon, 2016). Nevertheless, effective assessment practices in yielding SRL in higher education were still a neglected research focus (Bevitt, 2015).

Despite the promising link between classroom assessment strategies and SRL, existing literature has reported mixed findings. While assessment strategies have been found to positively influence students' capacity to regulate their learning (Hawe et al., 2021; Waluyo, 2018; Weldmeskel & Michael, 2016), some studies conveyed less than promising findings (Broadbent et al., 2016; Fraile et al., 2020; Simon, 2019). Hence, there is a need to understand salient features of assessment practices that could potentially lead to favourable impacts on SRL. Aiming to fill the gap in the existing literature, the critical focus of this paper is to explore assessment strategies and practices that promoted SRL. Drawing upon these discussions, a systematic review of influential and impactful formative and summative assessment tasks for promoting SRL is presented. The review involves six articles published between 2016 to 2022, with a specific focus on SRL practices in the context of higher education. The discussion on Methods details the scope, search procedures and criteria for inclusion of articles selected for the systematic review.

Definition

Literature focused on SRL has addressed the term under its many aliases: independent learning, autonomous learning, self-organized or self-directed (Steh & Saric, 2020). Panadero and Alonso-Tapia (2013) emphasized the link between assessment practices and SRL in addressing self-regulation and self-assessment, and the understanding of these complex overlap would enrich one's view of the interaction. While assessment activities are integrated within instructional and pedagogical components, SRL is internal and involves cognitive and affective processes. Zimmerman (2008), however, regarded SRL as also encompassing behaviours, and the interaction between cognitive and affective domains, as stressed by Panadero and Alonso-Tapia (2013). He viewed SRL as complex interactions between metacognition, motivation and behaviors framed by beliefs and active regulation of one's learning process. As such, learners are able to regulate their mental capacity into academic-related skills such as goal setting, monitoring, controlling and coordinating all three domains of learning to ensure meaningful learning engagement and outcomes (Zimmerman, 2002).

Zimmerman (2008, 2013) clarified the concept as consisting of three cyclical phases: forethought, performance and self-reflection. Grounded in social cognitive theory, the model is regarded as one of the most comprehensive models describing SRL strategies and highly referred to in scientific literature (Panadero, 2017). Zimmerman also produced two other SRL models: the triadic analysis of self-regulation (Zimmerman, 1989); and a multi-level model of self-regulation (Zimmerman, 2002); each with a slightly different focus and orientation (Zimmerman, 2002). The phases in Zimmerman's cyclical phase model (2008, 2013) refer to the efforts undertaken prior to learning, during learning and upon completion of learning. Forethought involves efforts undertaken prior to learning. In order to initiate learning, learners engage in task analysis which includes goal-setting and strategic planning, in addition to having a sufficient dose of self-motivation. While learning is taking place or the performance phase, learners activate self-control and self-observation which are significant factors in ensuring learning success. In the former, appropriate learning methods and strategies are employed in enabling sustained focus at a given task; whilst the latter refers to self-regulation of learners' learning process. To complete the loop is self-reflection, in which learners engage in self-evaluation that calls for the relationship between learning efforts and outcomes to be examined and reflected. This final phase of SRL heavily influences the forethought process of the subsequent learning engagement (Zimmerman, 2008; 2013).

METHODS

There was a significant mismatch in the number of literature on SRL in schools as opposed to higher education, with the latter receiving minimal research interest (Bevitt, 2015; Pintrich, 2000). The literature search had demonstrated that the relationship between assessment practices and SRL was one of the least explored areas in SRL studies in the higher education context. Within this minimal scope of available literature, most reported studies examining specific assessment strategies were found to have a heavier focus on the research framework, methods and findings; however, the strategies/interventions examined were not detailed sufficiently. The use of systematic review helped in filtering out articles with insufficient information on the presented intervention strategies and enabled articles that fulfilled the inclusion criteria to be highlighted in the discussions.

In order to ensure complete coverage, literature search was carried out involving major databases, namely, the web of science (WoS), Elsevier and Google Scholar. The terms *self-regulated learning* in connection to *educational assessment, formative assessment, assessment practice* and *higher education* were used. A total of 32 articles were gathered from this initial search. The inclusion criteria of the selected articles were based on currency, relevancy and sufficiency, and the article selection was based on two filtering processes. The first filter involved selecting articles that were current. Initially, only articles no older than five years were selected, this limited the selection to articles published between 2018 and 2022. Such criterion was set to ensure the selection of articles that depict the use of current and significant assessment strategies, particularly ones that are susceptible to reform, changes and volatility that have recently taken place in education. However, the search has resulted in a minimal selection of articles. Hence, the year of publications was adjusted to include articles published between 2015 to the most recent. The second inclusion criterion is relevancy, with relevant articles that conform to the context of higher education, research-based, peer-reviewed journal articles, and reported favourable findings of the approaches employed. Articles focusing on review and/or conceptual framework were omitted. The abstract review and concept scan performed based on the abovementioned inclusion criteria resulted in 18 articles being shortlisted.

The second filter was based on the inclusion criteria of sufficiency. Given the scope of the paper, the articles reviewed must consist of a sufficient explanation of the intervention strategies and/or the assessment activities employed. In addition, the course/context of the intervention must be adequately detailed. An in-depth review was conducted to narrow down articles that detailed the assessment tasks or strategies to a sufficient extent. The final criterion has resulted in the elimination of many compelling research papers with convincing findings, due to the lack of sufficient depth in the explanation of the interventions utilized. Similarly, the sole focus on higher education has ruled out high-quality articles that explored assessment strategies within the school context. Search parameters neither included articles based a specific region/geographical location nor specific areas/type of classroom assessments. Therefore, the articles yielded for review represented studies from several parts of the globe and sampled varying assessment strategies concerning SRL. Consequently, only six articles were selected for an in-depth review.

RESULTS

The review presented in this paper is based on six selected peer-reviewed, research-focused journal articles that ventured into studies that examined the connection between classroom assessment strategies in higher education and SRL. Search parameters were kept open for the type of assessment strategies used and the region in which the studies took place due to the limited availability of the articles. Two studies employed quantitative research design; two adopted qualitative design and the remaining two used mixed-methodology research design. Out of six, four focus on course assessments for undergraduate programs and the remaining two on master's degree programs. The details of the articles and the specific intervention strategies employed in measuring SRL are presented in Table 1.

Discussion

The reviewed literature has illuminated a spectrum of assessment designs, focus and features that would likely elicit learner engagement in SRL (Table 2 consists of detailed descriptions of each study). Five prominent features of assessment strategies that promoted SRL are salient across the reviewed literature. Central to the intervention/assessment activities investigated was a strong emphasis on feedback-driven and discussion-based activities structured around specific assessment designs that provided a different push for motivation and purpose to deploying SRL strategies. Educators' ability to use assessment data was at the core of successful implementation.

Feedback-Driven Assessment Activities

The element of feedback is integral in the assessment activities across the reviewed literature. Although feedback underpinned the design of the assessment activities, its function and emphasis in each study differed.

Feedback needs to be objective, clear, specific, personalized (Broadbent et al., 2021; Hawe & Dixon, 2016; Tian et al., 2022) and of multiple and varied sources (Tian et al., 2022) for students to see value in using them. Feedback should also be structured around the use of rubrics and the marking criteria (Broadbent et al., 2021; Teng, 2022).

All feedback systems addressed in the literature were interlayered into respective assessment structures (Broadbent et al., 2021; Tian et al., 2022). For example, the students in Tian et al.'s (2022) study engaged with multiple feedback in revising their ongoing essay development. This process was reflected in the course requirements, in which, in addition to submitting three essay assignments, students needed to complete three feedback revision tasks. The online and blended learners in Broadbent et al. (2021) study, on the other hand, were required to integrate educator feedback in their final work. The resubmission must consist of track changes, enabling the assessors to identify changes and improvements made to the essays before the final submission.

An emerging theme from the analysis is the systematic engagement in dialogue sessions structured around feedback, a process known as dialogic feedback (Hawe & Dixon, 2016). The authors believed that providing access to feedback might not be sufficient to exert the desired thought processes aligned with SRL strategies. Students needed to be prompted to use feedback. Both authors structured their feedback around dialogic sessions that stimulated discussions between educator-students and students with their peers. Educators assumed a proactive role during both educator-led and student-facilitated discussions by moving around groups and interjecting the discussions with provocative questions.

The synthesis of the key features of effective feedback is presented below. The reviewed literature has empirically demonstrated that these features have initiated and sustained learners' successful engagement in SRL activities.

i. Clear (Broadbent et al., 2021)
ii. Specific (Broadbent et al., 2021)
iii. Actionable (Broadbent et al., 2021)
iv. Objective (Hawe & Dixon, 2016)
v. Personalized to individual students (Broadbent et al., 2021; Hawe & Dixon, 2016; Teng, 2022)
vi. Task-focused (Broadbent et al., 2021; Teng, 2022)
vii. Multiple sources (Tian et al., 2022)
viii. Rubric-focused and structured around marking criteria (Broadbent et al., 2021; Hawe & Dixon, 2016; Teng, 2022)
ix. Diagnostic with a focus on weaknesses and specific areas for improvement (Broadbent et al., 2021; Hawe & Dixon, 2016; Wallin & Adawi, 2018)
x. Scaffold learning (Teng, 2022)
xi. Systematically integrated into course requirements (Broadbent et al., 2021; Tian et al., 2022)
xii. Structured with educator dialogue (dialogic feedback) (Hawe & Dixon, 2016).

Discussion-based Assessment Activities

The review also noted assessment activities integrated with discussion or dialogic elements. Discussions were held at various levels, from educator-led whole-class discussions to the group and pair discussions (Broadbent et al., 2021; Hawe & Dixon, 2016; Teng, 2022; Wallin & Adawi, 2018). Discussions were also continuous throughout the intervention or the implementation of assessment activities. They provided prolonged opportunities and motivation for students to regulate their learning. Teng (2022) integrated the component of discussion in stage 2 (educator-led discussion) as well as in stages 4 and 5 (group and pair discussions) of her six-stage instructional procedures. Discussions revolved around examining the quality of students' current work in progress using a self-revision checklist (Teng, 2022). Systematically and frequently organized discussions-oriented student readiness and compelled student participation. In the study by Hawe and Dixon (2016), weekly discussions where all learners were expected to be involved were found to have successfully engaged all students, including passive learners who were first hesitant to share their views.

The role of educators to guide students in activating specific SRL strategies for specific phases and purposes during the assessment activities is also well recognized in the reviewed literature. As evidenced in Teng's (2016) study, the instructional procedures deployed were directed by the educator-led discussion following a range of activities systematically introduced to instigate students' prior knowledge on essays of different genres. Discussions were diagnostic and capitalized on features of excellent essays and targeted SRL strategies applicable in each writing phase.

The analysis of reviewed literature has illuminated eight stimuli for discussions that initiated and sustained SRL strategies:

i. Assignment requirements and marking criteria (Broadbent et al., 2021; Hawe & Dixon, 2016; Teng, 2022)
ii. Feedback-based dialogic analysis (Hawe & Dixon, 2016; Teng, 2022; Wallin & Adawi, 2018)
iii. Evaluation of exemplars (Hawe & Dixon, 2016; Teng, 2022)
iv. Evaluation of work in progress (Broadbent et al., 2021; Hawe & Dixon, 2016)
v. Provocative questions on students' work (Hawe & Dixon, 2016)
vi. Self-assessment (Teng, 2022; Yan, 2022; Wallin & Adawi, 2018)
vii. Peer assessment (Hawe & Dixon, 2016; Teng, 2022; Tian et al., 2022)
viii. Series of prompts (Hawe & Dixon, 2016; Wallin & Adawi, 2018)

The key to effective discussions in stimulating SRL strategies rested on the educators' ability to facilitate the discussions. Non-researcher educators in the studies were provided with training in facilitating feedback provision and discussion-led activities. Discussions acted as stimuli for learners to elicit SRL strategies. Hence, lessons should not be dominated by educator talk but by sharing sessions that enable misconceptions, misunderstanding, and gaps to be highlighted (Broadbent et al., 2021; Hawe & Dixon, 2016; Teng, 2022; Tian et al., 2022; Yan, 2022).

Structure of Assessment Activities

In order to promote SRL, the employment of specifically designed assessment activities was salient across the reviewed literature. Broadbent et al. (2021), Hawe and Dixon (2016) and Tian et al. (2022) focused on a summative assessment with solid formative elements and the adoption of a task-based intervention component that students were required to complete prior to final submission. The authors hypothesized that engagement with the task during the intervention phase would exert the desired SRL strategies. In Broadbent et al.' (2021), the students were issued personalized written feedback following the first submission of their lab report. In contrast, in Tian et al.'s (2022) study, feedback from three different sources (an automated writing evaluation program, peer and educator feedback) was generated following the first submission. The students in both of these studies were provided with sufficient time to revise the feedback, regulate their learning and carry out improvements on their first draft before the final submission. The exposure to certain stimuli in the previously mentioned studies had effectively ignited and maintained SRL strategies among learners and functioned as one of the critical elements in the design of the assessment activities.

Some studies paid considerable attention to the duration of exposure to stimuli to facilitate learners' continuous engagement in SRL strategies. Hawe and Dixon (2016) adopted a similar format of assessment design to that of Broadbent et al. (2021) and Tian et al. (2021), in which students revised their ongoing work following the first submission. However, instead of feedback, the students were introduced to exemplars of excellent work samples based on a similar assignment from the previous semester. The students in the study were asked to bring in the first draft of their essays and examine them against the exemplars. In addition, students had to complete a weekly reading task and respond to weekly prompts, which served as a basis for educators to organize a dialogic feedback session in the upcoming week. Weekly prompts guided the students in Wallin and Adawi's (2018) study in the course of producing weekly reflective entries. Prompts were in the form of general and specific questions that served as stimuli for the reflection, with students being exposed to general prompts on odd weeks and specific prompts on even weeks. The prompts revolved around detailing aspects of learning, how they approached the situation, justifications for the approach employed, and their learning experience. The study by Teng (2002), presumably, consists of the most complex assessment design. Teng's six-stage instructional procedures provided ample opportunity for students to exercise SRL strategies in each stage. Furthermore, her assessment requirements were embedded with input emphasis that compelled learners to regulate their learning.

Drawing upon the assessment activities presented in the reviewed literature, several key considerations emerged. First, sufficient time was the essence to the effectiveness of the assessment strategies aimed at promoting SRL. All the investigated studies were conducted for at least one semester (except for Broadbent et al.'s, 2021 study, which was carried out for two semesters). In addition, studies that focused on summative assessments imposed an early start to accommodate the following process: draft development, submission, revision, improvement and final submission (Broadbent et al., 2021; Hawe & Dixon, 2016; Teng, 2022). Time was also significant in ensuring student development and growth in their learning (Broadbent et al., 2021). Second, personalization was emphasized in the feedback, dialogues, discussions and instructional procedures structured around the assessment activities. The intervention strategies integrated into the assessment activities were targeted at the individual level (Broadbent et al., 2021; Hawe & Dixon, 2016; Teng, 2022); only then feedback and dialogues would be specific, practical and actionable to the students (Broadbent et al., 2021). Feedback in Broadbent et al.'s (2021) study, for example, should be 25 minutes in length, rubric-focused and structured around the marking criteria with educators detailing the weaknesses and areas for improvement; targeted and actionable concerning aspects that students needed to improve to achieve higher level on the rubric; task-focused and devoid of emotive language. Teng's (2022) integrated model of SRL strategy instruction comprised of instructional and assessment strategies and activities developed for whole-class, small group, pair and individual levels; aimed to promote students' engagement in continuous SRL activities. At the individual level, educators provided personalized support, social scaffolding and motivational support, with feedback customized to individual students.

Various studies have attested to the significance of personalization in activating and sustaining SRL strategies among learners (Zerihun, Beishuizen & Van Os, 2012). Targeted feedback and information at the individual level would enable students' variability to be taken into consideration (Broadbent et al., 2021; Hawe & Dixon, 2016; Teng, 2022), and only then the information presented becomes actionable to the students and lead to the desired changes and improvements (Broadbent et al., 2021). This is also validated by the review of selected articles that emphasized the importance of assessment activities being built around individual learners (Broadbent et al., 2021; Hawe & Dixon, 2016; Teng, 2022; Tian et al., 2022; Wallin & Adawi, 2018; Yan, 2022). It is worth noting that personalising feedback and customizing assessment activities at an individual level is time-consuming and physically and mentally exhausting to educators. This leads to the third consideration of the vital effectiveness of assessment activities and SRL strategies in the reviewed studies: group size. The educators in the reviewed studies were able to accommodate personalised assessment and feedback activities due to the small number of participants. This presented a unique condition to the reviewed studies; however, their assessment models may not be able to be replicated by other higher learning institutions. Hawe and Dixon (2016) and Wallin and Adawi (2018) embarked on qualitative studies with nine and four students, respectively. Broadbent and his colleagues (2021), despite a focus on an assessment model with personalized feedback, gathered their data using a questionnaire. Similarly, Tian et al. (2022), who adopted a mixed methodology research design, analyzed their qualitative data involving only four participants. Only one study in the reviewed literature generated findings based on a higher number of participants involving an in-depth text exploration to determine SRL strategies. Teng (2022) employed a quasi-experimental design and gathered her data using 250-word writing tests (pre, post and delayed posttests) (n=59), a questionnaire (n=59), and a reflective journal (n=30). Nevertheless, the number of participants in Teng's study still pales compared to the typical number of students assigned to educators every semester, indicating the minimal possibility of duplicating her assessment design in higher education.

Motivation Behind and Purpose for Regulating Learning

The purpose and level of learners' engagement in SRL strategies differed between SRL dimensions, phases, context and tasks. The students were found to regulate their learning across the four SRL dimensions (cognitive, metacognitive, social and motivational strategies) (Tian et al., 2022); and phases of SRL (preparatory, performance and appraisal phases) (Yan, 2022), however, the degree of intensity was different between one dimension or phase to another. Tian and her co-authors (2022) discovered that students regulated their cognitive strategies more intensely when working with an automatic generated feedback and relied on their motivational strategies more upon revising educator feedback. Yan (2022), on the other hand, reported that students engaged in self-assessment strategies more vigorously during the preparatory and performance phases, as opposed to when they were in the appraisal phase. Yan's findings contradicted other SRL models that emphasized more effective learning regulations during the appraisal phase as a measure of self-reflection. He theorized that engagement in self-assessment strategies during preparatory and performance phases directly impacted task quality. In contrast, similar engagement in SRL activities during appraisal did not improve task quality as the phase signified task completion.

Learning context was a detrimental factor in students' employment of SRL strategies. In the case of Broadbent et al. (2021), online learners demonstrated a greater degree of SRL activities than blended learners. It was further reported that self-efficacy and time management were significant predictors for online learners in indicative formative and summative grades, respectively. Broadbent and his co-authors attributed this to the necessity for online learners to exercise a higher degree of learning ownership and self-regulation in achieving learning success. On the other hand, the blended learners had the opportunity to co-regulate their learning with lecturers and peers through traditional means of learning. Goal-directed and task-focused learning activities using appropriate assessment tools and activities (for example, self-assessment, revision checklist, reflection, and self-monitoring) also enhanced learners' regulation of learning (Broadbent et al., 2021; Teng, 2022).

The findings in these studies indicated that learners' motivation and purpose for regulating their learning differed and were influenced by their goals and context for engagement. It is significant for educators to have a clear understanding of these motivating factors and the context students are in to provide impactful assistance concerning effective deployment of SRL strategies.

Educators' Use of Assessment Data

Educators' assessment literacy and evidence interpretation skills are prerequisites to the effective implementation of formative and summative assessment strategies that promote SRL activities. The reviewed studies employed complex classroom assessment knowledge and skills focused on producing assessment information that can be used to inform the decision-making process and the planning and implementation of the subsequent intervention strategies. Hence, the interplay of a number of assessment components and skills was recognized: assessment literacy and pedagogical data literacy as subsets of data literacy and evidence-informed instruction within evidence-based practice. These served as an overarching framework that ensured the effectiveness of the assessment strategies developed in promoting SRL.

Assessment literacy refers to the knowledge and skills about 'how to assess what students know and can do, interpret the results of these assessments, and apply these results to improve student learning and program effectiveness' (Webb, 2002, p.2). The proponents of *data literacy* strongly viewed the significance of educators working with other types of data, in addition to assessment data, in making sound and impactful instructional decisions (Mandinach, 2012; Mandinach & Gummer, 2016; Wasson & Hansen, 2016). What is significant about data literacy is the emphasis on transforming data into meaningful information and using it to feed instructional decision-making, before subsequent intervention strategies are acted upon (Webb, 2002). The set of skills required to carry out the abovementioned process efficiently involved *pedagogical data literacy* (Mandinach & Jackson, 2012) described as the ability to transform raw and analyzed data which usually consists of numbers and statistics into actionable knowledge that can be utilized to impact teaching and learning processes (Cramer, Little & McHatton, 2015; Datnow & Hubbard, 2015). Central to data and assessment literacy is evidence-based practice, described as approaches that critically examine teaching practice in yielding solid evidence for what works with the aim of informing policy (Adolphus, 2019).

Studies examined required educators to critically evaluate evidence of learning in producing information that can assist decision-making in myriad ways. The educators involved produced diagnostic and personalized feedback based on the submission of students' first draft (Broadbent et al., 2021; Tian et al., 2022); accommodated the use of exemplars and prompts that targeted and scaffolded student learning (Hawe & Dixon, 2016; Teng, 2022; Wallin & Adawi, 2018); utilized dialogic feedback and facilitated task-oriented group discussions (Hawe & Dixon, 2016; Wallin & Adawi, 2018); and worked with evidence in structuring instructional and assessment activities at group, pair and individual levels (Hawe & Dixon, 2016; Teng, 2022). Educators' ability to use and interpret assessment data into valuable and actionable information that informed decision-making and subsequent intervention strategies served as underlying assessment skills that supported the implementation of the reviewed studies.

Implications

The implications of this review are threefold. The reviewed literature has revealed prominent characteristics of assessment practices that have successfully promoted SRL strategies among learners in higher education. Hence, the implication for policymakers and university leaders included the provision of learning context, assessment designs and requirements that potentially motivate learners to engage in SRL strategies and activities.

For educators, accommodation for a learning experience that stimulates continuous engagement in SRL strategies is necessary. Instructional and assessment activities should be directed towards utilising feedback, and the employment of appropriate assessment tools and monitoring strategies. Central to the compelling interplay between the implementation of assessment strategies and SRL activities is the educators' assessment knowledge and skills. Educators need to be assessment literate and frame their instructional activities within an evidence-based framework. Henceforth, this necessitates the need for trainings and professional development.

For researchers, there is an immense gap between research and practice concerning assessment strategies and activities that prospered learning regulations among students in tertiary institutions. The number of available studies is minimal - the database search generated underwhelming search results, with the same articles being recommended across different databases. Further research is needed to inform the body of knowledge and validate effective assessment practices.

Limitations

This study is limited to a small number of articles reviewed, consequently raising a concern that the assessment strategies discussed may not accurately represent or lack variability in the identification of assessment practices that propelled SRL. Nevertheless, the relatively small number of selected literature is unavoidable due to the limited availability of studies venturing into the research scope and topic. Notwithstanding, the review provides insights into the current assessment practice and points towards the need and direction for future research.

Several conditions were unique to the reviewed studies presenting less-than-ideal opportunities for studies of similar designs to be replicated by other institutions. The small sample size is a well-noted limitation and has been detailed extensively in the earlier discussion in this review. In addition, several reviewed studies measured assessment tools and mechanisms particularly unique to specific institutions (Broadbent et al., 2021; Tan et al., 2022). Further, the sample in Hawe and Dixon's (2019) study were teachers who enrolled in an undergraduate program to upgrade their qualifications. The participants' maturity may affect the generalisability of these findings, particularly in relation to writing quality, learning ownership and the capacity to deploy SRL strategies.

CONCLUSION

This systematic review involved the analysis of six articles delving into the overlap between educational assessment practice and SRL strategies in the higher education context. Several key features of effective assessment activities were recognized: instructional and assessment activities that centred on feedback and discussions; characterized by learners' engagement with educators and peers at whole-class and small group levels; alongside activities structured around reflection and self-assessments. Specific assessment designs with a solid emphasis on the prolonged opportunity to exercise SRL were critical, including the provision of conditions that created motivation and purpose to engage in SRL strategies. At the heart of this effective facilitation were the educators' sound knowledge and skills in assessment, mainly being assessment literate, motivated by pedagogical activities driven by assessment-informed instruction, and operating within an evidence-based framework. The implications to policymakers, university leaders, educators, and researchers, as well as the limitations of the review were presented and discussed.

Table 1. *Details of Reviewed Articles*

	Articles	Context	Research Design	Research Objectives	Assessment Strategy	Duration	Number of Participants
1	Broadbent et al. (2021)	Cognitive psychology course (undergraduate)	Quantitative: Questionnaire	1. To measure the impact of SRL characteristics on online and blended learners' engagement with formative and summative assessments	▪ Exemplar-focused activity	2 semesters	181 students (96 blended learners & 85 online learners)
2	Hawe and Dixon (2016)	Assessment for Learning (undergraduate)	Qualitative: Semi-structured interview and document analysis	1. To evaluate the experience and responses of undergraduate students in teacher-learning environment where students were expected to exercise responsibility for learning.	▪ Exemplar-focused activity	12 weeks	9 students
3	Wallin and Adawi (2018)	Master's degree course on tissue engineering (postgraduate)	Qualitative: Document analysis	1. To explore the roles of reflective diaries in supporting conceptions of knowledge, conceptions of learning, and strategies in regulating and monitoring learning.	▪ Reflective diary	5 months	4 students
4	Tian, Lu and Zhang (2022)	College English Writing II in a university in Beijing, China (undergraduate)	Mixed-methodology: Questionnaire, think-aloud protocol and stimulated recall interview	1. To investigate the SR writing strategies used during the three-stage feedback revision process. 2. To ascertain the manner students utilize SR writing strategies.	▪ Three-stage feedback revision	1 semester	52 first year students
5	Teng (2022)	English writing course for second year non-English major undergraduates (undergraduate)	Mixed-methodology: Quasi-experimental research design	1. To investigate the extent to which SRL affect writing quality. 2. To determine the extent to which SRL affect students' motivational beliefs in writing. 3. To explore students' perceptions of formative assessment embedded with SRL strategy instruction.	▪ Process-genre approach (writing task)	16 weeks	59 second year students
6	Yan (2020)	Master program in a teacher education institute in Hong Kong (postgraduate)	Quantitative: Questionnaire	1. To determine the characteristics of self-assessment practice for each of the three phases of SRL and its relationship with academic achievement.	▪ Self-assessment	13 weeks	63 students

Table 2. Summary of Studies

Article	Summary
Broadbent et al. (2021)	Broadbent et al. explored the impacts of SRL on performance, in particular, students' engagement in formative and summative assessments. The formative assessment strategy involved actionable and targeted feedback provided to 900-word lab report submitted on a cognitive psychology topic. Submissions were then followed by clear, specific, and actionable written feedback aimed at helping learners improve the report for resubmission. Students were expected to incorporate the suggested changes and to resubmit for official grade (summative assessment) in which they would receive an indicative grade, alongside a scored rubric and written feedback. They were also required to respond to the Motivated Strategies for Learning Questionnaire (MSLQ) prior to the final submission. The findings revealed that formative assessment strategy elicited positive improvements in learning, however, the use of SRL strategies was not a strong predictor on student performance in formative and summative assessments. Online learners were found to have higher confidence and utilize greater degree of SRL strategies in comparison to blended learners. It was further reported that self-efficacy and time management were significant predictors for online learners in indicative formative grade and summative grade respectively. Broadbent and his co-authors attributed this to the necessity for online learners to exercise higher degree of learning ownership and self-regulation in achieving learning success. The blended learners, on the other hands, had the opportunity to co-regulate their learning with lecturers and peers through traditional means of learning.
Hawe and Dixon (2016)	The authors investigated the employment of a formative assessment model in promoting SRL. The study involved 9 teachers who enrolled in an undergraduate program to upgrade their qualification from a diploma to a bachelor's degree. Students completed three 500-word essay and were introduced to exemplars produced based on the same assignment by students of the previous semester. Students brought in their own essays to the class and examined them against the exemplars. Exposure to and working with exemplars enabled the participants to significantly improve the substantive essay that needed to be submitted. Each week students completed one or two set readings and responded to a series of prompts. Responses to these prompts were brought in to the next session. Feedback that engaged students in a dialogue with the teacher and/or each other was integrated into every session. Together the teacher and students constructed information about what was understood or achieved and which aspects of learning needed further attention. The authors reported that the analysis and evaluation of exemplars contributed to the development of both students' confidence and their evaluative knowledge and skill. They came to understand what was required, what counted as quality and how to evaluate work in relation to these elements. In addition, peer feedback helped students to gather analytical look at their own work. Students took more responsibility and ownership of their own learning and became less dependent on their lecturer. The authors concluded that the AfL activities and strategies were able to improve students' self-regulation of their own learning.
Wallin and Adawi (2018)	Wallin and Adawi examined the impacts of the use of reflective diary as a formative assessment strategy on three aspects of SRL: conceptions of knowledge, conceptions of learning, and strategies in monitoring and regulating learning. Four tissue engineering students engaged in writing their reflections weekly over a period of five months. General and specific prompts served as stimuli for the reflection, with students being exposed to general prompts on odd weeks and more specific prompts on even weeks. The prompts revolved around detailing aspects of learning: the manner in which they approached the situation; justifications for the approach employed; and their learning experience. Wallin and Adawi posited that weekly prompts can be customized to scaffold student learning through tasks that extend learning and increase in level of complexity. The findings reported that students held different conceptions about knowledge and learning. The authors maintained the importance for teachers to understand these different conceptions and overtime work towards forming beliefs and conceptions of learning rooted on constructive epistemology. The findings also revealed that reflective entries enabled students to examine their strengths, motivations and weaknesses. Both authors stressed the significance for teachers to provide necessary support and scaffolding based on the information provided in the reflective entries.
Tian et al. (2022)	The authors investigated the three-stage feedback revision framework employed for an online writing course. The course focused on expository and argumentative writing and students were required to complete three essay assignments, in addition to fulfilling three feedback revision tasks for each of these essays. The three-stage feedback revision framework comprised of an automated writing evaluation (AWE) program, peer and educator feedback. The authors were interested in measuring the extent to which students exercised SR writing strategies during revision of the feedback; as well as the manner in which these SR writing strategies were deployed. Data was gathered through the utilization a mixed-method study involving questionnaire, think-aloud protocol and stimulated recall interview. The Writing Strategies for Self-Regulated Learning Questionnaire (WSSRLQ) by Teng and Zhang (2016) was adopted which measured SRL-related writing strategies pertaining to cognitive, metacognitive, social and motivational strategies. The findings indicated that participants utilized SR writing strategies across all four dimensions investigated. This is further supported by qualitative data that revealed similar findings in working with their feedback revision, regardless of the participants' proficiency levels. Two strategies were found to be more commonly referred to - students relied on cognitive strategies in regulating AWE-generated feedback more than other strategies, with heavier dependence on motivational strategies when working with teacher feedback. Qualitative date pointed out AWE feedback was mostly referred to in comparison to two other feedback sources. The authors reported the employment of motivational strategies by all participants particularly when students regulated their own motivation in sustaining interest and focus in doing their revision.
Teng (2022)	Teng examined the effectiveness of an integrated model of SRL strategy instruction developed for second language writing classroom through a quasi-experimental study. The multifaceted model is embedded with formative assessment and process genre approach focusing on process-oriented emphasis to writing with explicit instruction (such as planning, restructuring, problem solving). Goal-directed strategies and feedback strategies were emphasized with formative assessment forming an overarching principles of the instructional procedures. The treatment group was also made familiar with the four dimensions of SRL strategies: cognition, metacognition, social behavior and motivational regulation, in promoting their active use during the writing process. Data was collected through pretest, posttest and delayed posttest; questionnaire and reflective journals. The delayed posttest, carried out four weeks after intervention concluded, would enable changes in writing quality to be identified. The Motivated Strategies for Learning Questionnaire (MSLQ) by Pintrich et al. (1991) was administered to the participants in measuring their motivational dimension of SRL. The third measure, reflective journals, were submitted at the end of the instruction and provided a medium for students' perceptions of formative assessment rooted in SRL strategies to be determined. The posttest and delayed posttest results indicated that the treatment group performed significantly better than their comparative counterpart. The treatment group also reported to experience increase in motivational beliefs, in particular, self-efficacy of learning and performance; intrinsic and extrinsic goal orientation; task value; as well as control of learning beliefs
Yan (2020)	Yan explored characteristics of self-assessment practice during the process of SRL and the relationship between self-assessment and academic achievement. Participants responded to three surveys, each during specific SRL phase: preparatory phase (when students embark on a task and develop a working plan); performance phase (when students prepare the targeted task); and appraisal phase (when students engage in evaluation and reflection related to the intended learning outcome). These SRL phases are in accordance to Puustinen and Pulkinen's (2001) classification. The timeline of the survey administration as well as the focus of the study were tied to the final assessment for the course which made up 50 percent of the total course assessment scores. The study revealed that students engaged in self-assessment throughout the three phases of SRL. The preparatory phase enabled the students to set appropriate learning goals and justify the most effective working plan to approach the task; self-assessment strategies continued to monitor students' plan in action during performance phase whilst ensuring that the set goal would be met; and in appraisal phase, the self-assessment strategies provided opportunity for students to examine their strengths, weaknesses and their learning journey. Yan, however, discovered that self-assessment strategies were least employed in the appraisal phase, the findings that contradicted most SRL models which stressed the deployment of SRL strategies with the highest intensity and purpose. The author justified that such could be the findings due to the fact that the first two earlier SRL phases required heavier use of self-assessment strategies as they directly link to the betterment of the task, whilst the final phase did not have any direct influence to the targeted task.

REFERENCES

Adolphus, M. (2019). *Using evidence-based practice to inform decision making*. Emerald Publishing. https://www.emeraldgrouppublishing.com/librarians/info/viewpoints/evidence_based_practice.htm

Bevitt, S. (2015). Assessment innovation student experience: A new assessment challenge and call for a multi-perspective approach to assessment research. *Assessment & Evaluation in Higher Education*, *40*(1), 103–109. doi:10.1080/02602938.2014.890170

Broadbent, J., Sharman, S., Panadero, E., & Fuller-Tyszkiewicz, M. (2021). How does self-regulated learning influence formative assessment and summative grade? Comparing online and blended learners. *The Internet and Higher Education*, *50*, 100805. doi:10.1016/j.iheduc.2021.100805

Cramer, E. D., Little, M. E., & McHatton, P. A. (2014). Demystifying the data-based decision-making process. *Action in Teacher Education*, *36*(5-6), 389–400. doi:10.1080/01626620.2014.977690

Datnow, A., & Hubbard, L. (2015). Teachers' use of assessment data to inform instruction: Lessons from the past and prospect for the future. *Teachers College Record*, *117*(4), 1–26. https://eric.ed.gov/?id=EJ1056748. doi:10.1177/016146811511700408

Fraile, J., Zamorano-Sande, D., Izquierdo, M. G., & Sanchez-Iglesias, I. (2020). Self-regulated learning and formative assessment process on group work. *RELIEVE*, *26*(1). doi:10.7203/relieve.26.1.17402

Hawe, E., & Dixon, H. (2016). Assessment for learning: A catalyst for student self-regulation. *Assessment & Evaluation in Higher Education*. doi:10.1080/02602938.2016.1236360

Hawe, E., Dixon, H., & Hamilton, R. (2021). Why and how educators use exemplars. *Journal of University Teaching and Learning*, *18*(3), 136–149. doi:10.53761/1.18.3.10

Knight, S., Shibani, A., Abel, S., Gibson, A., Ryan, P., & Sutton, N. (2020). AcaWriter: A learning analytics tool for formative feedback on academic writing. *Journal of Writing Research*, *12*(1), 141–186. doi:10.17239/jowr-2020.12.01.06

Liacuna, H., & Mason, G. (2022). Promoting self-regulated learning in higher education. *Pacific Journal of Technology Enhanced Learning*, *4*(1), 19–25. doi:10.24135/pjtel.v4i1.143

Mandinach, E. B., & Gummer, E. (2016). What does it mean for teachers to be data literate: Laying out the skills, knowledge, and dispositions. *Teaching and Teacher Education*. https://www.sciencedirect.com/science/article/pii/S0742051X16301391

Mandinach, E. B., & Jackson, S. S. (2012). *Transforming teaching and learning through data driven decision-making*. Corwin Press. doi:10.4135/9781506335568

Panadero, E. (2017). A review of self-regulated learning: Six models and four directions for research. *Frontiers in Psychology*, *28*(8), 422–435. doi:10.3389/fpsyg.2017.00422 PMID:28503157

Panadero, E., & Alonso-Tapia, J. (2013). Self-assessment: Theoretical and practical connotations. When it happens, how is it acquired and what to do to develop it in our Regulated learning and evaluative judgment 35 students. *Electronic Journal of Research in Educational Psychology*, *11*(2), 551–576.

Panadero, E., & Alonso-Tapia, J. (2014). How do students self-regulate? Review of Zimmerman's cyclical model of self-regulated learning. *Anales de Psicología, 30*(2), 450–462.

Pintrich, P. R. (2000). The Role of Goal-Orientation in Self-Regulated Learning. In M. Boekaerts, P. R. Pintrich, & M. Zeidner (Eds.), *Handbook of Self-Regulation* (pp. 451–502). Academic Press. doi:10.1016/B978-012109890-2/50043-3

Puustinen, M., & Pulkkinen, L. (2001). Models of self-regulated learning: A review. *Scandinavian Journal of Educational Research, 45*(3), 269–286. doi:10.1080/00313830120074206

Simon, B. (2019). *The Effect of Formative Assessment on Student Motivation and Self-Regulation* [Thesis, Concordia University, St. Paul]. https://digitalcommons.csp.edu/teachereducation_masters/2

Steh, B., & Saric, M. (2020). Enhancing self-regulated learning in higher education. *Journal of Elementary Education, 13*, 129–150.

Teng, L. S. (2022). Explicit strategy-based instruction in L2 writing contexts: A perspective of self-regulated learning and formative assessment. *Assessing Writing, 53*, 100645. www.elsevier.com/locate/asw. doi:10.1016/j.asw.2022.100645

Tian, L., Liu, Q., & Zhang, X. (2022). Self-regulated writing strategy use when revising upon automated, peer, and teacher feedback in an online English as a foreign language writing course. *Frontiers in Psychology, 13*, 873170. www.frontiersin.org. doi:10.3389/fpsyg.2022.873170 PMID:35519626

Wallin, P., & Adawi, T. (2018). The reflective diary as a method for the formative assessment of self-regulated learning. *European Journal of Engineering Education, 43*(4), 507–521. doi:10.1080/03043797.2017.1290585

Waluyo, B. (2018). Promoting self-regulated learning with formative assessment and the use of mobile app on vocabulary acquisition in Thailand. *Indonesian Journal of English Language Teaching and Applied Linguistics, 3*(1), 105–124. http://studentsrepo.um.edu.my/8274/2/WAN_MOHD_ZUHAIRI_BIN_WAN_ABDULLAH.pdf

Wasson, B., & Hansen, C. J. S. (2016). Data literacy and use for teaching. In P. Reimann, S. Bull, M. D. Kickmeier-Rust, R. Vatrapu, & B. Wasson (Eds.), *Measuring and Visualizing Learning in the Information-Rich Classroom* (pp. 56–73).

Webb, N. L. (2002). *Assessment literacy in a standards-based urban education setting*. Paper presented at the Annual Meeting of the American Educational Research Association, New Orleans, Louisiana. http://archive.wceruw.org/mps/AERA2002/Assessment%20literacy%20NLW%20Final%2032602.pdf

Weldmeskel, F. M., & Michael, D. J. (2016). The impact of formative assessment on self-regulating learning in university classrooms. *Tuning Journal for Higher Education, 4*(1), 99–118. doi:10.18543/tjhe-4(1)-2016pp99-118

Yan, Z., Chiu, M. M., & Ko, P. Y. (2020). Effects of self-assessment diaries on academic achievement, self-regulation and motivation. *Assessment in Education: Principles, Policy & Practice, 27*(5), 562–583. doi:10.1080/0969594X.2020.1827221

Zerihun, Z., Beishuizen, J., & Van Os, W. (2012). Student learning experience as indicator of teaching quality. *Educational Assessment, Evaluation and Accountability, 24*(2), 99–111. doi:10.100711092-011-9140-4

Zimmerman, B. J. (1989). A social cognitive view of self-regulated academic learning. *Journal of Educational Psychology, 81*(3), 329–339. doi:10.1037/0022-0663.81.3.329

Zimmerman, B. J. (2002). Becoming a Self-Regulated Learner: An Overview. *Theory into Practice, 41*(2), 64–70. doi:10.120715430421tip4102_2

Zimmerman, B. J. (2008). Investigating self-regulation and motivation: Historical background, methodological developments, and future prospects. *American Educational Research Journal, 45*(1), 166–183. doi:10.3102/0002831207312909

Zimmerman, B. J. (2013). From Cognitive Modeling to Self-Regulation: A Social Cognitive Career Path. *Educational Psychologist, 48*(3), 135–147. doi:10.1080/00461520.2013.794676

Section 3
Related Matters in Responsive and Responsible Learning

Chapter 19
Ethics of Hybrid Learning in Higher Education

Lin Chen
https://orcid.org/0000-0002-7111-2806
Universiti Putra Malaysia, Malaysia

Nur Surayyah Madhubala Abdullah
Universiti Putra Malaysia, Malaysia

EXECUTIVE SUMMARY

The issue of unethical behavior in academic work is more severe in hybrid learning in the context of responsive and responsible learning. This study conducted a qualitative research method and a case study design. It used the semi-structured interview to determine the college students' understanding and motivations for unethical behavior in academic work in hybrid learning, in the context of responsive and responsible learning. The findings showed that participants noticed unethical behavior contrary to ethical norms but could not come up with a sound definition of unethical behavior in academic work. Participants pointed out some types of unethical behavior. Still, they were mainly unsure about the different types of unethical behavior. Besides, nine categories of motivations for students' unethical behavior were revealed.

INTRODUCTION

The global spread of COVID-19 poses unprecedented challenges to the field of higher education that haven't been witnessed since the advent of technology support and online education (Liguori & Winkler, 2020). Globally, a common trend among education systems is their response to COVID-19 through emergency e-learning protocols; this marks a rapid shift from face-to-face to online learning (Murphy, 2020). Indeed, COVID-19 in various countries is in the normalization stage and has entered a post-epidemic era. However, the advent of COVID-19's post-epidemic era does not mean that it has completely disappeared and every facet of life recovers to its pre-COVID state. On the contrary, this era

DOI: 10.4018/978-1-6684-6076-4.ch019

signifies that COVID-19 may occur at any time, such as during the migration of population to and from various countries. Here, small-scale outbreaks and lasts are more prolonged, with far-reaching impacts on humans (Zhuli, 2020).

Specifically, in this aforementioned era the higher-education learning methods in various countries have been concomitantly adjusted to a certain extent, with a visible shift from single offline/online learning to hybrid learning strategies (Fangfang & Hao, 2021). As hybrid learning is a new learning paradigm, the issue of unethical behavior in academic work presents new characteristics with respect to hybrid learning (Raes et al., 2020). In fact, COVID-19 has necessitated stricter requirements for hybrid learning, requiring students to show more responsive and responsible learning behaviors and also undertake such learning actions in higher education (Xiaobing & Jinxia, 2020). Hence, it is clear that higher education also faces novel issues related to unethical behavior in hybrid learning processes. However, there is a lack of adequate previous research on the ethics of learning in hybrid learning paradigms, despite its increased popularity and its salience in the delivery of higher education. Hence, educators and administrators are now interested in framing policies with regard to this new pedagogical shift in higher education.

Presently, the accepted perspective on the ethics of hybrid learning draws on the findings of a small exploratory study of Chinese college students' perspectives on unethical behavior in higher-education academic work. Therefore, this study sought to provide an initial perspective on the following question: What are some considerations with regard to developing an ethics of learning within a hybrid learning environment in higher education? It found that with hybrid learning, an ethic of responsive and responsible learning sincerely focuses on the ethical aspect of students' unethical behavior in concomitant academic work. Based on the exploration of students' perspectives on unethical behavior in higher-education academic work within hybrid learning environments, an initial observation of the important notions related to the ethics of hybrid learning for higher education was noted. Hence, this study framed these findings and considered the tentative features of hybrid learning ethics, focusing on what features should be articulated and further explored.

CONCEPT DEFINITIONS

For the purpose of this study, its authors defined unethical behavior regarding hybrid-learning academic work as follows: activities—e.g., academic research activities, academic evaluation activities, academic reward activities, etc., in offline modes outside a classroom setup (tutorials, courses in other institutions on campus, or peer-review seminars) and in computer-mediated learning (online courses)—where a researcher does not adhere to the ethics integral to exploring and developing knowledge. This concept was based on the previous definitions of ethical behavior, academic work, and hybrid learning. In this study, these three definitions (discussed below) allowed the authors to identify the contours of unethical behavior within academic work through hybrid learning.

First, ethical behavior is that which is initiated by individuals, groups, and organizations in the face of ethical dilemmas (Gülcan, 2015). It is the external embodiment of individual ethical quality, representing the practical action that is beneficial (or harmful) to individuals and society (Tangney et al., 2007). According to Treviño et al. (2006), ethical behavior is subject to (or judged according to) generally accepted norms. Thus, it is observed within the context of more extensive social scripts. Such a broad definition also accounts for behavior contrary to ethical norms that is typically deemed unethical, such as lying, cheating, and stealing. Also, behavior that exceeds some minimal ethical standard is typically considered ethical (or not unethical), such as obeying the law, showing honesty, and whistle-blowing. Moreover, ethical or unethical behaviors are learned through social reference groups and from significant others who share conceptions of norms, values, and attitudes with a given individual (Ferrell & Gresham, 1985). Notably, ethical behavior in academic work has always been the focus of higher education, which also places emphases on promoting ethical academic education and improving the quality of scientific research (Ke & Wuyuan, 2020). In this light, the present study focused on behavior contrary to ethical norms or unethical behavior.

Second, the abovementioned concept of academic work refers to a series of activities to explore and develop academic knowledge, such as research, evaluation, reward activities, etc. (Xinhua, 2005). In other words, academic work undertaken in higher education comprises written assignments, project papers, tests, dissertations, etc.

Third, the notion of hybrid learning involves using technology to create various learning environments for students (Linder, 2017), with specific learner-centered teaching objectives that organically integrate online learning, traditional face-to-face learning and modern network learning (Manli, 2015). However, hybrid learning is not a simple superposition of online and conventional offline learning but an organic integration of personalized learning and the various abovementioned learning elements. Some researchers (Paechter, 2004; Arnold, 2004; Bärenfänger, 2005; Pöysä et al., 2005) believe that hybrid learning is not simply a combination of classroom instruction and e-learning, but an amalgamation of standard instructional settings (classroom meetings), offline activities outside a classroom setup (tutorials, courses with other institutions on a campus, peer-reviewed workshops), and computer-mediated learning (online courses) (Bärenfänger, 2005, p. 15). To be precise, hybrid learning includes self-directed activities and blends traditional classroom and computer-assisted learning methods. In other words, hybrid learning involves not only phone calls and face-to-face interactions but also self-directed learning activities in classrooms or outside (Shams, 2013).

THE ISSUES OF UNETHICAL BEHAVIOR WITHIN ACADEMIC WORK IN HIGHER EDUCATION

It is an indisputable fact that unethical academic behavior by college students is a common occurrence, with some scholars calling considering this fact as an "epidemic" and a "long-term problem" (Jensen et al., 2002). Here, it must be noted that ethical behavior in academic work is related to the healthy development and the prosperity of academic endeavors, the rise or fall of educational quality, and the progress of social ethics (Ke et al., 2015). Thus, the issue of college students' unethical behavior in academic work has garnered widespread concern worldwide. Scholars have also noted an increase in the number of students resorting to unethical behavior in higher-education academic work at a global level (Park, 2019; Kassim et al., 2019). Such unethical academic behavior is mainly identified in terms of weak academic consciousness, cheating, plagiarism, data fraud, and other related actions (Yuanyuan & Xianxue, 2018).

In this vein, Ameen et al. (1996) conducted a study with 285 accounting students from four public universities in U.S.A., finding that 56% of its respondents admitted to being dishonest in exams and written assignments. Whitley (1998) also conducted a meta-study of 46 different studies on student cheating in U.S.A. and Canada, revealing that 70% of the surveyed students reportedly engaged in academically dishonest behavior in college. Moreover, McCabe et al. (2006) indicated that up to 86% of college students considered in their study were involved in dishonest behaviors in class, strongly suggesting that dishonesty was increasing among college-going students. Further, Yukhymenko (2014) explored Ukrainian students' beliefs about various forms of academic misconduct, and the results of this study were compared with those of similar studies on undergraduate students in U.S.A. (N = 270). The authors found that generally, students in Ukraine were less likely to believe that academic misconduct is wrong compared to students in U.S.A. In addition, Winardi et al.(2017) surveyed 342 accounting students regarding their perceptions on academic dishonesty and the motivational sources of their related behavior. They found that 77.5% of their respondents admitted to committing academically dishonest acts. Hu et al.(2020) also considered the changes within and outside the Chinese higher-education environment; as per their findings, academic dishonesty in the daily academic behaviors of Chinese college students, especially seniors, was consistently high.

RESPONSIVE AND RESPONSIBLE LEARNING IN HYBRID LEARNING

As mentioned, hybrid learning is not simply a superposition of offline learning and online learning. Actually, it is a product of the interaction between offline learning, disciplinary practice, structured knowledge, strict supervision and management, and the online development of teaching forms and resources to meet students' personalized needs and achieve precise teaching evaluations. Thus, hybrid learning gives precedence to the leading role of teachers in guiding, enlightening, and monitoring a given teaching process and facilitates the responsive and responsible learning of students as the subjects of this process (Wenbin et al., 2021).

Responsive Learning

Responsive learning in hybrid learning refers to the interaction between and influence of different branch of learning in real and virtual environments. This multi-dimensional and multi-level responsive process enriches students' knowledge and experience and also increases the depth and breadth of their learning (Xiaobin & Jinxia, 2020). There are many types of responsive learning for students in a hybrid learning environment, including students who are responsive to teachers, peers, teaching assistants, and the learning system (Rong et al., 2018). Indeed, responsive learning within hybrid learning is a complex process requiring comprehensive guidance from activity theory.

Activity theory is a powerful lens through which to evaluate socio-cultural and socio-historical mores, enabling the analysis of most forms of human activity (Jonassen & Rohrer-Murphy, 1999). It was developed initially by Leont'ev (1978, 1981) based on Vygotsky's (1978) socio-cultural learning theory. Engeström (1987), Cole (1988), Wertsch (1991), and Nardi (1996) apply activity theory to the study of social environments. Engeström, in particular, extends the theoretical dimension of activity theory to the entire activity system by representing the theory graphically (as a triangle) and applying it to various work and learning environments.

Creating the activity theory triangle (Figure 1), Engeström (1999) maintains that subjects are participants in an activity, and the object is the purpose or function of the activity. This division of labor outlines how tools, rules, and responsibilities are shared among active subjects. The uppermost triangle, involving the subject, object, tools, and signs, is the central point of mediation. However, human activity cannot be reduced to just the topmost triangle, because it is not an individual act but takes place in a specific community governed by specific rules and a particular division of labor (Engeström, 1987).

Ethics of Hybrid Learning in Higher Education

In other words, the triangle at the top is the tip of the iceberg regarding group activities (Engeström, 1990). This triangle also explains the role of actions in executing activities to achieve a specific outcome. Moreover, in work or learning environments, activity outcomes are often prescribed (Engeström, 2008) and may come under pressure with regard to a subject's objective or motive.

Based on activity theory, this study examined all kinds of activity related to hybrid learning by defining the subjects (students, teachers, teaching assistants, and the learning system), the objects (the focuses of the given learning activity), as well as the mediating tools (content teaching, learning activities, and discussion process) and the division of labor (the variegated tasks of students, teachers, and teaching assistants during instruction). Thus, activity theory was considered to analyze the complexity of the responsive learning process, including the following: the roles students play before, during, and after hybrid learning; the tools used before, during, and after hybrid learning; the design of hybrid learning activities; and the level of student engagement in hybrid learning activities.

Figure 1. The activity theory triangle. Source: Engeström (2001, 135; 2008, 257)

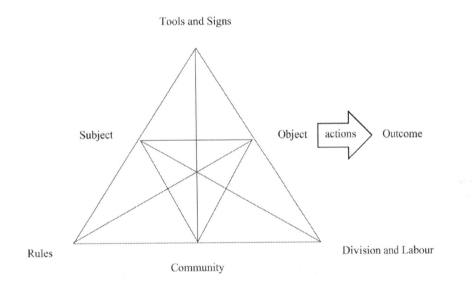

Responsible Learning

Under hybrid learning, responsible learning refers to learners' consciousness and their concept self-expressions with respect to their role as subjects in learning activities. Under hybrid learning, learners' subject consciousness is mainly reflected in their self-consciousness, practical consciousness, and relationship consciousness (Keding & Chaoqun, 2017). In this respect, Paris (2001) believes that responsible learning has seven distinctive characteristics: a) Choose your own learning goals and work towards them; b) Set your challenging goals, maximize your potential, strive to pursue success, and tolerate failure; c) Understand how to use learning resources in the classroom and freely regulate learning; d) Learn to work with others; e) Focus on the construction of meaning and creativity in learning; f) Acquire confidence and self-responsibility; g) Manage the learning process according to the predetermined learning standards and evaluate your learning performance.

In the context of Paris' (2001) research, it was important for this study to be guided by Zimmerman's self-regulated learning theory, so that it could exploring the complex process of responsible learning in hybrid learning settings. As per Zimmerman (2015), self-regulated learning involves metacognitive, motivational, and behavioral processes through which individuals acquire skills such as goal setting, planning, learning strategies, self-reinforcement, self-recording, and self-instruction. When students actively participate in learning using metacognition, motivation, and requisite behavior, their learning is termed responsible. To elaborate, in metacognition or autonomous learning, students can plan, organize, self-guide, self-monitor, and self-evaluate the different stages of their learning process. Regarding motivation, students who study independently are likely to regard themselves as competent, self-effective, and self-disciplined in terms of inspiration. In terms of behavior, students who study independently can choose, organize, and develop an environment that allows them to achieve the best learning results (Zimmerman, 1986).

In addition, Zimmerman's (2000) self-regulatory model of learning theory (Figure 2) divides self-regulated learning into three stages: forethought, performance/volitional control, and self-reflection. In the foresight stage, students analyze tasks, set goals, and plan how to achieve their objectives. Some self-motivation beliefs also motivate this process and influence the activation of learning strategies. Then, students perform their tasks in the performance/volitional control stage while monitoring their progress and using multiple self-control strategies to maintain their cognitive engagement and their motivation to complete the tasks. During the self-reflection stage, students self-judge how they have completed their tasks and attribute their success or failure. These attributions produce self-reactions and can positively or negatively impact how students shall complete tasks in their subsequent performances.

Therefore, the present study was based on Zimmerman's self-regulatory learning theory in order to analyze students' metacognitive, motivational, and behavioral processes and examine their responsible learning within hybrid learning settings. Using this theory, this study also explored the complexity of the responsive learning phases in hybrid learning (the anticipatory, performance/volitional control and self-reflective stages mentioned above).

Figure 2. Zimmerman's self-regulatory learning theory model. Source: Zimmerman (2000)

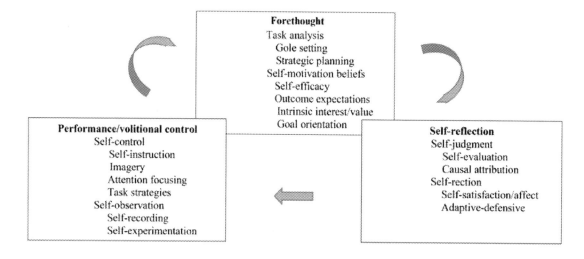

Ethics of Hybrid Learning in Higher Education

Further, this study assumed the following: in hybrid learning, students need to demonstrate responsive learning abilities and a conscious and clear understanding of their relationship with teachers and peers; students should clarify their equal relationship, mutual assistance relationship, mutual benefit relationship, and emotional interaction relationship in the process of seeking help from teachers and communicating with peers; students should be aware of their rights and responsibilities in a hybrid learning process; teachers' learning process and activity content can no longer be entirely controlled in hybrid learning settings; students will mainly learn as independent individuals not attached to teachers, parents, friends, classmates, and other objects, and they also need to have the requisite abilities to engage in responsible learning under hybrid learning settings.

RESEARCH GAPS AND RESEARCH QUESTIONS

In the context of a hybrid learning environment, there is a question about the nature of unethical behavior. The relevant literature suggests that the concomitant ethical behavior is evaluated in terms of (or judged according to) the generally accepted ethical norms of academic behavior. Thus, ethical behaviors are considered as occurring within the context of more extensive social prescriptions. This broad definition accounts for behaviors contrary to ethical norms that are typically deemed unethical, such as lying, cheating, and stealing (Reynolds & Ceranic, 2007). However, under hybrid learning, both the associated teaching and the learning methods have considerably changed (Ying, 2018; Mengya, 2022), and unethical behavior also acquires new characteristics. Still, in this regard there exists a lack of adequate definitions of ethical and unethical behavior, and only a few previous studies have been concerned with students' responsive and responsible learning.

One study conducted on students' responsive and responsible learning under hybrid learning settings (in higher education) reveals certain characteristics that are used in this chapter to discuss unethical behavior in hybrid learning. This study considers three questions:

1. What are students' understandings of unethical behavior in academic work within hybrid learning settings in the context of responsive and responsible learning?
2. What are the motivations for students' unethical behavior in academic work within hybrid learning settings in the context of responsive and responsible learning?

In summary, this study identifies students' unethical behavior in academic work within hybrid learning settings. These above questions particularly highlight the context that frames students' responsive and responsible learning. Still, most of the studies on students' unethical behavior in the available literature on academic work focuses on offline platforms rather than responsive and responsible learning regarding hybrid learning settings.

METHODOLOGY

Research Design

This study used a basic qualitative research approach and a case-study design. It mainly focused on understanding the world of hybrid learning and constructing the meanings of the world from group or individual perspectives (Merriam, 2014). Hence, semi-structured interviews were conducted to determine the students' understandings of and motivations behind unethical behavior in academic work within hybrid learning settings, in the context of responsive and responsible learning.

Participants

In light of this study's qualitative approach, the researchers considered it appropriate to created sample from an accessible population. This included current students at a college in Beijing, China. Moreover, this study used a purposive sampling strategy focused on "generating ideas and insights" (Churchill, 1995). The researchers advertised an invitation for students to participate in this study, at the abovementioned college. The participants' selection criteria included senior college students with the following credentials: those who had completed almost four years of study, those who possessed any experience related to unethical behavior in academic work and in hybrid learning settings, and those were willing to participate in a maximum of three interview sessions. Based on these criteria, five students who responded to the invitation were selected as part of a convenience sample. Thereafter, through semi-structured interviews, the participants were invited to contribute their understandings of and attitudes towards unethical behavior in academic work within hybrid learning settings.

Data Collection Procedures

The semi-structured interviews used in this study were voluntary and the participants received no monetary reward. Data were gathered during the students' respective second semesters (spring semesters) of the 2021–2022 season. Moreover, all interviews were conducted with each participant via email, as it is a contemporary form of streamlined communication that facilitates online and offline research opportunities (Burns, 2010). Due to the physical distances between interviewers and interviewees, an email-centered approach was indeed the most appropriate interview option; it offered several methodological possibilities of interviewing the participants individually. Specifically, it generated asynchronous written dialogues between the participants and researchers and transformed the virtual 'space' (and time). Indeed, rather than committing to immediate answers, our participants were able to reflect on our questions based on their own experiences (Bampton & Cowton, 2002). Additionally, due to the spread of COVID-19 widely across China, including Beijing, students from the abovementioned college (located in different provinces in China) were not allowed to return to campus in the spring semester, and seniors had to complete their graduation work online. Therefore, an email-centered approach was the most appropriate option regarding this study's interviews. Notably, the semi-structured interviews were conducted in China because all the participants hailed from this nation and their native language was Mandarin.

There were three main phases in this study's data collection process. First, the researchers explained the purpose of the interviews to the participants, obtained signed informed consent forms from them via email, and guaranteed their anonymity. Second, the researchers sent a semi-structured interview protocol to all the participants (via email) with regard to data collection. Then, the participants were asked to respond to the interview questionnaire in MS Word files within seven days; during these seven days, the researchers communicated with the participants via phone calls, WeChat, and email. Notably, each participant submitted her/his interview within the allotted time.

Data Analysis

The data obtained from the interviews were organized, coded, and interpreted based on qualitative data analysis procedures (Ary et al., 2010). As the most common type of thematic analysis in a qualitative study entails the exploration of interviewee responses (Guest et al., 2011), the researchers analyzed the obtained data via thematic analysis using the qualitative software analysis tool Nvivo12. Moreover, the emergent thematic analysis process comprises several steps, including iterative coding (Strauss & Corbin, 1998), identifying emergent themes (Strauss & Corbin, 1998; Weitzman, 2000), and classifying the identified themes. In this respect, the participants were assigned specific phone numbers to ensure their anonymity. In addition, Braun and Clarke (2006) reveal that themes (that represent the level or significance of response patterns in the dataset) are quite important in data analysis based on research questions, while sub-themes provide the structure for the broader themes. In this study, the results categorized the themes and subthemes identified as unethical behavior in academic work within hybrid learning settings.

Ethical Consideration

To ensure their adherence to research ethics, the researchers got the approval of the abovementioned college in Beijing to conduct this study. As mentioned, the researchers informed all the participants about the purpose of this study through a participant information form. Data collection began after participants had signed an informed consent form agreeing to participate. These participants voluntarily took part in the study; they were free to withdraw participation at any time and did not need to specify the reasons for withdrawal. All the written interview files were stored in the first author's email in a password-protected laptop, and only the first and second authors had direct access to the data. In other words, this study strictly abided by ethical considerations and prioritized the participants' well-being, privacy, safety, anonymity.

Validity and Reliability

Experienced researchers not involved in this study were invited to review the interview protocol, so that this study could ensure sufficient internal validity. Since the interview data (via email) were originally text-based, did not require transcription, and did not contain any potentially ambiguous paragraphs as per the researchers' verification, the participants were not asked to review their texts. For data analysis, the first author discussed with researchers from the abovementioned college the need to eliminate any potential bias during the thematic analysis. After the results indicated data saturation, the data were considered reliable or consistent; this was accomplished by simultaneously analyzing and collecting data. To ensure the trustworthiness of this qualitative study (Shenton, 2004), the first author triangulated the interview data using media research reports along with policy-related and legal documents.

RESULTS

Few published studies have hitherto examined the description of unethical behavior in hybrid learning settings or concerned themselves with students' responsive and responsible learning. Hence, this unique qualitative study on the ethics of hybrid learning in higher education provided much-needed knowledge to fill this research gap. It comprised semi-structured interviews with the participants to investigate the students' unethical behavior in higher-education academic work within hybrid learning settings, in the context of responsive and responsible learning. Specifically, this section delineates the coding of the interviews conducted by the researchers, as per the participants' responses identified and agreed upon by the authors in developing the findings-related frequencies and percentages. The findings were reported and discussed as per the order of the two research questions. Moreover, each participant's voice was maintained through frequent summaries of their accounts and examples from their quotes. The results of the present study are given below.

Students' Understanding of Unethical Behavior in Academic Work within Hybrid Learning Settings

In the first question of their interviews, the participants were explicitly asked how they defined and interpreted different types of ethical behavior in academic work within hybrid learning settings in the context of responsive and responsible learning. Analysis of the responses revealed a superficial understanding of the concomitant unethical behavior among the participants. Indeed, they could not come up with a sound definition of unethical behavior in academic work and were largely unsure about its different types.

The Definition of Unethical Behavior in Academic Work

Regarding the definition of unethical behavior in academic work within hybrid learning settings, all the participants noted unethical behavior as contrary to generally accepted ethical norms. Still, they could not come up with a sound definition of unethical behavior in academic work.

In hybrid learning settings, unethical behavior in academic work was deemed as referring to behavior that violates China's socialist ethical ideology, deviates from the mainstream ethical behavior advocated by the state and society, and does not conform to the core socialist values advocated by Chinese cultural scripts. Specifically, such behavior was considered as violating the relevant national laws and regulations, the provisions of college rules and regulations, or the provisions of hybrid learning integrity norms with respect to responsive and responsible learning in hybrid learning settings.

The Different Types of Unethical Behavior in Academic Work

Based on the definitions of unethical behavior in academic work within hybrid learning settings, the participants focused on the different types of such unethical behavior in the context of responsive and responsible learning. For this paper, the present study outlined certain authoritative judgment criteria to judge whether participants' understandings of unethical behavior in academic work was comprehensive and profound. According to the Handbook of Scientific Research Integrity Education for Colleges and Universities (Hui et al., 2020), the types of unethical behavior in academic work are the following: plagiarism, academic cheating, falsification, fabrication, repetitive publication, ghostwriting, dishonorable signature, and appropriation of others' academic achievements. However, since there was no authoritative definition of the concept and classification regarding the abovementioned unethical behavior, this study referred to the types of traditional learning, while still considering the characteristics of hybrid learning. To analyze the different types of such unethical behavior, this study focused on the participants' views on hybrid learning settings in the context of responsive and responsible learning. In turn, the participants did point out certain types of concomitant unethical behavior, but they were largely unsure about the different types of such behavior. The participants' views are given below.

Replace someone or find someone to replace you for class attendance: Although students' responsive and responsible learning requirements are high in related to hybrid learning, some students do not participate in hybrid learning but instead find others to complete the online learning portion instead of completing it themselves. In evaluating academic performance within hybrid learning settings, evaluating students' learning process is a primary aspect. The length and number of videos that students watch are used as the basis of assessment and are weighted by scores, which are reflected in their final academic evaluations. However, the students "virtually" use their corresponding user accounts in the hybrid learning platforms. Each of their learning statuses is mainly determined by checking whether the corresponding user account is completed. Therefore, some students take advantage of the loopholes in the rules to hand over their user accounts to others or obtain others' user accounts, let others replace themselves, or help others complete learning tasks and submit homework, etc.

Use illegal automatic substitute class software instead of attending class: For example, the given illegal software can simulate labor and allow automatic check-ins, along with learning and answering questions on behalf of students. Clearly, the type of responsible learning consciousness of a hybrid learning student can dominate the purpose, plan, scheme, and implementation of her/his hybrid learning activity. Also, one must consider that in hybrid learning, students are separated from the traditional classroom environment, thus lacking real-time guidance and correction; therefore, they need higher levels of consciousness and control to complete the learning processes. Although some students actively participate in hybrid learning, others may use illegal automatic substitute class software and not focus on learning. Further, students' attentions are free during the hybrid learning process; this counts as a deviation from the ongoing online learning environment, including activities such as browsing other websites, playing mobile phones, playing games, chatting, and eating during lectures.

Cheating: Students cheat while participating in daily tests or final exams within hybrid learning settings. As examination is one of the essential bases for hybrid learning evaluation, the examination results account for a critical proportion of students' final online academic evaluations. In hybrid learning examinations, because students usually do not get face-to-face supervision from teachers, they are prone to use mobile phones to check answers, copy answers, and find someone else to take their exams to obtain high scores. In turn, teachers cannot fix the factual learning evaluation basis and grasp the actual learning situation of students, which leads to the decline of students' learning effects. Thus, it is difficult to achieve the goal of improving students' problem-solving abilities.

Plagiarism: Hybrid learning gives students a more convenient opportunity to access online resources. However, to save time and trouble, some students can download relevant papers, search for materials and experimental results on the internet, and then download, copy, paste, learn, modify, and use others' academic works. Moreover, they may copy others' academic views and academic content, without annotating or adding quotes and explanations.

Motivations for Students' Unethical Behavior in Academic Work Within Hybrid Learning Settings

The participants in this study were explicitly asked a second question: what motivational factors do you think influence students' unethical behavior in academic work within hybrid learning settings, in the context of responsive and responsible learning? Analysis of the related data that were gathered from the semi-structured interviews revealed nine categories of motivations behind students' unethical behavior.

The prevalence of pursuing social profit: The participants maintained that money is supreme, efficiency is crucial, and confessed to blindly pursuing social profit in society. Such ideas erode the world of academia and makes scientific research goals increasingly focused on social profit. Pursuing social profit makes some college students only regard academic learning as a means and a tool of profit, which inevitably leads to the prevalence of unethical behavior in academic work.

Social pressure: Participants claimed that the exam results are the primary basis for students to obtain awards, academic degrees, and employment. Failure to get a good result means that one cannot subsequently obtain a scholarship or a degree and may even face challenges in finding jobs after graduation. As few employers welcome a student with low scores, such social pressures pose a significant burden to students' psychological well-being. Therefore, some students resort to unethical behavior in academic work within hybrid learning settings to obtain grades beyond their existing learning levels and reduce the associated social pressures.

Lack of academic integrity: The participants considered that their college does not pay enough attention to academic integrity education, does not offer standard academic courses, and does not effectively provide formal academic education, especially in hybrid learning settings. As a result, the students' definitions of unethical behavior in academic work remain vague. They lack adequate knowledge of academic norms even as they engage unethical behavior in academic work.

Insufficient academic research ability: The participants maintained that some students' insufficient academic research ability makes it impossible or at least difficult for them to conduct innovative research effectively. Without sufficient knowledge reserves, they want to acquire a high level of academic achievement; thus, they can only resort unethical behavior in hybrid learning settings to produce or "create" research results.

The sense of innovation is not strong: The participants considered that hybrid learning gives students more opportunities for responsive and responsible learning and puts forward higher requirements for such learning. However, some students still cannot shift from the traditional learning mode, leading to a lack of innovation consciousness, of the spirit of independent thinking, and of the due ideological and theoretical bases of academic research. These college students cannot find, ask, analyze, and solve problems, which makes them unable to undertake effective academic works. Thus, they resort to unethical behavior in completing their learning tasks.

The supervision mechanism is not perfect: The participants maintained that hybrid learning mainly relies on the network and platform. Still, their college has not developed an ideal supervision mechanism for unethical behavior in academic work in hybrid learning and lacks corresponding punishment measures. In hybrid learning, the supervision of the college and the teacher for students' unethical behavior in academic work regulation is difficult. For example, the college and teachers indeed find students' unethical behavior in academic work. Still, they worry that punishment would affect students' graduation and employment. Therefore, they only criticize students without letting them undergo the due punishment and thus, they cannot adequately play the role of supervisors.

Influence of peers: The participants thought that the more students see their classmates showing unethical behavior in academic work, the more likely they are to engage in unethical behavior themselves. The effects of hybrid learning include two aspects regarding the influence of peers. First, some good students in an exam find that many academically poor students, through unethical behavior in academic work, obtain good results; this makes the meritorious student feel a sense of injustice, leading them to also resort to unethical behavior in academic work. Second, some students with poor grades who see other students like themselves get high scores through such unethical behavior also feel a sense of unfairness and eventually participate in unethical behavior.

To maximize their interests: The participants believed that academic performance is an essential indicator that judges students' excellence, based on personal evaluation and award evaluation and bearing the heavy responsibility of successful graduation. Students with good academic performance can win the adulation of their peers, teachers, and parents. At the same time, academic advantages can create advantageous conditions for students in various evaluations, party memberships, employment opportunities, and other aspects. Therefore, some students are willing to violate disciplinary regulations, ignore ethical requirements, abandon ethical principles (including "integrity"), and engage in unethical behavior in hybrid learning settings.

Lack of academic preparation: The participants considered that adequate academic preparation is the basis and prerequisite for good grades. They thought that some students' insufficient academic preparation leads to unethical behavior in academic work within hybrid learning settings. First, some students lack learning goals and motivation, are lax in their requirements, or are late to lectures and leave early, or are keen on part-time businesses, or devote most of their time to non-academic personal activities, or are even addicted to the internet, with all of these factors resulting in the lack of time to prepare for their studies. Second, some students are used to the learning habits of their high school settings, lacking responsive and responsible learning ability or the learning methods appropriate for hybrid learning, enable to adapt to their college's learning requirements, and showing poor academic performance. Third, some students have weak learning foundations and cannot meet the responsive and responsible learning requirements within hybrid learning settings. The above findings are summarized in Table 1.

Table 1. Summary of codified results

Themes	Category
Societal	The prevalence of pursuing social profit
	Social pressure
Educational	Lack of academic integrity
	Insufficient academic research ability
	The sense of innovation is not strong
	The supervision mechanism is not perfect
Interpersonal	Influence of peers
Personal	To maximize their interests
	Lack of academic preparation

DISCUSSION

This study aimed to investigate Chinese college students' perspectives on unethical behavior in academic work within hybrid learning settings, in the context of responsive and responsible learning. The analysis of the first research question revealed that students had a shallow understanding of the definition of unethical behavior in academic work and were mainly unsure about its different types. Although some participants were familiar with the term unethical behavior in academic work, they could not accurately define what would count as unethical behavior.

Thus, this study claims that students need specific and explicit examples to understand the characteristics of unethical behavior in academic work, especially in hybrid learning. Thus, colleges should provide students with guidelines to understand the definition of unethical behavior in academic work. Only through this move will the colleges' integrity and reputation remain upheld, and they will be able to encourage students to demonstrate honesty and ethics in academic work.

Regarding the types of unethical behavior in academic work, the participants' responses indicated that they were primarily sure about certain types of unethical behavior, such as replacing someone or finding someone to as replacement for class attendance, using automatic substitute class software instead of attending class, cheating, and plagiarism. The participants also pointed out some types of unethical behavior in academic work by combining the responsive and responsible learning characteristics of hybrid learning and comparing the two templates. However, the participants' statements about the different types of unethical behavior in academic work were still missing.

In the participants' responses to the second question, they spoke about nine categories related to the motivations behind students' unethical behavior within hybrid learning settings. Indeed, this study found that these nine categories have a highly significant impact on educational factors and learning processes. Therefore, college authorities, students, and the larger society must seriously consider combating unethical behavior in academic work in its various forms. Some suggestions to overcome unethical behavior in academic work within hybrid learning settings are given below.

- Optimize the social integrity environment related to the integrity environment in higher education. Honesty and trustworthiness are essential cornerstones of building a modern civilization and creating a good environment of integrity. Foreground honesty and trustworthiness as integral to the code of conduct that most people can identify with and follow, and then establish a set of ethical systems, with integrity at their core, that meets the requirements of a social integrity environment related to the integrity environment in higher education.
- Improve the social evaluation system, create a fair social environment, and reduce students' social pressure that facilitate their unethical behavior in academic work. Whether a person is excellent should be considered in relation to ethical, intellectual, physical, and labor-related aspects, instead of taking academic performance as the only evaluation standard. Students should be encouraged to continue exploring the development modes and assessment systems of quality education. Parents, colleges administrations, and the whole society should move beyond considering students' scores as the only assessment criteria.
- In addition to a lack of academic integrity, strengthen honesty in education and cultivate students to establish a correct ethical outlook. First, colleges should add courses and offer resources related to integrity education and network ethics in hybrid learning and cultivate students' awareness of integrity regarding hybrid ethical education; this will help them establish the best values to face

hybrid learning correctly. Second, colleges should establish an integrity system network for students' learning behavior constraints and engage in supervision, rewards, punishments, and evaluations to maintain the entire environment of hybrid learning. Colleges can also build students' integrity files and record their dishonest hybrid learning behaviors, which can in turn help students become aware of the ethical concept of integrity.

- Change the teaching methods and improve college students' academic research ability. First, teachers should guide college students to adapt to the hybrid learning model. The adaptation here is not only technical but also psychological in kind. Colleges should shift from the traditional learning models, optimize their curricula, improve the teaching methods, serve as sources of inspiration, discussion, grouping, and other ways of flexible learning, stimulate students' interest and participation consciousness, and improve students' independent learning ability. These factors will enable students to master their domain knowledge and cultivate their interest in academic research. Moreover, they can improve students' ability to find, analyze, and solve problems, virtually enhancing their academic research ability.

- Enhance students' sense of innovation. The real significance of academic research lies in innovation. Unethical behavior in academic work runs counter to innovation. Therefore, college students should cultivate their innovation abilities while mastering theoretical knowledge. Academic seminars, academic innovation activities, or innovation competitions through hybrid learning platforms can facilitate students' interest in academic research and stimulate their innovative thinking, which can further allow students to cultivate their innovation ability.

- Strengthen hybrid teaching and technical management processes, pay attention to the unethical behavior in academic work within hybrid learning settings, and engage in timely interventions and corrections. First, colleges should strengthen the quality management of hybrid learning to provide students with better hybrid-learning content. They should actively use responsive and responsible learning within hybrid learning settings to improve the curricula and curricula quality and also closely follow the changes wrought by the hybrid learning environment to students' learning behavior, learning habits, and preferences. Second, they should strengthen the management of the hybrid learning process, actively pay attention to the feedback of students' learning data, and make timely adjustments to the teaching plans and guidance mechanisms. Third, they should strengthen technical management processes to monitor and prevent unethical behavior in academic work within a hybrid learning environment. For example, they can monitor abnormal I.P. addresses and lock a suspicious learning account to verify the log-in condition or conduct face-verification while completing the learning tasks, or develop an online invigilator program etc.

- To deal with the influence of peers, college students should set up a correct cognition mechanism and achieve self-management and restraint. For example, college students should know about and distinguish unethical behavior in academic work in the hybrid learning environment. Hybrid learning methods require students to take the initiative to adjust their learning behavior, actively control their learning process, and actively manage their own learning time. By strengthening self-control in their behavior, and refusing external temptation, flukes, or a utilitarian mentality, students can resist internal and external interference and reduce unethical behavior in hybrid learning settings.

- Finally, implement specific prevention strategies to maximize students' interests and the lack of academic preparation (as a personal factor). Stimulate students' independent learning motivations and correct hybrid learning attitudes. In hybrid learning, students need greater autonomy and self-management ability. Autonomy is manifested as students' interest in and need for hybrid learning. Then, their interest and needs will strongly show their thirst for knowledge and independent learning ability. When students have less interest in hybrid learning and think that participating in hybrid learning is the only way to escape punishment or external pressure or pursue other utilitarian values, their sense of autonomy is lower and they are more likely to engage in unethical behavior in hybrid learning settings. Therefore, there is a need to enhance their interest in and attraction towards hybrid learning, promote their attention to hybrid learning, and increase their interest in improving their independent learning and self-management ability. For example, in hybrid learning, students can be guided to establish learning goals, make self-learning plans, and maintain online punching records to strengthen self-supervision and self-promotion in their learning processes. Suppose the learning goal is achieved after a while. This will stimulate the leaners' sense of achievement and promote independent motivation so that students can enter a virtuous circle and avoid unethical behavior in academic work in hybrid learning settings.

Overall, it can be argued that college students' reasons for indulging in unethical behavior in academic work within hybrid learning settings are four in total: societal, educational, interpersonal, and personal reasons. This study, then, puts academics in a better position to implement the strategies used by society, college administrations, and college-going students that can be used to manage and decrease unethical behavior in academic work within hybrid learning settings. However, one must concomitantly consider contextual and situational factors.

CONCLUSION

This study shows that unethical behavior in academic work in hybrid learning is prevalent among college students in China. The motivations behind such behavior range from societal, educational, interpersonal, to personal factors. The current state of unethical behavior in academic work within hybrid learning settings needs to be given appropriate attention. This study highlights the need for immediate action by society, college authorities, and individual students.

The results of this study indicate that from a social point of view, colleges must optimize the social integrity environment and change the prevalence of attraction to social profit. They must also improve their social evaluation systems, create a fair social environment, and reduce students' social pressures to that lead unethical behavior in academic work. Colleges authorities should strengthen honest education and cultivate correct ethical outlooks in its students. Moreover, they should shift from the traditional teaching methods and improve college students' academic research ability in the hybrid learning settings. Further, they should enhance students' sense of innovation, strengthen the hybrid teaching and technical management, pay attention to unethical behavior in academic work within hybrid learning, and make timely intervention and correction in these regards. On their part, college students should cultivate correct cognition abilities and achieve self-management and restraint. Thus, implementing specific prevention strategies to maximize students' interests will lead to a significant reduction in their lack of academic preparation (as a personal factor lead to unethical behavior in hybrid learning settings).

REFERENCES

Ameen, E. C., Guffey, D. M., & McMillan, J. J. (1996). Gender differences in determining the ethical sensitivity of future accounting professionals. *Journal of Business Ethics*, *15*(5), 591–597. doi:10.1007/BF00381934

Arnold, R. (2004). *Blended learning in international human resource development, on the characteristic features and the comparative didactic advantages of face-to-face learning, distance learning and e-learning*. GIZ. https://www.gtz.de/en/dokumente/en-elearning-blendedlearning-in-international-human-resource-development.pdf

Ary, D., Jacobs, L. C., & Sorensen, C. (2010). *Introduction to research in education* (8th ed.). Wadsworth.

Bampton, R., & Cowton, C. J. (2002). The e-interview. *Forum Qualitative Social Research*, *3*(2). www.qualitatative-research.net/fqs/

Bärenfänger, O. (2005). Learning management: A new approach to structuring hybrid learning arrangements. *Electronic Journal of Foreign Language Teaching*, *2*(2), 14–35.

Braun, V., & Clarke, V. (2006). Using thematic analysis in psychology. *Qualitative Research in Psychology*, *3*(2), 77–101. doi:10.1191/1478088706qp063oa

Burns, E. (2010). Developing email interview practices in qualitative research. *Sociological Research Online*, *15*(4), 24–35. doi:10.5153ro.2232

Churchill, G. A. Jr. (1995). *Marketing research: Methodological foundations* (6th ed.). The Dryden Press.

Engeström, Y. (1990). *Learning, working and imagining: Twelve studies in activity theory*. Orienta-Konsultit.

Engeström, Y. (1999). Activity theory and individual and social transformation. In Y. Engestrom, R. Miettinen, & R.-M. Punamaki (Eds.), *Perspectives on activity theory* (pp. 19–38). Cambridge University Press. doi:10.1017/CBO9780511812774.003

Engeström, Y. (2001). Expansive learning at work: Toward an activity theory reconceptualization. *Journal of Education and Work*, *14*(1), 133–156. doi:10.1080/13639080020028747

Engeström, Y. (2008). Enriching activity theory without shortcuts. *Interacting with Computers*, *20*(2), 256–259. doi:10.1016/j.intcom.2007.07.003

Fangfang, T., & Hao, T. (2021). Research on the teaching mode of "dual-line hybrid integration" in the post-epidemic period. *Computer Knowledge and Technology*, *17*(10), 152–165.

Ferrell, O. C., & Gresham, L. G. (1985). A contingency framework for understanding ethical decision making in marketing. *Journal of Marketing*, *49*(Summer), 87–96. doi:10.1177/002224298504900308

Guest, G., MacQueen, K. M., & Namey, E. E. (2011). *Applied thematic analysis*. Sage Publication.

Gülcan, N. Y. (2015). Discussing the importance of teaching ethics in education. *Procedia: Social and Behavioral Sciences*, *174*, 2622–2625. doi:10.1016/j.sbspro.2015.01.942

Hui, L., Mingjun, W., & Li, Z. (2020). *Handbook of scientific research integrity education for colleges and universities* (1st ed.). Science Press.

Jensen, L. A., Arnett, J. J., Feldman, S. S., & Cauffman, E. (2002). It's wrong, but everyone does it: Academic dishonesty among high school and college students. *Contemporary Educational Psychology*, *27*(2), 210–211. doi:10.1006/ceps.2001.1088

Jian, H., Guangming, L., & Weijun, W. (2020). Perceptions, contexts, attitudes, and academic dishonesty in Chinese senior college students: A qualitative content-based analysis. *Ethics & Behavior*, *30*(7), 543–555. doi:10.1080/10508422.2020.1711758

Jonassen, D. H., & Rohrer-Murphy, L. (1999). Activity theory as a framework for designing constructivist learning environments. *Educational Technology Research and Development*, *47*(1), 61–79. doi:10.1007/BF02299477

Kassim, S. A., Nasir, N. F. M., Johari, N. R., & Razali, N. F. Y. (2021). Academic dishonesty intentions in the perspectives of higher education in Malaysia. *South Florida Journal of Development*, *2*(5), 7991–8000. doi:10.46932fjdv2n5-119

Ke, H., & Wuyuan, C. (2020). Governance of academic misconduct in colleges and universities—Takes Stanford University, Cambridge University, University of Tokyo for example. *Southeast Academic Research*, (6), 40–48.

Ke, W., Zhaobin, D., & Ming, X. (2015). Review, introspection and outlook on research of academic morality in Chinese universities. *Review of Higher Education*, *3*(10), 14–19.

Keding, Z., & Chaoqun, Y. (2017). Research on the development of learner's subjective consciousness in blended learning mode. *Modern Distance Education Research*, (6), 48–56.

Leont'ev, A. N. (1978). *Activity, consciousness, and personality*. Prentice-Hall.

Leont'ev, A. N. (1981). *Problems of the development of the mind*. Progress Publishers.

Liguori, E., & Winkler, C. (2020). From offline to online: Challenges and opportunities for entrepreneurship education following the COVID-19 pandemic. *Entrepreneurship Education and Pedagogy*, *3*(1), 346–351. doi:10.1177/2515127420916738

Linder, K. E. (2017). Fundamentals of hybrid teaching and learning. *New Directions for Teaching and Learning*, *2017*(3), 11–18. doi:10.1002/tl.20222

Manli, S. (2015). Evaluation of blended learning teaching mode in foreign universities. [Philosophy and Social Sciences Edition]. *Journal of Fujian Normal University*, (3), 153–172.

McCabe, D. L., Butterfield, K. D., & Treviño, L. K. (2006). Academic dishonesty in graduate business programs: Prevalence, causes, and proposed action. *Academy of Management Learning & Education*, *5*(3), 294–305. doi:10.5465/amle.2006.22697018

Mengya, W. (2022). A SWOT analysis of the hybrid learning patterns. *Heilongjiang Science*, *13*(5), 78–80.

Merriam, S. B. (2014). *Qualitative research: A guide to design and implementation*. Jossey-Bass.

Murphy, M. P. A. (2020). COVID-19 and emergency eLearning: Consequences of the securitization of higher education for post-pandemic pedagogy. *Contemporary Security Policy*, *41*(3), 492–505. doi:10.1080/13523260.2020.1761749

Nardi, B. (Ed.). (1996). *Context and consciousness: Activity theory and human-computer interaction.* MIT Press.

Paechter, M. (2004). Hybrid learning leads to better achievement and higher satisfaction than pure e-learning. Is it that easy? (pp. 584-591). I KNOW '04, Graz, Austria.

Paris, S. G., & Paris, A. H. (2001). Classroom application of research on self-regulated learning. *Educational Psychologist*, *36*(3), 89–113. doi:10.1207/S15326985EP3602_4

Park, S. (2019). Goal contents as predictors of academic cheating in college students. *Ethics & Behavior*, (3), 628–639.

Pöysä, J., Lowyck, J., & Häkkinen, P. (2005). Learning together "there"-hybrid "place" as a conceptual vantage point for understanding virtual learning communities in higher education context. *PsychNology Journal*, *3*(2), 162–180.

Raes, A., Vanneste, P., Pieters, M., Windey, I., Noortgate, W. V. D., & Depaepe, F. (2020). Learning and instruction in the hybrid virtual classroom: An investigation of students' engagement and the effect of quizzes. *Computers & Education*, *143*, 143. doi:10.1016/j.compedu.2019.103682

Reynolds, S. J., & Ceranic, T. L. (2007). The effects of moral judgment and moral identity on moral behavior: An empirical examination of the moral individual. *The Journal of Applied Psychology*, *92*(6), 1610–1624. doi:10.1037/0021-9010.92.6.1610 PMID:18020800

Rong, F., Yan, W., Xing, Y., & Yuan, L. (2018). Research on teacher-student interaction strategy in mixed learning from perspective of learners. *Vocational and Technical Education*, *39*(32), 43–46.

Shams, I. E. (2013). Hybrid learning and Iranian EFL learners' autonomy in vocabulary learning. *Procedia: Social and Behavioral Sciences*, *93*, 1587–1592. doi:10.1016/j.sbspro.2013.10.086

Shenton, A. K. (2004). Strategies for ensuring trustworthiness in qualitative research projects. *Education for Information*, *22*(2), 63–75. doi:10.3233/EFI-2004-22201

Strauss, A. L., & Corbin, J. M. (1998). *Basics of qualitative research*. Sage Publications.

Tangney, J. P., Stuewig, J., & Mashek, D. J. (2007). Moral emotions and moral behavior. *Annual Review of Psychology*, *58*(1), 345–372. doi:10.1146/annurev.psych.56.091103.070145 PMID:16953797

Treviño, L. T., Weaver, G., & Reynolds, S. J. (2006). Behavioral ethics in organizations: A review. *Journal of Management*, *32*(6), 951–990. doi:10.1177/0149206306294258

Vygotsky, L. S. (1978). *Mind in society: The development of higher psychological processes*. Harvard University Press.

Weitzman, E. A. (2000). Software and qualitative research. In N. K. Denzin & Y. S. Lincoln (Eds.), *Handbook of qualitative research* (pp. 803–820). SAGE.

Wenbin, H., Jun, M., Yang, C., Wuyi, M., & Yizhong, L. (2021). Analysis on open mixed teaching mode in the post-epidemic era- -Take CAD / CAM technology course as an example. *The Journal of Higher Education, 7*(35), 78–81.

Wertsch, J. (1991). *Voices of the mind: A sociocultural approach to mediated action.* Harvard University Press.

Whitley, B. E. (1998). Factors associated with cheating among college students: A review. *Research in Higher Education, 39*(3), 235–274. doi:10.1023/A:1018724900565

Winardi, R. D., Mustikarini, A., & Anggraeni, M. Z. (2017). Academic dishonesty among accounting students: Some Indonesian evidence. *Jurnal Akuntansi dan Keuangan Indonesia, 2*(14), 142–164.

Xiaobing, Y., & Jinxia, L. (2020). Inquiry on student interactive teaching strategies based on hybrid teaching. *Textile and Apparel Education, 35*(5), 377–381.

Xinhua, J. (2005). *Institutional analysis of why academic anomie and university academic ethics anomie* (1st ed.). Social Sciences Academic Press.

Ying, H. (2018). Research and exploration of online and offline mixed teaching modes under the background of "Internet +. *Business Story*, (10), 177–178.

Yuanyuan, Zh., & Xianxue, K. (2018). Analysis of the lack of academic morality of college students. *Modern Communication*, (16), 129–130.

Yukhymenko, M. A. (2014). Ethical beliefs toward academic dishonesty: A cross-cultural comparison of undergraduate students in Ukraine and the United States. *Journal of Academic Ethics, 12*(12), 29–41. doi:10.100710805-013-9198-3

Zhuli, W. (2020). How should education transform in the post-epidemic era? e-. *Education Research, 41*(3), 13–20.

Zimmerman, B. J. (1986). Becoming a self-regulated learner. *Contemporary Educational Psychology, 11*(4), 307–313. doi:10.1016/0361-476X(86)90027-5

Zimmerman, B. J. (2000). *Handbook of Self-Regulation* (M. Boekaerts, P. R. Pintrich, & M. Zeidner, Eds.). Academic Press.

Zimmerman, B. J. (2015). Self-regulated learning: Theories, measures, and outcomes. International Encyclopedia of the Social & Behavioral Sciences, 21, 541–546.

KEY TERMS AND DEFINITIONS

Academic: Methods and processes for exploring, learning, and discovering new knowledge.
Cheating: Using deception to achieve goals against the system or regulations.
College: Higher education institutions with fewer subjects and a high degree of specialization.

Ethics: The sum of behavioral norms that regulate people's relations with each other by the power of social opinion, traditional customs, and people's beliefs, with the evaluation of good and evil as the standard.

Falsification: Untruthfulness of language or behavior.

Ghostwriting: Writing for others or getting others to write for you.

Honest: Showing loyalty and honesty, frankness, no lies, no falsifications, no overstatements, no distortion of the truth, etc.

Plagiarism: Using other people's ideas, opinions, language, words, products etc., without crediting their sources.

Chapter 20
Factors to Consider When Moving a Cooperative Academic Literacy Activity Online

Chris Harwood
https://orcid.org/0000-0003-2789-8212
Sophia University, Japan

EXECUTIVE SUMMARY

This chapter focuses on cooperative learning in an undergraduate English for academic purposes context and discusses the pedagogical factors that educators should consider when moving a face-to-face cooperative learning activity online. In the discussion, a text-based academic literacy activity is used to illustrate how the principles of cooperative learning should incorporate pedagogic concepts and approaches from group-based online learning to facilitate cooperative learning online. Factors within task structure, and the importance of teaching presence and social presence in fostering cognitive presence in an online learning environment are discussed. Then, recommendations for how to cultivate positive interdependence, promotive interaction, individual accountability, interpersonal and small group skills, and group processing in online activities are proposed.

INTRODUCTION

Cooperative learning (CL) is an instructional method in which students, under the guidance of their instructor, work in small groups to achieve a shared learning goal. For over 70 years it has been integrated into the pedagogy of courses in educational contexts around the world. In their review of active learning, Johnson and Johnson (2018) note that, "cooperative learning is the foundation on which most active learning methods are built" (p. 62). The efficacy of CL is conclusive with research from over 1200 studies reporting that CL leads to higher achievement, greater productivity, more frequent new ideas and solutions, and higher-level reasoning than more competitive or individual methods of learning (Johnson & Johnson, 2018). The benefits of CL have been shown to transfer to online learning. Researchers report that online CL can enhance social presence (Flener-Lovitt et al. 2020; Rajaram, 2021); can have positive effects on communicative competence and student relationships (Estriegana et al., 2021); and can lead to higher self-esteem (Rajaram, 2021). Moreover, CL has been found to enable students to improve their problem-solving ability and increase online learning satisfaction (Wang & Wu, 2022).

In recent years there has been a migration of higher education courses to online environments. Online academic literacy, usually in the form of online text-based academic discussion, has become an essential skill to learn for undergraduate students who use English as a second language (Harwood & Brett, 2019). Although much of the pedagogic knowledge required to teach CL effectively in face-to-face classrooms can be transferred to teaching online, effective online teaching requires instructors to understand and adapt to the various affordances and constraints of online contexts (Ko & Rossen, 2017). Therefore, this chapter discusses the factors educators should consider when moving a cooperative English for academic purposes (EAP) classroom activity to an online text-based discussion context and outlines the implications these factors have for online course design and pedagogy. The activity discussed in this chapter is an academic reading activity that is part of the curriculum in an academic bridging program at a large urban North American University. First, the literature on cooperative learning (CL) and second language (L2) learning is reviewed. Second, the processes of a cooperative EAP learning activity are explained. Third, the literature related to building online communities and successfully structuring online group activities is reviewed and applied to recommendations for converting the CL activity to an online context.

Cooperative Learning

In 1949 Morton Deutsch wrote, 'A theory of co-operation and competition', in which he developed a detailed theory about the nature CL. Since this time Deutsch's CL theory has been highly influential in education and CL ideas and procedures have been researched and integrated into educational practices in schools, colleges, universities, and workplaces throughout the world. There are five key principals in CL:

1. **Positive interdependence:** Group members are dependent on each other, and each member cannot succeed unless the others succeed and/or that each member's work benefits the others (and vice versa).
2. **Promotive interaction:** Individuals encourage and help each other's efforts to reach the group's goals.
3. **Individual accountability:** All group members are held accountable for doing their share of the work and for mastery of all the material to be learned.
4. **Interpersonal and small-group skills:** Specific skills are needed when learners are learning within a group; students who have not been taught how to work effectively with others cannot be expected to do so must be developed.
5. **Group processing:** The group determines which behaviours should continue or change for maximizing success based upon reflection of how the group has performed so far.

(Adapted from Johnson & Johnson, 2009)

As noted earlier, the reasons for the popularity of CL are numerous. Johnson and Johnson (2002) conclude in their meta-analysis of CL that it can improve achievement, increase interpersonal interaction, self-esteem, and awareness of the perspectives of others as well as the use of higher-level cognitive skills and reasoning. Furthermore, these benefits are consistent across curriculums and student ability ranges (Stevens & Slavin, 1995). As Gillies and Boyle (2011, p.63) explain:

When students work cooperatively, they learn to listen to what others have to say, give, and receive help, share ideas, clarify concerns, and co-construct new understandings. It is this sense of working together that promotes group cohesion and creates the momentum to support each other's learning.

Johnson & Johnson (2009) assert that further benefits of CL include increased respect amongst group members, increased commitment to the group, increased adherence of group norms, and an increase in group members' collective identity. Next, to contextualize the discussion the relationship between language learning pedagogy and cooperative learning is explained.

Language Learning and Cooperative Learning

In the 1980s English language teaching (ELT) professionals began to integrate the social constructivist theories of thinkers such as Vygotsky, Dewey, Brunner, and education theories such as CL into their classroom pedagogy (Oxford, 1997). These theories helped inform the development of the *communicative approach,* an ELT methodology which seeks to capitalize on the collective intelligence of the group and give everyone a chance to interact and learn language from one another to improve their communicative competence (Canale & Swain, 1980). Group activities such as those using CL are implemented in second language (L2) learning contexts because they increase opportunities for peer interaction, facilitate a supportive learning environment, and improve intrinsic motivation (Ning & Hornby, 2014). More recently, CL language learning studies report that implementing CL tasks and pedagogy in ELT classrooms can, increase writing fluency (Pham, 2021); boost students' English oral proficiency (Namaziandost et al., 2020a), and enhance reading proficiency (Namaziandost et al., 2020b).

Because second language learning is situated in social contexts and L2 learners become part of the culture of the community they learn in, it is important to note that the culture of the learning context that CL is introduced into informs pedagogic decision making (Oxford,1997; Nomura & Yuan, 2019). However, integration into different learning cultures is a complex process that requires students to be prepared for CL and that educators be trained in syllabus design that is culturally accommodating (Baker & Clark, 2010; Zou & Yu, 2021). Students need to be trained in the use of interpersonal skills and group processing. Instructors must consider students English ability and scaffold their learning needs to enable students to express themselves in groups in respectful, non-threatening environments. Zou and Yu (2021) report on culture and CL and how cultural differences can affect how group work is perceived. They observe how the dialogic classroom in Western contexts can disadvantage Chinese students more used to individual competitive learning. L2 students require learner training about how CL works and how it can develop essential skills to enable them to study in English university communities. It is for these reasons EAP instructors include CL activities in their classrooms to support their student's development of academic literacy which includes practicing the interpersonal skills needed for group work in higher education contexts (Harwood, 2021).

Computer mediated communication (CMC) and computer assisted language learning (CALL) have been researched extensively. Although CL is implicit in the research the actual focus of much of it has focussed on how tools such as wikis, blogs (see Godwin-Jones, 2008; Lee, 2010; Blackstone & Harwood, 2011) and various software applications can be used to facilitate second language acquisition rather than the CL instruction method itself. In recent years more research has considered the pedagogy as well as the applications used in online CL (Huang, 2019). As Yanling et al. (2011) explain, CL is considered a

Factors to Consider When Moving a Cooperative Academic Literacy Activity Online

powerful instructional tool and motivational strategy in CALL. The research indicates that the benefits of using CL for language learning in offline contexts transfer to the online environment because they provide:

Opportunities to process complex information actively in a low-risk, low-anxiety situation. Social interaction is gradually developed. In this way, language and content learning is learnable and productive. Other benefits of cooperative learning with CALL for students include higher self-esteem and enhanced academic achievement (p.6971).

Moreover, as Blake (2009) reports, cooperative text-based CMC can improve oral and written skills fluency development. Next, the offline CL activity that will be discussed for online teaching and learning is outlined.

Academic Reading Circles (ARC)

ARC is a CL activity inspired by literature circles (see Daniels, 2002; Shelton-Strong, 2012) and developed by Seburn (2016). It is an activity that enables students to begin to read texts closely and critically. The activity is a blend of several CL methods including *Jigsaw* (Aronson, 1978), and *Group Investigation* (Slavin, 1983). An ARC is typically comprised of four or five students who have been given one of five roles, see Table 1. As an integrated learning activity, ARC enables students to practice their critical thinking, reading, writing and oral communication skills. In their different roles the students read and prepare notes about a controversial text for homework and discuss the text in class. For example, the student with the role of *connector* might connect a history text to their personal experience, other historical events or to other lectures they have attended (see Appendix 1 for other role examples). Each week students need to produce supporting information and arguments to support their role's perspectives. Structuring controversial discussions in this way creates a variety of expertise in the group, enabling each group member to maximize their learning (Johnson & Johnson;1994; Johnson & Johnson, 2018). This expertise can be deepened and consolidated by letting the same role members from different groups within the class share their homework learning prior to the discussion.

Table 1. ARC roles and responsibilities

ARC Roles	Responsibilities
Leader	Establishes group agreement on key points and facilitates discussion
Contextualizer	Explains why the author refers to people, dates, places, events, or outside sources of support
Visualizer	Uses graphical interpretations to improve understanding of challenging concepts or language used
Connector	Creates meaningful connections between text concepts and familiar situations
Highlighter	Facilitates lexical comprehension and raises awareness of topical vocabulary

Source: Seburn (2016)

In an ARC, group members are dependent on one another because each must bring critical new perspectives about the text to class to enable a successful discussion to take place. In an ARC, positive interdependence, promotive interaction, and individual accountability are increased and made stronger through assessment. As part of the activity students are required to take notes during the discussion and then produce graded synthesised written extended summaries of the discussion with possible solutions to the issues discussed. In addition, the class instructor checks student homework notes about the text for the activity prior to the discussion.

ARC is a challenging activity for L2 learners and a reoccurring problem for instructors is that some students do not prepare for the activity very thoroughly but still benefit from the discussion because of the work done by the other group members. At present, the way ill prepared students are penalised for this is through their class participation score for the year which is ten percent of their final grade. Interpersonal, small group and "conflict skills" (Johnson & Johnson, 1994, p. 80) such as active listening and polite disagreement are explicitly taught and reviewed prior to the ARC activity. These skills are both practiced by the students and monitored and modelled by the instructor during the discussion.

The group members then reflect on how they performed and interacted during the activity in their learning and verbally determine which behaviours they need to work on to maximize their success. Baker and Clark (2010) conclude, it is essential international students are prepared for CL activities and understand how teamwork is developed. Students need to be provided with explicit rationale for expected behaviour and outcomes as well as understand how their behaviour and outcomes will impact their assessment. At present the students are provided with rationale and expected behaviour and outcomes (see Appendix 1 and 2) but they are not explicitly stated in an assessment rubric.

MOVING COOPERATIVE LEARNING ACTIVITIES ONLINE

The research that informs online CL pedagogy and task design is well established. As with face-to-face learning, it is important that students understand the expectations of the instructor as well as the various processes involved in achieving intended learning outcomes. Therefore, instructors should carefully consider the type of online interactions they want their students to engage in and structure and evaluate learning processes accordingly.

Kreijns et al. (2003; 2014) discuss interaction in computer supported collaborative learning environments, asserting that collaboration does not naturally occur in online groups but must be explicitly structured within the groups. They present three ways of achieving this; through *cognitive*, *direct*, and *conceptual* approaches.

The cognitive approach promotes epistemic fluency, defined as "the ability to identify and use different ways of knowing, to understand the different forms of expression and evaluation, and to take perspectives of others who are operating within a different epistemic framework" (Kreijns et al., 2003, p. 338). This can be achieved by incorporating specific task requirements such as, defining key concepts, describing the context, explaining the process, predicting an outcome, arguing for/against, critiquing the text, evaluating the arguments within the group discourse.

The direct approach encompasses established collaborative techniques such as student achievement divisions (Slavin, 1996), Jigsaw (Aronson, 1978), and structured academic controversy (Johnson & Johnson, 1994), to structure a learning activity, such as writing an essay, designing a brochure, or organizing a class debate.

Factors to Consider When Moving a Cooperative Academic Literacy Activity Online

The conceptual approach is achieved by applying a set of conditions (such as the five key principles of CL) that enforce collaboration. All three approaches are compatible with the five tenets of cooperative learning and can be used in any subject area, for any age group, and can be adapted to the needs of the learning context. However, even with these structures in place, social interaction in a computer supported collaborative learning environment is unlikely to take place. It has been argued that collaborative and cooperative techniques support social interaction in online environments (Nam & Zellner, 2011; Graham & Misanchuk, 2004; Garrison & Arbaugh, 2007). But as Kreijns et al. (2003) assert, there is frequently an assumption that group members know one another, that they are willing to support one another, and that members have already progressed to the stage of a performing group.

There are two further assumptions common among instructors teaching in online environments: (1) instructors often take social interaction for granted and (2) they limit social interaction to cognitive tasks. It is common for instructors to assume that the ease of social interaction in face-to-face environments naturally transfers to an online space. This is simply not the case. Text-based CMC environments lack the amplitude of face-to-face interactions. The capacity for immediate feedback, the number of verbal and non-verbal cues reduces language variety and the personalization of communication (Krejins et al., 2003). There is also the potential for communication apprehension; anxiety experienced in real or anticipated communication encounters is something that is much more prevalent for second language learners (Horowitz et al.,1986). In addition, restricting social interaction to cognitive and educational tasks, neglects the socioemotional elements required for group formation and cohesion. Relationships do not form without an affective structure to facilitate affiliations, impression formation, and interpersonal bonding.

Conceptual Frameworks

Next, to better understand how CL can be optimized in online environments two established online learning conceptual frameworks are considered. Both the Community of Inquiry (COI) model (Garrison et al., 2000) and the framework for Computer Supported Group Based Learning (CSGBL) developed by Strijbos et al. (2004) are transactional or process oriented. The focus of both frameworks is on how interactions support learning. They emphasize the process of learning as opposed to learning outcomes. The COI offers a more global perspective while the CSGBL examines the interactions within the confines of tasks.

The Community of Inquiry Framework

Developed by Garrison et al. (2000) the COI framework recognizes that "effective online learning requires the development of a learning community which supports the meaningful inquiry and deep learning that is the hallmark of higher education" (Richardson et al., 2012, p.99). The framework envisions the online learning experience as an integration of three elements: *social presence, teaching presence*, and *cognitive presence*. Social presence, defined as the "degree to which participants feel connected one to another" (Richardson et al., 2012, p. 99), includes three dimensions: affective expression, open communication, and group cohesion.

Teaching presence is defined as the "design, facilitation, and direction of cognitive and social processes" (Garrison & Arbaugh, 2007, p. 163) and includes, instructional design and organization, facilitating discourse, and direct instruction. Cognitive presence is the extent to which students can construct and confirm meaning through sustained reflection and discourse in a critical community of inquiry (Garrison et al., 2000). Garrison et al. (2001) conceptualize cognitive presence as a four- phase process, the practical inquiry model, which encompasses:

1) triggering event, where some issue or problem is identified for further inquiry; 2) exploration, where students explore the issue, both individually and corporately through critical reflection and discourse; 3) integration, where learners construct meaning from the ideas developed during exploration and 4) resolution, where learners apply the newly gained knowledge to educational contexts or workplace settings" (p. 89).

Social, teaching, and cognitive presence are three interdependent variables. Without social presence it is unlikely that students will engage in the levels of interaction required to progress to a level of critical discourse (Garrison & Arbaugh, 2007). Teaching presence has been determined as a key factor in facilitating the progression to both the integration and resolution stages of the inquiry process and an indicator of the quality of cognitive presence. Seven design principles have been developed to help instructors support the development of both social and cognitive presence in online courses:

1. Design for open communication and trust
2. Design for critical reflection and discourse
3. Create and sustain a sense of community
4. Support purposeful inquiry
5. Ensure that students sustain collaboration
6. Ensure that inquiry moves to resolution
7. Ensure assessment is congruent with intended learning outcomes

(Richardson et al., 2012. p.10)

Research on the COI framework has been extensive; however, Rourke and Kanuka (2009) criticize much of the research for its focus on student perspectives and claim there is scant evidence to indicate that the framework results in deeper learning and higher student achievement. Of over two hundred reports which site the germinal work on COI, only five measure student learning. Many scholars, including Garrison and Arbaugh (2007) themselves, have documented the difficulty of moving students beyond the exploration stage of discourse. In a response to the critique Akyol et al. (2009) emphasize that though the framework is concerned with outcomes it is primarily a process model. The authors argue that low cognitive presence was related to the nature and design of the learning tasks as well as a lack of proper facilitation on the part of the instructors.

Furthermore, Richardson et al. (2012), suggest that the difficulty in establishing higher levels of cognitive presence may in fact be the result of disciplinary differences between hard disciplines which require "a progressive mastery of techniques in a linear sequence based upon factual knowledge" (p.115) and soft disciplines where learning is "more free ranging with knowledge building being a formative process and teaching and learning activities tend to be constructive and reiterative" (p.115). Instructors and designers must be mindful of the kinds of tasks they design if the goal of the task is to achieve high levels of interaction and critical discourse. Instructing students in critical thinking and ensuring that instructors have had the necessary training to scaffold students are also important considerations.

Factors to Consider When Moving a Cooperative Academic Literacy Activity Online

Group-Based Learning

The CSGBL framework focuses specifically on designing online tasks based on the kinds of interactions instructors wish to elicit (Strijbos et al., 2004). It is comprised of five variables: learning objectives, task type, level of pre-structuring, group size, and computer support. Learning objectives, the first variable, exist on a continuum between open and closed skills. Closed skills are relatively stable skills such as procedures for long division or basic concepts and are unlikely to elicit intensive interaction. Open skills are more complex skills such as negotiation or argumentation, with interaction being an essential component. Strijbos et al. (2004) argue that a continuum exists between well-structured and ill structured tasks. They conceive well-structured tasks as tasks that require the application of a set of rules and have only one correct answer. Ill-structured tasks, conversely, rarely have a clear-cut solution. They suggest that well-structured tasks elicit less interaction than ill-structured tasks and propose that there are varying degrees of interdependence implicit in the task impact interaction processes. For example, establishing common ground requires more interaction than reaching a pre-determined solution.

The third variable, the level of pre-structuring, is based on the observation that, collaboration occasionally occurs spontaneously, but often does not. The pre-structuring exists to establish both positive interdependence and individual accountability. However, instructors need to be cognizant that structuring activities can result in forced artificial interaction whereas too little structure might lead to inconsistent interaction or the perception that interaction could be viewed as optional rather than a required (Strijbos et al., 2004). It should be noted that these are general guidelines as there are exceptions. For instance, *structured academic controversy* (Johnson & Johnson, 1994) is a well-structured activity with high levels of pre-structuring that is used for the acquisition of open skills.

The other two variables that have to be considered during the design process are group size and computer support. For the group to be effective instructors should consider that as group size increases, the members must be able to take advantage of the affordance of the diversity of opinions and resources provided by the increased number of participants, while managing the higher demand for coordination and management processes. Computer support relates to how the affordances of the environment must support the kinds of intended interactions. However, as Strijbos et al. (2004) note, the task itself has the most impact on discourse and interactions.

Both the COI and CSGBL frameworks focus on facilitating interaction. The COI framework can be viewed as a more global perspective of all the interactions that take place in the online environment while CSGBL focuses on the tasks themselves and how decisions on task type and structure will influence the type of interactions that take place and how these relate to learning objectives. Both should be considered when shifting ARC to an online environment. Instructional designers need to ask: How are social presence, teaching presence, and cognitive presence supported in the environment? What interactions does the instructor wish to elicit and has she designed the task appropriately to support these kinds of interactions? Higher levels of critical discourse (i.e., cognitive presence), can be supported through the integration of properly structured tasks within an online environment that has integrated key supports to facilitate the development of a learning community.

Cooperative Learning and Online Pedagogy

As with face-to-face CL a key element of online CL is positive interdependence. In their study of online CL, Nam and Zellner (2011) report higher academic achievement for students working in a structured environment that emphasized positive interdependence. The study examined the effects of positive interdependence, group processing, and no interaction structure on Korean undergraduate student's attitudes and achievement in online CL environments. In the study, both instructors and students were coached in either positive interdependence or group processing techniques. The student participants showed increased achievement when working in cooperative online groups that incorporated structures supporting positive interdependence and group processing. Strategies for positive interdependence included using goal, reward, role, and resource dependence while those for group processing included encouraging and introducing, giving, and receiving feedback, and executing and evaluating group processing. Nam and Zellner (2011) argue that structuring positive interdependence addresses the common problem of low student participation in cooperative online learning environments and that fair and regular assessment by both instructors and peers during group processing increases meaningful interaction.

Structuring Learning Activities for Positive Interdependence

Three important aspects for successful computer-mediated group work are structuring the learning activities, facilitating group interactions, and creating the groups. Moreover, critical factors for successfully structuring group learning activities are establishing an appropriate level of interdependence and creating learner accountability. Interdependence is the type of dependence a member of a group has on the other members of the group to accomplish a task. Creating a successful level of interdependence is challenging due to the dichotomous relationship between efficiency and learning. For example, Graham and Misanchuk (2004) found that the groups in their study were able to decide their own level of interdependence which resulted in many groups simply splitting up the task for the sake of efficiency. Therefore, a fine balance must be struck between individual and group accountability as over emphasizing one or the other can lead to a lack of group cohesiveness for the former, and social loafing or free riding for the latter. Graham and Misanchuk (2004) suggest that assessment criteria can have a strong impact on learner accountability and recommend that instructors combine both process and product assessment criteria.

The Development of Cooperative Skills

Group interaction is an essential element in CMC environments to consider as group communication skills and norms in online contexts differ significantly from those in face-to-face environments. Instructors should not assume that group skills from face-to-face environments will simply transfer to online contexts. Students require opportunities to develop cooperative group skills otherwise a group culture can develop in which students are uncomfortable being critical at all. Conversely, as communication in online environments is more time consuming, students may adopt an approach that prioritizes efficiency where little attention is paid to the impact of the written post on other learners (Graham & Misanchuk, 2004).

In face-to-face interactions body language is used to acknowledge ideas, communicate agreement, and display engagement. Consequently, learning how to establish group norms, the shared expectations of how group members should act and interact, is another important online social skill. Although students will be familiar with informal online communication, they will often be new to formal online learning and will not be aware of the inherent differences in the medium compared to face-to-face learning interaction. Therefore, interactional group norms need to be established at the beginning of the CL activity or task. For instance, the mode of communication (e.g., e-mail, discussion boards, or instant messaging), acknowledging others communication so that other group members know that communication has been received and read, and detailing and sharing agreement or disagreement in a courteous and respectful tone. Establishing norms around these kinds of interactions will improve group cohesion in online CL activities. Acquiring these interactive skills will not only facilitate student learning at university but also provide students with workplace communication skills that will be highly beneficial when they graduate and begin their careers (Apte & Bhave-Gudipudi, 2020).

Group Size and Composition

Two of the challenges associated with creating groups are choosing the appropriate group size and determining group composition. Group size is an important factor to consider when thinking about the levels of interaction required by group members as there are several constraints to group work in online environments. These constraints include lengthier communication time, tighter schedules of many students who choose distance learning options, and the challenges of coordinating group members from different time zones. Although there is no optimal group number as the context a group is working in determines the appropriate group size, a balance should be found between the potential for increased interaction within a large group and the increased time required to manage these interactions.

Regarding group composition the main challenge is balancing efficiency with learning. Heterogeneous groups include diverse perspectives and increased conflict which often result in deeper learning (Johnson & Johnson, 1994). Graham & Misanchuk (2004), suggest groups should be heterogeneous whenever possible; however, they advise that instruction in conflict resolution as a necessary component heterogenous groupings. Furthermore, the use of optimal cooperative learning groups in which the instructor considers students' complementary competencies within the groups should also be considered (Liao et al., 2019). This is because, for example, grouping strong English writers who have weak speaking skills with strong English speakers who have weak writing skills can enable students to improve those skills they are stronger at as well as improve their weaker skills.

A misconception about cooperative learning is that it is a method in which students work individually then assemble their work without interacting. Johnson & Johnson, (1999) point out, cooperative learning is not a piecemeal process, "students discuss material with each other, help one another understand it, and encourage each other to work hard" (p.70). Indeed, as Nam and Zellner (2011) demonstrated, a proper understanding and implementation of positive interdependence in online environments results in increased student achievement. An outcome that would not have been possible if students had simply divided up the work.

Pedagogical Implications for ARC Online

Transferring the ARC activity online brings challenges for course designers and educators. These challenges revolve around how to structure the activity online to produce interdependent, positive interaction patterns that enable CL by making group members accountable for themselves and to the group. The asynchronous nature of online discussion threads allows students more time to reflect and compose their written thoughts which can result in highly focused exchanges of complex ideas and topics (Schellens & Valcke, 2005). Therefore, ARC online (ARCO) should span two weeks to provide L2 students with the processing and reflection time to prepare for the activity and to enable educators to scaffold learning from the preparation stage of the activity. This extra time is also beneficial for L2 learners who often require more time to prepare and compose their texts in English (Harwood & Brett, 2019) and it will also help reduce learner anxiety regarding the L2 composition process.

Instructors should be cognizant that the task itself has the most impact on discourse and interactions. Therefore, students should be engaged in a balance of well-structured and ill-structured tasks throughout the duration of the ARCO: Well-structured tasks will help maintain focus on the task, and ill-structured tasks will promote dialogue and interaction. Furthermore, tasks should result in a product e.g., in an online discussion: a summary of how the discussion progressed, what alternative viewpoints emerged and what supplementary sources were shared. Therefore, participation should be required in ARCO, and student assessment tied to explicit criteria intended for the evaluation of students' participation, posts, and interactions (see Appendix 3 for example criteria).

Students Roles in ARCO

ARC already has numerous elements that transfer directly to ARCO. Each student is given a role and is required to take notes about the reading to prepare for the role prior to discussion. Individual accountability can be increased in this important preparation stage of the activity by creating online space in the form of discussion threads for same role members from different groups to review and discuss their text interpretation. Students can be encouraged to create a group in *WhatsApp, LINE, Instagram, Facebook Groups*, or other social media platforms for this purpose. Online space of this kind provides L2 learners with time and space to review and consolidate their understanding of their role prior to the actual online group discussion. It enables peer learning with students outside of the cooperative learning group and reduces learner anxiety by allowing students to share their preliminary interpretations in a low-stakes environment. Allowing same role students to exchange ideas is also likely to positively impact their timeliness of response in the CL group, which is an important factor for student satisfaction in online CL contexts (Parsazadeh & Rezaei, 2018). It also allows the educator to see the process of learning, monitor it, and provide scaffolding and feedback where necessary. As noted earlier, tasks such as academic discussion should be assessed using process-based criterion (see Appendix 3 for an example rubric). Introducing the assessment of the process as well as a product increases individual and group accountability as well as meaningful interaction at each stage of the activity and can reduce incidents of students not preparing for the discussion.

Student Groups in ARCO

To encourage meaningful participation in asynchronous text-based online discussion, good online pedagogy should encourage cooperation among students. As previously stated, discussion groups should be as heterogenous as possible, and comprise of four or five students and be arranged, as far as possible, with a balance of genders and as much first language (L1) diversity (and complementary competencies) as possible. This should be done to promote online interaction in the L2 as students with the same L1 may transfer and translate many of their L1 writing conventions to English when trying to express themselves; a situation that may also cause pragmatic misunderstandings as L2 learners strive to improve their English pragmatic competence in preparation for writing online in North American university contexts. To mitigate misunderstandings regarding reading comprehension of student posts and related pragmatic miscommunication, instructors should provide guidelines regarding how to respond to peers' comments and posts that show clear misunderstanding and miscommunication (Huang, 2019). An effective instructor practice regarding student misunderstanding and miscommunication is for instructors to model the communication they expect of their students in their own online interactions in the ARCO.

The essential CL principle of group processing can be incorporated into the design of the ARCO activity by introducing a weekly online feedback survey that allows the group to determine which behaviours to retain and which to alter. The questionnaire ought to be short, and the results open to all group members. Appendix 4 provides an example of such a survey. Note, the last question can be open with the option to make the information public (with the group) or private (between the student and teacher). Group processing of this kind can help reduce group conflict and provide information to be used in other group processing spaces.

Cultivating Teaching and Social Presence in ARCO

In online CL in academic literacy contexts teaching and social presence have been found to be highly correlated with cognitive presence (Zhang, 2020). Therefore, cultivating teaching and social presence is of utmost importance for online CL instructors. Kreijns et al. (2014) note the importance of nurturing online contexts in which students perceive they can express themselves freely when they interact. The creation of social spaces for students to interact outside of task constraints can support social processes. Educators should therefore consider providing informal learning spaces to enable both on and off topic interaction. Providing informal learning spaces gives learners opportunities to share and socialize in informal online settings. These can take the form of café style chat rooms in formal learning environments such as *Blackboard* and *Moodle*, or class pages on established social media such as *Facebook* or *Instagram*. As Wu et al. (2021) point out, a large majority of all learning is informal; however, it is advisable that instructors require some formal participation within these informal spaces as simply providing them does not guarantee that they will be used. CL principles can be integrated into these informal spaces by, for example, asking groups to share web links and resources related to the topic they are leading in a given week. For instance, a discussion leader in an ARCO may find a useful *TED talk* related to a course reading and share it with their classmates on a class Facebook page. Another benefit of providing informal spaces is that they allow students to appreciate and practice both formal and informal text-based communication, an essential literacy distinction in academia and the modern workplace.

Social and teaching presence can also be facilitated by the instructor modelling appropriate pragmatic behaviour already taught in the course with polite, respectful, encouraging but critical posts and timely feedback. The instructor can also provide access to examples of previous student posts and other online work to guide students understanding and expectations of what is required in an ARCO. These expectations can be included the course rubric. Moreover, learner training regarding how to express opinions in a respectful and non-threatening manner should be provided and modelled by the instructor and these interpersonal skills can be added to the rubric (see Appendix 3). As part of this process, students ought to receive feedback on their interpersonal communication as well as their critical inquiry.

Furthermore, online space can be made available for students in which they can be encouraged to share biographical data and photographs of themselves and talk about their life experiences. Activities such as this can help online learners to see the person behind the text in online conversations and increase social presence throughout online courses. Another way to increase social and teaching presence is the use of video conference group meetings using applications such as *Zoom* or *Skype*. Video conferencing can provide a socially rich dimension to the online experience as it enables students and instructors to see and talk to each other. Therefore, complex group processing issues from the online survey (Appendix 4) can be addressed and teacher presence can be increased to deal with other complex course related issues through using videoconferencing. However, it should be noted that there can be scheduling issues for students in different time zones when synchronous communication of this kind is introduced into the activity.

CONCLUSION

This chapter has explored the criteria required to prepare a face-to-face cooperative activity for online learning. It is clear, online CL activities need to incorporate, positive interdependence, promotive interaction, individual accountability, interpersonal and small group skills, and group processing to be successful. To incorporate the tenets of CL effectively in online contexts, instructors need to carefully consider cognitive, direct, and conceptual approaches in their pedagogical decision making. Depending on the composition of the group and subject studied, instructors should decide how they want to scaffold students' ability to identify and apply forms of knowledge from different epistemic frameworks. In doing so, they should also determine which CL learning task, activity, or technique to employ, be it *student achievement divisions*, *jigsaw*, or *structured academic controversy*. Whichever task is employed, instructors should then ensure that the appropriate conditions for CL are embedded within the task and that the students are engaged in. Then students can be informed of the expectations regarding their participation and how they will be evaluated. Therefore, detailed task instructions with participation rubrics are an essential aspect of instructional online CL design. Not only because they inform student group processing, an important condition of CL, but because they help educators foster social, teaching, and cognitive presence and the development of a strong online learning community.

If instructors implementing ARCO combine these core CL principles with the practical application of the online theory and research discussed in this chapter, ARCO has the potential to be a fruitful online CL activity that can help prepare L2 learners for the online study demands of modern English medium universities. This is because the necessary online CL conditions will have been created in the learning environment. Conditions that have been designed to address the issue of low cognitive presence frequently observed in the research within courses using COI and knowledge building frameworks. Conditions in which students will be more likely to attain higher levels of discourse and inquiry.

REFERENCES

Akyol, Z., Arbaugh, J. B., Cleveland-Innes, M., Garrison, D. R., Ice, P., Richardson, J. C., & Swan, K. (2009). A response to the review of the community of inquiry framework. *Journal of Distance Education*, *23*(2), 123–135. https://files.eric.ed.gov/fulltext/EJ851908.pdf

Apte, M., & Bhave-Gudipudi, A. (2020). Cooperative learning techniques to bridge gaps in academia and corporate. *Procedia Computer Science*, *172*, 289–295. doi:10.1016/j.procs.2020.05.046

Aronson, E. (1978). The jigsaw classroom. *Sage (Atlanta, Ga.)*.

Baker, T., & Clark, J. (2010). Cooperative learning-a double-edged sword: A cooperative learning model for use with diverse student groups. *Intercultural Education*, *21*(3), 257–268. doi:10.1080/14675981003760440

Blackstone, B., & Harwood, C. (2011). Pedagogical blogging for university courses. In R. Jaidev, M. L. C. Sadorra, J. C. Wong, M., C. Lee, & B. Paredes-Lorente (Eds.), *Global perspectives, local initiatives: Reflections and practice in ELT* (pp. 67-82). National University of Singapore. https://nus.edu.sg/celc/research/books/3rdsymposium/067to084-blackstone.pdf

Blake, C. (2009). Potential of text-based internet chats for improving oral fluency in a second language. *Modern Language Journal*, *93*(2), 227–240. doi:10.1111/j.1540-4781.2009.00858.x

Canale, M., & Swain, M. (1980). Theoretical bases of communicative approaches to second language teaching and testing. *Applied Linguistics*, *1*(1), 1–47. doi:10.1093/applin/1.1.1

Daniels, H. (2002). *Literature circles: Voice and choice in book clubs and reading Groups*. Stenhouse.

Deutsch, M. (1949). A theory of co-operation and competition. *Human Relations*, *2*(2), 129–152. doi:10.1177/001872674900200204

Estriegana, R., Medina-Merodio, J.-A., Robina-Ramírez, R., & Barchino, R. (2021). Analysis of cooperative skills development through relational coordination in a gamified online learning environment. *Electronics (Basel)*, *10*(16), 2032. doi:10.3390/electronics10162032

Flener-Lovitt, C., Bailey, K., & Han, R. (2020). Using structured teams to develop social presence in asynchronous chemistry courses. *Journal of Chemical Education*, *97*(9), 2519–2525. doi:10.1021/acs.jchemed.0c00765

Garrison, D. R., Anderson, T., & Archer, W. (2000). Critical inquiry in a text-based environment: Computer conferencing in higher education. *The Internet and Higher Education*, *2*(2-3), 87–105. doi:10.1016/S1096-7516(00)00016-6

Garrison, D. R., Anderson, T., & Archer, W. (2001). Critical thinking, cognitive presence, and computer conferencing in distance education. *American Journal of Distance Education*, *15*(1), 7–23. doi:10.1080/08923640109527071

Garrison, D. R., & Arbaugh, J. B. (2007). Researching the community of inquiry framework: Review, issues, and future directions. *The Internet and Higher Education*, *10*(3), 157–172. doi:10.1016/j.iheduc.2007.04.001

Gillies, R., & Boyle, M. (2011). Teachers' reflections of cooperative learning (CL): A two-year follow-up. *Teaching Education*, *22*(1), 63–78. doi:10.1080/10476210.2010.538045

Godwin-Jones, R. (2008). Emerging technologies: Web-writing 2.0: Enabling, documenting, and assessing writing online. *Language Learning & Technology*, *12*(2), 7–13. https://www.lltjournal.org/item/10125-25195/

Graham, C. R., & Misanchuk, M. (2004). Computer-mediated learning groups: Benefits and challenges to using groupwork in online learning environments. In T. Roberts (Ed.), *Online collaborative learning: Theory and practice* (pp. 181–202). IGI Global. doi:10.4018/978-1-59140-174-2.ch008

Harwood, C. (2021). Active blended learning in an undergraduate english for academic purposes program. In B. C. Padilla Rodriguez & A. Armellini (Eds.), *Cases on Active Blended Learning in Higher Education* (pp. 122–148). IGI Global. doi:10.4018/978-1-7998-7856-8.ch007

Harwood, C., & Brett, C. (2019). Obuchenie online: The applicability of vygotskian pedagogy to online teaching and learning. *Technology, Instruction. Cognition & Learning*, *11*(2/3), 141–161.

Horwitz, E. K., Horwitz, M. B., & Cope, J. (1986). Foreign language classroom anxiety. *Modern Language Journal*, *70*(2), 125–132. doi:10.1111/j.1540-4781.1986.tb05256.x

Huang, K. (2019). Design and investigation of cooperative, scaffolded wiki learning activities in an online graduate-level course. *International Journal of Educational Technology in Higher Education*, *16*(11), 1–18. doi:10.118641239-019-0141-6

Johnson, D., & Johnson, R. (1994). Structuring academic controversy. In S. Sharan (Ed.), *Handbook of cooperative learning methods* (pp. 66–81). Greenwood Press.

Johnson, D., & Johnson, R. (1999). Making cooperative learning work. *Theory into Practice*, *38*(2), 67–73. doi:10.1080/00405849909543834

Johnson, D., & Johnson, R. (2002). Learning together and alone: Overview and meta-analysis. *Asia Pacific Journal of Education*, *22*(1), 95–105. doi:10.1080/0218879020220110

Johnson, D., & Johnson, R. (2009). An educational psychology success story: Social interdependence theory and cooperative learning. *Educational Researcher*, *38*(5), 365–379. doi:10.3102/0013189X09339057

Johnson, D. W., & Johnson, R. T. (2018). Cooperative learning: The foundation for active learning. In S. M. Brito (Ed.), *Active Learning: Beyond the Future*. IntechOpen. doi:10.5772/inMtechopen.81086

Ko, S., & Rossen, S. (2017). *Teaching online: A practical guide*. Routledge. doi:10.4324/9780203427354

Kreijns, K., Kirschner, P. A., & Jochems, W. (2003). Identifying the pitfalls for social interaction in computer-supported collaborative learning environments: A review of the research. *Computers in Human Behavior*, *19*(3), 335–353. doi:10.1016/S0747-5632(02)00057-2

Kreijns, K., Van Acker, F., Vermeulen, M., & Van Buuren, H. (2014). Community of inquiry: Social presence revisited. *E-Learning and Digital Media*, *11*(1), 5–18. doi:10.2304/elea.2014.11.1.5

Lee, L. (2010). Fostering reflective writing and interactive exchange through blogging in an advanced language course. *ReCALL*, *22*(2), 212–227. doi:10.1017/S095834401000008X

Liao, H.-C., Li, Y.-C., & Wang, Y. (2019). Optimal cooperative learning grouping to improve medical university students' English competencies. *SAGE Open*, *9*(3). doi:10.1177/2158244019861454

Nam, C. W., & Zellner, R. D. (2011). The relative effects of positive interdependence and group processing on student achievement and attitude in online cooperative learning. *Computers & Education*, *56*(3), 680–688. doi:10.1016/j.compedu.2010.10.010

Namaziandost, E., Homayouni, M., & Rahmani, P. (2020a). The impact of cooperative learning approach on the development of EFL learners' speaking fluency. *Cogent Arts & Humanities*, *7*(1), 1–13. doi:10.1080/23311983.2020.1780811

Namaziandost, E., Pourhosein Gilakjani, A., & Hidayatullah, H. (2020b). Enhancing pre-intermediate EFL learners' reading comprehension through the use of jigsaw technique. *Cogent Arts & Humanities*, *7*(1), 1–15. doi:10.1080/23311983.2020.1738833

Ning, H., & Hornby, G. (2014). The impact of cooperative learning on tertiary EFL learners' motivation. *Educational Review, 66*(1), 108–124. doi:10.1080/00131911.2013.853169

Nomura, K., & Yuan, R. (2019). Long-term motivations for L2 learning: A biographical study from a situated learning perspective. *Journal of Multilingual and Multicultural Development, 40*(2), 164–178. doi:10.1080/01434632.2018.1497041

Oxford, R. L. (1997). Cooperative learning, collaborative learning, and interaction: Three communicative strands in the language classroom. *Modern Language Journal, 81*(4), 443–456. doi:10.1111/j.1540-4781.1997.tb05510.x

Parsazadeh, N., Ali, R., & Rezaei, M. (2018). A framework for cooperative and interactive mobile learning to improve online information evaluation skills. *Computers & Education, 120*, 75–89. doi:10.1016/j.compedu.2018.01.010

Pham, V. P. H. (2021). The effects of collaborative writing on students' writing fluency: An efficient framework for collaborative writing. *SAGE Open, 11*(1). doi:10.1177/2158244021998363

Rajaram, K. (2021). *Evidence-based teaching for the 21st century classroom and beyond*. Springer. doi:10.1007/978-981-33-6804-0

Richardson, J. C., Arbaugh, J. B., Cleveland-Innes, M., Ice, P., Swan, K. P., & Garrison, D. R. (2012). Using the community of inquiry framework to inform effective instructional design. In L. Moller. & J. Huett (Eds.), The next generation of distance education. Springer. doi:10.1007/978-1-4614-1785-9_7

Rourke, L., & Kanuka, H. (2009). Learning in Communities of Inquiry: A Review of the literature. *Journal of Distance Education, 23*(1), 19–48. https://www.ijede.ca/index.php/jde/article/view/474

Schellens, T., & Valcke, M. (2005). Collaborative learning in asynchronous discussion groups: What about the impact on cognitive processing? *Computers in Human Behavior, 21*(6), 957–975. doi:10.1016/j.chb.2004.02.025

Seburn, T. (2016). *Academic reading circles*. Createspace Independent Publishing Platform.

Shelton-Strong, S. J. (2012). Literature circles in ELT. *ELT Journal, 66*(2), 214–223. doi:10.1093/elt/ccr049

Slavin, R. E. (1983). *Cooperative learning*. Longman.

Slavin, R. E. (1996). Research on cooperative learning and achievement: What we know, what we need to know. *Contemporary Educational Psychology, 21*(1), 43–69. doi:10.1006/ceps.1996.0004

Stevens, R. J., & Slavin, R. E. (1995). Effects of a cooperative learning approach in reading and writing on academically handicapped and nonhandicapped students. *The Elementary School Journal, 95*(3), 241–262. https://www.jstor.org/stable/1001933. doi:10.1086/461801

Strijbos, J. W., Martens, R. L., & Jochems, W. M. G. (2004). Designing for interaction: Six steps to designing computer-supported group-based learning. *Computers & Education, 42*(4), 403–424. doi:10.1016/j.compedu.2003.10.004

Wang, Y. P., & Wu, T. J. (2022). Effects of online cooperative learning on students' problem-solving ability and learning satisfaction. *Frontiers in Psychology, 13*, 817968. doi:10.3389/fpsyg.2022.817968 PMID:35756307

Wu, X., Kou, Z., Oldfield, P., Heath, T., & Borsi, K. (2021). Informal learning spaces in higher education: Student preferences and activities. *Buildings, 11*(6), 252. doi:10.3390/buildings11060252

Yanling, H., Peiwen, H., Shih-Jen, C., & Fu-Hau, H. (2011, September). The perceptions of cooperative learning in computer-assisted language learning environments. In *2011 International Conference on Electrical and Control Engineering* (pp. 6969-6972). IEEE 10.1109/ICECENG.2011.6056758

Zhang, R. (2020). Exploring blended learning experiences through the community of inquiry framework. *Language Learning & Technology, 24*(1), 38–53. 10125/44707

Zou, T. X., & Yu, J. (2021). Intercultural interactions in Chinese classrooms: A multiple-case study. *Studies in Higher Education, 46*(3), 649–662. doi:10.1080/03075079.2019.1647415

APPENDIX 1

Academic Reading Circles Guidelines

Purpose: Reading Circles refers to small groups of students gathered to discuss a text in depth. The purpose of the Reading Circles is to provide a way for students to engage in critical thinking and reading skills as they read, discuss, and respond to a variety of texts. Through structured discussion and written responses, Reading Circles guide students to a deeper understanding of what they read.

Table 2.

Schedule	Reading Topics	Writing Assignment
Week 1	Politics & Preservation	Expository Paragraph
Week 3	I Don't & Prayer in Schools	Argumentative Paragraph
Week 5	Falun Gong & Scientology	Comparison/Contrast Paragraph
Week 7	Islamophobia	Cause/Effect Paragraph
Week 9	TBA	TBA

Procedure: Reading Circles are made up of 4-5 five students each with a different role (please see the Reading Circles roles handout for a detailed description of the individual role responsibilities). Your instructor assigns groups; students perform each role. Though every role is not represented each week, every Reading Circle must have a discussion leader. The instructor also assigns the article to be read. Students are expected to come to class having thoroughly read the article following the duties of their role with printed handouts for each group member. The Reading Circles take approximately 90 minutes to complete in-class, and each has a mandatory writing assignment to complete.

Extended Readings: For each Reading Circle the instructor assigns a text; however, students are also responsible for reading 1-2 articles from an extended reading list. These articles provide different perspectives on the topic under study. Information from these articles should also be used to complete the writing assignments.

Writing Assignments and Reflections: A graded writing assignment is attached to each Reading Circle. These writing assignments give students the opportunity to critically respond to the issues presented in the readings. Instructors will announce the writing topics the day of the in-class Reading Circle and the writing assignment will be due the week after. All drafts and process documents for the writing assignment should be typed and printed by the due date, while final drafts will be posted to Blackboard student blogs. Students must also post a reflection for each writing assignment (see *Portfolio* handout for more information).

Source: Academic bridging program curriculum document

APPENDIX 2

Examples of Academic Reading Circles Roles and Responsibilities

Table 3.

Role	Process
Discussion Leader	**Lead the group in discussion, provide support for each role and coordinate the reports. It is wise for group members to email their preparation to DL before class discussion, so DL is prepared to help.** **Agenda** Create an agenda to give to each member which includes the names of group members, their roles, the order in which members participate in discussion and suggested time limit **Prepared questions** Create three comprehension questions about key elements for understanding (and identify the answers). Create three discussion questions about the ideas in the reading for a lively discussion in class Email all questions to instructor at least two days before class discussion for approval **Devil's Advocate** Independently source an article that presents information differently from the assigned reading (e.g., presents contrasting arguments, written from a different perspective, or from a different source). **Discussion management** Keep group members on task Ensure discussion is conducted in English Assist group members in their individual roles
Visualizer	**Organise or locate related information from the reading graphically in three ways (e.g., chart, timeline, meaningful photo, video clip, art, political cartoon, etc.) to help others understand it in a visual way.** Each graphic must be fully introduced to group in terms of source, why it was chosen and how it specifically relates to the reading content. Create three discussion questions about the visuals and reading content.

Source: Academic bridging program curriculum document

APPENDIX 3

ARCO Rubric Example

The following rubric is for online discussion assessment. Positive interdependence is created using reading roles, (discussion leader, contextualizer, etc), specific to the activity. Promotive interaction, social skills are explicitly taught in the course and are incorporated into criteria of the rubric. Individual accountability is created through individual assessment.

Group processing is made possible by a weekly online survey. Pragmatics will apply to all posts and critical discourse will be examined holistically. The group processing survey results are open to all group members, but the other comments section is private.

Table 4.

Pragmatic competence	Still developing	Developed	Highly developed
	Sometimes	Usually	Consistently
Politely acknowledges and notes author when replying			
Respectful, polite, and inclusive language			
Critical posts are constructive and supportive			
Contribution expectations			
Contributions are spread throughout the week and not last minute			
Contributions are on topic and concise			
Critical discourse: *Contributions combine the following:*			
Post demonstrates full comprehension of reading role			
Makes meaningful references to reading and other resources			
Builds on and connects with others' ideas			
Advances the topic discussion			
Demonstrates critical understanding through articulating multiple perspectives about the topic			
Asks a meaningful question to continue the conversation			

APPENDIX 4

Online Questionnaire for Group Processing

Table 5.

Group Processing	Strongly agree	Agree	Disagree	Strongly disagree
The other group members enhanced my learning				
I am happy with other group members contributions				
I am happy with my contributions				
I am in a supportive group environment				
Additional/Other comments (Private)				

Chapter 21
Exploring Lecturer and Student Readiness on Flexible Learning Pathways Toward SDG4

Rafidah Abd Karim
Universiti Teknologi MARA, Malaysia

Ramlee Mustapha
Sultan Idris Education University, Malaysia

EXECUTIVE SUMMARY

This chapter presents a study about flexible learning pathways towards SDG4 in Malaysian higher education. The purpose of the study was to explore the lecturers' perception on flexible teaching and the students' readiness for flexible learning pathways to achieve the Sustainable Development Goal 4 (SDG4) in Malaysian higher education institutions (HEIs). The study employed a survey method. An online questionnaire was designed and distributed to a total of 167 students and 60 lecturers from selected higher education institutions in Malaysia. Data were analysed using the SPPS version 27, and the findings were presented using descriptive statistics. The study found that the tertiary students were ready for flexible learning pathways. In terms of teaching, the lecturers agreed that they have implemented flexible teaching modes. Based on the empirical findings, several suggestions for future research are presented.

INTRODUCTION

In 2018, the International Institute for Educational Planning (IIEP) -- UNESCO has started the project "SDG4: Planning for flexible learning pathways in higher education." Flexible learning pathways (FLPs) refer to entry and re-entry points for people of all ages and educational levels. It is aimed to enhance the "educability" of an individual. Flexible learning can also be defined as pedagogical practice in which various learning modes, assessment, and certification are implemented. Flexible learning pathways could also include legislative and regulatory frameworks, credit transfer, and lifelong policies (Godonoga & Martin, 2020).

DOI: 10.4018/978-1-6684-6076-4.ch021

In today's complex and fast-changing world, flexible learning by youth and adults needs to be recognised (Yang, 2015). It can be part of life-long learning paradigm in which knowledge, skills and competencies gained through non-formal and informal education are all desirable goals (UNESCO, 2015). Hence, multiple entry points into learning institutions could be necessary to non-conventional students due to study-work intermittence. In the same token, flexible exit strategies from learning institutions could be crucial in assisting students with their transition to the workforce. To create these pathways, HEIs will need to organise their study programmes using innovative strategies that are based on productive collaboration with companies and the industry.

Through the flexible learning pathways, the educational profiles of students can be more effectively tailored to their learning preferences and the demands of the labour market by offering a more varied range of learning options (OECD, 2020). Therefore, higher education institutions and companies must collaborate to design higher education programmes to be more flexible. It will allow students to combine study and employment and it could increase graduates' employment opportunities and provide them more freedom to adapt to various learning styles. A fundamental input for the learning-teaching system is readiness, which is crucial in the education-instruction process (Bloom, 1995). In line with the above, it is crucial to research on the readiness on flexible teaching and flexible learning pathways among lecturers and students in the higher education. To gain an in-depth insight of the topic, the authors highlight research on related definitions and overview of the flexible learning pathways and quality education.

BACKGROUND

Flexible Teaching and Learning in Malaysian Higher Education

According to Taylor (1988) flexible teaching involves an attempt to change how we go about our teaching or how students engage in learning. Flexible learning as discussed by Cybinski & Selvanathan (2005) is an alternative to the traditional face-to-face instructional methods used in higher education. Flexible learning is a collection of educational approaches and philosophies that are concerned with by giving students more personalisation, convenience, and choice tailored to their needs (Shurville et al., 2008). Recently, several trendy flexible learning environments are being practiced in educational institutions such as e-learning, blended learning, flipped learning and mobile learning. Most students now use mobile devices for e-learning in their classrooms because they find the gadgets to be adaptable for learning (Karim et al., 2019). Flexible learning environments provide alternatives to address these issues in several ways, including altering the length of instruction, enabling imaginative learning activities, and providing useful assessments and resources (Naidu, 2017). Descriptions of learning environment characteristics include reduced traditional face-to-face time, flexibility in learning delivery mode, equivalence in learning regardless of delivery mode, design for student-centered and collaborative learning, and application of self-regulation and motivation for learning (Cybinski & Selvanathan, 2005). Lundin (1999) provided the characteristic and principles of open and flexible learning, for example external studies, distance education, distance learning, open learning, flexible delivery, flexible teaching and learning a distributed learning.

Malaysia's higher education system is going through a significant shift after years of development. To produce graduates who are prepared for the future, the curriculum and teaching strategies are being updated to include new essential components like experiential learning, an organic and adaptable curriculum, and a lifetime learning mindset. E-learning as a new learning ecosystem is a growing trend in technology that calls for digital literacy proficiency and offers the possibility of lifelong learning (Valverde-Berrocoso et al., 2020). This ecosystem has been developed in Malaysian higher education through various digital technologies such as mobile devices, immersive learning through virtual reality (VR), augmented reality (AR) and the internet of things (IoTs). To ensure that graduates and upcoming graduates would be employable in the workforce in the Industry 4.0 (IR.4.0) age, the Ministry of Education Malaysia (MOE) has begun to introduce changes to the landscape of the nation's higher education framework. Hence, the tertiary students need to develop the ten Industry 4.0 skillsets such as complex problem solving, critical thinking, creativity, cognitive flexibility and people management, emotional intelligence, judgement and decision making, coordinating with others, service orientation and negotiation. Creativity, critical thinking, communication, and cooperation abilities are among the essential competencies for educating students for the 21st century (Karim & Mustapha, 2020). For example, the TVET students in Malaysia were discovered to have the capability to promote their creativity and design thinking using the digital technology like digital mind map (Karim & Mustapha, 2022).

In response to the pandemic's new normal, higher education institutions in Malaysia have stepped up their efforts to incorporate e-learning methodologies, sometimes called as Open and Distance Learning (ODL) practices which provide access to high-quality education, encourage opportunities for lifelong learning, offer flexible learning methods, and create an atmosphere where learning may take place. Ahmad et al. (2015) revealed several benefits from e-learning such the learning approach seems to be more pleasant, efficient, and straightforward than traditional tutorials. In addition, the e-learning tutorial may be flexible at any time and from anywhere, which can lower the cost of learning. Mohamed (2011) who started the initial study on the e-learning implementation in Malaysia found that 90% of all the higher learning institutions with e-learning policies have also created their own implementation strategies for e-learning by their instructors and students. The optimal way to provide online course materials, engage students, and do evaluations has been discussed by many faculty (Mukhtar et al., 2020). Jaffar et al. (2022) discovered that the majority of students and staffs are at an intermediate level in e-learning skills due to the adaptation of new phenomenon but at the same time the study also found that the majority of students have shown their readiness for the implementation of e-learning. From the findings, it confirmed that there is a good potential for flexible learning to be continued in higher learning institutions.

SDG4- Quality Education in Malaysian Higher Education. Institutions

In today's world, education is important for individuals because it liberates the mind, frees the imagination, and fosters intellectual freedom. It is the secret to wealth and unlocks a world of possibilities, enabling each of us to contribute to a forward-thinking and healthy society. Quality education specifically entails issues such as appropriate skills development, gender parity, provision of relevant school infrastructure, equipment, educational materials and resources, scholarships or teaching force. Having access to education is beneficial to all individuals. In schools and tertiary institutions, it is also essentially important for preparing students for successful, satisfying lives anywhere in the world. Giving students engaging educational opportunities that encourage their interests, problem-solving skills, and higher order thinking abilities, such as creativity and critical thinking are one of the excellent approaches toward quality education. United Nations (2015) conveys the 2030 agenda for 17 sustainable development goals (SDGs). One of the goals is a Sustainable Development Goal 4 (SDG4) which aims to ensure inclusive and equitable quality education and promote lifelong learning opportunities for all. The objective consists of 10 targets covering a wide range of educational topics. In terms of achieving the SDGs, higher education institutions (HEIs) have a crucial role to play. Likewise, a specific emphasis on SDG4 was placed on expanding access to higher education in Malaysia. Pertaining to the agenda, which is to promote lifelong learning, the flexible learning pathways turn into the immediate objective in ensuring quality education specifically in the higher education. For example, in the era of the pandemics, many institutions have flexible teaching and learning which indicated a variety of advantages as well as obstacles and challenges in its implementation. Leal et al. (2019) stated that the foundation of the SDGs is education. The HEIs play an important role in SDG implementation through their experience of learning and teaching, which includes multiple degrees of education levels.

Malaysia offers top notch higher education programmes at private, international institutions of higher education for both undergraduate and graduate levels. Furthermore, the purpose of the Malaysian Education Blueprint 2013–2025 is to assist Malaysia in realising its vision of becoming a nation that provides high-quality education while adhering to global best practices. During that time, Massive Open Online Course (MOOCs) was also being introduced in 2015 as a one of the e-learning approach using technology to increase access to flexible learning and improve the quality education.

Figure 1. The 10 shifts of Malaysian Education Blueprint for higher education. 2013-2025
Source: Ministry of Education (MOE), 2015

In Figure 1, the Malaysian Education Blueprint is illustrated with 10 shifts: (1) holistic: entrepreneurial and balanced graduates, (2) talent excellence, (3) nation of lifelong learners, (4) quality TVET graduates, (5) financial sustainability, (6) empowered governance, (7) innovation ecosystem, (8) global prominence, (9) globalised online learning, and (10) transformed HE delivery. As in figure, the shifts revealed that the shift 3 (nation of lifelong learners) and the shift 9 (globalised online learning) agendas link up with the flexible learning pathways in Malaysian higher education. Thus, the precise strategies are planned to provide equitable, quality education for all have been specified through the shifts. Based on the blueprint, the plan is divided into three waves - Wave 1 (2013-2015): Supporting teachers and focusing on core skills; Wave 2 (2016-2020): Accelerate system improvement; and Wave 3 (2021-2025): Move towards excellence with increased operational flexibility. The Wave 3 also demonstrates that there will be an increase in flexibility approaches to be implemented in Malaysian higher learning institutions in future.

In making sure students are ready for the future, all institutions and colleges need to follow a set of guidelines. Universities in Malaysia are renowned for implementing a more comprehensive approach to academic excellence. The Malaysian Qualifications Agency (MQA) was founded in 2007 implemented the Malaysian Qualifications Framework (MQF) to guarantee that the public and private higher education sectors uphold top-notch standards. The objective of the framework is to ensure that all programmes provided by the Malaysian system continue to be affordable and appealing to both domestic and foreign students. Evidently, the framework designed well for streamlining Malaysia's educational system's quality. Besides, the Accreditation of Prior Experiential Learning (APEL), which has been designed as a road to various levels of credentials set under the MQF, is supported by the MQF. In addition to teaching students about industry best practices, this institution mentors its students to develop stronger social responsibility, leadership, critical thinking, teamwork, problem-solving, entrepreneurialism, values, ethics, and effective communication abilities.

PROBLEM STATEMENT

SDG4 expresses a vision to 'Ensure inclusive and equitable quality education and promote lifelong learning opportunities for all' (UN 2015). While education is most explicitly formulated as a standalone goal (SDG4) in the 2030 Agenda for Sustainable Development, it also has reciprocal links throughout the 2030 Agenda. SDG4 progress has been made, and there are new knowledge horizons and opportunities for strengthened solidarity and partnerships centred on providing quality education and lifelong learning for all. However, the environment is changing because of new technologies and skill demands, as well as economic shocks and environmental degradation. Many barriers to education access and educational outcomes remain, as do challenges to progress monitoring. Education must be included in national development plans and strategies for achieving all the SDGs because it is not only an integral part of, but also a key enabler of, sustainable development.

. Lacking logical connectors, their ideas may be jumping around and they may experience flights of ideas. Furthermore, using pen and paper technique is not too effective in improving the university students' writing skills because the students need some time to produce their ideas. Therefore, students need an advanced technique to create and generate ideas for their writing. Therefore, the purpose of this study was to examine the use of digital mind map to stimulate creativity and critical thinking in students' writing course.

There is a lack of literature and inadequate documentation on flexible learning pathways and its practices in Malaysia. Thus, the purpose and objectives of the study are specified as in the following section.

PURPOSE OF THE STUDY

In this study, the authors aim to explore the lecturers' perception on flexible teaching pathways and students' readiness for flexible learning pathways toward Sustainable Development Goal 4 (SDG4) in Malaysian higher education. The specific objectives of the study are as the following:

1. To identify the lecturers' perception on flexible teaching pathways toward SDG4 in Malaysian higher education.
2. To identify students' readiness for flexible learning pathways toward SDG4 in Malaysian higher education.
3. To determine the relationship between the lecturers' perception on flexible teaching pathways and the quality education
4. To determine the relationship between the students' readiness on flexible learning pathways and the quality education

THE CONCEPTUAL FRAMEWORK

The authors designed two conceptual frameworks for the study to explore the lecturers' perception on flexible teaching pathways and students' readiness on flexible learning pathways toward SDG4 in Malaysian higher education. as in the following section.

Conceptual Framework 1

In Figure 2, the authors demonstrated the first conceptual framework of the study. The framework for flexible teaching pathways for lecturers' perception toward SDG4 in Malaysian higher education. showed the two main variables based on the past research: (i) flexible teaching pathways and (ii) SDG4 quality education. For the independent variable, the flexible teaching pathways was based on Joan (2013) and Rands-Gandsemer–Topf (2017) models. The independent variable was consisted of four elements which are flexible teaching structures, flexible teaching activities and engagement, flexible course design and flexible peer teaching. The quality education (SDG4) was decided as the dependent variable and it was based on UNICEF (2000). Similarly, there were four elements for this conceptual framework: learners, environment, content and learning process. The moderator variables for the framework were gender, age, location, and flexible teaching background.

Conceptual Framework 2

Figure 3 displayed the second conceptual framework of the study for the flexible learning pathways for students' readiness toward SDG4 in Malaysian higher education. The independent variable was flexible learning pathways which was based on UNESCO (2015) research. There were three main elements: (i) flexible entry points (ii) flexible learning structures and (iii) accreditation which were derived from the research. The dependent variable for this framework was quality education (SDG4) which was established from UNICEF (2000). The variable consisted of four elements: learners, environments, content and learning process same as the elements for the conceptual framework 1.

Figure 2. Conceptual framework for lecturers' perception for flexible teaching pathways toward SDG4 in Malaysian higher education

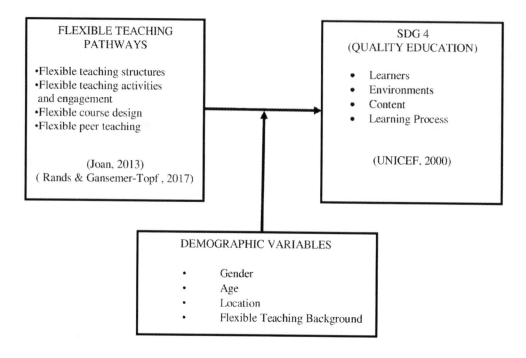

Figure 3. Conceptual Framework for students' readiness for flexible learning pathways toward SDG4 in Malaysian higher education

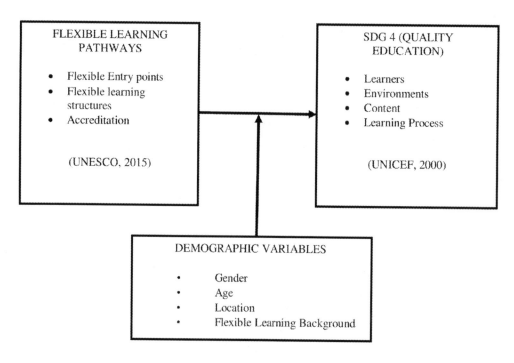

METHODOLOGY

A survey research design was employed for the study. To answer the research objectives of the study, the researchers conducted an online survey for two main groups of participants. The groups involved in the study were the lecturers and the students in Malaysian higher education. The first objective was conducted for lecturers to identify the lecturers' perception on flexible teaching pathways toward quality education in Malaysian higher education. In this study, the researchers also think it is necessary to study find out about the students' readiness for flexible learning pathways toward quality education in Malaysian higher education as revealed in the second objective.

Participants

Lecturers

For the first group, the lecturers from various public and private higher learning institutions in Malaysia were involved in the study. There were about 40 lecturers from the higher learning institutions who responded to the online questionnaire.

Students

The students were the second group involved in this study. The participants involved were 171 male and female students from various public higher learning institutions in Malaysia. The participants were the tertiary students who came from various course of programmes from several institutions in Malaysia. Their ages mostly ranged from 17-19 years old.

Sampling

The number of respondents was randomly selected based on sample size table formula of Krejcie and Morgan (1970). A random sample of 40 lecturers and 171 students from public higher learning institutions in Malaysia were selected from the overall population.

Instrument

The quantitative data of the study was collected by the online questionnaire. Two online questionnaires were designed differently for the two groups which were lecturers and students. The questionnaire items for lecturers' group were adapted from Joan (2013), Rands- Gandsemer – Topf (2017) and UNICEF (2000) research. The questionnaire items included flexible teaching structures, flexible teaching activities and engagement, flexible course design, flexible peer teaching for flexible teaching pathways elements whereas for quality education (SDG4) elements were learners, environments, content and learning process. The items were designed for the purpose of identifying their readiness on flexible teaching pathways toward quality education in Malaysian higher education. The online questionnaire which had 63 items consisted of four parts: (A) Lecturer profile (6 items), (B) Flexible teaching pathways (24 items), (C) Quality education (30 items) and (D) Open-ended (3 items). The participants also answered three open-ended items in the questionnaire. In this section, they needed to give reasons why they like flexible teaching, list the barriers that suppress flexible teaching pathways in their institution and state the suggestions to improve the quality education in their institution.

For the students' online questionnaire, the questionnaire was designed from UNESCO (2015) and UNICEF (2000) research. The items included in the questionnaire were based on the four elements: flexible entry points, flexible learning structures, accreditation. Quality education (SDG4) elements consisted of learners, environments, content and learning process. 56 items of the questionnaire were divided into four parts: (A) Student profile (7 items), (B) Flexible learning pathways (15 items), (C) Quality education (31 items) and (D) Open-ended (3 items). The open-ended items included three items that asked the students to answer in the final part. The first question asked the students about why they like flexible learning. Next, the students were also needed to list what challenges that restrain the flexible learning pathways in their institution. Finally, they requested to suggest how to improve the quality education in their institution. The items for both questionnaires were measured by using 5-point Likert scale: strongly agree (5), agree (4), uncertain (3), disagree (2) and strongly disagree (1).

Data Analysis

After the data collection process was completed, data was analysed using the SPSS software version 27. The open-ended items for both groups were analysed using thematic analysis method (Miles & Huberman,1994). The online questionnaire was developed and validated by three experts in the field. The reliability of the instrument for lecturers' group was established by using Cronbach Alpha coefficient, $\alpha = 0.98$ whereas the results of Cronbach Alpha coefficient, $\alpha = 0.97$ for students' group.

RESULTS AND DISCUSSION

In the results and discussion part, the findings of the study were presented into four main sections of items analysed for this study: (1) profile (2) lecturers' perception on flexible teaching pathways and (3) students' readiness on flexible learning pathways and (4) open-ended items. First, the profile analysis was presented for each section followed by these two data analyses. Findings for the items for these two sections were interpreted into the mean values and the results were divided into sections: Strongly agree (4.21-5.00), Agree (3.41-4.20), Uncertain (2.61-3.40), Disagree (1.81-2.60) and Strongly disagree (1.00-1.80). Next, the results were described based on the three highest means and the three lowest means of the items. For open-ended items results, the items were analysed and ranked using the thematic analysis.

Lecturers' Perception on Flexible Teaching Pathways

Table 1 shows lecturer profile for the lecturers' data analysis for exploring lecturers' perception on flexible teaching pathways. Based on gender, male respondents showed a higher percentage (52.4%) than female respondents (47.6%). Majority of respondents (42.9%) came from the age group of 50 years and above, followed by the age group of 40-50 years which was 31%. The respondents were involved in the study in age group of 30-40 years was 23.8%. Only 2.4% of the respondents involved were in the age group of 20-30 years. In terms of location, most of the respondents (52.4%) live in the city. The table showed the respondents mostly live in suburban as the second highest percentage (38.1%), followed by the lowest percentage 9.5% for rural area. The respondents were asked whether they know about the term of flexible teaching. Most of respondents (100%) said they know about this term. Similarly, they also said they know about flexible learning and quality education which the percentage showed 100% from the table. This result showed that the lecturers are well-informed with the flexible teaching and learning environment.

Table 1. Lecturer profile (n = 42)

Characteristics	Frequency	%
Gender		
Female	20	47.6
Male	22	52.4
Age (years)		
20-30 years	1	2.4
30-40 years	10	23.8
40-50 years	13	31.0
50 years and above	18	42.9
Location		
City	22	52.4
Rural	4	9.5
Suburban	16	38.1
Do you know what is flexible teaching?		
Yes	42	100
No	0	0
Do you know what is flexible learning?		
Yes	42	100
No	0	0
Do you know what is quality education?		
Yes	42	100
No	0	0

Regarding the lowest mean data, the respondents agreed (M=3.80, SD=0.72) that they know how to design varied learning activities for flexible course teaching in flexible course design aspect (item 5). Based on the same aspect, the respondents also agreed (M=3.85, S.D=0.85) that they know how to design the course for a hybrid environment in item 3. In terms of flexible teaching structures, the respondents also agreed (M=3.83, S.D=0.80) that they plan their flexible teaching activities which suits their students' interest and enthusiasm.

To fulfill the first objective, Table 2 described the lecturers' perception on flexible teaching pathways. With regards to flexible course design aspect, the first highest mean was for item 1 which showed that the respondents were strongly agreed (M=4.39, SD=0.63) that they prefer to teach students using the flexible mode of teaching. Next, majority of respondents largely agreed (M=4.22, S.D=0.73) that they integrate digital technology to engage students in learning activities (item 16) for flexible teaching activities. This result was in line with Anderton et al. (2021) who claimed that online teaching has improved student learning and engagement as well as how best to use technology. In item 6, the respondents mostly believed (M=4.20, S.D=0.72) that the flexible course design will enhance student-centered multi modal learning experience.

Table 2. Lecturers' perception on flexible teaching pathways

No	Item	Mean	S.D	Interpretation
Flexible Course Design				
1.	I prefer to teach students using the flexible mode of teaching	4.39	0.63	Strongly agree
2.	I manage my time designing the flexible course design	4.07	0.85	Agree
3.	I know how to design the course for a hybrid environment	3.85	0.85	Agree
4.	I accommodate the students' needs, interest and ability to suit my flexible teaching mode	4.05	0.71	Agree
5.	I know how to design varied learning activities for flexible course teaching	3.80	0.72	Agree
6.	I believe flexible course design will enhance student-centered multi-modal learning experience.	4.20	0.72	Agree
Flexible Teaching Structures				
7.	I plan my teaching activities according to my students' interest and enthusiasm through flexible teaching	3.83	0.80	Agree
8.	My flexible teaching structures allow lessons to have a much flexible structure	3.93	0.69	Agree
9.	I design flexible teaching environment for my students	3.93	0.76	Agree
10.	I accommodate my students' curiosity into meaning in my class	3.90	0.77	Agree
11.	I prefer flexible teaching over one fixed method of teaching	4.17	0.80	Agree
12.	I believe flexible teaching can increase student participation and engagement	4.15	0.73	Agree
Flexible Teaching Activities and Engagement				
13.	I believe flexible teaching activities and engagement are important structures for creating flexible classrooms	4.17	0.63	Agree
14.	I design flexible teaching activities and engagement to suit my students' needs	3.88	0.71	Agree
15.	I modify teaching activities to demonstrate the flexibility in the classroom	3.95	0.74	Agree
16.	I integrate digital technology to engage students in learning activities	4.22	0.73	Strongly agree
17.	I believe engagement through active and flexible teaching enhance students' achievement in my class	4.15	0.70	Agree
18.	I believe by using flexible lecturer's approach, the students' participation and engagement will increase	4.15	0.73	Agree
Flexible Peer Teaching				
19.	I prefer flexible peer teaching method	4.07	0.65	Agree
20.	My flexible peer teaching is suited to my students' needs and interests	4.00	0.60	Agree
21.	I encourage students to give and receive feedback and evaluate each other's learning for flexible peer teaching	3.98	0.61	Agree
22.	I believe flexible peer teaching enhances students' engagement and independence skills	4.15	0.62	Agree
23.	I believe flexible peer teaching promotes critical thinking and problem-solving based learning.	4.17	0.63	Agree
24.	I believe flexible peer teaching establishes an environment where students can learn in small groups and learn how to work as a team	4.15	0.63	Agree
Total		4.05	0.48	Agree

Exploring Lecturer and Student Readiness on Flexible Learning Pathways Toward SDG4

Results for lecturers' perceptions on quality education were as shown in Table 3. The highest means were depicted in content aspect. The respondents were strongly believed (M=4.56, S.D=0.63) that the appropriate teaching content is important to achieve quality education (item 38) followed by item 40 which showed the respondents also strongly believed (M=4.46, S.D=0.71) that the quality contents will help the students to succeed in the future life. Concerning the teaching process, the respondents were strongly agreed (M=4.45, S.D=0.71) that that the quality teaching helps their students to succeed in life (item 43).

Table 3. Lecturers' perceptions on quality education

No	Item	Mean	S.D	Interpretation
Learners				
31.	I believe the lecturers in my learning institutions are focusing on student-centered approach	4.12	0.72	Agree
26.	The curricular in my institution have focused on student-centered pedagogy	4.12	0.64	Agree
27.	My students' program has included various aspects of spiritual, social, emotional, mental, physical, cognitive development and co-curricular activities	4.05	0.71	Agree
28.	I am expert and knowledgeable of my subject-matter for quality education	4.10	0.77	Agree
29.	I have used quality learning philosophy to enhance my students' understanding of education	4.10	0.70	Agree
30.	I engage students in rigorous, meaningful activities that foster quality learning for all students	4.05	0.77	Agree
Environment				
31.	I am well-trained in pedagogy to ensure conducive learning environment for my students	3.93	0.85	Agree
32.	I apply green environment philosophy into my teaching	3.68	0.85	Agree
33.	I ensure safe learning environment in my classes	4.20	0.68	Agree
34.	My institution makes it compulsory to design pleasant learning environment	3.93	0.82	Agree
35.	I believe I have a supportive teaching environment in my institution	3.95	0.77	Agree
36.	I believe making conducive learning environment is a must in my institution	4.12	0.71	Agree
37.	I believe the teaching environment influences my teaching performance	4.24	0.73	Agree
Content				
38.	I believe appropriate teaching content is important for quality education	4.56	0.63	Strongly agree
39.	I believe my teaching materials are based on the educational goals	4.34	0.73	Strongly agree
40.	I believe the quality contents will help the students to succeed in the future life	4.46	0.71	Strongly agree
41.	I believe my teaching contents of classes are a good quality	4.22	0.73	Strongly agree
42.	I design teaching materials to suit my students' learning needs	4.22	0.73	Strongly agree
Teaching Process				
43.	I believe quality teaching helps my students to succeed in life	4.45	0.71	Strongly agree
44.	I always look for ways to integrate independent, critical, and creative thinking in my classroom	4.43	0.73	Strongly agree

continues on following page

Table 3. Continued

No	Item	Mean	S.D	Interpretation
45.	I always find new materials to enhance the quality of my teaching	4.17	0.80	Agree
46.	I often give feedback for my students' work and assessments to enhance the quality of teaching	4.41	0.70	Strongly agree
47.	I work hard to facilitate my students' learning	4.20	0.72	Agree
48.	My institution has a good lifelong learning programme to promote quality education	4.20	0.84	Agree
Outcomes				
49.	I believe quality education will produce quality graduates	4.34	0.69	Strongly agree
50.	I teach students to think critically	4.34	0.73	Strongly agree
51.	I teach students to be creative	4.32	0.72	Strongly agree
52.	I teach students to maintain sustainability like use green skills and technology	3.90	0.86	Agree
53.	I teach students the proper attitude to deal with people and situations	4.34	0.76	Strongly agree
54.	I believe proper learning outcomes is important to achieve quality education	4.44	0.67	Strongly agree
	Total	4.20	0.53	Agree

Based on Table 3, the lowest mean data mostly showed in the environment aspect. First, the respondents agreed (M=3.68, S.D=0.85) that they apply green environment philosophy into their teaching (item 32). Next, the respondents agreed (M=3.93, S.D= 0.85) that they are well-trained in pedagogy to ensure conducive learning environment for their students (item 31). Likewise, the respondents also said (M=3.93, S.D=0.82) that the institution makes it compulsory to design a pleasant learning environment (item 34). Finally, the respondents were also just agreed (M=3.90, S.D=0.86) that they teach students to maintain sustainability like green skills and technology in terms of teaching process aspect (item 52).

To examine the relationship between the lecturers' perception on flexible teaching pathways and their perceptions on quality education, the results were as shown in Table 4 and Table 5. Table 4 showed the overall mean for both constructs. The overall mean for flexible teaching pathways was (M=4.05, S.D = 0.48) whereas for the overall mean for quality education was (M= 4.20, S.D =0.53).

Table 4. Mean and standard deviations for constructs

Construct	Mean	Standard Deviation
Flexible Teaching Pathways	4.05	0.48
Quality Education	4.20	0.53

Table 5 illustrated the correlation of each construct between the flexible teaching pathways and the quality education. The findings showed that there was a strong positive relationship (r= 0.78, p<0.05) between the flexible teaching pathways and the quality education constructs. The positive relationship demonstrates that the lecturers' perceptions on flexible teaching pathways will contribute toward the quality education (SDG4).

Table 5. Flexible teaching pathways and quality education relationship toward SDG4

Variable	Quality Education	Significance
	r	p-value
Flexible Teaching Pathways	0.78	0.00

Table 6 described the final part of the questionnaire which is the open-ended items analysis (Part D). There were three items constructed for exploring lecturers' perception on flexible teaching pathways. Item A asked the lecturers the main reasons they like flexible teaching. Three themes emerged from the item were flexible time, enhance teaching strategies and independent teaching. The highest rank for the theme emerged from this item was the flexible time. Naidu (2017) in his study stated that flexible teaching may involve decisions for the instructors regarding how they spend their time, how they communicate with students, and how they interact with the educational setting.

Most of respondents said that the flexible teaching has provided them with flexible time to teach the students. The respondents also said that the flexible teaching can enhance their teaching strategies in terms of using digital technology makes the teaching more creative and innovative. Moreover, the final theme was about independent teaching. The respondents believed that the flexible teaching makes them more independent in practice teaching outside of the traditional walls of universities.

Table 6. Open-ended items analysis

Item	Rank	Main Theme	Frequency (f)
A. List 3 main reasons that I like flexible teaching	1	Flexible time	27
	2	Varied teaching strategies	14
	3	Independent teaching	6
B. List 3 barriers that suppress flexible teaching pathways in my institution	1	Technological barriers	17
	2	Lack of internet access	16
	3	Lack of knowledge and training	8
C. List 3 main suggestions to improve the quality education in my institution	1	Upgrade Internet access	14
	2	Improve technological infrastructure	13
	3	Provide more trainings	7

The second item (item B) required the respondents to list three barriers that suppress flexible teaching pathways in their institution. The first theme emerged was the technological barriers. Most of the respondents believed that technological barriers acts as a challenge towards adopting flexible teaching pathways in the institution. Another factor was lack of internet access in the most of institutions that impede the process of flexible teaching. The respondents also identified that they need more knowledge and trainings especially on information and communications technology trainings to apply flexible teaching in the universities. Finally, the respondents also were asked to give suggestions on how to improve the quality education. Most of respondents answered the internet access should be improved for quality education in the institutions. Besides, the institutions also need to improve the technological infrastructure for achieving quality education. In addition, additional training can be provided to lecturers to enhance the quality of education in higher education.

Students' Readiness on Flexible Learning Pathways

Student Profile

The online survey was also conducted for the students for exploring their readiness on flexible learning pathways. The sample size *(n =171)* was used for the study. Table 7 shows the student profile analysis which are gender, age location, flexible learning and quality education. From the analysis, there were 58.5% female respondents and 41.5% male respondents who answered the questionnaire. There were four age groups of students who involved in the study. Most of the respondents (42.1%) were in the 17-19 years, followed by 20-22 years of age group which was 32.2%. There were 20.5% of respondents from 23-25 years whereas only 5.3% respondents were from 26 years and above. Regarding the location where the respondents stayed showed that the majority of respondents (56.1%) came from a city. 23.4% of the respondents came from suburban area whereas only 20.5% of the respondents lived in rural area. The study also needed to find about the students' background knowledge on flexible learning and quality education Most of respondents (93%) said that they know what the flexible learning is. However, only a few of respondents (15.2%) did not know about the flexible learning. Likewise, many respondents said that they know what the quality education is whereas only 7% responded 'No' for this item.

Table 7. Student profile (n =171)

Characteristics	Frequency	%
Gender		
Female	100	58.5
Male	71	41.5
Age (years)		
17-19 years	72	42.1
20-22 years	55	32.2
23- 25 years	35	20.5
26 years and above	9	5.3
Location		
City	96	56.1
Rural	35	20.5
Suburban	40	23.4
Do you know what is flexible learning?		
Yes	145	84.8
No	26	15.2
Do you know what is quality education?		
Yes	159	93.0
No	12	7.0

To answer the second objective of the study which was to identify students' readiness for flexible learning pathways toward quality education in Malaysian higher education.higher education.. Thus, the researchers presented the data analysis of items into two tables: Table 7 for students' readiness on flexible learning pathways and Table 8 for quality education.

Table 8 indicates the items about the students' readiness on flexible learning pathways. The items were divided into three main components: (i) Flexible entry points (ii) Flexible learning structures and (iii) Accreditation. In terms of the flexible learning aspect, the highest mean (M=4.46, SD=0.64) showed that most of the respondents strongly agreed that they prefer flexible learning because it is not limited by time, place, and pace of study (item 11). In a study conducted by Soffer et al., (2019), the different pattern of learning time, place, and content access among students show that flexibility was heavily utilized. Similarly, they also strongly agreed (M=4.45, SD=0.70) that the teaching and learning process was more pleasant and it gave them more freedom in their learning process as stated in Item 9. For flexible entry points, the third highest means showed (M=4.32, SD=0.70) that the respondents strongly believed that the entry points and re-entry points at all educational levels are important for flexible learning pathways (item 3).

Table 8. Students' readiness on flexible learning pathways

No	Item	Mean	S.D	Interpretation
Flexible Entry Points				
1.	Flexible entry points for higher education admission should be implemented for flexible learning pathways	4.29	0.66	Strongly agree
2.	I think that entry points and re-entry points should depend on the students' readiness	4.21	0.72	Strongly agree
3.	I think that entry points and re-entry points at all educational levels are important for flexible learning pathways	4.32	0.70	Strongly agree
4.	I found that flexible entry points can create opportunities for flexible learning pathways	4.29	0.65	Strongly agree
5.	Flexibility in learning may include choices in relation to entry and exit points	4.20	0.63	Agree
6.	Working adults will have more opportunities to be admitted for furthering study at higher education with flexible entry points	4.15	0.81	Agree
Flexible Learning Structures				
7.	I can plan my learning activities according to my interest and enthusiasm through flexible learning	4.27	0.67	Strongly agree
8.	I prefer the method of flexible learning environment	4.25	0.72	Strongly agree
9.	I prefer learning with freedom and pleasant through flexible learning	4.45	0.70	Strongly agree
10.	I prefer learning using hybrid mode because it reflects flexible learning method	4.16	0.86	Agree
11.	I prefer flexible learning because it is not limited by time, place, and pace of study	4.46	0.64	Strongly agree
Accreditation				
12.	I believe flexible learning modes are required to be implemented by educational institutions to be accredited by accreditation agency	4.27	0.69	Strongly agree
13.	I believe the accreditation should be awarded for courses that allow individuals to learning in flexible ways	4.29	0.65	Strongly agree
14.	I believe flexible learning should be measured by the flexible assessment	4.22	0.69	Strongly agree
15.	I believe flexible learning outcomes is required for accreditation	4.24	0.70	Strongly agree
	Total	4.27	0.47	Strongly agree

The three lowest means for this component were displayed in item 5, item 6, and item 10. The lowest mean (M=4.15, SD=0.81) in item 6 illustrated that the students believed that the flexible entry points will be able to help the adult learners to further their study at the tertiary institutions. Regarding the hybrid learning mode, the respondents prefer to apply a hybrid mode because it reflects flexible learning method (item 10). The results of the item showed the mean (M=4.16, S.D=0.86). In item 5, the respondents also agreed (M=4.20, SD=0.63) that the flexibility in learning may include choices in relation to entry and exit points. In general, the findings revealed that the students at higher learning institutions in Malaysia are strongly agreed with the application of the flexible learning pathways and they have a positive perception on this learning approach.

Based on Table 9, the results illustrate the respondents' perceptions on quality education. The items analysis was divided into five main components: (i) Learners, (ii) Environment, (iii)Content, (iv) Learning process and (v) Outcomes. Concerning the outcome component, the highest mean (M=4.53, S.D=0.59) in item 41 showed that the majority of the respondents believed that quality graduates will be produced through quality education. The respondents also considered the content component is an important factor for the quality education. Thus, they strongly agreed that (M=4.51, S. D=0.59) that appropriate learning content is important for quality education (item 29). With regards to learning process, item 35 revealed that the respondents believed (M=4.49, S. D=0.62) that they can succeed in life if they have a quality learning.

Table 9. Students' perceptions on quality education

No	Item	Mean	S.D	Interpretation
Learners				
16.	I believe the lecturers in my learning institutions had focused on student-centered approach	4.24	0.67	Strongly agree
17.	The curricular in my institution have focused on student-centered pedagogy	4.05	0.75	Agree
18.	My program has included various aspects of spiritual, social, emotional, mental, physical, cognitive development and co-curricular.	4.22	0.74	Strongly agree
19.	I interact with my friends and lecturers effectively for quality education	4.29	0.69	Strongly agree
20.	My lecturers provided me with quality materials as learning resources.	4.34	0.70	Strongly agree
21.	I am active participant in my learning and less dependent on my lecturer	4.00	0.79	Agree
Environment				
22.	I believe my lecturers were well-trained to conduct the classes	4.46	0.70	Strongly agree
23.	I believe my lecturers well-managed the classroom for conducting students' learning	4.35	0.71	Strongly agree
24.	I have safe learning environments in my institution	4.40	0.65	Strongly agree
25.	I am motivated to learn because my institution has a pleasant learning environment	4.22	0.74	Strongly agree
26.	I believe I have a supportive learning environment in my institution	4.34	0.74	Strongly agree
27.	I have a conducive learning environment in my institution	4.29	0.68	Strongly agree
28.	I believe the learning environment influences my learning performance	4.40	0.67	Strongly agree

continues on following page

Table 9. Continued

No	Item	Mean	S.D	Interpretation
Content				
29.	I believe appropriate learning content is important for quality education	4.51	0.59	Strongly agree
30.	I believe my learning materials are based on the educational goals	4.34	0.65	Strongly agree
31.	I believe the quality contents will help the students to succeed in the future life	4.44	0.62	Strongly agree
32.	The learning contents of my programme are of good quality	4.33	0.65	Strongly agree
33.	The learning materials in my programme suited my learning needs	4.32	0.64	Strongly agree
34.	I have quality lecturers in my programme	4.48	0.65	Strongly agree
Learning Process				
35.	I believe quality learning helps me to succeed in life	4.49	0.62	Strongly agree
36.	My prior knowledge is helpful to succeed to my present programme	4.36	0.68	Strongly agree
37.	The materials presented by lecturers are good quality	4.34	0.68	Strongly agree
38.	I obtained feedback from lecturers when I sent my assignments	4.11	0.78	Agree
39.	My lecturers are well-trained, and they facilitate my learning	4.35	0.68	Strongly agree
40.	My institution has a good lifelong learning programme	4.40	0.67	Strongly agree
Outcomes				
41.	I believe quality education will produce quality graduates	4.53	0.59	Strongly agree
42.	My lecturers have taught me to think critically	4.27	0.71	Strongly agree
43.	My lecturers have taught me to be creative	4.31	0.73	Strongly agree
44.	My lecturers have taught me to maintain sustainability like use green skills and technology	4.22	0.76	Strongly agree
45.	My lecturers have taught me the proper attitude to deal with people and situations	4.33	0.69	Strongly agree
46.	I believe proper learning outcomes is important to achieve quality education	4.47	0.62	Strongly agree
Total		4.33	0.47	Strongly agree

The findings in the table reveal three items with the lowest means for the quality education. With regards to learners' aspect, the lowest mean (M=4.00, S. D=0.79) showed that the respondents agreed that they are an active participant in their classes, and they are not very dependent on their lecturer (item 21). Likewise, they agreed (M= 4.05, S.D=0.75) that the curricular in their institution have focused on student-centered pedagogy. In terms of the learning process, the respondents agreed (M=4.11, S.D=0.78) that they received feedback from their lecturers when they sent the assignments. Thus, the findings concluded that most of the respondents perceived the learners, environment, content, learning process and outcomes components shaped the quality education for the students.

Table 10 and Table 11 showed the findings for the final research objective. Table 10 showed the overall mean and standard deviation for the flexible learning pathways was (M=4.27, S. D=0.47) whereas the overall mean and standard deviation for quality education was (M=4.33, S.D=0.47).

Table 10. Mean and standard deviations for variables

Construct	Mean	Standard Deviation
Flexible Learning Pathways	4.27	0.47
Quality Education	4.33	0.47

Table 11. Flexible learning pathways and quality education relationship toward SDG4

Variable	Quality Education	Significance
	r	p-value
Flexible Learning Pathways	0.71	0.00

In Table 11, the findings showed that there was a strong positive relationship (r=0.71; p <0.05) between the flexible learning pathways and the quality education constructs. The positive relationship demonstrates that the students' readiness on flexible learning pathways will contribute toward the quality education (SDG4).

For open-ended items, the respondents were asked to answer three questions in the final part (Part D). Table 12 showed the items analysis for students' readiness on flexible learning pathways. Data was gathered and analysed using thematic analysis. From the items analysis, the themes emerged were ranked from one to three based on the highest to the lowest frequency. The first open-ended item (Item A) asked the respondents to list three main reasons why they like flexible learning. The highest rank for the first item based on the theme emerged was they like flexible learning due to flexible time and place followed by the second theme emerged was reduce stress. The students agreed that the flexible learning can reduce their stress compared to face-to-face learning style. This concurs with a study done Cremer et al (2021) who found that during flexible learning, stress lowers both model-based and model-free brain computations during flexible learning (Cremer et al., 2021). Another reason they believed that the flexible learning offers an experiential learning because they mostly use the digital technology for their learning, and they also experience how to learn independently.

Table 12. Open-ended items analysis for students' readiness on flexible learning pathways

Items	Rank	Main Themes	Frequency (f)
A. List 3 main reasons that I like flexible learning	1	Flexible time and place	118
	2	Reduction of stress	38
	3	Experiential learning	29
B. List 3 barriers that suppress flexible learning pathways in my institution	1	Lack of social interaction	31
	2	Lack of Internet access	30
	3	Lack of motivation	22
C. List 3 main suggestions to improve the quality education in my institution	1	Innovative teaching methods	53
	2	Upgrading facilities and infrastructures	51
	3	Qualified and well-trained lecturers	13

The next item (Item B) asked the respondents to list three barriers that suppress flexible learning pathways. There were three themes emerged from the items analysis which are lack of social interaction, internet problem and lack of motivation. The students mostly agreed that lack of social interaction was the highest obstacle for flexible learning pathways because this learning approach use the virtual platform as the learning environment which they were not be able to meet their friends and lecturers physically. Next, the students also agreed that the internet connectivity problems can impede flexible learning pathways. They also believed that the flexible learning may reduce their motivation for learning.

Finally, the respondents also were asked to give their suggestions on how to improve the quality of education in their institution. The results of open-ended item revealed that the highest rank for the theme emerged for Item C was the innovative teaching methods. They agreed that the effective teaching methods using the modern technologies are required to enhance the quality education in the institution. Moreover, the institution also needs to improve facilities and infrastructures in the institution to ensure the quality education for the students. For the final theme, the students suggested that they must have qualified and well-trained lecturers for assisting them to achieve good grades and success in their studies. Thus, it will help to improve the quality education in their institutions.

FUTURE RESEARCH DIRECTIONS

This chapter posits the findings of an empirical study on flexible learning pathways of lecturers and students in Malaysia. The study provides a modest contribution to an understanding of the issue of flexible learning pathways toward SDG4 in Malaysian higher education. The empirical data from the study can be used for future higher education policymakers specifically for directing the flexible learning pathways in Malaysian higher education.higher education. and other countries. Furthermore, the discussions on the quality education perceived by lecturers' and students in higher education were highlighted in this chapter. The barriers and challenges revealed in the study such as lack of internet access, technological difficulties, lack of trainings, lack of social interaction and lack of motivation that impede the flexible learning pathways were also discussed in this chapter. Therefore, providing quality education in higher education and the barriers and challenges of flexible learning pathways will provide more opportunities for the future research to decipher more on the sustainability of adult education and propose a new model of life-long learning. To this end, the proposed conceptual frameworks may offer the new dimensions required for embarking on the flexible learning pathways toward achieving SDG4 in higher education.

CONCLUSION

The purpose of the study was to explore the lecturers' perceptions on the flexible teaching pathways and the students' readiness on flexible learning pathways toward SDG4 in Malaysian higher education. Based on the results of the study, the empirical findings confirmed on lecturers' perception on flexible teaching pathways. The lecturers generally prefer to employ flexible teaching mode in the higher learning institutions. Moreover, the lecturers agreed that using digital technology enhances the student' learning and engagement in the classroom. Besides, they agreed that the flexible course design will enhance student-centered multi modal learning experience. The findings also showed that there was a strong and positive relationship between the flexible teaching pathways and the quality of education.

The open-ended items results showed that the lecturers agreed that the flexible teaching provided them more flexible time, enhance teaching strategies and independent teaching.

Regarding the students' results of the study, the empirical data showed that a majority of students believed that they practiced flexible learning pathways. The students also prefer flexible learning due to flexible time, place and pace of study. Furthermore, they have a sense of freedom, and the learning process is more pleasant. They also believed that the flexible entry points are critical for realizing flexible learning pathways. In addition, there was a strong and positive relationship between the flexible learning pathways and quality education. Based on the open-ended items, the students mostly agreed that they like flexible learning because they will have more time to study, and they can study anywhere. Through flexible learning, the students also believed that they will be able to ease stress and they can practice the experiential learning. However, challenges and barriers from both groups of participants have also been discussed in the chapter to illustrate how the flexible learning pathways can be suppressed for achieving the quality education in Malaysian higher education. In conclusion, the overall findings showed that the lecturers have positive perceptions on flexible teaching mode and the students confirmed their readiness for flexible learning pathways in Malaysian higher education. It is clear from the current study, these findings might provide the lecturers and policymakers with insights on how to improve the flexible teaching and learning environment toward quality education in higher education.

REFERENCES

Ahmad, N., & Lay, N. C. (2015). Technology and higher education: Using E-learning tutorial as a pedagogy for innovation and flexible learning. *Malaysian Journal of Distance Education*, *17*(1), 21–31.

Anderton, R. S., Vitali, J., Blackmore, C., & Bakeberg, M. C. (2021). Flexible teaching and learning modalities in undergraduate science amid the COVID-19 pandemic. *Frontier Education*, *5*, 608703. doi:10.3389/feduc.2020.609703

Bloom, B. (1995). *Human qualities and learning at school*. National Education Printing House.

Cremer, A., Kalbe, F., Gläscher, J., & Schwabe, L. (2021). Stress reduces both model-based and model-free neural computations during flexible learning. *NeuroImage*, *229*, 117747. doi:10.1016/j.neuroimage.2021.117747 PMID:33454417

Cybinski, P., & Selvanathan, S. (2005). Learning experience and learning effectiveness in undergraduate statistics: Modelling performance in traditional and flexible learning environments. *Decision Sciences Journal of Innovative Education*, *3*(2), 251–271. doi:10.1111/j.1540-4609.2005.00069.x

Godonoga, A., & Martin, M. (2020). *SDG 4 - Policies for flexible learning pathways in higher education: Taking stock of good practices internationally.* IIEP Working paper.

Jaafar, M. N., Mahmud, N. H., Amran, M. F., Abdul Rahman, M. H., Abd Aziz, N. H., & Che Noh, M. A. (2022). Online learning and teaching technology services: USIM's experience during COVID-19 pandemic. *Front Education*, *7*, 813679. doi:10.3389/feduc.2022.813679

Joan, R. (2013). Flexible learning as a new learning design in classroom process to promote quality education. *I-managers Journal on Social Educational Technology, 9*.

Karim, R.A., Idris, N., Ismail, I., Saad, N.H.M. & Abu, A.G. (2019). The impact of utilizing Mobile-assisted Mind Mapping technique (MAMMAT) on the development of undergraduate students' writing performance. *Journal of Advanced Research in Dynamic & Control Systems, 11*(12), 674-68.

Karim, R. A., & Mustapha, R. (2020). Students' perception on the use of digital mind map to stimulate creativity and critical thinking in ESL writing course. *Universal Journal of Educational Research, 8*(12A), 7596–7606. doi:10.13189/ujer.2020.082545

Karim, R. A., & Mustapha, R. (2022). TVET Student's Perception on Digital Mind Map to Stimulate Learning of Technical Skills in Malaysia. *Journal of Technical Education and Training, 14*(1), 1–13.

Krejcie, R. V., & Morgan, D. W. (1970). Determining Sample Size for Research Activities. *Educational and Psychological Measurement, 30*(3), 607–610. doi:10.1177/001316447003000308

Leal, F., Shiel, W., Paco, A., Mifsud, M., Avilia, L., Brandli, L., Molthan-Hill, P., Pace, P., Azeiteiro, U., Vargas, V., & Caiero, S. (2019). Sustainable development goals ans sustainability teaching at universities falling behind or getting ahead of the pack? *Journal of Cleaner Production, 232*, 285–294. doi:10.1016/j.jclepro.2019.05.309

Lundin, R. (2012). *Flexible Teaching and Learning: Perspectives and Practices*. The University of Sydney Library.

McGarry, B., Theobald, K. A., Lewis, P. A., & Coyer, F. M. (2015). Flexible learning design in curriculum delivery promotes student engagement and develops metacognitive learners: An integrated review. *Nurse Education Today, 35*(9), 966–973. doi:10.1016/j.nedt.2015.06.009 PMID:26169287

Miles, M. B., & Huberman, A. M. (1994). *Qualitative data analysis: An expanded sourcebook* (2nd ed.). Sage Publications, Inc.

Ministry of Education. (n.d.). *Malaysia Education Blueprint 2015-2025 (higher education.)*.

Mohamed, A. E. (Ed.). (2011). E-learning in Malaysian higher education institutions. Klang Ministry of higher education., Malaysia.

Mukhtar, K., Javed, K., Arooj, M., & Sethi, A. (2020). Advantages, limitations, and recommendations for online learning during COVID-19 pandemic era. *Pakistan Journal of Medical Sciences, 36*(COVID19-S4), 27–31. doi:10.12669/pjms.36.COVID19-S4.2785 PMID:32582310

Naidu, S. (2017). How flexible is flexible learning, who is to decide and what are its implications? *Distance Education, 38*(3), 269–272. doi:10.1080/01587919.2017.1371831

OECD. (2020). *The role of labour market information in guiding educational and occupational choices*. OECD Publishing.

Rands, M., & Gansemer-Topf, A. (2017). "The room itself is active": How classroom design impacts student engagement. *Journal of Learning Spaces, 6*(1).

Shurville, S., O'Grady, T., & Mayall, P. (2008). Educational and institutional flexibility of Australian Educational Software. Campus-wide information systems. *Emerald Group Publishing Limited*, *25*(2), 74–84.

Soffer, T., Kahan, T., & Nachmias, R. (2019). Patterns of students' utilization of flexibility in online academic courses and their relation to course achievement. *The International Review of Research in Open and Distributed Learning*, *20*(3), 3. doi:10.19173/irrodl.v20i4.3949

Taylor, P. (1998). Supporting Students for Flexible Learning, Teaching Through Flexible Learning Resources. Griffith Institute for higher education, 2-5.

UN. (2015). *Transforming Our World: The 2030 Agenda for Sustainable Development, 2nd August 2015*. United Nations.

UNESCO. (2015). *Education 2030 Incheon Declaration and Framework for Action for the Implementation of Sustainable Development Goal 4. United Nations Educational, Scientific and Cultural Organization*. UNESCO.

UNICEF. (2000). *Curriculum report card. Working Paper Series, Education Section, Programme Division*. UNICEF.

United nations (2015). *Transforming Our World: The 2030 Agenda For Sustainable Development*. UN.

Valverde-Berrocoso, J., Garrido-Arroyo, M. del C., Burgos-Videla, C., & Morales-Cevallos, M. B. (2020). Trends in educational research about e-learning: A systematic literature review (2009–2018). *Sustainability*, *12*(12), 5153. doi:10.3390u12125153

Yang, J. (2015). *Recognition, validation and accreditation of non-formal and informal learning in UNESCO member states*. UNESCO Institute for Lifelong Learning.

KEY TERMS AND DEFINITIONS

Accreditation: The external recognition of your adherence to a set of standards to perform an activity or hold a certain status. Typically, accreditation is held by education institutions or organisations.

Flexible Learning Environment: The school or institution adapts the use of resources such as staff, space, and time to best support a combination of different structures, instructional strategies, and curricular approaches.

Flexible Learning Pathways: Nontraditional programs and learning experiences that allow students to earn credit inside or outside of schools or institutions.

Flexible Learning: A set of educational philosophies and systems, concerned with providing. learners with increased choice, convenience, and personalisation to suit the learner. In. particular, flexible learning provides learners with choices about where, when, and how. learning occurs.

Flexible Teaching: An approach to course design and delivery that helps students learn and succeed in any mode: face-to-face, online, or hybrid.

Higher Education Institutions (HEIs): Universities, colleges, and further education institutions offering and delivering higher education.

Quality Education: An education that is well designed to provide the recipient with an all-round development of skills and potential to achieve success in their future endeavors in a society.

Readiness: The quality or state of being ready. Readiness is the state of being prepared to act.

Sustainable Development Goals (SDGs): The blueprint to achieve a better and more sustainable future for all. They address the global challenges we face, including poverty, inequality, climate change, environmental degradation, peace and justice.

Chapter 22
SoTL for Responsive Teaching:
Managing Issues and Challenges

Nurahimah Mohd. Yusoff
Universiti Utara Malaysia, Malaysia

Aizan Yaacob
Universiti Utara Malaysia, Malaysia

EXECUTIVE SUMMARY

While many studies have acknowledged the positive impact of the scholarship of teaching and learning, also known as SoTL, issues and challenges in implementing SoTL at public universities, particularly in Malaysia, are not fully understood. Building on this gap, it is felt that there is a need to conduct a study on the SoTL grant recipients in Universiti Utara Malaysia (UUM). This study chose the samples who could provide "rich and relevant information" to answer the research questions. The findings include issues related to (1) time constraints, (2) understanding SoTL concept, (3) SoTL inquiry, (4) student learning, (5) publication as an output, (6) difficulty in convincing others to change, (7) workload and (8) reflective practice. It is recommended that more trainings be given to SoTL recipients from various discipline areas, to ensure completion of the project and continuous mentoring be provided for them to ensure sustainability of SoTL. SoTL in UUM, it can be concluded, has empowered academicians in pursuing their academic endeavor.

INTRODUCTION

What Is SOTL

Boyer's *Priorities of the Professoriate* (1990) called for efforts to broaden the scope of scholarship to include discovery, integration, application, and teaching (Boyer, 1990). The integration of research and teaching is the key towards enhancing, developing, and informing the teaching practice both within and beyond an institution of higher education (Dobbins, 2008; Hutchings & Shulman, 1999). The above definition for the Scholarship of Teaching and Learning known as SoTL was echoed by Darling (2003),

DOI: 10.4018/978-1-6684-6076-4.ch022

who viewed SoTL as tasks taken to encourage empirical examination of teaching in relation to student learning. Bernstein (2010) claimed that the true method of SoTL is to have every teacher treats every course as an opportunity to learn how to create better learning environments and generate richer educational experiences. He called upon the faculty to re-assert the inherent value of teaching as a mission of the university in which effective teaching should be rewarded and honoured because it is important, not because it resembled discovery research. Besides that, institutions might better improve the learning of our students by making the faculty's intellectual work in teaching visible for discussion and collaboration by inviting colleagues to discover new frontiers in educational practice or theory. Similarly, Gayle et al. (2013) used a variety of faculty development activities at campuses engaged in the Carnegie Campus Cluster programme to enhance the participation in SoTL where the main focus was on faculty learning of distinctive developmental stages that lead to both cognitive and affective transformation for the professors' and students' learning. The findings of Gayle et al.'s study indicated that it provided professors with advanced strategies for engaging students in their own learning. Additionally, it promoted reflection, awareness of common goals, and public dissemination of SoTL practices which should be the basis of on-going professional growth. Besides that, practice in discovery, co-creating, learning by doing, application of skills, training, developing muscle-memory, and engaging in activities beyond the classroom context.

Why Do SOTL

Based on a study by McNiff (2017), it is to connect instruction to scholarship, to learn about how others have approached teaching as a scholarly activity through the SoTL literature, and to become more reflective and intentional teachers as they embark on their careers. The advantage is it is more engaged and dedicated teaching. Besides that, it promotes reflecting on effective teaching, testing new approaches, and focusing on student learning. Moreover, it makes teaching more transparent. The impact of SoTL on teachers is the critical reflection on teaching where it is carried out to identify and test their teaching assumptions. The impact of SoTL among students is it familiarizes students with a branch of study of which they may have been unaware of. Besides that, it gives students a way to think about teaching as a scholarly act and become advocates for scholarly teaching. Moreover, it helps prepare students for the teaching in higher education. Additionally, students become more critically reflective and intentional teachers.

How Can SOTL Benefit Instructors

The role of university and higher education is changing and will continue to change in unexpected and unforeseen ways. Academicians need to realize that the role as teachers in higher education has shifted from being the providers of knowledge to the facilitators of students' learning. The fundamental processes of knowledge creation, preservation, integration, transmission, and application will continue to change. It is argued that the new focus of teaching and learning in higher education is on designing less traditional classroom teaching and relying more on students' learning experiences, processes, and environments. Huber (2006) claimed that "undertaking complex classroom research to enhance practice can be both epistemologically challenging and empowering" (as cited in Hubball and Clarke, 2009, p. 2). On the one hand, it is challenging as an academician must carry over arching responsibilities in teaching, research, publication and consultation. On the other hand, the experience can be empowering as the faculty members engage and collaborate with students to improve their teaching and learning experiences.

SOTL for Responsive Teaching

Responsive teaching receives different understanding in literature. Some scholars (Bennett, 2011; Reis, 2007) view it as a form of providing feedback to students whereby using real-time evidence as a formative assessment. In this manner, the instructors make time to adapt changes or adjustments to their instructional inputs and activities in respond to students' levels of performance. Other scholars (Wood, 2018; Coffey et al., 2011) noted that when students bring different experiences, understanding, strengths, and areas for growth to the classroom, instructors need the tools to observe and respond to those differences. Thus, instructors need to do reflective and responsive teaching.

With regards to SoTL, during the critical incident stage, the instructor becomes sensitive to the issue of how students are doing in the classroom. He/she will attend as much as possible in providing help to the students. The extra miles given to students in supporting as well as adapting teaching to meet their needs are considered as part of responsive teaching. Hence, for a teacher-scholar, the art of responsive teaching can take place in three steps. Firstly, the instructor can set clear goals and plan learning carefully. Secondly, the instructor can identify what students have understood and where they are struggling. And finally, the instructor can respond and adapt teaching to support students to do better.

ISSUES AND CHALLENGES IN CONDUCTING SOTL INQUIRY

There are many issues and challenges highlighted by researchers on SoTL. Among them are: (1) Lack award in the tenure system or research valued more than teaching (Louie et al., 2016; Arellano & Jones, 2018; Bartling, 2009; Marckettin & Freeman, 2016); (2) SoTL is not encouraged or embraced at institutions (Bartling, 2009; Marckettin & Freeman, 2016); (3) Lack of SoTL training, and (4) lack of understanding on SoTL. The first issue mentioned was the lack of award in the tenure system for teaching. In other words, in many western countries, research is valued more than teaching and it cannot be used for promotion or tenureship. This line of researchers mentioned that they found it disturbing to have research valued more than teaching. Besides that, it battles around tenure and the defeat of individuals whose teaching-oriented research was considered as inadequate for academic promotion (Louie et al., 2016). In a similar vein, Arellano & Jones (2018) argued that institutional practices and policies still appear to favour research in the faculty's discipline than within their teaching and learning in the service-learning pedagogy. It also challenges the traditional practices in higher education of focusing on teaching, learning, and research, by supporting practices that are deeply engaging, local, and impactful. Moreover, they highlighted the failure for institutions to view their faculty's work with the service-learning pedagogy as "scholarly work". Besides that, the higher education prevents their faculty from contributing to the literature of the scholarship of teaching and learning and engaged research (Arellano and Jones, 2018). Similarly, Anjum (2019) also mentioned some issues regarding limited teaching awards, tenure, or promotion in her study (Anjum, 2019). She claimed that the lack of reward in the tenure system was a major impediment for the growth of scholarship in this area amongst the fourteen participating accounting academics. In other words, the disadvantage of SoTL is that it limits teaching awards, tenure, or promotion. Besides that, the complete lack of training in educational research available to any of the academic members in the accounting field becomes a constraint to them. Besides that, they employed "wisdom of practice" to improve their teaching instead of the scholarship of teaching and learning which is worrying. Besides that, someone engaging in the scholarship of teaching and learning would have only a limited impact on their earning a teaching award, promotion or tenure. Additionally, she argues that it suffers from an underdeveloped definition of high-quality teaching (Anjum, 2019).

While many studies have acknowledged the positive impact of SoTL on teaching and learning, issues, and challenges in implementing SoTL at public university particularly in Malaysia are not fully understood. Studies conducted in addressing this issue are still scarce. Issues and challenges the researchers face while conducting SoTL research need to be understood fully, so that continuous monitoring can be implemented. Building on this gap, it is felt that there is a need to conduct a study on the SoTL grant recipients in one public higher institution so as to provide an 'audit trail' of SoTL practitioners as well as to analyze how they transfer their SoTL research skills into their teaching and learning practices. Hence, a more dynamic understanding of SoTL needs to be further developed to redefine the relationship between research and teaching.

The following findings indicated that there are a few issues and challenges reported by the participants which include: (1) Time constraints, (2) Understanding SoTL concept, (3) SoTL inquiry, (4) Student learning, (5) Publication as an output, (6) Difficulty in convincing others to change, (7) Workload and (8) Reflective practice.

Time Constraints

One of the major constraints in conducting SoTL research is time. Many participants mentioned that they did not have enough time to complete the research and it has somehow demotivated them. P10. P3, P9, P14 stated the issue regarding time management. Meanwhile participants P27, 30 and 38 mentioned that they had difficulty during the planning and implementation of the intervention. P27 stated that she had to take more time to integrate the 'buddy system' into the course syllabus, while P 30 mentioned that she had to conduct series of meetings with the team members to develop new games in her teaching.

Understanding SoTL Concept

Another issue mentioned by the participants was related to understanding of the SoTL concept and teaching inquiry as they were from different disciplines. P2 mentioned that she had difficulty understanding the concept of SoTL research. P16 mentioned that she had difficulty conducting SoTL research because her colleagues were not interested to do classroom inquiry, because they thought that it was in the field of Education. However, she claimed that after looking at her students' improved engagement in her class, she continued with the research.

Participants in general understood that conducting SoTL research is basically part of the teaching-learning inquiry whereby instructors reflect and collect evidence in their classroom practice to improve students' learning.

SoTL Inquiry

The next issue concerned SoTL inquiry which includes collecting and managing the qualitative data, as well as analysing them. Some of them who were from different fields felt that they were overwhelmed by the richness of qualitative data and did not know how to manage them and analyse them. P24 stated that she was frustrated in getting an experienced research assistant who could help her with the data analysis. Some participants also stated that they found it challenging to collect the classroom data during pandemic. P15, P17 and P20 claimed that they could not meet face-to-face for data collection as they were forced to conduct classes online during Pandemic. To them online classes were difficult as only a few students were active in the discussion.

Student Learning

SoTL research somehow made them aware of the students' abilities and their learning. P4 mentioned that she needed to be prepared with the various abilities that students brought with them into the classroom. In addition, P5 mentioned that she had to learn to adept to the new ways of teaching and learning. At the same time, she had to give enough room for her students to adapt to her new way of teaching. Therefore, she mentioned that the planning stage was difficult as she had to consider her students' abilities.

Publication as An Output

SoTL research requires publication as an output. As such, the participants mentioned that they had difficulty searching for the right sources and writing in the field of education as many of them are not from educational field and they were not familiar with classroom inquiry and qualitative research. P12 mentioned that she was not confident in publishing a journal article in a field different from her field.

Difficulty in Convincing Others to Change

One of the participants mentioned that it was difficult to convince her colleagues to 'buy in' with the idea of SoTL research.

Workload

Some participants who were doing some administrative tasks, would find it difficult to enhance new teaching strategy as it should be done continuously.

Reflective Practice

One of the participants mentioned about getting used to writing reflection in teaching and learning and felt that reflective practice takes time to be turned into a habit. Therefore, it was a challenge for her to complete the research on time, as Action Research cycles must be conducted continuously to see continuous improvements in students' learning.

OTHER ISSUES RELATED TO SOTL

Mentoring Programmes in SoTL

Lack of mentoring and coaching training on SoTL has also become an issue (Larsson et al, 2020; Anjum, 2019). According to Larsson et al. (2019), those who are engaged in SoTL lack adequate training and some of them had never heard of SoTL. They mentioned that it was found some considerable overlaps and commonalities between the SoTL and Educational Research (Larsson et al., 2020). The result showed that novice members have never heard of SoTL. Hence, causes overlapping of practices between SoTL and educational research. Besides that, in terms of membership, those who did not belong in their community and their membership cannot be considered as education researcher. The beneficiaries are that it should not rush too quickly to the practical improvement of education, members of the educational research field (primary) rather than students (secondary aim). Both may focus on the same direct object which is student learning in specific contexts. However, arguably, they perceive different things as meaningful because of a variation in the indirect object where SoTL improves students' learning locally and educational research adds to literature. The issues portrayed in the study is that those who are engaged in SoTL lack adequate training. Besides that, they had never heard of SoTL although there were considerable overlaps and commonalities between the SoTL and educational research. The challenges found is the observation reflects that distance from the students and their context: Dual relationship, as a researcher and as a teacher (Larsson et al., 2020). Anjum (2019) also claimed that there was a complete lack of training in educational research available to any of the academic members in the accounting field (Anjum, 2019).

Hence, it is pertinent to have a structured and coordinated mentoring programme at the various levels from department to faculty levels and then followed by the institutional and national levels. As such the mentoring programmes can be coordinated by the central teaching and learning centre of the respective institution. This will assist academicians to have opportunities to learn and share knowledge and skills in conducting SoTL activities gradually and continuously.

Publishing SoTL Research

Another issue mentioned by the researchers is the pressure to publish (Bartling, 2009). Pressure to publish and a low value given to teaching in institutional policies and procedures are highlighted by Bartling (2019). Moreover, the university allowed teaching development to occur, there were few intentional instances where this was encouraged and supported. Additionally, the scholarship of teaching and learning has not been embraced at institutions. The pattern of the study shows the faculty perceptions of the institutional context where institutional influence on faculty approach to teaching, and therefore on student learning, was the finding that the more student-centred faculty members' approaches to teaching were, the more likely those faculty members recognized their need for improvement in teaching, pursued development opportunities and engaged in the scholarship of teaching (Bartling, 2009).

Leadership in SoTL

A line of researchers claimed that SoTL is not encouraged or embraced at many institutions (Bartling, 2009; Marckettin & Freeman, 2016). Bartling (2009) for example, argues that scholarship of teaching and learning has not been embraced at institutions whereby the university allowed teaching development to occur, but there were few intentional instances where this was encouraged and supported. In addition, Marcketting and Freeman (2016) conducted a study which focuses on the participation of SoTL by faculty members in Iowa State University. They found that there was a disconnect between tenured and tenure-track faculty, where the non-tenured faculty were more likely to judge teaching activities that were less likely to undergo the peer-review process of SoTL. Besides that, the criterion for tenure requires faculty members to establish a national reputation in their disciplinary field. Moreover, greater number of SoTL grants received as compared to presentations and publications. The challenges and findings show that some departments and colleges value and are more supportive of SoTL than others. Additionally, the faculty may be interested in teaching related grants for curriculum improvement, but do not consider the additional effort required to produce SoTL presentations and publications worth their time (Marckettin & Freeman, 2016).

In addition, some researchers claimed that academics who are not from the educational fields had to grapple with new literature and new genres (Matthews & Cook-Sather, 2019). They had to work on unfamiliar methods and genres. Since scholarship focused on teaching and learning, they may also find it difficult to make sense of new research expectations in a different discipline. Matthews and Cook-Sather (2019) mentioned that the disadvantage of the study is the forging of their identities within this field as they will need to place their work in the context of a broader literature and address the interests of a wider audience. The issue found in the study is that they have become interested in exploring issues in higher education alongside their disciplinary interests. The challenges portrayed are that they have to grapple with a new literature and sometimes unfamiliar methods and genres in encouraging scholarship focused on teaching and learning which can also find it difficult to make sense of new research expectations in a different discipline (Matthews & Cook-Sather, 2019).

This indicated the need for SoTL leadership to be part of the system so that all academicians may benefit in improving their classroom practices whether they are those from tenured, non-tenured and/or academics who are not from the educational fields.

CONCLUSION AND RECOMMENDATION

In this paper, we have highlighted a few issues and challenges reported by the SoTL recipients from one public university in Malaysia. Our findings include issues related to (1) time constraints, (2) understanding SoTL concept, (3) SoTL inquiry, (4) student learning, (5) publication as an output, (6) difficulty in convincing others to change, (7) workload and (8) reflective practice.

These issues and challenges are also highlighted by other researchers on SoTL from past studies. Among them are: lack of award in the tenure system /research valued more than teaching (Louie et al., 2016; Arellano & Jones, 2018; Bartling, 2009; Marckettin & Freeman, 2016); SoTL is not encouraged or embraced at institutions (Bartling,2009; Marckettin & Freeman, 2016); lack training on SoTL, and lack of understanding of SoTL. Some researchers also claimed that academics which are not from the educational fields had to grapple with new literature and new genres (Matthews & Cook-Sather, 2019).

This unfamiliarity with SoTL literature could lead to research results that are not optimal (Kim et al, 2020). Therefore, they need more time to familiarize themselves with systematic review and analysis through published documentation as this is what differentiates SoTL from any other research. Another issue mentioned by the researchers is the pressure to publish (Bartling, 2009). The academics' unfamiliarity a field which is different to theirs can make the idea of publishing and making their work public to be intimidating for some (Chng & Martensson, 2020). Time constraint is a barrier for academics to complete and achieve SoTL expectations as they find it challenging to manage the pressure of workload (Flavell et al., 2018). It was clear in this study that academics found that all the workloads including the teaching and administrative tasks have made it difficult for them to manage their time to engage in SoTL more effectively. This agrees with another study that found that participants struggled to manage their workload while at the same time finding that extra time for SoTL research (Kim et al., 2020). Another issue concerned is the SoTL inquiry where the participants found difficulty in collecting, managing and analysing the qualitative data. Kim et al. (2020) described the participants' unfamiliarity in the field led to struggles in the research process.

In conclusion, even though SoTL research is bound to have some issues and challenges, it has somehow empowered teaching and learning among the SoTL recipients. We have provided evidence that it has brought some positive impacts on teaching and learning, not only for the teachers but also for the students' learning. We have also provided evidence that best practices among SoTL recipients include a combination of teaching and learning and SoTL attributes, with students' outcome as a central concern, and SoTL goes a step further in turning the process into a scholarly work through systematic review, analysis and published documentations. It is recommended that more trainings be given to SoTL recipients from various discipline areas, to ensure completion of the project and continuous mentoring be provided for them to ensure sustainability of SoTL. Indeed, SoTL has empowered academicians in pursuing their academic endeavor.

How SOTL Plays a Role In Responsive Teaching

Some academics were found to misunderstand the concept of SoTL (Bartling, 2009). Bartling (2009) argues that the scholarship of teaching and learning remains a misunderstood phenomenon whereby the culture of SoTL is unapologetically teaching. A study conducted by Bartling (2009) uses approaches to Teaching Inventory which are contextual, and faculty may hold a specific conception of teaching, their approach to teaching within courses may vary. The method is a highly teacher-focused approach to the scholarship of teaching. The disadvantages are larger class sizes limited the amount of discussion, group work, and other conceptual change activities they could use in the classroom. Besides that, the scholarship of teaching and learning remains a misunderstood. Moreover, the culture of SoTL is unapologetically teaching-focused. The issues found are that the traditional activities such as research and keeping current as the scholarship of teaching. Besides that, pressure to publish and a low value given to teaching in institutional policies and procedures. Moreover, the university allowed teaching development to occur, there were few intentional instances where this was encouraged and supported. Additionally, the scholarship of teaching and learning has not been embraced at institutions. The pattern of the study shows the faculty perceptions of the institutional context where institutional influence on faculty approach to teaching, and therefore on student learning, was the finding that the more student-centred faculty members' approaches to teaching were, the more likely those faculty members recognized their need for improvement in teaching, pursued development opportunities and engaged in the scholarship of teaching (Bartling, 2009).

We have provided evidence that best practices among SoTL recipients include a combination of teaching and learning and SoTL attributes, with students' outcome as a central concern, and SoTL goes a step further in turning the process into a scholarly work through systematic review, analysis and published documentations. It is recommended that more trainings be given to SoTL recipients from various discipline areas, to ensure completion of the project and continuous mentoring be provided for them to ensure sustainability of SoTL in an institution. In a nutshell, SoTL has empowered academicians in pursuing their academic endeavour. It is a catalyst for Responsive Teaching. The major benefits include facilitating learning, motivating and engaging students, as well as cultivating students' transferable skills.

REFERENCES

Anjum, S. (2019). *The status of Scholarship of Teaching and Learning in the accounting discipline: A case study of academics' perspectives.* (Order No. 13859998) [Doctoral dissertation, University of Calgary]. ProQuest Dissertations and Theses Global.

Arellano, I., & Jones, S. J. (2018). Exploration of university faculty perceptions and experiences of service-learning as engaged Scholarship of Teaching and Learning. *The Journal of Scholarship of Teaching and Learning, 18*(4), 111–129. doi:10.14434/josotl.v18i4.23178

Bartling, J. D. (2009). *Faculty and administrator perceptions of teaching, the Scholarship of Teaching and Learning, and culture at a teaching university.* (Order No. 3344920) [Doctoral dissertation, Capella University]. ProQuest Dissertations and Theses Global.

Bennett, R. (2011). Formative assessment: A critical review. *Assessment in Education: Principles, Policy & Practice, 18*(1), 5–25. doi:10.1080/0969594X.2010.513678

Bernstein, D. (2010). Finding your place in the Scholarship of Teaching and Learning. *International Journal for the Scholarship of Teaching and Learning, 4*(2). doi:10.20429/ijsotl.2010.040204

Boyer, E. L. (1990). The scholarship of teaching from: Scholarship reconsidered: Priorities of the professoriate. *College Teaching, 39*(1), 11–13. doi:10.1080/87567555.1991.10532213

Braun, V., & Clarke, V. (2013). *Successful qualitative research: A practical guide for beginners. sage.*

Chng, H. H., & Martensson, K. (2020). Leading change from different shores: The challenges of contextualizing the Scholarship of Teaching and Learning. *Teaching & Learning Inquiry, 8*(1), 24–41. doi:10.20343/teachlearninqu.8.1.3

Coffey, J., Hammer, D., Levin, D., & Grant, T. (2011). The missing disciplinary substance of formative assessment. *Journal of Research in Science Teaching, 48*(10), 1109–1136. doi:10.1002/tea.20440

Creswell, J. W., & Creswell, J. D. (2005). Mixed methods research: Developments, debates, and dilemmas. *Research in organizations: Foundations and methods of inquiry, 2*, 315-326.

Creswell, J. W., & Garrett, A. L. (2008). The "movement" of mixed methods research and the role of educators. *South African Journal of Education, 28*(3), 321–333. doi:10.15700aje.v28n3a176

Creswell, J. W., & Poth, C. N. (2017). *Qualitative inquiry and research design: Choosing among five approaches*. Sage publications.

Darling, A. L. (2003). Scholarship of Teaching and Learning in Communication: New Connections, New Directions, New Possibilities. *Communication Education*, 52(1), 47–49. doi:10.1080/03634520302458

Denzin, N. K. (2012). *Triangulation 2.0. Journal of mixed methods research*, 6(2), 80-88. doi:10.1177/1558689812437186

Dobbins, K. (2008). Enhancing the Scholarship of Teaching and Learning: A Study of the Factors Identified as Promoting and Hindering the Scholarly Activities of Academics in One Faculty. *International Journal for the Scholarship of Teaching and Learning*, 2(2). doi:10.20429/ijsotl.2008.020217

Felton, P., & Binnix, T. (2013). *Engaging Students as partners in Teaching, Learning, and SoTL*. Wiley.

Flavell, H., Roberts, L., Fyfe, G., & Broughton, M. (2018). Shifting goal posts: The impact of academic workforce reshaping and the introduction of teaching academic roles on the Scholarship of Teaching and Learning. *Australian Educational Researcher*, 45(2), 179–194. doi:10.100713384-017-0247-6

Fletcher, H. R. (2018). What is responsive teaching? *Improving Teaching*.

Gayle, B. M., Randall, N., Langley, L., & Preiss, R. (2013). Faculty learning processes: A model for moving from scholarly teaching to the Scholarship of Teaching and Learning. *The International Society for the Scholarship of Teaching and Learning*, 1(1), 81–93. doi:10.20343/teachlearninqu.1.1.81

Hubball, H., Clarke, A., & Poole, G. (2010). Ten-year reflections on mentoring SoTL research in a research-intensive university. *The International Journal for Academic Development*, 15(2), 117–129. doi:10.1080/13601441003737758

Hutchings, P., & Shulman, L. S. (1999). The Scholarship of Teaching:New Elaborations, New Developments. *Change: The Magazine of Higher Learning*, 31(5), 10–15. doi:10.1080/00091389909604218

Kim, A. S. N., Popovic, C., Farrugia, L., Saleh, S. A. F., Maheux-Pelletier, G., & Frake-Mistak, M. (2020). On nurturing the emergent SoTL researcher: Responding to challenges and opportunities. *The International Journal for Academic Development*, 26(2), 163–175. doi:10.1080/1360144X.2020.1842743

Larsson, M., Mårtensson, K., Price, L., & Roxå, T. (2020). Constructive friction? Charting the relation between educational research and the Scholarship of Teaching and Learning. *Teaching & Learning Inquiry*, 8(1), 61–75. doi:10.20343/teachlearninqu.8.1.5

Louie, B. Y., Drevdahl, D. J., Purdy, J. M., & Stackman, R. W. (2003). Advancing the Scholarship of Teaching through collaborative self-study. *The Journal of Higher Education*, 74(2), 150–171. doi:10.1353/jhe.2003.0016

Marcketti, S. B., & Freeman, S. (2016). SoTL evidence on promotion and tenure vitas at a research university. *The Journal of Scholarship of Teaching and Learning*, 16(5), 19–31. doi:10.14434//josotl.v16i5.21152

Matthews, K. E., Cook-Sather, A., Acai, A., Dvorakova, S. L., Felten, P., Marquis, E., & Mercer-Mapstone, L. (2019). Toward theories of partnership praxis: An analysis of interpretive framing in literature on students as partners in teaching and learning. *Higher Education Research & Development, 38*(2), 280-293. doi:10.14264/uql.2018.519

McNiff, L., & Hays, L. (2017). SoTL in the LIS classroom: Helping future academic librarians become more engaged teachers. *Communications in Information Literacy, 11*(2), 366–377. doi:10.15760/comminfolit.2017.11.2.8

Merriam, S. B., & Tisdell, E. J. (2015). *Qualitative research: A guide to design and implementation.* John Wiley & Sons.

Patton, M. Q. (2002). Two decades of developments in qualitative inquiry: A personal, experiential perspective. *Qualitative Social Work: Research and Practice, 1*(3), 261–283. doi:10.1177/1473325002001003636

Reis, H. (2007). Steps toward the ripening of relationship science. *Personal Relationships, 14*(1), 1–23. doi:10.1111/j.1475-6811.2006.00139.x

Stake, R. E., & Schwandt, T. A. (2006). On discerning quality in evaluation. The Sage handbook of evaluation, 404-418. .

Yin, R. K. (2013). Validity and generalization in future case study evaluations. *Evaluation, 19*(3), 321–332. doi:10.1177/1356389013497081

Compilation of References

Abdullah, S., Alias, N. A., Elias @ Mayah, A., & Jusoh, C. R. (2019) *Buku panduan amalan pendidikan berimpak tinggi (High-Impact Educational Practices-HIEPs) dalam matapelajaran pengajian umum*. Jabatan Pendidikan Tinggi, Wilayah Persekutuan Putrajaya.

Abrams, S. S. (2021). Game-Informed Cooperative Assessments and Socially Responsible Learning in Public School Math Classes. In M. Harvey & R. Marlatt (Eds.), *Esports Research and Its Integration in Education* (pp. 168–184). IGI Global. doi:10.4018/978-1-7998-7069-2.ch010

Academy of Sciences Malaysia. (2020). *10-10 Malaysian Science, Technology, Innovation and Economy (MySTIE) Framework: Trailblazing the way for prosperity, societal well-being & global competitiveness*. Academy of Sciences Malaysia. www.akademisains.gov.my/10-10-mystie

Acar, B., & Yaman, M. (2011). The effects of context-based learning on students' levels of knowledge and interest. *Hacettepe University Journal of Education, 40*, 1–10.

Adam, N. L., Alzahri, F. B., Cik Soh, S., Abu Bakar, N., & Mohamad Kamal, N. A. (2017). Self-regulated learning and online learning: A systematic review. In H. Badioze Zaman, P. Robinson, A. F. Smeaton, T. K. Shih, S. Velastin, T. Terutoshi, A. Jaafar, & N. Mohamad Ali (Eds.), *Advances in visual informatics* (pp. 143–154). Springer International Publishing. doi:10.1007/978-3-319-70010-6_14

Adolphus, M. (2019). *Using evidence-based practice to inform decision making*. Emerald Publishing. https://www.emeraldgrouppublishing.com/librarians/info/viewpoints/evidence_based_practice.htm

Advance, H. E. (2011). *The UK Professional Standards Framework (PSF) for Teaching and Supporting Learning in Higher Education*. Advance HE. Available at: www.advance-he.ac.uk/guidance/teaching-and-learning/ukpsf

Ag-Ahmad, N. (2020). Open and Distance Learning (ODL): Preferences, issues and challenges amidst Covid-19 Pandemic. *Creative Practices in Language Learning and Teaching, 8*(2), 1-14.

AGCAS. (2009). *At the Assessment Centre*. Sheffield, UK: Association of Graduate Careers Advisory Services. Available at: www.agcas.org.uk/Knowledge-Centre/a752384c-02f5-434c-b8e1-802b151652ab

Aghakhani, S. (2022). *Developing reflective practice among teachers of mathematics: A case study of four teachers* [Doctoral dissertation]. University of Toronto.

Agustan, S., Juniati, D., & Siswono, T. Y. E. (2017). Reflective thinking in solving an algebra problem: A case study of field independent-prospective teacher. *Journal of Physics: Conference Series, 893*(1), 012002. doi:10.1088/1742-6596/893/1/012002

Ahmad, N., & Lay, N. C. (2015). Technology and higher education: Using E-learning tutorial as a pedagogy for innovation and flexible learning. *Malaysian Journal of Distance Education, 17*(1), 21–31.

Airasian, P. W., & Walsh, M. E. (1997). Constructivist cautions. *Phi Delta Kappan, 78,* 444–449. https://www.ncbi.nlm.nih.gov/pmc/articles/PMC8448099/

Ajzen, I. (1991). The theory of planned behavior. *Organizational Behavior and Human Decision Processes, 50*(2), 179–211. doi:10.1016/0749-5978(91)90020-T

Akbari, M., Ardekani, Z. F., Pino, G., & Maleksaeidi, H. (2019). An extended model of Theory of Planned Behavior to investigate highly-educated Iranian consumers' intentions towards consuming genetically modified foods. *Journal of Cleaner Production, 227,* 784–793. doi:10.1016/j.jclepro.2019.04.246

Akpınar, İ. A., & Özkan, E. (2010). *Kimya dersi çözünürlük konusunda 5E modeline uygun etkinlikler geliştirme [Develop appropriate activities to 5 models in chemistry resolution].* Paper presented at IX. National Science and Mathematics Education Congress, Izmir, Turkey.

Akyol, Z., Arbaugh, J. B., Cleveland-Innes, M., Garrison, D. R., Ice, P., Richardson, J. C., & Swan, K. (2009). A response to the review of the community of inquiry framework. *Journal of Distance Education, 23*(2), 123–135. https://files.eric.ed.gov/fulltext/EJ851908.pdf

Alahmad, A., Stamenkovska, T., & Gyori, J. (2021). Preparing Pre-service Teachers for 21st Century Skills Education: A Teacher Education Model. *GiLE Journal of Skills Development, 1*(1), 67–86. doi:10.52398/gjsd.2021.v1.i1.pp67-86

Al-Ansi, A., Suprayogo, I. & Abidin, M. (2019). *Impact of Information and Communication Technology (ICT) on Different Settings of Learning Process in Developing Countries.* doi:10.5923/j.scit.20190902.01

Aleksandrov, A. D. (1956). *Mathematics, its essence, methods and role.* USSR Academy of Sciences.

Ali, A., Siddiqui, A. A., Arshad, M. S., Iqbal, F., & Arif, T. B. (2022, June). Effects of COVID-19 pandemic and lockdown on lifestyle and mental health of students: A retrospective study from Karachi, Pakistan. *Annales Médico-Psychologiques, 180*(6), S29–S37. doi:10.1016/j.amp.2021.02.004 PMID:33612842

Ali, G., Jaaffar, A. R., & Ali, J. (2021). STEM Education in Malaysia: Fulfilling SMEs' Expectation. *Modeling Economic Growth in Contemporary Malaysia,* (February), 43–57. doi:10.1108/978-1-80043-806-420211005

Alkan, F., & Yücel, A. S. (2019). Investigation of epistemological beliefs and creativity fostering behaviours of prospective teachers' in terms of various variables. *Journal of Educational Studies Trends and Practices, 9,* 212–226.

Allen, K., & Friedman, B. (2010). Affective Learning: A Taxonomy for Teaching Social Work Values. *Journal of Social Work Values and Ethics.*

Al-Maatouk, Q., Othman, M. S., Alsayed, A. O., Al-Rahmi, A. M., Abuhassna, H., & Al-Rahmi, W. M. (2020). Applying Communication Theory to Structure and Evaluate the Social Media Platforms in Academia. [IJATCSE]. *International Journal of Advanced Trends in Computer Science and Engineering, 9*(2), 1505–1517. doi:10.30534/ijatcse/2020/92922020

Almarshad, S. O. (2017). Adopting sustainable behavior in institutions of higher education: A study on intentions of decision makers in the MENA region. *European Journal of Sustainable Development, 6*(2), 89–89. doi:10.14207/ejsd.2017.v6n2p89

Almulla, M. A. (2020). The Effectiveness of the Project-Based Learning (PBL) Approach as a Way to Engage Students in Learning. *SAGE Open, 10*(3). Advance online publication. doi:10.1177/2158244020938702

Amabile, T. M. (1983). Motivation and Creativity: Effects of Motivational Orientation on Creative Writers. *Journal of Personality and Social Psychology, 48*(2), 393–399. doi:10.1037/0022-3514.48.2.393

Compilation of References

Ameen, E. C., Guffey, D. M., & McMillan, J. J. (1996). Gender differences in determining the ethical sensitivity of future accounting professionals. *Journal of Business Ethics*, *15*(5), 591–597. doi:10.1007/BF00381934

American Association of School Administrators. (2010). *2011 district excellence award for digital learning*. AASA. http://www.aasa.org/uploadedFiles/Programs_and_Events/Awards_ and_Scholarships/Technology_Award/2011_Technology_Award/2011_Technology_Award2011_ AASA_LS_App_procedure_082410.pdf

Anastasakis, M., Triantafyllou, G., & Petridis, K. (2021). *Undergraduates' barriers to online learning during the pandemic in Greece*. Tech Know Learn. doi:10.100710758-021-09584-5

Anderton, R. S., Vitali, J., Blackmore, C., & Bakeberg, M. C. (2021). Flexible teaching and learning modalities in undergraduate science amid the COVID-19 pandemic. *Frontier Education*, *5*, 608703. doi:10.3389/feduc.2020.609703

Andrée, M. (2003). *Everyday-life in the science classroom: A study on ways of using and referring to everyday-life*. Paper presented at the ESERA Conference, Noordwijkerhout, The Netherlands.

Andreoni, J. (1990). Impure altruism and donations to public goods: A theory of warm-glow giving. *Economic Journal (London)*, *100*(401), 464–477. doi:10.2307/2234133

Anjum, S. (2019). *The status of Scholarship of Teaching and Learning in the accounting discipline: A case study of academics' perspectives*. (Order No. 13859998) [Doctoral dissertation, University of Calgary]. ProQuest Dissertations and Theses Global.

Anthonysamy, L., Koo, A. C., & Hew, S. H. (2020). Self-regulated learning strategies in higher education: Fostering digital literacy for sustainable lifelong learning. *Education and Information Technologies*, *25*(4), 2393–2414. doi:10.100710639-020-10201-8

Antoniadou, M. (2020). From euphoria to letting go: experiences of cross-cultural adaptation of international academics in UK higher education. In M. Antoniadou & M. Crowder (Eds.), *Modern Day Challenges in Academia: Time for a Change* (pp. 82–98). Edward Elgar Publishing. doi:10.4337/9781788119191.00014

Antoniadou, M., Crowder, M., & Andreakos, G. (2021). Emotional Intelligence in Engineering Management Education: The Missing Priority. In D. Ktoridou (Ed.), *Cases on Engineering Management Education in Practice* (pp. 92–104). IGI Global. doi:10.4018/978-1-7998-4063-3.ch005

Antoniadou, M., & Quinlan, K. M. (2020). Thriving on challenges: How immigrant academics regulate emotional experiences during acculturation. *Studies in Higher Education*, *45*(1), 71–85. doi:10.1080/03075079.2018.1512567

Antoniadou, M., & Quinlan, K. M. (2022). Holding true or caving in? Academics' Values, Emotions, and Behaviors in Response to Higher Education Reforms. *Higher Education Policy*, *35*(2), 522–541. doi:10.105741307-021-00225-1

Apodaca-Orozco, G. U. G., Ortega-Pipper, L. P., Verdugo-Blanco, L. E., & Reyes-Barribas, L. E. (2017). Modelos educativos: Un reto para la educación en salud. *Ra Ximhai*, *13*(2), 77–86. doi:10.35197/rx.13.02.2017.06.gg

Apte, M., & Bhave-Gudipudi, A. (2020). Cooperative learning techniques to bridge gaps in academia and corporate. *Procedia Computer Science*, *172*, 289–295. doi:10.1016/j.procs.2020.05.046

Arasaratnam-Smith, L. A., & Northcote, M. (2017). Community in online higher education: Challenges and opportunities. *Electronic Journal of e-Learning*, *15*(2), 188–198.

Araujo, M. & Campos, M. (2006). La praxis pedagógica en la educación física y los estilos de enseñanza predominantes en los docentes de educación básica. *Revista EDUCARE-UPEL-IPB-Segunda Nueva Etapa 2.0*, *10*(3).

Arbaugh, J. B. (2013). Does academic discipline moderate CoI-course outcomes relationships in online MBA courses? *Internet High. Educ*, *2013*(17), 16–28. doi:10.1016/j.iheduc.2012.10.002

Archer, E. (2017). The assessment purpose triangle: Balancing the purposes of educational assessment. *Front. Educ.*, *2*(41), 41. Advance online publication. doi:10.3389/feduc.2017.00041

Arellano, I., & Jones, S. J. (2018). Exploration of university faculty perceptions and experiences of service-learning as engaged Scholarship of Teaching and Learning. *The Journal of Scholarship of Teaching and Learning*, *18*(4), 111–129. doi:10.14434/josotl.v18i4.23178

Aris, S. R. S., Salleh, M. F. M., & Ismail, M. H. (2020). Guided Cooperative Flipped Classroom Approach in Learning Molecular Orbital Theory. *International Journal of Academic Research in Business & Social Sciences*, *10*(14), 200–212. doi:10.6007/IJARBSS/v10-i14/7689

Aristovnik, A., Keržič, D., Ravšelj, D., Tomaževič, N., & Umek, L. (2020). Impacts of the COVID- 19 pandemic on life of higher education students: A global perspective. *Sustainability*, *12*(20), 8438. doi:10.3390u12208438

Arizabaleta, S. L., & Ochoa, A. F. (2016). Hacia una educación superior inclusiva en Colombia. *Pedagogía y saberes*, (45), 41-52.

Arnold, D. Y., & Yapita, J. D. (2000). *El rincón de las cabezas: Luchas textuales, educación y Tierras en los Andes*. Instituto de Lengua y Cultura aymara IICA.

Arnold, R. (2004). *Blended learning in international human resource development, on the characteristic features and the comparative didactic advantages of face-to-face learning, distance learning and e-learning*. GIZ. https://www.gtz.de/en/dokumente/en-elearning-blendedlearning-in-international-human-resource-development.pdf

Aronson, E. (1978). The jigsaw classroom. *Sage (Atlanta, Ga.)*.

Arslan, M. Ö., & Bayrakçı, M. (2006). Metaforik düşünme ve öğrenme yaklaşımının eğitimöğretim açısından incelenmesi. *Millî Eğitim*, *171*, 100.

Ary, D., Jacobs, L. C., & Sorensen, C. (2010). *Introduction to research in education* (8th ed.). Wadsworth.

Aslanidou, S., & Menexes, G. (2008). Youth and the Internet: Uses and practices in the home. *Computers & Education*, *51*(3), 1375–1391. doi:10.1016/j.compedu.2007.12.003

Au, K. H. (1998). Social constructivism and the school literacy learning of students of diverse backgrounds. *Journal of Literacy Research*, *30*(2), 297–319. doi:10.1080/10862969809548000

Ausubel, D. (1961). In Defense of Verbal Learning. *Educational Theory*, *11*(1), 15–25. doi:10.1111/j.1741-5446.1961.tb00038.x

Ausubel, D. (1963). *The psychology of meaningful verbal learning*. Grune & Stratton.

Ausubel, D. (1968). *Educational psychology. A cognitive view*. Holt Rinehart and Winston.

Ausubel, D. (1978). *Educational Psychology: A Cognitive View*. Holt, Rinehart and Winston.

Ausubel, D., Novak, J., & Hanesian, H. (1978). *Educational psychology: A cognitive view*. Holt, Rinehart & Winston.

Awang, M. M., Ahmad, A. R., Bakar, N. A. A., Ghani, S. A., Yunus, A. N. M., Ibrahim, M. A. H., & Rahman, M. J. A. (2013). Students' attitudes and their academic performance in nationhood education. *International Education Studies*, *6*, 21–28.

Compilation of References

Ayas, A. (1995). Fen bilimlerinde program geliştirme ve uygulama teknikleri üzerine bir çalışma: İki çağdaş yaklaşımın değerlendirilmesi. [A study on curriculum development and application techniques: Evaluation of two modern approaches]. *Hacettepe University Journal of Education, 11*, 149–155.

Aydın-Günbatar, S., Öztay, E. S., & Ekiz-Kıran, B. (2021). Examination of pre-service chemistry teachers' STEM conceptions through an integrated STEM course. *Turkish Journal of Education*, 251-273.

Aznar, P. (1992). *Constructivismo y educación*. Tirant lo Blanch.

Baker, T., & Clark, J. (2010). Cooperative learning-a double-edged sword: A cooperative learning model for use with diverse student groups. *Intercultural Education, 21*(3), 257–268. doi:10.1080/14675981003760440

Balasubramanian, K., Jaykumar, V., & Fukey, L. N. (2014). A study on "Student preference towards the use of Edmodo as a learning platform to create responsible learning environment". *Procedia: Social and Behavioral Sciences, 144*, 416–422. doi:10.1016/j.sbspro.2014.07.311

Baliga, S. S., Walvekar, P. R., & Mahantshetti, G. J. (2021). Concept map as a teaching and learning tool for medical students. *Journal of Education and Health Promotion, 10*(1), 35. doi:10.4103/jehp.jehp_146_20 PMID:33688544

Bampton, R., & Cowton, C. J. (2002). The e-interview. *Forum Qualitative Social Research, 3*(2). www.qualitatative-research.net/fqs/

Bandura, A. (1986). *Social Foundations of Thought and Action: A Social Cognitive Theory*. Prentice Hall.

Bao, L., & Koenig, K. (2019). Physics education research for 21st century learning. *Discip Interdscip Sci Educ Res, 1*(1), 2. Advance online publication. doi:10.118643031-019-0007-8

Bärenfänger, O. (2005). Learning management: A new approach to structuring hybrid learning arrangements. *Electronic Journal of Foreign Language Teaching, 2*(2), 14–35.

Barker, V., & Millar, R. (1999). Students' reasoning about basic chemical reactions: What changes occur during a context-based post-16 chemistry course? *International Journal of Science Education, 21*(6), 645–665. doi:10.1080/095006999290499

Barker, V., & Millar, R. (2000). Students' reasoning about basic chemical thermodynamics and chemical bonding: What changes occur during a context - based post-16 chemistry course? *International Journal of Science Education, 22*(11), 1171–1200. doi:10.1080/09500690050166742

Bartling, J. D. (2009). *Faculty and administrator perceptions of teaching, the Scholarship of Teaching and Learning, and culture at a teaching university*. (Order No. 3344920) [Doctoral dissertation, Capella University]. ProQuest Dissertations and Theses Global.

Basir, S.N.M., & Bakar, M. Z. A., Hassan, Junainor., & Hassan, H. (2018). Persepsi terhadap penawaran Mata Pelajaran Umum Hubungan Etnik dalam meningkatkan kefahaman patriotisme di Universiti Malaysia Perlis. [Perception of the offering of the General Subject of Ethnic Relations in improving the understanding of patriotism at Universiti Malaysia Perlis]. *Journal of Human Development and Communication, 7*, 143–154.

Başol, G., & Evin-Gencel, İ. (2013). Yansıtıcı Düşünme Düzeyini Belirleme Ölçeği: Geçerlik ve güvenirlik çalışması [Reflective thinking level determination scale: valitidy and reliability study]. *Kuram ve Uygulamada Eğitim Bilimleri [Educational sciences in theory and practice], 13*(2), 929–946.

Bastable, E., McIntosh, K., Falcon, S. F., & Meng, P. (2022). Exploring educators' commitment to racial equity in school discipline practice: A qualitative study of critical incidents. *Journal of Educational & Psychological Consultation, 32*(2), 125–155. doi:10.1080/10474412.2021.1889194

Baytiyeh, H. (2021). Social Media Tools for Educational Sustainability in Conflict-Affected Regions. *Education Sciences*, *11*(11), 662. doi:10.3390/educsci11110662

Beck, E., Sollbrekke, T., Sutphen, M., & Fremstad, E. (2015). When mere knowledge is not enough: The potential of building as self-determination, co-determination, and solidarity. *Higher Education Research & Development*, *34*(3), 445–457. doi:10.1080/07294360.2014.973373

Becker, G. S. (1993). Nobel lecture: The economic way of looking at behavior. *Journal of Political Economy*, *101*(3), 385–409. doi:10.1086/261880

Becker, H. J. (1983). Eine empirische untersuchung zur beliebtheit von chemieunterricht. [An empirical investigation on the popularity of chemistry teaching]. *Chimica Didactica*, *2*, 97–123.

Beghetto, R. A. (2019). Structured uncertainty: How creativity thrives under constraints and uncertainty. In C. A. Mullen (Ed.), Creativity under duress in education? (Vol. 3, pp. 27–40). Springer Nature.

Beghetto, R. A. (2020). Uncertainty. In V.P. Glăveanu (Ed.), The Palgrave encyclopaedia of the possible (pp. 1-7). Palgrave Macmillian.

Beghetto, R. A. (2016). Creative openings in the social interactions of teaching. *Creativity. Theories Research-Applications*, *3*(2), 261–273. doi:10.1515/ctra-2016-0017

Beghetto, R. A. (2017). Creativity and Conformity: A Paradoxical Relationship. In J. A. Plucker (Ed.), *Creativity & Innovation* (pp. 267–275). Prufrock Press Inc.

Beghetto, R. A. (2021). There is no creativity without uncertainty: Dubito ergo creo. *Journal of Creativity*, *31*, 1–5. doi:10.1016/j.yjoc.2021.100005

Beghetto, R. A., & Kaufman, J. (2007). The genesis of creative greatness: Mini-c and the expert performance approach. *High Ability Studies*, *18*(1), 59–61. doi:10.1080/13598130701350668

Bell, S. (2010). Project-Based Learning for the 21st Century: Skills for the Future. *The Clearing House: A Journal of Educational Strategies, Issues and Ideas*, *83*(2), 39–43. doi:10.1080/00098650903505415

Belth, M. (1993). *Metaphor and thinking*. University Press.

Bennett, J., & Lubben, F. (2006). Context-based chemistry: The Salters approach. *International Journal of Science Education*, *28*(9), 999–1015. doi:10.1080/09500690600702496

Bennett, J., Lubben, F., & Hogarth, S. (2006). Bringing science to life: A synthesis of the research evidence on the effects of context-based and sts approaches to science teaching. *Science Education*, *91*(3), 347–370. doi:10.1002ce.20186

Bennett, R. (2011). Formative assessment: A critical review. *Assessment in Education: Principles, Policy & Practice*, *18*(1), 5–25. doi:10.1080/0969594X.2010.513678

Ben-Peretz, M., Mendelson, N., & Kron, F. W. (2003). How teachers in different educational contexts view their roles. *Teaching and Teacher Education*, *19*(2), 277–290. doi:10.1016/S0742-051X(02)00100-2

Bergdahl, N., Nouri, J., & Fors, U. (2020). Disengagement, engagement and digital skills in technology-enhanced learning. *Education and Information Technologies*, *25*(2), 957–983. doi:10.100710639-019-09998-w

Bernard, P., & Mendez, J. (2020). Low-Cost 3D-Printed Polarimeter. *Journal of Chemical Education*, *97*(4), 1162–1166. doi:10.1021/acs.jchemed.9b01083

Compilation of References

Bernstein, D. (2010). Finding your place in the Scholarship of Teaching and Learning. *International Journal for the Scholarship of Teaching and Learning*, *4*(2). doi:10.20429/ijsotl.2010.040204

Berryman, T. (2002). Éco-ontogenèse et éducation: les relations à l'environnement dans le développement humain et leur prise en compte en éducation relative à l'environnement durant la petite enfance, l'enfance et l'adolescence [Eco-ontogeny and education: relations to the environment in human development and their consideration in environmental education during infancy, childhoos, and adolescence]. *Open Edition Journals*.

Besser, A., Flett, G. L., & Zeigler-Hill, V. (2022). Adaptability to a sudden transition to online learning during the COVID-19 pandemic: Understanding the challenges for students. *Scholarship of Teaching and Learning in Psychology*, *8*(2), 85. doi:10.1037/stl0000198

Béteille, T., & Evans, D. (2021). *Successful Teachers, Successful Students: Recruiting and Supporting Society's Most Crucial Profession*. World Bank. Retrieved from https://policycommons.net/artifacts/2445925/successful-teachers-successful-students/3467666/

Bevitt, S. (2015). Assessment innovation student experience: A new assessment challenge and call for a multi-perspective approach to assessment research. *Assessment & Evaluation in Higher Education*, *40*(1), 103–109. doi:10.1080/02602938.2014.890170

Bhat, S. (2021). *An Evaluative Study of Educational Philosophy of Swami Vivekananda*. doi:10.31426/ijamsr.2021.4.7.4511

Biggs, J. (2014). Constructive alignment in university teaching. *HERDSA Review of Higher Education*, *1*, 5–22.

Biggs, J., & Tang, C. (2011). *Teaching for Quality Learning at University*. McGraw-Hill/Society for Research into Higher Education / Open University Press.

Bjarne, I. (1992). *Frivilligt Arbejde i idrætsforeninger*. DHL/Systime.

Black, P., & Wiliam, D. (1998). 'Assessment and Classroom Learning, Assessment in Education: Principles. *Policy & Practice*, *5*, 1.

Blackshields, D. (2016). Encountering the 'unknown knowns': Scaffolding contemplative reading to cultivate a creative inquiry disposition in 21st century undergraduate economics students. In N. Alias & J. Luaran (Eds.), Student driven Learning in the 21st Century (pp. 217-238). IGI Global.

Blackshields, D. (2019). Songs in the key of life: Designing a deep dive learning journey to employability. *Guidance Matters*, (3), 42-49.

Blackshields, D. (2021, December 12). *Within you, without you: The imperative to cultivate the creative promise of thinking together* [Powerpoint slides]. UCC, Cork, Ireland.

Blackshields, D. (2022a, April 8). *Provocating competence to provoke strategic conversations* [course document]. UCC, Cork, Ireland.

Blackshields, D. (2022b, February 3). *Embracing the potentiality of a post-covid 19 future* [course document]. UCC, Cork, Ireland.

Blackshields, D. (2022c, October 25). *Research assistant: Interview guide* [course document]. UCC, Cork, Ireland.

Blackshields, D. (2010). Making connections for mindful inquiry: using reflective journals to scaffold an autobiographical approach to learning in economics. In B. Higgs, S. Kilcommins, & T. Ryan (Eds.), *Making connections: Intentional teaching for integrative learning* (pp. 45–64). NAIRTL.

Blackshields, D. (2014). Yes, and... cultivating the art of conversation through improvisational classroom experiences. In *Integrative learning: International research and practice* (pp. 68–82). Routledge. doi:10.4324/9781315884769

Blackshields, D., & McCarthy, M. (2013). The game is afoot – playing the sleuth in creative problems solving performances by business economics students. In *Innovative business school teaching: Engaging the millennial generation* (pp. 109–127). Routledge.

Blackstone, B., & Harwood, C. (2011). Pedagogical blogging for university courses. In R. Jaidev, M. L. C. Sadorra, J. C. Wong, M., C. Lee, & B. Paredes-Lorente (Eds.), *Global perspectives, local initiatives: Reflections and practice in ELT* (pp. 67-82). National University of Singapore. https://nus.edu.sg/celc/research/books/3rdsymposium/067to084-blackstone.pdf

Blake, C. (2009). Potential of text-based internet chats for improving oral fluency in a second language. *Modern Language Journal*, *93*(2), 227–240. doi:10.1111/j.1540-4781.2009.00858.x

Bloom, B. (1956). *Taxonomy of Educational Objectives. Book I: Cognitive Domain*. David Mckay.

Bloom, B. (1995). *Human qualities and learning at school*. National Education Printing House.

Böcher, J. (2005). *Halogenverbindungen im alltag. [Halogen compounds in everyday life]* CHIDS. http://www.chids.de/dachs/expvortr/719Halogenverbindungen_Boecher.pdf .

Bockman, D. J., & Kroth, M. (2010). Immunity to transformational learning and change. *The Learning Organization*, *17*(4), 328–342. doi:10.1108/09696471011043090

Bonwell, C. C., & Eison, J. A. (1991). Active learning: creating excitement in the classroom. *ASH#-ERIC Higher Education Report No. 1*. The George Washington University.

Bonwell, C. C., & Eison, J. A. (1991). Active Learning: Creating Excitement in the Classroom. *ASHE-ERIC Higher Education Report*, *1*(1), 16–17.

Boostrom, R. (1998). Safe spaces: Reflections on an educational metaphor. *Journal of Curriculum Studies*, *30*(4), 397–408. doi:10.1080/002202798183549

Borden, R. J. (1977). One more look at social and environmental psychology: Away from the looking glass and into the future. *Personality and Social Psychology Bulletin*, *3*(3), 407–411. doi:10.1177/014616727700300309

Borup, J., & Stevens, M. (2016). Parents' perceptions of teacher support at a cyber charter high school. *Journal of Online Learning Research*, *2*(3), 227–246. https://files.eric.ed.gov/fulltext/EJ1148409.pdf

Borup, J., West, R. E., & Graham, C. R. (2012). Improving online social presence through asynchronous video. *Internet High. Educ.*, *2012*(15), 195–203. doi:10.1016/j.iheduc.2011.11.001

Boucher, A. (2010). Les usages politiques des politiques publiques et des enquêtes sociologiques. L'instrumentalisation d'une politique sportive départementale et de son évaluation. *Sciences sociales et sport*, *3*, 157-192.

Boudreau, I. (1997). *Attitude des adolescents et des jeunes adultes à l'égard de la pratique de comportements sécuritaires en planche à neige [Attitudes of adolescents and young adults toward practicing safe snowboarding behaviors]*. [Doctoral dissertation, Université du Québec à Trois-Rivières].

Boyd, M. P. (2016). Calling for Response-Ability in Our Classrooms. *Language Arts*, *93*(3), 226–233.

Boyd, M., Mykula, V., & Choi, Y. (2020). Responsive and responsible teacher telling: An across time examination of classroom talk during whole group writing workshop minilessons. *Research Papers in Education*, *35*(5), 574–602. doi:10.1080/02671522.2019.1601761

Compilation of References

Boyer, E. L. (1990). The scholarship of teaching from: Scholarship reconsidered: Priorities of the professoriate. *College Teaching*, *39*(1), 11–13. doi:10.1080/87567555.1991.10532213

Brady, P., & Bowd, A. (2005). Mathematics anxiety, prior experience and confidence to teach mathematics among preservice education students. *Teachers and Teaching*, *11*(1), 37–46.

Bransford, J. D., Brown, A. L., & Cocking, R. R. (Eds.). (1999). *How people learn: Brain, mind, experience, and school*. National Academy Press.

Braun, V., & Clarke, V. (2013). *Successful qualitative research: A practical guide for beginners*. sage.

Braun, V., & Clarke, V. (2006). Using thematic analysis in psychology. *Qualitative Research in Psychology*, *3*(2), 77–101. doi:10.1191/1478088706qp063oa

Brayshaw, M., Gordon, N. A., & Grey, S. (2019). Smart, Social, Flexible and Fun: Escaping the Flatlands of Virtual Learning Environments. In K. Arai, R. Bhatia, & S. Kapoor (Eds.), *Intelligent Computing. CompCom 2019. Advances in Intelligent Systems and Computing* (Vol. 998, pp. 1047–1060). Springer. doi:10.1007/978-3-030-22868-2_70

Broadbent, J., Sharman, S., Panadero, E., & Fuller-Tyszkiewicz, M. (2021). How does self-regulated learning influence formative assessment and summative grade? Comparing online and blended learners. *The Internet and Higher Education*, *50*, 100805. doi:10.1016/j.iheduc.2021.100805

Brookfield, S. D. (2015). *The skillful teacher: On technique, trust, and responsiveness in the classroom*. John Wiley & Sons.

Brown, T. (2008). Design Thinking: Harvard Business Review. *Academia (Caracas)*.

Broza, O., Lifshitz, A., & Atzmon, S. (2022). Exploring a Model to Develop Critical Reflective Thought Among Elementary School Math Preservice Teachers. *Journal of Education*, *202*(4), 406–415. doi:10.1177/0022057421998336

Bryant, W. K., Jeon-Slaughter, H., Kang, H., & Tax, A. (2003). Participation in philanthropic activities: Donating money and time. *Journal of Consumer Policy*, *26*(1), 43–73. doi:10.1023/A:1022626529603

Bubeck, P., Wouter Botzen, W. J., Laudan, J., Aerts, J. C., & Thieken, A. H. (2018). Insights into flood-coping appraisals of protection motivation theory: Empirical evidence from Germany and France. *Risk Analysis*, *38*(6), 1239–1257. doi:10.1111/risa.12938 PMID:29148082

Budiarto, M. K. (2020). Identification of students' needs for multimedia development in craft and entrepreneurial topic: Information technology-assisted learning. *COUNS-EDU: The International Journal of Counseling and Education*, *5*(4), 153–162. doi:10.23916/0020200525740

Burke, K., & Larmar, S. (2021). Acknowledging another face in the virtual crowd: Reimagining the online experience in higher education through an online pedagogy of care. *Journal of Further and Higher Education*, *45*(5), 601–615. doi:10.1080/0309877X.2020.1804536

Burns, E. (2010). Developing email interview practices in qualitative research. *Sociological Research Online*, *15*(4), 24–35. doi:10.5153ro.2232

Burns, L. D., & Botzakis, S. (2016). *Teach on purpose! Responsive teaching for student success*. Teachers College Press.

Burton, R. (2022). Nursing Students Perceptions of Using YouTube to Teach Psychomotor Skills: A Comparative Pilot Study. *SAGE Open Nursing*, *8*. doi:10.1177/23779608221117385 PMID:35923914

Busker, M., & Flint, A. (2022). Neue Zugänge zu chemischen Reaktionen: Das Basiskonzept des Chemieunterrichts [New approaches to chemical reactions: the basic concept of chemistry teaching]. *Unterricht Chemie*, *2022*(190), 2–5.

Cabi, E. (2018). The impact of the flipped classroom model on students' academic achievement. *International Review of Research in Open and Distance Learning, 19*(3), 203–221. doi:10.19173/irrodl.v19i3.3482

Cadoret, I., Benjamin, C., Martin, F., Herrard, N., & Sandré, T. (2004). Économétrie appliquée: méthodes, applications, corrigés. De Boeck University.

Calvo, R., Arbiol, A., & Iglesias, A. (2014). Are all chats suitable for learning purposes? A study of the required characteristics. *Procedia Computer Science, 27*, 251–260. doi:10.1016/j.procs.2014.02.028

Canale, M., & Swain, M. (1980). Theoretical bases of communicative approaches to second language teaching and testing. *Applied Linguistics, 1*(1), 1–47. doi:10.1093/applin/1.1.1

Carpenter, T. P., Fennema, E., Peterson, P. L., Chiang, C. P., & Loef, M. (1989). Using knowledge of children's mathematics thinking in classroom teaching: An experimental study. *American Educational Research Journal, 26*(4), 499–531. https://doi.org/10.3102/00028312026004499

Carroll, J. B., & Eifler, K. E. (2002). Servant, master, double-edged sword: Metaphors teachers use to discuss technology. *Journal of Technology and Teacher Education, 10*, 235–246.

Carr, R., Palmer, S., & Hagel, P. (2015). Active learning: The importance of developing a comprehensive measure. *Active Learning in Higher Education, 16*(3), 173–186. doi:10.1177/1469787415589529

Carrus, G., Scopelliti, M., Fornara, F., Bonnes, M., & Bonaiuto, M. (2014). Place attachment, community identification, and pro-environmental engagement. *Place attachment: Advances in theory, methods and applications*, 156-162.

Carson, E. D. (1993). On race, gender, culture, and research on the voluntary sector. *Nonprofit Management & Leadership, 3*(3), 327–335. doi:10.1002/nml.4130030311

Carter, K. (1990). Meaning and metaphor: Case knowledge in teaching. *Theory into Practice, 29*(2), 109–115. doi:10.1080/00405849009543440

Casaló, L. V., & Escario, J. J. (2018). Heterogeneity in the association between environmental attitudes and pro-environmental behavior: A multilevel regression approach. *Journal of Cleaner Production, 175*, 155–163. doi:10.1016/j.jclepro.2017.11.237

Cavanagh, S. R. (2016). *The spark of online learning: energizing the college classroom with the science of emotion*. West Virginia University Press.

Cerratto Pargman, T., McGrath, C., Viberg, O., Kitto, K., Knight, S., & Ferguson, R. (2021). Responsible learning analytics: creating just, ethical, and caring. In *Companion Proceedings 11th International Conference on Learning Analytics & Knowledge (LAK21)*.

Chakraborty, P., Mittal, P., Gupta, M. S., Yadav, S., & Arora, A. (2021). Opinion of students on online education during the COVID-19 pandemic. *Human Behavior and Emerging Technologies, 3*(3), 357–365. doi:10.1002/hbe2.240

Chang, C.-C., & Wang, Y.-H. (2021). Using Phenomenological Methodology with Thematic Analysis to Examine and Reflect on Commonalities of Instructors' Experiences in MOOCs. *Education Sciences, 11*(5), 203. doi:10.3390/educsci11050203

Charney, R. S. (1993). Teaching children to care: Management in the responsive classroom. Northeast Foundation for Children.

Chatzara, E., Kotsakis, R., Tsipas, N., Vrysis, L., & Dimoulas, C. (2019). Machine-Assisted Learning in Highly-Interdisciplinary Media Fields: A Multimedia Guide on Modern Art. *Education Sciences, 9*(3), 198. doi:10.3390/educsci9030198

Compilation of References

Chen, F., Chen, H., Guo, D., & Long, R. (2017). Analysis of undesired environmental behavior among Chinese undergraduates. *Journal of Cleaner Production, 162*, 1239–1251. doi:10.1016/j.jclepro.2017.06.051

Cheng, J. (2017). Learning to attend to precision: The impact of micro-teaching guided by expert secondary mathematics teachers on pre-service teachers' teaching practice. *ZDM Mathematics Education, 49*(2), 279–289. doi:10.100711858-017-0839-7

Cheng, M.-M., Lacaste, A. V., Saranza, C., & Chuang, H.-H. (2021). Culturally Responsive Teaching in Technology-Supported Learning Environments in Marine Education for Sustainable Development. *Sustainability, 13*(24), 13922. doi:10.3390u132413922

Chen, J., Zhang, L. J., Wang, X., & Zhang, T. (2021). Impacts of Self-Regulated Strategy Development-Based Revision Instruction on English-as-a-Foreign-Language Students' Self-Efficacy for Text Revision: A Mixed-Methods Study. Journal. *Frontiers in Psychology, 12*, 2609. https://www.frontiersin.org/article/10.3389/fpsyg.2021.670100

Chen, M. P., Wang, L. C., Zou, D., Lin, S. Y., & Xie, H. R. (2019). Effects of caption and gender on junior high students' EFL learning from iMap-enhanced contextualized learning. *Computers & Education, 140*(103602). Advance online publication. doi:10.1016/j.compedu.2019.103602

Chiu, T. (2022). Applying the self-determination theory (SDT) to explain student engagement in online learning during the COVID-19 pandemic. *Journal of Research on Technology in Education, 54*(1), S14–S30. doi:10.1080/15391523.2021.1891998

Chng, H. H., & Martensson, K. (2020). Leading change from different shores: The challenges of contextualizing the Scholarship of Teaching and Learning. *Teaching & Learning Inquiry, 8*(1), 24–41. doi:10.20343/teachlearninqu.8.1.3

Choi, N. G., & Bohman, T. M. (2007). Predicting the changes in depressive symptomatology in later life: How much do changes in health status, marital and caregiving status, work and volunteering, and health-related behaviors contribute. *Journal of Aging and Health, 19*(1), 152–177. doi:10.1177/0898264306297602 PMID:17215206

Choo, Y. B., Abdullah, T., & Nawi, A. M. (2018). Learning to teach: Patterns of reflective practice in a written journal. *LSP International Journal, 5*(2). Advance online publication. doi:10.11113/lspi.v5n2.80

Chua, Y. P. (2022). *Mastering Research Methods*. McGraw-Hill Education.

Chu, K. K., Lee, C. I., & Tsai, R. S. (2011). Ontology technology to assist learners' navigation in the concept map learning system. *Expert Systems with Applications, 38*(9), 11293–11299. doi:10.1016/j.eswa.2011.02.178

Churchill, G. A. Jr. (1995). *Marketing research: Methodological foundations* (6th ed.). The Dryden Press.

Coates, H. B. (2008). *Australasian Survey of Student Engagement.* Institution Report.

Cocco, S. (2006). *Student leadership development: The contribution of project-based learning* [Unpublished Master's thesis]. Royal Roads University, Victoria, BC. https://www.collectionscanada.gc.ca/obj/thesescanada/vol2/002/MR17869.PDF?oclc_number=271429340

Coffey, J., Hammer, D., Levin, D., & Grant, T. (2011). The missing disciplinary substance of formative assessment. *Journal of Research in Science Teaching, 48*(10), 1109–1136. doi:10.1002/tea.20440

Cohen, L. (1992). Anthem [Recorded by L. Cohen]. On *The future* [CD]. Columbia.

Cohen, L., & Robinson, S. (2001). In my secret life [Recorded by L. Cohen]. On *Ten new songs* [CD]. Columbia.

Collingwood, R. G. (1938). *The principles of art*. Oxford University Press.

Collins, E. C., & Gren, J. L. (1990). Metaphors: The construction of a perspective. *Theory into Practice*, *29*(2), 71–77. doi:10.1080/00405849009543435

Cook, J., & Burchell, J. (2018). Bridging the gaps in employee volunteering: Why the third sector doesn't always win. *Nonprofit and Voluntary Sector Quarterly*, *47*(1), 165–184. doi:10.1177/0899764017734649

Cooperrider, D. L., & Srivastva, S. (1987). Appreciative Inquiry. *Research in Organizational Change and Development*, *1*, 129–169.

Cotter, R., Kiser, S., Rasmussen, J., & Vemu, S. (2022). Supporting biology education research at community colleges: Implementing and adapting evidence-based practices. *New Directions for Community Colleges*, *2022*(199), 201–213.

Covey, S. (2004). The Seven Habits of Highly Effective People. Free Press. (Original publication 1989)

Cramer, E. D., Little, M. E., & McHatton, P. A. (2014). Demystifying the data-based decision-making process. *Action in Teacher Education*, *36*(5-6), 389–400. doi:10.1080/01626620.2014.977690

Cremer, A., Kalbe, F., Gläscher, J., & Schwabe, L. (2021). Stress reduces both model-based and model-free neural computations during flexible learning. *NeuroImage*, *229*, 117747. doi:10.1016/j.neuroimage.2021.117747 PMID:33454417

Crespo, S. (2003). Learning to pose mathematical problems: Exploring changes in preservice teachers' practices. *Educational Studies in Mathematics*, *52*, 243–270.

Creswell, J. W. (2011). Controversies in mixed methods research. The Sage Handbook of Qualitative Research, 4(1), 269-284.

Creswell, J. W., & Creswell, J. D. (2005). Mixed methods research: Developments, debates, and dilemmas. *Research in organizations: Foundations and methods of inquiry, 2*, 315-326.

Creswell, J. W., & Garrett, A. L. (2008). The "movement" of mixed methods research and the role of educators. *South African Journal of Education*, *28*(3), 321–333. doi:10.15700aje.v28n3a176

Creswell, J. W., & Poth, C. N. (2017). *Qualitative inquiry and research design: Choosing among five approaches*. Sage publications.

Cross, N. (1982). Designerly Ways of Knowing. *Design Studies*, *3*(4), 221–227. doi:10.1016/0142-694X(82)90040-0

Crowder, M., Antoniadou, M., & Stewart, J. (2019). To BlikBook or not to BlikBook: Exploring student engagement of an online discussion platform. *Innovations in Education and Teaching International*, *56*(3), 295–306. doi:10.1080/14703297.2018.1502091

CSEFRS. (2017). Rapport sur l'éducation non formelle. Author.

Csikszentmihalyi, M. (2013). *Creativity: the psychology of discovery and invention*. Harper Perennial Modern Classics.

Cybinski, P., & Selvanathan, S. (2005). Learning experience and learning effectiveness in undergraduate statistics: Modelling performance in traditional and flexible learning environments. *Decision Sciences Journal of Innovative Education*, *3*(2), 251–271. doi:10.1111/j.1540-4609.2005.00069.x

Dahar, R. W. (2011). *Teori belajar dan pembelajaran*. Erlangga.

Daley, B. J., & Torre, D. M. (2010). Concept maps in medical education: An analytical literature review. *Medical Education*, *2010*(44), 440–448. doi:10.1111/j.1365-2923.2010.03628.x PMID:20374475

Dall'Alba, G. (2012). Re-imagining the university: Developing a capacity to care. In R. Barnett (Ed.), *The future university: Ideas and possibilities* (pp. 112–122). Routledge.

Compilation of References

Dang, H., Li, E., & Bruwer, J. (2012). Understanding Climate Change Adaptive Behaviour of Farmers: An Integrated Conceptual Framework. *International Journal of Climate Change: Impacts & Responses, 3*(2), 255–272. doi:10.18848/1835-7156/CGP/v03i02/37106

Daniels, H. (2002). *Literature circles: Voice and choice in book clubs and reading Groups.* Stenhouse.

Darby, F. (2020). *Emotions in online teaching: A powerful tool for helping online students engage, persist, and succeed.* https://www.facultyfocus.com/articles/online-education/online-student-engagement/emotions-in-online-teaching-a-powerful-tool-for-helping-online-students-engage-persist-and-succeed/

Darling, A. L. (2003). Scholarship of Teaching and Learning in Communication: New Connections, New Directions, New Possibilities. *Communication Education, 52*(1), 47–49. doi:10.1080/03634520302458

Dasgupta, S. (2019). *A Cognitive Historical Approach to Creativity.* Routledge. doi:10.4324/9780429032363

Datnow, A., & Hubbard, L. (2015). Teachers' use of assessment data to inform instruction: Lessons from the past and prospect for the future. *Teachers College Record, 117*(4), 1–26. https://eric.ed.gov/?id=EJ1056748. doi:10.1177/016146811511700408

Day, K. M., & Devlin, R. A. (1996). Volunteerism and crowding out: Canadian econometric evidence. *The Canadian Journal of Economics. Revue Canadienne d'Economique, 29*(1), 37–53. doi:10.2307/136150

De Leeuw, A., Valois, P., Ajzen, I., & Schmidt, P. (2015). Using the theory of planned behavior to identify key beliefs underlying pro-environmental behavior in high-school students: Implications for educational interventions. *Journal of Environmental Psychology, 42*, 128–138. doi:10.1016/j.jenvp.2015.03.005

Degli Antoni, G. (2009). Intrinsic vs. extrinsic motivations to volunteer and social capital formation. *Kyklos, 62*(3), 359–370. doi:10.1111/j.1467-6435.2009.00440.x

Del Campo, S. (2000). *Análisis del manejo de la autoevaluación de los alumnos por parte de los profesores que imparten cursos transferidos con el nuevo modelo de rediseño creado en la misión del ITESM para el año 2005 en el campus Cd. Juárez* [Tesis de maestría]. Instituto Tecnológico y de Estudios Superiores de Monterrey. https://repositorio.tec.mx/bitstream/handle/11285/628762/EGE00000007633.pdf?sequence=1

Delgado, A. M., & Oliver, R. (2010). Interacción entre la evaluación continua y la autoevaluación formativa: La potenciación del aprendizaje autónomo. *Revista de Docencia Universitaria, 4*, 2-13. https://revistas.um.es/redu/article/view/92581

DeLuca, C., LaPointe-McEwan, D., & Luhanga, U. (2016). Approaches to Classroom Assessment Inventory: A New Instrument to Support Teacher Assessment Literacy. *Educational Assessment, 21*(4), 248–266. Advance online publication. doi:10.1080/10627197.2016.1236677

Denton, C. A., Fletcher, J. M., Anthony, J. L., & Francis, D. J. (2006). An evaluation of intensive intervention for students with persistent reading difficulties. *Journal of Learning Disabilities, 39*(5), 447–466. doi:10.1177/00222194060390050601 PMID:17004676

Denzin, N. K. (2012). Triangulation 2.0. *Journal of mixed methods research, 6*(2), 80-88. doi:10.1177/1558689812437186

Desfitri, R. (2018). Pre-service teachers' challenges in presenting mathematical problems. *Journal of Physics: Conference Series, 948*(1), 012035.

Deutsch, M. (1949). A theory of co-operation and competition. *Human Relations, 2*(2), 129–152. doi:10.1177/001872674900200204

Dewey, J. (1916). *Democracy and education: an introduction to the philosophy of education.* The Free Press.

Dewey, J. (1938). Experience & Education. *Touchstone (Nashville, Tenn.)*.

Dewsbury, B., & Brame, C. J. (2019). Inclusive teaching. *CBE Life Sciences Education*, *18*(2), fe2.

Dhamija, A., & Dhamija, D. (2020). Impact of Innovative and Interactive Instructional Strategies on Student Classroom Participation. In M. Montebello (Ed.), Handbook of Research on Digital Learning (pp. 20–37). IGI Global. doi:10.4018/978-1-5225-9304-1.ch002

Dias, A. (2009). Technology Enhanced Learning and Augmented Reality: An Application on Multimedia Interactive Books. *International Business & Economics Review*, *1*(1), 69–79.

Dimoulas, C. A., Veglis, A. A., & Kalliris, G. (2019). Semantically Enhanced Authoring of Shared Media. In M. Khosrow-Pour, D.B.A. (Ed.), Advanced Methodologies and Technologies in Media and Communications (pp. 277–289). IGI Global. doi:10.4018/978-1-5225-7601-3.ch022

Dimoulas, C., Veglis, A., & Kalliris, G. (2015). Audiovisual Hypermedia in the Semantic Web. In M. Khosrow-Pour, D.B.A. (Ed.), Encyclopedia of Information Science and Technology, Third Edition (pp. 7594–7604). IGI Global.

Dimoulas, C., Veglis, A., & Kalliris, G. (2014). Application of Mobile Cloud-Based Technologies in News Reporting: Current Trends and Future Perspectives. In J. Rodrigues, K. Lin, & J. Lloret (Eds.), *Mobile Networks and Cloud Computing Convergence for Progressive Services and Applications* (pp. 320–343). IGI Global. doi:10.4018/978-1-4666-4781-7.ch017

Djoub, Z. (2018). *Assessment for learning: Key principles and strategies*. Edulearn2change. https://edulearn2change.com/article-assessment-for-learning-key-principles-strategies/

Dobbins, K. (2008). Enhancing the Scholarship of Teaching and Learning: A Study of the Factors Identified as Promoting and Hindering the Scholarly Activities of Academics in One Faculty. *International Journal for the Scholarship of Teaching and Learning*, *2*(2). doi:10.20429/ijsotl.2008.020217

Dombal, R. (2011, November 9). Achtung baby (super deluxe edition). *Pitchfork*. Retrieved from https://pitchfork.com/reviews/albums/16022-achtung-baby-super-deluxe-edition/

Domunco, C. F. (2011). Social media and the social (re)construction of the educational reality. *Journal of Educational Sciences & Psychology*, *1*(2).

Dung, N. T. (2022). Challenges of Online Learning and Some Recommendations for University Students in Vietnam. *Journal of Algebraic Statistics, 13*(2), 350-358. https://publishoa.com

Dyer, E. B., & Sherin, M. G. (2016). Instructional reasoning about interpretations of student thinking that supports responsive teaching in secondary mathematics. *ZDM*, *48*(1), 69–82.

Ellinger, A. D. (2004). The concept of self-directed learning and its implications for human resource development. *Advances in Developing Human Resources*, *6*(2), 158–177. doi:10.1177/1523422304263327

Ellis, R. (2015). *Understanding second language acquisition* (2nd ed.). Oxford University Press.

Embi, M. A., Hamat, A., & Sulaiman, A. (2012). The Use of Learning Management Systems Among Malaysian University Lecturers. *International Journal of Learning*, *18*(4), 61–70. doi:10.18848/1447-9494/CGP/v18i04/47554

Endut, N. A., Amin, R., Mohamad, A. N., & Din, H. A. M. (2019). Impak Mata Pelajaran Umum dari kaca mata Kolej Universiti Islam Antarabangsa Selangor (KUIS) [Impact of general sucjects from the eyes of Selangor international Islamic university college (KUIS)]. *e-Bangi, 16*(2) 1-18.

Engeström, Y. (1990). *Learning, working and imagining: Twelve studies in activity theory*. Orienta-Konsultit.

Engeström, Y. (1999). Activity theory and individual and social transformation. In Y. Engestrom, R. Miettinen, & R.-M. Punamaki (Eds.), *Perspectives on activity theory* (pp. 19–38). Cambridge University Press. doi:10.1017/CBO9780511812774.003

Engeström, Y. (2001). Expansive learning at work: Toward an activity theory reconceptualization. *Journal of Education and Work*, *14*(1), 133–156. doi:10.1080/13639080020028747

Engeström, Y. (2008). Enriching activity theory without shortcuts. *Interacting with Computers*, *20*(2), 256–259. doi:10.1016/j.intcom.2007.07.003

Engeström, Y., & Glaveǎnu, V. (2012). On Third Generation Activity Theory: Interview with Yrjö Engeström. *Europe's Journal of Psychology*, *8*(4), 515–518. doi:10.5964/ejop.v8i4.555

Ernawati, R., Rahman, F. F., Khoiroh, M. S., Rahmah, F. D., Sulistiawan, J., & Moslehpour, M. (2021). The Effectiveness of Web-Based Audiovisual Media Applications in Monitoring Children's Growth to Prevent Stunting. *Advances in Decision Sciences*, *25*(3), 1–11.

Espejo, R. M. (2016). ¿Pedagogía activa o métodos activos? El caso del aprendizaje activo en la universidad. *Revista Digital de Investigación en Docencia Universitaria*, *10*(1), 16. doi:10.19083/ridu.10.456

Estonian Ministry of the Interior. (2006). *Civic initiative action plan 2007-2010/Development plan of voluntary action 2007 - 2010*. Author.

Estriegana, R., Medina-Merodio, J.-A., Robina-Ramírez, R., & Barchino, R. (2021). Analysis of cooperative skills development through relational coordination in a gamified online learning environment. *Electronics (Basel)*, *10*(16), 2032. doi:10.3390/electronics10162032

Evans, K., & Kersh, N. (2014). Training and workplace learning. In K. Kraiger, J. Passmore, N. R. Santos, & S. Malvezzi (Eds.), *The Wiley-Blackwell handbook of the psychology of training, development and performance improvement* (pp. 50–67). Wiley. doi:10.1002/9781118736982.ch4

Eyler, J. R. (2018). *How humans learn: The science and stories behind effective college teaching*. West Virginia University Press.

Faisal, F. A., & Ali, M. M. (2022). Cabaran Pembelajaran Atas Talian Di Rumah: Tinjauan Ibu Bapa Murid Berkeperluan Khas Bermasalah Pembelajaran [Challenges Of Online Learning At Home: A Survey Of Parents Of Students With Special Needs With Learning Disabilities]. *International Journal of Advanced Research in Islamic Studies and Education*, *2*(1), 129–141.

Falcione, S., Campbell, E., McCollum, B., Chamberlain, J., Macias, M., Morsch, L., & Pinder, C. (2019). Emergence of Different Perspectives of Success in Collaborative Learning. *The Canadian Journal for the Scholarship of Teaching and Learning*, *10*(2), n2. doi:10.5206/cjsotl-rcacea.2019.2.8227

Fangfang, T., & Hao, T. (2021). Research on the teaching mode of "dual-line hybrid integration" in the post-epidemic period. *Computer Knowledge and Technology*, *17*(10), 152–165.

Farrington, C. A., Roderick, M., Allensworth, E., Nagaoka, J., Keyes, T. S., Johnson, D. W., & Beechum, N. O. (2012). *Teaching Adolescents to Become Learners. the Role of Noncognitive Factors in Shaping School Performance: A Critical Literature Review*. University of Chicago Consortium on Chicago School Research.

Feist, G. J. (2010). The Function of Personality in Creativity. In J. C. Kaufman & R. J. Sternberg (Eds.), *The Cambridge Handbook of Creativity* (pp. 113–130). Cambridge University Press. doi:10.1017/CBO9780511763205.009

Felton, P., & Binnix, T. (2013). *Engaging Students as partners in Teaching, Learning, and SoTL*. Wiley.

Fenwick, T. (2016). Social media, professionalism and higher education: A sociomaterial consideration. *Studies in Higher Education*, *41*(4), 664–677. doi:10.1080/03075079.2014.942275

Ferrell, O. C., & Gresham, L. G. (1985). A contingency framework for understanding ethical decision making in marketing. *Journal of Marketing*, *49*(Summer), 87–96. doi:10.1177/002224298504900308

Fiorillo, D., & Nappo, N. (2020). Volunteering and self-perceived individual health: Cross-country evidence from nine European countries. *International Journal of Social Economics*.

Fishbein, M., & Ajzen, I. (1974). Attitudes towards objects as predictors of single and multiple behavioral criteria. *Psychological Review*, *81*(1), 59–74. doi:10.1037/h0035872

Fishbein, M., Jaccard, J., Davidson, A. R., Ajzen, I., & Loken, B. (1980). Predicting and understanding family planning behaviors. In *Understanding attitudes and predicting social behavior*. Prentice Hall.

Fitzsimmons, C. J., & Thompson, C. A. (2022). Developmental differences in monitoring accuracy and cue use when estimating whole-number and fraction magnitudes. *Cognitive Development*, *61*, 101148. https://doi.org/10.1016/j.cogdev.2021.101148

Flavell, H., Roberts, L., Fyfe, G., & Broughton, M. (2018). Shifting goal posts: The impact of academic workforce reshaping and the introduction of teaching academic roles on the Scholarship of Teaching and Learning. *Australian Educational Researcher*, *45*(2), 179–194. doi:10.100713384-017-0247-6

Flener-Lovitt, C., Bailey, K., & Han, R. (2020). Using structured teams to develop social presence in asynchronous chemistry courses. *Journal of Chemical Education*, *97*(9), 2519–2525. doi:10.1021/acs.jchemed.0c00765

Fletcher, H. R. (2018). What is responsive teaching? *Improving Teaching*.

Fletcher, T., & Chróinín, D. N. (2021). Pedagogical principles that support the prioritisation of meaningful experiences in physical education: Conceptual and practical considerations. *Physical Education and Sport Pedagogy*, *27*(5), 455–466. doi:10.1080/17408989.2021.1884672

Flores, G., De Alba, R., & Caicedo, E. (2020). Recomendaciones básicas de competencias docentes para la modalidad no escolarizada en tiempos de la pandemia. *Humanidades, Tecnología y Ciencia, del instituto Politécnico Nacional*, *22*(25). http://revistaelectronica-ipn.org/ResourcesFiles/Contenido/23/HUMANIDADES_23_000877.pdf

Florescu, O. (2014). Positive and Negative Influences of the Mass Media upon Education. *Procedia: Social and Behavioral Sciences*, *149*, 349–353. doi:10.1016/j.sbspro.2014.08.271

Forget, E. L. (2011). The town with no poverty: The health effects of a Canadian guaranteed annual income field experiment. *Canadian Public Policy*, *37*(3), 283–305. doi:10.3138/cpp.37.3.283

Foutsitzi, A. (2022). Images in Educational Textbooks and Educational Audiovisual Media. *European Journal of Language and Literature*, *8*(2), 26–32.

Fraile, J., Zamorano-Sande, D., Izquierdo, M. G., & Sanchez-Iglesias, I. (2020). Self-regulated learning and formative assessment process on group work. *RELIEVE*, *26*(1). doi:10.7203/relieve.26.1.17402

Franada, J. M. (2018). 2C-2I-1R Pedagogical Approaches in Teaching Technology and Livelihood Education Exploratory Courses and the Academic Performance of Grade 8 Students in the Division of Lipa. *Ascendens Asia Journal of Multidisciplinary Research Abstracts*, *2*(6).

Frisen, N., & Kuskis, A. (2013). Modes of Interaction. In M. G. Moore (Ed.), *Handbook of Distance Education* (pp. 351–371). Routledge. doi:10.4324/9780203803738.ch22

Compilation of References

Frolova, E. V., Rogach, O. V., & Ryabova, T. M. (2020). Digitalization of Education in Modern Scientific Discourse: New Trends and Risks Analysis. *European Journal of Contemporary Education*, *9*(2), 313–336.

Frolova, E. V., Ryabova, T. M., & Rogach, O. V. (2019). Digital Technologies in Education: Problems and Prospects for "Moscow Electronic School" Project Implementation. *European Journal of Contemporary Education*, *8*(4), 779–789.

Fuller, K. S., & Rivera, C. T. (2021). A Culturally Responsive Curricular Revision to Improve Engagement and Learning in an Undergraduate Microbiology Lab Course. *Frontiers in Microbiology*, *2021*, 577852. Advance online publication. doi:10.3389/fmicb.2020.577852 PMID:33519726

Galatsopoulou, F., Kenterelidou, C., Kotsakis, R., & Matsiola, M. (2022). Examining Students' Perceptions towards Video-Based and Video-Assisted Active Learning Scenarios in Journalism and Communication Courses. *Education Sciences*, *12*(2), 74. doi:10.3390/educsci12020074

Galdames, V., Walqui, A., & Gustafson, B. (2011). *Enseñanza de la lengua indígena como Lengua Materna*. PROEIB Andes.

Gallup. (2017). *How millennials want to work and live*. Gallup. https://www.gallup.com/workplace/238073/millennials-work-live.aspx

Gallup. (2019). *Forging pathways to meaningful work – The role of Higher Education*. https://www.gallup.com/education/248222/gallup-bates-purposeful-work-2019.aspx

García-Crespo, F. J., Fernández-Alonso, R., & Muñiz, J. (2021). Academic resilience in European countries: The role of teachers, families, and student profiles. *PLoS One*, *16*(7), e0253409. Advance online publication. doi:10.1371/journal.pone.0253409 PMID:34214094

Garrison, D. R., Anderson, T., & Archer, W. (2000). Critical inquiry in a text-based environment: Computer conferencing in higher education. *The Internet and Higher Education*, *2*(2-3), 87–105. doi:10.1016/S1096-7516(00)00016-6

Garrison, D. R., Anderson, T., & Archer, W. (2001). Critical thinking, cognitive presence, and computer conferencing in distance education. *American Journal of Distance Education*, *15*(1), 7–23. doi:10.1080/08923640109527071

Garrison, D. R., & Arbaugh, J. B. (2007). Researching the community of inquiry framework: Review, issues, and future directions. *The Internet and Higher Education*, *10*(3), 157–172. doi:10.1016/j.iheduc.2007.04.001

Garrote, D., Garrote, C., & Jiménez Fernández, S. (2016). Factores Influyentes en Motivación y Estrategias de Aprendizaje en los Alumnos de Grado. *REICE. Revista Electrónica Iberoamericana sobre Calidad, Eficacia y Cambio en Educación*, *14*(2). Advance online publication. doi:10.15366/reice2016.14.2.002

Gayle, B. M., Randall, N., Langley, L., & Preiss, R. (2013). Faculty learning processes: A model for moving from scholarly teaching to the Scholarship of Teaching and Learning. *The International Society for the Scholarship of Teaching and Learning*, *1*(1), 81–93. doi:10.20343/teachlearninqu.1.1.81

Georgiou, H., & Sharma, M. D. (2012). University students' understanding of thermal physics in everyday contexts. *International Journal of Science and Mathematics Education*, *10*(5), 1119–1142. doi:10.100710763-011-9320-1

Gérard-Varet, L. A., Kolm, S. C., & Mercier Ythier, J. (2000). *The Economics of Reciprocity, Giving and Altruism*. Palgrave Macmillan. doi:10.1007/978-1-349-62745-5

Gerdes, K. E., & Segal, E. (2011). Importance of empathy for social work practice: Integrating new science. *Social Work*, *56*(2), 141–148. doi:10.1093w/56.2.141 PMID:21553577

Gibbs, G. (1988). *Learning by doing: A guide to teaching and learning methods*. Further Education Unit.

Gillies, R., & Boyle, M. (2011). Teachers' reflections of cooperative learning (CL): A two-year follow-up. *Teaching Education*, 22(1), 63–78. doi:10.1080/10476210.2010.538045

Ginestie, J. (2002). The industrial project method in French industry and in French schools. *International Journal of Technology and Design Education*, 12(2), 99–122. doi:10.1023/A:1015213511549

Giomelakis, D., Karypidou, C., & Veglis, A. (2019). SEO inside Newsrooms: Reports from the Field. *Future Internet*, 11(12), 261. doi:10.3390/fi11120261

Glasser, W. (1998). *Choice theory in the classroom*. HarperCollins Publishers.

Glăveanu, V. P. (2013). Rewriting the language of creativity: The five A's framework. *Review of General Psychology*, 17(1), 69–81. doi:10.1037/a0029528

Glynn, T., Wearmouth, J., & Berryman, M. (2006). *Supporting students with literacy difficulties: A responsive approach*. Open University Press/McGraw Hill.

Godonoga, A., & Martin, M. (2020). *SDG 4 - Policies for flexible learning pathways in higher education: Taking stock of good practices internationally*. IIEP Working paper.

Godwin-Jones, R. (2008). Emerging technologies: Web-writing 2.0: Enabling, documenting, and assessing writing online. *Language Learning & Technology*, 12(2), 7–13. https://www.lltjournal.org/item/10125-25195/

Gómes, C., & Gargallo, B. (1993). Las bases de una concepción constructivista de la educación. Implicaciones pedagógicas. In *Construcción humana y procesos de estructuración: propuestas de intervención pedagógica* (pp. 35–65). Quiles Artes Gráficas.

González-Salamanca, J. C., Agudelo, O. L., & Salinas, J. (2020). Key Competences, Education for Sustainable Development and Strategies for the Development of 21st Century Skills. A Systematic Literature Review. *Sustainability*, 12(24), 10366. doi:10.3390u122410366

Gooch, D., Vasalou, A., & Benton, L. (2015, July). Exploring the use of a gamification platform to support students with dyslexia. In *2015 6th international conference on information, intelligence, systems and applications (IISA)* (pp. 1-6). IEEE. 10.1109/IISA.2015.7388001

Goodell, J. (2000). Learning to teach Mathematics for understanding: The role of reflection J. Math. *Teacher Education and Development*, 2, 48–60.

Gordon, N., & Brayshaw, M. (2014). Technology-Enhanced Learning in Higher Education: Tribes and Territories. In V. Zuzevičiūtė, E. Butrimė, D. Vitkutė-Adžgauskienė, V. Vladimirovich Fomin, & K. Kikis-Papadakis (Eds.), *E-Learning as a Socio-Cultural System: A Multidimensional Analysis* (pp. 224–236). IGI Global. doi:10.4018/978-1-4666-6154-7.ch013

Gounaridou, A., Siamtanidou, E., & Dimoulas, C. (2021). A Serious Game for Mediated Education on Traffic Behavior and Safety Awareness. *Education Sciences*, 11(3), 127. doi:10.3390/educsci11030127

Gouvea, J., & Appleby, L. (2022). Expanding Research on Responsive Teaching. *CBE Life Sciences Education*, 21(2), 1–3. https://doi.org/10.1187/cbe.22-03-0064

Gowin, D. B. (1990). *Educating* (2nd ed.). Cornell University Press.

Goyette, Y. (2019). *Le développement de la conscience écologique dans un cours d'éducation par l'aventure [The development of ecological awareness in an adventure education course]* (Doctoral dissertation, Université du Québec à Chicoutimi).

Compilation of References

Graham, C. R., & Misanchuk, M. (2004). Computer-mediated learning groups: Benefits and challenges to using groupwork in online learning environments. In T. Roberts (Ed.), *Online collaborative learning: Theory and practice* (pp. 181–202). IGI Global. doi:10.4018/978-1-59140-174-2.ch008

Graham, S., Harris, K. R., & Mason, L. (2005). Improving the writing performance, knowledge, and self-efficacy of struggling young writers: The effects of self-regulated strategy development. *Contemporary Educational Psychology*, *30*(2), 207–241. doi:10.1016/j.cedpsych.2004.08.001

Grant, M., & Ferguson, S. (2021). Virtual microteaching, simulation technology & curricula: A recipe for improving prospective elementary mathematics teachers' confidence and preparedness. *Journal of Technology and Teacher Education*, *29*(2), 137–164. https://www.learntechlib.org/primary/p/218262/

Grapragasem, S., Krishnan, A., & Mansor, A. (2014). Current Trends in Malaysian Higher Education and the Effect on Education Policy and Practice: An Overview. *International Journal of Higher Education*, *3*(1). Advance online publication. doi:10.5430/ijhe.v3n1p85

Gravel, H., & Pruneau, D. (2004). Une étude de la réceptivité à l'environnement chez les adolescents [A study of environmental responsiveness in adolescents]. *Revue de l'Université de Moncton*, *35*(1), 165–187. doi:10.7202/008767ar

Greenhill, V. (2010). 21st Century Knowledge and Skills in Educator preparation. *Partnership for 21st Century Skills*.

Griffith, P. L., & Laframboise, K. L. (1998). Literature case studies: Case method and reader response come together in teacher education. *Journal of Adolescent & Adult Literacy*, *41*(5), 364–375.

Guerrero Castañeda, A., Rojas Morales, C., & Villafañe Aguilar, C. (2019). Impacto de la Educación Virtual en Carreras de Pregrado del Área de Ciencias de la Salud. Una Mirada de las Tecnologías Frente a la Educación [Trabajo de Grado presentado como requisito parcial para optar al título de: Especialización en Docencia Universitaria Línea de Investigación]. Monografía Universidad Cooperativa de Colombia Facultad de Educación Especialización en docencia universitaria.

Guerrero, M. C. M., & Villamil, O. S. (2002). Metaphorical conceptualizations of ESL teaching and learning. *Language Teaching Research*, *6*(2), 95–120. doi:10.1191/1362168802lr101oa

Guest, G., MacQueen, K. M., & Namey, E. E. (2011). *Applied thematic analysis*. Sage Publication.

Guglielmino, L. M. (1977). *Development of the self-directed learning readiness scale* [Unpublished doctoral dissertation, The University of Georgia, Athens, Georgia].

Guilford, J. P. (1950). Creativity. *The American Psychologist*, *5*(9), 444–454. https://doi.org/10.1037/h0063487

Guilford, J. P. (1956). The Structure of Intellect. *Psychological Bulletin*, *53*(4), 267–293. doi:10.1037/h0040755 PMID:13336196

Gülcan, N. Y. (2015). Discussing the importance of teaching ethics in education. *Procedia: Social and Behavioral Sciences*, *174*, 2622–2625. doi:10.1016/j.sbspro.2015.01.942

Gutierez, S. B. (2019). Teacher-practitioner research inquiry and sense making of their reflections on scaffolded collaborative lesson planning experience. *Asia Pacific Science Education*, *5*(1), 1–15. doi:10.118641029-019-0043-x

Haase, J., Hoff, E. V., Hanel, P., & Innes-Ker, A. (2018). A Meta-Analysis of the Relation between Creative Self-Efficacy and Different Creativity Measurements. *Creativity Research Journal*, *30*(1), 1–16. doi:10.1080/10400419.2018.1411436

Hall, R. (2021). Students as Partners in University Innovation and Entrepreneurship. *Education + Training*, *63*(7–8), 1114–1137. doi:10.1108/ET-01-2021-0003

Hambrock, H., Villiers, F. d., Rusman, E., MacCallum, K., & Arrifin, S. A. (2020). *Seamless Learning in Higher Education: Perspectives of International Educators on its Curriculum and Implementation Potentia*. PRESSBOOK. Retrieved from https://pressbooks.pub/seamlesslearning/

Hamid, M. Z. B. S. A., & Karri, R. R. (2021). Overview of Preventive Measures and Good Governance Policies to Mitigate the COVID-19 Outbreak Curve in Brunei. In I. Linkov, J. M. Keenan, & B. D. Trump (Eds.), COVID-19: Systemic Risk and Resilience. Risk, Systems and Decisions. Springer. https://doi.org/10.1007/978-3-030-71587-8_8.

Hamid, M. Z. B. S. A., Karri, R. R., & Karri, Y. (2022). Status quo of outbreak and control of COVID19 in the Southeast Asian Nations during the first phase: A case study of sustainable cities and communities. In COVID-19 and the Sustainable Development Goals. Elsevier.

Hamid. (2020). An Analysis of the success in suppressing COVID-19 cases in Brunei Darussalam. *International Journal of Advanced Research, 8*(6), 718-725.

Hammer, D., Goldberg, F., & Fargason, S. (2012). Responsive teaching and the beginnings of energy in a third grade classroom. *Review of Science, Mathematics and ICT Education, 6*(1), 51-72.

Hammer, D., Goldberg, F., & Fargason, S. (2012). Responsive teaching and the beginnings of energy in a third-grade classroom. *Review of Science, Mathematics, and ICT Education, 6*(1), 51–72.

Hanani, N. (2020). Meaningful Learning Reconstruction for Millennial: Facing competition in the information technology era. *IOP Conference Series. Earth and Environmental Science, 469*(1). doi:10.1088/1755-1315/469/1/012107

Handy, F., & Mook, L. (2011). Volunteering and volunteers: Benefit-cost analyses. *Research on Social Work Practice, 21*(4), 412–420. doi:10.1177/1049731510386625

Hanley, T., Winter, L. A., & Burrel, K. (2019). Supporting emotional well-being in schools in the context of austerity: An ecologically informed humanistic perspective. *The British Journal of Educational Psychology, 90*(1), 1–18. doi:10.1111/bjep.12275 PMID:30912121

Hare, C. (2019). *An introduction to humanistic learning theory*. Age of Awareness. https://medium.com/age-of-awareness/an-introduction-to-humanistic-learning-theory-1489cdde6359

Hargie, O. (2006). *The Handbook of Communication Skills* (3rd ed.). Routledge. doi:10.4324/9780203007037

Haruna, & Ibrahim, U. (2015). The Need for an Effective Collaboration Across Science, Technology, Engineering & Mathematics (STEM) Fields for a Meaningful Technological Development in Nigeria. *Journal of Education and Practice, 6*(25), 16-21.

Harwood, C. (2021). Active blended learning in an undergraduate english for academic purposes program. In B. C. Padilla Rodriguez & A. Armellini (Eds.), *Cases on Active Blended Learning in Higher Education* (pp. 122–148). IGI Global. doi:10.4018/978-1-7998-7856-8.ch007

Harwood, C., & Brett, C. (2019). Obuchenie online: The applicability of vygotskian pedagogy to online teaching and learning. *Technology, Instruction. Cognition & Learning, 11*(2/3), 141–161.

Hashem, M. E., Hashem, J., & Hashem, P. (2017). Role of new media in education and corporate communication: Trends and prospects in a middle Eastern context. In M., Friedrichsen, Y. Kamalipour (Eds.), Digital Transformation in Journalism and News Media: Media Management, Media Convergence and Globalization (pp. 443–466). Media Business and Innovation. Springer.

Hashim, A. M., Aris, S. R. S., & Chan, Y. F. (2019). Promoting empathy using design thinking in project-based learning and as a classroom culture. *Asian Journal of University Education, 15*(3), 14–23. doi:10.24191/ajue.v15i3.7817

Hawe, E., & Dixon, H. (2016). Assessment for learning: A catalyst for student self-regulation. *Assessment & Evaluation in Higher Education*. doi:10.1080/02602938.2016.1236360

Hawe, E., Dixon, H., & Hamilton, R. (2021). Why and how educators use exemplars. *Journal of University Teaching and Learning*, *18*(3), 136–149. doi:10.53761/1.18.3.10

Hawkins, P. (1999). *The Art of Building Windmills: Career Tactics for the 21st Century*. Graduate into Employment Unit, University of Liverpool.

Hed, N. M., Hussin, N. I., Yaacob, N. H., & Boyman, S. N. (2020). The impacts of the nationhood course on students' political engagement in Malaysia: A Comparative analysis. *Journal of Critical Reviews*, *7*, 877–883.

Helfensteller, R., & Flint, A. (2022). POLARIO–A simple low-cost-polarimeter for the chemistry lesson. *CHEMKON*.

Hendrix, J. (1971). Room Full of Mirrors [Recorded by J. Hendrix]. On *Rainbow bridge* [CD]. Reprise.

High Commission for Plan. (2007). *Summary Report National Survey of Non-Profit Institutions*. ISBL.

High Commission for Planning. (2011). Enquête Nationale sur les jeunes 2011. Author.

Hiley, T. J. (2006). Finding one's voice: The poetry of reflective practice. *Management Decision*, *44*(4), 561–574. doi:10.1108/00251740610663081

Hill, H. C., Blunk, M. L., Charalambous, C. Y., Lewis, J. M., Phelps, G. C., Sleep, L., & Ball, D. L. (2008). Mathematical knowledge for teaching and the mathematical quality of instruction: An exploratory study. *Cognition and Instruction*, *26*(4), 430–511.

Hillman, A. L. (2003). *Public finance and public policy: responsibilities and limitations of government*. Cambridge University Press.

Holdsworth, C., & Quinn, J. (2010). Student volunteering in English higher education. *Studies in Higher Education*, *35*(1), 113–127. doi:10.1080/03075070903019856

Horsch, P., Chen, J.-Q., & Wagner, S. (2002). The Responsive Classroom Approach. *Education and Urban Society*, *34*(3), 365–383. doi:10.1177/0013124502034003006

Horvathova, M. (2019). *Study on employability skills in the ib diploma programme and career-related programme curricula*. Center for Curriculum Redesign. Retrieved from https://www.ibo.org/globalassets/publications/ib-research/employability-skills-full-report.pdf

Horwitz, E. K., Horwitz, M. B., & Cope, J. (1986). Foreign language classroom anxiety. *Modern Language Journal*, *70*(2), 125–132. doi:10.1111/j.1540-4781.1986.tb05256.x

Howland, J. L., Jonassen, D. H., & Marra, R. M. (2011). *Meaningful Learning with Technology* (4th ed.). Pearson.

Huang, K. (2019). Design and investigation of cooperative, scaffolded wiki learning activities in an online graduate-level course. *International Journal of Educational Technology in Higher Education*, *16*(11), 1–18. doi:10.118641239-019-0141-6

Huang, S. Y. L. (2012). Learning environments at higher education institutions: Relationships with academic aspirations and satisfaction. *Learning Environments Research*, *15*(3), 363–378. doi:10.100710984-012-9114-6

Hubball, H., Clarke, A., & Poole, G. (2010). Ten-year reflections on mentoring SoTL research in a research-intensive university. *The International Journal for Academic Development*, *15*(2), 117–129. doi:10.1080/13601441003737758

Hudzik, J. K. (2011). Comprehensive Internationalization: From Concept to Action. NAFSA. doi:10.100710734-013-9696-7

Hughes, P. (2019). The Churches' Role in Volunteering in Urban and Rural Contexts in Australia. *Rural Theology*, *17*(1), 18–29. doi:10.1080/14704994.2019.1585111

Hui, L., Mingjun, W., & Li, Z. (2020). *Handbook of scientific research integrity education for colleges and universities* (1st ed.). Science Press.

Husain, F. C., & Kadir, F. A. (2012). Contribution of the Islamic and Asia Civilization (TITAS) towards Holistic Formation of Students. *Journal of Al-Tamaddun, 7*, 15–35. .

Hutchings, P., & Shulman, L. S. (1999). The Scholarship of Teaching:New Elaborations, New Developments. *Change: The Magazine of Higher Learning*, *31*(5), 10–15. doi:10.1080/00091389909604218

Ibrahim, R. (2018). 'Ethnic Relations' Course for National Integration among Malaysian Universities' Students: Some Reflections. *JATLaC Journal, 12*, 4–14.

Idris, F., Yaacob, M., & Taha, M. (2012). Teaching and learning methods of ethnic relations course: Interactive or destructive? *Procedia: Social and Behavioral Sciences*, *59*, 105–109. doi:10.1016/j.sbspro.2012.09.252

Ikramina, A. F. (2020). Teachers'set Induction And Closure In Efl Young Learners Classroom. *Eeal Journal*, *3*(3), 226–231.

Iksan, Z. H., Zakaria, E., & Daud, M. (2014). Model of lesson study approach during micro teaching. *International Education Studies*, *7*(13), 253–260. https://doi.org/10.5539/ies.v7n13p253

Inbar, D. (1996). The free educational prison: Metaphors and images. *Educational Research*, *28*(1), 77–92. doi:10.1080/0013188960380106

International Labour Office. (2011). *Global employment trends 2011: The challenge of a jobs recovery*. International Labour Office.

International Labour Organisation. (2021). *Volunteer work measurement guide*. ILO Department of Statistics.

Ishak, N. A., & Jamil, H. (2020). Pedagogies towards enhancing students' intellectual capital in Malaysian secondary schools. *Asia Pacific Journal of Educators and Education*, *35*(2), 57–76. doi:10.21315/apjee2020.35.2.4

Jaafar, M. N., Mahmud, N. H., Amran, M. F., Abdul Rahman, M. H., Abd Aziz, N. H., & Che Noh, M. A. (2022). Online learning and teaching technology services: USIM's experience during COVID-19 pandemic. *Front Education*, *7*, 813679. doi:10.3389/feduc.2022.813679

Jaber, L., Herbster, C., & Truett, J. (2019). Responsive Teaching. *Science and Children*, *57*(2), 85–89. https://orcid.org/0000-0003-1523-3889

Jamali, S. M., Ale Ebrahim, N., & Jamali, F. (2022). The role of STEM Education in improving the quality of education: A bibliometric study. *International Journal of Technology and Design Education*, 1–22. doi:10.100710798-022-09762-1

Janmaimool, P. (2017). Application of protection motivation theory to investigate sustainable waste management behaviors. *Sustainability*, *9*(7), 1079. doi:10.3390u9071079

Janoski, T. (1998). *Citizenship and civil society: A framework of rights and obligations in liberal, traditional, and social democratic regimes*. Cambridge University Press. doi:10.1017/CBO9781139174787

Jarrah, A. M. (2020). The challenges faced by pre-service mathematics teachers during their teaching practice in the UAE: Implications for teacher education programs. *International Journal of Learning. Teaching and Educational Research*, *19*(7), 23–34.

Compilation of References

Jarvis, P. (2002). *Career Management Paradigm Shift: Prosperity for Citizens, Windfall for Governments*. National Life/Work Centre.

Jayabalan, S. (2017). Teaching Law: The Learner in the Driver's Seat. In *Student-Driven Learning Strategies for the 21st Century Classroom*. IGI Global. . doi:10.4018/978-1-5225-1689-7

Jensen, L. A., Arnett, J. J., Feldman, S. S., & Cauffman, E. (2002). It's wrong, but everyone does it: Academic dishonesty among high school and college students. *Contemporary Educational Psychology*, *27*(2), 210–211. doi:10.1006/ceps.2001.1088

Jian, H., Guangming, L., & Weijun, W. (2020). Perceptions, contexts, attitudes, and academic dishonesty in Chinese senior college students: A qualitative content-based analysis. *Ethics & Behavior*, *30*(7), 543–555. doi:10.1080/10508422.2020.1711758

Joan, R. (2013). Flexible learning as a new learning design in classroom process to promote quality education. *I-managers Journal on Social Educational Technology, 9.*

Johnson, A. P. (2014). *Educational psychology: Theories of learning and human development*. National Science Press. www.nsspress.com

Johnson, D. W., & Johnson, R. T. (2009). An Educational Psychology Success Story: Social Interdependence Theory and Cooperative Learning. *Educational Researcher*, *38*(5), 365–379. doi:10.3102/0013189X09339057

Johnson, D. W., & Johnson, R. T. (2018). Cooperative learning: The foundation for active learning. In S. M. Brito (Ed.), *Active Learning: Beyond the Future*. IntechOpen. doi:10.5772/inMtechopen.81086

Johnson, D., & Johnson, R. (1994). Structuring academic controversy. In S. Sharan (Ed.), *Handbook of cooperative learning methods* (pp. 66–81). Greenwood Press.

Johnson, D., & Johnson, R. (1999). Making cooperative learning work. *Theory into Practice*, *38*(2), 67–73. doi:10.1080/00405849909543834

Johnson, D., & Johnson, R. (2002). Learning together and alone: Overview and meta-analysis. *Asia Pacific Journal of Education*, *22*(1), 95–105. doi:10.1080/0218879020220110

Joksimovic, S., Gasevic, D., Kovanovic, V., Adesope, O., & Hatala, M. (2014). Psychological characteristics in cognitive presence of communities of inquiry: A linguistic analysis of online discussions. *Internet High. Educ*, *2014*(22), 1–10. doi:10.1016/j.iheduc.2014.03.001

Jonassen, D. (2003). *Learning to Solve Problems with Technology: A Constructivist Perspective* (2nd ed.). Merrill.

Jonassen, D. H., & Rohrer-Murphy, L. (1999). Activity theory as a framework for designing constructivist learning environments. *Educational Technology Research and Development*, *47*(1), 61–79. doi:10.1007/BF02299477

Jonathan, W. K., & Michael, K. Ponton. (2006). Understanding Responsibility: A Self-Directed Learning Application Of The Triangle Model Of Responsibility. *New Horizons in Adult Education and Human Resource Development*, *16*, 16–27.

Joo, Y. J., Lim, K. Y., & Kim, E. K. (2011). Online university students' satisfaction and persistence: Examining perceived level of presence, usefulness and ease of use as predictors in a structural model. *Computers & Education*, *2011*(57), 1654–1664. doi:10.1016/j.compedu.2011.02.008

Julca, F. (2000). *Uso de las lenguas quechua y castellano en la escuela urbana: un estudio de caso* [Tesis de maestría]. Universidad Mayor de San Simón. http://bvirtual.proeibandes.org/bvirtual/docs/tesis/proeib/Tesis_Felix_Julca.pd

Kalliris, G., Dimoulas, C. A., & Matsiola, M. (2019). Media Management, Sound Editing and Mixing. In M. Filimowicz (Ed.), *Foundations in Sound Design for Linear Media: A Multidisciplinary Approach* (pp. 82–112). Routledge. doi:10.4324/9781315106335-3

Kalliris, G., Dimoulas, C., Veglis, A., & Matsiola, M. (2011). Investigating quality of experience and learning (QoE & QoL) of audiovisual content broadcasting to learners over IP networks. *IEEE Symposium on Computers and Communications (ISCC 2011)*, 836-841. 10.1109/ISCC.2011.5983946

Kalliris, G., Matsiola, M., Dimoulas, C., & Veglis, A. (2014). Emotional Aspects and Quality of Experience for Multifactor Evaluation of Audiovisual Content. [IJMSTR]. *International Journal of Monitoring and Surveillance Technologies Research*, 2(4), 40–61. doi:10.4018/IJMSTR.2014100103

Kanellopoulou, C., & Giannakoulopoulos, A. (2021). Internet-Assisted Language Teaching: The Internet as a Tool for Personalised Language Exploration. *Creative Education*, 12(03), 625–646. doi:10.4236/ce.2021.123043

Kaplan, A. E., & Hayes, M. J. (1993). What we know about women as donors. *New Directions for Philanthropic Fundraising*, 1993(2), 5–20. doi:10.1002/pf.41219930203

Karim, R.A., Idris, N., Ismail, I., Saad, N.H.M. & Abu, A.G. (2019). The impact of utilizing Mobile-assisted Mind Mapping technique (MAMMAT) on the development of undergraduate students' writing performance. *Journal of Advanced Research in Dynamic & Control Systems*, 11(12), 674-68.

Karim, N. A., & Yin, K. Y. (2013). Outcome-based Education: An Approach for Teaching and Learning Development. *Journal of Research. Policy & Practice of Teachers and Teachers Education*, 3(1), 26–35.

Karim, R. A., & Mustapha, R. (2020). Students' perception on the use of digital mind map to stimulate creativity and critical thinking in ESL writing course. *Universal Journal of Educational Research*, 8(12A), 7596–7606. doi:10.13189/ujer.2020.082545

Karim, R. A., & Mustapha, R. (2022). TVET Student's Perception on Digital Mind Map to Stimulate Learning of Technical Skills in Malaysia. *Journal of Technical Education and Training*, 14(1), 1–13.

Kartal, B., & Çınar, C. (2022). Preservice mathematics teachers' TPACK development when they are teaching polygons with geogebra. *International Journal of Mathematical Education in Science and Technology*, 1-33. doi:10.1080/0020739X.2022.2052197

Kassim, S. A., Nasir, N. F. M., Johari, N. R., & Razali, N. F. Y. (2021). Academic dishonesty intentions in the perspectives of higher education in Malaysia. *South Florida Journal of Development*, 2(5), 7991–8000. doi:10.46932fjdv2n5-119

Katsaounidou, A. N., & Dimoulas, C. A. (2019). Integrating content authentication support in media services. In M. Khosrow-Pour, D.B.A. (Ed.), Advanced Methodologies and Technologies in Digital Marketing and Entrepreneurship (pp. 395–408). IGI Global. doi:10.4018/978-1-5225-7766-9.ch031

Katsaounidou, A., Vrysis, L., Kotsakis, R., Dimoulas, C., & Veglis, A. (2019). MAthE the Game: A Serious Game for Education and Training in News Verification. *Education Sciences*, 9(2), 155. doi:10.3390/educsci9020155

Kaufmann, J. C., & Beghetto, R. A. (2009). Beyond big and little: The four c model of creativity. *Review of General Psychology*, 13(1), 1–12. doi:10.1037/a0013688

Kavanagh, E., & O'Kane, A. (2014). Developing the self in economics: The role of developmental space in an integrated undergraduate education. In *Integrative learning: International research and practice* (pp. 130–142). Routledge.

Kay, D., & Kibbl, J. (2016). Learning theories 101: Application to everyday teaching and scholarship. *Advances in Physiology Education*, 40(1), 17–25. doi:10.1152/advan.00132.2015 PMID:26847253

Compilation of References

Keding, Z., & Chaoqun, Y. (2017). Research on the development of learner's subjective consciousness in blended learning mode. *Modern Distance Education Research*, (6), 48–56.

Ke, F. (2010). Examining online teaching, cognitive, and social presence for adult students. *Computers & Education, 2010*(55), 808–820. doi:10.1016/j.compedu.2010.03.013

Kefala, A. (2021). Social Media Effects and Self-Harm Behaviors Among Young People: Theoretical and Methodological Challenges. *Journal of Education. Innovation and Communication, 3*(2), 13–25.

Kefalaki, M., & Karanicolas, S. (2020). Communication's rough navigations: 'fake' news in a time of a global crisis. *Journal of Applied Learning and Teaching, 3*(1), 29–41.

Kegan, R., & Lahey, L. (2009). *Immunity to change*. Harvard Business Press.

Ke, H., & Wuyuan, C. (2020). Governance of academic misconduct in colleges and universities—Takes Stanford University, Cambridge University, University of Tokyo for example. *Southeast Academic Research*, (6), 40–48.

Kember, D., Leung, D. Y. P., Jones, A., Loke, A. Y., McKay, J., Sinclair, K., Tse, H., Webb, C., Yuet Wong, F. K., Wong, M., & Yeung, E. (2000). Development of a questionnaire to measure the level of reflective thinking. *Assessment & Evaluation in Higher Education, 25*(4), 381–395. doi:10.1080/713611442

Kember, D., McKay, J., Sinclair, K., & Frances, Y. W. (2008). A four-category scheme for coding and assessing the level of reflection in written work. *Assessment & Evaluation in Higher Education, 33*(4), 369–379. doi:10.1080/02602930701293355

Kementerian Pendidikan Tinggi. (2016). *Buku Garis Panduan Matapelajaran Pengajian Umum (MPU) Edisi Ke-2*. Kementerian Pendidikan Tinggi.

Kempke, T., & Flint, A. (2021). The introduction of the particle concept in inclusive chemistry lessons based on the concept of "Chemistry for Life". *CHEMKON, 28*, 1–5. doi:10.1002/ckon.202100049

Kemp, N., & Grieve, R. (2014). Face-to-face or face-to-screen? Undergraduates' opinions and test perfor- mance in classroom vs. online learning. *Frontiers in Psychology, 5*, 1278. doi:10.3389/fpsyg.2014.01278 PMID:25429276

Keshavarz, M., & Karami, E. (2016). Farmers' pro-environmental behavior under drought: Application of protection motivation theory. *Journal of Arid Environments, 127*, 128–136. doi:10.1016/j.jaridenv.2015.11.010

Ke, W., Zhaobin, D., & Ming, X. (2015). Review, introspection and outlook on research of academic morality in Chinese universities. *Review of Higher Education, 3*(10), 14–19.

Khalek, A. K. (2012). Exploring the use of project-based learning on students' engagement at Taylors' University, Malaysia. *Jurnal BITARA UPSI, 5*, 17–29.

Khatib, M., Sarem, S. N., & Hamidi, H. (2013). Humanistic education: Concerns, implications and applications. *Journal of Language Teaching and Research, 4*(1), 45–51. doi:10.4304/jltr.4.1.45-51

Kholdarvovna, T. M. (2021). The Role Of Information And Communication Technologies In The Global Environment. *The American Journal of Social Science and Education Innovations, 3*(1), 564–570. doi:10.37547/tajssei/Volume03Issue01-99

Kholid, M. N., Telasih, S., Pradana, L. N., & Maharani, S. (2021). Reflective thinking of mathematics prospective teachers' for problem solving. []. IOP Publishing.]. *Journal of Physics: Conference Series, 1783*(1), 012102. doi:10.1088/1742-6596/1783/1/012102

Khvilon, E., & Patru, M. (2004). *Technologies de L'Information ET de la Communication en éDucation: Un Programme D'Enseignement ET un Cadre Pour la Formation Continue Des Enseignants* [Information and Communication Technologies in Education: A Curriculum AND Framework for Continuing Teacher Education.]. UNESCO.

Killpack, T. L., & Melón, L. C. (2016). Toward inclusive STEM classrooms: What personal role do faculty play? *CBE Life Sciences Education*, *15*(3), es3.

Kim, A. S. N., Popovic, C., Farrugia, L., Saleh, S. A. F., Maheux-Pelletier, G., & Frake-Mistak, M. (2020). On nurturing the emergent SoTL researcher: Responding to challenges and opportunities. *The International Journal for Academic Development*, *26*(2), 163–175. doi:10.1080/1360144X.2020.1842743

Kim, J., Kwon, Y., & Cho, D. (2011). Investigating factors that influence social presence and learning outcomes in distance higher education. *Computers & Education*, *2011*(57), 1512–1520. doi:10.1016/j.compedu.2011.02.005

Kim, J., & Pai, M. (2010). Volunteering and trajectories of depression. *Journal of Aging and Health*, *22*(1), 84–105. doi:10.1177/0898264309351310 PMID:19920207

Kim, M., Yoon, H., Ji, Y. R., & Song, J. (2012). The dynamics of learning science in everyday contexts: A case study of everyday science class in Korea. *International Journal of Science and Mathematics Education*, *10*(1), 71–97. doi:10.100710763-011-9278-z

Kim, S., Jeong, S. H., & Hwang, Y. (2013). Predictors of pro-environmental behaviors of American and Korean students: The application of the theory of reasoned action and protection motivation theory. *Science Communication*, *35*(2), 168–188. doi:10.1177/1075547012441692

Kirschner, P. A. (2001). Using integrated electronic environments for collaborative teaching/learning. *Learning and Instruction*, *10*, 1–9. doi:10.1016/S0959-4752(00)00021-9

Knight, S., Shibani, A., Abel, S., Gibson, A., Ryan, P., & Sutton, N. (2020). AcaWriter: A learning analytics tool for formative feedback on academic writing. *Journal of Writing Research*, *12*(1), 141–186. doi:10.17239/jowr-2020.12.01.06

Knowles, M. S. (1975). *Self-Directed Learning: A Guide for Learners and teachers*. Association Press.

Knowles, M. S. (1989). *The Making of an Adult Educator: An Autobiographical Journey*. Jossey-Bass.

Koçak, C. (2013). Metaphorical perceptions of teacher candidates towards the school concept: Lotus flower model. [MIJE]. *Mevlana International Journal of Education*, *3*(4), 43–56. doi:10.13054/mije.13.61.3.4

Koehler, M. J., & Mishra, P. (2005). What Happens When Teachers Design Educational Technology? The Development of Technological Pedagogical Content Knowledge. *Journal of Educational Computing Research*, *32*(2), 131–152. doi:10.2190/0EW7-01WB-BKHL-QDYV

Kolm, S. C. (2000). Introduction: the economics of reciprocity, giving and altruism. In The economics of reciprocity, giving and altruism (pp. 1-44). Palgrave Macmillan. doi:10.1007/978-1-349-62745-5_1

Kordoutis, P., & Kourti, E. (2016). Digital Friendship on Facebook and Analog Friendship Skills. In *Proceedings of the European Conference on Social Media Research*, Caen, France 2016 (pp. 109–115).

Ko, S., & Rossen, S. (2017). *Teaching online: A practical guide*. Routledge. doi:10.4324/9780203427354

Kostaris, C., Sergis, S., Sampson, D. G., Giannakos, M. N., & Pelliccione, L. (2017). Investigating the potential of the flipped classroom model in K-12 ICT teaching and learning: An action research study. *Journal of Educational Technology & Society*, *20*(1), 261–273.

Kostiainen, E., Ukskoski, T., Ruohotie-Lyhty, M., Kauppinen, M., Kainulainen, J., & Mäkinen, T. (2018). Meaningful learning in teacher education. *Teaching and Teacher Education*, *2018*(71), 66–77. doi:10.1016/j.tate.2017.12.009

Kotsakis, R., Dimoulas, C., Kalliris, G., & Veglis, A. (2014). Emotional Prediction and Content Profile Estimation in Evaluating Audiovisual Mediated Communication. [IJMSTR]. *International Journal of Monitoring and Surveillance Technologies Research*, 2(4), 62–80. doi:10.4018/IJMSTR.2014100104

Kourti, E., Kordoutis, P., & Anna, M. (2018). Social perception of Facebook friendship among Greek students. *Psychology: The Journal of the Hellenic Psychological Society*, 23(2), 53–68. doi:10.12681/psy_hps.22603

Kozan, K., & Caskurlu, S. (2018). On the Nth presence for the Community of Inquiry framework. *Computers & Education*, 2018(122), 104–118. doi:10.1016/j.compedu.2018.03.010

Krause, N. (1987). Life stress, social support, and self-esteem in an elderly population. *Psychology and Aging*, 2(4), 349–356. doi:10.1037/0882-7974.2.4.349 PMID:3268227

Kreijns, K., Kirschner, P. A., & Jochems, W. (2003). Identifying the pitfalls for social interaction in computer-supported collaborative learning environments: A review of the research. *Computers in Human Behavior*, 19(3), 335–353. doi:10.1016/S0747-5632(02)00057-2

Kreijns, K., Van Acker, F., Vermeulen, M., & Van Buuren, H. (2014). Community of inquiry: Social presence revisited. *E-Learning and Digital Media*, 11(1), 5–18. doi:10.2304/elea.2014.11.1.5

Krejcie, R. V., & Morgan, D. W. (1970). Determining Sample Size for Research Activities. *Educational and Psychological Measurement*, 30(3), 607–610. doi:10.1177/001316447003000308

Ku Samsu, K. H., Adnan, Z. H., Ismail, M. M., Lee, Y. F., Ab Majid, A., & Razak, Ab. R. R. (2017). Kaedah menangani kebosanan mahasiswa terhadap subjek Kenegaraan Malaysia. [Methods of dealing with the boredom of students on the subject of Malaysia Nationality. In Persidangan Antarabangsa Sains Sosial & Kemanusiaan Kali ke-2 PASAK2017, Kolej Universiti Islam Selangor.

Kumar, A. (2015). *Enabling All Learners to SOAR for Employability: An Inclusive, Integrative Pedagogy*. Advance HE. www.advance-he.ac.uk/knowledge-hub/enabling-all-learners-soar-employability-inclusive-integrative-pedagogy

Kumar, A. (2022) *Personal, Social Academic and Career Development in Higher Education – SOARing to Success*. Routledge Taylor & Francis. www.routledge.com/9780367648053 (Original publication 2007)

Kumar, A. (2009). 'Using Assessment Centre Approaches to Improve Students' Learning. In C. Nygaard & C. Holtham (Eds.), *Understanding Learning centred Higher Education*. Copenhagen Business School.

Kumar, A. (2013). SOARing to Success: Employability Development from the inside out. In T. Bilham (Ed.), *For the Love of Learning: Innovations from Outstanding University Teachers* (pp. 221–227). Palgrave Macmillan. doi:10.1007/978-1-137-33430-5_32

Laal, M., & Laal, M. (2012). Collaborative learning: What is it? *Procedia: Social and Behavioral Sciences*, 31, 491–495. doi:10.1016/j.sbspro.2011.12.092

Lakoff, G., & Johnson, M. (1980). *Metaphors we live by*. University of Chicago Press.

Lampert, M., Franke, M. L., Kazemi, E., Ghousseini, H., Turrou, A. C., Beasley, H., ... Crowe, K. (2013). Keeping it complex: Using rehearsals to support novice teacher learning of ambitious teaching. *Journal of Teacher Education*, 64(3), 226–243.

Lamprou, E., Antonopoulos, N., Anomeritou, I., & Apostolou, C. (2021). Characteristics of Fake News and Misinformation in Greece: The Rise of New Crowdsourcing-Based Journalistic Fact-Checking Models. *Journalism and Media*, 2(3), 417–439. doi:10.3390/journalmedia2030025

Larsson, M., Mårtensson, K., Price, L., & Roxå, T. (2020). Constructive friction? Charting the relation between educational research and the Scholarship of Teaching and Learning. *Teaching & Learning Inquiry*, *8*(1), 61–75. doi:10.20343/teachlearninqu.8.1.5

Latif, B., Ong, T. S., Meero, A., Abdul Rahman, A. A., & Ali, M. (2022). Employee-Perceived Corporate Social Responsibility (CSR) and Employee Pro-Environmental Behavior (PEB): The Moderating Role of CSR Skepticism and CSR Authenticity. *Sustainability*, *14*(3), 1380. doi:10.3390u14031380

Lau, H. (2020). Comparing the Effectiveness of Student-Centred Learning (SCL) Over Teacher-Centred Learning (TCL) of Economic Subjects in a Private University in Sarawak. *International Journal of Innovation, Creativity, and Change*, *10*(10), 147–160.

Law, N., Yuen, A., & Fox, R. (2011). *Educational Innovations Beyond Technology: Nurturing Leadership and Establishing Learning Organizations*. Springer. doi:10.1007/978-0-387-71148-5

Leal, F., Shiel, W., Paco, A., Mifsud, M., Avilia, L., Brandli, L., Molthan-Hill, P., Pace, P., Azeiteiro, U., Vargas, V., & Caiero, S. (2019). Sustainable development goals ans sustainability teaching at universities falling behind or getting ahead of the pack? *Journal of Cleaner Production*, *232*, 285–294. doi:10.1016/j.jclepro.2019.05.309

Leander, K. M., Phillips, N. C., & Taylor, K. H. (2010). The changing social spaces of learning: Mapping new mobilities. *Review of Research in Education*, *34*(1), 329–394. doi:10.3102/0091732X09358129

Lee, P. (2020, November 9). *Achtung baby: A second listen*. Hooks and Harmony. Retrieved from https://hooksandharmony.com/achtung-baby-a-second-listen/

Lee, J. H., & Segev, A. (2012). Knowledge maps for e-learning. *Computers & Education*, *59*(2), 353–364. doi:10.1016/j.compedu.2012.01.017

Lee, L. (2010). Fostering reflective writing and interactive exchange through blogging in an advanced language course. *ReCALL*, *22*(2), 212–227. doi:10.1017/S095834401000008X

Lee, L., Liang, W.-J., & Sun, F.-C. (2021). The Impact of Integrating Musical and Image Technology upon the Level of Learning Engagement of Pre-School Children. *Education Sciences*, *11*(12), 788. doi:10.3390/educsci11120788

Lee, M. N. (1997). Education and the State: Malaysia After the NEP. *Asia Pacific Journal of Education*, *17*(1), 27–40. doi:10.1080/02188799708547741

Leonard, M. (2021, April 14). *The genius of…Achtung baby by U2*. Guitar.com. Retrieved from https://guitar.com/review/album/the-genius-of-achtung-baby-by-u2/

Leong, Y., Cheng, L., & Toh, W. (2021). Teaching students to apply formula using instructional materials: a case of a Singapore teacher's practice. *Math Ed Res J.*, *33*, 89–111. doi:10.1007/s13394-019-00290-1

Leont'ev, A. N. (1978). *Activity, consciousness, and personality*. Prentice-Hall.

Leont'ev, A. N. (1981). *Problems of the development of the mind*. Progress Publishers.

Levin, B. (2010). Leadership for evidence-informed education. *School Leadership and Management*, *30*(4), 303-315. https://doi/abs/ doi:10.1080/13632434.2010.497483

Liacuna, H., & Mason, G. (2022). Promoting self-regulated learning in higher education. *Pacific Journal of Technology Enhanced Learning*, *4*(1), 19–25. doi:10.24135/pjtel.v4i1.143

Liao, H.-C., Li, Y.-C., & Wang, Y. (2019). Optimal cooperative learning grouping to improve medical university students' English competencies. *SAGE Open*, *9*(3). doi:10.1177/2158244019861454

Compilation of References

Liedtka, J., & Ogilvie, T. (2011). *Designing for Growth: A design thinking tool kit for managers.* Columbia Business Press.

Liguori, E., & Winkler, C. (2020). From offline to online: Challenges and opportunities for entrepreneurship education following the COVID-19 pandemic. *Entrepreneurship Education and Pedagogy, 3*(1), 346–351. doi:10.1177/2515127420916738

Li, J., & Che, W. (2022). Challenges and coping strategies of online learning for college students in the context of COVID-19: A survey of Chinese universities. *Sustainable Cities and Society, 83*, 103958. doi:10.1016/j.scs.2022.103958 PMID:35620298

Lillo, V. (2014). Salud y Educación: Dos Vocaciones Al Servicio De Los Derechos Humanos. *Revista Médica Clínica Las Condes, 25*(2), 357–362. doi:10.1016/S0716-8640(14)70047-1

Lin, Fu, & Hsung. (1998). Position Generator: A Measurement for Social Capital. In *Social Networks and Social Capital.* Duke University.

Lincoln, Y. S., Guba, E. G., & Pilotta, J. J. (1985). Naturalistic inquiry. *Sage (Atlanta, Ga.), 9*(4), 438–439. Advance online publication. doi:10.1016/0147-1767(85)90062-8

Linder, K. E. (2017). Fundamentals of hybrid teaching and learning. *New Directions for Teaching and Learning, 2017*(3), 11–18. doi:10.1002/tl.20222

Livingstone, S., Mascheroni, G., & Stoilova, M. (2021). The outcomes of gaining digital skills for young people's lives and well-being: A systematic evidence review. *New Media & Society.* Advance online publication. doi:10.1177/14614448211043189

Li, Y., Huang, R., & Yang, Y. (2011). Characterizing expert teaching in school mathematics in China: A prototype of expertise in teaching mathematics. In Y. Li & G. Kaiser (Eds.), *Expertise in mathematics instruction: An international perspective* (pp. 167–195). Springer.

Looi, C. K., So, H. J., Chen, W., Zhang, B., Wong, L. H., & Seow, P. (2012). Seamless learning. In: Seel N.M. (eds) Encyclopaedia of the Sciences of Learning. Springer.

López-Vargas, A., Fuentes, M., & Vivar, M. (2020). Challenges and opportunities of the internet of things for global development to achieve the united nations sustainable development goals. *IEEE Access: Practical Innovations, Open Solutions, 8*, 37202–37213. doi:10.1109/ACCESS.2020.2975472

Lorenzo-Lledó, A., Lledó, A., Lorenzo, G., & Gilabert-Cerdá, A. (2022). Outside Training of Spanish University Students of Education for the Didactic Application of Cinema: Formal, Non-Formal, and Informal Perspectives. *Education Sciences, 12*(1), 38. doi:10.3390/educsci12010038

Louie, B. Y., Drevdahl, D. J., Purdy, J. M., & Stackman, R. W. (2003). Advancing the Scholarship of Teaching through collaborative self-study. *The Journal of Higher Education, 74*(2), 150–171. doi:10.1353/jhe.2003.0016

Loyens, S., & Gijbels, D. (2008). Understanding the efects of constructivist learning environments: Introducing a multi-directional approach. *Instructional Science, 36*(5-6), 351–357. doi:10.100711251-008-9059-4

Lui, A. M., & Bonner, S. M. (2016). Preservice and inservice teachers' knowledge, beliefs, and instructional planning in primary school mathematics. *Teaching and Teacher Education, 56*, 1–13. doi:10.1016/j.tate.2016.01.015

Lundin, R. (2012). *Flexible Teaching and Learning: Perspectives and Practices.* The University of Sydney Library.

MacArthur, C. A. (2015). Instruction in evaluation and revision. In C. A. MacArthur, S. Graham, & J. Fitzgerald (Eds.), *Handbook of Writing Research* (pp. 272–287). Guilford Publications.

MacArthur, C. A. (2018). Evaluation and revision. In S. Graham, C. A. Charles, M. Hebert, & J. Fitzgerald (Eds.), *Best Practices in Writing Instruction* (pp. 287–308). Guilford Publications.

MacCormac, E. (1990). *A cognitive theory of metaphor*. MIT Press.

Mahzan, M. S. W., Alias, N. A., & Abdullah, N. (2019). Infusing Engagement into Digital Game-based Learning Design for Orang Asli Learners. In Improving Educational Quality Toward International Standard (ICED-QA 2018) (pp. 178–184). SCITEPRESS.

Maki, A., & Snyder, M. (2017). Investigating similarities and differences between volunteer behaviors: Development of a volunteer interest typology. *Nonprofit and Voluntary Sector Quarterly*, *46*(1), 5–28. doi:10.1177/0899764015619703

Makri, A., & Vlachopoulos, D. (2019). Professional development for school leaders: A focus on soft and digital skills. In L. G. Chova, A. L. Martínez, & I. C. Torres (Eds.), *Proceedings of EDULEARN19 Conference,* (pp. 6200–6209). IATED Academy. 10.21125/edulearn.2019.1492

Malaysian Qualifications Agency. (2021). *Malaysian Qualifications Framework (MQF)* (2nd ed.). Retrieved 10 9, 2022, from Malaysian Qualifications Agency: https://www.mqa.gov.my/pv4/document/mqf/2021/MQF%20Ed%202%20 02102019%20updated%2017022021.pdf

Mandinach, E. B., & Gummer, E. (2016). What does it mean for teachers to be data literate: Laying out the skills, knowledge, and dispositions. *Teaching and Teacher Education*. https://www.sciencedirect.com/science/article/pii/S0742051X16301391

Mandinach, E. B., & Jackson, S. S. (2012). *Transforming teaching and learning through data driven decision-making*. Corwin Press. doi:10.4135/9781506335568

Manli, S. (2015). Evaluation of blended learning teaching mode in foreign universities. [Philosophy and Social Sciences Edition]. *Journal of Fujian Normal University*, (3), 153–172.

Manolika, M., Kotsakis, R., Matsiola, M., & Kalliris, G. (2021). Direct and Indirect Associations of Personality With Audiovisual Technology Acceptance Through General Self-Efficacy. *Psychological Reports*, *125*(2), 1165–1185. doi:10.1177/0033294121997784 PMID:33632017

Mantovan, N., Wilson, J., & Sauer, R. M. (2020). The economic benefits of volunteering and social class. *Social Science Research*, *85*, 102368. doi:10.1016/j.ssresearch.2019.102368 PMID:31789200

Marchand, G. C., & Gutierrez, A. P. (2012). The role of emotion in the learning process: Comparisons between online and face-to-face learning settings. *The Internet and Higher Education*, *15*(3), 150–160. doi:10.1016/j.iheduc.2011.10.001

Marcketti, S. B., & Freeman, S. (2016). SoTL evidence on promotion and tenure vitas at a research university. *The Journal of Scholarship of Teaching and Learning*, *16*(5), 19–31. doi:10.14434//josotl.v16i5.21152

Marshall, C. (2013, July 2). Jump start your creative process with Brian Eno's "oblique strategies" deck of cards (1975). *Open Culture*. Retrieved from https://www.openculture.com/2013/07/jump_start_your_creative_process_with_brian_eno_oblique_strategies.html

Marshall, H. H. (1990). Beyond the workplace metaphor: The classroom as a learning setting. *Theory into Practice*, *29*, 94–101.

Martin, F., Ahlgrim-Delzell, L., & Budhrani, K. (2017). Systematic review of two decades (1995 to 2014) of research on synchronous online learning. *American Journal of Distance Education*, *31*, 3–19. .1264807 doi:10.1080/08923647.2017

Martin, A. D., & Strom, K. J. (2016). Toward a linguistically responsive teacher identity: An empirical review of the literature. *International Multilingual Research Journal*, *10*, 239–253.

Compilation of References

Martinez, M. A., Sauleda, N., & Huber, G. L. (2001). Metaphors as blueprints of thinking about teaching and learning. *Teaching and Teacher Education, 17*, 965–977.

Martin, F., & Bolliger, D. U. (2018). Engagement matters: Student perceptions on the importance of engagement strategies in the online learning environment. *Online Learning, 22*(1), 205–222. doi:10.24059/olj.v22i1.1092

Martyushev, N., Shutaleva, A., Malushko, E., Nikonova, Z., & Savchenko, I. (2021). Online Communication Tools in Teaching Foreign Languages for Education Sustainability. *Sustainability, 13*(19), 11127. doi:10.3390u131911127

Matsiola, M. (2008). *New Technological Tools in Contemporary Journalism: Study Concerning Their Utilization by the Greek Journalists Related to the Use of the Internet as a Mass Medium* [Unpublished Ph.D. Thesis, School of Journalism and Mass Communications, Aristotle University of Thessaloniki, Thessaloniki, Greece].

Matsiola, M., Dimoulas, C., Kalliris, G., & Veglis, A. A. (2015). Augmenting User Interaction Experience through Embedded Multimodal Media Agents in Social Networks. In J. Sahlin (Ed.), *Social Media and the Transformation of Interaction in Society* (pp. 188–209). IGI Global. doi:10.4018/978-1-4666-8556-7.ch010

Matsiola, M., Spiliopoulos, P., Kotsakis, R., Nicolaou, C., & Podara, A. (2019). Technology-Enhanced Learning in Audiovisual Education: The Case of Radio Journalism Course Design. *Education Sciences, 9*(1), 62. doi:10.3390/educsci9010062

Matsiola, M., Spiliopoulos, P., & Tsigilis, N. (2022). Digital Storytelling in Sports Narrations: Employing Audiovisual Tools in Sport Journalism Higher Education Course. *Education Sciences, 12*(1), 51. doi:10.3390/educsci12010051

Matthews, K. E., Cook-Sather, A., Acai, A., Dvorakova, S. L., Felten, P., Marquis, E., & Mercer-Mapstone, L. (2019). Toward theories of partnership praxis: An analysis of interpretive framing in literature on students as partners in teaching and learning. *Higher Education Research & Development, 38*(2), 280-293. doi:10.14264/uql.2018.519

Mayer, R. E. (2004). Should there be a three-strikes rule against pure discovery learning? *The American Psychologist, 59*(1), 14–19. doi:10.1037/0003-066X.59.1.14 PMID:14736316

Mayer, R. E. (2014). *The Cambridge Handbook of Multimedia Learning* (2nd ed.). Cambridge Handbooks in Psychology—Cambridge University Press. doi:10.1017/CBO9781139547369

McCabe, D. L., Butterfield, K. D., & Treviño, L. K. (2006). Academic dishonesty in graduate business programs: Prevalence, causes, and proposed action. *Academy of Management Learning & Education, 5*(3), 294–305. doi:10.5465/amle.2006.22697018

McGarry, B., Theobald, K. A., Lewis, P. A., & Coyer, F. M. (2015). Flexible learning design in curriculum delivery promotes student engagement and develops metacognitive learners: An integrated review. *Nurse Education Today, 35*(9), 966–973. doi:10.1016/j.nedt.2015.06.009 PMID:26169287

McKernan, J. (2010). A Critique of Instructional. *Education Inquiry, 1*(1), 57–67. doi:10.3402/edui.v1i1.21929

McKown, C., & Weinstein, R. S. (2008). Teacher expectations, classroom context, and the achievement gap. *Journal of School Psychology, 46*(3), 235–261. https://doi.org/10.1016/j.jsp.2007.06.001

McLaughlin, M., & Talbert, J. (1993). *Contexts That Matter for Teaching and Learning: Strategic Opportunities*. Academic Press.

McLeod, S. A. (2018, May 21). *Maslow's hierarchy of needs*. https://www.simplypsychology.org/maslow.html

McMahon, M., Patton, W., & Tatham, P. (2003). *Managing Life, Learning and Work in the 21st Century*. Miles Morgan Australia.

McNiff, L., & Hays, L. (2017). SoTL in the LIS classroom: Helping future academic librarians become more engaged teachers. *Communications in Information Literacy, 11*(2), 366–377. doi:10.15760/comminfolit.2017.11.2.8

Meijer, H., Brouwer, J., Hoekstra, R., & Strijbos, J. W. (2022). Exploring Construct and Consequential Validity of Collaborative Learning Assessment in Higher Education. *Small Group Research*. Advance online publication. doi:10.1177/10464964221095545

Mengya, W. (2022). A SWOT analysis of the hybrid learning patterns. *Heilongjiang Science, 13*(5), 78–80.

Merriam, S. B. (2014). *Qualitative research: A guide to design and implementation*. Jossey-Bass.

Michelson, E. (1996). Usual suspects: Experience, reflection, and the (en)gendering of knowledge. *International Journal of Lifelong Education, 15*(6), 438–454. doi:10.1080/0260137960150604

Middleton, N., Koliandri, I., Hadjigeorgiou, E., Karanikola, M., Kolokotroni, O., Christodoulides, V., Nicolaou, C., & Kouta, C. (2020). Mixed-method study on internet use and information seeking during transition to motherhood. *European Journal of Public Health, 30*(Supplement_5), ckaa165.905.

Miles, M. B., & Huberman, A. M. (1994). *Qualitative data analysis: An expanded sourcebook* (2nd ed.). Sage Publications, Inc.

Miller, K. D., Schleien, S. J., Brooke, P., Frisoli, A. M., & Brooks, W. T. (2005). Community for all: The therapeutic recreation practitioner's role in inclusive volunteering. *Therapeutic Recreation Journal, 39*(1), 18–31.

Miller, R. (1997). *What are schools for? Holistic education in American culture* (3rd ed.). Holistic Education Press.

Miller, S. (1987). Some comments on the utility of metaphors for educational theory and practice. *Educational Theory, 37*, 219–227.

Ministerial Council on Education Employment Training and Youth Affairs. (2008). Learning spaces framework: Learning in an online world. Author.

Ministry of Education. (n.d.). *Malaysia Education Blueprint 2015-2025 (higher education.)*.

Ministry of Higher Education Malaysia. (2016). *Guidelines of General Studies*.

Min, M., Lee, H., Hodge, C., & Croxton, N. (2022). What empowers teachers to become social justice-oriented change agents? Influential factors on teacher agency toward culturally responsive teaching. *Education and Urban Society, 54*(5), 560–584.

Mintzes, J., & Wandersee, J. (2000). Reforma e Inovação no Ensino da Ciência: uma visão construtivista. In Ensinando Ciência para a compreensão – uma visão construtivista. Plátano Edições Técnicas.

Mioduser, D., & Betzer, N. (2008). The contribution of Project-based-learning to high-achievers' acquisition of technological knowledge and skills. *International Journal of Technology and Design Education, 18*(1), 59–77. doi:10.100710798-006-9010-4

Mohamed, A. E. (Ed.). (2011). E-learning in Malaysian higher education institutions. Klang Ministry of higher education., Malaysia.

MOHE. (2015). *Malaysia Education Blueprint, 2015-2025 (Higher Education)*. Retrieved 10 September, 2022, from Kementerian Pengajian Tinggi: https://www.mohe.gov.my/muat-turun/penerbitan-jurnal-dan-laporan/pppm-2015-2025-pt/102-malaysia-education-blueprint-2015-2025-higher-education/file

Montuori, A. (1996). The art of transformation: Jazz as a metaphor for education. *History of Education Review, 9*(4), 57–62.

Compilation of References

Montuori, A. (2006). The quest for a new education: From oppositional identities to creative inquiry. *ReVision*, *28*(3), 4–20. doi:10.3200/REVN.28.3.4-20

Moore, A. (2015). *Understanding the school curriculum: Theory, politics and principles*. Routledge.

Morales-Cevallos, M. B. (2020). Trends in Educational Research about e-Learning: A Systematic Literature Review (2009–2018). *Sustainability*, *2020*(12), 5153. doi:10.3390u12125153

Moreau, C. S., Darby, A. M., Demery, A. J. C., Arcila Hernández, L. M., & Meaders, C. L. (2022). A framework for educating and empowering students by teaching about history and consequences of bias in STEM. *Pathogens and Disease*, *80*(1), ftac006.

Moreira, M. A. (2011). Why Concepts, Why Meaningful Learning, Why Collaborative Activities and Why Concept Maps? *Aprendizagem Significativa em Revista/Meaningful Learning Review*, *6*(3), 5.

MOSTI. (2022). *Pelan hala tuju teknologi diperkenalkan bagi menjadikah Malaysia negara pembangun teknologi teknologi*. YouTube. https://www.youtube.com/watch?v=v5TPh-lEizk

Mother, L. E., Halim, L., Rahman, N. A., Maat, S. M., Iksan, Z. H., & Osman, K. (2019). A model of interest in STEM careers among secondary school students. *Journal of Baltic Science Education*, *18*(3), 404–416.

Mukhtar, K., Javed, K., Arooj, M., & Sethi, A. (2020). Advantages, limitations, and recommendations for online learning during COVID-19 pandemic era. *Pakistan Journal of Medical Sciences*, *36*(COVID19-S4), 27–31. doi:10.12669/pjms.36.COVID19-S4.2785 PMID:32582310

Mulcahy, D. (2015). Re/assembling spaces of learning in Victorian government schools: Policy enactments, pedagogic encounters and micropolitics. *Discourse (Abingdon)*, *36*(4), 500–514. doi:10.1080/01596306.2014.978616

Murphy, M. P. A. (2020). COVID-19 and emergency eLearning: Consequences of the securitization of higher education for post-pandemic pedagogy. *Contemporary Security Policy*, *41*(3), 492–505. doi:10.1080/13523260.2020.1761749

Murtafiah, W., & Lukitasari, M. (2019). Developing Pedagogical Content Knowledge of Mathematics Pre-Service Teacher through Microteaching Lesson Study. *Online Submission*, *13*(2), 201–218.

Musick, M. A., & Wilson, J. (2003). Volunteering and depression: The role of psychological and social resources in different age groups. *Social Science & Medicine*, *56*(2), 259–269. doi:10.1016/S0277-9536(02)00025-4 PMID:12473312

Musick, M. A., Wilson, J., & Bynum, W. B. Jr. (2000). Race and formal volunteering: The differential effects of class and religion. *Social Forces*, *78*(4), 1539–1570. doi:10.2307/3006184

Mutalib, H. (2022). *72.1% lepasan SPM tidak sambung belajar*. Utusan Malaysia. https://www.utusan.com.my/nasional/2022/07/72-1-lepasan-spm-tidak-sambung-belajar/

Mutch, C., & Peung, S. (2021). 'Maslow before Bloom': Implementing a caring pedagogy during Covid-19. *New Zealand Journal of Teachers' Work*, *18*(2), 69–90. doi:10.24135/teacherswork.v18i2.334

Mystakidis, S. (2019). *Motivation Enhanced Deep and Meaningful Learning with Social Virtual Reality*. University of Jyväskylä.

Mystakidis, S., Berki, E., & Valtanen, J. (2019). The Patras Blended Strategy Model for Deep and Meaningful Learning in Quality Life-Long Distance Education. *Electron. J. e-Learning*, *17*, 66–78.

Mystakidis, S. (2021). Deep Meaningful Learning. *Encyclopedia*, *2021*(1), 988–997. doi:10.3390/encyclopedia1030075

Nagy, J. T. (2018). Evaluation of online video usage and learning satisfaction: An extension of the technology acceptance model. *The International Review of Research in Open and Distributed Learning*, *19*(1), 160–185. doi:10.19173/irrodl.v19i1.2886

Naidu, S. (2017). How flexible is flexible learning, who is to decide and what are its implications? *Distance Education*, *38*(3), 269–272. doi:10.1080/01587919.2017.1371831

Naismith, L., Lonsdale, P., Vavoula, G. N., & Sharples, M. (2004). *Mobile technologies and learning*. University of Leicester.

Namaziandost, E., Homayouni, M., & Rahmani, P. (2020a). The impact of cooperative learning approach on the development of EFL learners' speaking fluency. *Cogent Arts & Humanities*, *7*(1), 1–13. doi:10.1080/23311983.2020.1780811

Namaziandost, E., Pourhosein Gilakjani, A., & Hidayatullah, H. (2020b). Enhancing pre-intermediate EFL learners' reading comprehension through the use of jigsaw technique. *Cogent Arts & Humanities*, *7*(1), 1–15. doi:10.1080/23311983.2020.1738833

Nam, C. W., & Zellner, R. D. (2011). The relative effects of positive interdependence and group processing on student achievement and attitude in online cooperative learning. *Computers & Education*, *56*(3), 680–688. doi:10.1016/j.compedu.2010.10.010

Nardi, B. (Ed.). (1996). *Context and consciousness: Activity theory and human-computer interaction*. MIT Press.

Nasar, A., & Kaleka, M. B. U. (2020). The effect of distance learning with Learner Center Micro Teaching Model On student' teaching confidence and teaching skills. *Jurnal Ilmu Pendidik. Fisika*, *5*(3), 159-168. https://journal.stkipsingkawang.ac.id/index.php/JIPF

Nasir, M. F. M., Ridzuan, M. I. M., Hock, A. T. Y., Pei, O. S., Jamaludin, A. L., Hamidi, N. H. A., & Maswan, N. A. M. (2019). Keberkesanan subjek Matapelajaran Umum (MPU) dalam memperkasa Bahasa Melayu: Satu tinjauan awal. [The effectiveness of General Subjects (MPU) in strengthening the Malay language: A preliminary survey] *International Journal of Education. Psychology and Counselling*, *4*, 85–96.

National Centre for Social Research and the Institute for Volunteering Research. (2007). *Helping out: A national survey of volunteering and charitable giving*. Prepared for the UK Cabinet Office.

National Council of Teachers of Mathematics (NCTM). (2000). *Principles and standards for school mathematics*. NCTM.

National Writing Project. (n.d.). *National Writing Project, What Is Connected Learning?* National Writing Project. https://lead.nwp.org/knowledgebase/what-is-connected-learning/

NCTM. (2000). *Principles and Standards for School Mathematics*. NCTM.

Nesbit, J. C., & Adesope, O. O. (2013). Concept maps for learning: Theory, research, and design. In G. Schraw, M. T. McCrudden, & D. Robinson (Eds.), *Current perspectives on cognition, learning, and instruction. Learning through visual displays* (pp. 303–328). Information Age Publishers.

Newby, T. J., Stepich, D. A., Lehman, J. D., Russell, J. D., & Leftwich, A. T. (2019). *Educational Technology for Teaching and Learning* (4th ed.). Pearson Education.

Newman, F. M., Marks, H. M., & Gamoran, A. (1996). Authentic pedagogy and student performance. *American Journal of Education*, *104*(4), 280–312. doi:10.1086/444136

Newton, C., & Gan, L. (2012). Revolution or missed opportunity. *Architecture Australia*, *101*(1), 74–78.

Compilation of References

Ngah, R., Junid, J., & Osman, C. A. (2019). The Links between Role of Educators, Self-Directed Learning, Constructivist Learning Environment and Entrepreneurial Endeavor: Technology Entrepreneurship Pedagogical Approach. *International Journal of Learning. Teaching and Educational Research, 18*(11), 414–427. doi:10.26803/ijlter.18.11.25

Ngubane-Mokiwa, S. A., & Khoza, S. B. (2021). Using Community of Inquiry (CoI) to Facilitate the Design of a Holistic E-Learning Experience for Students with Visual Impairments. *Education Sciences, 11*(4), 152. doi:10.3390/educsci11040152

Nguyen, Q. N. (2022). Teachers' scaffolding strategies in internet-based ELT classes. *Teaching English as a Second Language Electronic Journal, 26*(1). doi:10.55593/ej.25101a1

Nicolaou, C. (2011a). *Public Relations and New Technologies* [Unpublished CIPR Professional PR Diploma Thesis, Chartered Institute of Public Relations, London, UK].

Nicolaou, C. (2015, June). *Modern trends in teaching methodology in adult education* [Paper presentation]. The 1st Panhellenic Scientific Conference on Lifelong Learning on Lifelong Learning and Modern Society: Local Government, Education and Work, Thessaloniki, Greece.

Nicolaou, C. (2017, June). *Modern theoretical approaches to adult education* [Paper presentation]. The 5th Student Excellence Conference 2017 of the Mediterranean College (Thessaloniki), Thessaloniki, Greece.

Nicolaou, C. (2019a, March). *Audiovisual media of mass media in the teaching methodology* [Paper presentation]. The 18th Pancyprian Scientific Conference of the Educational Group of Cyprus on RE-view of the Public School of Cyprus in a World of Constant Changes and Challenges, Limassol, Cyprus.

Nicolaou, C. (2020). Communication Skills through Audiovisual Media and Audiovisual Content. *ΣΚΕΨΥ, 7*(1), 166–174.

Nicolaou, C. (2021a). Development of Business Through the Internet and Social Media: The Professional Use of Audiovisual Media Technologies Through Strategic Tactics and Practices. In H. El-Gohary, D. Edwards, & M. Ben Mimoun (Eds.), Handbook of Research on IoT, Digital Transformation, and the Future of Global Marketing (pp. 193–211). IGI Global.

Nicolaou, C. (2021c, October). *Outlining the profile and professional identity of the Greek and Cypriot Adult Educators through a phenomenological approach in the era of the three dimensions* [Paper presentation]. The 4th Annual International Symposium of the International Network of Vignette and Anecdotes Research Symposium on "Learning as Experience: Phenomenological Approaches in Educational Research", Thessaloniki, Greece.

Nicolaou, C. (2021e, July). *The description of the profile and the professional identity of Greek and Cypriot Adult Educators in the era of the triptych dimension* [Paper presentation]. The 7th International Scientific Conference of the Institute of Humanities and Social Sciences, Heraklion, Crete, Greece.

Nicolaou, C. A. (2011b). *Public Relations: Future and New Technologies* [Δημόσιες Σχέσεις: Μέλλον και Νέες Τεχνολογίες of Greek language] [Unpublished Bachelor's Thesis, University of Nicosia, Nicosia, Cyprus].

Nicolaou, C. A. (2014). Life Skills: The Importance of Non-Verbal Communication. In M. Tzekaki, M. Kanatsouli (Eds.), Panhellenic Conference with International Participation: Re-Reflections on Childhood (pp. 1544–1546). TEPAE, AUTh.

Nicolaou, C. (2019b). The use of audiovisual media in adult education. In *Proceedings of the 5th International Scientific Conference on Communication, Information, Awareness and Education in Late Modernity* (vol. A, pp. 155-163). Institute of Humanities and Social Sciences.

Nicolaou, C. (2021b). Media Trends and Prospects in Educational Activities and Techniques for Online Learning and Teaching through Television Content: Technological and Digital Socio-Cultural Environment, Generations, and Audiovisual Media Communications in Education. *Education Sciences, 11*(11), 685. doi:10.3390/educsci11110685

Nicolaou, C. (2021d). Qualitative methods research through the Internet Applications and Services: The contribution of audiovisuals media technology as technology-enhanced research. *International Research in Higher Education*, 6(1), 1. Advance online publication. doi:10.5430/irhe.v6n1p1

Nicolaou, C. (2022a). Information and Communications Technologies Through Technology-Enhanced Learning in Adult Education: The Re-Approach of the Adult Educator and the Adult Learners. In C. Krishnan, F. Al-Harthy, & G. Singh (Eds.), *Technology Training for Educators From Past to Present* (pp. 73–94). IGI Global. doi:10.4018/978-1-6684-4083-4.ch004

Nicolaou, C. (2022b). Methodological Approaches utilizing Information and Communication Technologies (ICTs): Trends and Perspectives of Research Methods from and through the Internet. *Open Education: The Journal for Open and Distance Education and Educational Technology*, 18(1), 290–315.

Nicolaou, C. (2022c). The Secret Power of Digital Storytelling Methodology: Technology-Enhanced Learning Utilizing Audiovisual Educational Content. In J. DeHart (Ed.), *Enhancing Education Through Multidisciplinary Film Teaching Methodologies* (pp. 235–246). IGI Global. doi:10.4018/978-1-6684-5394-0.ch013

Nicolaou, C. (2023). Generations and Branded Content from and through the Internet and Social Media: Modern Communication Strategic Techniques and Practices for Brand Sustainability—The Greek Case Study of LACTA Chocolate. *Sustainability*, 15(1), 584. doi:10.3390/su15010584.

Nicolaou, C., & Kalliris, G. (2020). Audiovisual Media Communications in Adult Education: The case of Cyprus and Greece of Adults as Adult Learners. *European Journal of Investigation in Health, Psychology and Education*, 10(4), 967–994. doi:10.3390/ejihpe10040069 PMID:34542430

Nicolaou, C., & Kalliris, G. (2021). The (Non-Verbal) Communication and the use of Audiovisual Media. In *Proceedings of the 6th International Scientific Conference on Communication, Information, Awareness and Education in Late Modernity* (vol. A, pp. 303–311). Institute of Humanities and Social Sciences.

Nicolaou, C., & Karypidou, C. (2021). Generations and Social Media: The case of Cyprus and Greece. In *Proceedings of the 7th International Scientific Conference* (vol. A, pp. 592–601). Institute of Humanities and Social Sciences.

Nicolaou, C., Matsiola, M., & Kalliris, G. (2019). Technology-Enhanced Learning and Teaching Methodologies through Audiovisual Media. *Education Sciences*, 9(3), 196. doi:10.3390/educsci9030196

Nicolaou, C., Matsiola, M., & Kalliris, G. (2022). The Challenge of an Interactive Audiovisual-Supported Lesson Plan: Information and Communications Technologies (ICTs) in Adult Education. *Education Sciences*, 12(11), 836. doi:10.3390/educsci12110836

Nicolaou, C., Matsiola, M., Karypidou, C., Podara, A., Kotsakis, R., & Kalliris, G. (2021b). Medias Studies, Audiovisual Media Communications, and Generations: The case of budding journalists in radio courses in Greece. *Journalism and Media*, 2(2), 155–192. doi:10.3390/journalmedia2020010

Nicolaou, C., Podara, A., & Karypidou, C. (2021a). Audiovisual media in education and Generation Z: Application of audiovisual media theory in education with an emphasis on radio. In *Proceedings of the 6th International Scientific Conference on Communication, Information, Awareness and Education in Late Modernity* (vol. A, pp. 294–302). Institute of Humanities and Social Sciences.

Ning, H., & Hornby, G. (2014). The impact of cooperative learning on tertiary EFL learners' motivation. *Educational Review*, 66(1), 108–124. doi:10.1080/00131911.2013.853169

Nomura, K., & Yuan, R. (2019). Long-term motivations for L2 learning: A biographical study from a situated learning perspective. *Journal of Multilingual and Multicultural Development*, 40(2), 164–178. doi:10.1080/01434632.2018.1497041

Novak, J. (1990). Human Construtivism: A Unification of Psychological and Epistemological Phenomena in Meaning Making. *Dalam Fourth North American Conference on Personal Construct Psychology, 15*.

Novak, J. D. (1993). A view on the current status of Ausubel's assimilation theory of learning. In *Proceedings of the Third International Seminar on Misconceptions and Educational Strategies in Science and Mathematics*. Misconceptions Trust.

Novak, J. D., & Cañas, A. J. (2008). *The theory underlying concept maps and how to construct them*. Technical report IHMC CmapTools 2006-01 Rev 01-2008.

Novak, J., & Gowin, D. (2006). *Learning How to Learn*. Cambridge University Press.

Novakovich, J., Miah, S., & Shaw, S. (2017). Designing curriculum to shape professional social media skills and identity in virtual communities of practice. *Computers & Education, 104*, 65–90. doi:10.1016/j.compedu.2016.11.002

Nugraini, S. H., Choo, K. A., & Hin, H. S. (2009, November). *The proposed conceptual framework of e-audio visual biology for teaching and learning in Indonesia senior high schools* [Paper presentation]. CoSMEd 2009 Third International Conference, Penang, Malaysia.

Nusrat, M., & Sultana, N. (2019). Soft skills for sustainable employment of business graduates of Bangladesh. *Higher Education. Skills and Work-Based Learning, 9*(3), 264–278. doi:10.1108/HESWBL-01-2018-0002

O'Donnell, A. M., Dansereau, D. F., & Hall, R. H. (2002). Knowledge maps as scaffolds for cognitive processing. *Educational Psychology Review, 14*(1), 71–86. doi:10.1023/A:1013132527007

O'Leary, E. S., Shapiro, C., Toma, S., Sayson, H. W., Levis-Fitzgerald, M., Johnson, T., & Sork, V. L. (2020). Creating inclusive classrooms by engaging STEM faculty in culturally responsive teaching workshops. *International Journal of STEM education, 7*(1), 1-15.

O'Sullivan, M. K., & Dallas, K. B. (2010). A collaborative approach to implementing 21st century skills in a high school senior research class. *Education Libraries, 33*(1), 3–9.

OECD. (2020). *The role of labour market information in guiding educational and occupational choices*. OECD Publishing.

Olt, P. A. (2018). Virtually there: Distant freshmen blended in classes through synchronous online education. *Innovative Higher Education, 43*, 381–395. https://dx.doi.org/10.1007/s10755-018-9437-z

Oostdam, R. J., Peetsma, T. T. D., & Blok, H. (2007). *Het nieuwe leren in basisonderwijs en voortgezet onderwijs nader beschouwd* [New learning in primary and secondary education reconsidered]. SCO-Kohnstamm Instituut.

Osborne, M., & Freyberg, P. (1985). *Learning in science: Implications of children's knowledge*. Heinemann.

Owusu-Ansah, A., & Kyei-Blankson, L. (2016). Going back to the basics: Demonstrating care, connectedness, and a pedagogy of relationship in education. *World Journal of Education, 6*(3). Advance online publication. doi:10.5430/wje.v6n3p1

Oxford, R. L. (1997). Cooperative learning, collaborative learning, and interaction: Three communicative strands in the language classroom. *Modern Language Journal, 81*(4), 443–456. doi:10.1111/j.1540-4781.1997.tb05510.x

Oxford, R. L., Tomlinson, S., Barcelos, A., Harrington, C., Lavine, R. Z., Saleh, A., & Longhini, A. (1998). Clashing metaphors about classroom teachers: Toward a systematic typology for the language teaching field. *System, 26*, 3–50.

Öztürk, M., & Çakıroğlu, Ü. (2021). Flipped learning design in EFL classrooms: Implementing self-regulated learning strategies to develop language skills. *Smart Learn. Environ., 8*(1), 2. doi:10.118640561-021-00146-x

Padgett, D. (2012). *Qualitative and mixed methods in public health*. SAGE. Retrieved from http://ezproxy.deakin.edu.au/login?url=http://search.ebscohost.com/login.aspx?direct=true&db=cat00097a&AN=deakin.b3657335&authtype=sso&custid=deakin&site=eds-live&scope=site

Paechter, M. (2004). Hybrid learning leads to better achievement and higher satisfaction than pure e-learning. Is it that easy? (pp. 584-591). I KNOW '04, Graz, Austria.

Palioura, M., & Dimoulas, C. (2022). Digital Storytelling in Education: A Transmedia Integration Approach for the Non-Developers. *Education Sciences*, *12*(8), 559. doi:10.3390/educsci12080559

Panadero, E. (2017). A review of self-regulated learning: Six models and four directions for research. *Frontiers in Psychology*, *28*(8), 422–435. doi:10.3389/fpsyg.2017.00422 PMID:28503157

Panadero, E., & Alonso-Tapia, J. (2013). Self-assessment: Theoretical and practical connotations. When it happens, how is it acquired and what to do to develop it in our Regulated learning and evaluative judgment 35 students. *Electronic Journal of Research in Educational Psychology*, *11*(2), 551–576.

Panadero, E., & Alonso-Tapia, J. (2014). How do students self-regulate? Review of Zimmerman's cyclical model of self-regulated learning. *Anales de Psicología*, *30*(2), 450–462.

Papastergiou, M., & Solomonidou, C. (2005). Gender issues in Internet access and favourite Internet activities among Greek high school pupils inside and outside school. *Computers & Education*, *44*(4), 377–393. doi:10.1016/j.compedu.2004.04.002

Papatheodorou, T., & Moyles, J. R. (Eds.). (2009). *Learning Together in the Early Years - Exploring Relational Pedagogy*. Routledge.

Paris, S. G., & Paris, A. H. (2001). Classroom application of research on self-regulated learning. *Educational Psychologist*, *36*(3), 89–113. doi:10.1207/S15326985EP3602_4

Park, S., Lee, S., Oliver, J. S., & Cramond, B. (2006). Changes in Korean science teachers' perceptions of creativity and science teaching after participating in an overseas professional development program. *Journal of Science Teacher Education*, *17*, 37–64. doi:10.1007=s10972-006-9009-4

Park, S. (2019). Goal contents as predictors of academic cheating in college students. *Ethics & Behavior*, (3), 628–639.

Parsazadeh, N., Ali, R., & Rezaei, M. (2018). A framework for cooperative and interactive mobile learning to improve online information evaluation skills. *Computers & Education*, *120*, 75–89. doi:10.1016/j.compedu.2018.01.010

Patahuddin, P., Syawal, S., Esnara, C., & Abdullah, M. (2022). Characterizing the Ideal Audio-Visual Learning Content of Writing Course Learned in Distance. *Lingua Cultura*, *16*(1).

Patnaik, C., & Mortensen, P. (2009). *Wired to care: How companies prosper when they create widespread empathy*. FT Press.

Patrick, S., & Sturgis, C. (2015). *Maximizing competency education and blended learning: Insights from experts*. iNACOL

PattonI. (2014). *Embedding sustainability in universities*. https://www.universityworldnews.com/post.php?story=20140513111222724

Patton, M. Q. (2002). Two decades of developments in qualitative inquiry: A personal, experiential perspective. *Qualitative Social Work: Research and Practice*, *1*(3), 261–283. doi:10.1177/1473325002001003636

Patton, W., & McMahon, M. (1999). *Career development and systems theory: A new relationship*. Thomson Brooks/Cole Publishing Co.

Compilation of References

Pavla, S., Hana, V., & Jan, V. (2015). Blended learning: Promising strategic alternative in higher education. *Procedia: Social and Behavioral Sciences*, *171*, 1245–1254. doi:10.1016/j.sbspro.2015.01.238

Pekrun, R. (2019). Inquiry on emotions in higher education: Progress and open problems. *Studies in Higher Education*, *44*(10), 1806–1811. doi:10.1080/03075079.2019.1665335

Pellikka, J., Ruuskanen, J., & Suazo de Kontro, P. R. (2021). Fostering commercialization of innovation and student entrepreneurship in innovation ecosystems: The case of the Business Center of North Savo in Finland. *Revista Nacional de Administración*, *12*(1), e3556. Advance online publication. doi:10.22458/rna.v12i1.3556

Périer, F. (2005). *Study on volunteering and volunteering in Morocco*. UNDP Rabat.

Perifanou, M., Tzafilkou, K., & Economides, A. A. (2021). The Role of Instagram, Facebook, and YouTube Frequency of Use in University Students' Digital Skills Components. *Education Sciences*, *11*(12), 766. doi:10.3390/educsci11120766

Perry, C., & Cooper, M. (2001). Metaphors are good mirrors: Reflecting on change for teacher educators. *Reflective Practice*, *2*, 41–52.

Pettinger, L., Forkert, K., & Goffey, A. (2018). The Promises of Creative Industry Higher Education: An Analysis of University Prospectuses in Malaysia. *International Journal of Cultural Policy*, *24*(4), 466–484. doi:10.1080/10286632.2016.1223644

Pham, V. P. H. (2021). The effects of collaborative writing on students' writing fluency: An efficient framework for collaborative writing. *SAGE Open*, *11*(1). doi:10.1177/2158244021998363

Piaget, J. (2001). *The Psychology of Intelligence* (M. Piercy & D. E. Berlyne, Trans.). Routledge Classics.

Piccinin, S., Cristi, C., & McCoy, M. (2006). The impact of individual consultation on student ratings of teaching. *The International Journal for Academic Development*, *4*(2), 78–88. doi:10.1080/1360144990040202

Pierson, J. L. (2008). *The relationship between patterns of classroom discourse and mathematics learning*. The University of Texas at Austin.

Piliavin, J. A., & Siegl, E. (2007). Health benefits of volunteering in the Wisconsin longitudinal study. *Journal of Health and Social Behavior*, *48*(4), 450–464. doi:10.1177/002214650704800408 PMID:18198690

Pintrich, P. R. (2000). The Role of Goal-Orientation in Self-Regulated Learning. In M. Boekaerts, P. R. Pintrich, & M. Zeidner (Eds.), *Handbook of Self-Regulation* (pp. 451–502). Academic Press. doi:10.1016/B978-012109890-2/50043-3

Plagnol, A. C., & Huppert, F. A. (2010). Happy to help? Exploring the factors associated with variations in rates of volunteering across Europe. *Social Indicators Research*, *97*(2), 157–176. doi:10.100711205-009-9494-x

Platz, L., Jüttler, M., & Schumann, S. (2021). Game-Based Learning in Economics Education at Upper Secondary Level: The Impact of Game Mechanics and Reflection on Students' Financial Literacy. In C. Aprea & D. Ifenthaler (Eds.), *Game-based Learning Across the Disciplines* (pp. 25–42). Advances in Game-Based Learning. Springer. doi:10.1007/978-3-030-75142-5_2

Plucker, J. A., Beghetto, R. A., & Dow, G. T. (2004). Why isn't creativity more important to educational psychologists? Potential, pitfalls, and future directions in creativity research. *Educational Psychologist*, *39*, 83–96. doi:10.1207=s15326985ep3902_1

Podara, A., Giomelakis, D., Nicolaou, C., Matsiola, M., & Kotsakis, R. (2021). Digital Storytelling in Cultural Heritage: Audience Engagement in the Interactive Documentary New Life. *Sustainability*, *13*(3), 1193. doi:10.3390u13031193

Podara, A., & Kalliris, G. (2022). How Digital Poverty Affects Television Viewing Habits. In N. E. Myridis (Ed.), *Poverty and Quality of Life in the Digital Era* (pp. 105–123). Springer. doi:10.1007/978-3-031-04711-4_5

Podara, A., Matsiola, M., Nicolaou, C., Maniou, T. A., & Kalliris, G. (2019, November). *Audiovisual consumption practices in post-crisis Greece: An empirical research approach to Generation Z* [Paper presentation]. The International Conference on Filmic and Media Narratives of the Crisis: Contemporary Representations, Athens, Greece.

Podara, A., Matsiola, M., Nicolaou, C., Maniou, T. A., & Kalliris, G. (2022). Transformation of television viewing practices in Greece: Generation Z and audio-visual content. *Journal of Digital Media & Policy*, *13*(2), 157–179. doi:10.1386/jdmp_00034_1

Polman, J., Hornstra, L., & Volman, M. (2021). The meaning of meaningful learning in mathematics in upper-primary education. *Learning Environments Research*, *24*(3), 469–486. doi:10.100710984-020-09337-8

Popham, W. J. (2006, October 10-13). *Defining and enhancing formative assessment* [Paper presentation]. Annual Large-Scale Assessment Conference, Council of Chief State School Officers, San Francisco, CA, United States.

Porritt, J. (2013). *The World We Made: Alex McKay's story from 2050*. Phaidon.

Pöysä, J., Lowyck, J., & Häkkinen, P. (2005). Learning together "there"-hybrid "place" as a conceptual vantage point for understanding virtual learning communities in higher education context. *PsychNology Journal*, *3*(2), 162–180.

Prater, M. A., & Devereaux, T. H. (2009). Culturally responsive training of teacher educators. *Action in Teacher Education*, *31*(3), 19–27. https://doi.org/10.1080/01626620.2022.2058641

Presmeg, N. C. (1986). Visualization in high school mathematics. *For the Learning of Mathematics*, *6*(3), 42–46.

Prouteau, L. (2002). Le bénévolat sous le regard des économistes. *Revue Française des Affaires Sociales*, (4), 117–134.

Prouteau, L., & Wolff, F. C. (2006). Does volunteer work pay off in the labor market? *Journal of Socio-Economics*, *35*(6), 992–1013.

Psomadaki, O., Matsiola, M., Dimoulas, C. A., & Kalliris, G. M. (2022). The Significance of Digital Network Platforms to Enforce Musicians' Entrepreneurial Role: Assessing Musicians' Satisfaction in Using Mobile Applications. *Sustainability*, *14*(10), 5975. doi:10.3390u14105975

Pun, J., & Jin, X. (2021). Student challenges and learning strategies at Hong Kong EMI universities. *PLoS One*, *16*(5), e0251564. doi:10.1371/journal.pone.0251564 PMID:33961675

Puustinen, M., & Pulkkinen, L. (2001). Models of self-regulated learning: A review. *Scandinavian Journal of Educational Research*, *45*(3), 269–286. doi:10.1080/00313830120074206

Quinn-Allan, D. (2010). Public relations, education, and social media: Issues for professionalism in the digital age. *Asia Pacific Public Relations Journal*, *11*(1), 41–55.

Quinn, K. (2018). Congnitive Effects of Social Media Use: A case Case of Older Adults. *Social Media + Society*, *4*(3). doi:10.1177/2056305118787203

Radzali, U. S., Mohd-Yusof, K., & Phang, F. A. (2018). Changing the conception of teaching from teacher-centered to student-centered learning among engineering lecturers. *Global Journal of Engineering Education*, *20*(2), 120–126.

Raes, A., Vanneste, P., Pieters, M., Windey, I., Noortgate, W. V. D., & Depaepe, F. (2020). Learning and instruction in the hybrid virtual classroom: An investigation of students' engagement and the effect of quizzes. *Computers & Education*, *143*, 143. doi:10.1016/j.compedu.2019.103682

Rahimi, S., & Shute, V. J. (2021). First inspire, then instruct to improve students' creativity. *Computers & Education*, *174*(January), 104312. https://doi.org/10.1016/j.compedu.2021.104312

Rainear, A. M., & Christensen, J. L. (2017). Protection motivation theory as an explanatory framework for proenvironmental behavioral intentions. *Communication Research Reports*, *34*(3), 239–248. doi:10.1080/08824096.2017.1286472

Rajaram, K. (2021). *Evidence-based teaching for the 21st century classroom and beyond*. Springer. doi:10.1007/978-981-33-6804-0

Ramli, N. F., & Talib, O. (2017). Can education institution implement STEM? From Malaysian teachers' view. *International Journal of Academic Research in Business & Social Sciences*, *7*(3), 721–732. doi:10.6007/IJARBSS/v7-i3/2772

Ramsey, L. R., Betz, D. E., & Sekaquaptewa, D. (2013). The effects of an academic environment intervention on science identification among women in STEM. *Social Psychology of Education*, *16*(3), 377–397. https://doi.org/10.1007/s11218-013-9218-6

Rands, M., & Gansemer-Topf, A. (2017). "The room itself is active": How classroom design impacts student engagement. *Journal of Learning Spaces*, *6*(1).

Rao, M. S. (2018). Soft skills: Toward a sanctimonious discipline. *On the Horizon*, *26*(3), 215–224. doi:10.1108/OTH-06-2017-0034

Rayner, V., Pitsolantis, N., & Osana, H. (2009). Mathematics anxiety in preservice teachers: Its relationship to their conceptual and procedural knowledge of fractions. *Mathematics Education Research Journal*, *21*(3), 60–85.

Reddan, G., & Rauchle, M. (2012). Student Perceptions of the Value of Career Development Learning to a Work-Integrated Learning Course in Exercise Science. *Australian Journal of Career Development*, *21*(1), 38–48. doi:10.1177/103841621202100106

Reddan, G., & Rauchle, M. (2017). Combining quality work-integrated learning and career development learning through the use of the SOAR model to enhance employability. *Asia-Pacific Journal of Cooperative Education, Special Issue*, *18*(2), 129–139.

Reimagining the Role of Technology in Education (2017). *National Education Technology Plan Update January 2017*. U.S. Department Of Education http://tech.ed.gov

Reis, H. (2007). Steps toward the ripening of relationship science. *Personal Relationships*, *14*(1), 1–23. doi:10.1111/j.1475-6811.2006.00139.x

Reynolds, S. J., & Ceranic, T. L. (2007). The effects of moral judgment and moral identity on moral behavior: An empirical examination of the moral individual. *The Journal of Applied Psychology*, *92*(6), 1610–1624. doi:10.1037/0021-9010.92.6.1610 PMID:18020800

Rhodes, M. (1961). An Analysis of Creativity. *Phi Delta Kappan*, *42*(7), 305–310.

Richardson, J. C., Arbaugh, J. B., Cleveland-Innes, M., Ice, P., Swan, K. P., & Garrison, D. R. (2012). Using the community of inquiry framework to inform effective instructional design. In L. Moller. & J. Huett (Eds.), The next generation of distance education. Springer. doi:10.1007/978-1-4614-1785-9_7

Richardson, G. M., & Liang, L. L. (2008). The use of inquiry in the development of preservice teacher efficacy in mathematics and science. *Journal of Elementary Science Education*, *20*(1), 1–16.

Rieger, A., Radcliffe, B. J., & Doepker, G. M. (2013). Practices for developing reflective thinking skills among teachers. *Kappa Delta Pi Record*, *49*(4), 184–189.

Rissanen, I., Kuusisto, E., Hanhimäki, E., & Tirri, K. (2018). The implications of teachers' implicit theories for moral education: A case study from Finland. *Journal of Moral Education*, *47*(1), 63–77. https://doi.org/10.1080/03057240.2017.1350149

Riyanti, A., Nurgiyantoro, B., & Suryaman, M. (2021, December). The Use of Cartoon Film Media in Narrative Writing Skills for Elementary School Students. In *2nd International Conference on Innovation in Education and Pedagogy (ICIEP 2020)* (pp. 22–27). Atlantis Press.

Robertson, A. D., Atkins, L. J., Levin, D. M., & Richards, J. (2015). What is responsive teaching? In *Responsive teaching in science and mathematics* (pp. 1–35). Routledge. doi:10.4324/9781315689302

Robertson, A. D., Scherr, R. E., & Hammer, D. (2016). *Responsive teaching in Science and Mathematics*. Routledge.

Robinson, C., & Hullinger, H. (2008). New benchmarks in higher education: Student engagement in online learning. *Journal of Education for Business*, *84*, 101–109. .84.2.101-109. doi:10.3200/JOEB

Robotham, D. (1995). Self-directed learning: The ultimate learning style? *Journal of European Industrial Training*, *19*(7), 3–7. doi:10.1108/03090599510092918

Roelofs, E., & Terwel, J. (1999). Constructivism and authentic pedagogy: State of the art and recent developments in the Dutch national curriculum in secondary education. *Journal of Curriculum Studies*, *31*(2), 201–227. doi:10.1080/002202799183232

Roelofs, E., Visser, J., & Terwel, J. (2003). Preferences for various learning environments: Teachers' and parents' perceptions. *Learning Environments Research*, *6*(1), 77–110. doi:10.1023/A:1022915910198

Rogers, R. W. (1983). Cognitive and psychological processes in fear appeals and attitude change: A revised theory of protection motivation. *Social psychophysiology: A sourcebook*, 153-176.

Rogers, E. M. (2003). *Diffusion of Innovations* (5th ed.). Free Press.

Rohana, N. A. M., Hashim, S. N. I., Hamid, N. A. P., Rameli, M. F., & Mohamed, N. (2020). Pelaksanaan subject Hubungan Etnik tanpa peperiksaan akhir di UiTM cawangan Melaka. [Implementation of Ethnic Relations subject without final exam at UiTM Melaka branch]. *E-Journal of Islamic Thought and Understanding*, *1*, 18–34.

Røkenes, F. M., & Krumsvik, R. J. (2014). Development of student teachers' digital competence in teacher education - A Literature Review. *Nordic Journal of Digital Literacy*, *9*(4), 250–280. doi:10.18261/ISSN1891-943X-2014-04-03

Rolfe, G. (2002). Reflective practice: Where now? *Nurse Education in Practice*, *2*(1), 21–29. doi:10.1054/nepr.2002.0047 PMID:19036272

Romero Juárez, M. G. (2020). *Enseñanza de programación de estructuras de datos aplicando estrategias didácticas basadas en la teoría de carga cognitiva* [Tesis de maestría en informática y tecnologías computacionales]. Universidad Autónoma de Aguascalientes. Centro de Ciencias Básicas. http://hdl.handle.net/11317/1857

Rong, F., Yan, W., Xing, Y., & Yuan, L. (2018). Research on teacher-student interaction strategy in mixed learning from perspective of learners. *Vocational and Technical Education*, *39*(32), 43–46.

Rosano, S. (2007). *La cultura de la diversidad y la educación inclusiva*. http://benu.edu.mx/wp-content/uploads/2015/03/La_cultura_de_la_diversidad_y_la_educacion_inclusiva.pdf

Rösken, B., & Rolka, K. (2006, July). A picture is worth a 1000 words–the role of visualization in mathematics learning. In *Proceedings 30th conference of the International Group for the Psychology of mathematics education* (Vol. 4, pp. 457-464). Charles University.

Compilation of References

Rourke, L., & Kanuka, H. (2009). Learning in Communities of Inquiry: A Review of the literature. *Journal of Distance Education*, *23*(1), 19–48. https://www.ijede.ca/index.php/jde/article/view/474

Rubin, B., Fernandes, R., & Avgerinou, M. D. (2013). The effects of technology on the Community of Inquiry and satisfaction with online courses. *Internet High. Educ*, *2013*(17), 48–57. doi:10.1016/j.iheduc.2012.09.006

Rubinstein, M. (2006). Le développement de la responsabilité sociale de l'entreprise. Une analyse en termes d'isomorphisme institutionnel [The development of corporate social responsibility, an analysis in terms of institutional isomorphism]. *Revue d'Economie Industrielle*, (113), 83–105. doi:10.4000/rei.295

Ruey, S. (2010). A case study of constructivist instructional strategies for adult online learning. *British Journal of Educational Technology*, *41*(5), 706–720.

Runco, M. A., & Albert, R. S. (1986). The Threshold Theory Regarding Creativity and Intelligence: An Empirical Test With Gifted and Nongifted Children. *The Creative Child and Adult Quarterly*, *11*(4), 212–218.

Runco, M. A., & Chand, I. (1995). Cognition and Creativity. *Educational Psychology Review*, *7*(3), 243–267. doi:10.1007/BF02213373

Runco, M. A., & Jaeger, G. J. (2012). The Standard Definition of Creativity. *Creativity Research Journal*, *24*(1), 92–96. doi:10.1080/10400419.2012.650092

Rutherford, A., & Woolvin, M. (2013). *Volunteering and public service reform in rural Scotland*. SRUC Rural Policy Centre.

Ryabova, T., Frolova, E., & Rogach, O. (2018). Interaction of educational process participants in network online-space: The trends of new media reality development. *Media Education (Mediaobrazovanie)*, *58*(3), 140–146.

Saeed, M. A., Ghazali, K., & Aljaberi, M. A. (2018). A review of previous studies on ESL/EFL learners' interactional feedback exchanges in face-to-face and computer-assisted peer review of writing. *International Journal of Educational Technology in Higher Education*, *15*(1), 6. doi:10.118641239-017-0084-8

Said Hashim, K., Abdul Majid, R., & Alias, A. (2018). Gender and Ability Differences on the Profile of Purpose in Life among Adolescents. *Journal of Advance Research in Dynamical & Control Systems*, *10*(12).

San Pedro, T., & Kinloch, V. (2017). Toward Projects in Humanization: Research on Co-Creating and Sustaining Dialogic Relationships. *American Educational Research Journal*, *54*(1), 373S–394S. doi:10.3102/0002831216671210

Sani, K., & Adiansha, A. A. (2021). Smartphone: Bagaimana Pengaruh terhadap Motivasi Belajar Siswa Sekolah Dasar? [Smartphone: How does it influence elementary school students' learning motivation?]. *Jurnal Ilmiah Mandala Education*, *7*(2).

Santrock, J. W. (2018). *Educational Psychology* (6th ed.). McGraw-Hill Education.

Sardar, Z. (2010). Welcome to postnormal times. *Futures*, *42*(5), 435–444. doi:10.1016/j.futures.2009.11.028

Sarridis, I., & Nicolaou, C. (2015, December). *Social Media: (Correct) Professional Use* [Paper presentation]. The 2nd Student Conference of the Department of Applied Informatics—University of Macedonia on Modern Entrepreneurship & Informatics Technologies, Thessaloniki, Greece.

Scharmer, C. O. (2009). *Theory U: Leading from the future as it emerges*. The Society for Organizational Learning.

Schellens, T., & Valcke, M. (2005). Collaborative learning in asynchronous discussion groups: What about the impact on cognitive processing? *Computers in Human Behavior*, *21*(6), 957–975. doi:10.1016/j.chb.2004.02.025

Schiff, J. (1990). *Charitable Giving and Government Policy. An Economic Analysis*. Greenwood Press.

Schneider, K. J., Pierson, J. F., & Bugental, J. F. T. (2014). *The Handbook of Humanistic Psychology: Theory, Research, and Practice* (2nd ed.). SAGE Publications Inc.

Schrage, M. (1999). *Serious play: How the world's best companies simulate to innovate*. Harvard Business Press.

Schwartz, P. (1991). *The art of the long view*. Doubleday.

Schwartz, S. H. (1977). Normative influences on altruism. In Vol. 10, pp. 221–279). Advances in experimental social psychology. Academic Press.

Scott, D., & Friesen, S. (2013). Inquiry-Based Learning: A Review of the Research Literature. *Alberta Education*, *1*, 1–29.

Seburn, T. (2016). *Academic reading circles*. Createspace Independent Publishing Platform.

Şentürk, C. (2021). Effects of the blended learning model on preservice teachers' academic achievements and twenty-first century skills. *Education and Information Technologies*, *26*(1), 35–48. doi:10.100710639-020-10340-y PMID:33020691

Seshaiyer, P. (2021). Novel frameworks for upskilling the mathematics education workforce. In *Mathematics Education for Sustainable Economic Growth and Job Creation* (pp. 90–107). Routledge. doi:10.4324/9781003048558-8

Seshaiyer, P., & McNeely, C. L. (2020). Challenges and Opportunities From COVID-19 for Global Sustainable Development. *World Medical & Health Policy*, *12*(4), 443–453. doi:10.1002/wmh3.380 PMID:33362943

Shaari, S. S., Besar, J. A., & Jali, M. F. M. (2017). Analisis keberkesanan subjek Hubungan Etnik sebagai pencetus literasi politik: Kajian ke atas mahasiswa. [Analysis of the effectiveness of the Ethnic Relations subject as a trigger for political literacy: A study on undergraduates] *e-Bangi*, *14*, 26-33.

Shafiei, A., & Maleksaeidi, H. (2020). Pro-environmental behavior of university students: Application of protection motivation theory. *Global Ecology and Conservation*, *22*, e00908. doi:10.1016/j.gecco.2020.e00908

Shams, I. E. (2013). Hybrid learning and Iranian EFL learners' autonomy in vocabulary learning. *Procedia: Social and Behavioral Sciences*, *93*, 1587–1592. doi:10.1016/j.sbspro.2013.10.086

Shanti, S. (2019). Swami Vivekananda's Perspective on Education. *JETIR*, *6*(5). Retrieved from http://www.jetir.org

Sharan, Y. (2015). *Meaningful Learning in the Co-operative Classroom. Education 3-13: International Journal of Primary, Elementary and Early Years Education, 43(1), 83-94.*

Shea, P., & Bidjerano, T. (2009). Community of inquiry as a theoretical framework to foster "epistemic engagement" and "cognitive presence" in online education. *Computers & Education*, *2009*(52), 543–553. doi:10.1016/j.compedu.2008.10.007

Shea, P., & Bidjerano, T. (2012). Learning presence as a moderator in the community of inquiry model. *Computers & Education*, *2012*(59), 316–326. doi:10.1016/j.compedu.2012.01.011

Shelton-Strong, S. J. (2012). Literature circles in ELT. *ELT Journal*, *66*(2), 214–223. doi:10.1093/elt/ccr049

Shenton, A. K. (2004). Strategies for ensuring trustworthiness in qualitative research projects. *Education for Information*, *22*(2), 63–75. doi:10.3233/EFI-2004-22201

Shurville, S., O'Grady, T., & Mayall, P. (2008). Educational and institutional flexibility of Australian Educational Software. Campus-wide information systems. *Emerald Group Publishing Limited*, *25*(2), 74–84.

Compilation of References

Shutaleva, A., Martyushev, N., Nikonova, Z., Savchenko, I., Bovkun, A., & Kerimov, A. (2021). Critical thinking in media sphere: Attitude of university teachers to fake news and its impact on the teaching. *Journal of Management Information and Decision Sciences*, *24*, 1–12.

Shutaleva, A., Martyushev, N., Starostin, A., Salgiriev, A., Vlasova, O., Grinek, A., Nikonova, Z., & Savchenko, I. (2022). Migration Potential of Students and Development of Human Capital. *Education Sciences*, *12*(5), 324. doi:10.3390/educsci12050324

Sidiropoulos, E., Vryzas, N., Vrysis, L., Avraam, E., & Dimoulas, C. (2019). Growing media skills and know-how in situ: Technology-enhanced practices and collaborative support in mobile news-reporting. *Education Sciences*, *9*(3), 173. doi:10.3390/educsci9030173

Simon, B. (2019). *The Effect of Formative Assessment on Student Motivation and Self-Regulation* [Thesis, Concordia University, St. Paul]. https://digitalcommons.csp.edu/teachereducation_masters/2

Simonton, D. K. (2017). Domain-general Creativity: On Generating Original, Useful, and Surprising Combinations. In J. C. Kaufman, V. P. Glăveanu, & J. Baer (Eds.), The Cambridge Handbook of Creativity Across Domains (pp. 41-60). Cambridge University Press.

Simonton, D. K. (2017). Big-C Versus Little-c Creativity: Definition, Implications, and Inherent Educational Contradictions. In R. Beghetto & B. Sriraman (Eds.), *Creative Contradictions in Education. Creativity Theory and Action in Education* (Vol. 1, pp. 3–19). Springer. doi:10.1007/978-3-319-21924-0_1

Slavin, R. E. (1983). *Cooperative learning*. Longman.

Slavin, R. E. (1996). Research on cooperative learning and achievement: What we know, what we need to know. *Contemporary Educational Psychology*, *21*(1), 43–69. doi:10.1006/ceps.1996.0004

Smart, K. L., & Cappel, J. J. (2006). Students' perceptions of online learning: A comparative study. *Journal of Information Technology Education*, *5*(1), 201–219.

Smith, K., Gamlem, S. M., Sandal, A. K., & Engelsen, K. S. (2016). Educating for the future: A conceptual framework of responsive pedagogy. *Cogent Education*, *3*(1).

Smith, L., & Cotten, M. (1980). Effect of lesson vagueness and discontinuity on student achievement and attitude. *Journal of Educational Psychology*, *72*, 670–675.

Soffer, T., Kahan, T., & Nachmias, R. (2019). Patterns of students' utilization of flexibility in online academic courses and their relation to course achievement. *The International Review of Research in Open and Distributed Learning*, *20*(3), 3. doi:10.19173/irrodl.v20i4.3949

Spady, W. G. (1994). *Outcome-Based Education: Critical Issues and Answers*. American Association of School Administrators.

Spencer, S. J., Logel, C., & Davies, P. G. (2016). Stereotype threat. *Annual Review of Psychology*, *67*(1), 415–437. https://doi.org/10.1146/annurev-psych-073115-103235

Spyropoulou, N., & Kameas, A. (2021). A holistic framework of STE(A)M educators competences. *13th annual International Conference of Education, Research and Innovation*, 504-514.

Sriraman, B. (2010). *Theories of Mathematics Education*. Springer-Verlag Berlin Heidelberg. doi:10.1007/978-3-642-00742-2

Stake, R. E., & Schwandt, T. A. (2006). On discerning quality in evaluation. The Sage handbook of evaluation, 404-418. .

Stake, R. (1995). *The art of case study research.* SAGE Publications.

Statistics Canada. (2003). *Cornerstones of Community: Highlights from the National Survey of Nonprofit and Voluntary Organizations, 2003.* Author.

Steg, L., & Vlek, C. (2009). Encouraging pro-environmental behaviour: An integrative review and research agenda. *Journal of Environmental Psychology, 29*(3), 309–317. doi:10.1016/j.jenvp.2008.10.004

Steh, B., & Saric, M. (2020). Enhancing self-regulated learning in higher education. *Journal of Elementary Education, 13,* 129–150.

Stein, D. (1998). *Situated learning in adult education* . ERIC Clearinghouse on Adult, Career, and Vocational Education, Center on Education and Training for Employment, College of Education, the Ohio State University. http://www.edpsycinteractive.org/files/sitadlted.html

Sternberg, R. (2006). The nature of creativity. *Creativity Research Journal, 18*(1), 87–98. doi:10.120715326934crj1801_10

Stevens, R. J., & Slavin, R. E. (1995). Effects of a cooperative learning approach in reading and writing on academically handicapped and nonhandicapped students. *The Elementary School Journal, 95*(3), 241–262. https://www.jstor.org/stable/1001933. doi:10.1086/461801

Strahan, D. (2008). Successful Teachers Develop Academic Momentum with Reluctant Students. *Middle School Journal, 39*(5), 4–12.

Strauss, A. L., & Corbin, J. M. (1998). *Basics of qualitative research.* Sage Publications.

Strijbos, J. W., Martens, R. L., & Jochems, W. M. G. (2004). Designing for interaction: Six steps to designing computer-supported group-based learning. *Computers & Education, 42*(4), 403–424. doi:10.1016/j.compedu.2003.10.004

Stukas, A. A., Hoye, R., Nicholson, M., Brown, K. M., & Aisbett, L. (2016). Motivations to volunteer and their associations with volunteers' well-being. *Nonprofit and Voluntary Sector Quarterly, 45*(1), 112–132.

Suci, W., Muslim, S., & Chaeruman, U. A. (2022). Use of Social Media for Collaborative Learning in Online Learning: A Literature Review. *Al-Ishlah: Jurnal Pendidikan, 14*(3), 3075-3086. Doi:10.35445/alishlah.v14i3.833

Sucipto, S., Ihsan, M. I., & Wiyono, B. B. (2019). Fostering Curiosity to Form Self-Directed Learning Traditions. *SAR Journal.* http://www.sarjournal.com/content/22/SARJournalJune2019_61_67.pdf

Sueb, R., Hashim, H., Hashim, K. S., & Izam, M. M. (2020). Excellent Teachers' Strategies in Managing Students' Misbehaviour in the Classroom. *Asian Journal of University Education, 16*(1), 46–55. doi:10.24191/ajue.v16i1.8982

Suh, J., Seshaiyer, P., Lee, K. H., Peixoto, N., Suh, D., & Lee, Y. (2014, October). Critical learning experiences for Korean engineering students to promote creativity and innovation. In 2014 IEEE Frontiers in Education Conference (FIE) Proceedings (pp. 1-6). IEEE. doi:10.1109/FIE.2014.7044438

Sumamol, N. S. (2019). *Strategies for reflective teaching practices.* Laxmi Book Piblication.

Suyatno. (2009). *Menjelajah Pembelajaran Inovatif.* Bumi Aksara.

Talbert, R., & Mor-Avi, A. (2019). A space for learning: An analysis of research on active learning spaces. *Heliyon, 5*(12). doi:10.1016/j.heliyon.2019.e02967

Tangney, J. P., Stuewig, J., & Mashek, D. J. (2007). Moral emotions and moral behavior. *Annual Review of Psychology, 58*(1), 345–372. doi:10.1146/annurev.psych.56.091103.070145 PMID:16953797

Compilation of References

Taylor, P. (1998). Supporting Students for Flexible Learning, Teaching Through Flexible Learning Resources. Griffith Institute for higher education, 2-5.

Tekkol, İ. A., & Demirel, M. (2018). An investigation of self-directed learning skills of undergraduate students. *Frontiers in Psychology*, *23*(9), 2324. doi:10.3389/fpsyg.2018.02324 PMID:30532727

Teng, L. S. (2022). Explicit strategy-based instruction in L2 writing contexts: A perspective of self-regulated learning and formative assessment. *Assessing Writing*, *53*, 100645. www.elsevier.com/locate/asw. doi:10.1016/j.asw.2022.100645

Thanavathi, C. (2021). Teachers' Perception On Digital Media Technology. [TURCOMAT]. *Turkish Journal of Computer and Mathematics Education*, *12*(10), 6972–6975.

The Doors. (1967). Strange Days [Recorded by The Doors]. On Strange days [CD]. Elektra.

Thomas, R. A., West, R. E., & Borup, J. (2017). An analysis of instructor social presence in online text and asynchronous video feedback comments. *Internet and Higher Education*, *2017*(33), 61–73. doi:10.1016/j.iheduc.2017.01.003

Thomas, W. (2016, August 1). The Education Revolution. Academic Press.

Tian, L., Liu, Q., & Zhang, X. (2022). Self-regulated writing strategy use when revising upon automated, peer, and teacher feedback in an online English as a foreign language writing course. *Frontiers in Psychology*, *13*, 873170. www.frontiersin.org. doi:10.3389/fpsyg.2022.873170 PMID:35519626

Tobin, K. (1990). Changing metaphors and beliefs: A master switch for teaching? *Theory into Practice*, *29*, 122–127.

Toffler, A. (1974). *Learning for tomorrow: The role of the future in education*. Vintage Books.

Tomlinson, C. A., & Moon, T. R. (2013). *Assessment and Student Success in a Differentiated Classroom*. Association for Supervision and Curriculum Development.

Tomyuk, O., Dyachkov, M., Shutaleva, A., Fayustov, A., & Leonenko, E. (2019). Social networks as an educational resource. In *SHS Web of Conferences* (*vol. 69*, p. 00105). EDP Sciences. 10.1051hsconf/20196900105

Tousignant, J. (2001). *Gifts of time, gifts of money: An econometric analysis of the determinants of Quebec behavior in 1997* [Unpublished Master dissertation]. Université de Montréal, Montréal, Canada.

Trettenero, S. (2020). *Human beings are emotional creatures*. Psychreg. https://www.psychreg.org/human-beings-are-emotional-creatures/

Treviño, L. T., Weaver, G., & Reynolds, S. J. (2006). Behavioral ethics in organizations: A review. *Journal of Management*, *32*(6), 951–990. doi:10.1177/0149206306294258

Trujillo, K. M., & Hadfield, O. D. (1999). Tracing the roots of mathematics anxiety through in-depth interviews with preservice teachers. *College Student Journal*, *33*(2), 219–232.

Tsimane, T. A. & Downing, C. (2019). Transformative learning in nursing education: A concept analysis. *International Journal of Nursing Sciences*, *7*(1), 91-98. doi:10.1016/j.ijnss.2019.12.006

Tugtekin, E. B., & Koc, M. (2020). Understanding the relationship between new media literacy, communication skills, and democratic tendency: Model development and testing. *New Media & Society*, *22*(10), 1922–1941. doi:10.1177/1461444819887705

Turan, Z., & Cetintas, H. B. (2020). Investigating university students' adoption of video lessons. *Open Learning*, *35*(2), 122–139. doi:10.1080/02680513.2019.1691518

Turdieva, N. S. (2021). Didactic conditions for the formation of attitudes toward education as a value among primary school pupils. *Middle European Scientific Bulletin, 10*. Retrieved from http://cejsr.academicjournal.io/index.php/journal/article/view/368

Tyson, P. A. (1995). *The metaphor of students as mathematicians: issue and implications* [Unpulished Doctorial Thesis, Stanford University].

U2. (1991). Acrobat [Recorded by U2]. On Achtung baby [CD]. Island.

U2. (1993). Zooropa [Recorded by U2] On Zooropa [CD]. Island.

U2. (2014). California (There is no End to Love); Cedarwood Road; Every Breaking Wave; Iris (Hold Me Close); Lucifer's Hands; Song for Someone; The Troubles; The Miracle (of Joey Ramone); This is Where you Can Reach Me Now; Raised by Wolves; Volcano [Recorded by U2]. On Songs of innocence [CD]. Island.

UN. (2015). *Transforming Our World: The 2030 Agenda for Sustainable Development, 2nd August 2015*. United Nations.

UNDP. (2005). Human Development Report 2005: International cooperation at a crossroads: Aid, trade and security in an unequal world. UNDP.

UNESCO & UNODC. (2019). *Strengthening the Rule of Law through Education: A Guide for Policymakers*. Author.

UNESCO. (2015). *Education 2030 Incheon Declaration and Framework for Action for the Implementation of Sustainable Development Goal 4. United Nations Educational, Scientific and Cultural Organization*. UNESCO.

UNESCO. (2020). *Education: From disruption to recovery*. UNESCO. https://en.unesco.org/covid19/educationresponse

UNESCO/OREALC. (2007). El derecho de una educación de calidad para todos en América Latina y el Caribe. *Revista Electrónica Iberoamericana sobre Calidad, Eficacia y Cambio en Educación, 5*(3), 1–21.

UNICEF. (2000). *Curriculum report card. Working Paper Series, Education Section, Programme Division*. UNICEF.

United nations (2015). *Transforming Our World: The 2030 Agenda For Sustainable Development*. UN.

Untari, L. (2016, January-June). An epistemological review on humanistic education theory. *Leksema, 1*(1), 59–72. Advance online publication. doi:10.22515/ljbs.v1i1.26

US Bureau of Labor Statistics. (2008). *May 2008 national industry-specific occupational employment and wage estimates*. https://www.bls.gov/oes/current/oessrci.htm

Uusimaki, L., & Nason, R. (2004). Causes underlying pre-service teachers' negative beliefs and anxieties about mathematics. In M. J. Høines & A. B. Fuglestad (Eds.), *Proceedings of the 28th conference of the International Group for the Psychology of Mathematics Education* (Vol. 4, pp. 369-376). Bergen University.

Vaillancourt, F. (1994). To volunteer or not: Canada, 1987. *The Canadian Journal of Economics. Revue Canadienne d'Economique, 27*(4), 813–826.

Vaillancourt, F., & Payette, M. (1986). The supply of volunteer work: The case of Canada. *Journal of Voluntary Action Research, 15*(4), 45–56.

Van Oers, B. (1998). From context to contextualizing. *Learning and Instruction, 8*(6), 473–488. doi:10.1016/S0959-4752(98)00031-0

Van Oers, B. (2009). Developmental education: Improving participation in cultural practices. In M. Fleer, M. Hedegaard, & J. Tudge (Eds.), *Childhood studies and the impact of globalization: Policies and practices at global and local levels* (pp. 213–229). Routledge.

Compilation of References

Van Rijk, Y., Volman, M., de Haan, D., & Van Oers, B. (2017). Maximizing meaning: Creating a learning environment for reading comprehension of informative texts from a Vygotskian perspective. *Learning Environments Research, 20*(1), 77–98. doi:10.100710984-016-9218-5

VandenBos, G., Knapp, S., & Doe, J. (2001). Role of reference elements in the selection of resources by psychology undergraduates. *Journal of Bibliographic research*. http://jbr.org/articles.html

Veglis, A., & Avraam, E. (2001, July). Using the Web in supplementary teacher education. In *EUROCON'2001. International Conference on Trends in Communications. Technical Program, Proceedings* (Cat. No. 01EX439) (*Vol. 2*, pp. 274–277). IEEE. 10.1109/EURCON.2001.938112

Veglis, A., Saridou, T., Panagiotidis, K., Karypidou, C., & Kotenidis, E. (2022). Applications of Big Data in Media Organizations. *Social Sciences, 11*(9), 414. doi:10.3390ocsci11090414

Vergara, I., Travieso, N., & Crespo, M. (2014). Dinámica del proceso enseñanza-aprendizaje de la Química en tecnología de la salud. *Educación Médica Superior, 28*(2), 272–281.

Verner, I., & Betzer, N. (2001). Machine control – a design and technology discipline in Israel's senior high schools. *International Journal of Technology and Design Education, 11*(3), 263–272. doi:10.1023/A:1011256612709

Verschafel, L., & Greer, B. (2013). Mathematics education. In J. M. Spector, M. D. Merrill, J. Elen, & M. J. Bishop (Eds.), *Handbook of research on educational communications and technology* (pp. 553–563). Springer. doi:10.1007/978-1-4614-3185-5_43

Vicente-Molina, M. A., Fernández-Sainz, A., & Izagirre-Olaizola, J. (2018). Does gender make a difference in pro-environmental behavior? The case of the Basque Country University students. *Journal of Cleaner Production, 176*, 89–98. doi:10.1016/j.jclepro.2017.12.079

Villegas, A. M., & Lucas, T. (2002). Preparing culturally responsive teachers: Rethinking the curriculum. *Journal of Teacher Education, 53*(1), 20–32. https://doi.org/10.1177%2F0022487102053001002

Villegas, A. M., & Lucas, T. (2007). The culturally responsive teacher. *Educational Leadership, 64*(6), 28.

Ville, P. A. (2010). Mentoring reflective thinking practice in pre-service teachers: A reconstructions through the voices of australian science teachers. *Journal of College Teaching and Learning, 7*(9).

Vincent-Lancrin, S., Urgel, J., Kar, S., & Jacotin, G. (2019). *Measuring Innovation in Education 2019: What Has Changed in the Classroom? Educational Research and Innovation*. Paris: OECD Publishing. https://www.oecd-ilibrar

Volman, M., & Ten Dam, G. (2015). Critical thinking for educated citizenship. In M. Davies & R. Barnett (Eds.), *The Palgrave handbook of critical thinking in higher education* (pp. 593–603). Palgrave Macmillan. doi:10.1057/9781137378057_35

von Glasersfeld, E. (1985). Reconstructing the concept of knowledge. *Archives de Psychologie, 53*(204), 91–101.

Vu, T., & Dall'Alba, G. (2014). Authentic assessment for student learning: An ontological conceptualisation. *Educational Philosophy and Theory, 46*(7), 778–791. doi:10.1080/00131857.2013.795110

Vygotsky, L. (1978). *Mind in society: The development of higher psychological processes*. Harvard University Press.

Vygotsky, L. S. (1978). *Mind in society*. Harvard University Press.

Vygotsky, L. S. (1978). *Mind in Society: the Development of Higher Psychological Processes*. Harvard University Press.

Wagoner, B. (2013). Bartlett's concept of schema in reconstruction. *Theory & Psychology, 23*(5), 553-575. doi:https://doi.org/10.1177/09593543500166

Wallace, S. (2001). Guardian angels and teachers from hell: Using metaphor as a measure of schools' experiences and expectations of General National Vocational Qualifications. *International Journal of Qualitative Studies in Education: QSE*, *14*, 727–739.

Wallin, P., & Adawi, T. (2018). The reflective diary as a method for the formative assessment of self-regulated learning. *European Journal of Engineering Education*, *43*(4), 507–521. doi:10.1080/03043797.2017.1290585

Waluyo, B. (2018). Promoting self-regulated learning with formative assessment and the use of mobile app on vocabulary acquisition in Thailand. *Indonesian Journal of English Language Teaching and Applied Linguistics*, *3*(1), 105–124. http://studentsrepo.um.edu.my/8274/2/WAN_MOHD_ZUHAIRI_BIN_WAN_ABDULLAH.pdf

Wang, H., Tlili, A., Lehman, J. D., Lu, H., & Huang, R. (2021). Investigating feedback implemented by instructors to support online competency-based learning (CBL): A multiple case study. *Int J Educ Technol High Educ*, *18*(1), 5. doi:10.118641239-021-00241-6

Wang, J., Mendori, T., & Xiong, J. (2014). A language learning support system using course-centered ontology and its evaluation. *Computer Education*, *78*, 278–293. doi:10.1016/j.compedu.2014.06.009

Wang, J., Ogata, H., & Shimada, A. (2017). A meaningful discovery learning environment for e-book learners. *IEEE Global Engineering Education Conference*, 1158–1165. 10.1109/EDUCON.2017.7942995

Wang, J., Shimada, A., Oi, M., Ogata, H., & Tabata, Y. (2020). Development and evaluation of a visualization system to support meaningful e-book learning. *Interactive Learning Environments*, 1–18. Advance online publication. doi:10.1080/10494820.2020.1813178

Wang, Y. P., & Wu, T. J. (2022). Effects of online cooperative learning on students' problem-solving ability and learning satisfaction. *Frontiers in Psychology*, *13*, 817968. doi:10.3389/fpsyg.2022.817968 PMID:35756307

Wang, Y., Liang, J., Yang, J., Ma, X., Li, X., Wu, J., Yang, G., Ren, G., & Feng, Y. (2019). Analysis of the environmental behavior of farmers for non-point source pollution control and management: An integration of the theory of planned behavior and the protection motivation theory. *Journal of Environmental Management*, *237*, 15–23. doi:10.1016/j.jenvman.2019.02.070 PMID:30776770

Wardekker, W., Boersma, A., Ten Dam, G., & Volman, M. (2012). Motivation for school learning: Enhancing the meaningfulness of learning in communities of learners. In M. Hedegaard, A. Edwards, & M. Fleer (Eds.), *Motives in children's development: Cultural–historical approaches* (pp. 153–170). Cambridge University Press.

Wasson, B., & Hansen, C. J. S. (2016). Data literacy and use for teaching. In P. Reimann, S. Bull, M. D. Kickmeier-Rust, R. Vatrapu, & B. Wasson (Eds.), *Measuring and Visualizing Learning in the Information-Rich Classroom* (pp. 56–73).

Watts, A. (2008). Review: 'Personal, Academic and Career Development in Higher Education: SOARing to Success'. *British Journal of Guidance & Counselling*, *36*(3).

Watts, A. G. (1999). *Reshaping Career Development for the 21st Century*. Centre for Guidance Studies, University of Derby.

Watts, A. G., & Hawthorn, R. (1992). *'Careers Education and the Curriculum in Higher Education'. NICEC Project Report*. Careers Research and Advisory Centre.

Weade, R., & Ernst, G. (1990). Pictures of life in classrooms, and the search for metaphors to frame them. *Theory into Practice*, *29*, 133–140.

Webb, N. L. (2002). *Assessment literacy in a standards-based urban education setting*. Paper presented at the Annual Meeting of the American Educational Research Association, New Orleans, Louisiana. http://archive.wceruw.org/mps/AERA2002/Assessment%20literacy%20NLW%20Final%2032602.pdf

Compilation of References

Weiss, S., Steger, D., Schroeders, U., & Wilhelm, O. (2020). A Reappraisal of the Threshold Hypothesis of Creativity and Intelligence. *Journal of Intelligence*, *8*(4), 38. doi:10.3390/jintelligence8040038 PMID:33187389

Weitzman, E. A. (2000). Software and qualitative research. In N. K. Denzin & Y. S. Lincoln (Eds.), *Handbook of qualitative research* (pp. 803–820). SAGE.

Weldmeskel, F. M., & Michael, D. J. (2016). The impact of formative assessment on self-regulating learning in university classrooms. *Tuning Journal for Higher Education*, *4*(1), 99–118. doi:10.18543/tjhe-4(1)-2016pp99-118

Wenbin, H., Jun, M., Yang, C., Wuyi, M., & Yizhong, L. (2021). Analysis on open mixed teaching mode in the post-epidemic era- -Take CAD / CAM technology course as an example. *The Journal of Higher Education*, *7*(35), 78–81.

Werth, E. P., & Werth, L. (2011). Effective training for millennial students. *Adult Learning*, *22*(3), 12–19. doi:10.1177/104515951102200302

Wertsch, J. (1991). *Voices of the mind: A sociocultural approach to mediated action*. Harvard University Press.

What is humanistic learning theory in education? (2020, July 21). Teaching & Education. Western Governors' University. https://www.wgu.edu/blog/what-humanistic-learning-theory-education2007.html#close

Whitley, B. E. (1998). Factors associated with cheating among college students: A review. *Research in Higher Education*, *39*(3), 235–274. doi:10.1023/A:1018724900565

Wilson, S. M., & Peterson, P. L. (2006). *Theories of Learning and Teaching: What Do They Mean for Educators?* Working Paper.

Wilson, J. (2000). Volunteering. *Annual Review of Sociology*, *26*, 215–240.

Winardi, R. D., Mustikarini, A., & Anggraeni, M. Z. (2017). Academic dishonesty among accounting students: Some Indonesian evidence. *Jurnal Akuntansi dan Keuangan Indonesia*, *2*(14), 142–164.

Wiske, M. S. (1998). *Teaching for understanding: Linking research with practice*. Jossey-Bass Publishers.

Wolf, A., & Kolb, D. A. (1980). Career development, personal growth, and experimental learning. In J. W. Springer (Ed.), *Issues in Career and Human Resource Development*. American Society for Training and Development.

Wong, L. H., & Looi, C. K. (2011). What seams do we remove in mobile-assisted seamless learning? A critical review of the literature. *Computers & Education*, *57*(4), 2364–2381. doi:10.1016/j.compedu.2011.06.007

Wong, Y. L., & Siu, K. W. M. (2018). The curriculum development and project-based assessment of design education in Singapore and Hong Kong secondary schools. In V. X. Wang (Ed.), *Handbook of research on program development and assessment methodologies in K-20 education* (1st ed., pp. 220–243). IGI Global., doi:10.4018/978-1-5225-3132-6.ch011

Wu, H., & Krajcik, J. S. (2006). Inscriptional practices in two inquiry-based classrooms: A case study of seventh graders' use of data tables and graphs. *Journal of Research in Science Teaching*, *43*(1), 63–95.

Wulf, A., & Dudis, P. (2005). Body partitioning in ASL metaphorical blends. *Sign Language Studies*, *5*(3), 317–332.

Wu, W. C. V., Hsieh, J. S. C., & Yang, J. C. (2017). Creating an online learning community in a flipped classroom to enhance EFL learners' oral proficiency. *Journal of Educational Technology & Society*, *20*(2), 142–157.

Wu, X., Kou, Z., Oldfield, P., Heath, T., & Borsi, K. (2021). Informal learning spaces in higher education: Student preferences and activities. *Buildings*, *11*(6), 252. doi:10.3390/buildings11060252

Xiao, H., Li, S., Chen, X., Yu, B., Gao, M., Yan, H., & Okafor, C. N. (2014). Protection motivation theory in predicting intention to engage in protective behaviors against schistosomiasis among middle school students in rural China. *PLoS Neglected Tropical Diseases, 8*(10).

Xiaobing, Y., & Jinxia, L. (2020). Inquiry on student interactive teaching strategies based on hybrid teaching. *Textile and Apparel Education, 35*(5), 377–381.

Xinhua, J. (2005). *Institutional analysis of why academic anomie and university academic ethics anomie* (1st ed.). Social Sciences Academic Press.

Yaacob, N. H., & Kassim, F. (2020). Inovasi terhadap pengajaran dan pembelajaran bagi penerapan kemahiran insaniah dalam mata kuliah Tamadun Islam Dan Asia (TITAS) di Universiti Malaya Kuala Lumpur Malaysia. [Innovation in teaching and learning for the application of soft skills in Islamic and Asian Civilizations (TITAS) subjects at Universiti Malaya Kuala Lumpur Malaysia]. *Jurnal Pendidikan Ilmu Pengetahuan Sosial Indonesia, 7*(1), 1–21. doi:10.21831/jipsindo.v7i1.30844

Yalçın, M. (2011). İlköğretim okullarında okul müdürüne ilişkin metaforik algılar [Metaphorical perceptions of the school principal in primary schools] [Master's Thesis, Gaziosmanpaşa Üniversitesi].

Yang, J. (2015). *Recognition, validation and accreditation of non-formal and informal learning in UNESCO member states*. UNESCO Institute for Lifelong Learning.

Yanling, H., Peiwen, H., Shih-Jen, C., & Fu-Hau, H. (2011, September). The perceptions of cooperative learning in computer-assisted language learning environments. In *2011 International Conference on Electrical and Control Engineering* (pp. 6969-6972). IEEE 10.1109/ICECENG.2011.6056758

Yan, Z., Chiu, M. M., & Ko, P. Y. (2020). Effects of self-assessment diaries on academic achievement, self-regulation and motivation. *Assessment in Education: Principles, Policy & Practice, 27*(5), 562–583. doi:10.1080/0969594X.2020.1827221

Yee, T. Y., & Baskaran, V. (2017). The effectiveness of encouraging learning among the Gen Z students. In Farrah Dina Yusop · Amira Firdaus (Ed.), Alternative assessments in Malaysian higher education voices from the field (pp. 259-268). Springer Nature.

Yee, C. P., Yean, T. S., & Yi, A. K. J. (2018). verifying international students' satisfaction framework for the development of MISS-Model in Malaysia. *Pertanika Journal of Social Science & Humanities, 26*, 1–17.

Yeromin, M. B. (2021). *Universal Codes of Media in International Political Communications: Emerging Research and Opportunities*. IGI Global. doi:10.4018/978-1-7998-3808-1

Yeung, J. W., Zhang, Z., & Kim, T. Y. (2018). Volunteering and health benefits in general adults: Cumulative effects and forms. *BMC Public Health, 18*(1), 1–8.

Yeung, M. W., & Yau, A. H. (2022). A thematic analysis of higher education students' perceptions of online learning in Hong Kong under COVID-19: Challenges, strategies and support. *Education and Information Technologies, 27*(1), 181–208. https://doi.org/10.1007/s10639-021-10656-3

Ying, H. (2018). Research and exploration of online and offline mixed teaching modes under the background of "Internet +. *Business Story*, (10), 177–178.

Yin, R. (1994). *Case study research: Design and methods* (2nd ed.). Sage Publishing.

Yin, R. K. (2013). Validity and generalization in future case study evaluations. *Evaluation, 19*(3), 321–332. doi:10.1177/1356389013497081

Compilation of References

Yip, N. M., & Burhanuddin, I. H. (2017, August). Matapelajaran Umum peneraju transformasi pendidikan holistik, [General subjects leading the transformation of holistic education] In N*ational Pre-University Seminar 2017 (NpreUS2017)*, Kolej Universiti Islam Antarabangsa Selangor.

Yob, I. M. (2003). Thinking constructively with metaphors. *Studies in Philosophy and Education*, *22*, 127–138.

Yuanyuan, Zh., & Xianxue, K. (2018). Analysis of the lack of academic morality of college students. *Modern Communication*, (16), 129–130.

Yücel, A.S. & Koçak, C. (2008, September). *The mental images of preservice teachers related to teacher concept: forming imaginary metaphor groups.* The Current Trends in Chemical Curricula, Praque.

Yukhymenko, M. A. (2014). Ethical beliefs toward academic dishonesty: A cross-cultural comparison of undergraduate students in Ukraine and the United States. *Journal of Academic Ethics*, *12*(12), 29–41. doi:10.100710805-013-9198-3

Yung, B. H. W. (2001). Examiner, policeman or students' companion: Teachers' perceptions of their role in an assessment reform. *Educational Review*, *53*, 251–260.

Yusoff, A. N. M., & Ali, N. (2018). Kaedah MOOC (Massive Open Online Course) dalam Pengajaran dan Pembelajaran Tamadun Islam dan Tamadun Asia (TITAS), Hubungan Etnik (HE), Kenegaraan dan Pengajian Islam Alaf 21 di Universiti Awam dan Swasta. In *Proceeding of INSIGHT 2018 1st International Conference on Religion, Social Sciences and Technological Education, Universiti Sains Islam Malaysia* (pp. 18-19). Academic Press.

Yusoff, A. N. M., & Ali, N. (2018, April). Penerapan model kolaboratif e-learning dalam kursus TITAS MOOC dan aplikasinya dalam platform Open Learning versi 02. [Application of the e-learning collaborative model in the TITAS MOOC course and its application in the Open Learning platform version 02.] In *e-Prosiding Persidangan Antarabangsa Sains Sosial dan Kemanusiaan 2018.* Kolej Universiti Islam Selangor. .

Zerihun, Z., Beishuizen, J., & Van Os, W. (2012). Student learning experience as indicator of teaching quality. *Educational Assessment, Evaluation and Accountability*, *24*(2), 99–111. doi:10.100711092-011-9140-4

Zhang, R. (2020). Exploring blended learning experiences through the community of inquiry framework. *Language Learning & Technology*, *24*(1), 38–53. 10125/44707

Zhang, Y., & Mi, Y. (2010, September). Another look at the language difficulties of international students. *Journal of Studies in International Education*, *14*(4), 371–388. doi:10.1177/1028315309336031

Zhan, Z., & Mei, H. (2013). Academic self-concept and social presence in face-to-face and online learning: Perceptions and effects on students' learning achievement and satisfaction across environments. *Computers & Education*, *2013*(69), 131–138. doi:10.1016/j.compedu.2013.07.002

Zhu, G., & Chen, M. (2022). Positioning preservice teachers' reflections and I-positions in the context of teaching practicum: A dialogical-self theory approach. *Teaching and Teacher Education*, *117*, 103734.

Zhuli, W. (2020). How should education transform in the post-epidemic era? e-. *Education Research*, *41*(3), 13–20.

Zimmerman, B. J. (2015). Self-regulated learning: Theories, measures, and outcomes. International Encyclopedia of the Social & Behavioral Sciences, 21, 541–546.

Zimmerman, B. J. (1986). Becoming a self-regulated learner. *Contemporary Educational Psychology*, *11*(4), 307–313. doi:10.1016/0361-476X(86)90027-5

Zimmerman, B. J. (1989). A social cognitive view of self-regulated academic learning. *Journal of Educational Psychology*, *81*(3), 329–339. doi:10.1037/0022-0663.81.3.329

Zimmerman, B. J. (2000). *Handbook of Self-Regulation* (M. Boekaerts, P. R. Pintrich, & M. Zeidner, Eds.). Academic Press.

Zimmerman, B. J. (2002). Becoming a Self-Regulated Learner: An Overview. *Theory into Practice*, *41*(2), 64–70. doi:10.120715430421tip4102_2

Zimmerman, B. J. (2008). Investigating self-regulation and motivation: Historical background, methodological developments, and future prospects. *American Educational Research Journal*, *45*(1), 166–183. doi:10.3102/0002831207312909

Zimmerman, B. J. (2013). From Cognitive Modeling to Self-Regulation: A Social Cognitive Career Path. *Educational Psychologist*, *48*(3), 135–147. doi:10.1080/00461520.2013.794676

Zimmermann, W., & Cunningham, S. (1991). Editor's introduction: What is mathematical visualization. In W. Zimmermann & S. Cunningham (Eds.), *Visualization in Teaching and Learning Mathematics* (pp. 1–8). Mathematical Association of America.

Žižek, S. (2014). *Event*. Penguin Books.

Zou, T. X., & Yu, J. (2021). Intercultural interactions in Chinese classrooms: A multiple-case study. *Studies in Higher Education*, *46*(3), 649–662. doi:10.1080/03075079.2019.1647415

About the Contributors

Nor Alias a Professor of Instructional Technology and currently an Honorary Professor at the Faculty of Education, Universiti Teknologi MARA Malaysia. I graduated with a B Sc Physics and M Sc Physics from Indiana University, Bloomington and later pursued a Graduate Certificate in Open and Distance Learning (USQ, Australia) before my doctoral study in online learning. My current research interest and activities are in the field of e-learning, open distance learning, learning design and design and development research(DDR). I have been awarded the Edu Tech Leadership Award (Higher Education) in 2019 and have recently been acknowledged as one of the Academic Icons by the Ministry of Higher Education, Malaysia (in conjunction with the National Academia Day).

Sharipah Syed-Aris is an Assoc. Prof Ts Dr Sharipah Ruzaina Syed Aris is currently the Dean at the Faculty of Education, Universiti Teknologi MARA (UiTM). She received her B.Sc. (Hons.) in Chemistry in 1995 from the University of Malaya. Her passion and deep interest in the value of education have led her to pursue her master's and PhD in Chemistry Education at the same alma mater. She was a director at the Curriculum Affairs Unit, Academic Affairs Division, at UiTM from 2015 to 2019 with 11 years of experience in curriculum development. Apart from her contribution as an academic administrator and educator, she also participated and contributed at national level, as a member of technical committee for NOBLe (Noble Outcome Based Learning), Strategic Committee for 2U2i industry mode, Strategic Committee of Service-Learning Malaysia-University for Society (SULAM) and Task Force for 4.0 Educators. DR Sharipah Ruzaina has conducted 3 research projects for the Malaysian Ministry of Higher Education, namely on the study of Outcome-Based Education, the impact of the mode industry academic program, and the impact of the My3S instrument on students. Her vast experience in curriculum development and hybrid programmes has made her a frequently invited speaker at workshops and conferences. She is also recognised by the Malaysian Board of Technology (MBOT) as a professional technologist in the field of Chemical Technology and is currently a panel member of the MBOT and Malaysian Qualification Agency (MQA).

Hamimah Hashim obtained a PhD in Educational Psychology from International Islamic University,Malaysia (IIUM), Master of Education in Preschool Education (UKM) and first degree in Psychology (IIUM) . Started as a lecturer at UiTM in 2004 and most recently she held the position of Deputy Dean of Academic at the Faculty of Education, UiTM. Active in conducting various research and consultancy grants from KPM and UiTM. Also active in the field of academic writing and received the "Best paper award" at the International Conference on Social Sciences Studies 2019. She was invited as a keynote speaker at the International Conference on Education held in Bukiitinggi, Indonesia in 2020.

In addition, she gave lot of talks and motivational programs with students and teachers. Dr Hamimah has received the Outstanding Service Award in 2009 and 2018. In the field of teaching, she actively supervises undergraduate and postgraduate students and supervises international students. She is also active in participating in Innovation competitions and has several products registered as "Intellectual Property". Her most recent award was the Aspiring Innovator Award 2020 in producing items for online teaching evaluation. In addition, she was also invited as Jury in several National and International Level in Innovation Competitions based on her experiences and involvements in the field of innovation.

* * *

Aiedah Abdul Khalek is a Senior Lecturer and Convenor for General Studies at the Malaysia Immersion and Pathways, Monash University Malaysia. She leads the General Studies Units at the Malaysia Immersion and Pathways. Her research interest lies broadly in the study of religion, Muslim societies, ethnicities, and nation-building. She investigates the dynamic interaction between religion, cultures and society in various contexts and she is currently works on multidisciplinary research which is established on the intersection of medicine, religion, and social sciences. She also works on educational research with the aim to improve her teaching practices and students' learning experience.

Adibah Abdul Latif is an Assoc Prof Dr. Adibah Binti Abdul Latif is a senior lecturer in the School of Education, Faculty of Social Sciences and Humanities, Universiti Teknologi Malaysia. Her Ph.D. and Master's are in Educational Measurement and Evaluation. She joined the university in 2003 and held the position of Manager (Standard and Quality Academic Enhancement) from 2017 to 2020. Now, she is a research fellow (education and global wellness) at the Center of Fiqh Science and Technology. Some of her achievements in education are she was the winner of Transformative Teaching: Alternative Assessment. She also received the teaching award at the faculty level and is now actively involved as a panel and speaker in government, agencies, industries, and the community. She has had 65 publications with 19 WoS publications and has been involved in 80 research grants as principal investigator and member. Up to 2021, 25 PhD and seven master's students have graduated under her supervision, and she is currently supervising 18 postgraduate students. Now, she is also actively involved in pedagogical innovation and manages to commercialize the services and products locally and internationally.

Nur Surayyah Madhubala Abdullah is an Associate Professor in Moral Education with background in Philosphy of Education (Moral and Political Philosopy related to moral education). Area of interest is on issues related to moral education for plural societies specialising in issues in moral education for Malaysia's plural society.

Zaim Azizi Abu Bakar is a lecturer at the School of Liberal Arts & Sciences, Taylor's University, teaching Mata Pelajaran Umum(MPU)and Social Sciences modules such as Tamadun Islam & Tamadun Asia, Penghayatan Etika & Peradaban, Introduction to Ethics and Social Innovation Projects. He holds a Master's degree in Teaching and Learning from Taylor's University and a Bachelor's degree in Human Sciences from International Islamic University, Malaysia. Zaim was involved in scholarly and industry experience; being an expert reviewer for Oxford Fajar, and reviewing Higher Education (IPT) textbooks. He received a TRGS grant under Emerging arch Funding Scheme and actively presented in conferences and published articles in journals. He won several national awards in E-Content Development for MPU

About the Contributors

modules and under Social Sciences & Humanities Category. He grabbed Gold Awards in ECONDEV 2021 for MOOC and Pitching Category. Recently, Zaim has won the Gold Award for Invention, Innovation & Design on E-Learning (IUCEL)2022. Zaim has been involved in several national projects with government agencies such a sPEMANDU and the Department of National Unity & Integration (JPNIN).

Mohd Hafnidzam Adzmi graduated with a Degree in Computer Graphic Design in 2006 from Wanganui School of Design, New Zealand. He further his studies in Universiti Teknologi Mara, graduating with a Masters in VIsual Communication and new media in 2009 and completed his PhD in Education at University of Malaya, Kuala Lumpur in 2022 with his dissertation on Creativity in the Graphic Design Process. His main interests are the psychology of creativity and how it intersects with the fields of Design. He has over 10 years of experience in teaching Graphic Design. Currently, he is a senior lecturer at Universiti Teknologi Mara teaching undergraduate and postgraduate courses.

Nadia Ainuddin Dahlan has been teaching at the Faculty of Education, Universiti Teknologi MARA (UiTM), Puncak Alam Campus since 2009. She received her Master's of Education in Educational Psychology from the International Islamic University Malaysia. Some of the courses she has taught include Educational Psychology, Educational Sociology, History and Philosophy of Education, Educational Testing and Assessment and Professional Development in Education. She is interested in areas of research pertaining to Educational Assessment, Educational Psychology, Gender Studies, underachievement of boys and education in general.

Canan Koçak Altundağ is currently an Associate Professor in the Department of Mathematics and Science Education at Hacettepe University, Ankara, Turkey. Dr. Altundağ received B.Sc., M.Sc., and Ph.D. degree from the Faculty of Education at Hacettepe Univer- sity. Her research interests include daily life chemistry, context based learning and chemistry education. She has teaching experience of more than 10 years in the area of chemistry education. Dr. Altundağ published a number of papers in preferred Journals and participated in a range of conferences.

Amaghouss Jabrane is a Professor of Economics, his researches focus on inequalities in education and labor markets. He conducted several empirical works related to economics of education

Rene Babiera graduated from The University of the Iimmaculate Conception (UIC) with Master of Education in Educational major in Physical Education. His research interests include International Education, Student Affairs and Services, Culture and Arts, Sports, Physical Education and Teacher training. Rene is currently working as the Coordinator of the International Affairs and Linkages and at the College of Teacher Education, UIC Davao City Philippines teaching Professional PE courses and service PE for undergraduate students. Besides teaching, Rene is a also the Coordinator of UIC's Culture and Arts Office since 2013.

Serit Banyan is a lecturer and Stream Coordinator for MPU modules in the School of Liberal Arts and Sciences at Taylor's University, where he has been a school member since 2011. His expertise is online learning, technology in education, and pedagogy. Serit is also a multi-award-winning lecturer as he received numerous awards and recognitions for his teaching and learning innovations. At the university level, Serit received awards and recognitions for his excellence in teaching and learning, such

EMAS Award, Taylor's President Award and Taylor's Distinguish e-Learning Educator Award. He is also a three-time award winner at the International University Carnival on e-Learning, where in 2018 he received the Best e-Learning Facilitator Award, 2019 he received the Best e-Learning Product Award and 2021 he received Best Trend-Setter Award. He also one of the winners of Anugerah Pemikiran Semula dan Rekabentuk Kurikulum Pengajian Tinggi Malaysia in 2017. In 2018, Serit is selected as a finalist of QS-Wharton Reimagine Education Award organized by QS Quacquarelli Symonds. Serit also selected as a finalist of Anugerah Akademik Negara ke-14. In addition, Serit also won numerous medal awards from IUCEL and ECONDEV. As an expert in redesigning higher education, Serit was appointed by the Ministry of Higher Education to be a national committee member for several committees such as MPU, SULAM and AKRI. He also appointed as a jury for several competitions related to innovation in teaching and learning such as ECONDEV, AKRI, IUCEL and QS-Wharton Reimagine Education Award.

Kriscentti Exzur P. Barcelona graduated with the degree Doctor of Philosophy in English with concentration on Language at the University of San-Jose Recoletos, Cebu City, Philippines. He is presently the Dean of Teacher Education Program, Master of Arts in Education, and Master of Arts in Home Economics of Lourdes College, Inc. Cagayan de Oro City, Philippines. He is also the present president of the Council of Deans of Teacher Education in Region 10, Philippines, and the Vice-chair of the RVM Teacher Education Institutions Network. He is a member of various professional organizations and serves as a local and international lecturer, quality assessor, adjudicator, and internal auditor. His primary research interests include linguistics, educational technology, pedagogy, and assessment.

Daniel Blackshields lectures at the Department of Economics in University College, Cork. I am also the Centre for the Integration of Research, Teaching and Learning in UCC Teaching Fellow for Reflective Practice. I have presented and published on teaching for understanding, integrative learning, reflection, arts-based learning and creativity. I have won the President's Award for Excellence in Teaching and President's Award for Research on Innovative Forms of Teaching and Learning in Higher Education. With colleagues from UCC Career Service we won the Association of Higher Education Careers Services Excellence in Employability Award. I have been nominated for a UCC Staff Recognition Award: Enhancing the Student Experience; NAIRTL National Excellence in Teaching Award; National Teaching Experts: learning Impact Award from the National Forum for the Enhancement of Teaching and Learning in Higher Education and (with colleagues from UCC Career Service) nominated for the Irish Education Awards – Best Career Impact Strategy.

Lin Chen specializes in moral education with an area of interest in issues related to academic ethics in higher education.

Younes Elguerch is a specialist in environmental economics

Chris Harwood is an associate professor in rhetoric and composition in the Faculty of Liberal Arts at Sophia University in Japan. He has over 20 years of experience in language and academic literacies education, and is highly experienced in curriculum design, development, and administration. Chris has taught in a variety of contexts in Europe, North America, Asia, and the Middle East. His research interests include sociocultural theory, academic discourse socialization, online learning, computer-mediated communication, L2 writing, and language policy and planning.

About the Contributors

Aomar Ibourk, is a professor of quantitative methods and social economics at the Cadi Ayyad University in Marrakech, an economist, as well as Senior Fellow at the Policy Center for the New South, who focuses on Applied econometrics, labor market, economics of education and development economics

Norezan Ibrahim is Senior lecturer of Science Education from Science Department, Faculty of Education, Universiti Teknologi MARA (UiTM), Malaysia. She received her B.Sc. Education (Physics) and M.Sc. Physics (Research) degrees from Universiti Teknologi MARA (UiTM). She has been serving at the Faculty of Education, UiTM since 2014.Her research areas are Dielectric, STEM education, Physics education and Teaching and learning in Physics education. To date, she has received 1 research grant as a Principal Investigator plus 2 grants as a co-investigator. Within the Faculty of Education, UiTM, she teaches a number of courses related to her expertise and research. Since arriving at the Faculty of Education, she has taught more than six courses from the bachelor degree levels. Her goal in teaching is to share her knowledge and skills with her students, while at the same time learning from them. Norezan Ibrahim has written and co-authored at least 7 Scopus-indexed and 5 indexed articles in journals and proceedings. She was also a recipient of Anugerah Perkhidmatan Cemerlang (APC) at the UiTM in 2018. From the aspect of management and administration of the faculty, she was appointed as Coordinator of Science Programmes for 5 years beginning in 2018 until early of 2023.

Zainuddin Ibrahim graduated with an honours degree in Graphic Design from Universiti Teknologi MARA (UiTM) in 2002. Later, he pursued a Master's Degree in Visual Communication and New Media in 2008 from the same university. Finally, the University of Malaya awarded him a PhD in Curriculum and Instructional Technology in 2016. In terms of working experience, he worked for two years in the creative industry before joining UiTM as a tutor in 2004. In 2006, he was promoted to young lecturer and, after that, became a senior lecturer. His teaching philosophy is based on knowledge, student preferences, different ways of learning, and technology. First, as academicians, we are responsible for imparting knowledge, especially in our area of expertise. Second, knowledge is a valuable asset, and education is vital to ensure that knowledge is taught well. Third, all students have the same right to learn. Felder and Silverman (2002) say that the challenge is to give students an education that fits their different learning styles and preferences. Lastly, using the right kinds of technology will help students learn more. Thanks to Felder and Solomon for creating the Index of Learning Styles, which helps identify students' learning styles and preferences.

Leele Susana BT Jamian is an Associate Professor attached at the Faculty of Education Universiti Teknologi MARA (UiTM), Malaysia. Currently, she is heading the Educational Management and Leadership Department at the Faculty of Education UiTM. Her 28 years of teaching experiences at various government institutions ranging from school to university, has given her a strong determination to develop students at university in becoming future educational managers, leaders, trainers and educators in various fields of studies. Her research interests lie in the areas of Educational Management and Leadership in Higher Education, and Language Learning amongst ESL learners in both public and private learning institutions in Malaysia. She has published in numerous international journals and chapters in books and became an international plenary speaker in the area of her specialization. She can be contacted via email at leele@uitm.edu.my

About the Contributors

Sakinatul Ain Jelani has over six years of experience in teaching English in Universiti Teknologi MARA (UiTM), areas of expertise include TESL, Applied Linguistics, and Grammar. She has conducted research on trainee teachers' sense of efficacy in teaching English and semiotic analyses of myths in Malaysian magazine advertisements. Other related academic involvement includes carrying out duties as the Resource Person for Fundamentals of Academic Reading as well as training and preparing modules for kindergarten teachers' English proficiency training programmes.

Rafidah Abd Karim is a Senior Lecturer at Academy of Language Studies, Universiti Teknologi MARA, Malaysia. She holds a PhD in TESL which specialized in Mobile Learning and Digital Mind Mapping from Sultan Idris Education University. She writes and presents widely on issues of mobile technology, digital mind mapping, language learning, gender and indigenous studies published by various publishers. She published more than 60 publications such as journals, proceedings, book chapters and research books at both national and international level published by various publishers. She is also an innovator of multiple innovative products mainly in language learning and digital technologies, and she won more than 50 awards in various innovation competitions. She is a member of professional organisations at national and international level. She is also actively leads and involves in two international research projects and three national research grant projects.

Adlet Kariyev is a Candidate of Pedagogical Sciences, Program Leader of the Department of Preschool and Primary Education of the Kazakh National Women's Teacher Training University, Republic ok Kazakhstan, Almaty city.

Koo Ah-Choo is an Associate Professor at Faculty of Creative Multimedia (FCM), Multimedia University (MMU). She received her B.Sc. (Hons) from the Universiti Teknologi Malaysia (UTM) and her PhD from MMU. Her research specialization is mainly on technology enhanced learning, communication and quality of life. She is active in the research of media usage, design and creation, media methods especially in the promotion of wellness, education and lifelong learning. She led recent research projects on eHealth modality for mental wellness among digital talents (funded by Ministry of Higher Education, FRGS); Designing mobile services for ageing women in Malaysia (funded by IDRC, Carleton University), Joint Research of six other universities on Digital Futures under RIPHEN initiative, and Empathic e-mental health awareness and 5R model for final year students (Internal Knowledge Transfer Grant). She is currently served as the Deputy Director for Government Liaison and Industry Engagement (GLIE) Division, under the Vice President Office of Market Exploration, Engagement and Touchpoint at Multimedia University.

Sheela Jayabalan is an Associate Professor at the Faculty of Law, Universiti Teknologi Mara, Shah Alam, Selangor. She has been teaching law for the last thirty years. She is very passionate about teaching and learning pedagogies. Her areas of expertise are E-Commerce Contracts and the Law of Contract. She has authored books on e-commerce and contract law as well as chapters in books in the field of education and written articles on diverse areas. She has also presented at both national and international conferences.

Arti Kumar MBE is the former Associate Director of the Centre for Excellence in Learning and Teaching at the University of Bedfordshire and is an Honorary Research Fellow. Her awards include

About the Contributors

a National Teaching Fellowship, AGCAS Lifetime Achievement Award, and MBE 'for services to higher education'. The SOAR model she developed and authored offers an innovative approach that has proved to be highly beneficial in developing career maturity and employability in the UK and abroad. Its methodology is available primarily in the book / e-book: Kumar, A. (2008; 2022) Personal, Social, Academic and Career Development in Higher Education – SOARing to Success: Routledge Taylor and Francis, available with eResources. SOAR enables individuals to develop holistically, to become effective, productive and regenerative in the diverse contexts of learning, work, and life. Arti currently writes, mentors and works independently on projects with universities.

Fadhilah Raihan Lokman is a lecturer of Bachelor of Social Science (International Relations) programme and Mata Pelajaran Umum (MPU) in the School of Liberal Arts and Sciences at the Taylor's University where she has been a school member since 2015. Fadhilah has completed her International Master In ASEAN Studies at the University of Malaya and Post Graduate Certification in Teaching and Learning at Taylor's University, Malaysia. Prior to that, Fadhilah has studied at the University of Nebraska-Lincoln for her Bachelor of Degree in Political Science and minors in Mathematics and Global Studies. Fadhilah has taught several MPU modules, including the Social Innovation Project, for which she served as the module leader and contributed to the development of the module's instructional design and content. Since she entered her first competition for teaching and learning in 2018 and took home the first gold medal in the eCONDEV competition that year for Pengajian Malaysia 2, Fadhilah has been driven to identify the best practices in education. At the university level, Fadhilah has also received recognition as Silver Award Recipient for Immersive Learning Category of Exemplary Meritorious Academic Staff (EMAS) Award in 2020. At the national level, Fadhilah has continued to lead her team and actively took part as a team member in winning the first place in AKRI 2019 under the area of Immersive Learning for Pengajian Malaysia 3 module, Gold Award in Econdev 2021(MOOC) for Social Innovation Project, Gold Award in Econdev 2021 (Pitching), also for Social Innovation Project module, a Gold award in ECONDEV 2022 (MOOC) for a newly developed module, the Falsafah dan Isu Semasa and lastly another Gold award in the recent International University Carnival on e-Learning 2022.

Melissa Malik has always been fascinated with educational issues and is currently working at Centre for Foundation Studies, UiTM Kampus Dengkil, Sepang in Selangor, teaching language courses to TESL Foundation students. She graduated from University of Auckland, New Zealand with Master of Arts in Language Teaching and Learning. Her research interests include Second Language Acquisition, Individual Differences in Language Learning, Teacher Beliefs and Teacher Education.

Nurshamshida Md Shamsudin is an active researcher in advanced education related to safety and health, teacher's training, and educational research analysis. She embraces the latest technology for classroom and instruction research and practices.

Nur Hidayah Md Yazid as 10 years of teaching English, and more than 6 years of experience as an Asasi TESL lecturer under the Faculty of Education, Universiti Teknologi MARA with areas of interest of Grammar, Second Language Acquisition and Teaching English as a Second Language. Presented several conference papers since 2013 and published a few articles in refereed journals. In 2017, the innovative co-curriculum at the Asasi TESL program won the Anugerah Pemikiran & Rekabentuk Semula Pendidikan (APRS 2017): Redesigning and Rethinking Higher Education Award organized by MOHE and awarded a RM10,000 grant. The Resource Person of Grammar I course since 2018. A recipient of Anugerah Perkhidmatan Cemerlang (APC) in 2020. A speaker at a sharing session in Best Practices in Online/Flexible Delivery and Assessments in 2020 and an invited speaker for APB Collaborative Teaching (Special Series): A Guide to Polishing Your Grammar in 2022. A recipient of the Best Presenter Award at the International Conference on Research and Practices in Science, Technology and Social Sciences (I-CReST) 2022.

Mawarni Mohamed obtained her Master Science in Sport Science from New South Wales University, Australia, and her PhD from University Malaya in Leisure Studies (Management & Policy). She obtained her Associate Professorship in 2019. Before joining the Insitution Mawarni worked as an English teacher. Since joining Universiti Teknologi MARA (UiTM), Mawarni has carried out projects involving students in schools and other institutions and centers of different backgrounds. Her research interests focus on young adolescents and their time use, physical activities and leisure studies. She has won several medals for teaching innovations, presented papers nationally and internationally, and published papers in preferred Journals and chapters in books

Fatin Aliana Mohd Radzi is a senior lecturer in the Department of Educational Studies, Faculty of Education, Universiti Teknologi MARA. She has 15 years experience in teaching courses such as Sociology of Education, Research Methodology and Early Childhood Education. She received a PhD in Early Childhood Education from The Ohio State University, USA and a master's degree in Sociology of Education from Universiti Malaya, Malaysia. Being a mother of three, her research interest includes Early Childhood Education, parental involvement, and children in the marginalized groups.

Nor Syazwani is a senior lecturer at the Faculty of Education, Universiti Teknologi Mara, Malaysia. I graduated from Universiti Teknologi Mara in 2010 with a bachelor's degree in Science Education (Mathematics). Then, I furthered study at Universiti Teknologi Malaysia for a Master in Science (Mathematics) in 2012. I am teaching Mathematics Education subjects for the past ten years until the present. I also enjoy conducting research related to mathematics education and STEM education.

Nurahimah Mohd. Yusoff is a Professor of Curriculum and Instruction at the School of Education, College of Arts and Sciences, Universiti Utara Malaysia (UUM). Her research interests include Curriculum Design and Development, Scholarship of Teaching and Learning in Higher Education, Educational Evaluation and Assessment, and Qualitative Research. She is very passionate about teaching and was a recipient of the UUM Distinguished Teacher Award in 2010. She has engaged in many research projects, receiving grants from both local and international agencies, including the Malaysian Ministry of Higher Education (MoHE), and the Higher Education Leadership Academy of MoHE (AKEPT). She has published many refereed journal articles and presented papers at local and international conferences. Over the last 34 years at UUM, she had served as the Director of the University Teaching and Learning Centre (UTLC) and was the Head of Taskforce for the UUM Teach for Malaysia (PGDE) and the Doctor of Education programmes. From 2010 - 2016, she has been involved in the training of Master Trainers in the areas of Scholarship of Teaching and Learning (SoTL), Curriculum Design, Management and Development (CDMD), Student Supervision (SSV) and Instructional Design and Strategies (IDS) for higher education academic leaders. In these Training of Trainers (ToT) programmes at AKEPT, she and her colleagues integrate theory, research, and practice to empower academic leaders to improve their

About the Contributors

teaching-learning and supervision skills. Professor Dr. Nurahimah was also the former Director of two important Units: the UUM Self-Accreditation Unit and the Academic Excellence Development Unit at the Department of Academic Affairs.

Khalid Mustafa is an assistant professor at the Faculty of Education, Koya University, Iraq. He holds a PhD in Instructional Technology from the International Islamic University Malaysia. He was the Deputy dean for academic affairs at the Faculty of Education Koya University and was also the former director of the postgraduate unit. He has published in the field of instructional technology as well as on the topics of academic resilience of students and quality of life of university instructors. He has also researched other social psychological factors among students and instructors alike. Dr Khalid has received awards from various departments including the Ministry of Education.

Ramlee Bin Mustapha is a Professor of Technical and Vocational Education at the Faculty of Technical and Vocational Education, Universiti Pendidikan Sultan Idris (UPSI) [the Sultan Idris Education University]. In 2010, he was appointed as the Dean for Post-Graduate Studies at UPSI. A year later, he is appointed as the Dean of the Faculty of Technical and Vocational Education at UPSI. In 2017, he was appointed as the 5 th President of the Asian Academic Society for Vocational Education and Training (AASVET). Dr. Ramlee Mustapha holds a Bachelor degree in Chemical Engineering (BSChE) from University of Alabama, USA. His first Masters degree in Educational Administration (M.Ed) from Eastern New Mexico University, USA and his second Masters degree in Industrial Technology (M.Sc) from Purdue University, USA. He earned a doctoral degree in Technical and Vocational Education (Ph.D) also from Purdue University, USA.

Priyadarshini Muthukrishnan is a research enthusiast, and she is passionate to explore new areas of educational research. Her research is focused on teacher education and professional development. Her recent research interests are e-learning, growth mindset teaching practices, postgraduate students' graduation on time, open and distance education and eye-tracking research.

Teoh Sian Hoon is a BSc graduate from Universiti Teknologi Malaysia, Malaysia and obtained her MSc in Statistics and PhD in Information Technology with Education from Universiti Sains Malaysia, Malaysia. Her fields of interest are Information Technology in Education, Statistics Education and Mathematics Education. Her doctoral thesis was on developing and testing of effectiveness of an interactive mathematical courseware using three different learning strategies.

Constantinos Nicolaou is a researcher at the Laboratory of Electronic Media, School of Journalism and Mass Communications, Faculty of Economic and Political Sciences, Aristotle University of Thessaloniki (Greece). His research interests are focused on non-verbal communication, music/radio and TV production, television and audiovisual branded content, digital storytelling, audiovisual-supported teaching methodologies and methods, curricula, technology-enhanced learning, adult and high education, ICTs, social media, heritage, generations and generational cohorts, media studies, technology-enhanced research as well as research from and through the Internet.

About the Contributors

Nor Azah has been in the teaching field for more than twenty-five years. Her research interests are on Intercultural Communication, Teaching and Learning Practices, Online Learning and Curriculum Development.

Khadijah Said Hashim earned her Master's of Education in Educational Psychology from the International Islamic University Malaysia and PhD from Universiti Kebangsaan Malaysia. She is currently a senior lecturer at the Faculty of Education, UiTM Puncak Alam Campus in Selangor, teaching Research Methodology and Educational Psychology for undergraduate level, and Human Development for Postgraduate students. Besides teaching, Khadijah has been a speaker and trainer for new lecturers at UiTM since 2007. She is also actively engaged in collaborative work with international universities. Her research interests include Pedagogy and Andragogy, Educational Psychology, Special Education and Teacher training.

Suriati Saidan is a lecturer at Universiti Teknologi Mara in Shah Alam, Selangor Malaysia. She has experience in teaching fashion design since 2009 at the undergraduate level. She graduated with a Degree in Fashion Design in 2008 and a Master's Degree in Design technology in 2013 from Universiti Teknologi Mara. Currently, she taught fashion design with specific courses in pattern and garment, fashion illustration, Malaysian Traditional costume and hand embroidery.

Norshiha Saidin has over thirty years of Academic experience as a senior lecturer at the Faculty of Education, with areas of expertise in Classroom Management, Teacher Education and Language Education for Boys. Pioneered research into investigating boys as the new disadvantaged group. Presented numerous conference papers, authored 3 books and several publications in refereed journals. Spent the last twelve years in various leadership post in UiTM as Head of UiTM and KPM Twinning Program (2002-2006), Head of TESL Program (2007-2009), Head of UiTM Community Networking, ICAN (2012-2014), and currently Head of Asasi TESL in CFS UiTM Dengkil. In 2011 was granted a one year Sabbatical tenure at University of South Adelaide, Australia. Posesses vast exposure in training and consultancy, regular speaker at UiTM KAP training for young lecturers in IlQAM and ILD courses, as well as invited speaker on various topics such as Motivation, Teacher Education and Social Entrepreneurship to Universities and schools in the Klang Valley. Developed competencies in Social Entrepreneurship, Humanitarian Aid and Volunteerism. Promotes youth philanthropy projects in UiTM and established international collaborations with NGO's and humanitarian organisations such as MERCY Malaysia, Syria Care, Al Itisam Relief Project, Aman Palestin, Asian Development Relief Fund (ADRF) and South East Asian Social Innovation Network (SEASIN). Initiated the establishment of UiTM MERCY Malaysia chapter in UITM and spearheaded various international humanitarian projects in Cambodia, Vietnam and Indonesia. The International Humanitarian Mission to Kampung Ampal, Cambodia in 2012 successfully raised funds for the construction of 44 wells and distribution of education kits to communities in need. This project won UiTM a gold medal in the Innovative Practices in Higher Education Expo 2015 (IPHEX), organized by AKEPT. In 2017 the innovative co-curriculum at the Asasi TESL program won an Award from YB Dato Idris Jusoh Anugerah Pemikiran & Rekabentuk Semula Pendidikan (APRS 2017) Redesigning and Rethinking Higher Education Award organized by MOHE and awarded a RM10,000 grant. Founding member of PRIZMA, New Zealand Malaysian Student Alumni and served as Exco and Secretary General of UiTM Academic Staff Association (MITASA) since 2009.

About the Contributors

Padmanabhan Seshaiyer is a tenured Full Professor in the Department of Mathematical Sciences and the Director of the Center for Outreach in Mathematics Professional Learning and Educational Technology (COMPLETE) at George Mason University, Fairfax, Virginia, USA. During the last decade, Dr. Seshaiyer has initiated and directed a variety of educational programs including graduate and undergraduate research, K-12 outreach, teacher professional development, and enrichment programs to foster the interest of students and teachers in STEM at all levels.

Malai Zeiti Hamid is Assistant Professor with the Centre for Communication, Teaching and Learning and Head of the Wellness Research Thrust at Universiti Teknologi Brunei (UTB). She graduated with a PhD in English Language and Literacy Education (Bath), Masters of Education in Applied Linguistics and TESOL (Leicester) and Bachelors in Education in Teaching English as a Second Language (Brunei). Dr Zeiti has a Teaching Certificate in Higher Education (Harvard) and completed the Women's Leadership Development Programme (Oxford). Dr Zeiti was awarded the Royal Charter Qualification of Chartered Teacher of English (CTE) by the English Association (EA, UK). She is a Chartered Linguist of Education from the UK Chartered Institute of Linguists (CIL, UK). In addition, she is also a Fellow of the UK Chartered College of Teaching (UK CCT) and Fellow of the UK Society of Education and Training (UK SET). During her career, she had been an award recipient of the US - ASEAN Fulbright Scholarship Program and received the UTB Teaching Excellence Award Special Mention at her university. She was a Visiting Scholar at the Harvard Graduate School of Education (HGSE) and is currently pursuing her postdoctoral programme at Harvard University. Dr Zeiti is the President of the Brunei Reading and Literacy Association (ReLA), and is the international ambassador for Brunei for the UK Literacy Association (UKLA). She is Founder and Curator of TEDxBandarSeriBegawan. Her current research interests are Cultural Literacy and Digital Literacy. She has presented widely in numerous international conferences as keynote speaker, moderator and chair to various webinar and presentations including the UK, USA and ASEAN countries. She is a published author for children's book for Brunei. More recently, Dr Zeiti has been writing stories for promoting children's literature internationally through a collection of stories entitled, "Cultural Stories Around the World", and scheduled to be launched this year.

Geetha Subramaniam is an educationist for more than 37 years. A research enthusiast, she actively researches on teaching and learning, online learning, collaborative learning as well as business & management topics and SDG.

Omar Vargas-González is Professor and Head of Systems and Computing Department at Tecnologico Nacional de Mexico Campus Ciudad Guzman, professor at Telematic Engineering at Centro Universitario del Sur Universidad de Guadalajara with a master degree in Computer Systems. Has been trained in Innovation and Multidisciplinary Entrepreneurship at Arizona State University (2018) and a Generation of Ecosystems of Innovation, Entrepreneurship and Sustainability for Jalisco course by Harvard University T.H. Chan School of Health. At present conduct research on diverse fields such as Entrepreneurship, Economy, Statistics, Mathematics and Information and Computer Sciences. Has colaborated in the publication of over 15 scientific articles and conducted diverse Innovation and Technological Development projects.

José Vargas-Hernández is a Research Professor Professor José G. Vargas-Hernández, M.B.A.; Ph.D. Member of the National System of Researchers of Mexico and a research professor at Tecnológico Mario Molina Unidad Zapopan formerly at University Center for Economic and Managerial Sciences, University of Guadalajara. Professor Vargas-Hernández has a Ph. D. in Public Administration and a Ph.D. in Organizational Economics. He has undertaken studies in Organisational Behaviour and has a Master of Business Administration, published four books and more than 200 papers in international journals and reviews (some translated to English, French, German, Portuguese, Farsi, Chinese, etc.) and more than 300 essays in national journals and reviews. He has obtained several international Awards and recognition.

Farhana Wan Yunus is a senior lecturer at the Faculty of Education, Universiti Teknologi MARA in Puncak Alam, Malaysia. She also holds a position of practicum coordinator at the faculty. With more than 10 years experience in various areas of education subjects, she teaches future teachers and handles their practicum experience at secondary schools all over Malaysia. Farhana received her PhD in Education (specifically ECE) from Victoria University of Wellington, New Zealand in 2019. Her research areas include Early Childhood Education, Educational Psychology and teaching and learning in schools. She loves traveling, reading and swimming in her free time.

Aizan Yaacob obtained her PhD in English Language Teaching (ELT) and Applied Linguistics from the University of Warwick, United Kingdom. She gained her Master of Arts in Language Studies from the University of Lancaster, United Kingdom and her Bachelor of Education with a double major in TESL and English Literature from the University of Winnipeg, Manitoba, Canada. Her areas of specialization include ELT, Applied Linguistics, Bilingualism, Teaching English to Young Learners, and qualitative research. Associate Professor Dr Aizan Yaacob did her post-doctoral study at the University of Warwick in 2007 and became a visiting scholar at Higher Education Department Centre, Otago University, New Zealand and International Islamic University Malaysia in 2017- 2018 in the areas of Scholarship of Teaching and Learning (SoTL) and English Language Teaching (ELT) respectively. She was the module writer for AKEPT SoTL and university trainer for SoTL. She is currently the Editor-in-Chief for Practitioner Research. She has published widely in national and international journals in her field.

Zuraimi Zakaria is a senior lecturer with the Department of Educational Studies, Faculty of Education, Universiti Teknologi MARA (UiTM), Malaysia. She graduated with Bachelor Degree in Education (Hons.) Teaching of English as a Second Language (TESL) from the same faculty she is currently attached to before pursuing her Master in Assessment and Evaluation with the University of Melbourne, Australia. Specializes in educational assessment, particularly assessments within constructivist framework and evidence-based practice; she used to serve Melbourne Graduate School of Education, University of Melbourne as an assessment coach. Working with a team under the assessment project, she had directly assisted 15 schools in the state of Victoria, Australia, to develop an assessment system which focuses on teaching and assessment activities that scaffold learning at group and individual levels. She is currently pursuing her doctoral degree in Educational Measurement and Evaluation at the Universiti Teknologi Malaysia.

Index

21st Century Learning 6, 66, 95

A

Academic 1-2, 5, 7, 13, 16, 19-22, 25, 32-33, 35, 38-41, 47-48, 50-53, 58, 60, 64-66, 71-72, 74, 77, 81, 85, 90, 94, 106, 132, 136, 151, 185, 197, 199, 234, 251, 257, 260, 268, 270, 304, 308, 317, 319-320, 335-337, 339-342, 345-354, 356-358, 360-364, 367, 370-375, 377-378, 384, 402, 404, 406, 409, 411-414
Accreditation 384-385, 388, 395, 402
Actionable Uncertainty 144-145, 147, 163-164, 171-172, 175
Active Learning 9, 54, 59, 62, 66, 92, 95, 97, 101, 107, 130, 224, 270, 307-308, 310, 318-319, 360, 374
adult education 197, 257-258, 261, 266, 274-276, 320, 399
Appreciative Inquiry 15, 27-28, 35-36, 38-39, 41
Assessment 3, 10, 14, 20, 23, 28-29, 31, 33-34, 39-40, 48-49, 51-53, 64, 73-74, 82, 85-91, 107, 113, 119, 122, 136, 145, 148-151, 157, 161-162, 164-165, 172, 175, 179, 188, 239, 246, 253, 255, 285-286, 291, 305, 307-318, 321-332, 335-337, 349, 352, 364, 366, 368, 370, 378, 380, 406, 412
audiovisual content 256-258, 263, 266, 271, 274, 279
Audiovisual Media Communications (AMCs) 257, 279
audiovisual media technologies 256-258, 266, 274, 279
Authenticity 144-145, 147, 149, 163, 166, 170-172, 175, 303

B

Becoming 27, 32, 37, 115, 144-145, 153, 163, 172, 185, 337, 358, 383
Behavior 46, 48, 55, 89, 200-201, 203, 213, 216, 271, 280-281, 285-287, 289-290, 293-304, 339-342, 344-354, 356-357, 359, 374-375
Behavioural Competencies 15-16, 23, 29, 38
Being 1-3, 6-8, 11, 17, 25, 27, 31, 35, 42, 47, 49-50, 55, 57, 65, 76, 80, 83, 85-86, 91, 95, 97, 100, 104, 116, 121-123, 129-130, 137, 144, 147, 149, 153, 156, 161-163, 165-167, 169-170, 172, 175, 178, 185-186, 189-191, 199, 202, 204, 209, 218, 222, 237, 242, 249, 256, 266, 284, 311, 325, 328-329, 332, 341, 366-368, 381, 383, 403, 405
Books 53, 92-97, 99-100, 175, 257, 269, 312, 373

C

Care 28, 47, 52, 73, 75, 80-83, 89-91, 144, 147, 153, 163, 166, 171-172, 174, 178, 184, 197, 284
Care Pedagogy 73, 80-82, 91
Caring Classroom 73
Cheating 341, 345, 348-349, 352, 357-358
Chemistry for Life 236, 242-243, 253
Collaborative Learning 9, 30, 59, 95, 97, 103-109, 111-119, 125, 180-181, 190, 229, 316-317, 364-365, 373-375, 381
Collaborative Pedagogy 103-109, 111, 113-114, 117
Collaborative Teaching 120, 122, 125-126, 131, 197
College 8, 89, 103, 109-110, 119, 144-145, 197, 231, 234, 254, 274, 311, 319, 335, 339-342, 346-348, 350-354, 356-358, 412
community of inquiry 69, 71, 274, 360, 365, 372-376
Constructive Alignment 24-25, 27, 29, 39
Content 2-3, 6, 9, 16-17, 20, 42, 55-59, 61, 64-65, 73-74, 80-81, 83, 91, 101, 107, 120-124, 139, 147, 150, 159, 170, 218-222, 224-226, 228, 230, 233, 236-237, 242-243, 251, 256-261, 263-266, 271-272, 274-277, 279, 307, 311-312, 316, 343, 345, 349, 353, 363, 380, 385, 387-388, 391, 395-397
Creative Self 134, 136-137, 139-140
Creativity 25, 44, 46, 51-52, 58, 92, 113-114, 117, 121-122, 131-132, 134-139, 141-147, 150, 156-159, 172-175, 177, 180, 182, 196, 219-221, 232-234, 251, 259, 261-262, 264, 343, 382, 384, 401

D

Determinants 37, 198-202, 209, 212, 216, 280, 282, 284, 293, 296-297, 299
Didactic Strategies 54-56, 61-64
Digital Transformation 257, 271, 274, 279

E

education 1-6, 8-9, 11-19, 21, 23, 32, 36, 38-60, 62-63, 65-74, 78, 80-81, 89-92, 94-95, 100, 104, 107, 109, 113, 116, 118-123, 125-126, 129-132, 134-137, 139, 141-143, 146, 151, 158, 173-174, 178-181, 184-185, 196-199, 201, 203, 206, 209, 211-213, 218, 220-222, 226, 228, 230-234, 236-239, 242, 244-245, 248-259, 261, 264-278, 280, 298, 300-303, 305-308, 311, 313, 315, 317-321, 323-326, 330-332, 335-336, 339-341, 345, 348, 350, 352, 354-358, 361-362, 365, 372-376, 380-389, 391-394, 396-410, 412-414
Emotional Support 73-74, 81, 85, 88
Environmental commitment 280-283, 299-300
Environments 4-5, 10, 12-14, 23, 25, 27-28, 38, 56, 59-60, 63, 65, 69-72, 74, 76, 115, 135, 177, 190, 197, 221, 250, 256-258, 264, 268-269, 284, 303, 308, 320, 340-343, 356, 361-362, 364-365, 368-369, 371, 373-374, 376, 380-381, 385, 387-388, 400, 405
Ethical Conversation 152, 175
Ethics 17, 51, 110, 146, 339-341, 347-348, 352, 355-359, 384
Expression 5, 10, 144, 157, 163, 171-172, 175, 242, 249-250, 364-365

F

Falsification 348, 359
Flexi Scaffolding 83, 91
Flexible Entry Points 380, 385, 388, 395-396, 400
Flexible Learning 4, 353, 380-389, 394-402
Flexible Learning Environment 402
Flexible Learning Pathways 380-381, 383-388, 394-400, 402
Flexible Learning Structures 380, 385, 388, 395
Flexible Teaching 380-381, 383, 385-386, 388-390, 392-393, 399-402
Formative Assessment 14, 48-49, 85, 90, 323, 325, 335-336, 406, 412
Foundation Program 92

G

General Studies 178, 305-308, 312, 318, 320, 322
Ghostwriting 348, 359
Global Learners 103-107, 109-111, 113-115, 117
group-based learning 360, 367, 375

H

Higher Education 1-2, 4-5, 11-14, 21, 39-41, 43, 45, 52, 54-55, 57, 66, 68, 71-72, 81, 89-90, 92, 100, 107, 113, 118-119, 122, 131, 134-137, 139, 141-142, 151, 158, 179, 199, 211, 213, 253, 256, 258, 266, 268, 270-271, 273, 275-276, 278, 280, 302, 305-306, 308, 319-321, 323-326, 330-332, 335-336, 339-341, 345, 348, 352, 356-358, 361-362, 365, 373-374, 376, 380-387, 393-394, 399-406, 410, 413-414
Higher Education Institutions (HEIs) 21, 380, 383, 403
Holistic 5-6, 15-16, 25, 30, 32, 38, 42-43, 47, 49, 52, 73-74, 83, 122-123, 125, 132, 140, 146, 172, 274, 305-306, 318, 320-321, 383
Holistic Development 30, 73, 172
Holistic Personalised Development 15
Honest 83, 354, 359
Humanism 73
Humanistic Learning Theory 74-75, 90-91
Hybrid 258, 339-351, 353-358, 389, 396, 402

I

ICTs 62, 256, 258, 261-263, 265-266, 275-276, 279
Immunity to Change 144, 148, 174-175
Industrial Revolution 1-2, 42-43, 121, 136
Information and Communications Technologies (ICTs) 258, 276, 279
Internet of Things (IoT) 120, 124
Issues and Challenges 89, 105, 111-112, 404, 406-407, 410-411

L

Learning 1-25, 27-28, 30, 32-35, 37, 39-40, 42-56, 58-97, 99-101, 103-129, 131-132, 134-142, 145, 148-150, 158, 160, 162-165, 172-175, 177-184, 187-190, 192-194, 196-197, 214, 218-222, 224, 226-239, 242-245, 248, 250-251, 253-254, 256-280, 305-325, 327-332, 335-337, 339-351, 353-358, 360-376, 380-389, 392, 394-402, 404-414
Learning and Teaching 50, 53, 89, 141, 222, 226, 238, 272, 274-275, 305, 307, 383, 400

Index

Learning Process 2, 8, 47, 50, 56, 61, 65, 73, 88, 90, 95, 104, 107, 122, 124, 140, 180, 237, 251, 309-310, 316-318, 324, 343-345, 349, 353, 385, 387-388, 395-397, 400
Learning Spaces 58, 92-95, 100-101, 150, 371, 376, 401
Life-Long 42, 69, 381, 399
Literacy Skills 92, 259, 265

M

Malaysian Higher Learning Institution 305
Maslow 73-75, 90-91
Mathematics 11, 14, 45, 53, 68-72, 120-122, 124, 126, 128, 130-132, 134, 217-219, 221-222, 224-235, 251, 253-254, 278
Meaningful Learning 3, 54-65, 68-71, 75, 88, 179, 324
Metacognitive Model 15
Metaphor 150, 170-172, 174, 236, 238-240, 248-250, 252-255
Microteaching 217-218, 220-227, 230, 232-233
Morocco 198, 200, 212-213, 215-216, 280-281
Motivation 7, 16, 32-33, 46, 48, 59-60, 63-64, 69, 72-75, 77, 80-83, 91, 105, 111-117, 137-138, 141, 145-147, 151-152, 158, 162, 165-166, 171-172, 178, 203, 208, 212, 224, 237, 250, 257, 265, 278, 280-282, 285-286, 297, 300, 302-304, 308-309, 311, 318, 323-324, 326-327, 330, 332, 336-337, 344, 351, 354, 362, 375, 381, 399
Multiple-Multimodal Skills 256, 258, 261-262, 265-267, 279

O

Online Assessments 85, 91
online communities 360-361
Online Learning 4, 47, 62, 65, 72, 74, 77, 79-81, 86, 88-89, 103-107, 109-113, 115-119, 123-124, 179, 181, 197, 221, 231, 260, 274, 339-342, 349, 360-361, 365, 368, 372-373, 383, 400-401
Online pedagogy 89, 360, 367, 370
Open and Distance Learning (ODL) 73-74, 80, 89, 382

P

Pandemic Teaching 80-81, 88, 91
Pedagogy 9-11, 13, 15-17, 19, 27-28, 32, 40-42, 44, 48, 50, 55, 61, 67, 70, 73, 75, 80-82, 89-91, 103-109, 111, 113-114, 117, 123, 172, 176, 218, 251, 254, 277, 356-357, 360-362, 364, 367, 370, 374, 392, 397, 400, 406
Plagiarism 47, 341, 348-349, 352, 359

Post-COVID-19 Pandemic 103
Postnormality 146, 172, 175
pragmatic competence 370
Preservice Teacher (PST) 217
Pre-University 321
pro-environmental behavior 280, 285, 287, 289-290, 293-304
Project-Based Assessment 305, 307-313, 315-318, 321-322
Project-Based Learning 65, 121, 177, 180-181, 196, 271, 307-310, 319, 322

Q

Quality Education 46, 56, 59, 123, 352, 381-385, 387-389, 391-394, 396-401, 403

R

Readiness 1-2, 45, 320, 327, 380-382, 385-388, 394-395, 398-400, 403
Reading 63, 71, 75, 92, 94, 96-97, 100, 150, 173, 201, 214, 310, 328, 361-363, 370-371, 373-375, 377-378
reading circles 363, 375, 377-378
Reflection 18, 31, 110, 123, 153, 165-166, 169, 171, 184-185, 187, 224, 236, 246, 248, 250-251, 253, 273, 277, 285, 308, 312-313, 323, 328, 330, 332, 361, 365-366, 369, 377, 405, 408
Responsible 1-2, 6-13, 42-43, 45, 47, 49-51, 59-61, 92-93, 95-97, 120-122, 124-131, 161, 163, 221, 236-237, 239, 242-245, 248, 250-252, 256-259, 261, 263-269, 280, 305-308, 310-312, 317-319, 339-340, 342-346, 348-353, 377
Responsive 1-14, 19, 21, 27, 36, 38, 42-45, 47-53, 68, 81, 92-96, 100, 104, 120-122, 124-131, 134-135, 141, 217-234, 236-237, 239, 242-245, 248, 250-252, 254-259, 261, 263-267, 269, 305, 307-308, 310, 312, 315, 318-319, 339-340, 342-346, 348-353, 404, 406, 411-413
Responsive and Responsible Learning 1-2, 6, 8-11, 42-43, 45, 47, 50-51, 92, 95-96, 120-122, 125, 131, 236-237, 239, 242-245, 248, 250-251, 256-259, 261, 263-266, 305, 310, 312, 339-340, 342, 345-346, 348-353
Responsive Learning Environment 1-5, 92, 130, 134-135
Responsive Teaching 1-3, 5-6, 11-14, 47-48, 53, 68, 81, 217-218, 220-234, 236, 245, 251, 269, 404, 406, 411-413

S

Scaffolding 32, 83-85, 90-91, 108-109, 113, 148, 172-173, 329, 370
SDG4 380, 382-388, 392-393, 398-399
Seamless Learning 127, 129-131, 311, 316, 320-322
Self-Directed Learning 13, 92, 95, 100-101, 261, 272, 274, 315, 320, 341
Self-Regulated Learning 4, 6, 12, 70, 118, 268, 323, 325, 335-336, 344, 357-358
Skill 17, 37, 103, 131, 136, 138, 147, 149, 218, 222, 279, 305, 361, 368, 384
skills 3, 5, 12, 16-17, 19-21, 23-33, 35-36, 42-48, 51, 57-59, 61-65, 70-71, 80, 88-89, 92, 95-97, 101, 103-104, 106-107, 113, 116, 121, 123-124, 130-131, 134, 138, 140, 146, 151-152, 158-159, 165, 174, 177-180, 185, 190-192, 195, 199-201, 217-219, 221-222, 224-227, 229-230, 232-233, 236-239, 243, 248, 251, 254, 257-259, 261-274, 276-279, 306, 308-312, 315-316, 318-321, 323-324, 330-332, 335, 344, 360-364, 367-369, 371-373, 375, 377-378, 381-382, 384, 392, 401, 403, 405, 407, 409, 412
Social Innovation Project Module 177, 181-183, 192
social media 119, 259, 263, 268, 270-278, 311, 370-371
Social Medias (SMs) 279
SoTL, 404, 406, 410
STEM Education 5, 13, 120-123, 125-126, 129-131, 218, 220, 231, 233
Storying 75-77, 91
structural equation modelling 280
Structured Uncertainty 144-145, 147, 149-150, 158, 172-173, 175
Student 2, 4-5, 8-9, 11, 13-14, 20-25, 32, 34, 38-44, 48-51, 53, 55-60, 62-65, 70, 74-76, 78-84, 86-87, 89-91, 93-95, 100, 106-107, 109, 112, 119, 122, 138, 140-141, 144-145, 150-152, 156-157, 170, 172-173, 175, 179, 184, 187, 196-199, 204, 207, 209, 211-212, 217, 220, 222, 226, 228-231, 233-234, 237, 243, 249, 268-269, 274, 277-278, 280, 299, 305, 310, 312-319, 327, 329, 331, 335-337, 339, 341, 343, 349-351, 358, 361-364, 366, 368-372, 374, 376-377, 380, 388-389, 394, 399, 401, 404-405, 407-411
Student Engagement 64, 89, 91, 107, 109, 112, 119, 151-152, 157, 229, 269, 299, 310, 319, 343, 401
Students 4-7, 9-11, 13-38, 40-46, 48-68, 72-89, 92-101, 103-107, 109-122, 124-132, 135, 138-141, 144-145, 147-153, 156-160, 162-166, 170-173, 177-196, 198-199, 202-207, 209, 211-214, 217-222, 224-234, 236-238, 249-255, 269-270, 272, 274, 277-283, 285-286, 289-290, 293-322, 324, 326-332, 335-336, 339-346, 348-354, 356-358, 360-372, 374-377, 380-382, 384-389, 391-402, 405-409, 411-414
Summative Assessment 31, 48-49, 85, 323-324, 328, 330
Sustainable Development Goals (SDGs) 17, 22, 35, 121, 382, 403
Systematic Review, 323, 411-412

T

Teaching 1-6, 9-14, 16, 20-21, 23, 25, 38-39, 42-55, 57-60, 62, 64-66, 68-69, 73-74, 78-83, 85, 87-91, 95, 103-106, 108-109, 113-114, 118, 120-122, 124-126, 130-131, 138, 141-142, 172-173, 175-176, 178-181, 196-197, 217-223, 225-238, 245, 249-258, 261-266, 269-276, 278-279, 283, 305, 307-308, 312, 314-315, 320-321, 331, 335-337, 341-343, 345, 353-356, 358, 360-363, 365-367, 371-375, 381-386, 388-393, 395, 399-402, 404-414
Teaching Strategies 9-10, 54, 62, 221, 307, 358, 381, 393, 400
Technology-Enhanced Learning (TEL) 257, 279

U

Unethical 339-341, 345-354

V

Value-Based Innovation 177
Volunteering 10, 100, 198-203, 206-207, 209-216
Žižekian Event 175

Recommended Reference Books

IGI Global's reference books are available in three unique pricing formats:
Print Only, E-Book Only, or Print + E-Book.

Shipping fees may apply.

www.igi-global.com

ISBN: 9781522589648
EISBN: 9781522589655
© 2021; 156 pp.
List Price: US$ 155

ISBN: 9781799840756
EISBN: 9781799840763
© 2021; 282 pp.
List Price: US$ 185

ISBN: 9781799855989
EISBN: 9781799856009
© 2021; 382 pp.
List Price: US$ 195

ISBN: 9781799864745
EISBN: 9781799864752
© 2021; 271 pp.
List Price: US$ 195

ISBN: 9781799875710
EISBN: 9781799875734
© 2021; 252 pp.
List Price: US$ 195

ISBN: 9781799857709
EISBN: 9781799857716
© 2021; 378 pp.
List Price: US$ 195

Do you want to stay current on the latest research trends, product announcements, news, and special offers?
Join IGI Global's mailing list to receive customized recommendations, exclusive discounts, and more.
Sign up at: www.igi-global.com/newsletters.

Publisher of Timely, Peer-Reviewed Inclusive Research Since 1988

www.igi-global.com   Sign up at www.igi-global.com/newsletters   facebook.com/igiglobal   twitter.com/igiglobal   linkedin.com/igiglobal

Ensure Quality Research is Introduced to the Academic Community

Become an Evaluator for IGI Global Authored Book Projects

 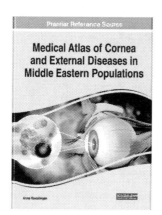 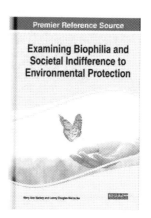 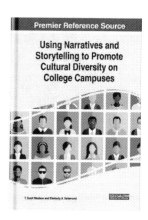

The overall success of an authored book project is dependent on quality and timely manuscript evaluations.

Applications and Inquiries may be sent to:
development@igi-global.com

Applicants must have a doctorate (or equivalent degree) as well as publishing, research, and reviewing experience. Authored Book Evaluators are appointed for one-year terms and are expected to complete at least three evaluations per term. Upon successful completion of this term, evaluators can be considered for an additional term.

If you have a colleague that may be interested in this opportunity, we encourage you to share this information with them.

Easily Identify, Acquire, and Utilize Published Peer-Reviewed Findings in Support of Your Current Research

IGI Global OnDemand

Purchase Individual IGI Global OnDemand Book Chapters and Journal Articles

For More Information:
www.igi-global.com/e-resources/ondemand/

Browse through 150,000+ Articles and Chapters!

Find specific research related to your current studies and projects that have been contributed by international researchers from prestigious institutions, including:

- Accurate and Advanced Search
- Affordably Acquire Research
- Instantly Access Your Content
- Benefit from the InfoSci Platform Features

" It really provides an excellent entry into the research literature of the field. It presents a manageable number of highly relevant sources on topics of interest to a wide range of researchers. The sources are scholarly, but also accessible to 'practitioners'. "

- Ms. Lisa Stimatz, MLS, University of North Carolina at Chapel Hill, USA

Interested in Additional Savings?

Subscribe to
IGI Global OnDemand Plus

Learn More

Acquire content from over 128,000+ research-focused book chapters and 33,000+ scholarly journal articles for as low as US$ 5 per article/chapter (original retail price for an article/chapter: US$ 37.50).

6,600+ E-BOOKS.
ADVANCED RESEARCH.
INCLUSIVE & ACCESSIBLE.

IGI Global e-Book Collection

- **Flexible Purchasing Options** (Perpetual, Subscription, EBA, etc.)
- Multi-Year Agreements with **No Price Increases** Guaranteed
- **No Additional Charge** for Multi-User Licensing
- No Maintenance, Hosting, or Archiving Fees
- Transformative **Open Access Options** Available

Request More Information, or Recommend the IGI Global e-Book Collection to Your Institution's Librarian

Among Titles Included in the IGI Global e-Book Collection

Research Anthology on Racial Equity, Identity, and Privilege (3 Vols.)
EISBN: 9781668445082
Price: US$ 895

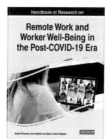

Handbook of Research on Remote Work and Worker Well-Being in the Post-COVID-19 Era
EISBN: 9781799867562
Price: US$ 265

Research Anthology on Big Data Analytics, Architectures, and Applications (4 Vols.)
EISBN: 9781668436639
Price: US$ 1,950

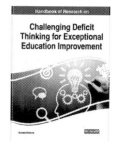

Handbook of Research on Challenging Deficit Thinking for Exceptional Education Improvement
EISBN: 9781799888628
Price: US$ 265

Acquire & Open

When your library acquires an IGI Global e-Book and/or e-Journal Collection, your faculty's published work will be considered for immediate conversion to Open Access *(CC BY License)*, at no additional cost to the library or its faculty *(cost only applies to the e-Collection content being acquired)*, through our popular **Transformative Open Access (Read & Publish) Initiative**.

For More Information or to Request a Free Trial, Contact IGI Global's e-Collections Team: eresources@igi-global.com | 1-866-342-6657 ext. 100 | 717-533-8845 ext. 100

Have Your Work Published and Freely Accessible
Open Access Publishing

With the industry shifting from the more traditional publication models to an open access (OA) publication model, publishers are finding that OA publishing has many benefits that are awarded to authors and editors of published work.

Freely Share Your Research

Higher Discoverability & Citation Impact

Rigorous & Expedited Publishing Process

Increased Advancement & Collaboration

Acquire & Open

When your library acquires an IGI Global e-Book and/or e-Journal Collection, your faculty's published work will be considered for immediate conversion to Open Access *(CC BY License)*, at no additional cost to the library or its faculty *(cost only applies to the e-Collection content being acquired)*, through our popular **Transformative Open Access (Read & Publish) Initiative**.

- Provide Up To **100%** OA APC or CPC Funding
- Funding to Convert or Start a Journal to **Platinum OA**
- Support for Funding an **OA Reference Book**

IGI Global publications are found in a number of prestigious indices, including Web of Science™, Scopus®, Compendex, and PsycINFO®. The selection criteria is very strict and to ensure that journals and books are accepted into the major indexes, IGI Global closely monitors publications against the criteria that the indexes provide to publishers.

Learn More Here: For Questions, Contact IGI Global's Open Access Team at openaccessadmin@igi-global.com

Are You Ready to Publish Your Research?

IGI Global offers book authorship and editorship opportunities across 11 subject areas, including business, computer science, education, science and engineering, social sciences, and more!

Benefits of Publishing with IGI Global:

- Free one-on-one editorial and promotional support.
- Expedited publishing timelines that can take your book from start to finish in less than one (1) year.
- Choose from a variety of formats, including Edited and Authored References, Handbooks of Research, Encyclopedias, and Research Insights.
- Utilize IGI Global's eEditorial Discovery® submission system in support of conducting the submission and double-blind peer review process.
- IGI Global maintains a strict adherence to ethical practices due in part to our full membership with the Committee on Publication Ethics (COPE).
- Indexing potential in prestigious indices such as Scopus®, Web of Science™, PsycINFO®, and ERIC – Education Resources Information Center.
- Ability to connect your ORCID iD to your IGI Global publications.
- Earn honorariums and royalties on your full book publications as well as complimentary copies and exclusive discounts.

Join Your Colleagues from Prestigious Institutions, Including:

Australian National University

Massachusetts Institute of Technology

Johns Hopkins University

Harvard University

Tsinghua University

Columbia University in the City of New York

Learn More at: www.igi-global.com/publish
or Contact IGI Global's Aquisitions Team at: acquisition@igi-global.com

Easily Identify, Acquire, and Utilize Published Peer-Reviewed Findings in Support of Your Current Research

IGI Global OnDemand

Purchase Individual IGI Global OnDemand Book Chapters and Journal Articles

For More Information:
www.igi-global.com/e-resources/ondemand/

Browse through 150,000+ Articles and Chapters!

Find specific research related to your current studies and projects that have been contributed by international researchers from prestigious institutions, including:

- Accurate and Advanced Search
- Affordably Acquire Research
- Instantly Access Your Content
- Benefit from the InfoSci Platform Features

"It really provides an excellent entry into the research literature of the field. It presents a manageable number of highly relevant sources on topics of interest to a wide range of researchers. The sources are scholarly, but also accessible to 'practitioners'."

- Ms. Lisa Stimatz, MLS, University of North Carolina at Chapel Hill, USA

Interested in Additional Savings?

Subscribe to

IGI Global OnDemand *Plus*

Learn More

Acquire content from over 128,000+ research-focused book chapters and 33,000+ scholarly journal articles for as low as US$ 5 per article/chapter (original retail price for an article/chapter: US$ 37.50).